London's South Bank
The History

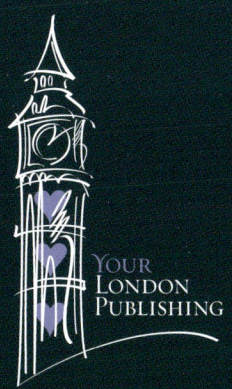

London's South Bank

The History

Mireille Galinou

Illustrations by Stephen Conlin

First published by Your London Publishing in 2023

Text copyright © Mireille Galinou © Simon Thurley for the Foreword

Reconstruction Drawings © Stephen Conlin unless specified otherwise

All right reserved. Except as permitted under current legislation no part of this work may be photocopied, stored in a retrieval system, published, performed in public, adapted, broadcast, transmitted, recorded or reproduced in any form or by any means, without the prior permission of the copyright owners.

ISBN 978-0-9933610-2-9

Editor: Valerie Cumming
Designer: Tom Keates-Miles
Printed and bound in Italy by L.E.G.O.S.p.A.

This book is dedicated to the memory of Xavier Baron (1941–2020) from Milwaukee, United States

Front cover

This highly atmospheric photograph of the Shard in Southwark was taken from the roof of One New Change shopping centre in the City of London. Chris Dalton's image was timed at 19.21 on 2 May 2019 (www.chrisjdalton.com).
(© Chris Dalton)

Frontispiece:

'View of London with Pale Horse', painted in 2020, is a collage of memories – one based on a 1980s sketch the artist, Michael Johnson, made of a rag and bone man's horse, the other a recollection of a spectacular low flight over the river Thames. Of his muse, London, the artist wrote: 'London's a vessel, a vehicle for so much of ourselves. And for me and others the contact with this ever-changing mirror through looking, sketching, grounding, then dreaming through mark making'.

The artist admits there is a pervading sense of foreboding and this may be detected in the painting's detail: the horse's red eyes and placement of its ears, appear demonic – a working horse which, despite its gigantic scale, still bears the badge of its enslavement to man with its feed bag. The group of crows underneath its belly fuels unease as does the city with its sulphuric sky – as if devastated by some powerful event. The choice of words in the title 'Pale Horse' may also suggest the fourth horseman of the Apocalypse, the carrier of death.

The harsh, gloomy side of London has often been associated with the South Bank, and although this painting, a beautiful nightmare, floats above practical, realistic interpretations, it offers a deeply symbolic image of London and its two banks.

(Private collection, © Michael Johnson)

In the beginning
of this book
was the idea
of a quest

CONTENTS

Foreword by Simon Thurley — 8

Acknowledgements — 10

1. Prologue — **14**
    The Quest — 17
    The Centre of gravity of London — 19
    How big is the South Bank in this book? — 21

2. The Eye of London – the artists' chapter — **22**
    2.1 Going back in time — 25
    2.2. The legacy of the Middle Ages — 30
    2.3 The sixteenth century — 31
    2.4 The seventeenth century — 46
    2.5 Later remarkable panoramas taken from the south — 56

3. The Sweep of History — **64**
    3.1 In the beginning of the South Bank — 68
    3.2 The South Bank around 1600 — 84
    3.3 The South Bank around 1770 — 142
    3.4 The South Bank around 1845 — 220
    3.5 The South Bank now — 294

4. The 'Quest' – soul searching in the South Bank's neighbourhoods — **356**
    4.1 Vauxhall and Lambeth – Paradise regained — 360
    4.2 Waterloo – Fall and redemption — 400
    4.3 Borough and Bankside – Sinners and saints, life and death — 442
    4.4 Southwark and Bermondsey – The highs and lows of a strategic neighbourhood — 484

5. Answers to the Quest — **524**
    5.1 Dialogue with the past — 527
    5.2 Becoming increasingly disconnected from our environment — 544
    5.3 Looking for the soul of London — 546
    5.4 The South Bank – a mirror of the north? — 557

List of Subscribers — 562

Bibliography — 563

Index — 573

Foreword

In 2000 Mireille Galinou and I were both working at the Museum of London. At the time we were undergoing one of those periodic interrogations of what the museum was for and how we would present London to our visitors. The debate raged and, at one point, one of our brilliant colleagues said 'London is not a place, it's a concept'. I've remembered that observation over the years as my own career interacted with the capital in various ways.

The fact is that London is both a tangible place and a bundle of ideas; it means something different to everybody who lives, works or visits. Capturing the meaning of London is consequently immensely difficult, if not impossible, but in this book Mireille has approached the problem by triangulating past, present and future to find the essence of place.

The place in question, is the South Bank, a huge tract of amorphous development that only became part of modern London after it was tied to the north bank, by roads, bridges, tunnels and eventually the sinews of government and administration. It is now hard to imagine how separate the south bank was until the nineteenth century. Since Roman times London Bridge had been the only land link; in 1750 Westminster bridge made a second crossing and it took another 16 years for Blackfriars bridge to make a third.

But of course, the place that grew up on the banks of the Thames opposite Westminster and the City is no more homogenous than the places that make up the north

bank. It is a federation of waterways, wharfs, roads, bridges, buildings, parks, gardens and of course all the intangible capital that goes into making a space a place. Untangling all this, questioning and probing has been Mireille's task over the last five years. It has involved the dissection of maps and images, immersion in the thoughts of writers and engagement with people who live and work there today; but most of all pounding the pavements, intimately tracing and understanding the urban fabric and making it come alive in print.

This is a new kind of urban history, one that makes little distinction between then and now, where Renzo Piano and Canaletto sit side by side on a page; it is a history that rightly portrays past and present as a continuum, as inseparable and equal parts of the human condition. That is why we care about historic places and want to make sure that, as they change, and as we change as a society, they continue to resonate and connect us with our ancestors.

Some recent developments on the South Bank have traversed this territory with skill and sensitivity adding to the richness and interest of the place; others have aggressively turned their backs on the past and our successors will judge whether the area is better or worse off as a result. Either way this book provides the context in which we can think about the future. Let's hope it will be bright.

Simon Thurley

Simon Thurley is an historian who is currently the Chair of the National Lottery Heritage Fund; he was for thirteen years the Chief Executive of English Heritage and before that the Director of the Museum of London soon to be renamed The London Museum. Many of his twelve books have been about London and its buildings, most recently *From Leper Hospital to Palace – The History of St. James' Palace*.

Julian Bell's 'Flightpath' was exhibited at the Meunier Gallery in 2019 as part of his solo show 'When the City is Built'. The exhibition was devised around a loose narrative – the arrival in London of Ibrahim, an elderly foreigner 'from the east', looking for his grand-daughter, a North London nanny. A number of paintings in that series focus on the Elephant and Castle area. Without always being topographically correct, this plausible view of the capital gives prominence to the South Bank, blending reality with a dream-like cityscape.
(Private collection; © Julian Bell)

Acknowledgements

This book has taken just over five years to complete, the sign of a demanding project. Since 2013 Your London Publishing has relentlessly pursued its agenda of investigating residential neighbourhoods; because they are consistently overlooked by residents and tourists alike. The South Bank, the capital's original suburb, is now regarded as part of Central London, and has recently turned into a magnet for tourists: so where is the residential bias might you ask? Mostly in the flourishing of the area's residential component – despite seeming likely to be eradicated in the twentieth century – though of course there are many other dimensions and layers to examine. Hence the absolute reliance of the project on the research and good will of many, many people –alive and dead.

My first massive thank you has to go to the small but wonderful team behind this project: the designer Tom Keates-Miles has surpassed himself as he shaped and enhanced this long and challenging publication; Valerie Cumming, Your London Publishing's loyal and patient editor, has been confronted with never ending reams of text, and this over and over again; finally, Stephen Conlin without whose beautiful reconstructions, the book would simply not work at all. Their work has inspired me and filled me with gratitude.

Then there are the friends and former colleagues who have helped by reading sections of the text, correcting mistakes and suggesting improvements which have clearly benefited the project – Richard Woollard was the most involved, followed by Peter Barber (British Library), Caroline Barron (Royal Holloway, University of London), Jon Cotton, Polly Freedman, Karen Hearn (University College London), Elizabeth New (Aberystwyth University), Cathy Ross (Museum of London), Edward Town (Yale Center for British Art), Alex Werner (Museum of London). Thank you all very much and thank you too, to those who have granted me access to unpublished research: Martha Carlin (University of Wisconsin-Milwaukee), Adam Dennett (CASA, University College, London); or granted lengthy interviews: Chris Constable (Borough of Southwark) and Graham Morrison (Allies and Morrison architects), the latter ably recorded by Vicky Woollard.

The picture research, as it is called in the book trade, represents to my eyes a completely intrinsic part of the book; and I would not dream of 'delegating' it, even if I were encouraged to do so. I think visually, often ahead of the linguistic tools, but the 'nailing down' of images represents hours and hours of toil – part chore, part inspiring. I am therefore immensely grateful to all those who have helped me on the way – particularly so to those who have reduced or waived the sometimes eye-watering fees that may still be charged in a world that is increasingly switching to 'images in the public domain' and where it is almost impossible to make any money out of well-illustrated non-fiction books. A massive thank you to all the artists and rare institutions who have chosen to be collaborators rather than business driven. And thank you, too, to the institutions who have opened their doors to me when I was researching in the long shadow of the pandemic. I will always remember with affection the print rooms of the Ashmolean Museum and Hatfield House. To the long list of people and institutions who have made a contribution to this book, I owe you a considerable debt: Allies and Morrison (Graham Morrison, Romy Berlin, Alfredo Caraballo), Ashmolean Museum (Caroline Palmer, An van Camp and Erica Martin), Sharon Beavan, Julian Bell, Bodleian Libraries (Martin Kauffmann), British Museum, British Library, John and Ann Bryce, Canterbury Cathedral Archives (Toby Huitson), John

Chase, Julian Cooper, Chris Dalton Photography, Ann Desmet, Arturo Di Stefano, Dulwich Archives (Calista Lucy), Gethin Evans, Torla Evans, Flowers Gallery, Dorian Gerhold, Antony Gormley Studio (Ann Chow Thomas), Guildhall Art Gallery (Elizabeth Scott), Hatfield House (Sarah Whale), Michael Heindorff, David Hepher, Timothy Hyman, Lambeth Archives (Zoe Darani, Jon Newman, Len Reilly), Lambeth Palace Library (Camille Koutoulakis), Andrew Lawson Photography, Pete Le May Photography, Paul Liss (Liss Llewellyn Gallery), London Metropolitan Archives (Steph Eeles, Jakub Rutkiewicz, Jeremy Smith), London Topographical Society (Bridget Cherry and Roger Cline), Manna (Paddy Boyle), Peter Marshall, Sarah Medway, Graeme Miller, MOLA (Andy Chopping, Maggie Cox), Museum of London (Nikki Braunton, John Clark, Dan Nesbitt), Dan Pearson Studio (Huw Morgan), Pre-Construct Archaeology (Cate Davies, Douglas Kinnock, Kevin Rielly, Vicki Ridgeway), Sarah O'Kane Contemporary Fine Art, Jiro Osuga, Mike O'Dwyer, Michael Richardson (Art Space Gallery), SE1 Community News, Mike Seaborne, Robert Soden, Southwark Archives, Southwark Museum (Judy Aitken), Kay Staniland, Woburn Abbey. The list is not exhaustive, as there is a full bibliography at the back of the book and the captions to images deliberately carry detailed credit lines which will make the images easy to find.

Last, but not least, I am also deeply indebted to our printing team – Jeremy Snell and the staff of L.E.G.O. our brilliant Italian printers who have overseen all three books published by Your London Publishing. Finally, new onto the scene, I am thrilled to introduce our partner-distributor, Unicorn Publishing. Your London Publishing is entering a new era and I am deeply grateful to its chairman, Lord Strathcarron, for responding so positively to my initial approach.

Map Disclaimer

The zones of Vauxhall and Lambeth (green), Waterloo (blue), Borough and Bankside (red) and Southwark and Bermondsey (grey) have been created for the purpose of this book; they are useful tools to organise the substantial amount of data in London's South Bank. Although there is nothing scientific about these divisions, to a large extent they capture the distinctive qualities of each area.

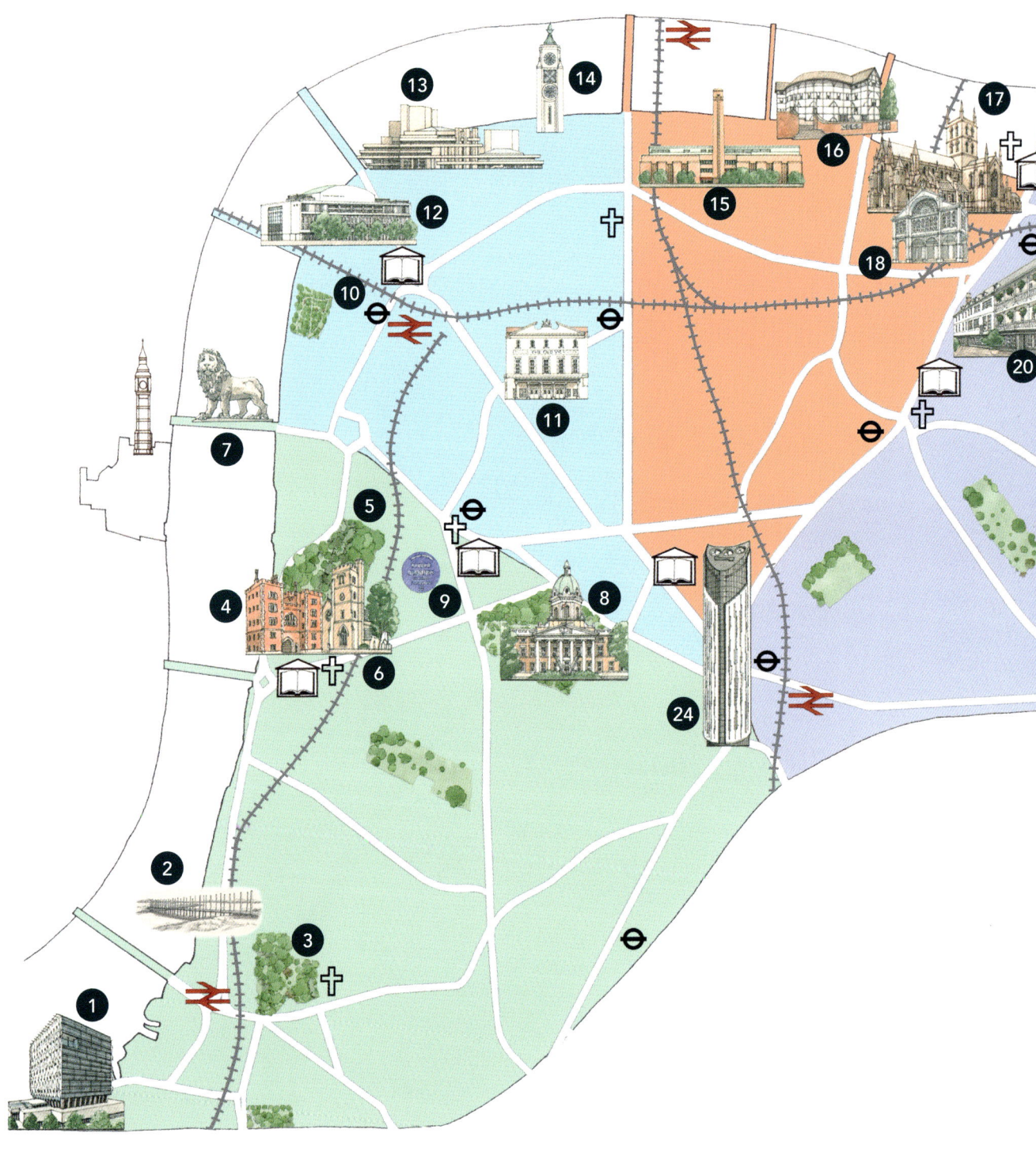

MAP & KEY   13

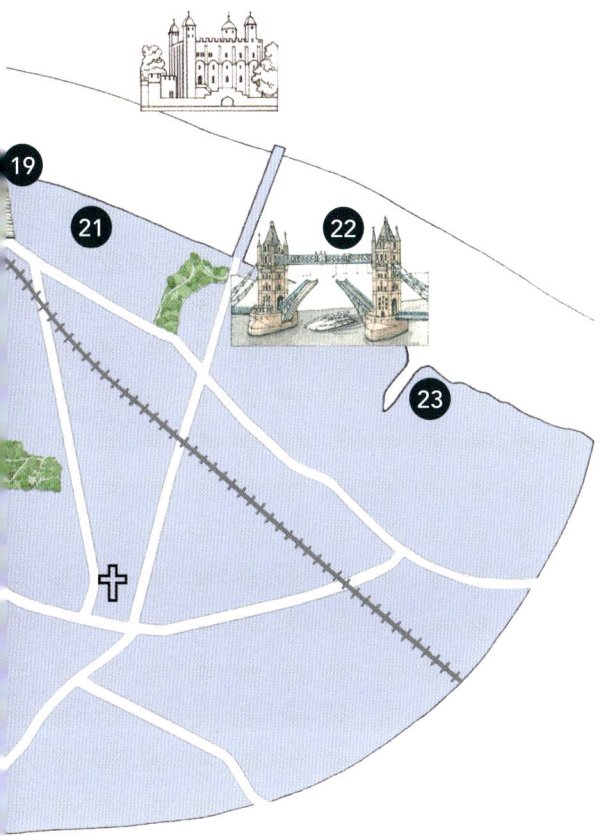

This navigational map for the South Bank has been prepared by Mireille Galinou and drawn by the illustrator Stephen Conlin. © Stephen Conlin

Key

1	US Embassy
2	Vauxhall prehistoric jetty
3	Vauxhall Gardens
4	Lambeth Palace and the church of St Mary
5	Archbishop's Park
6	Garden Museum (= St Mary's Lambeth)
7	Westminster Bridge lion
8	Imperial War Museum
9	William Blake lived there
10	South Bank Place
11	Old Vic
12	Royal Festival Hall
13	National Theatre
14	Oxo Tower
15	Tate Modern
16	Shakespeare's Globe
17	Southwark Cathedral
18	Borough Market
19	The Shard Quarter
20	The George Inn
21	More London
22	Tower Bridge
23	Saint Saviour's Dock
24	Strata building

Vauxhall and Lambeth
Waterloo
Borough and Bankside
Southwark and Bermondsey

☦ Churches
📖 Libraries
⇌ Stations
⊖ Tube stations

Previous and above:
Jiro Osuga, 'Metropolis', 2017,
oil on canvas, 104 x 129 cm.

The artist painted this London picture in the year that I visited India and it encapsulates perfectly the cross-fertilisation of cultures and ideas that I experienced as a result of this revelatory trip: spiritual India versus multi-cultural London.

Jiro Osuga, after admitting he is more comfortable painting buildings than people, writes: 'Buildings are a feast to the eye, and each one of them has a different personality just like people … But much as I love buildings, I have never felt that depictions of architecture without any human presence made for entirely satisfactory paintings.'

His solution? 'I tried to circumvent this difficulty by adopting an alternative approach to painting architecture. I created a quasi-religious altarpiece to the architectural delights of the city, piling up the characteristic building types of London to form a throne, a dais, and a lectern. These host big figures clad in colourful robes, who could be personifications of the spirit of the city.'

(© The artist)

The Quest

I was profoundly moved by a visit to India in October 2017. In Madurai (south India) the Minakshi Sundareshvara Temple dominates the busy city. It is a vibrant and popular institution with a life of its own, a city within the city. The temple, its oldest building, represents layer upon layer of human history. You could argue that it gives this place a soul. A local woman who was there to pay homage to the gods, befriended me and placed between my eyebrows a spot of reddish brown surmounted by a dash of yellow. I felt I was brought within the sacred fold.

I next went to Auroville near Pondicherry (south east India); there I was confronted with another more recent manifestation of a city's soul.

A team of 'seekers' led by Mirra Alfassa (known as 'The Mother') and inspired by the spiritual work of British-educated Sri Aurobindo, founded an ideal city in 1968 based around a magnificent Mandir/Temple. At the heart of it, in the Inner Chamber, a serene circular space, was placed an enormous crystal which captures and reflects the sunlight through a unique roof opening: this crystal represents the soul of Auroville. The town, which is still largely unfinished, was conceived around a natural landmark – an old banyan tree – its geographic centre, while Auroville's spiritual centre was placed nearby – the Matrimandir, dedicated to the Universal Mother, and the repository of the city's soul.

The crystal was installed in April 1991, and in The Mother's words: 'The Matrimandir will be the soul of Auroville. The sooner the soul is there, the better it will be for everybody'.

This led me to my quest for London's own soul. London's geographic centre – the equivalent of Auroville's banyan tree – has been investigated by others (see below) and although final thoughts on London's soul will only be pulled together at the end of this volume, readers are encouraged to keep this important thread uppermost in their minds.

The London Stone, across the river in Cannon Street has sometimes been considered London's 'crystal'. The author Peter Ackroyd hailed it as such in his London *The Biography*: 'It was once London's guardian spirit, and perhaps it is still'. There has indeed been some attempt at turning the ancient 'London stone' into a significant symbol for the capital – A Roman relic to tie us back to London's Roman origins? Or as John Carter described it in 1798 'the symbol of this great city's quiet state'? (*Gentleman's Magazine*). But the medieval historian John Clark's detailed investigation into its story has instead thrown light on to the human creation of a legend rather than the uncovering of a historic truth. In the latest instalment of a long saga, John Clark examines the association of the London stone with the Roman senator Brutus who is supposed to have founded London. This story was manufactured in the fourteenth century, its outcome teetering between fake history and literature. The story comes close to mythic resonance when in 1450, the rebel Jack Cade crossed London Bridge to ride into the City and struck the stone with his sword, identifying himself with John Mortimer, the enemy of Henry VI, he uttered: 'Now is Mortimer Lord of the City'. Ackroyd remarks that this episode suggests that 'this ancient object came somehow to represent the power and authority of the city'. Readers may perceive a faint echo of the sword in the stone, the Arthurian legend which, incidentally, is found in the same manuscript as the Brutus story with the Stone (see John Clark in biblio). Another interpretation recorded in the sixteenth century associates the Stone with another

Above & below:

The crystal-soul of Auroville is inside the Matrimandir temple in a large, sacred and empty room at the top of the sphere. Access is by appointment only. By contrast, the London Stone has always been outside, in the street, inside a walled cavity protected by bars and readily accessible to anyone who notices it.

We could not obtain permission to reproduce the Auroville crystal here, but are reproducing a detail from a 2019 photograph by Ethan Doyle White on Wikimedia Commons to stand for the heart of the Matrimandir and Auroville. (© The author, 2017; Crystal image in the public domain)

legendary figure, King Lud. The names vary but what these stories have in common is the search for *sacred* legitimacy.

For centuries places were made sacred through religion – official, poetic or popular: the miraculous survival of one of London's great symbolic landmarks, St Paul's Cathedral during the Second World War, or William Blake's Peckham vision of angels in a tree or the popular heroes celebrated in Postman's Park in the City (one of its heroines is discussed on pp. 464 ff). But the upheaval of the Reformation in the 1530s and 1540s when all Roman Catholic religious establishments were abolished or changed in use, partially compromised this natural outlet.

Unlike Auroville which obtained its crystal from Germany, the South Bank would probably have once been able to forge its own crystal (see p. 119) while the concept of the Universal Mother finds echo in one of the South Bank's most tragic figures – Alice Ayres (see p. 466). The structure of Auroville into four zones – the International, Cultural, Residential and Industrial – fits the history of the South Bank surprisingly well. The South Bank's theatres and concert halls combine 'international' and 'cultural' appeal while housing has long been an important issue which, in our own times, continues to draw our attention with vertiginous high-rise constructions in the boroughs of Lambeth and Southwark. From the sixteenth to the twentieth century the South Bank was heavily industrial – glassmaking, printing, tanning and brewing representing some of the most significant activities. Peter Ackroyd, as always, has sensed and described the intangible nature of our capital city when writing about Victorian London: 'So great was London that it seemed to contain within itself all previous civilizations'. Still mindful of a spiritual agenda, this is what

P D James wrote in *The Lighthouse* (2005):

> 'London withheld some part of her mystery even from those who loved her. London was history solidified in brick and stone, illuminated in stained glass, celebrated in monument and statue, and yet to Emma it was more a spirit than a place, a vagrant air which breathed down the hidden alleyways, possessed the silence of empty city churches, and lay dormant under her most raucous streets'.

London's South Bank invites readers to dwell on the complexity of a neighbourhood which started life as London's original suburb before becoming an integral part of central London, albeit with a tarnished reputation – often unfair and unjustified.

The book charts the past through a series of panoramic map-views which will give you glimpses, snapshots of the South Bank in history. But we should be mindful not to deal solely with the shell of the past rather than its beating heart. The chapters on individual neighbourhoods try to capture something of the old villages' heart and use a narrative, thematic and interpretative approach rather than simply providing an impersonal survey and catalogue of facts.

For Justine Simons OBE, Deputy Mayor for Culture and Creative Industries in the Mayor of London office, the soul of a London neighbourhood is its culture: she says so in the well-presented *London Bridge Culture Strategy* published by Team London Bridge on 26 February 2018:

> Having great transport and efficient roads alone isn't enough – cities also need a soul, so threading culture through all aspects of city life is key.

But I should not like to take Justine Simons' words at face value. It is dangerous to make or trust assumptions when you go on a quest. The search for truth is sometimes well hidden.

The centre of gravity for London

> London is bent around the Thames; however much the north bank might wish to forget it, the south holds the centre of gravity. The shortest way from Pimlico to the City is via Southwark, not Charing Cross.
> Ian Nairn, *Nairn's London*, 1966

Or put more simply – London wraps around the South Bank and thereby makes it the geometric centre of London. In May 2014, the estate agent Knight Frank issued a press release claiming they had used 'techniques developed by Army cartographers' to reveal the new centre of London – a bench on Victoria Embankment. This infuriated Dr Adam Dennett from CASA (Centre for Advanced Spatial Analysis, UCL) who was approached by London Live TV for comment. Unable to make the interview slot he was offered, he exploded in his personal blog: 'No it's bloody well not the new centre of London!!! I'm not too happy with defining the centre of a massive city like London just by some arbitrary chosen section of road, that just happens to be sort of circular and sort of in the middle.

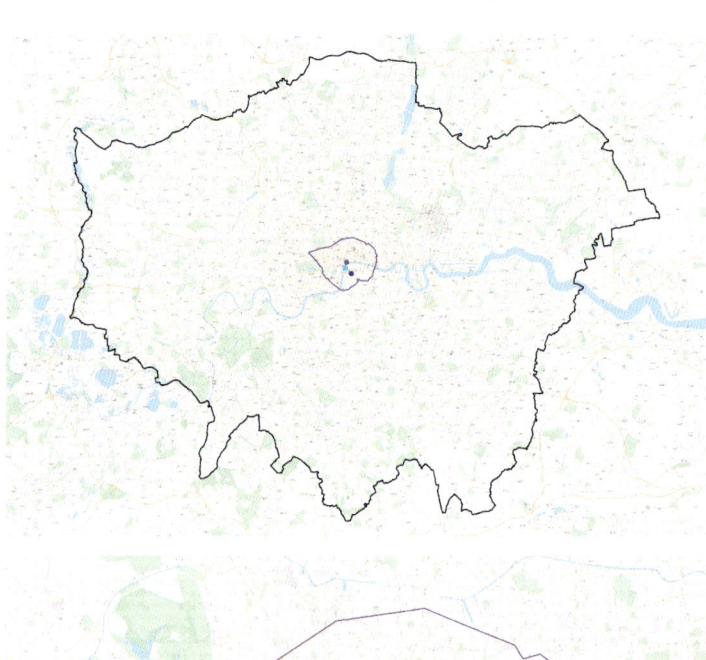

I think we can be a little more sophisticated with our advanced army technique'. Adam Dennett went on to describe the correct way of finding the geographical centre of London.

Four years later ESRI UK (Environmental Systems Research Institute, based in Aylesbury) issued another press release about the 'Exact' geometric centre of the UK's ten largest cities, 'using the latest boundary data released by the ONS [Office for National Statistics] in December 2017'. The result for London was 'on Baylis Road, opposite De-Lady Hair and Beauty Salon, Lambeth SE1'. They explained: 'the geometric centre is a shape's centre of gravity or where it would balance on a pin … Locations have been calculated to 1 metre'. The 'shape' for London is thirty three boroughs including the City of London which, combined, create the Greater London area.

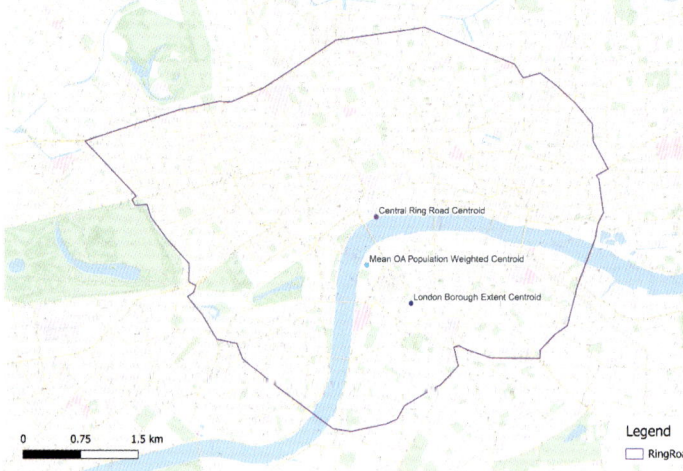

But what would happen if instead of the 'shape' we were to add people to the equation? Adam Dennett explained:

'Us geographers quite often use …. 'Population Weighted Centroids' [which] take account of where people actually live'. And this is how it can be done: 'Results from the 2011 Census are released for zones of around 300 people called Output Areas … What I have done is calculate the mean centre of all the population weighted centroids for all of the Output Areas in all of the London Boroughs … if we take population into account the centre of London moves to … somewhere in the Shell Centre just off the entrance ramp to Waterloo Bridge'.

Be it shape or population driven, the centre of London is firmly on the South Bank, close to Waterloo Station – which, with London Bridge station, represent the South Bank's two beating hearts.

How big is the South Bank in this book?

Nowadays most people think of the South Bank* as the area in and around the South Bank Centre but this view is far too restrictive to be left unchallenged. No-one on the north bank has appropriated the expression to describe a fraction of its natural spread. The South Bank should be restored to its full dimensions, as it will be worth dwelling on the great London north/south divide.

The area under discussion is shown on the map reproduced at p. 12 and is formed of the northern parts of the London Boroughs of Southwark and Lambeth. It stretches from Vauxhall (south west) to Jacob's Island beyond Tower Bridge (east), is bordered by the Thames on the north and west sides and goes down to the Elephant & Castle (south). The area is roughly shaped like a fan with its main articulation point at the Elephant & Castle. Within the shape of the fan, it forms four areas defined by main roads and bridges. These areas are Vauxhall & Lambeth, Waterloo, Bankside & Borough, Southwark & Bermondsey. The divisions are not arbitrary but they are not 'scientific' either – this working solution simply helps us look at a strategic area – what is across the river from the main foundation of London, namely the City, Westminster and the West End. The partitioning works as a whole and it neatly divides into neighbourhoods, which more or less correspond to the original villages which first took shape on the South Bank.

Historically all these neighbourhoods were once unified, forming part of the County of Surrey. Our stretch of the South Bank is delimited by the following topographical markers: the Thames; St Saviour's dock on the east side, a natural indentation which has survived from waterworld days, was used as a dock by the monks of Bermondsey Abbey and is now the heart of the St Saviour's conservation area; the remains of a small prehistoric jetty or 'bridge' at Vauxhall; finally, at the Elephant & Castle – a major road junction which first took shape in the eighteenth century.

I have adopted capital letters throughout the book whenever the phrase is used to denote the area under review, lower case when it is used to denote a wider geographical term.

Opposite:
These maps show the three calculations mentioned in the text for obtaining London's centre of gravity. The purple dot relates to Knight Frank's partial result (Embankment), based on the central ring road. The turquoise blue dot shows the geographical centre of gravity in Pearman Street, using all thirty-three London boroughs, while the dark blue dot based on London's population shows 'the average centroid of all population-weighted output areas [OAs] (small census-based geographies)' explains Professor Dennett. With the last calculation the dot moves to the river bank immediately north of Jubilee Gardens.
(Maps prepared by Professor Adam Dennett, Bartlett Centre for Advanced Spatial Analysis (CASA), University College London. © OpenStreetMap contributors)

Above and previous:
Timothy Hyman, 'Utopian thoughts while crossing Waterloo Bridge' (detail), oil on canvas, 2009. The artist is looking at the South Bank from the northern end of Waterloo Bridge. His thoughts have been painted upside-down in a bubble placed next to his self-portrait in the foreground – the ten dancing female figures come from Lorenzetti's mid-fourteenth-century fresco 'Allegory of Good Government' in Siena's Palazzo Publico (Italy), Hayman's favourite. Few artists have followed Timothy Hyman's example and turned 'their eye' onto the South Bank. This painting captures in all its glory the magnificent, the exhilarating panoramic sweep afforded by Waterloo Bridge, taking in the City of London (left) and Westminster (right). The South Bank's main landmarks are the London Eye and County Hall, the Royal Festival Hall and the Shell Centre.

(© The artist, Private Collection)

The eye of London is both the eye of the artist and its chosen viewpoint for depicting London. For centuries the eye of London has been based on the south bank – the most satisfactory viewpoint for capturing the City of London bristling with church steeples and overlooking the Thames – 'the most loved of all the Ocean's Sons' the poet John Denham tells us. This chapter unpacks, chronologically, the birth, growth and full development of London in art and the persistent dominance of the south bank as the artist's favoured viewpoint.

Going Back in Time

Some readers will be familiar with the name of John Stow (1525–1605), London's first historian. I suspect far fewer will recognize the name of Edmund Howes (working between 1602 and 1631), an English chronicler who lived quite literally in the shadow of John Stow; spending his working life revising and expanding two of Stow's publications including Stow's final book, *The Annales of England*. Howes published two further editions, the last edition, in 1631, contained this phrase:

> 'After the Royal Exchange, which is now called the
> Eye of London …'

The Royal Exchange had been in existence for sixty years when this was written but by then, it should have been clear to all that the real 'eye' of London was not in the City but on the South Bank. This has hardly changed in several centuries – from artists climbing up the stairs of St Mary Overie's tower in the sixteenth century (now Southwark Cathedral) to artists climbing up the London Eye (Timothy Hyman) – the temporary structure which so impressed London that it became a permanent fixture. London's best viewpoint for artists intent on capturing the city, is the South Bank; and there is an exciting new platform – 'the view from the Shard', this venue's marketing slogan.

Is it a coincidence if the image of London was forged, true to life, in the middle of the sixteenth century, shortly after Henry VIII's own version of Brexit – England's separation from the Church of Rome and the dissolution of the monasteries? And is it a coincidence if the first and most influential images of London were created by foreigners?

The past, the present and indeed the future are so inextricably connected that it may seem futile to even think of disentangling all the different strands. However, it is possible to enter this extraordinary world of connections, 'correspondances' as Baudelaire described them, which echo down the centuries.

Opposite:
Jiro Osuga, 'Window' 2016, oil on board
This tiny, postcard-size, painting offers bold intentions: 'Eyes are often referred to as the windows to the soul. In a child's drawing of anthropomorphized houses, the eyes are always represented by windows. People often speak of ancient buildings as having borne witness to history as if they had a pair of eyes', wrote the artist who also highlighted the tension unleashed by a clash of scale – a giant trapped inside a window? Whatever their handicap, painters continue to be our eyes on the world and this is particularly true of the relationship between artists and the subject of London. For this artist's version of London from the South Bank, see pp. 532–535
(© Jiro Osuga, Flowers Gallery)

To see and be seen

We will start in 2007, seven years into the new millennium. Were you in London then? Do you remember seeing the naked life-size casts of British sculptor Antony Gormley RA? They had been placed along the South Bank, on top of high buildings and with one at ground level on Waterloo Bridge. They acted as an intriguing device to draw attention to the Gormley exhibition on show at the Hayward Gallery, 'Blind Light'. But a simple marketing ploy, they certainly were not. Antony Gormley had been 'placing his body' in the environment for at least three decades before the Hayward Gallery show gave the artist his first proper urban outing. And it was on the South Bank.

Gormley's urban outing had been a long gestation – from the 1974 'Sleeping Place' when the artist, foetus or cocoon-like, was enveloped in a white sheet, before gradually assuming a standing pose in 1982 in 'A View Land Sea and Air II'. In 1997 the project reached heroic dimensions with 'Another Place' first exhibited in Germany, then Norway and Belgium before finding a permanent resting place – not without controversy – at Crosby Beach in Merseyside. It is also the body of Antony Gormley, blown up to a gigantic scale, which rests on the gentle hill of Low Eighton in Gateshead: there 'the Angel of the North' has been radiating benevolent and spiritual vibes since 1998.

But the South Bank Gormley figures were not made to confront the natural elements of their predecessors – tidal sea and wind. On Waterloo Bridge Gormley mingled with the tide of commuters and tourists, and the Gormleys perched on top of the South Bank Centre, the National Theatre and other neighbouring blocks, cast a non-judgemental eye on the horizon of north and south London. The installation was called 'Event Horizon' and consisted of thirty one bodies (twenty seven in fibreglass and four in cast iron). Their quiet, determined and innocent appearance seemed real enough from a distance and the statues were occasionally mistaken for potential suicides, in London where they were first exhibited and also in New York, Sao Paolo, Rio de Janeiro, and Hong Kong. The South Bank 'bodies' were taken down many years ago but for those who saw them and were moved by them, their haunting presence resonates to this day.

When the local turns global

Antony Gormley RA has long enjoyed the status of 'international artist' – both in outreach and in content. His art does not appear to be limited by time or location and he was the perfect presenter of the fascinating BBC television programme 'How art began' first broadcast on 26 January 2019 – a project

Above:
Antony Gormley – birth of the artist as a standing figure
'Sleeping Place', 1974, Plaster and linen, 55 x 91 x 106 cm.
(© The artist)
'Land Sea and Air II', 1982, 45 x 103 x 50 cm – Land (crouching), 191 x 50 x 32 cm; Sea (standing), 118 x 69 x 52 cm; Air (kneeling).
(© The artist)
'Another Place', installation view, Crosby Beach, Merseyside, England, 1997, Cast iron, 189 x 53 x 29 cm (100 elements). Photograph by Stephen White, London.
(© The artist)

Opposite:
Antony Gormley's 'Event Horizon' at the Hayward Gallery, 2007. The cast of the artist's naked body stands, imperturbable, on top of the South Bank Centre.
(Chris Deeney/Alamy Stock Photo)

Antony Gormley, 'Event Horizon' 2007, twenty seven fibreglass and four cast iron figures, 189 x 53 x 29 cm, installation view, Hayward Gallery, London, England. This general view shows Waterloo Bridge and includes two solitary Gormley casts standing on the roofs of the South Bank Centre's Queen Elizabeth Hall and Purcell Room. (Photograph by Richard Bryant, © The artist)

which unexpectedly blended very local themes with global ones. This has a particular resonance with London's South Bank where the international remit of the South Bank Centre, Tate Modern or the Globe echoes the powerful local impact made by William Shakespeare and other contemporaries. Antony Gormley travelled across the globe and thousands of years back in time to discover that the 'local' exists spontaneously at opposite ends of the globe – prehistoric art in French and Spanish caves echoes that newly discovered in caves in Indonesia and of course Australia, where the continuity of art between past and present is awe inspiring. Now that the vexed question of dating those ancient drawings has been partially solved by scientists, there have been major breakthroughs in interpreting these first manifestations of human art. Anthony Gormley summed it up in a phrase which merged the incredibly distant past with the here and now when he was filming at Sulewesi in Indonesia:

> Here we are in a completely different culture, latitude, different side of the world … [and here we have] the same idea of leaving a mark [stencilled hands] …. On the one hand you're invited to put your hand and say: I've just hi-fived somebody from 30,000 years ago, and then on the other it's saying … here is what will be, long after the person who made it has gone, but also long after I who come after him will be gone.

These connections across time and place become even more tangible if we turn to another artist, Timothy Hyman RA.

As part of his London Eye residency 'Taking on London', Timothy Hyman also drew from the top of Guy's Hospital tower (2003-04). Charcoal drawing. (© The artist, Trustees of the British Museum)

The London Eye

In 2002 Timothy Hyman secured a residency, 'Taking on London' with the London Arts Café (see 'Art and Cities' in bibliography). It enabled him to pursue his passion for panoramic views, this time based on the views afforded by the London Eye and also Guy's Hospital. By contrast with Antony Gormley's impassive figures Timothy's wish was 'to internalise the totality of the city – to be able to grasp it, in a way that a medieval cosmographer might grasp "the world"'. He described the Eye as 'a modified spaceship, by which we visit Planet London'.

London has been Hyman's muse all his life and it can be traced back to a single powerful moment: falling in love with Lorenzetti's fourteenth-century frescoes of Good and Bad Government in Siena, Italy, hence the use of one of its details in the painting which opens this chapter (see caption on p. 24). This revelatory work has fired up the artist's imagination ever since – he is arguably a modern version of Lorenzetti for London. His attachment to Sienese painting in general runs very deep and led him to write a book on this topic in the Thames and Hudson World of Art series (about to be re-issued at the time of writing).

Both Gormley and Hyman are firmly connected to London's north bank: Gormley was born in Hampstead Garden Suburb and despite an early studio in Peckham – close to Bellenden Road where he contributed an interesting group of street bollards – his large studio is now to be found on the streets of regenerated and fashionable King's Cross. Hyman's childhood was spent in west London and his chosen home in later life has been in Clerkenwell/Islington. He describes the South Bank as 'terra incognita' in his painting 'My London Cosmos' (reproduced in this publisher's *The Streatham Sketchbook*) though possibly the best painting he made of the South Bank (rather than from the South Bank) was not from the London Eye but from the north end of Waterloo Bridge (see pp. 22–23).

The artistic search for high viewpoints along the South Bank, is immensely interesting, as a way of understanding London for Hyman, or placing oneself within the urban environment for Gormley. This is precisely where the image of London started, some five hundred years ago, in the sixteenth century. This London story is rarely told though it describes the vital role played by the South Bank in providing a viewpoint for artists wishing to capture London's essence, or even its soul.

The Legacy Of The Middle Ages

The birth of the London cityscape in the sixteenth century was underpinned by the medieval interest in defining this city. The sense of civic identity which developed in the twelfth and thirteenth centuries encouraged city leaders to commission suitable imagery for town seals. Writers, too, sought to describe their cities (*descriptiones*) – the earliest for Milan dates from the eighth century, the first in a long list of descriptions and the longest for any city! The most influential description was written for Rome in 1143. This interest in representing towns/cities in words and pictures was a European-wide phenomenon and the two outstanding London examples are William Fitzstephen's 'Description of the Most Noble City of London' which prefaces his Life of Thomas Becket (1170s) and also the breathtaking images found on the City Common Seal (dated around 1214 by Elizabeth New). Both the description and the seal are connected to Becket when the trend for venerating saints – particularly those who died a violent death – was gathering momentum.

The interpretation of European cities in words and pictures has been researched by scholars who appear to reach a similar conclusion: they note the move away from symbolic and idealized cities and the gradual introduction of increasingly realistic details. For J K Hyde, the common trend in the *Descriptiones* was 'away from generalized literary *laudes* [praise] … towards a concentration on specific details often of a statistical nature'. Brigitte M Bedos-Rezak who researched medieval city seals, noted that the monuments and people depicted, gradually acquired realistic features. So a greater sense of realism was where all this was leading, perhaps culminating in Geoffrey Chaucer's famous *Canterbury Tales* – one of the first literary works to be written in spoken English (not French or Latin), set in a real setting – Southwark's Tabard Inn and with characters or types familiar to all Londoners at the end of the fourteenth century.

The City of London Common Seal

This seal is so unusual in its imagery and so perfectly executed that many, to this day, have puzzled over its correct interpretation.

On the obverse side: St Paul, London's patron saint, stands in the middle of the walled city, ready to defend London, lifting his sword to the sky and strategically positioned behind the main city gate. The spiky cityscape – more swords rather than steeples – echoes the saint's own lifted weapon. Scholars have suggested that the city represented could be made to match the topography of medieval London. But there are many features which elude this interpretation and the extraordinary symmetry alone, on both sides of the seal, suggests other priorities. It is possible to observe that the obverse is taken from the south bank as it shows the flowing Thames licking the foot of the walled city.

Whereas Archbishop Thomas Becket on the reverse is seated, Christ-like, on a semi-circular arc which later artists, in the fifteenth century, will represent as a rainbow. The saint is shown risen above the city which gave birth to him, London reclaiming its vital place in the saint's life whose martyrdom in Canterbury was drawing pilgrims to that site instead. Becket's origins are firmly on the north bank and his birthplace, in Cheapside, soon became a shrine after the archbishop's violent death. Becket also has a strong association with London Bridge: many historians believe it was his death and the meteoric rise of his cult as a saint which gave the final impetus to rebuilding the bridge in stone rather than timber. And on this bridge of stone, a chapel dedicated to St Thomas was erected (see p. XX).

Elizabeth New has pointed out how exceptional it was to find such a blend of buildings and people on city seals; and how ambitious to represent a small crowd on a matrix of just over seven centimetres in diameter! The figure of Becket is framed by a group representing the civic elite on the left and clerics on the right. This is unique in Europe and puts a (temporary) stop to the puzzling question – is a city represented by its walls or its people? Isidore of Seville was the first to formulate it in the seventh century. Here, it is clearly both, though from the eighteenth century onwards artists tend to fall into one camp or the other, sometimes striking deals with fellow artists to produce totally accomplished pictures. The most famous collaboration within a London context is Pugin and Rowlandson for *The Microcosm of London* (1808-10): Augustus Charles Pugin responsible for the architecture and Thomas Rowlandson bringing life to his settings with lively figures.

The Sixteenth Century

There was a sombre conjunction of events in mid-sixteenth-century London which engendered new ideas and new subjects for painters. The destruction of religious images and the prosecution of those who ignored the royal edict ensured that the seismic change initiated by Henry VIII was serious. At the King's death in 1547, the nine-year-old Edward VI succeeded his father and barely six months into his reign, in the words of art historian Margaret Aston:

> a royal visitation authorized the clergy to "take away, utterly extinct and destroy" all shrines, pictures, paintings and monuments of superstition and idolatry in their churches and to encourage parishioners to do the same in their own houses.

Three years later in 1550 the city which had long sought control over Southwark finally struck a deal with Edward VI and his advisers;

The City Common Seal dates from around 1214 and shows (obverse) the City's patron saint St Paul inside the walled City, armed with an uplifted sword, in a protective gesture and (reverse) St Thomas Becket, seated on an all-embracing arc above London, his native city, whose spiritual protector he is. The inscriptions on the City Common Seal place great emphasis on the people rather than the walls of the city. (obverse) 'Seal of the Barons of London' who are at the top of the social ladder and (reverse) 'Do not cease, Thomas, to protect me who gave you birth' – the city itself, personified, addressing her saint, Thomas Becket, asking for his protection.
(British Library Board. All Rights reserved/ Bridgeman Images)

large swathes of Southwark lost their independence and the city acquired a new alderman and a new ward: London Bridge without.

The destruction of pictures/the creation of pictures

The Reformation is not simply about the separation of the English church from Rome or the abolition of monasteries, it is also about the destruction of pictures – on panel, inside books, on walls or on stained glass windows.

There is a late but vivid episode of this intolerance at Lambeth Palace when it was the home of Archbishop Laud (1633–1645). It is related in detail in Michael Archer's article on the glass-painter 'Richard Butler of Southwark'.

> **The accuser** challenged the archbishop who 'caused these demolished superstitious Pictures in the Glasse windows to be repaired, furbished, beautified … so as no chapel in Rome could be more Idolatrous, Popish, superstitious in regard of such offensive pictures, than his at Lambeth'.
>
> **Laud's response:** 'The truth is, they [the windows] were all shameful to look on, all diversely patched, like a Poor Beggar's Coat … The windows contain the whole story from the creation of the Day of Judgment: I know no Crime, or Superstition in this History: And though Calvin do not approve Images in Churches, he doth approve very well of them which contains a History; and says plainly, that these have their use … in Teaching and Admonishing the People …
>
> But here the Statute of Ed.6 [Edward VI] was charged against me, *which requires the Destruction of all Images as well in Glass-windows,* as elsewhere to which I answered … First, that the Statute of Ed.6 spake of other images; and that Images in Glass-windows, were neither mentioned, nor meant in that Law: The words of the Statute are, *Any Images of Stone, Timber, Alabaster or Earth; Graven, Carved or Painted,* taken out of any Church, &c shall be *Destroyed,* etc and not reserved to any Superstitious Use. So there's not a word of Glass-windows.

The most extreme bouts of iconoclasm occurred during the reign of Edward VI (1547–1553) and the Protectorate of his uncle the duke of Somerset who set out to reorganize religion along firmly Protestant lines; it was followed by regular outbursts of anti-papal sentiment such as the overzealous arguments made at Lambeth Palace above, or the destruction of the medieval Eleanor cross in Cheapside in 1643 during the English Civil Wars.

Despite religious upheaval, the image of cities emerged in Europe, though a little later in London than in Italy, France or Germany. After the pioneering but not necessarily reliable *Nuremberg Chronicles* of 1493, follows the breathtaking map-view of Venice by Jacopo de Barbari (1500). The status of artists in Europe started to rise – first in Italy, a little more slowly elsewhere. In 1550 Vasari published his *Lives of the Artists*. Before him, the names of artists were barely recorded. The London example which comes to mind in this context is the *Self-Portrait* of 1579 by gentleman-artist George Gower. The art historian

'Antwerpia in Brabancia': A view of Antwerp from across the river Schelde, by an anonymous painter, oil on panel, c.1540. This large and extraordinary painting shows how sophisticated the art of capturing cities in paint had become in the Low Countries.
(Museum aan de Stroom (MAS), Antwerp; image in the public domain, Wikimedia Commons)

Karen Hearn writes that 'Gower … proclaims his status as an artist to be greater than his status as a gentleman by birth … [and] he depicts himself holding a brush and palette'.

Antwerp and London

The growing commercial links and migration between London and Antwerp at this time is documented in John Wheeler's 1601 pamphlet 'A Treatise of Commerce'. It explains that at first there were only twelve to sixteen Low Countries merchants in England but by 1560 their number had increased to one hundred (source: Puttevils). The close links with Antwerp in particular, led to the building of Thomas Gresham's Royal Exchange in 1569, on the model of Antwerp's *Bourse*.

Both Richard III and Henry VIII had encouraged alien migration, particularly craftsmen – Henry VIII through a series of official statutes in the 1520s. This clashed with the City of London's own goals: the encouragement of *English* trade. Tension gradually mounted on the streets of London leading to Evil May Day on 30 April 1517 when around 1000 English youths gathered in Cheapside and ransacked the homes of aliens. Some of the instigators were put to death and immigration continued, leading to many more complaints. To appease citizens the Privy Council ordered three surveys of London aliens and foreigners in 1568 and 1571. This census is known as 'The Return of Aliens' and has been published by the Huguenot Society. It has proved an invaluable source of information for foreign artists based in London, including the South Bank.

These commercial links played a pivotal role in art because Antwerp artists had long been engaged in the practice of realistic portraiture – of people of course but also of cities (the earliest prospect of Antwerp, an anonymous woodcut in the Plantin-Moretus Museum, dates from 1515). From the 1540s Flemish merchants but also artists were coming to London in increasing numbers. The community of artists on the north bank is better known, but there was a large and substantial 'Doche' community in Southwark which consisted of French, Dutch, German and Flemish immigrants loosely grouped around the churches of St Olave in Tooley Street and St Mary Magdalen in Bermondsey Street. Whether settled on the north or south banks, all, eventually, were made to register.

The art historian Hope Walker gave the number of alien painters in London as thirty nine. I have scoured 'The Return of Aliens' for entries in Surrey, in search of artists living in Vauxhall, Lambeth, Bankside, Southwark and Bermondsey, and cross-referencing with Edward Town's research. The outcome is disappointing – a mere three or four names with only one, Hans Eworth, from Southwark, who is both documented on paper and with a body of work which can be ascribed to him – predictably linked to royal or aristocratic patronage (right).

Independently from 'The Return of Aliens' the art historian Erna Auerbach identified 'a group of craftsmen and artists in the royal employment, partly of foreign origin, who lived in the parish of Bermondsey … [and] were on terms of friendship, intermarried and were efficient and versatile in their respective crafts'. This early artists' community was pieced together: Henry/Harry Blankston from Cologne and denizened by the King in 1534, was employed by Henry VIII at Hampton Court; and left a will. Garrard Hone, his son-in-law, was also a painter and the son of Galyon Hone, the King's glazier; followed by Robert Schynk painter, of the same parish of St Mary Magdalen. The former Victoria and Albert Museum curator Michael Archer independently established that 'Southwark was the area where a large number of glass-painters lived in the first half of the sixteenth century including Galyon Hone, James Nicholson, Francis Williamson and Richard Butler'. We know from a 1535 complaint made against the master and brothers of St Thomas' Hospital that Galyon Hone, one of the victims, lived within the hospital's precinct.

Since religious painting had become controversial and demand ceased, portraiture became a safe and increasingly popular outlet for artists. This has been widely acknowledged, but not the development of urban imagery, a subject which has remained neglected.

The gradual emergence of London as a subject for artists was not simply a response to the loss of religious subjects. The historian J A van Dorsten has explained that following the disillusionment caused by the shortcomings of the Roman Catholic church, the ideas which grew in Europe and spread to London, often via Antwerp, led to the creation in 1540 of a spiritual but non-religious movement – the Family of Love. Its message of charity and inner light could be achieved through understanding the world, whether it be of local, national or global significance. This conciliatory movement hoped to rid Europe of the divisions between Catholics and Protestants. A number of Antwerp artists belonged to the new 'geographical school' which sought to understand man's urban or rural environment.

According to Van Dorsten:

> Theology as the traditional science of revelation had failed visibly to unite mankind in one indisputably "true" perception of God's plan … The Antwerp geographers and cosmographers attempted to reveal God's creation scientifically and reconstruct the pageant of man's history.

The role played by Antwerp in the sixteenth century, further consolidated by Amsterdam in the seventeenth century, cannot be overestimated. However strange this may seem to us now, the first image of London, one that still resonates with us today, was unquestionably created by a foreigner or, in the language of the day, an 'alien'.

The first long view of London and other contemporary works

Dated 1544, this is the earliest known work by the poorly documented Flemish artist Anthonis van den Wyngaerde (c. 1525–1571). There is no firm date for his birth or even place of birth though

This double portrait of Queen Mary and her husband Philip II of Spain, by Hans Eworth (c. 1520–1574) is interesting in this context for it merges the two types of portraiture which thrived in the sixteenth century after the religious split – people and cities. The view glimpsed through the window is frequently described as showing Old St Paul's Cathedral from across the Thames, i.e., taken from the south bank. The cathedral's outline is convincing enough but the presence of a dome on the right, seen through the partially opened window, discredits this identification. A date of c. 1554 has been suggested for this painting.
(From the Woburn Abbey Collection)

Detail from Prospect of London, unfinished drawing by Anthonis van den Wyngaerde, 1544. This is the first long view of London, a unique document which records the capital in the mid-sixteenth century, before the arrival of theatres on Bankside (1580s) and before the impressive spire of St Paul's Cathedral came tumbling down after being hit by lightning in 1561. With details showing Suffolk House in Long Southwark above and a Bermondsey cottage right.
(© Ashmolean Museum, University of Oxford)

one Anthonis van den Wyngaerde is documented in Antwerp in 1510 – a little too early but possibly a relative. Van den Wyngaerde's best documented work belongs to the period when he was in the service of Philip II of Spain, from around 1557 (Philip was king of England between 1554-58 when he was married to Mary Tudor). But for his London period and in the words of art historian Susan Foister: 'no record of Wyngaerde's presence in England survives, and his career is a blank for most of the next decade'. Who was van den Wyngaerde's patron when he was walking up and down the South Bank to draw his London view? Foister finds it hard 'to conceive that a very young artist would have been in a position to take on such an ambitious piece of work … or that he would have found the necessary support to enable him to do so.'

By contrast, Peter Barber, who has extensively researched the collections of Henry VIII, is convinced that the young Wyngaerde had to be one of the many artists the King attracted to his court in the 1540s when, after the dissolution of the monasteries, he was, briefly, fabulously wealthy. Barber is convinced that the long view was a preparatory drawing for a mural at Whitehall Palace which he thinks could have been sited in the Privy Chamber, perhaps facing the famous Holbein family portrait? Since Whitehall Palace burnt down in 1698 and murals do not appear in inventories, there is no direct way to substantiate this suggestion.

However, this supposition is backed up by two facts: Wyngaerde's later career at the Escorial near Madrid where he produced numerous murals of cities, for his royal patron Philip II (some have survived). Philip was not alone in showing an interest in city views – consider for instance the cycle of city murals at the Palazzo Vecchio in Florence. Secondly, closer to home, the

programme of murals carried out by Holbein for Cowdray Castle, destroyed by fire in 1793, but after they were recorded in great detail by the Society of Antiquaries. They contained several representations of cities, mostly connected to historical events except for the 'straight' view of Calais in the Dining Parlour.

The visualizing of cities in Europe was well under way by the time Wyngaerde produced his long view. There were two separate strands – one connected to royal patronage and the fashion for picturing cities, battles and maps in large murals. The other, northern European, produced paintings or pictorial maps of cities on a more domestic scale. Wyngaerde's long view of London followed closely the formula developed at Antwerp and many artists would have been aware or indeed practiced at creating sophisticated portraits of cities (see p. 33). Both Marcus Gheeraerts the Elder and Lucas de Heere who will be discussed below produced prospects of their native city – Bruges for Gheeraerts and Ghent for de Heere; both were in London in the second half of the sixteenth century.

There are earlier images of London hidden in manuscripts but nothing on the scale of van den Wyngaerde's extraordinary drawing. It set the full extent of the long view of London – from Westminster to well beyond the Tower of London with a partial view of the South Bank. It is a very sketchy affair but is particularly informative about Borough High Street in Southwark, prompting historian Howard Colvin to note: 'shown in somewhat greater architectural detail than the buildings on the north side of the river', a significant remark linked to the viewpoint but perhaps, too, patronage? Wyngaerde has also drawn buildings not otherwise recorded such as Suffolk House and a Bermondsey cottage. One of the view's most remarkable

'Civitas Londini', Prospect of London by John Norden, engraving on four sheets, 1600 and the only complete copy now in existence. The detail with the inscription 'Statio Prospectiva' shows the artist's viewpoint – the tower of St Saviour's church, now Southwark Cathedral.
(National Library of Sweden, Stockholm; image in the public domain, Wikimedia Commons)

features is the depiction of Old St Paul's with its spire, one of the loftiest in Europe at 149 metres. For comparison, the spire of Mechelen's Cathedral was planned in the fourteenth century as 'the tallest spire in the world' at 167 metres but was left unfinished at 97 metres, while the spire of Antwerp's cathedral is 123 metres and that of Cologne's cathedral stretches to 157 metres, just overtaken by Ulm's at 161 metres. Old St Paul's lost its spire in a storm in 1561 and it was never replaced.

How influential would this long view have been? Not very much if we consider the points made by Susan Foister. The London prospect was acquired by the Ashmolean Museum in the nineteenth century as part of the Sutherland collection and the Wyngaerde drawings appear to have been purchased by Mrs Sutherland from the London art dealer Colnaghi in 1823, who in turn had purchased

the drawings at auction in Antwerp. If Wyngaerde took his drawings with him when he left England – this is suggested by Susan Foister – and the drawings remained abroad until the 1820s, this leaves little room for opportunities to see and be influenced by the work; unless of course these drawings were turned into a large mural at the King's Palace which many would have seen?

The next important prospect of London from the South Bank is that of John Norden (c.1547–1625); it dates from 1600 and is the second earliest printed long view (the first being the view from the north described below) with the charming detail of the artist's viewpoint (right). In the seventeenth century Dulwich College purchased a copy of another version of this print and a rare near-contemporary witness, John Bagford, described how it was displayed there: 'on the staircase, I had a sight of it … Mr Secretary Pepys went afterwards to view it by my recommendation and was very desirous to have purchased it. But since it is decayed and quite destroyed by means of the moisture on the walls … I have not met with any other of the like kind' (source: Hyde 1985).

The first maps of London

One of the artists of the 'geographical movement' in the sixteenth century was Frans Hogenberg (1535–1590), the author of many plates in the groundbreaking publication *Civitates Orbis Terrarum* (1572–1617) – an atlas of world cities which was a collaboration between George Braun's texts and Frans Hogenberg's maps. London was the first pictorial map in this ambitious project, where the mapmaker adopted a bird's eye view, positioning himself above the South Bank, looking north. However, on this occasion, the map was not one of Hogenberg's creations. We owe it to the 1550s anonymous mapmaker who produced the large and masterly Copperplate map – so called because no printed copy of it exists and only three out of the original fifteen sections of this map have come to light as copperplates (the best account is Peter Barber's

This map of London was the very first city to feature in the groundbreaking Cologne publication *Civitates Orbis Terrarum*, a series of six volumes of town plans (1572–1617) compiled by Georg Braun and Frans Hogenberg. For London, the authors produced a miniature version of the 'lost' Copperplate map (1550s). It was first published in 1572 but this edition dates from 1574 when the Royal Exchange, missing from the first edition, was inserted in its proper place. For the 'beere house' on the right-hand side of the print (see SB26 on p.138).
(Universitätsbibliothek Heidelberg – [VD16-B7188]; Image in the public domain, Wikimedia Commons)

in Saunders & Schofield 2001). The *Civitates Orbis Terrarum* project simply published a miniature version of this map in 1572.

A map detective would not fail to notice several peculiarities about this map – at least two of these should be highlighted here. In the 1550s when the very first map of London was published – the Copperplate map – the Royal Exchange had not yet been built; it therefore did not feature on this map, and was also missing from the 1572 miniature version. But the new interest in accuracy – and the Royal Exchange was not a landmark which could be ignored – meant that in the 1574 edition of the map this mistake had been corrected. There is another glaring mistake in the Braun and Hogenberg map – the presence of the spire of St Paul's Cathedral which was lost in 1561 and never replaced. This was not corrected, perhaps because it would have meant taking away from the view something which was perceived as symbolic and which many people thought might be reinstated in due course. As for the figures in the foreground they represent, in the words of the historian Van Dorsten, the 'pageant of man's history': a group of wealthy Londoners standing on a convenient but imaginary hill.

This map and the Wyngaerde drawing were used extensively in the reconstruction of London around 1600 on pp. 86–87.

The first London landscape – A fête at Bermondsey

> The [English] inventories examined … reveal a clear change in English collecting habits over the Tudor period as a whole, from the predominance of alabasters, gilded sculpture and devotional paintings, to *a new emphasis on painted pictures with secular subjects including portraits.*
> Susan Foister, 'Paintings and other works of art in sixteenth century English inventories, *Burlington Magazine* (vol. XXIII, No 938, May 1981)

The painting, 'A fête at Bermondsey', sometimes called 'A marriage fête at Bermondsey' is a perfect illustration of what Susan Foister observed when she reviewed almost seventy English inventories in search of works of art. One of these was for a Southwark resident named 'Sent' though he only possessed a Head of St John – apparently a popular subject before the Reformation.

'A fête at Bermondsey', is the first London landscape painting, and as the art historian Edward Town states: 'one of the earliest, if not the earliest, depictions of a landscape in British art'. It is dated 1571 and is remarkable for including the Tower of London in the background, identifying the locality depicted – Bermondsey, across the Thames, south of the Tower. Edward Town has recently reassessed the painting, particularly in the light of the discovery of a second painting, 'A Village Festival', closely related to this fête but not featuring the Tower of London (both paintings now at Hatfield House, see bibliography). 'A fête' has probably been in the collection of Hatfield since at least 1611, the date of the first inventory, possibly 'the picture of the solemnities of a marriage'. The painting's inscription which for years could not be properly deciphered has recently revealed the date to be 1571 and also the name of the artist – Marcus Gheeraerts the Elder, and not Joris Hoefnagel as was previously thought. The analysis also revealed that the name Hoefnagel which misled art historians into thinking the artist was Joris Hoefnagel

These two oil panels by Marcus Gheeraerts the Elder (c. 1520 – c. 1590) – 'A Fête at Bermondsey' (1571) and 'A Village Festival' were recently reunited. They are clearly by the same artist and depict the same scene. The former was previously thought to be by Joris Hoefnagel but new research has shown this was a misattribution. The details all come from the painting above and show
1. The Maypole near the artillery ground, with the Tower of London;
2. The church of St Mary Magdalen;
3. The wedding procession;
4. The Bridal Cup;
5. The central group;
6. Yeoman of the Guard.

(The Marquess of Salisbury, Hatfield House, Hertfordshire)

1   2

THE EYE OF LONDON 43

3   4   5   6

turned out to be Jacques Hoefnagel, Joris' father, an Antwerp merchant trading in London. A great deal of detective work went into establishing the pictorial sources for the various elements of the painting – Lucas de Heere/Joris Hoefnagel for the people and clothing, Hans Bol's etchings for one of the houses. However, the most remarkable aspect of this painting has not yet been discussed since it is described as an 'imaginary landscape', the houses belonging 'to a Netherlandish rather than an English tradition of building' (Town). While we should expect the nationality of artists to affect their interpretation of London (for instance their insistence on depicting London Bridge with round instead of Gothic arches, see p. 50), there are several elements which point to a reasonably realistic rendering of the scene:

- The presence of the very recognizable Tower of London.
- The presence of a Maypole – documented near the Artillery ground (depicted here) by William Rendle in his book *Old Southwark and its people* – its disappearance recorded for 1617.
- The presence of a church on the right-hand side where we would expect to find one – St Mary Magdalen's, previously thought, to have been unrecorded (see p. 139).
This represents a unique painted image which roughly fits the 1658 visual record which has come down to us.
- The depiction of the 'wedding procession' from the church to the banquet hall matches reasonably well the almost contemporary description found by the cataloguers of the Hatfield painting (Erna Auerbach and C Kingsley Adams): 'Then was there a faire Bride cup of silver and gilt carried before her, wherein was a goodly braunch of Rosemarie gilded very faire, hung about with silken Ribonds of all colours; next was there a noyse of Musitians that played all the way before her; after her came all the chiefest maydens of the Countrie, some bearing great Bride Cakes …'
From Thomas Deloney's 1597 novel: *The Pleasant History of John Winchcomb*.
- The houses may be re-interpreted as Flemish, but the well-known London long view by Anthonis van den Wyngaerde (1544) shows a single house in Bermondsey (see p. 37) which is very much in the spirit of those shown in 'A fête'.
- The dress historian Valerie Cumming also pointed out that 'the figures in the foreground … look outwards/pose as if to be recognized and possibly, at the time, were identifiable to viewers of the image'.
- There is a further detail which was first observed by the Hatfield House cataloguers in 1971 and is worth reiterating here: 'the 'bride' whom most would agree does not convince as a bride, was tentatively identified as Queen Elizabeth – in 1571 she would have been thirty eight. Valerie Cumming who recently re-examined the different types of clothing worn by all the participants, reached the same conclusion and was also struck by the presence, ahead of the procession in the middle foreground, of a Yeoman of the Guard aka 'beefeater' (= personal bodyguard to the Monarch since 1485) wearing the royal coat of arms – a comparison with the rubbing of the brass effigy of beefeater Robert Brampston, formerly in the church of All Saints at Chingford will show how closely related the two uniforms are. Brampston was a Yeoman of the Chamber during the reigns of Edward VI, Mary I and Elizabeth I.

There are several vivid references to Queen Elizabeth crossing the river at Lambeth to ride cross-country to Bermondsey to visit her friend Thomas Radcliffe, the Earl of Sussex. At first the latter rented the house built by Thomas Pope on the site of Bermondsey Abbey (see p. 140), before buying it outright in 1561 (MOLA 2009 in bibliography). In Lambeth churchwardens' account for the year 1571 – when this painting was made – Elizabeth is thus recorded: 'the Queen's Ma[jes]tie going to my Lord of Sissix 2 times'. Other entries in the same document record her as '[she] rode about the fields' and she was in 'St George's Fields', no doubt having crossed the river at Lambeth stairs before switching to horseback or carriage.

Might the Earl of Sussex, Thomas Radcliffe (c.1525–1583) be the glamorous man in centre foreground, perhaps wearing his Knight of Garter medal which often features on his portraits? In our painting, the 'bride' leads an austere procession, the Hatfield House cataloguers noting that 'the members of the party being honoured are dressed in black', as are the three ladies accompanying our glamorous gentleman in the middle. The austere and dignified group has emerged from the church and greatly contrasts with the men and women dancing, laughing and chatting in the foreground, dressed in bright colours – 'altogether a crowd including people of all classes of society'.

This painting was almost certainly at Hatfield House in 1610, and possibly before. The Earl acquired his Bermondsey/Rotherhithe property in 1607 in exchange, along with Hatfield House, for the Theobalds property he had gallantly ceded to King James I. Clearly, the acquisition of land in Bermondsey would have prompted his interest in the Gheeraerts painting. This may also explain the involvement of Richard Butler of Southwark in the making of stained-glass for the Earl's chapel at Hatfield. Historian Lawrence Stone describes the Earl's estate as 'amongst the very best-run aristocratic estates in England', arguing that the Cecils paid particular attention to surveying, alongside rigorous record keeping (see p. 510). The Cecil estate was the object of a complete survey in 1609 while Bermondsey itself was surveyed in 1626 and again in 1632-34. Some of that land was sold in the late seventeenth and early eighteenth centuries. Historian Dorian Gerhold catalogued three of the deeds in his book *London Plotted*: East Lane and Salisbury Lane (sold in 1711); wharves in Bermondsey (sold around 1670); Whiting ground (sold in 1701).

But since the painting has now also been connected to the Flemish merchant Jacques Hoefnagel, it was thrilling to discover that this merchant was actually based in *Tower* Ward across the river (Return of Aliens); the presence of the Tower of London suddenly acquiring a new significance. Although the twin painting 'A Village Festival' (see p. 43) has been dated c. 1575, four years later than 'A fête' it contains so many of the same elements, but in a more confused composition, that it is tempting to suggest it might have come first rather than second: the crowd is considerably larger and its organization across the picture is not as crisp and effective as in 'A fête'. Did Jacques suggest to the artist a second version of this work, simplified, more 'geographic' and therefore more realistic, bringing to the fore the fascinating detail of procession and banquet? This is of course speculative.

Anon,
'London from Southwark', c. 1630
Oil on panel

When this work, the first oil painting of London, entered the collection of the Museum of London in 1992, it encouraged new research into the origins of the image of London and the adoption of the South Bank as the best viewpoint for depicting the capital.

(© Museum of London)

The Seventeenth Century

The first oil painting of London

The birth of London in art made a gentle start in the sixteenth century but came to full bloom in the seventeenth century. In 1991 I was working as Curator of Paintings at the Museum of London when the extraordinary 'London from Southwark' painting came onto the market. It was acquired for the Museum's collections and provided a fantastic opportunity to understand how the image of London was created and how it developed.

'London from Southwark' is arguably the first surviving oil painting which attempts to show the whole of London. With the help of colleagues, I was able to date the picture to around 1630 – using topographical landmarks, dendrochronology (tree-ring dating the panel) and expert input from Antwerp to decipher the panel maker's mark on the back of the painting. The detailed account of this research was published in the Tate Gallery's *Dynasties* catalogue, edited by Karen Hearn (1995) and also in the Museum's own catalogue of oil paintings *London in Paint* (Galinou & Hayes). So what are this painting's most salient features?

- The viewpoint is the tower of Southwark Cathedral even though the cathedral is actually shown in the picture – an artist's trick! The engraver/publisher John Norden makes this perfectly clear when he labels the tower of Southwark Cathedral 'Statio Prospectiva' (viewpoint) in his groundbreaking printed prospect (see p. 39).
- The view is taken from the south looking north. We will shortly examine the other viewpoints which were tried but not generally adopted.
- The view is organized around the Thames and the most prominent landmarks are Old St Paul's Cathedral, London Bridge, the Tower of London and the church of St Saviour (Southwark Cathedral).
- The east/west panoramic view is squeezed to the point of distortion because the artist wants to include Westminster (left) and the area east of the Tower (right), which in reality is quite impossible.
- The wood panel for this painting bears a panel maker's mark from Antwerp.

This particular way of depicting London dominated artistic practice in the sixteenth, seventeenth and early eighteenth centuries. We saw earlier that it made its first appearance with Antwerp-born artist Anthonis van den Wyngaerde. But the most popular and most reproduced long view is that prepared by the Bohemian artist Wenceslaus Hollar (1607–1677). This one was actually drawn from life and published in Amsterdam in 1647 (see overleaf). In summary, between 1600 and 1666, out of 110 versions of what became the standard view (mostly prints), only two were actually drawn from life: those of Norden and Hollar. Many were published abroad (sixty three) rather than in London (around twenty four). The figure rises to three if you include Anthonis van den Wyngaerde's long view (see p. 39) from the sixteenth century.

For almost two centuries the image of London was locked into this composition. Yet there were artists who experimented with alternative viewpoints, particularly from the east. Peter Barber made an interesting case for the earliest viewpoint having been from the east (Barber 1995). The best example is a Flemish manuscript illumination found in a book of poems written by the Duc d'Orleans. But the view of London from the north is extremely rare and there is only one known

Illumination to a Flemish edition of the Duc d'Orleans poems, c. 1500
The French Duke was captured at the battle of Agincourt in 1415 and spent twenty-five years imprisoned in the Tower of London. In this picture he is shown three times: inside the Tower reading a document, at one of the windows and saying goodbye prior to leaving the Tower. The view is looking west towards London Bridge with a very good rendition of St Thomas Becket's chapel on the bridge (also see p. 128). The colonnaded building above the Tower is Billingsgate.
(British Library, London, Royal Ms 16 F II. f.73, Image in the public domain, Wikimedia Commons)

Wenceslaus Hollar, London, 1647. This prospect was taken from the tower of St Saviour's church, the future Southwark Cathedral. This inclusive panoramic view stretches from Salisbury House in the Strand (left) to well beyond the Tower of London.
(Image in the public domain; Wikimedia Commons)

Two views of Southwark taken from the tower of St Saviour's church (now Southwark Cathedral) by Wenceslaus Hollar, pen and ink drawings dated around 1638; one looking east (right), the other looking west (left).
(Yale Center for British Art, Paul Mellon Collection)

Hollar and the South Bank

These three images give a fascinating insight into Wenceslaus Hollar's methods of working. The two pen and ink drawings were clearly drawn in situ, from the tower of St Saviour's church in Southwark, as preparatory drawings for the final etching – the panorama above. They are probably more accurate than the panorama itself which is a 'reconstruction' – an intellectual exercise which needs to make different life-drawings work within a wider context, sometimes leading to distortions. An example is the inclusion of Westminster on the far-left hand side, as this neighbourhood could not and still cannot be seen from the viewpoint in question.

One major mistake in the depiction of the Thames in the seventeenth century is the sudden inclusion, east of the Tower of London, of a non-existent bend. It makes its first appearance in print about 1620. It was an error made by one of the engravers in Claes Visscher's workshop who had the task of copying this publisher's 1616 prospect when a new edition was needed (Scouloudi). The mistake is clearly visible on the first oil painting of London (previous spread), which suggests it derived from an earlier print. Hollar, however, is one of the rare artists to work from life so the topography of his 1647 London may be trusted.

London Bridge viewed from the West, Claude de Jongh, oil on panel, c. 1632. This most vivid rendering of the inhabited bridge adopts a strip composition. By eliminating most of the sky the picture is able to concentrate on one of London's 'wonders'. The painting, inaccurate in places, presents a most atmospheric vision of the famous bridge.

(© Historic England Archive)

Richard Garth signed this unusual illumination in Emanuel van Meteren's *album amicorum*. It depicts London in 1578, from the west, with London Bridge and the tower of St Saviour's on the right. The bundle of hay hanging from a pole is a striking device partly explained by the title: '*Omnis caro foenum*' which means 'all flesh is grass'.

(Photo: author, Courtesy: Bodleian Libraries, Ms Douce 68, f. 047r)

example – a print dating from the late sixteenth century of which only two copies survive (Saunders & Schofield). However, it was almost as if the viewpoint was tried, found unsatisfactory and never used again.

There are also images taken from a western viewpoint. For example: Richard Garth's truly original composition with its bundle of hay hanging from a pole dates from 1575; the artist looks at London Bridge from the west, with the tower of St Mary Overie on the right. Claude de Jongh's magnificent painting of London Bridge is also taken from the west. Art lovers will enjoy this vivid image but topographers have long dismissed the picture for its lack of accuracy. Both these pictures display the classic mistake artists made with London Bridge. The bridge, originally a timber structure, was finally built in stone between 1176 and c.1209 (see p. 126); but Old London Bridge had nineteen pointed arches of different sizes, not round arches of the same size. This mistake has been attributed to the Netherlandish nationality of early artists who were brought up with bridges made up of round arches, not gothic ones. As early methods of making pictures were often based on copying other pictures, rather than working from the original, mistakes spread quickly.

Dissemination

Long views of London from the south made between 1600 and 1666 were conscientiously catalogued by Irene Scouloudi and she recorded well over one hundred pictures. The majority of these views – many published abroad – were not drawn from life but copied from a handful of prototypes which themselves derived from earlier sources.

What impact did this group of pictures have on ordinary Londoners of the sixteenth and seventeenth centuries? These works were made for those who could afford them – wealthy or comfortable households, antiquarians or historians obsessed with collecting data. However, through the medium of theatre and pageantry, the new image of London quickly spread to all classes: Inigo Jones used it in one of his royal masques – performed to an aristocratic audience but able to inspire fellow theatre professionals, friends of Jones, such as those who ran the Bankside theatres and their counterparts, north of the river. From the same period, one of the seven triumphal arches erected in the City of London for the 1604 Coronation procession of James I, displayed a model of London also taken from the south.

Painting South London out of the picture

The only major disadvantage to depicting London from Southwark was that South London was literally painted out of the picture. Bankside and Tooley Street were included, as was a section of Borough High Street, and sometimes Lambeth Palace and village, but it is clear that historically, South London has been in a position of secondary significance from at least the sixteenth century: a traumatic pictorial start from which South London may not have fully recovered. In addition, shortly after the image of London was first created by van den Wyngaerde, large swathes of Southwark lost their independence, becoming one of the City wards – another blow to this neighbourhood's sense of identity and one which they had resisted for a long time (see p. 82–83).

At the close of the nineteenth century this is what London historian and novelist Walter Besant (1836–1901) wrote about South London:

> In South London there are two millions of people. It is therefore one of the great cities of the world … it is a city without a municipality, without a centre, without a civic history … it has no intellectual artistic, scientific, musical, literary centre … its residents have no local patriotism or enthusiasm. One cannot imagine a man proud of New Cross … It is argued that although it has none of these things, yet it has them all by right of being part of London.

It is hard to think of a more dismissive and inaccurate statement but Walter Besant continues to be admired and his judgement resonates to this day. On 30 April 2018, the *Evening Standard* reported on a variety of readers' opinions on the north/south London divide, including:

- One person insisted: 'Well, South London is best London'.

This is Inigo Jones' set design for the opening scene of a 1637 masque, *Britannia Triumphans*, which was performed at Whitehall Palace. Jones has placed St Paul's Cathedral in the centre of the composition (he was appointed surveyor of the cathedral in 1633). The stage directions specify that the nearer parts express the suburbs. In scene 2 the whole contraption turned into a 'horrid hell' and 'a flaming precipice'.
(© The Devonshire Collections, Chatsworth. Reproduced by permission of Chatsworth Settlement Trustees)

'Londinium', one of the seven temporary triumphal arches designed by Stephen Harrison and erected for the Coronation procession of James I on 15 March 1604. This particular arch was sited in Fenchurch Street in the City where many people would have seen it. Engraving by William Kip.
(© The Trustees of the British Museum)

- To which a north London fan retorted: 'unless you like having a tube nearby'.
- Another added: 'London stops at the river'. Another retorted 'London does indeed end at the river. Everything north of it is 'The North'.
- and moving on to plain unfair contributions such as: 'I get a nosebleed if I go south of the river'.

This exchange of viewpoints may make us smile but it is not necessarily friendly and Londoners will all be aware of the classic South London slurs.

London is not alone in neglecting one of its river banks; Bordeaux and Vienna have privileged their west banks, leaving the east sides with a diminished status. While Paris and Prague have shown that both sides of a river can have different personalities and equal status; historic images of these cities adopt a middle position in their aerial view showing both sides of the river.

By adopting the South Bank as *the* viewpoint for London, the identity of the South Bank was left in a precarious state. 'Chercher le South Bank' in pictures of London is a revealing exercise, and no one should be entirely surprised to find that the Buck Brothers' classic and important engraved prospect of London and Westminster, published in 1749, omits the South Bank altogether. However, the historian Ralph Hyde worked out in detail all the South Bank viewpoints used by the brothers in making their groundbreaking five-sheet prospect. The London historian Hugh Phillips who systematically studied pictures of London's Thames banks wrote of the Canaletto picture reproduced overleaf, 'An interesting topographical feature of Canaletto's picture is the unique view it gives us of the southern shore'. Although it was not unique, it was certainly rare.

Another classic example of omitting the South is Joseph Mead's volume *London Interiors* published in 1841 which does not include a single South London interior. More recent examples include Peter Ackroyd's 2000 text *London – A Biography*. Three years after publication, the book was repackaged, edited down to make room for pictures and renamed *Illustrated London*: the chapter on Southwark and Lambeth 'The south work' was almost entirely eliminated. Even the scholarly maps of Medieval and Tudor London by the British Historic Towns Atlas, almost completely omit the South Bank.

Breaking the mould

So how did artists move on from depicting London from Southwark? They had to abandon the idea of showing London in a single picture. So first they split London into two, then three then more sections. It happened around the middle of the seventeenth century and this may have been encouraged by the fight between Royalists and Parliamentarians. This conflict put into clear focus the separate identities of Royal Westminster and the Parliamentary City. Politically, they sat in opposite camps.

The first hint of a shift may be spotted in 'View from the top of Arundel House' by Prague-born Wenceslaus Hollar (1607–1677). In 1636 he had joined the retinue of Thomas Howard, 14th Earl of Arundel. The Arundels once had land on the South Bank and also a house – Norfolk House, Lambeth (see p. 97, VL7). But soon after 1549 their main London residence switched to the north bank overlooking the Thames, hence Hollar's etched views taken of and from Arundel House. Also dating from the 1640s are the two river views taken from outside Arundel House: looking east 'London viewed from Milford Stairs' and looking

THE EYE OF LONDON

west 'View of Lambeth from Whitehall Stairs'. Rather unusually, the view of Arundel House from the South includes Hollar's studio – a rare depiction of an artist's London studio of that time (right).

Antwerp-born Cornelis Bol (1589–1666), a little-known Flemish artist, appears to have been the first *painter* to move his viewpoint near Somerset House on the north bank. From here he produced a view looking east with Old St Paul's in the middle ground, then the artist looked the other way towards Westminster. A third view focused on the Pool of London. All three works (overleaf) were painted for the diarist John Evelyn and are in private hands. These early prototypes effectively led the way to the famous Canaletto paintings of the eighteenth century now in the Royal Collection: 'The Thames from the Terrace of Somerset House, the City in the Distance' and 'The Thames from the Terrace of Somerset House, Westminster in the Distance'. The painting reproduced overleaf, also remarkable, is 'The View of the Thames from Richmond House' a rare early glimpse of the South Bank (also see p. 169).

These etchings are by Wenceslaus Hollar – 'London viewed from Milford Stairs' (1643) and 'View of Lambeth from Whitehall Stairs' (1650). In Hollar's view of Arundel House from the south, there is a rare depiction of his studio on the right-hand side of the print, with pictures leaning against the wall and a large window above.
(Yale Center for British Art (left) and © The Trustees of the British Museum (above))

54 LONDON'S SOUTH BANK

1

2

3

Great Fires

The Great Fire of London was memorable and life-changing, but it did not substantially alter the image of London, except perhaps for one important detail. The fire only affected the City of London, so artists would have been encouraged to focus on this particular stretch of the urban landscape. The field was still dominated by Flemish and Dutch artists who used all the viewpoints already mentioned: from the south, from the west and from the east. But a fire is such a fascinating thing that some artists naturally sought to depict it as a close-up view. A painting in the Paul Mellon collection includes, on its right-hand side, one of the earliest painted street scenes (overleaf). This is a by-product of the artist homing in on his subject, and in due course street scenes went on to become a subject in their own right.

In Southwark the 1676 fire which started in an oil shop close to the George Inn, was particularly devastating. There are no pictures of it while the Great Fire of London across the Thames has been the subject of endless pictures and has been chronicled in countless publications – the Southwark fire has remained a footnote in most books; though not in William Rendle's *Old Southwark*, who noted 'especially fatal to the inns'. This author must have relied on the contemporary pamphlet in the British Museum: 'A True Narrative of the Great and Terrible Fire in Southwark' (online at Google books). The conflagration started on Friday 26 May 1676 in the 'house of a Colourman, or Oyl shop', moving northwards and destroying the

Cornelis Bol (1589–1616), the little-known Antwerp painter, made (visual) history with this split view of London into three oil canvases:
1. Looking west towards Westminster;
2. Looking east towards St Paul's Cathedral and the City;
3. The Pool of London, east of London Bridge.
(Private collection)

Canaletto's 'A View of the Thames from the house of the Duke of Richmond', 1746. Also see p. 169 (Goodwood House; image in the public domain, Wikimedia Commons)

Unknown artist, The Great Fire of London, with Ludgate and Old St. Paul's, around 1670, oil on canvas. This bold close-up view of the fire allowed the artist to focus on the part of the City which was affected; combining a symbolic vision of the 'Gates of Hell' alongside a vignette on the Blackfriars district, an early street scene.
(Yale Center for British Art, Paul Mellon Collection, B1976.7.27; image in the public domain, Wikimedia Commons)

Queen's Head, Talbot, George, White Hart, King's Head, Green Dragon, 'the prison of the 'Counter', the 'meal-market' and about five hundred dwellings. St Thomas' Hospital and St Saviour's church were saved when the wind changed course. Another serious Southwark fire in 1689, which started near King's Bench prison, brought the total loss of houses by fire in the last decades of the seventeenth century to around 700.

Later remarkable panoramas taken from the South

The Scottish portrait painter Robert Barker made history when he exhibited, in 1794, his 360 degrees panorama in Leicester Square, in a circular building which had been specially designed for this purpose. He first tested the idea in his native Edinburgh where in the mid-1780s he created a panorama of his city from the observatory at Calton Hill. He exhibited it at Edinburgh, then at 28 Haymarket, London where he won the admiration of the great Sir Joshua Reynolds and obtained the required capital for building a purpose-built panorama building in Leicester Square. The word 'panorama' was coined in 1791 and Barker's discovery unleashed what Ralph Hyde has described as 'Panoramania!'.

Barker's panorama building may have been erected in the West End but the first panorama he exhibited there was actually created in South London, the brainchild of an adopted South Londoner living

in St George's Fields. The American historian Richard Altick gives an excellent summary of Barker's invention: 'Drawing upon two older artistic techniques – the portrayal of landscapes on interior walls and of wide outdoor scenes in engraved 'prospects' – he added his own discovery – the trick of painting a broad scene on a cylindrical canvas and the result was the panorama'.

In the winter of 1790–91 Robert Barker sent his son Henry Aston to make sketches from the roof of the Albion Flour Mills at the southern end of Blackfriars Bridge (see p. XX). The viewpoint was further west than the historic tower of Southwark Cathedral at the southern end of London Bridge. But since the city had grown west, it was a good choice. The resulting panorama was first exhibited a year later, in Castle Street. This was a semi-circular panorama; the full 360 degrees panorama was finally exhibited in 1794 when Barker's new premises in Leicester Square were ready.

The first true panorama of London, taken from the South Bank, became the talk of the town and was visited by King George III and Queen Charlotte (who felt seasick!). Blackfriars Bridge had pride of place as did the smart new Albion Place leading to Surrey Street, with the steeple of Christchurch emerging from the regular development. The roof of Albion Mills (see p. XX) obscured much of what was on the riverside, but the smoking potteries behind Albion Mills and the mills themselves suggest that industry was an important component.

Barker's first panorama was followed by many showing other geographical areas but all were manufactured on the South Bank – they were painted in a large circular wooden building which Barker had erected close to his home at 14 West Square, St George's Fields. Henry Aston Barker, Robert's son, took over the business at his father's death in 1806 and set up in partnership with John Burford. This was one of London's most successful commercial shows, lasting until 1863.

Robert Barker's ground-breaking 360 degrees panorama of London was taken from the roof of Albion Flour Mills at the southern end of Blackfriars Bridge (preliminary sketches taken by Barker Junior) and exhibited in 1794. The massive canvases were exhibited in the Panorama building erected in Leicester Square for that purpose. Unfortunately, the large roof of the Albion Mills, the viewpoint for the panorama, substantially obstruct the view of the South Bank. These aquatints by Frederick Birnie provide a lasting record of Barker's popularity and success.
© London Metropolitan Archives (City of London)

The inscription on this watercolour reads: 'Building for Painting the Panoramas near West Square'. The Barkers' rotunda was recorded by J C Buckler in 1827 and it can also be spotted in the background of the large Rhinebeck panorama (see pp 206–207). It was used for around twenty years to paint the works which were exhibited at Leicester Square.
© London Metropolitan Archives (City of London)

Thomas Girtin's 'Eidometropolis' (from the Greek, namely the image of the capital) was a 360 degrees panorama which was exhibited in Spring Gardens between August 1802 and March 1803 – briefly interrupted by the artist's death in November 1802, aged 27. Unlike Barker's panorama, it was never recorded in a set of prints; what survives are working drawings made around 1801 and only partially reproduced here – Albion Mills (looking towards Southwark) and Lambeth. The artist's viewpoint was almost the same as the Barkers' – across the road from the Albion Mills. By that date the Mills were a mere shell, having gone up in smoke in 1791 (see p. 185); but the new viewpoint afforded a fine prospect of Lambeth, contrasting older buildings in the foreground with taller newer ones in the middle ground (same juxtaposition in the Albion Mills view).
(© The Trustees of the British Museum)

Art versus topography

Barker's panoramas inspired a whole generation of artists, including Thomas Malton (his 'Sketches for a Panorama of London' alas came to nothing) and the young Thomas Girtin … though his panoramic adventure – the Eidometropolis – also taken from the southern end of Blackfriars bridge – now strikes a tragic note. Greg Smith's excellent study of this project describes it thus: 'Girtin's drawings may have been produced for a 'connoisseur's panorama', with complex light and weather effects, but at the heart of the project was a solid core of topographical fact'. The Eidometropolis was a commercial failure and Smith, who discovered yet another touring panorama of London taken from the top of the ruined Albion Mills ('touring Scotland and England between 1798-1803') summed up: 'the London public by 1802 was clearly sated with views of their city near Blackfriars bridge.' The early prospects from the south had endured for almost two centuries but their existence and resilience did not depend on a mass market as the late Georgian panoramas did.

After a gap of almost two hundred years the young artist Sharon Beavan (b. 1956) would also be drawn to the view of London

from Blackfriars Bridge. She explains in an interview published in the London Arts Café's *Newsletter* No8 (summer 2001):

> I started the view from Blackfriars Bridge to Westminster Bridge just as I would start any painting; by seeing something that compelled me to put it down on canvas. When a painting has started, it makes its own demands and requires the painter to make detours that must be followed. Two years and many sketch books later I realised that I had begun what could become a very long-term project.

What is remarkable about Sharon's painting is that unlike the artists who preceded her, she has not used the south bank to focus on the north bank; by placing herself half way across the bridge she presents a more balanced view of both banks. The south bank is shallower but treated with the same care as the north bank. Will Sharon Beavan's panorama of London take its place alongside those great unfinished works of art over which art historians ponder, puzzled as to why the artist did not feel able to finish the work? The View from Blackfriars Bridge was started in 1990, almost thirty-five years ago at the time of writing. It is still unfinished (overleaf).

'The View from Blackfriars Bridge to Westminster Bridge' by Sharon Beavan was started in 1990, here photographed at the exhibition 'Meeting Points' held at the Royal Drawing School in February 2020. Alongside the central photograph are two details from the left-hand side of the painting depicting the South Bank. On the left, the IPC tower dominates the composition with a diminutive Oxo Tower, Bernie Spain Gardens and Gabriel's Wharf at bottom right. On the right, it is the turn of the LWT tower to dominate the composition with a diminutive National Theatre at its foot; Waterloo Bridge is in the centre, then the white Royal Festival Hall, with the Hayward, the Queen Elizabeth Hall and Purcell Room all jumbled up together, before moving onto to Jubilee Gardens and County Hall at the top. Oil on canvas.

(Collection of the artist. Photos: The author)

THE EYE OF LONDON 61

'H G', Robert Wilson and
Hans Peter Kuhn, 1996.
(Artangel. Photo: Stephen White)

The view from the Shard

The view from the south bank continues to be a defining feature of this part of London, both at ground level thanks to the excellent and almost uninterrupted Thames path, and at high level, thanks to places such as the London Eye, Oxo Tower and now the Shard. The extraordinary height and position of this building offer a near cosmic experience at its summit (see chapter 4.4). It is more than just the view, it is about atmospheric effects, light, sky. But the prohibitively high entrance fee discourages return visits while the 'ride' at the very top ('Are you a Screamer?') will, for some, intrude on the quiet meditative time this view could afford with your head in the sky – literally.

Soulful art

So … have the artists who gave birth to the image and landscape of London, succeeded in capturing the city's soul? Or have they fractured it? They depicted a pristine and orderly city by the side of the Thames, glowing in silvery light and punctuated at regular intervals by the steeples of dense churches. It was a spiky, uplifting city for Londoners whose lives were dominated by the church. The south bank existed in the shadow of this idealized city ('paved with gold'!) and for all its vitality the 'wrong side' gradually acquired a bad reputation. Then, the city and its citizens' aspirations changed and the ever-growing capital exploded into a kaleidoscope of thousands of pictures. Did that shatter the soul of London? Did it, too, fragment into thousands of pieces? Or did it create a large community of souls singularly attached to 'mother London' wherever she was? Or was it a return to pagan times where there were gods on every corner of human paths?

Have you ever experienced a glimpse of London's soul on the South Bank? I felt it rampant at my feet and tugging at my heart when in 1995, I was one of the first visitors to the extraordinary 'H G' exhibition staged by Artangel in the dark and damp vaults off Clink Street. This remarkable collaboration between Artangel (Michael Morris and James Linwood), Robert Wilson (art director) and Hans-Peter Kuhn (musician) is described by James Linwood:

> The Clink Street vaults were like a huge underground street,
> in a part of London very near the City and very near the River

Thames, but which every development boom had passed by (until the last one). From the street outside, it was impossible to have any idea of the scale of the spaces behind the facade.

The title 'H G' (for H G Wells) came later when someone noticed this author's *Time Machine* was celebrating its 100th anniversary since publication. The location on Bankside was crucial: 'The space was the starting point, rather than the book' (James Linwood). It was an emotional, sensory evocation of history – all the fears, hang-ups, implanted memories, dramatically lit arrangements of rooms visitors explored in semi-darkness, supplying with their imagination what they couldn't see. At that moment London's soul was in Bankside, touching the hearts of whoever moved around this extraordinary installation. But it was so short-lived! The site was taken over by wine merchant Duncan Vaughan-Arbuckle who opened his 'Vinopolis' on 23 July 1999. That, too, was short-lived.

By focusing on a single house in time, the playwright Paul Mercier coolly dissects the slow degradation of a soulful dream. The action of his poignant play *Buddleia* (Donmar Theatre, 1995) unfolds around a house and its successive residents – from the early days when deeply caring owners lavished love and attention on their home, then moving on to a series of tenants who could not care less and stood as mindless witnesses to the slow decay and death of the house. At the end of the play the house is demolished to build a road and a service station. One of the characters utters:

> At the end of the day, Les, we're all just passin' through. Tell ye this much, it's gonna be some road out there when they're finished. And there like an oasis in the wilderness is your service station.

Jordan, a homeless kid who keeps returning to this house because it means shelter and a shadow of long-lost kindness, is accidentally killed on the building site. It was as if the soul of the place had finally died.

Mercier's play is set in Dublin but this could be happening in any city. Have you ever wondered what happened to the small community of homeless people who huddled in the Ring next to Waterloo Station, now transformed into an Imax cinema? (See pp. 552–553)

But the arts, which have been so central to this chapter, are uniquely placed to capture the depth of humanity in all its glory and all its sadness. They make us see; to see is to understand and remember, and perhaps, perhaps … transcend.

Sources (see bibliography for abbreviated entries):

William Fitzstephen's Description of London (*c.* 1190) in Stow 1598; J K Hyde 'Medieval Descriptions of Cities' in *Bulletin of the John Rylands Library Manchester*, Vol.48, 1965-66, pp. 308-340; Brigitte M Bedos-Rezak, *When Ego Was Imago: Signs of Identity in the Middle Ages*, 2011; New; Caroline Barron, 'Thomas Becket and London' in *London Topographical Society Newsletter,* Number 93, November 2021; Michael Archer, 'Richard Butler, glass-painter' in the *Burlington Magazine*, May 1990; Walker; J A van Dorsten, *Radical Arts*, 1970; Barber 2012; LTS 1996; Scouloudi; Hyde 1988; Hyde 1985; Altick; Smith.

Previous & above
Jiro Osuga, 'The Growth of London', 2017 – Roman, Tudor, Georgian, Victorian and Modern London, from a series of four pen and ink drawings showing the development of London.
(© The artist)

'Secret London' is not simply a clever marketing ploy for attracting tourists and Londoners to sites of historical interest. At Vauxhall for instance, it takes the shape of a massive building, MI6, or more correctly, the Headquarters of the Secret Intelligence Service. The building, designed by Terry Farrell, was completed in 1995. Five years later, on 21 September 2010, *The Guardian's* headline must have shocked many: 'Graham Greene, Arthur Ransome and Somerset Maugham all spied for Britain admits MI6'.

In this book, the Vauxhall site has been placed under the microscope, revealing many historical layers – a prehistoric jetty – transport hub or a place for votive offerings to the river gods, no one knows for certain; a medieval royal manor house – Faux Hall – with a grand and elaborate mansion nearby – Copped Hall. In the eighteenth and nineteenth centuries industry arrived – guns, sugar, vinegar, gin, oil works, and finally cars, each took their turn. Then came the bridge, finally solidified – an echo of the early prehistoric timber jetty or bridge.

In some ways, this follows the pattern of a number of sites along the South Bank but Vauxhall's occupation is very ancient and it demonstrates ambition. Will these layers reveal the character of Vauxhall? We will find out in Chapter 4.1 and the final chapter.

This section of the book provides visual snapshots of the South Bank at various periods of history. Such 'visions' of times past, modelled on maps, prints, drawings and paintings represent the sum of thousands of personal experiences, from the down-to-earth archaeologist and mapmaker to the artist, writer, historian

or the musician – all those who have aspired to capture the spirit of times past and present, however fleetingly. The reconstructions have also been used in this book, as building blocks for interpreting, applauding, sometimes deploring the paths travelled so far and those yet to be travelled.

These witnesses and researchers are there to make sense of the formidable amount of data available. 'The South Bank around 1600' aims to catch a last glimpse of the ephemeral – yet influential – Elizabethan playhouses, but also pays homage to a time when living on the South Bank was quite glamorous. The next section 'around 1770' captures the South Bank at a great moment of change – more bridges, more industry and more architectural aspirations than ever before. Exceptionally for the period, the South Bank is caught in its full Victorian apparel by the balloon artist J H Banks in the 1840s. Our own times are featured using an aerial photograph.

The task of producing these reconstructions and other graphic material was immensely difficult and labour intensive. Stephen Conlin rose to the challenge; he is not only a highly experienced illustrator, he is also extremely knowledgeable about London – a rare combination of skills which recalls the work of the late Peter Jackson (1922–2003).

IN THE BEGINNING
of the South Bank

Waves   **70**

Dawn   **70**

The Romans and the South Bank   **72**
    Islands in the stream   73
    Temples   75
    Sacred water   77
    City of the Dead   77

Coming back from the dead   **78**

Domesday   **80**

How Southwark came to be ruled by the City   **81**

Previous:
This Roman boat, recovered in 1910 during the construction of County Hall, was previously believed to have been a Roman galley which sank in a hard-fought battle. But this opinion was revised: 'her timbers were too lightly jointed for a sea-going vessel and … it was unlikely that she ever possessed a mast. It seems probable that she was a ferry boat plying across the river' concludes the *Survey of London*.
(From *Wonderful London*, John Adcock (ed), Volume two of three)

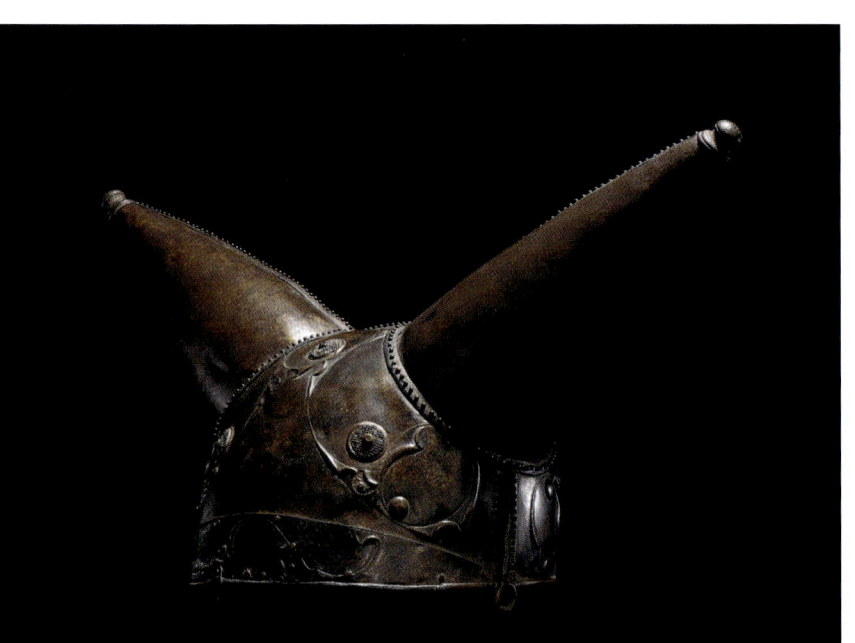

The Waterloo helmet dates from c. 150–50 BC and was probably used for ceremonial purposes. It is the only example of an Iron Age horned helmet to be found in Europe.
(© The Trustees of the British Museum)

Waves

The image of the wave is a useful way of visualising the role played by humans in the original, stark, flat and muddy Thames valley. The Celts, the Romans, the Saxons and the Vikings, then the Normans all congregated on the shores of the Thames. People think of the Normans as the last great wave of colonisation – but less insidious and with roots of deep inheritance, Christianity might be an equally strong candidate. It came to be the cement which held people and nations together, until of course it splintered in the sixteenth century, opening the gates to deep divisions, with religious refugees pouring into London and elsewhere. Christian beliefs have considerably weakened in recent times but are likely to prevail as long as there is nothing of substance to replace them.

Dawn

The South Bank, as defined in this book, lies in a flood plain that stretches from Vauxhall to Deptford and all the way down to Peckham. Two rivers – the Neckinger and the Earl's Sluice – drained it naturally, but as often happens with 'lost' rivers, there are contradictory accounts of their route – I have followed Barton's and Gibberd's accounts. Archaeologists have demonstrated that the Thames was a multi-channel river which ran significantly further south than it does now and that Southwark and Lambeth are the results of sand accretion which formed dunes, which went on to attract sediments. The close study of the Bermondsey Lake – further east than our designated area – yielded woodland data, perhaps reflecting the ecology of wider Southwark. Prehistoric expert Jon Cotton thus summed up the site's findings: 'Some of the earliest activity, which includes an important hunter-gatherer site dating back some 10,000 years, was sited to exploit a late glacial lake – part of whose shoreline ran along the Old Kent Road in Bermondsey.'

The only other book to adopt a similarly broad definition of the South Bank as this one is *The prehistory and topography of Southwark and Lambeth*. This specialised publication provides evidence that all four landmarks used here to delimit the area covered by *London's South Bank*, showed very early signs of human settlement.

- 'The Lower Thames valley is justly famous for the spectacular sequence of objects dredged from THE THAMES'. For instance, the Iron Age horned helmet found near Waterloo Bridge in 1868, now in the British Museum collections (left).

- Evidence for early cultivation, rare in a British context, was recovered in Bermondsey, close to ST SAVIOUR'S DOCK (at Lafone Street, Wolseley Street and Phoenix Wharf). At Phoenix Wharf in 1988, archaeologists also found an early Bronze Age boiling pit and burnt mound. 'The interpretation of burnt mounds has mostly related to boiling or dry roasting of meat'.

- At VAUXHALL, the remnants of a four-metre-wide timber structure was discovered in 1993 after two spearheads were found on the site (above). The structure, dated to around 1500 BC, is made up of twenty 'piles' (driven by force into the mud) over a distance of fifteen metres and it is partially visible at low tide. The spearheads had been pushed into the foreshore between two of these wooden piles.

- The Southwark Castle Leisure Centre at the ELEPHANT AND CASTLE was one of several sites excavated which revealed the presence of Bronze Age peat. Pollen analysis at that site (and also at Wilson's Wharf close to Hay's Galleria) showed the presence of agriculture, similar to that near St Saviour's Dock.

This reconstruction of the Vauxhall jetty or bridge of around 1500 BC can prove disappointing if you catch the actual stumpy remains at very low tides in January or very early spring, on the shore in front of the MI6 building. It is evidence not of a building but of a possible causeway, jetty or platform structure. Its overall appearance was first reconstructed for the 2007 BBC Time Team programme, working alongside historians and archaeologists from the Museum of London and elsewhere.
(© Stephen Conlin)

All these sites, mapped on pp. 12–13, help us place lively touches of humanity onto the portrait of prehistoric South Bank. The circle of life would not be complete without the findings at Fennings Wharf, on the site of 1 London Bridge. There, a Bronze Age ring ditch highlighted ceremonials around death; it 'represents the truncated remains of a small circular earthen barrow, used and subsequently reused for up to a thousand years after its construction'. The ditch included 'identifiable remains of at least one adult and ?seven [sic] children'.

The Romans And The South Bank

'From the very beginning London was a town that spanned the Thames. The south bank settlement was confined to two of the islands that rose above the river channels' wrote Francis Grew in *London – The Illustrated History*. They were the Northern and Southern islands of Southwark and at eighty acres, 'it was not much less than the entire Roman town of Silchester [in Hampshire]'.

Islands in the Stream

> In Esmeralda, city of water, a network of canals and a network of streets span and intersect each other. To go from one place to another you have always the choice between land and boat'.
>
> Italo Calvino, *Invisible Cities*, 1972

And so it was for Southwark during the Roman period. Southwark Street was a water channel between the northern and southern islands of Southwark. There was topographical fragmentation – the isles of Rotherhithe, Bermondsey, Horsleydown, Southwark, Lambeth, Battersea were low lying and prone to flooding. In Southwark water was everywhere: Thames on the north side, 'Borough channel' on the south side and 'Guy's channel' on the east side. A second-century boat was recovered from Guy's Channel, just north of our contemporary Guy's Hospital Cancer Centre. Long Lane and large areas north and east of it were under water, probably creating the kind of dreamy, watery landscape reproduced on p. 76.

The Romans pursued a sustained campaign of works to protect Southwark from flooding, building embankments and waterfronts – archaeologists believe this was likely to have been a collective action, perhaps initiated by the town's administrators. Most of the perimeter of the northern and southern islands of Southwark were probably revetted.

What of Lambeth? Historian Hannah Renier summarises its circumstances: 'Lambeth, as an unhealthily marshy, sparsely inhabited sprawl of hovels several miles upriver from London, was of little interest to the Roman incomers … So far as we know the Romans largely ignored Lambeth … and yet, they did use it as a local through route … across Lambeth from Southwark to the ferry to Thorney Island [Westminster]'. There is a splendid artefact in the Museum of London to help visitors measure the significance of river crossing at the ancient location of Stangate (which means stone lane): a Roman galley was found during the construction of County Hall in 1910 (see p. 68). It provided a memorable piece of propaganda for the newly formed London Museum at Kensington Palace. Its director led it across London to the delight of the newspapers and public.

Opposite:

Artist's reconstruction of the northern temple which stood at Tabard Square in Southwark in the second century. When excavated, the overall ground plan of the (almost) square building was clear: 'an inner square within a larger square, the classic form for a Romano-Celtic temple'. The measurements were around 4.85 square metres for the inner cell and around 10.45 square metres for the larger square. The scene includes a reasonably well documented type of animal sacrifice: a ram, a pig and a bull – or *suovetaurilia* – known to us from contemporary sculptures (Illustration: Chris Mitchell for Douglas Killock et al's *Temples and Suburbs – Excavations at Tabard Square, Southwark*, Pre-Construct Archaeology Monograph 18, 2015)

Temples

Where would you look for Roman temples in Southwark? The Museum of London *Londinium* map will show you two of them: the *temenos* or sacred enclosure, was sited at modern Tabard Square, formerly the junction of Stane and Watling Streets (now Borough High Street and Great Dover Street) next to a vast cemetery lining both sides of Watling Street. Whether approaching London from the east (Kent) or the west (Chichester), travellers 'would have passed through a landscape of cemeteries and temples, crossing the islands along a busy thriving street, lined with domestic and commercial properties, market areas and bathhouses, on their way to the city' (PCA 2015).

But in 2010–11, the News Building archaeological site near the Shard probably contained at least one further temple; in the 2012 MOLA's post-excavation assessment, Building 2 is dated to 120–160 AD and its plan reminiscent of many Romano-British temples. One of the significant Roman finds at that site, contemporary with the temple, was an inscribed stone base referring to the god Silvanus:

> The column base probably supported a votive statue of Silvanus, a woodland god explicitly associated with hunting … [so] it may be a statue pedestal and analysis of its provenance may be worthwhile as it may be made from the same source of stone as the Hunter god statue found nearby. (Left)

But Tabard Square remains the best documented site and when Pre-Construct Archaeology (PCA) was preparing their 2015 publication, archaeologists, researchers and illustrators were determined to bring back to life the temenos and the two small temples which once graced the junction of Southwark's two main Roman roads – now at 34–70 Long Lane or Tabard Square for short. The patient and meticulous excavation work was carried out by a team from PCA. Berkeley Homes who have since built new flats there, financed the excavation (between 17 July 2002 and 25 July 2003) and the publication which followed (PCA 2015). Those responsible for laying out the sacred enclosure did not choose a virgin site. Archaeologists concluded that there was 'evidence of persistent, if not intense occupation from the Neolithic to late Bronze periods … the recovery of blade ends of two axe heads might allude to the symbolic or ritual importance of this particular locale from an early date'.

As for the Romans, the earliest sign of their presence on this site dates from around AD 80, with the reclamation of low-lying damp areas; seventy years later they prepared the site for construction. The large number of animal bones suggests it had become a religious precinct by then – the sacrifice of animals being one of the most characteristic religious practices of the Romans. The temples were built a little later in AD 160.

Killock explains: 'the presence of open spaces around or adjacent

Opposite:

Hunter God with dog and deer, probably fourth century AD. Recovered in 1977 from a well filled with Roman artefacts, found in a crypt inserted in 1703 under Southwark Cathedral, and sealed in the 1840s. The goddess Diana is normally associated with a deer and a dog, but the nearest male equivalent might be Apollo. The MOLA assessment report mentioned in the text below explained that the late Ralph Merrifield suggested there was 'a cult shrine to Apollo Cunomaglos (an alternative identification of Silvanus) near the road junction south of London Bridge'. (Cuming museum collection, Southwark Council. Photo: Museum of London)

Reconstruction of both Southwark temples within their natural setting: 'a vista looking south-eastwards directly down the main axis of the Bermondsey eyot with the southern channel separating the Southwark islands [left] from the mainland [the rest] … and, just to the right, the expanse of tidal marsh between Bermondsey eyot and the mainland, with Watling Street extending off to the south east [right] … Nowhere would such a dramatic and spiritually uplifting view be visible from any part of the urban or, for that matter, suburban areas so close to Londinium.'
(Quote and illustration by Chris Mitchell for Douglas Killock et al's *Temples and Suburbs – Excavations at Tabard Square, Southwark*, Pre-Construct Archaeology Monograph 18, 2015)

to these religious buildings is of great significance in our understanding of how the buildings were used and what went on or was placed inside them'. At Tabard Square a well-preserved inscription from after AD 161, enabled Dr Roger Tomlin to conjure up a portrait of the man who commissioned it, Tiberius Celerianus, a citizen of Bellovaci – a tribe from Gaul based north of Paris (what is now Beauvais).

Tiberius was a sea farer who

probably traded and travelled regularly with that region but whose home seems to have become London … His choice of god, Mars Camulus, was entirely in keeping with the dual tradition of a Romano-Celtic temple. The Celtic god Camulus, twinned with the Roman god Mars, was a popular deity in the homeland of the Bellovaci.

One of the temples, but we don't know which one, would have been dedicated to Mars Camulus. The other remarkable thing about this inscription is that it contains the word 'Londiniensi' translated as 'Londoners'. The full inscription translated by Dr Tomlin reads:

To the Divinities of the Emperors (and) to the god Mars Camulus. Tiberinius Celerianus, a citizen of the Bellovaci, moritix, of Londoners the first … [text missing].

Moritix is apparently a Gaulish word for sea-farer. But to return to the word 'Londiniensi', Dr Tomlin's remark helps us measure its enormous significance: 'This is the first stone inscription found with the name of the city or in this case the inhabitants of the city, carved into it.' This dedication plaque was carefully buried in the fourth century when the temples fell out of fashion and use.

Some of the most useful information about this religious complex came from the northern temple: measurements, internal arrangement and interior decoration. The two temples were aligned, but the northern temple was slightly smaller than the southern temple. The northern temple also had the best view (opposite). The placing of two or more temples within a *temenos* is not unusual. Springhead near Gravesend is a case in point. Douglas Killock was even tempted to suggest that the sites of Tabard Square, Greenwich Park (another possible temple site) and Springhead, all sited along Watling Street form 'a chain as part of a route of pilgrimage or, at the very least, convenient wayside locations for any necessary and regular devotions irrespective of one's destination.' This was long before its more famous successor: the medieval Canterbury pilgrims' route, and the link between the distant past and the future may also be observed at the ancient church of St George on Borough High Street (or Stane Street) which is literally a stone's throw from this *temenos*. Once a sacred neighbourhood ...

Sacred Water

Water was regarded as a dwelling place for the gods. Roman Londoners kept small shrines in their homes and made regular votive offerings often involving water. There is a healthy debate amongst archaeologists about the large amount of objects which have been recovered from the Thames (for instance p. 70 helmet) – some favouring a strong link to ritual activities to honour the gods (MoLAS 2002); others arguing that 'if we regard the Thames in the Pre-Roman Iron Age as being a boundary between competing tribal groups, it is just as possible that the loss of military equipment could be accidental skirmish or battle loss, rather than devotional deposition of valued items' (PCA 2015).

City of the Dead

Excavations in 2002/3 revealed just how extensive Southwark's role as a Roman burial ground really was. From a position of substantial ignorance, London archaeologists were suddenly confronted with the realisation that 'extensive cemeteries ... would have occupied much of the suburb in the Roman period' (PCA 2013). The same report also points out: 'until recently little was known about the southern 'cemetery' of Roman London'. In 1996 there was evidence for eighty-six bodies and by 2013 this figure had jumped to 460. In 2022 it stands at around 600.

Great Dover Street became south London's cemetery for the wealthy classes, while Lant Street seemingly catered for more ordinary people – though 35% of all burials there contained grave goods (overleaf). But at Lant Street there was no evidence for coffins while 48% of burials at Great Dover Street involved coffins (identification of coffins rely on the presence of nails; the coffins themselves do not survive). The burials near Southwark Bridge Road were 'densely clustered' and bodies superimposed; archaeologists admitted this pattern was difficult to interpret but suggested the lack of tomb markers or restrictive topography.

It is easy to forget that the soil of our cities is abundantly streaked with the bones of

Reconstruction of roadside mausoleums found in Southwark, 2009.
(© MOLA, painted by Kikar Singh)

the thousands of men, women and children who died long ago. And this despite Cicero's famous injunction: 'Do not bury or burn a dead body in the city' (*On the Laws*, this Roman statesman and philosopher lived in the first century before Christ). And so, in *Londinium*, as elsewhere in the Roman empire, cemeteries were placed outside the walls of cities. Southwark was outside the walls, had no walls of its own despite its thriving community, and so the dead were placed at a little distance – two on the northern and southern island, and two at the important road junction of Stane and Watling Streets (see map on p. 455). But these areas are now right in the middle of the city – north and south of Southwark Street; at Borough Station; and on both sides of Great Dover Street, close to the junction with Borough High Street.

The excellent exhibition on the 'Roman Dead' held at Docklands Museum in 2018 focused on the large, delicate but massively heavy sarcophagus recovered from Harper Road in June 2017 by PCA (overleaf). The sarcophagus contained the skeleton of a woman, some bones from an infant and two fragments – one from a gold necklace or earring, the other a small oval of jasper, carved with a figure of a satyr and which may have been mounted on a ring. A large amount of the evidence presented in the exhibition came from Southwark where six separate sites have yielded artefacts around this theme: Lant Street, Union Street, Southwark Bridge Road, St Thomas Street, Swan Street and Great Dover Street.

City of Westminster guide and blogger Sheldon K Goodman, co-founder of the Cemetery Club, wrote an informative post about the 'Roman Dead' exhibition on 25 May 2018 and described his personal ambition with eloquence: 'to challenge the perception of cemeteries; not as mournful places but as museums of people and libraries of the dead. Fascinating catalogues of lives long gone!'

Coming back from the dead

In the first half of the fourth century AD, *Londinium* was still a capital but in long term decline. When Roman rule ended in 410, the army left and London slowly fell into ruins. Historian Martha Carlin writes: 'occupation at Southwark evidently ceased at the end of the fourth century … there is no archaeological evidence of human activity at Southwark for the next 450 years or more.' Chris Constable, Borough Archaeologist for Southwark, thinks the overall picture is not fully understood and not so clear-cut. There was a level of occupation, as evidenced at the Pickle Factory site, Trinity Church Square. Coins and bodies were recovered from the 'dark earth' which in the past has been interpreted as proof of cessation of human activity.

The Saxons invaded the country in 467 and Wessex was founded in AD 519, gradually consolidating the idea of the Thames as frontier: the South Bank belonged to Wessex, and London to Mercia from 656,

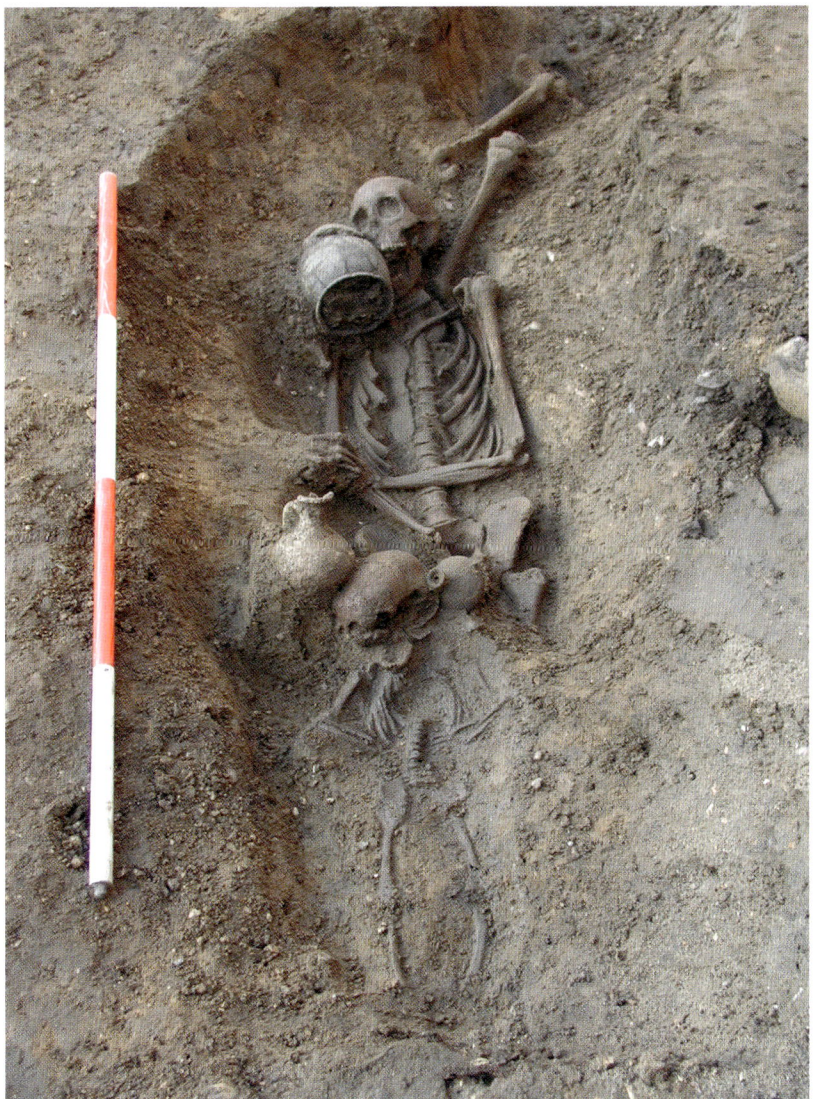

Mercia's foundation date. In 595 the Pope Gregory I sent Augustine, the prior of a Rome monastery, to Britain to convert King Aethelberht to Christianity. Augustine was successful, became the first Archbishop of Canterbury, was canonised and is now regarded as founder of the English church. Christianisation slowly followed its course and the authorities in Rome thought it worthwhile to send a mission in 604 – as a result, Mellitus, the new Bishop of London founded the church of St Paul, but was soon driven out and London relapsed into paganism. The Thames continued to encourage trade and economic prosperity: 'the mart of many nations resorting to it by land and sea' wrote the historian Bede around 730 – referring to Lundenwic, sited near the Aldwych since the Roman city of

Lant Street's triple grave contained the remains of a male teenager, a baby nestled against his leg and a child at his feet. The analysis of the teenager's tooth enamel revealed that the first five years of his life were spent in a Mediterranean country. Three pottery vessels were also placed close to the bodies. The grave has been dated 130–200 AD.
(Pre-Construct Archaeology)

This Roman Sarcophagus, made of Ancaster stone from Lincolnshire, is a rare find – it is one of only thirty which have been recovered in Greater London since the sixteenth century. It was excavated by Pre-Construct Archaeology from a site in Harper Road (at the junction with Swan Street) and it contained the body of a thirty-year-old woman. The tomb appeared to have been robbed but small fragments of precious materials were found inside.

(Pre-Construct Archaeology)

London had been abandoned. The Thames was good for trade but also facilitated Viking attacks – a permanent threat between 834 and 1016.

Books on London history contain snippets of information about traces left by the Vikings on the South Bank but there is no comprehensive survey. Countless attacks of the Vikings on London usually focused on the wharves and London Bridge. Historian Richard Tames summed up the *Olaf Saga*, a thirteenth-century text mentioning Southwark (*Suthvirki*) as 'a great trading place' which was protected by 'large ditches' – this feature was confirmed by archaeologists who found them to be four metres wide. In 1014 King Olaf II of Norway, who had recently converted to Christianity and had switched sides, was now helping King Aethelred II regain control over London. At the famous London Bridge battle Olaf did not hesitate to tear down houses in Southwark to fit his men's boats with protective roofs against missiles. It was also on this occasion that he and his men succeeded in bringing down London Bridge – the source of the nursery rhyme: 'London Bridge is falling down, falling down' – crushing the attacking Danes in the process. Olaf was killed by his countrymen in 1030 and canonised a year later. Londoners did not forget his dramatic intervention in the fight against the Danes and, in awe of his sainthood, dedicated no less than five churches to him – four on the north bank and one in Tooley Street on the South Bank.

The Danish leader Cnut recaptured London in 1016 and was eventually accepted as King of all England; his family reigned for about twenty-five years. King Harhacnut, son of Cnut, died suddenly at a wedding feast held in Lambeth in June 1042 'as he stood at his drink'.

Domesday

The Norman invasion and the systematic and thorough stocktaking of all lands under their control, provided a lasting hold on administering the kingdom.

William I ordered 'The Great Survey' of England and Wales for tax purposes. This was the best way to establish what taxes his predecessor, Edward the Confessor, should have claimed and what he could legitimately levy. The Survey was complete in 1086 and the resulting two volumes became known as the Domesday Book – Domesday as in the Day of Judgement 'because its decisions, like those of the Last Judgment, are unalterable' specified a twelfth-century text *Dialogus of Scaccario*. London and several other towns are not included but the Domesday Book gives the earliest glimpse of the South Bank with four entries, here organized according to their population, recording 'other resources' and the area's tax value:

- Southwark – there is no recorded population, which is not unusual with large towns; however, it would clearly have the highest figure. Other resources: one church. £16
- Lambeth – seventy-nine households. Other resources: meadow of six acres. £4
- Bermondsey (two entries) – seventy-two households. No 'Other resources'. £0.4
- Kennington – eight households. Other resources: meadow of four acres. £3

Lambeth and Kennington had one slave each (listed under households). The king was the only true owner of land in England, sometimes named the lord and sometimes the overlord, then came the church (bishops, religious houses) followed by the Tenants-in-Chief. The chapter dealing with the South Bank around 1600 (p. 85) will present the neighbourhoods in their medieval and post-medieval state but there is one key event which topography cannot account for. It is:

Southwark manors in 1550, based on the work of Martha Carlin (see bibliography) and redrawn by Stephen Conlin. The three manors in the hands of the City were: 'the Guildable' at the southern foot of London Bridge, the 'King's Manor', mostly on the west side of the main road going south from London Bridge, and finally 'the Great Liberty' made up of large tracts of land on the east side. The manors of Paris Garden (top left) and the Clink next to it remained independent.

(© Stephen Conlin)

How Southwark came to be ruled by the city – in ten key events

Southwark controlled London's entrance and exit across the Thames. The bridge itself had always been the responsibility of the City. But as Southwark showed initiative and independence, its reputation grew: as a haven for people who, to the eyes of the City, were guilty of anti-social crimes – from prostitution to escaping control exercised by the City guilds, and the general unruliness which came from a neighbourhood with an unusually high number of taverns.

One of the early signs of Southwark's independence and significance was its representation in 1295 at Edward I's 'Model Parliament'. For this assembly each county sent two knights and each town two burgesses. So Southwark was regarded as 'a town'. Richard Tames noted that it was 'the first part of London outside the City proper to be recognised as worthy of representation in its own right'. Southwark's status was confirmed by an Italian visitor, Dominic Mancini, who thought as early as 1483 that Southwark had so many streets and buildings that if it were surrounded by walls, it would be called a city.

One: Edward II's proclamation in 1326 set the scene: 'malefactors after their offences flee to Southwark … out of the city, because the ministers of the city cannot attack [arrest] them there'.

Two: In 1327 the new King, Edward III, granted the fee farm of Southwark to London.

Three: Several royal charters issued in 1406, 1442, 1462 enabled the City to acquire extensive rights within the central portion of Southwark – known as the Guildable Manor.

Four: During the fifteenth century the City established a weekly market in the High Street in direct competition with the existing market associated with St Thomas' Hospital in a side street off the High Street, probably causing the latter's decline.

Five: Shortly before the suppression of St Thomas' Hospital at the Reformation (1537–38) the Mayor of London, Sir Richard Gresham, petitioned the King to allow the City to have the governance of St Thomas and three other London hospitals. This was unsuccessful.

Six: In 1549, the twelfth-century Lock Hospital for lepers at the junction of Tabard and Great Dover Streets was taken over by the Hospital of St Bartholomew in the City. By the eighteenth century, leprosy had disappeared so it dealt with venereal diseases before its closure in 1760.

Seven: Most of Southwark was brought into the City fold in 1550. This is how the historian John Stow described the event in his 1598 *Survey of London*:

> King Edward VI., for the sum of six hundred and forty-seven pounds two shillings and one penny, paid into his court of augmentations and revenues of his crown, granted to the mayor and commonalty all his lands and tenements in Southwark, except, and reserved, the capital messuage, two mansions called Southwark Place, late the Duke of Suffolk's, and all the gardens and lands to the same appertaining, the park, and the messuage called the Antelope. Moreover, he gave them the lordship and manor of Southwark, with all members and rights thereof, late pertaining to the monastery of Bermondsey … He also granted unto them his manor and borough of Southwark, with all the members, rights, and appurtenances, late of the possession of the Archbishop of Canterbury and his see in Southwark … [continues below]

Eight: Later that year, the alderman for Southwark was directly nominated by the City Aldermen. Stow continues:

> And the same year, in the Whitsun week, in a court of aldermen kept at the Guildhall of London, Sir John Ayloffe, knight, was sworn the first alderman of Bridge Ward Without, and made up the number of twenty-six aldermen of London.

Bankside and Lambeth were not included and that gave the South Bank more than enough independence to escape City rules and develop its own original identity.

Nine: St Thomas's Hospital was closed between 1540 and 1551 as a result of the Dissolution of the Monasteries. It was sold to the City in 1552. This is how a contemporary, the chronicler L. Grenade, summarised what happened to hospitals at the Reformation; he credited 'the good king Edward VI' for this breakthrough:

> [he] wrote to the … Lord Mayor … [who] assembled a common council … [They] made a distinction between poor and poor, and divided them into 3 classes: the first was the sick and helpless; the second orphans and the elderly; the third, vagabonds and idlers … For the first category, Saint Thomas of Southwark was chosen and it was ruled it would receive the sick and elderly. With regard to orphans and other poor abandoned children, the aforementioned home of the so-called Franciscans was selected [Grey Friars, i.e. Christ's Hospital]. And for vagabonds and idlers, the lavish and magnificent residence of Bridewell was chosen.

The Singularities of London, 1578

Ten: The existence of Bridge Ward Without lasted from 1550 to 1899; but in practice the system continued until 1978. In the words of John William Pinder, the historian of St George's church: 'The original intention was that Southwark should have full civic rights but these were never granted despite several attempts to obtain them. Consequently, Southwark has always been a kind of poor relation' (1965).

Sources used (see bibliography for abbreviated entries)

Barton; Gibberd; Carlin; Tames; 'The Place, formerly New London Bridge House, 25 London Bridge Street, London SE1' LBN08 Post-excavation report © MOLA 2012; MoLAS 2002; PCA 2013; PCA 2015; Ross & Clark, *London, The Illustrated Story*; Domesday website; Pinder

THE SOUTH BANK AROUND 1600

Lambeth

The landlords north and south of the river were very different; north of the river they were dukes and earls whilst in Lambeth ... the landlords never changed, being the Archbishop of Canterbury and the Duchy of Cornwall ... North of the river the landlords exploited their land with speculative developments but in Lambeth Marsh the two ground landlords never built; only tenants built and they were always small developments.

Graham Gibberd

Southwark

In 1327 the City acquired its charter from Edward III and took authority over the Guildable Manor, the original Southwark burh settlement ... This began the steady encroachment of the City's authority, not merely ownership, into the transpontine area.

Tony Sharp

The reconstruction on the previous page illustrates how royal and religious establishments dominated the South Bank until around 1600. It shows the residual impact of an outgoing medieval culture – for instance the sprawling mass of Lambeth House (later Palace) or Winchester Palace; but it also hints at the changes brought about by royal decree with the Dissolution of the Monasteries (1536-41). Bermondsey Abbey has been partially demolished and is in private hands; the former Priory of St Mary Overie, is now a parish church, renamed St Saviour's; its famous hospital, once run by the Priory, is rebuilt further south and owned by the City of London; the homes of bishops and abbots in Southwark are ordinary inns such as those of the Prior of Lewes or the Abbot of Battle Abbey. The theatres may still be glimpsed but are soon to be wiped away by the South Bank's changing fortunes.

The land is still largely split between the Crown and the Church but the latter has suffered. Tim Tatton-Brown, the historian of Lambeth Palace, writes 'the late sixteenth and early seventeenth centuries saw a considerable diminution of the status of the Archbishop of Canterbury. This started in a big way in 1577 when Edmund Grindal … was sequestered (suspended) by Queen Elizabeth. He spent the rest of his life effectively in internal exile on his estates'.

The Crown also partially stepped back from the scene; royal seats such as Suffolk Place, Kennington Palace and Fox Hall have either gone or been reduced to a ghostly presence. With the departure of the royals from the South Bank and the Church in disarray, the scene is set for a new order. What will happen next?

Sources in brackets under each entry (full references in bibliography)

1600 or thereabouts is a useful date for contemporary sources as the image of London took shape from the mid-sixteenth century onwards (see Chapter 2). In the reconstruction we were able to lean on the 1542 map of Southwark, Anthonis van den Wyngaerde's extraordinary panorama of London (see pp. 36–37); the late sixteenth-century map of London by Braun and Hogenberg – a miniature version of the intricately detailed 'Copperplate map' (see p. 40); as well as the so-called Agas map, a later full-size version also deriving from the 'Copperplate map'. Even the map of Tudor London in 1520 was useful for sites on the border of the Thames, as were the mid-seventeenth century engravings by Wenceslaus Hollar and the late seventeenth-century Restoration map by William Morgan have helped fill some of the gaps. Finally, the antiquary and first historian of London, John Stow (1525–1605), published his *Survey of London* in 1598, two years before our chosen date. His text may be unreliable at times but it unquestionably breathes life into the streets of South London.

I have also used contemporary sources such as the relevant volumes of the *Survey of London*, the publications of Julian Bowsher, Martha Carlin, Dorian Gerhold, Graham Gibberd, Jennifer Potter, Tim Tatton Brown, Warwick Wroth.

Manors

(dates in brackets show when first mentioned in the records)

- Manor of South Lambeth (1263)
- Manors of Kennington and Vauxhall: in 1337, Edward III granted these two manors to his eldest son Edward.
- Manor of Lambeth (1042) made up of Water Lambeth and quite distinct from Lambeth Marsh further north. This was the 'Lambhythe' of the 1086 Domesday Survey. Its heart was Lambeth High Street. William II granted the manor of Lambeth to the convent of St Andrew, Rochester in the eleventh century; a hundred years or so later it entered the portfolio of the Archbishop of Canterbury.
- Paris Garden, a liberty (former name 'the Wilys' i.e. Willows) – First mentioned in 1113, this small manor of around 100 acres had first belonged to Cluniac monks followed by the Templars, then the Hospitallers, until 1536. In May 1589, it was bought by the developer Francis Langley.
- Guildable Manor, belonged to the Crown but was acquired by the City in 1327.
- The Clink was the manor of the Bishop of Winchester, known as the 'liberty of the Clink' from the sixteenth century.
- King's Manor, described in Domesday (1086), belonged to the powerful Warenne family and their successors. This manor was sold to the City in 1550.
- Manor of Walworth granted to the Prior and Convent of Christ Church, Canterbury in 1052. From the thirteenth century it became synonymous with the parish of St Mary's Newington.
- Great Liberty (its sixteenth-century name) was the Archbishop of Canterbury's manor.
- Manor of Bermondsey: William II granted lands there to the Priory around 1094, a grant confirmed by Henry I in 1127.

Parishes

In 1600 there were seven parishes: those of St Mary's Lambeth, St Saviour's Southwark, St Thomas's Southwark, St George's Southwark, St Mary Newington, St Olave's Southwark and St Mary Magdalen Bermondsey.

VAUXHALL AND LAMBETH

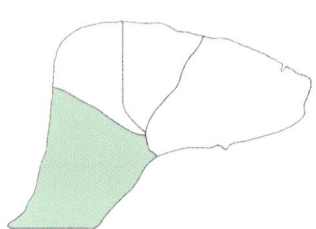

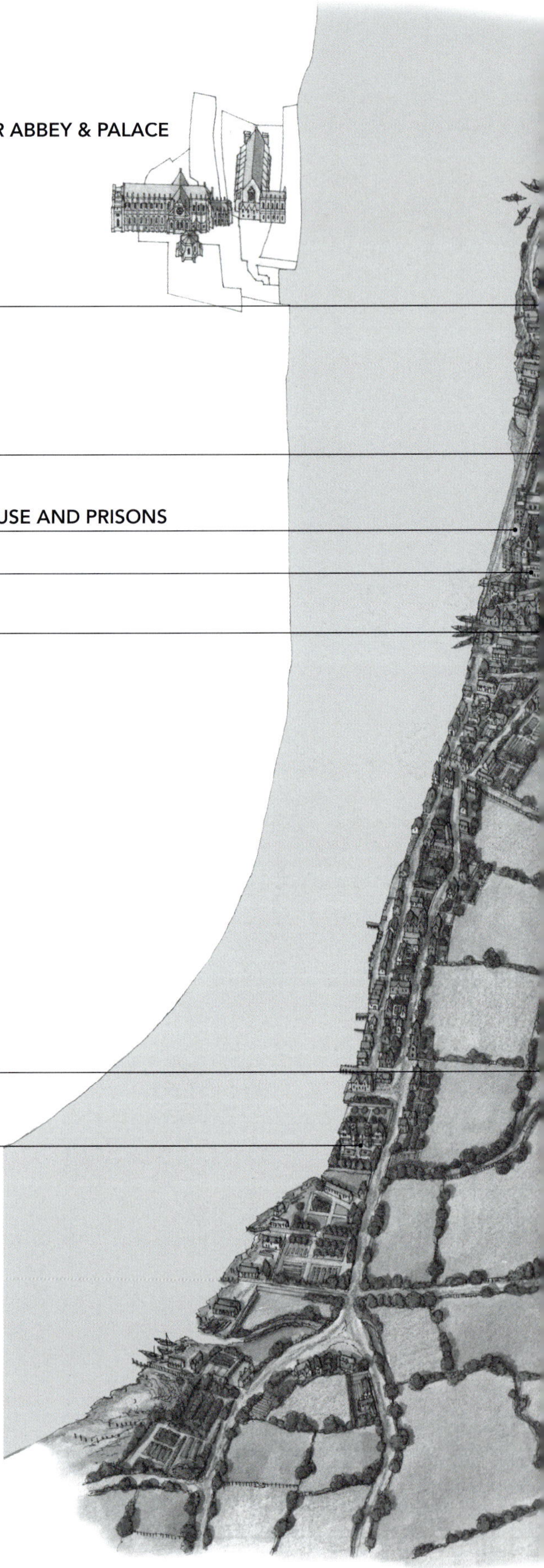

WESTMINSTER ABBEY & PALACE

VL11 CARLISLE HOUSE

VL9 GARDEN OF LAMBETH HOUSE

VL9 & VL10 LAMBETH HOUSE AND PRISONS

VL8 CHURCH OF ST MARY, LAMBETH

VL7 NORFOLK HOUSE

VL3 KENNINGTON PALACE

VL6 COPT HALL (LATER FOX HALL)

VL4 TRADESCANT HOUSE
VL5 CARON HOUSE
See pages 94 and 96

Above:

Thomas Hill's 1681 map of the Manor of Vauxhall. This is the earliest surviving map for Vauxhall – an important document which records the essentially rural character of this neighbourhood and the arrival of industry in the seventeenth century. John Baker's glasshouse by the side of the Thames just above Spring Garden (the future Vauxhall Gardens) is recorded, but not its more famous predecessors (see p. 154). The blown-up detail at the bottom left corner, helps us understand the layout of the glasshouse. The map also includes the South Lambeth 'gardens' enclave: Caron House and the Tradescants' site to its left. See p. 96 for a reconstruction using correct orientation - north at the top.

(Canterbury Cathedral Archives, map 18; by permission of the Dean & Chapter of Canterbury).

(VL1) Church of St Mary, Newington: little is known about the medieval church, not even its precise site! However, the list of rectors is almost complete from 1212 onward which suggests a thirteenth-century building. The first description to have come down to us is that of John Aubrey in 1718 who said the church was about 150 years old, i.e. around 1570, except for the north aisle which was built in 1600:

> very small and built of brick and boulder ... a double Roof covered with Tile, and the Walls with a rough Cast; the Windows are of a modern Gothick; the Floor is paved with Stone, the Body being one Step lower than the Chancel. Here are three Iles, and the Roof is supported with wooden Pillars, partly of the Tuscan Order, formed octogonally.

Aubrey noted that the tower had five bells. No picture exists. Continues on p. 163

(*Survey of London* 25)

(VL2) Newington Butts playhouse. In 1566, the owners of the land – the Dean and Chapter of Canterbury Cathedral leased a field at Newington Butts (on the site of today's Elephant & Castle massive road junction) to Richard Hicks, a 'yeoman of her Majesty's guard'. In 1596, the landowners described the property: 'one messuage or tenement heretofore by one Richard Hicks, deceased, erected and built upon parcel of the said lands, now called the playhouse, with 'all houses gardens or orchards thereto adjoining'.

The Elizabethan actor Jerome Savage, from the Warwick's Men company, is believed to have leased the 'messuage or tenement' around 1576, converting the house into a playhouse (an indoor theatre). When the company dissolved in 1580, various other companies are recorded there, probably involving theatre impresario Philip Henslowe. We know for instance that the great actor Edward Alleyn was working there in 1593 when the plague was raging in London.

Documents show that the new lease holder, Paul Buck, planned to 'convert the playhouse to some other use'. Julian Bowsher adds: 'it is also the first playhouse to be built, albeit converted, by a player'.
(Bowsher; Jan Piggott, *Dulwich College – A History* 1616-2008, 2008)

(VL3) Kennington Palace stood near the junction of Kennington Lane and Kennington Road. The site of the Palace is marked on a Kennington Estate map of 1636. The site had been occupied by a manor house from the eleventh century – probably then a timber construction. In the fourteenth century Edward III granted Kennington Palace to his son, Edward of Woodstock (1330-1376) the first Duke of Cornwall, known from the sixteenth century as the Black Prince. The estate has been in the hands of the monarch's eldest son ever since, as part of the Duchy of Cornwall; it was the Duke's chief residence near London.

The young Edward partly demolished the old Palace to rebuild it along more ambitious lines using one of the best architects of the time – Henry Yevele, one of this country's main exponents of the Perpendicular style. The Prince was known to be impressed by the castle of John, Duke of Berri (Chateau de Lusignan in Poitou, France). No plans or images of Kennington Palace exist but Yevele's contract mentions two spiral staircases and three chimneys at the end of the hall – an arrangement which recalls what was built for the Duke of Berri. A 1399 roll of 'particulars' refers to a 'painted chamber' at Kennington and a 'great garden' planted with vines … and a royal barge lay at Lambeth for the King's visits.

When Prince Edward wed Joan of Kent in 1361, Kennington Palace was almost ready. In the accounts the buildings mentioned were: the great hall, the great chamber, the chapel and the small chapel. Both the Prince's sons – Edward who died in childhood, and Richard, the future Richard II were brought up here.

The Palace subsequently faced years of neglect and in 1531, Henry VIII is believed to have demolished part of the structure to re-use its materials when building Whitehall Palace. In 1589 when Queen Elizabeth granted a lease of the estate to Richard Beamond, the description of the land read: 'demesne lands of our manor of Kennington. And all houses, buildings, structures, barns, stables, dovecotes, yards, orchards, gardens, land, meadow, feed, leasowes and pasture… containing by estimation, 122 acres'. (Dulwich College) Edward Alleyn was a subsequent lease holder, followed by 'Ambassador' Caron (see below).

Some have claimed the palace had completely disappeared by 1607 but William Faden's map of 1785 clearly shows a long rectangular structure with a central projection at the back labelled 'Black Prince', seemingly on the same site as the contemporary 'Black Prince Court'. This was probably the 'long barn' or stables which survived into the nineteenth century (see the 1636 plan in Lambeth Archives – ref. 01939).

The reconstruction takes inspiration from Lusignan castle in France – its ghostly outline indicates the missing presence of what was once a remarkable landmark.
(HM Colvin (editor), *The History of the King's Works*, 1962–83; *Survey of London* 23)

(VL4) Tradescant House, South Lambeth Road. This property was situated on the Vauxhall Escheat, a portion of land from a manor which is leased, sold or given/granted (illustrated overleaf). The *Survey of London* charted the list of tenants who occupied this land from 1592 onwards, creating a useful map. The Tradescants' house and garden were sited on part of the land which had been purchased from the Foster family by the Flemish national, Sir Noel Caron (in 1618, see below). Historian David Sturdy has identified the site of the house as the present 113–119 South Lambeth Road.

There John Tradescant the Elder (1570/75–1638), botanist and gardener, developed his garden and 'museum' – the Ark. Caron died in 1624 and barely five years later Tradescant's plants were recorded at the southern end of the site. The land reverted back to the Dean and Chapter of Canterbury in 1632, but John the Elder opened up his garden to the public as early as 1634 when the first plant catalogue was published – 'Catalogus', listing 750 different plants. In 1638 John the Elder died, handing over his royal gardener post to son John (1608–1662), who continued the work at the South Lambeth garden and the Ark.

Around 1650, John Tradescant the Younger met the great antiquary, botanist and alchemist Elias Ashmole (1617–1692), of Ashmolean Museum fame and two years later Ashmole published a catalogue of Tradescant's plants at Vauxhall/Lambeth. Both men were inveterate collectors – Tradescant, like his father whose frequent travels had led him to form 'the Ark', one of this country's earliest Cabinet of Curiosities – the precursors of museums. Continues on p. 152
(*Survey of London* 26; Potter)

(VL5) Caron House (overleaf) was the home of Noel Caron (before 1530–1624), Lord of Schoonewale in his native Flanders. He came to London in 1585 when he tried,

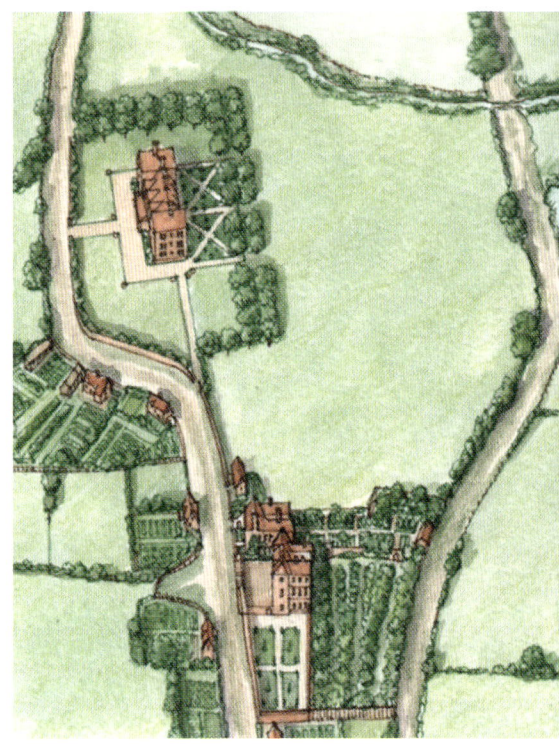

Above:

Caron House. Lewis Frederick, Prince of Württemberg described the location of this house in 1610: '… After dinner he went to see the resident Ambassador of the States [of the Netherlands], Mr Carron who lives out of the city, opposite Westminster, in a very fine house of his own, well furnished, and with beautiful gardens round about: it is called South Lambeth. On repassing through the suburb of Water Lambeth, where the Archbishop of Canterbury resides, his Excellency met at the Thames ferry the Prince, and the Prince of Brunswick, with whom he crossed the water and went to see the tombs of the Kings at Westminster'. (Detail taken from Thomas Hill's 1681 map on p. 94)

Right:

Reconstruction of the Vauxhall Escheat (VL4–VL5) with Caron House at the top and the Tradescant/Ashmole houses at the bottom. (© Stephen Conlin, 2021; based on Thomas Hill's 1681 map)

unsuccessfully, to persuade Queen Elizabeth to claim sovereignty of his country under Spanish occupation. He eventually elected to settle in London and purchased in two parts his large estate at South Lambeth – 'most of the freehold land available at Vauxhall Manor at the onset of the seventeenth century' says the *Survey of London*. First in 1602, 70 acres with a 'greate howse' and a dairy. He built himself a new, lavish residence and also attended to the garden, which was celebrated. In 1618, he purchased more land adjoining his estate. It became an unofficial focus for Flemish diplomats and other important visiting dignitaries. John Aubrey wrote that the house was pulled down around 1687.
(*Survey of London* 26; Potter; Aubrey)

(VL6) Fox Hall on the site of MI6 building. The building of Fox Hall or Fauxhall and even Fulke's Hall was the outcome of an unhappy marriage ordered by King John in the early thirteenth century – that of the widow Margaret de Redvers (South Lambeth Manor) to an Anglo-Norman soldier Sir Fulk of Brent (various spellings, including Falkes de Breauté). When he fell from favour in 1224, his wife Margaret requested a divorce from the King (by then it was Henry III). She was not successful but recovered some of her lands. Sir Fulk went into exile and died in Rome in 1226. When Margaret died the contemporary historian Matthew Paris (1200–1259) wrote in his *Chronica Majora*: 'noble though she was, she was married to this ignoble creature, the pious to the impious, beauty to the foul, unwilling and coerced'.

There is no known view of the aristocratic Fulke's Hall. It was close to, but separate from, the large mansion depicted here – Copped Hall or Copt Hall which at the beginning of the seventeenth century came to assume the name of Faux Hall when the original manor house was no longer in existence.

Shortly after the accession of James I (1603), a plot financed by Spain was uncovered and Lady Arabella Stuart, one of Henry VIII's descendants, was thought

ready to usurp the throne. She was placed under house arrest at Fox Hall under the watchful eye of its resident, Sir Thomas Parry. She eloped to meet and marry William Seymour in Calais but she was caught and sent to the Tower.
(Wilkinson; Walter Thornbury & Edward Walford, *Old & New London*, 1878, Vol. 6; *Survey of London* 26)

(VL7) **Norfolk House**, sited opposite St Mary's church, Lambeth, on the south side.

By 1600, the heyday of Norfolk House and its estate was over. One of the earliest records for the site ownership dates from 1397 when Richard Fitzalan, 4th Earl of Arundel and Surrey, beheaded in that year, lost this land on his attainder. The *Survey of London* tells us it is not known how long the Fitzalans had held land in Lambeth though Richard's son managed to recover the estate two years later

The Arundel estates were eventually transferred to the Howard family, one of the most powerful recusant families in England. Thomas Howard (1536–1572), 4th Duke of Norfolk, was soon 'the greatest landowner in the kingdom' writes the historian John Martin Robinson, later giving rise to the popular comment that the Duke could ride from Arundel in Sussex to his house in Lambeth without ever leaving his estate. His son, Philip Howard, was the future St Philip, a canonized saint (1970). The property acquired notoriety earlier in the sixteenth century for it was where Catherine Howard, the fifth wife of Henry VIII was born and brought up (born around 1523, executed in 1542).

This is how the estate was described when it sold in the 1570s:
two inns, formerly called the George and the Bell, the former being annexed to the mansion house on the west and the Bell, on the east; Bell Close, at the rear of the Bell, containing two acres, two perches; 23½ acres in "Cottmansfeld," an acre of pasture in St. George's Field, a close lying near the Bishop of Rochester's House (later Carlisle House) containing four acres, three acres of meadow near Prince's Meadows, and eight acres of marsh called "The Hopes" (see pp. 430–431).

The property was divided into three parts: two thirds went to Thomas Cure (see BB14) and the rest, which included Norfolk House, was sold and re-sold, then also divided into three. The western portion, the site of most of the original mansion, was sold to Archbishop Whitgift in 1590. Sir George Paule bought the house from Whitgift's son in 1608 and lived there until his death in 1635. The 1608 sale gives details about Norfolk House.

A great gate from 'the King's highway leading from Lambeth Town to St. George's Fields' [Lambeth Road] then a paved yard. The Duke's chapel on the west side had been converted into a hall, buttery and parlour by 1590, 'a greate chamber' on the first floor, a gallery, oratory and several closets, with the hall opening on to the garden on the south. The total width of the garden was 125 feet, and it is a reasonable assumption that the street frontage was approximately the same.

In 1990, part of the site was excavated and the footings of the original house found. Also see St Mary's entry below.
(*Survey of London* 23; Gibberd; John Martin Robinson, *The Dukes of Norfolk*, 1995)

(VL8) **Church of St Mary, Lambeth**: the foundation of this church pre-dates the Norman Conquest. The church is listed in the Domesday book (1086) as belonging to King Edward the Confessor's sister, Countess Goda. After being administered by the Bishops of Rochester, it was handed over to the Archbishop of Canterbury in 1197. The church was rebuilt in stone in the fourteenth century (1374–77 for the nave; the tower followed). More building work followed in the sixteenth century and parish records began in 1504.

The description found in John Aubrey's *Natural history of Surrey* (1719) documents the Leigh and Norfolk chapels built in the 1520s: 'that at the East End of the North Ile, is called HOWARD'S Chapel, from the Interment of some of the *Norfolk* Family, and one at the East End of the South Ile, called *LEIGH'S* Chapel, where lye buried Sir *John Leigh*, Son of *Ralph Leigh*, Esq.; Lord of the Manor of *Stockwell*, and his Wife. The Inside of this Church is light and pleasant'. The Howard and Leigh chapels were built in 1522; both families were most generous in their patronage of the church.
(Wyngaerde; Braun & Hogenberg; *Survey of London* 23)

(VL9) **Lambeth House (later Palace)**: In 1600, the occupant of Lambeth House was Archbishop John Whitgift (1530–1604) from Lincolnshire. He was followed by Archbishop Richard Bancroft (1544–1610) who bequeathed his great library to his successors, 'England's first public library … today the principal library for the history of the Church of England' (Edwards).

The manor of Lambeth was in royal hands by the time of the

Domesday Survey. William II granted it to the church of St Andrew in Rochester who in 1190 exchanged this manor with the Archbishop of Canterbury for land in Darenth, Kent – minus the retention of enough land for the bishop of Rochester's London residence. Apart from one exception in 1648–1650, during the Commonwealth, when the manor of Lambeth was sold for just over £7000, with the intention to pull down the palace, the manor has remained in ecclesiastical hands ever since.

The existence of Lambeth House arose from the twelfth-century conflict between two religious factions: Archbishop Baldwin of Forde (c.1125–1190) was fighting the monks of Christ Church for ecclesiastical supremacy and the situation became so tense that the Archbishop sought relief from interference. First, he set up a collegiate chapel just outside Canterbury before finally planning a site further away, close to London at the manor of Lambeth. He died on crusade and it was his successor Archbishop Hubert Walter (1160–1205) who built the collegiate chapel in 1197 on the site Archbishop Baldwin had intended for it. This was opposed by the Priory of Christ Church in Canterbury; two years later, backed by the Pope, they succeeded in having the chapel razed to the ground. Soon after, a resolution to this impasse was found and Archbishop Walter was allowed to build a house of Praemonstratensian canons (from the order founded in Premontré in northern France) at Lambeth with accommodation for his own residence.

Walter's successor, the renowned Biblical scholar, Archbishop Stephen Langton (c.1150–1228) developed and consolidated the project when he was elected in 1207. He is believed to have been the first archbishop to live at Lambeth House. Part of the chapel crypt may date from this time; no remnants of the previous chapel have been found. The residential/ecclesiastical complex was ready by 1300. The guard room, which has survived, probably dates from the second half of the fourteenth century with its roof, 'one of the finest surviving medieval roofs in London' according to Tim Tatton Brown.

In the fifteenth century Lambeth House acquired two towers which added a defensive character to the overall structure and consolidated its status as London's most magnificent ecclesiastical house – Lollards' tower, started by Archbishop Henry Chichele (completed in 1435), followed by Morton's Tower at the main entrance in the 1450s. Two further towers followed in the sixteenth and seventeenth centuries: the so-called Laud's tower, early sixteenth-century and built before Laud's time, afforded four floors of lodging chambers. Both Laud's and Morton's towers incorporated prisons (see below). Archbishop William Laud (1573–1645) could not resist the addition of a third tower in 1635 – a staircase tower against the Lollards' tower.

Archbishop William Warham (c.1450–1532), who had crowned Henry VIII in 1509, welcomed the Dutch humanist and scholar Erasmus and the famous painter Hans Holbein the Younger (1497–1543). He was followed by Thomas Cranmer (1489–1556), a leader of the English Reformation, and the author of the Book of Common Prayer. In the mid-1550s Cardinal Reginald Pole (1500–1558) became the last Roman Catholic archbishop of Canterbury. Much of his life was spent in Italy and this may have prompted him to add a Gallery to Lambeth Palace. It is also in the mid-sixteenth century that the first post-reformation Archbishop

Above:
Lollard's Tower also known as Chichele's or even Water Tower, Lambeth Palace. It was one of archbishop Chichele's projects, built in Kentish ragstone in 1434-35. The prison at the top of this tower is believed to have imprisoned 'the Lollards', the followers of John Wycliffe who challenged the religious establishment but predated the Reformation. (Photos courtesy of Lambeth Palace Library)

was consecrated: Matthew Parker (1504–1575). Parker and his wife were particularly interested in the garden and the gardeners' duties were set down at that time:

> to see the garden, orchard and walks to be kept well weeded and rolled, the grass walks not suffered to be much grown, but kept low with the scythe. To see that there be planted in the grounds flowers, herbs and roots, both for the provision of the kitchen and chambers; and with all sorts of good fruits, herbs, plants and flowers for use and pleasure (cited in Huelin).

The library was created in

Opposite top:
The Lambeth Apocalypse, 1260s; written in Latin and produced in England. This folio represents the black horse of the Apocalypse according to St John (6: 5–6): 'And I beheld, and lo a black horse; and he that sat on him had a pair of balances in his hand.' Commentators have suggested this indicated approaching famine when foods were so scarce, they had to be weighed and rationed.
(Lambeth Palace Library, Ms 209, f. 5v. Image in the public domain; Wikimedia Commons)

Opposite below:
This is the portrait of St Matthew, the Evangelist; from the MacDurnan Gospels, about 888–927.
(Lambeth Palace Library, MS 1370, folio 4 verso; image in the public domain. Wikimedia Commons)

1610, England's first public library noted David Edwards, when Archbishop Bancroft bequeathed his great collection of books to Lambeth House. Now it holds 4000 manuscripts, including 600 medieval documents.

The reconstruction has relied heavily on Hollar's 1647 views of the Palace. His view of Lambeth House from the Thames (above) is the only record of the later medieval great hall before it was pulled down around 1650. This print also includes a group of houses in Water Lambeth and the long landing stage described in the records as 'The Great Bridge'. Continues on p. 157.
(Wyngaerde II; Braun & Hogenberg; LTS 1988; *Survey of London* 23; Huelin; Edwards; Tatton Brown)

(VL10) Lambeth House prisons: Archbishop Henry Chichele was the first to add a prison to Lambeth House; in 1425 he built his 'Lollards' tower, so-called after the name given to the followers of 'heretic' John Wycliffe (d. 1384), the reformer seminary professor based at the University of Oxford. He advocated restraint on the part of the clergy and for religion to be more accessible to all. The prison was on the upper floor. The building of Morton's Tower (1450s) added a second prison cell. Historian Hannah Renier gives a vivid description of the rising discontent which led to the arrival of prisons at Lambeth House; there

> lived men who wore ermine and sable, richly dyed warm wool and silk and linen and jewels. They spent their days in prayer and intrigue. Outside the gates, paupers in hessian and fustian and rabbit fur shivered and scratched and died in intermittent plagues. Anger slowly mounted.

(VL11) Carlisle House, formerly La Place. La Place was the name of the Bishop of Rochester's London home from 1197. It was sited a little further north from Lambeth Palace and parallel to it. It ran its own ferry across the Thames, delivering passengers but not horses, much closer to Westminster than the Horseferry at

Lambeth House seen from the river, etching by Wenceslaus Hollar, 1647.
(Fisher Hollar Collection, University of Toronto. Picture in the public domain; Wikimedia Commons)

Lambeth Palace. At the Reformation, the Bishop of Rochester fell out of favour with Henry VIII and his property was confiscated and handed over to the more compliant Bishop of Carlisle; it was rebuilt in 1540 and became known as Carlisle House; modern day Carlisle Street is on the site of this property. The Bishop of Rochester who escaped with his life, relocated to Southwark (see p. 120). The house was sold in 1647 but reverted back to the see of Carlisle in 1660. Continues on p. XX.
(*Survey of London* 23, Gibberd 71)

(VL12) **Stangate and Stangate Stairs** now on the site of St Thomas' Hospital. Stangate, meaning 'stone lane', is a name which probably dates back to Roman times. Its site, which was approached by Lambeth Marsh, is associated with crossing the Thames – an early visual representation of this is found in Wyngaerde's long view of London; Braun and Hogenberg's 1572 map-view of London depicts it too (see p. 40) though it is not named.
(Wyngaerde II; Braun & Hogenberg; *Survey of London* 23)

WATERLOO

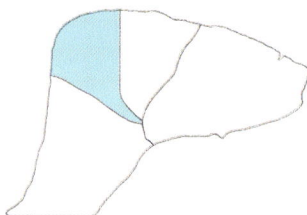

W6 HOLLAND'S LEAGUER IN PARIS GARDEN

W5 OLD BARGE HOUSE

W4 [A]SPARAGUS GARDEN

W3 LAMBETH MARSH

W2 BISHOP BONNER'S HOUSE

LOWER MARSH (See page 169)

W1 BISHOP BONNER'S HOUSE

ST. GEORGE'S FIELDS (See pages 172–173)

Despite its title 'Lambeth Marsh as it appeared about the year 1670', this nineteenth-century engraving by J Barnett shows the Marsh just before the Great Fire of 1666 and is based on Hollar's Prospect of London from Lambeth (pp. 392–393). Taken from a viewpoint close to Lambeth House (bottom left, not shown), it is looking towards the area which would later become Waterloo, and beyond, towards the City. It shows Norfolk House in the left foreground.
(© The Trustees of the British Museum)

(W1–W2) **The somewhat mysterious Bishop Bonner's House,** on the south side of Lower Marsh became a local landmark – perhaps because it had once been a splendid Tudor style building before turning into a picturesque ruin. The 1806 enclosure map for the Manor of Lambeth (Lambeth Archives) shows it close to the junction with Westminster Bridge Road, as a large building set back from the road which corresponds to the image (bottom right) reproduced here.

At first Bishop Edmund Bonner (c. 1500–1569) sided with Henry VIII's schism from the Church but later returned to the Catholic cause. This earned him the nickname of 'Bloody Bonner' as he was an enthusiastic supporter of Queen Mary, 'Bloody Mary', when she pursued her relentless purge of protestants. The association of this house with Bonner is puzzling. The only source to mention the two together is John Strype's *Memorials of Cranmer* which records an ordination 'in the chapel of my lord the Bishop of London in the Lower Marsh'. When Elizabeth I came to the throne, Bishop Bonner was imprisoned in the Marshalsea and threatened with execution; although briefly released, he spent the last year of his life in the Marshalsea where he died on 5 September 1569. He is buried in St George's Southwark. This house was demolished in July 1823.

However, a second, much smaller house, was also labelled 'Bishop Bonner's house' by artists and local historians, and sometimes called 'the old house' (top right). It stood on what is now 19 Lower Marsh – a sixteenth century structure with picturesque

windows but also in ruins in the nineteenth century (see Sandby on p. 173).
(Lambeth Archives; Gibberd; Allen; I am grateful to Richard Woollard for his help with this entry)

(W3) **Lambeth Marsh**: the name goes back to 1332 (Lay subsidy returns) and describes the wedge-shaped area found between Lambeth and Blackfriars Bridges. Until the eighteenth century the words 'Lambeth Marsh' tended to designate a landscape – the whole of the area of North Lambeth. Later it came to designate the street split between Upper and Lower Marsh. The word 'Marsh' has survived to this day but not the association of 'Lambeth' and 'Marsh' which was dropped in 1889 when the Borough of Lambeth was formed. Graham Gibberd ascribes this to the wish 'to forget the less salubrious part of their new-found borough'. The administrative name North Lambeth dates from 1900.
(*Survey of London* 23; Gibberd)

(W4) [A]**Sparagus Garden**, Lambeth Marsh. The playwright Richard Brome (?1590–1652) set his eponymous play of 1635 in this otherwise poorly documented Lambeth pleasure garden, though its site is clearly marked on Morgan's late seventeenth-century map. The garden was so named because the refreshments served included asparagus and strawberries. Pepys was there on 22 April 1668 hoping to meet friends who turned out to be in Covent Garden where he headed next, without describing the said garden. Curiously, he mentioned eating asparagus in Guildford on the very same day, 22 April, six years previously: 'there passed our time in the garden, cutting of sparagus for supper, the best that ever I eat in my life'.

The connection between Brome's play and a real-life location marked the introduction in literary circles of geographic realism. It offers a distant echo – a century later – of the 'geographic school' described in the

Eye of London chapter. Some have argued that in poetry it first manifested itself in John Denham's poem 'On Cooper's Hill' (1642) but clearly plays came earlier with Ben Jonson's *Bartholomew Fair* (1614, performed at the Hope theatre, but only published in 1631), Shackerley Marmion's *Holland's Leaguer* (1631, see overleaf) and Brome's *Sparagus Garden* in 1635. The dates relate to the works when they were first performed; publication came later.(Morgan 1682, Plan 32; Gibberd 26; Wikipedia 12 November 2020)

(W5) **Old Barge House.** The sloping beach on this spot was ideal for landing barges and the Old Barge House was first recorded as Henry VIII's in the sixteenth century – recalled today as Barge House Stairs. The barge itself was described in 1593 as containing 'two splendid cabins beautifully ornamented with glass windows, painting and gilding.' By the seventeenth century the area was sheltering several barge houses including those of the Merchant Taylors, the Woodmongers and the Lord Mayor of London. Further south between Stangate ferry and Horseferry were the barge houses of the Armourers Company, the Goldsmiths,

Bishop Bonner's House in Lower Marsh was frequently depicted by artists and topographers. It was picturesque, ancient and a little mysterious – no one could piece its history together. The association with Bishop Bonner has never been satisfactorily explained and when a second house, in a slightly different location, was also designated Bishop Bonner's House, the plot simply thickened.

1. Watercolour by Sir Thomas Gage, 1809 (Lambeth Archives)
2. Anonymous watercolour, 1820s © London Metropolitan Archives (City of London)

the Grocers, the Barber-Surgeons and the Royal Barge when it moved from Lower Marsh. In the late sixteenth century the actor-entrepreneur Edward Alleyn and his father-in-law, theatre impresario Philip Henslowe, owned the Old Barge House Alley where royal barges were kept and was also the site of the fourth Bear Garden – 'the Hope' which mixed, unsuccessfully, theatre and bear baiting – another of their ventures (see p. 448).
(Morgan 21; *Survey of London* 22; *VCH 4*)

(W6) Paris Garden (former name: Wideflete manor or Wylis) granted to Henry Cary by Elizabeth I in 1578, it was acquired by Thomas Cure junior in 1580 (son of Thomas Cure, see BB14) before selling it to Francis Langley when it was described as: 'four messuages, two tofts, four gardens, ten acres of land, fifty acres of meadow, thirty acres of pasture and one acre of woodland'.

A high-class brothel, the Holland's Leaguer (right), was housed in Paris Garden's former manor house. It was eventually besieged by the law in December 1631 and January 1632. The owner, Elizabeth Holland, avoided conviction and was able to move her business elsewhere. The affair was so well known that it inspired a play by Shackerley Marmion (1631), a ballad by Lawrence Price and a 1632 pamphlet written by Nicholas Goodman. The last contains a rare and elliptical early seventeenth-century description of Paris Garden and Bankside, with occasional exaggerations such as 'delicate river' when referring to the Thames. The heroine, Britanica (sic) Hollandia alias Elizabeth Holland, is looking for a new home:

> It was out of the Citie, yet in the view of the Citie, only divided by a delicate River, there was many handsome buildings, and many hearty neighbours … she was brought to a fort, citadel, or mansion house, so fortified and environed with all manner of fortifications that ere any foe could approach it, hee must march … on a narrow banke between two dangerous ditches … she was most taken with the report of three famous amphytheators, which stood so neere scituated, that her eye might take a view of them from her lowest turret – one was the Continent of the World [= the Globe theatre] … , the other was a building of excellent Hope [= the Hope Theatre], and though wild beasts and gladiators did most possesse it, yet the gallants that came to behold those combats, though they were of a mixt society, yet were many noble worthies amongst them. The last which stood … being in times past as famous as any of the others, was now fallen to decay, and like a dying swanne [the Swan Theatre], hanging down her head, seemed to sing her own dierge [sad song].

In the sixteenth century Paris Garden was also widely known for animal baiting; for instance, the actor-manager Edward Alleyn kept the following at Paris Garden: 120 mastiffs, three bulls, twenty bears, three polar bears, and the lions; a leopard and a wolf were also mentioned in the records. Animal baiting predated theatre, with the full approval of royalty since it was a royal monopoly, in particular Richard III who established the post of 'Maister, Guyder and Ruler of all our Beres and Apes' in 1484.

Towards the middle of the sixteenth century, William Baiseley, Bailiff of Southwark opened Paris Garden to the public as a recreational place for bowling and gambling.

Graham Gibberd has traced the outlines of the former Paris Garden on London streets now:
West: Barge House Stairs (near Oxo Tower) down to The Cut along Hatfields
South: Boundary Row/Pocock Street up to Great Suffolk Street
East: up Great Suffolk Street to the river (near the Founder's Arms pub)
North: along the river
Continues on p. 184.

Paris Garden is split across two of this book's neighbourhoods – 1. Waterloo and 2. Bankside & Borough. When described as a single neighbourhood it has been placed under Waterloo.
(Agas; Grenade; *Survey of London* 22; Gibberd; Jan Piggott, *Dulwich College – A History 1616–2008*, 2008)

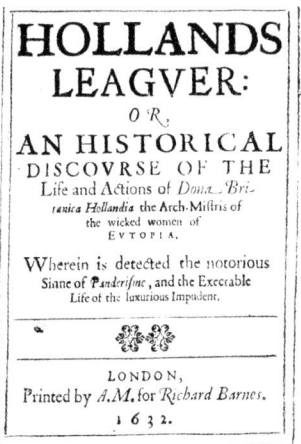

Above:
Holland's Leaguer at Paris Garden: this notorious brothel occupied the old manor house of Paris Garden, close to the bank of the Thames. The house was the object of a 1632 play by Shackerley Marmion (1603–39), a protégé of Ben Jonson: *Hollands Leaguer: or An Historical Discourse of the Life and Actions of Dona Britanica Hollandia the Arch-Mistris of the wicked women of Eutopia*. This print was used in several publications linked to this affair, including Marmion's play which has it as its frontispiece.
(Wikimedia Commons, in the public domain).

Opposite:
This mid seventeenth century painting by an anonymous artist from the South Netherlands, depicts an elegant company walking on a causeway leading to a small manor house. Its moated situation is strongly reminiscent of Holland's Leaguer in Paris Garden and the reconstruction on pp.104–105 draws inspiration from this painting. This blend of land and water would also be prevalent in this marshy part of the South Bank.
(Rijksmuseum, Image in the public domain, Wikimedia Commons)

BOROUGH AND BANKSIDE

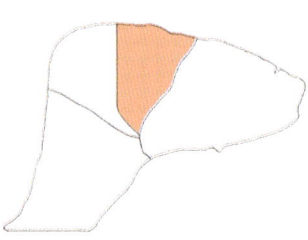

BB5 BANKSIDE & ITS THEATRES

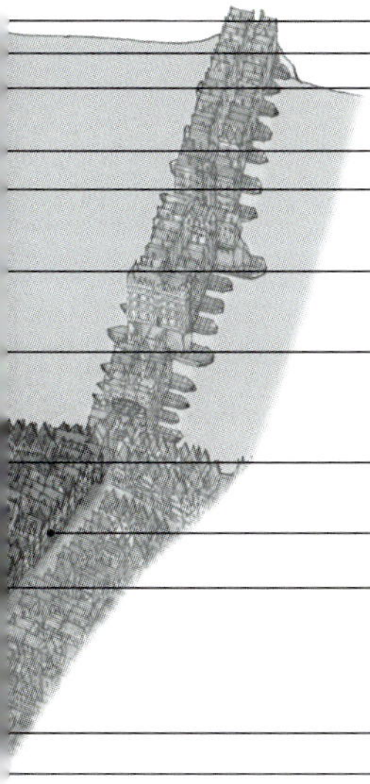

BB6 THE SWAN
BB2 UPPER GROUND
BB18 CARDINAL'S HAT INN
BB1 & BB7 BEAR GARDEN
BB8 THE ROSE
BB9 THE GLOBE
BB16 DEADMAN'S PLACE
BB15 WINCHESTER PALACE
BB10 CHURCH OF ST SAVIOUR
BB11 MONTAGUE CLOSE
BB17 ROBERT HARVARD'S BUTCHER'S SHOP
BB12 ST. SAVIOUR'S GRAMMAR SCHOOL
BB19 SOUTHWARK COMPTER (PRISON) AND SESSIONS HOUSE
BB13 CALVERT'S BUILDINGS
BB14 CURE'S COLLEGE
BB3 CROSS BONES YARD
BB21 SUFFOLK PLACE
BB4 ST. GEORGE'S FIELDS

Above:
Bear Baiting, 1330s. Frederick, Duke of Württemberg, wrote a vivid description, in German, of bear and bull baiting in London in 1592: 'At such times you can perceive the breed and mettle of the dogs, for although they receive serious injuries from the bears, are caught by the horns of the bull, and tossed into the air so as frequently to fall down again upon the horns, they do not give in [but fasten on the bull so firmly] that one is obliged to pull them back by the tails, and force open their jaws'.
(Luttrell Psalter Ms 42130, f.161r, 1330s, © British Library Board. All Rights Reserved/Bridgeman Images)

(BB1) Bull and Bear Baiting. The origins of bull baiting (unlike bear baiting, see BB7) was not as a 'cruelty sport' but as a method to tenderise meat before its consumption. The so-called Agas map showing London in the mid-sixteenth century records 'the bolle bayting' arena next to that of 'The Beare bayting' (a royal monopoly). At first the Manor of Paris was the traditional venue for animal baiting though it seemed later to spread to Bankside. The French visitor L Grenade recorded in 1578 that 'the pleasure of a bull fight comes from when the bull is able to seize a mastiff using its horns; it throws the mastiff high up into the air and the mastiff, falling to the ground, either dies or breaks a limb, and so is no longer of any worth'.
(Braun & Hogenberg; Grenade; Bowsher)

(BB2) Upper Ground – this naturally raised foreshore, formerly known as 'Narrow Wall', was described by Graham Gibberd as 'supposedly the Roman wall'. The name 'Upper

Ground' clearly features on William Morgan's 1682 map of London which it would have predated.

I came across an early reference to it in Philip Henslowe's Account Book for the year 1597 (see p. XX): [I] Lente unto Frances Henslow the 15 desembz 1597 when he went to tacke his howsse one the bancksyd [Bankside] called the vper grovne [upper ground] the some of …'.
(Gibberd; Dulwich Archives)

(BB3) Cross-Bones burial ground, now at the corner of Redcross Way and Union Street, is an unconsecrated burial ground on land which once belonged to the Bishop of Winchester (the Clink Liberty). It is estimated to contain remains of some 15,000 Londoners – men, women and children. It *may* owe its origins to the notorious 'Winchester geese' or whores who operated freely in this part of Southwark. John Stow wrote about 'these single women [who] were forbidden the rites of the church so long as they continued that sinful life, and were excluded from Christian burial if they were not reconciled before their death. And therefore, there was a plot of ground called the Single Woman's Churchyard, appointed for them far from the parish church.' This was written in 1598 and there is a 'long established tradition' that this burial ground was Cross-Bones Yard.

The Survey of London has argued that 'the only possible proof for 'the truth of this tradition is the fact that the ground remained unconsecrated, although from the middle of the 17th century until 1853 it was used as a parish burial ground.' Archaeologists who excavated the site in the 1990s pointed out that the land was leased from the Bishop of Winchester and 'it was customary only to consecrate freehold land', nevertheless adding that the burial ground of St Saviour's Workhouse in Pepper Street, also leased from the Winchester Park estate, was consecrated. Finally, it might be argued that Stow's words – 'a plot of ground … far from the parish church' – does not describe Cross-Bones Yard, a few minutes-walk from the parish church of St Saviour. Continues on p. 194.
(Stow 1598; *Survey of London* 22; MoLAS 1999)

(BB4) St George's Fields was the common field of the manor and borough of Southwark in medieval times. This plot of about 144 acres lay between Lambeth Marsh and Blackman Road (the southern continuation of Borough High Street). In 1550, Edward VI granted the King's Manor (Southwark), the Great Liberty and St George's Fields to the City, to be administered by the Bridge House Estates. St George's Fields was marshy and used by all as common land. The first survey of the Fields in 1555 shows the earliest path to become a recognised right of way – from Newington Butts to Church Street in Lambeth. It was made into a 'road' in the seventeenth century – roughly along the axis made by Lambeth Road and St George's Road. Graham Gibberd points out: 'the Fields, seemingly an empty space, were often used by map publishers to put their ornate labels or keys, making it even more difficult for historians to know what little went on there.'

The *Survey of London* reconstructed the ownership of St George's Fields: in 1621, seventy of 144 acres belonged to the City. The four principal freeholders of the remainder were, in order of acreage – the Wells family; Sir John Lade (later Rolls' estate); the Revd Thomas Clarke; Hayle's (later amalgamated with the Walcot estate).
(*Survey of London* 25; Gibberd)

(BB5) Bankside and its theatres: 'For at least five hundred years, Bankside was the red-light district of London' according to Barker and Jackson in *The Pleasures of London*. The 'entertainment' included visiting whores, drinking in the numerous taverns, going to the theatre and animal baiting – temptations for Londoners and visitors alike.

Historian Martha Carlin explained that 'the Bankside area had been established in 1390 as the only legal brothel district in Southwark. Of the other English cities, only Sandwich seems to have followed London in appointing a sanctioned brothel area'.

By the late sixteenth century, Philip Henslowe owned a number of properties and businesses in the area including taverns. He described in his Account Book/Diary (1576-1609) some of the furnishing of the James Head tavern he had bought on 14 August 1595, giving us a rare glimpse of the interior of a tavern: 'wainscot and painted cloths' in the hall and parlour and 'turnde pellers' [turned pillars] in the parlour.

Shakespeare was living on Bankside from 1598 until 1604, possibly near the Bear Garden (see BB7). Fellow actor Edward Alleyn was there too – in 1592 his friend John Griggs, who built the Rose Theatre and Philip Henslowe's house, built him a house facing the Thames on Bankside. In his Account Book Henslowe – Alleyn's father-in-law and the owner of the Rose theatre – conjures up a picture of new, comfortable wainscoted homes for himself (he lived opposite the Clink Prison), his brother Edmond, Frances Henslowe and Alleyn.
(Dulwich College Archive)

Theatres – London historian and archaeologist Julian Bowsher is the principal source for the theatre and animal baiting entries; he states unequivocally that 'London [was] the first home of professional theatre'.

Strictly speaking, the Rose and the Hope theatres could not be shown in the same picture because the former had been taken down a few years before the Hope was built. Equally the Bear Garden and the Hope could not be shown in the same picture because the Bear Garden had to be

Above:
Interior of the Swan playhouse, copied by Aernout van Buchell (1565-1641) from a drawing by the Dutch humanist scholar Johannes de Witt when he visited London in 1595/6. He described the Swan as the most magnificent of London's four theatres, adding that the two theatres in Bankside (the Rose and the Swan) were finer than the two Shoreditch playhouses (The Theatre and the Curtain). The Swan could accommodate an audience of 3000 people.
(From Arnoldus Buchelius' *Adversaria*, Ms. 842 f.132r in the Special Collections of Utrecht University Library. Image in the public domain, Wikimedia Commons)

demolished before the Hope could be built on the same site. So our reconstruction of around 1600 only shows the Rose and the Bear Garden.

(BB6) The Swan 1595 in the Manor of Paris Garden, was Bankside's second theatre and the only Elizabethan theatre to have had its interior recorded (left). From 1597, it was the home of the Earl of Pembroke's Company. Their first year was memorable because they staged the controversial satirical comedy *The Isle of Dogs* by Thomas Nashe and Ben Jonson. The play was reported to the authorities as containing 'seditious and slanderous matter' and was immediately suppressed. No copy of it has survived. Three of the players, including one of the authors – Ben Jonson –, were arrested and sent to the Marshalsea prison. This setback appears to have stopped activities there for the next decade or so. After that it was used intermittently until the 1630s – the last recorded use being in 1634.
(Bowsher)

(BB7) The Bear Garden. This Bear Garden was built in 1583 to replace the third ring built in the manor of Paris Garden, where it had been used as a 'Games Place' or animal place since 1526. Thirty years later Thomas Fluddie, the Yeoman of the King's Bears was granted a licence for bear baiting on Bankside; it was soon followed by a similar licence to John Allen, the Yeoman of the Prince's Bears in Southwark. Both licences were only valid for Sundays. The earliest 'ring', was recorded in Long Southwark (Southwark High Street) on the 1542 map of Southwark (see p. 129).

According to the Reverend John Field who raged against bear baiting when the third Bear Garden collapsed in 1583 – with loss of life –, there really was no difference between this cruel sport and the theatre: 'Beeing thus ungodly assembled, to so unholy a spectacle [bear baiting] … For surely it is to be feared, beesides the distruction of bothe of bodye and soule, that many are brought unto, by frequenting the *Theater*, the *Curtin* and such like …'.
(Norden 1600; 'Bear Garden 3A' in Bowsher)

(BB8) The Rose 1587 is now 'one of the most intrinsically important playhouses of the "Shakespearean" period' for its exceptionally good historical and archaeological evidence wrote Julian Bowsher in 2012. The theatre's 'partnership document', dated 10 July 1587, is in the Dulwich College archive; its owner, the entrepreneur Philip Henslowe kept detailed accounts, many of which have survived, including a list of more than 200 plays performed between 1592 and 1603 by five different companies of actors. The most celebrated, the Admiral's Men, arrived here in 1592 after its leading actor Edward Alleyn – the Queen's favourite – fell out with James Burbage at The Theatre. Its principal playwright was Christopher Marlowe. The 1989 archaeological excavation uncovered nearly three quarters of the Rose, yielding rich pickings for theatre historians. The playhouse was thatched and made up of fourteen sides – not all of equal lengths. After 1600 the Admiral's Men left for the Fortune Theatre on the north bank, on the fringe of today's Barbican estate. The lease of the Rose expired in 1605 and Philip Henslowe chose not to renew it. By April 1606 the theatre was described as 'the Late playhouse in maidelane called the Rose'. Archaeological evidence suggests the Rose was dismantled rather than demolished.
(Norden 1600; Bowsher)

(BB9) The Globe, 1599 and 1614, the most famous playhouse, because William Shakespeare's plays were first performed there, was located a hundred yards from the Rose. The first Globe is clearly depicted on John Norden's 1600 panorama of London (see pp. 38–39), but when the thatched roof caught fire on 29 June 1613 during a performance, 'it burn't … down to the ground in less than two hours, with a dwelling house-adjoining, and it was a great marvaile and fair grace of God, that the people had so little harm, having but two narrow doors to get out' recalled Sir John Chamberlain. The theatre was rebuilt on the foundations of the old one. In the 1630s disputes broke out with the landowner, Sir Matthew Brent. The Globe finally closed its doors in 1642 at the outbreak of the Civil War though the lease only ran out in 1644. Brent probably demolished the building soon after he recovered the property. The Globe's long career ensured that the artist Wenceslaus Hollar was able to include the building in his Prospect of London – the sole pictorial representation which can be trusted (see pp. 48–49). (Norden 1600; Bowsher; Hollar 1647; Barker & Jackson 2008)

(BB10) Church of St Saviour (formerly St Mary Overie): By 1600, this building was the fourth one on the site. The first 'of old time, long before the conquest' in the words of John Stow, is connected to a story he narrates in his *Survey of London*: that of a convent founded by a maiden called Mary, the daughter of a local ferryman. This building was replaced by the Saxon minster, listed in the Domesday Book as a 'monasterium', believed to have been built by St Swithun Bishop of Winchester, a prolific builder, in the 850s. In 1106 this church was reconstituted as an Augustinian Priory soon to acquire a hospital in the 1170s. The whole complex was destroyed in a major fire in 1212. The hospital was moved to a different site (see SB17 on p. 135) and reconstruction of the church followed, very slowly, over a century. This fourth church was consecrated in 1260 by the Bishop of London but not completed until the first decades of the fourteenth century when the church became known as St Mary Overie, in the words of Stow 'St Mary over the Tir or Overie; that is over the water'.

The tower, familiar from countless panoramic views, was only completed in 1520 by Bishop Richard Foxe (c.1448–1528), a few years after he founded Oxford's Corpus Christi College. He was Bishop of Winchester between 1501 and 1528 and donated the great altar screen which survives, but much altered.

At the suppression of the monasteries (1536–41) the Priory was abolished and the building became the largest parish church in England. Dedicated to St Saviour it headed a new parish (by Act of Parliament) which merged with the parishes of St Margaret's (the early twelfth-century church on an island in the middle of the High Street) and St Mary Magdalen's (attached to the south side of the former Priory and founded in the 1220s and 30s) to serve lay residents living in the precinct of St Mary Overie's. Continues on p. 193. (Wyngaerde VI; Stow 1598; Carlin)

(BB11) Montague Close, wrapped around the north and west sides of St Saviour's church, was formerly

Above:

Medieval roof bosses at the Priory of St Mary Overie. In 1469 the nave collapsed and a wooden roof was installed. Some of the large bosses hanging from the ceiling have survived and may be seen at ground level in the nave of Southwark Cathedral.

(© The author, 2016)

Below:

The parish church of St Saviour, formerly the Priory of St Mary Overie. The graphic artist Wenceslaus Hollar who has produced the landmark long view for the seventeenth century (see pp. 48–49) is the author of this print.

(Yale Center for British Art; image in the public domain, Wikimedia Commons)

Above:
Montague Close. "A North-west View of the House of William Parker, Lord Monteagle", 1825
(Yale Center for British Art; image in the public domain, Wikimedia Commons)

Above:
This jug of tin-glazed earthenware is believed to have been made by Jacob Prynn at the Montague Close Pottery around 1620.
(© The Trustees of the British Museum)

the site of the cloisters and convent of St Mary Overie's Priory. At the Reformation this area entered private hands, initially those of Sir Anthony Browne. The name commemorates his eldest son's title – Anthony junr (1528-1592) who was ennobled as the first Viscount Montague in 1554 and probably lived in the Prior's house. At his death he left his mansion house 'of St Mary Overies' to his (second) wife Magdalen Dacre, with reversion to his grandson Anthony.

In 1625 the family sold the close to Robert Bromfield and Thomas Overman who replaced the area's 'meane cottages and habitacons for the poorer sort of people that crouded themselves there together' with houses 'fit for men of better ability'. In a 1692-93 chancery case we learn that the 'capital messuage' (Montague House) was used as a pothouse. Abutting on the church wall were: a shed for soap making, 'a colour house' and 'a kilnehouse of old building'.

Archaeological excavations carried out in 1969 and 1970 revealed two delftware kilns. The Montague Close Pottery which started around 1613 has been described as 'the first tin-glazed earthenware pottery to be established in Southwark and the second in London after Aldgate'. It lasted until around 1755. Continues on p. 193.
(*Survey of London* 22; MoLAS 2008)

(BB12) St Saviour's Grammar School for boys was founded in 1559, initially operating from the church house of the old parish of St Margaret. It moved to nearby Green Dragon Court after 1585, a site south of St Saviour's church which owed its name to a house/inn called Green Dragon (marked on Southwark's oldest map of 1542). It received a charter from Queen Elizabeth in 1562. It burnt down in the 1676 fire but was rebuilt on the same site. It was intended for a maximum number of 100 pupils; its most famous pupil was John Harvard (1607–1638) – one of the founders of Harvard University in America. Continues on p. 193.
(1542 Southwark map; Rendle 1878; *Survey of London* 22; R C Carrington

(BB13) Calvert's Buildings, behind No 50 Borough High Street, is a timber-framed building, Grade II listed, with access through an arched opening. It is the former Goat Inn, later the Brew House, 'reputed to be c1542' says Historic England, but seventeenth century according to the *Survey of London*. It has a twin-gabled roof, an overhanging first floor; inside there are a number of original beams.
(*Survey of London* 22; Historic England listing website)

(BB14) Cure's College, Park Street: almshouses for sixteen poor parishioners, founded by Thomas Cure in 1584 and sited at the southwest end of Deadman's Place (now Park Street). The excavation of its burial ground was carried out in 2009-11; Cure's was one of nine burial grounds in the parish of St Saviour's.

In 1579 Thomas Cure bought Waverley House (in the hands of the Abbot of Waverley prior to the Dissolution) and adjoining lands including St Margaret's new churchyard which had declined in use after 1540. By 1580 the wardens of the parish of St Saviour's had already built six almshouses on part of the new churchyard. In 1584 Thomas Cure commissioned the building on his land of a hospital or college for poor and sick people. Another ten almshouses were built alongside the existing six.

Thomas Cure (d.1588) was Master of the Horse to King Edward VI, Queen Mary and Queen Elizabeth and a member of parliament for Southwark in 1563, 1571 and 1586. He was a wealthy man who seemed to have benefited when property was in rich supply after the Dissolution of the Monasteries. He purchased land and property in Lambeth ('three acres of medowe' in 'the bishopp of Canterburyes marshe'), Southwark and East Grinstead. His will, prepared shortly before his death, provided £100 towards the purchase of land for Southwark grammar school (presumably St Saviour's) and 20s 'to make all the scholars a little recreation after my burial'. Continues on p. 193. (1542 map for 'Waverley'; *Survey of London* 22 & 23, History of Parliament online)

(BB15) Winchester House (or Palace or Place), Bankside. The land, between the Manor of Paris Garden and St Mary's Priory (St Saviour's church by 1600) was a gift, in the early twelfth century, from the priory of Bermondsey to the Bishops of Winchester. By the thirteenth century it was referred to as 'Southwark Marsh' and large tracts of land remained open meadow until well after the Reformation. In Tudor times, the open ground was known as the Bishop of Winchester's park. The house or palace was built by William Gifford, Bishop of Winchester between 1107 and 1129. The earliest mention of hospitality at Winchester House is found in William FitzStephen's *Life of St Thomas Becket* (around 1170); it was during Becket's last visit to London before his murder, first processing to the abbey church of St Mary (Overie) before visiting the Bishop of Winchester and finally making his way to Canterbury. From the fourteenth century to around 1550 the Bishops of Winchester held important positions at court and their residence was the scene of splendid hospitality. The hall was enlarged and acquired its striking rose window in the mid-fourteenth century. The Bishops' House's glorious days came to an abrupt end in 1551 when Bishop Gardiner was thrown into the Tower after he tried to resist changes to religious doctrine. Winchester House was granted to the Marquess of Northampton the following year who added a gallery to it. Bishop Gardiner was reinstated to his house and bishopric at the accession of Mary I in 1553. From around 1560 there are few references to Winchester House. House and grounds were sold in 1649. (1542 map; Wyngaerde VI; *Survey of London* 22; Carlin)

Glassmaking – glass historian Eleanor Godfrey has described in detail how in the seventeenth and eighteenth centuries Winchester House became a centre for glassmaking. It started in 1608 with a furnace set up and operated by Edward Salter. Salter and his five partners brought in glass workers from Murano near Venice and they began making cruets, trenchers, plates, salts and stills in 'cristello', which would become London's speciality. Sir Edward Zouch and his partners leased the Winchester House factory from Salter around 1610. They succeeded in switching from wood to coal. The glasshouses of Winchester House and Vauxhall shared the market – Vauxhall meeting the demand in plate-glass while Winchester House cornered the market for crystal. Winchester stopped making glass in 1624.

Continues on p. 191.
(Eleanor S Godfrey, *The Development of English Glassmaking 1560–1640*, 1975)

The Clink prison, Bankside: while Lambeth House developed as a fortified enclave within a rural environment, only acquiring its prison in 1425, Winchester Palace, by contrast, was sited in the midst of urban life – with a red-light district, with theatres and drinking establishments, while nearby Kent Street and the Mint were described later as 'bad spots in a squalid district'. So it is no surprise that the Bishop of Winchester decided to set up a prison in the grounds of his palace. Cardinal Henry Beaufort (Bishop of Winchester, 1404–47) gave £400 to be distributed among London's prisoners including those of Marshalsea, the King's Bench and those 'in confinement within my manor of Southwark'. But the Clink prison was first mentioned by name in 1509, despite existing from 'an early period', says the *Survey of London*. At the end of the sixteenth century, Stow explained there were five prisons in Southwark, a substantial number, and all feature in this gazetteer – the other four sited along 'Long Southwark' i.e. the High Street. Stow adds 'for such as should break the peace on the said bank, or in the brothel-houses'. However, unmentioned by Stow, were those prisoners who were victims of religious persecutions under the reigns of Mary and Elizabeth.
(Carlin; *Survey of London* 22)

(BB16) Deadman's Place: now Park Street, a sinister designation or a corrupted name for a local property owner such as 'Desmond'? Historian Richard Tames seems to favour the latter on the basis that people's names were often at the root of place names. On the 1572 Braun and Hogenberg map it is not named but shown as a wide path with water running in the middle. William Morgan's 1682 map names the street 'Deadman's Place' which runs south from the Thames before turning back in the direction of St Saviour's, creating the characteristic square angle which has survived to this day. By 1600 Thomas Cure had set up his college in that kink where there was a burial ground, the 'new' churchyard of the church of St Margaret. Could that have been responsible for the name? (Braun & Hogenberg; Morgan 1682; *Survey of London* 22)

(BB17) Robert Harvard's butcher shop. We know that John Harvard's father, Robert, had a butcher's shop on the west side of Long Southwark immediately opposite the Boar's Head Inn (see SB15). This was just north of the Southwark market. SB6, an illustration of the market, contrasts market stalls on the east side of the road with regular shops on the west side of the road. All those shops sell meat and give some idea of what Harvard's butcher's shop, on the same side of the road but further up, closer to the bridge, would have looked like. (Hugh Alley; Rendle 1878)

(BB18) Cardinal's Hat Inn is believed to have been built by 'Hugh Browker, later the owner of the Manor of Paris Garden, [who] was in possession of ground there in 1579'; the alley alongside has survived to this day, and is believed to date from that ancient time. The name 'Cardinal's Hat' may indicate a connection with Cardinal Wolsey (Bishop of Winchester in 1529–30) and not, as previously suggested, Cardinal Beaufort who died in 1447, long before the inn had been built. Continues on p. 188.
(*Survey of London* 22; Tindall)

(BB19) Southwark Compter (prison) and Sessions House: between the Dissolution of the Monasteries and 1598 when John Stow published his *Survey*, the parish of St Margaret had merged with St Saviour's and its church, of ancient date, was given over to legal matters: part of it was 'a court, wherein the assizes and sessions be kept, and the court of admiralty is also there kept. One other part … is now a prison, called the Compter'. In 1583 Sessions Hall was sold to the City of London though Surrey's justices of the peace continued using these premises. The Compter was in operation by around 1562, originally housed in the old church of St Margaret then moved to one of the houses built on St Margaret's churchyard by landowner William Emerson. Continues on p. XX. (Stow; *Survey of London* 22 & 25)

(BB20) Bishop of Rochester's Inn. It was situated next to Winchester House, and was the Bishop's second home on the South Bank after being ousted from La Place in Lambeth which went to the Bishop of Carlisle (see VL11). John Stow did not know when this inn was built but described it as 'lyeth ruinous for lack of reparations' in 1598. (Not shown in the reconstruction)

We also know from Stow that the Abbot of Waverley's house was in the immediate neighbourhood of the Bishop of Rochester's house (1542 map). See BB14.
(Wyngaerde IV & VI; Stow 372)

(BB21) Suffolk Place (also known as Brandon or Southwark Place). Soon after the artist Anthonis van den Wyngaerde recorded Suffolk

Place in its full glory (see p. 36), it was gradually demolished – between 1557 and 1562 – and replaced by 'many small cottages of great rents … to the encreasing of beggers in that Borough,' John Stow tells us. However, Stow is unreliable about when the mansion was constructed and by whom. He ascribed it to the correct family – the Brandons – but to the wrong family member. It was built by William, not Charles. The historian Martha Carlin established that Sir William Brandon was living in Southwark by 1460 in the house which would soon be known as Brandon's Place. William enlarged his residence turning it into an urban palace. It passed to Sir Thomas Brandon in 1497 who created a park on adjoining land belonging to the Bishop of Winchester. After his death in 1510 Brandon Place was inherited by his nephew Charles, brother-in-law of Henry VIII who was made Duke of Suffolk in 1514, hence the change of name. At that time Charles Brandon was appointed marshal of the King's Bench prison.

Included as a ghost outline, this important mansion stood on the west side of Borough High Street. An early visitor was Sir John Howard (c.1425–1485), the first duke of Norfolk who stayed at 'Brandennes Place in Sothwerke'. Sir William Brandon (1456–1485) and his father – also Sir William, probably lived at 'Brandennes Place'. In 1536 Charles Brandon exchanged his Southwark property for the Bishop of Norwich's house near Charing Cross. Suffolk Place became part of Queen Jane's jointure and after her death in 1537, it was occasionally used to house distinguished visitors, but from 1545 to 1551, a royal mint was based there.

In February 1556 Queen Mary gave the property, fourteen acres in total, to the Archbishop of York, Nicholas Heath; he sold it a year later and it was quickly dismantled with some of the materials being used for the 'Lodging of the Poor Knights' in Windsor. Anthony Cage, a salter and London citizen, covered the site with 'small cottages of great rent' and bequeathed them to his third son

Edward in 1584. When surveyed by Parliamentary Commissioners in 1651 it was described as '16 tenements with gardens and grounds amounting to about 13 acres'. From the seventeenth century onwards it was known as the Mint. (Wyngaerde IV & VI; Stow 374 & 381; *Survey of London* 25; Carlin; *VCH*); Terence Paul Smith, Bruce Watson, Claire Martin and David Williams, 'Suffolk Place, Southwark, London: a Tudor palace and its terracotta architectural decoration, *Post Medieval Archaeology* 48/1, 2014)

This head of a girl, with plaits and wings, is the best example from a group of fifteen terracottas which were recovered from the site of Suffolk Place in 1937 – when 170–192 Borough High Street (Moser's Iron, Steel and Hardware Merchants) was redeveloped. It would have formed part of the elaborate external decoration of Suffolk Place. This terracotta has been dated 1518–1522. Terracotta work was also excavated from nearby sites in the late nineteenth century, including from St George's Church in 2006, all likely to be connected to Suffolk Place.
(© Victoria and Albert Museum, London)

SOUTHWARK AND BERMONDSEY

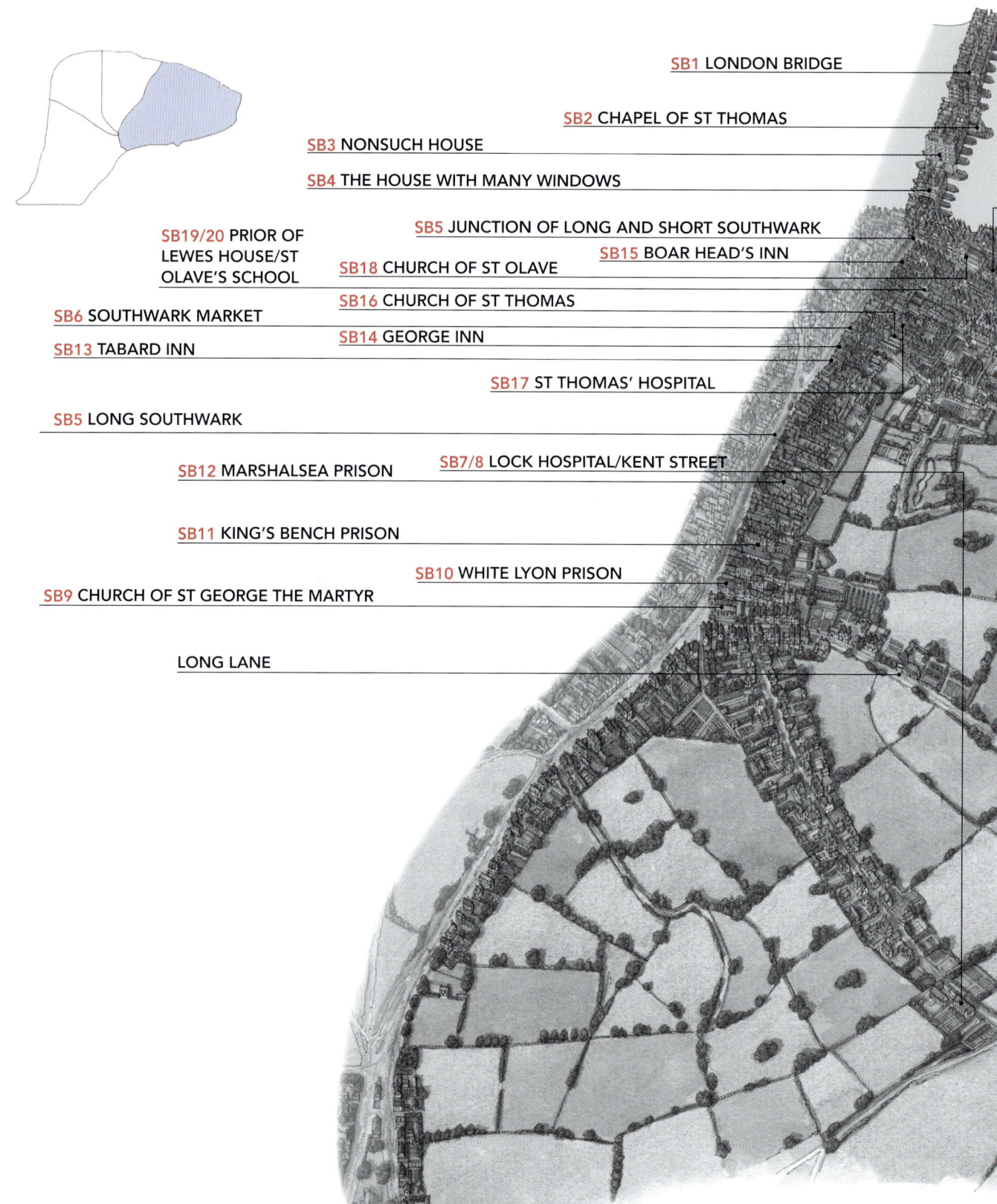

SB1 LONDON BRIDGE
SB2 CHAPEL OF ST THOMAS
SB3 NONSUCH HOUSE
SB4 THE HOUSE WITH MANY WINDOWS
SB19/20 PRIOR OF LEWES HOUSE/ST OLAVE'S SCHOOL
SB5 JUNCTION OF LONG AND SHORT SOUTHWARK
SB15 BOAR HEAD'S INN
SB18 CHURCH OF ST OLAVE
SB6 SOUTHWARK MARKET
SB16 CHURCH OF ST THOMAS
SB14 GEORGE INN
SB13 TABARD INN
SB17 ST THOMAS' HOSPITAL
SB5 LONG SOUTHWARK
SB12 MARSHALSEA PRISON
SB7/8 LOCK HOSPITAL/KENT STREET
SB11 KING'S BENCH PRISON
SB10 WHITE LYON PRISON
SB9 CHURCH OF ST GEORGE THE MARTYR
LONG LANE

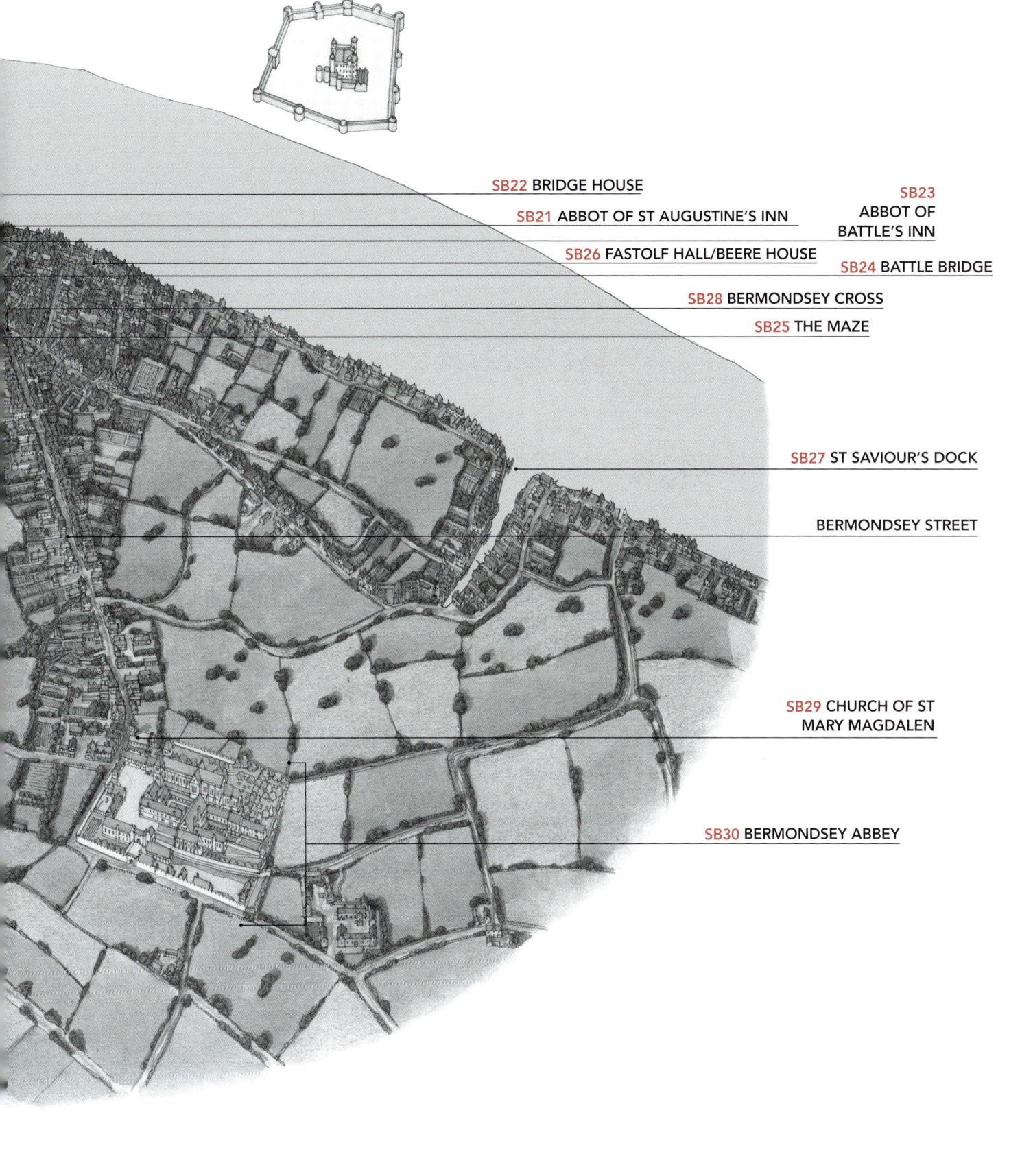

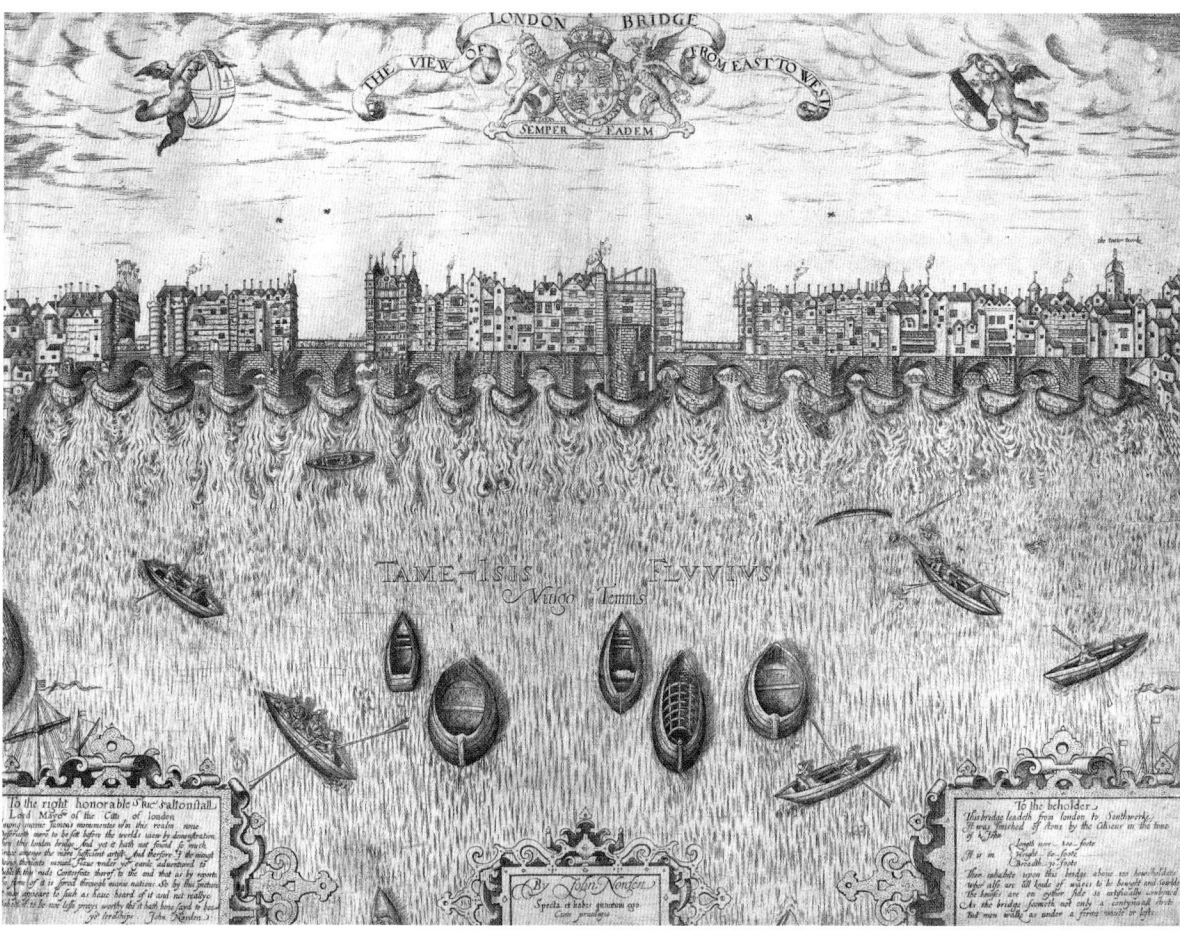

Above:
London Bridge seen from the east (Southwark is left, the City right), 1597–98 engraving by John Norden who described the bridge as one of the 'wonders of the world'. London Bridge, made up of nineteen arches of different widths boasted several landmark buildings: the old Stone Gate at the southern end of the Bridge, and the Drawbridge, positioned a third way of the bridge from the Southwark end; its use compromised the stability of its gate so it stopped being used after 1497. The Drawbridge gate was taken down in 1577 in a state of disrepair and replaced by the fine Nonsuch House in 1579. The grim spiked heads which used to 'decorate' its battlements were moved further south to the Old Stone Gate.
© London Metropolitan Archives (City of London)

(SB1) London Bridge: the first bridge was built by the Romans around 50 AD. At least three more followed before the structure fell into disrepair and collapsed. Peter Jackson described the legendary origins of the medieval bridge as recorded in a 1637 broadsheet in his collection: in the tenth century, the Thames cross-ferry was kept by the Ferry-man John Overy. His daughter Mary, grief-stricken at the death of her father, founded a convent which later became the priory of St Mary Overie. Its sisters looked after the ferry crossing. Swithin, a noble lady, was credited with converting the site into a college of priests, apparently responsible for replacing the ferry by a timber bridge. This version of events is close to that of John Stow. Ferrymen were very significant people in medieval and post-medieval London.

There are three references to a bridge (rather than a ferry) in the eleventh century though there may have been a bridge as early as c. 990. London Bridge was rebuilt in timber in 1163 and repaired and re-built later. Between 1176 and 1209 Peter, the chaplain of St Mary Colechurch in the City, oversaw the rebuilding of London Bridge in stone; Peter died in 1205 before the completion of this project.

The latest research on London Bridge's records was carried out by Dorian Gerhold: 'Houses on the bridge seem to have been envisaged from the start, probably drawing on precedents from France … All three

Left:
Late medieval pilgrim badge depicting St Thomas Becket returning from exile. This badge was excavated at Billingsgate and may have been associated with St Thomas' shrine in Cheapside.
(© The Trustees of the British Museum)

of the bridge's major buildings are mentioned within sixty years of the bridge's completion and all seem to have been part of the original plan'. These were the chapel – the first chapel was destroyed in the 1212/3 Southwark fire; the stone gate, first mentioned c. 1250 and the Drawbridge tower, first mentioned in 1258. All the buildings on London Bridge belonged to the Bridge House Estates and brought in revenue which helped maintain the bridge. There were waterworks and public latrines at both ends of the bridge. The first waterworks at the northern end (first arch, west side) was set up by a Dutchman, Peter Morris, in 1578–82. There were doubters but it was a success so was followed by another wheel under the second arch in 1582–83 and one under the fourth arch in 1701. At the southern end waterwheels for grinding corn were set up in 1590 (also attached to the west side of the bridge). The waterworks at both ends of the bridge were in use until 1822.

In the Middle Ages the building of a bridge was a labour of piety and devotion, comparable to the building of a cathedral. The famous twelfth-century Pont d'Avignon in Provence, an important precedent,

This detail from John Norden's London Bridge (see previous page) shows that by around 1600, the chapel of St Thomas Becket which stood near the centre of the bridge, projecting to the east – had been stripped of its dedication and Catholic associations and turned into a grocer's shop in 1553. It contrasts with the detail below from a c.1500 manuscript associated with the Duke of Orleans showing the chapel of St Thomas Becket as rebuilt in the late fourteenth-century (1384–97), very probably by Henry Yevele a warden of the bridge and England's most famous medieval architect. See p. 47 for the full image.

was dedicated to St Bénézet. In London there was a strong association with St Thomas Becket. For medieval historians the construction of the stone bridge 'was associated with the development of the cult of Thomas Becket', murdered in Canterbury Cathedral in 1170, and canonised in 1173. The Southwark/Canterbury pilgrimage started almost immediately after the murder and received added impetus with the canonisation of Becket. Numerous pilgrim badges were recovered from the Thames at the London Bridge site. (previous page).

The first recorded gift to the 'Colechurch' bridge came from the earliest known Mayor of London, Henry Fitz-Ailwyn; he was the first in a long line of benefactors. As a result, the Bridge House Estates (see SB22) were and still are astonishingly wealthy. In 1578 the diarist L Grenade praised this special bridge:

> From this suburb [Southwark], one enters the city by means of a great and powerful bridge, the most magnificent that exists in the whole of Europe. It is built entirely of ashlar and is completely covered with houses which are all like big castles. And the shops are great storehouses, full of all sorts of very opulent merchandise. And there is nowhere in London which is more commercial than this bridge … If a traitor has been decapitated, his head is placed at the end of a pike and displayed on this bridge for all to see. I reiterate that there is no bridge in the whole of Europe which is on a great river like the Thames and as formidable, as spectacular and as bustling with trade as this bridge in London.

The gruesome tradition of displaying traitor's heads on the drawbridge tower had started from at least 1305 but was disrupted in 1577 when the tower was demolished; the thirteenth-century drawbridge, rebuilt in 1426, had stopped working. After 1577 the heads were displayed on the stone gate instead. In 1684 the display moved to Temple Bar. (Wyngaerde; Stow; Jackson; Grenade; Gerhold 2019)

(SB2) The Chapel of St Thomas on London Bridge (left). The completion/consecration of the stone chapel dated from around 1200. It stood almost in the middle of the bridge, on the ninth pier from the north bank. It was dedicated to St Thomas Becket, the martyred archbishop of Canterbury whose cult is connected to the building of London Bridge. Its chaplains lodged in Bridge House Yard in Tooley Street. Their number varied but at the Reformation there were three chaplains and six clerks – mostly attending to the Canterbury pilgrims, chantries to benefactors and obits (obituaries). Between 1384 and 1396 the chapel was rebuilt in the perpendicular style by the most famous exponent of this style – Henry Yevele, also architect at Kennington Palace (VL3).

The chapel on the bridge and the priory of St Mary Overie, later St Saviour's church, were important stations in the pilgrimage which would have also involved a visit to Becket's birthplace in Cheapside.

The chapel was Peter Colechurch's last resting place. A casket in the Museum of London collections is intriguingly labelled 'Remains of Peter the Engineer of Old London Bridge who died in 1205'. On close inspection of the contents, the verdict disappointingly read: 'it seems probable that the claim made on the casket label is fraudulent'.

At the Reformation the dedication of the chapel was changed to that of St Thomas the Apostle, and the chantries were abolished. In 1553 it was leased to a grocer, William Bridger and by 1600 the chapel had been turned into a residential/commercial unit.
(Wyngaerde; Jackson; Gerhold)

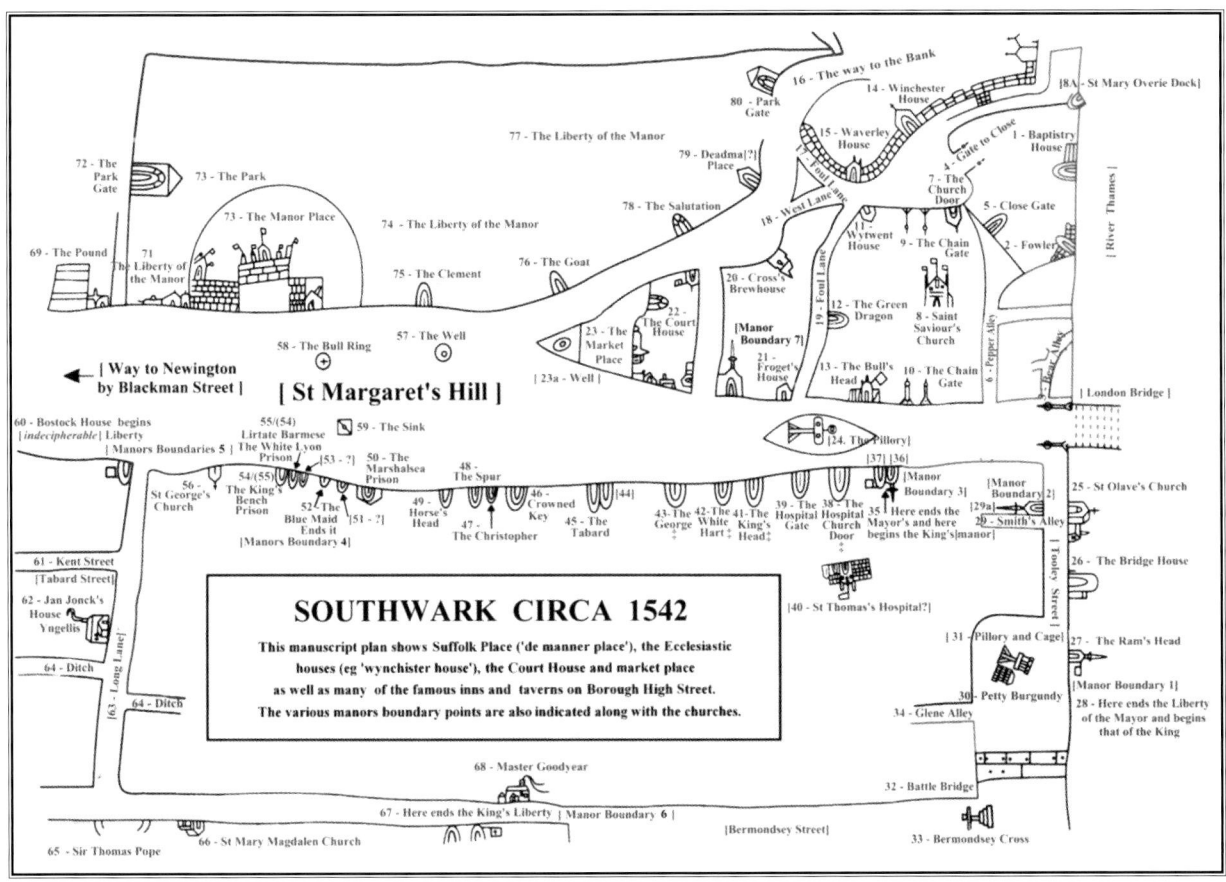

(SB3) **Nonsuch House**, built in 1577–79, replaced the original drawbridge tower which is shown on the Wyngaerde drawing (see pp. 36–37) but its fragile state in the early 1570s alarmed tenants and authorities alike. Along with 'the house with many windows' and despite the name 'Nonsuch House' (singular), it was made up of two houses. Designed by Lewis Stockett, the Bridge House master carpenter, its name meant 'no other such house' and it was the largest structure on the bridge. Dorian Gerhold believes the Pepys Library view in Cambridge gives the best rendering of its elaborate decoration. However, the building was noted as one of the earliest classical facades in England. Nonsuch House was built in Bridge House yard in Tooley Street and did not come in pre-fabricated sections from Holland as was previously believed.
(Gerhold 2019)

(SB4) **'The house with many windows'**: Dorian Gerhold coined this phrase in the absence of a name for the striking house with four semi-circular projections. It is in fact made up of two separate houses and is reminiscent of Nonsuch Palace. It was long thought to be Elizabethan but is in fact earlier, dating from 1539-45 in Henry VIII's reign.
(Gerhold 2019)

(SB5) **Long Southwark** and **Short Southwark** which ran south from London Bridge was the original name for Borough High Street, as distinct from Short Southwark which became Tooley Street. Both these

Above:

The 1542 pictorial map of Southwark is remarkable for its early date; the north is on the right-hand side. To the uninitiated, the original document is difficult to read, therefore this is a redrawn and annotated copy prepared by the historian Tony Sharp. It contains a substantial number of landmarks including Bermondsey Cross, the pillory (south of the bridge), St Saviour's church, Winchester Palace, the Manor House i.e. Suffolk Place – the largest landmark – and a bullring in the middle of St Margaret's Hill to name just a few.

(Courtesy of Tony Sharp, see bibliography)

Southwark Market in 1598, from Hugh Alley's small volume *A Caveat for the City of London, OR a forewarnining of offences against penal Lawes*, pen and wash drawing. The view is contemporary with the publication of Stow's *Survey of London*. It is taken from the east of 'Long Southwark' (the High Street), looking west, so London Bridge would be on the right. The market looks like a picture of orderliness with stalls arranged according to the provenance of the produce: London, Mid[d]lesex], Essex, Kent and Surri [Surrey]. The presence of a pillory (there from at least the 1530s and probably earlier) echoes various attempts by the City authorities to control overcrowding and impeding traffic; it also suggests a certain amount of unruliness. In 1606, the Bridgewardens replaced the pillory and also purchased stocks (the pillory was finally dismantled in 1620 and taken to the Bridge House). It seems there had always been a bell (rung to close the market) but the market hall was a new addition probably from the last quarter of the sixteenth century and probably erected on the site of the former bell; so a new bell was placed on top of the market hall.

(*The Folger Shakespeare Library, Washington DC*)

names feature on the 1542 map of Southwark (previous page).
(1542 map; Braun & Hogenberg; Stow)

(SB6) Southwark Market, Borough High Street (above). The original thirteenth century market was linked to the medieval Hospital of St Thomas and thrived alongside the hospital in Trenet Lane, the future St Thomas Street. But in the fifteenth century the market had to compete with another, weekly, street market in 'Long Southwark', closer to and under the control of the City of London. The old market was adversely affected by it and declined. While the new market grew in popularity, causing traffic congestion which led to further regulations from the City. On the west side it went as far as the church of St Margaret and on the east as far down as the new Hospital compound. After 1550 when the City increased its hold over Southwark, the market could be held four days a week, a fee was charged to stallholders while two City bailiffs oversaw market operations. The pillory at that site was an important component for keeping peace on market days.
(Hugh Alley; *Survey of London* 22)

(SB7–SB8) The Lock Hospital, Kent Street (now Tabard Street): John Stow tells us that in 1347 Edward III isolated lepers from healthy subjects by removing them 'into some out places of the fields, from the haunt or company of sound people, whereupon certain lazar-houses … were then built without the city some good distance' – one in the east, one in the north, one in the west and the Lock in the south in Kent Street, Southwark. Lepers were forbidden from entering the city.

Stow's information does not match the evidence that has come down to us. The first mention of the Lock Hospital in Kent Street was in 1315 though it probably dated back to the twelfth century. It stood on what is now Bartholomew Street. From 1375 the City, who feared the presence of lepers, became involved in the running of the leper hospital in Kent Street (south) and in Kingsland Road (east). Leper hospitals were not affected by the Reformation and in 1549 the City appointed trustees of St Bartholomew's Hospital to be directly responsible for running the Lock Hospital. There is a plan of the hospital in their archives, which helps interpret the only picture of the site which has come down (both on the right). By the beginning of the seventeenth century, leprosy was almost extinct in England.

With Long Southwark and Margaret's Hill (Borough High Street), **Kent Street** (now Tabard Street and the Old Kent Road) was roughly aligned with the Roman Road which led from London to Greenwich, then to Canterbury and Dover. It was rural, with two streams crossing the road, occasional country inns and also, suitably isolated, the Lock Hospital. In 1565 an Act ordered that Kent Street be paved with hard stone up to the Lock Hospital. Continues on p. 213.
(Morgan 35 & 47; Stow 381; *Survey of London* 25)

(SB9) Church of St George the Martyr, Southwark. Its first incarnation, of which almost nothing is known, was probably in the early twelfth century. It is first documented in 1122 when it was presented to the

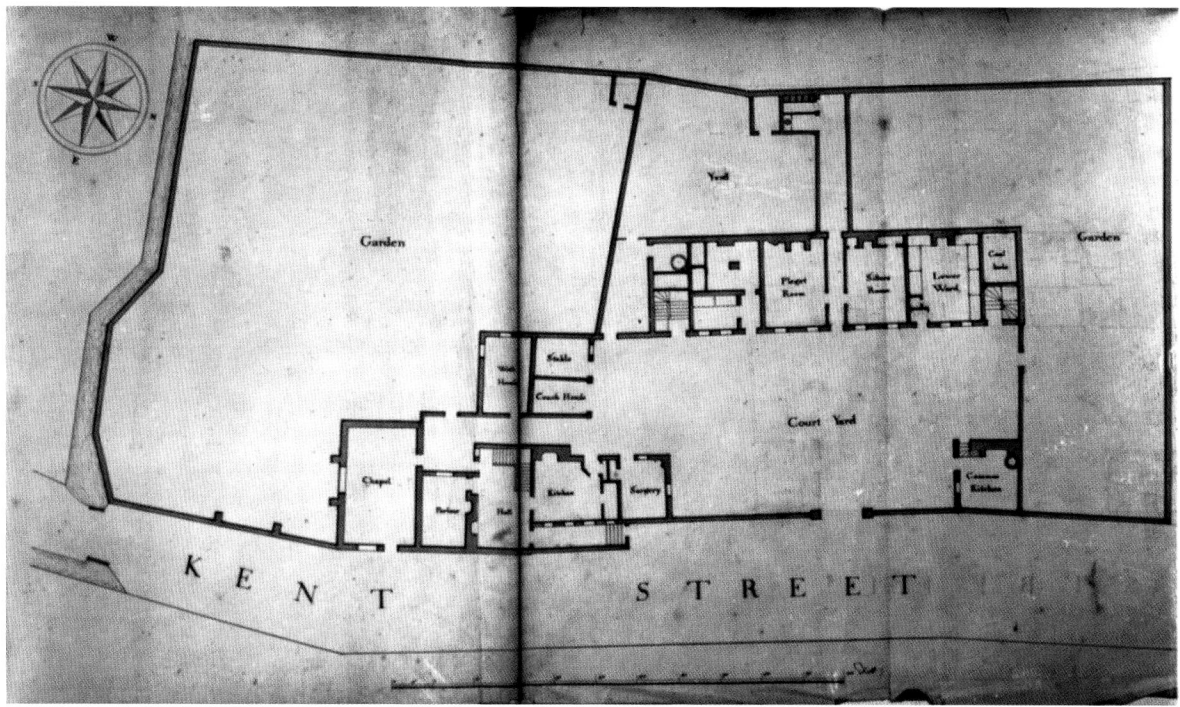

Abbey of Bermondsey by Thomas de Ardern and his son. It was rebuilt at the end of the fourteenth century and traditionally associated with four of the top twelve City Livery companies: the Grocers', Drapers', Fishmongers' and Skinners'. At the bottom of the present eighteenth-century tower, two inscribed stones bear witness to the likely chantry chapel left by Sir Edward Hastings (1382–1438), who spent eighteen years in the Marshalsea for refusing to pay the cost of an unsuccessful claim. From the Reformation onwards, the church has been in the hands of the Crown.

Stow's *Survey of London* strikes a sad note when it points out: 'St. George's was the nearest church to the prisons in Borough High Street and many of those who died in prison were buried there.' This was probably the fate of Sir Edward Hastings in 1438 but certainly that of Bishop Bonner (1500–1569), who died in the Marshalsea. Continues on p. 214. (Wyngaerde; Stow; *Survey of London* 25)

Prisons

The most important fact about prisons was that they were run as private concerns and their staff were paid out of money raised from the prisoners themselves. This led to untold cruelty and harsh living conditions for some of the inmates. This system was only abolished in the nineteenth century).

For Morton's and Lollard's prisons – see Lambeth House and for the Clink prison, see Winchester House.

(SB10) White Lyon prison or County Gaol: according to Stow, the White Lyon Inn, situated immediately north of St George's church, became a prison from around 1550 'the appointed Gaole for the Countie of Surrey'. The county did not own this prison, which was run as a private concern. Before becoming a gaol, it was described (in 1535) as 'a great tenement or inn with a tenement and shop on either side and a barn, stables etc., in the tenure of Robert Faireman, barber, and an acre of pasture ground lying in common

This original plan of the Lock Hospital, comes from the Archives of St Bartholomew's Hospital which administered this institution from 1549. The chapel (left on the plan and above) was built in 1636; around 1820 it was almost all that was left of the hospital. The buildings were organised around a large 'Court Yard'.

(Plan: Wellcome Collection. Attribution 4.0 International (CC BY 4.0). Etching: from Robert Wilkinson's *Londina Illustrata*, 1819–1825)

Below:
'Remember the poor prisoners' – from the series *The Cryes of London* (74) drawn by Marcellus Laroon (or Lauron), and published in 1688 by Pierce Tempest. None of Laroon's cries are associated with specific London locations yet the imprint makes clear they were 'Drawn after the Life'. The annotated set which was in the possession of Samuel Pepys confirms its veracity.

(© The Trustees of the British Museum)

in St George's Field'. In Protestant Elizabethan times many recusants were incarcerated here. It was not until 1654 that the trustees for the county purchased the White Lyon and the House of Correction it had set up. Continues on p. 213.
(not shown on 1542 map of Southwark; Stow 375; Rendle 1878; *Survey of London* 25)

(SB11) King's/Queen's Bench prison: from the documented arrival of the Marshalsea in 1373 (below), both the Marshalsea and the King's Bench prisons seemed to have been operating in Southwark – the former for the Court of Marshalsea and the latter for the Court of King's Bench (on the site of 201–205 Borough High Street).

The *Survey of London* notes that the earliest surviving list of prisoners, dated 1561, included 13 debtors, 3 recusants, 1 priest, and 2 persons accused of "inconjuracion" out of a total of 71, the remainder of whom were charged with felonies or misdemeanours. The prisoners were kept in two houses – the Angel and the Crane, the former giving its name to Angel Place on the south side of the prison.

In 1576 a commission was set up to relieve 'poor prisoners confined for debt in the Queen's Bench' which lasted until the end of Elizabeth's reign (1603), despite fierce opposition to it from the prison authorities themselves. The *Survey of London* noted that 'there were a number of private charities for the relief of prisoners, but it is doubtful if at any time more than a small proportion of the proceeds reached them'. But the 1601 Statute – a series of Acts dealing with social welfare – saw the early development of state encouragement for charities for the poor: by providing legal protection for charitable giving and encouraging donations, the state hoped the burden of care could be met by charity – specifically providing for the relief of poor prisoners in the King's Bench and Marshalsea. The (unpublished) history of the Charity Commission notes there was a significant increase in charitable giving as a result – philanthropy had become secularised and the many institutions endowed by London merchants were a matter of local and national pride.

The life of debtors in particular could be particularly harsh; their 1624 petition to the King reveals that eighty debtors had died of starvation in King's Bench prison in that year alone. Continues on p.215.
(Stow 375; *Survey of London* 25)

(SB12) Marshalsea prison: this prison was built in the year 1373: 'the good men of the town of Suthwerk' received a licence 'to build in the high street leading from the church of St. Margaret towards the south, a house, 40 feet long and 30 feet wide, in which to hold the pleas of the Marshalsea of the king's household and to keep the prisoners of the Marshalsea while in the said town, and to hold all other the king's courts.'

Perhaps the most poignant indication that the world of prisons was extremely tough came from one of the earliest musical 'Cries of London' – Richard Dering's lyrics for five voices published around 1610: 'Bread and meat for the poor prisoners of the Marshalsea'. This was echoed in print at the end of the seventeenth century by Marcellus Laroon's London cry: 'Remember the poor prisoners' (left). The feeding of prisoners was not the responsibility of the state or the parish/local authority. They could either pay for their meals or beg from passers-by from the barred windows. Continues on p. 215.
(Stow 375; *Survey of London* 25)

Inns

For a list of Southwark's inns in the sixteenth century and their location see the 1542 map on p.129. Here are three of the most interesting and best documented. Two out of the three were destroyed in Southwark's great fire of 1676 and rebuilt. We have used 'generic' inns in our reconstruction.

(SB13) The Tabard Inn stood on the east side of Borough High Street, opposite the former St Margaret's church. It is described by John Stow as 'the most ancient' of the 'many fair inns' which lined this side of the street, built around 1306. The most famous of Southwark's innumerable inns because it was immortalised as the starting point for the pilgrims of Chaucer's *Canterbury Tales* (above and boxed text). Stow also explained the pictorial significance of its name and its sign – a 'sleeveless coat … open on both sides … a stately garment of old time, commonly worn of noblemen and others'. This implies higher social status and adds weight to Stow's description: 'within this inn was also the lodging of the abbot of Hide, by the city of Winchester, a fair house for him and his train when he came to that city to parliament, &c.'. Stow makes an important point because the modern meaning of 'inn' detracts from its historic meaning as a desirable, comfortable environment, described as such by William Harrison (1577):

> '[they] abound in beer, ale and wine, and some of them are so large that they are able to lodge two or three hundred persons and their horses at ease … Each owner contended with other for goodnesse of entertainement of their guests, as about finesse and change of linen, furniture, of bedding, beautie of rooms, service at the table, costliness of plate, strength of drinke, varietie of wines, or well-using of horses'.

However, in this instance, the residence of the Abbot of Hyde came before the inn. The abbot purchased this site in 1304 with two houses from the Archbishop of Canterbury. There he built a town mansion and probably at the same time a hostelry for the convenience of travellers. In 1307 he obtained a licence from the Bishop of Winchester to build himself a chapel at or by the inn. In 1599 the group of buildings was thus described: 'The Abbott's lodgeinge was wyninge to the

Above:
This is a much later illustration of Geoffrey Chaucer's *Canterbury Tales* which was first published between 1387 and 1400; it is unusual for the way it blends pilgrims with their surroundings – here their departure from Tabard Inn in Southwark. In the early eighteenth century when this engraving was made, Southwark would have still retained a flavour of its medieval past. The Tabard – a sleeveless coat – features prominently on the sign erected across the road. William Blake's more famous illustration pays tribute to this print.
(From John Urry's edition of the *Works of Geoffrey Chaucer*, London, 1721)

When the soft sweet showers of April reach the roots of all things, refreshing the parched earth, nourishing every sapling and every seedling, then humankind rises up in joy and expectation. The west wind blows away the stench of the city … the trees themselves are bathed in song … It so happened that in April I was lodging at Southwark. I was staying at the Tabard Inn, ready to take the way to Canterbury and to venerate the saint. There arrived one evening at the inn twenty-nine other travellers and, much to my delight, I discovered that they were all Canterbury pilgrims.

From Peter Ackroyd, *A Retelling of Geoffrey Chaucer's The Canterbury Tales* (General Prologue), 2009

Below:
The façade of the former Boar's Head Inn, Borough High Street, anonymous wash drawing, around 1800.
© London Metropolitan Archives (City of London)

backside of the inn called the Tabarde, and had a garden attached'. The Elizabethan inn was thus described in Rendle and Norman: 'On the ground floor looking onto the street, was a room called "the darke parlor", a hall, and a general reception-room called "the parlor". This was probably the dining-room … as it opened on to the kitchen … The parlour sat on a cellar. The bedrooms were upstairs. A warehouse, coal hole, oven house and double stable (with an oat loft over it) were outside'.

In Chancery Proceedings of 27 June 1599, the inn was alternatively referred to as Tabard or Talbot but it only changed its name to Talbot after the fire of 1676 when it burnt down. It was rebuilt on the old plan.
(1542 map; Stow; Rendle & Norman; *Survey of London* 22)

(SB14) The George Inn: next to the Tabard on the north side, is the only London galleried inn to have partially survived to our own times. It is now the property of the National Trust.

The date of construction of the original 'St George' is unknown. It was still the 'St George' in 1554 but after that date and in post-Reformation times, the offensive 'St' was dropped. Humphrey Colet, a bowyer, and member of parliament in 1553 and 1555 (as the wealthiest tradesman in the borough) described the George as his principal house in his will of 1558.

Rendle and Norman mention 'a return … made [in 1634] by the Wardens to the Earl of Arundel that the George Inn, or tenements within it, was built of brick and timber in 1622'. This suggests that the land may have been part of the Arundel estates (encountered in Lambeth). The inn was totally destroyed in the 1676 fire and rebuilt by the tenant.
(1542 map; Rendle & Norman; *Survey of London* 22)

(SB15) Boar's Head Inn (left); opposite St Saviour's church and the butcher's shop of Robert Harvard (see BB17). It stood on the east side of Borough High Street and was first recorded in 1393. It was purchased by Sir John Fastolf in 1450. Rendle and Norman pointed out the uncanny way in which it echoed the site and name of the Boar's Head in Eastcheap on the north side of London Bridge, made famous by Shakespeare's *Henry IV* play:

> The City Inn looked upon the burying-ground of St Michael's Crooked Lane, as this other [the Southwark Boar's Head] upon the Flemish burying ground in Southwark. At the former was laid the scene of the revelries of Prince Hal and his fat friend Sir John Falstaff – the latter was curiously enough the property of Sir John Fastolfe,

the historic character believed to have been the inspiration for Falstaff (see SB26). It was Fastolfe's property in the 1450s. Later leases (in 1674 and 1694) describe the property in some detail; this inn escaped the devastating fire of 1676. Continues on p. 219. (1542 map of Southwark; Rendle and Norman; Gerhold 2016 No 98)

(SB16) Church of St Thomas: Probably originated as the chapel for St Thomas' Hospital; the date of building on the present site is not known but a tablet in the church apparently stated its foundation by Edward VI as 1552 (Manning & Bray). The tower came later in the early seventeenth century. The nave was used as a hospital ward. Martha Carlin points out that, as was usual in medieval hospitals, the brothers' function was purely religious while the sisters were responsible for the physical daily care of patients. (Morgan; Manning & Bray; Carlin)

(SB17) St Thomas' Hospital appears to have originated in the infirmary of the Priory of St Mary Overie, founded around 1106; it was completely destroyed by fire in 1212. But three years later it had been re-founded by Peter Des Roches, Bishop of Winchester, and relocated to the east side of Borough High Street. It was one of 1000 hospitals built in England between c. 1070 and the Dissolution of the Monasteries. The hospital became independent from the Priory of St Mary Overie but remained an Augustinian house. Its name originally paid tribute to St Thomas Becket who was canonised in 1173. At the Reformation the dedication to Thomas Becket was swapped for the less controversial figure of St Thomas the Apostle.

In the early fifteenth century the hospital was extended by Lord Mayor Richard (Dick) Whittington: 'a new chamber with eight beds for young women that had done amiss, in trust

Above:
St Elizabeth of Hungary bringing food for the inmates of a hospital, oil painting by Adam Elsheimer of around 1598. The painting gives a detailed rendering of the work of hospitals in the sixteenth century; no such image exists for London or England. In its early days St Thomas's church would have been used as a ward for hospital patients which would offer strong parallels with this painted scene. (Wellcome Collection, London, image in the public domain, Wikipedia).

Above:
The Oratory of the Inn of the Prior of Lewes, opposite St Olave's church in Tooley Street, survived into the nineteenth century and was published by Robert Wilkinson in his *Londina Illustrata* in 1819.

Church of St Olave, Tooley Street

of a good amendment', Whittington specifying 'that all things that happened in that chamber should be kept secret … for he would not shame no young woman in no wise, for it might be cause of their letting [hindering] of their marriage'. In 1535 Thomas Cromwell disparagingly referred to 'the bawdy hospital of St Thomas in Southwark'.

In Tudor times the hospital had operated like a busy creative hub – its premises being used for glassmaking (the Southwark School of Glaziers between 1526 and 1531), printing (the first complete translation of the Bible into English by Miles Coverdale was 'imprinted in Southwarke in Saint Thomas Hospitale by James Nycolson, 1537') and residential quarters where lived, among others, John Gower, the poet laureate and hospital benefactor (buried in St Saviour's).

The hospital's activities were briefly interrupted at the time of the Dissolution of the Monasteries (between 1540 and 1551) but it was re-founded in the mid-sixteenth century by Edward VI, who in 1552 sold it to the City Mayor and the citizens of London: 'the house and site of the late hospital, its church, belfry and churchyard, all the houses, buildings and land in its precinct, and the rectory called the parsonage of St. Thomas, with tithes, oblations and profits'. Continues on p. 217. (Stow; Morgan 35; Carlin; *Survey of London* 23)

(SB18) Church of St Olave, Tooley Street: This eleventh-century church was first mentioned by name in a 1096 record referring to its priest 'Peter of St Olavo' but its foundation may have been much earlier if it is the church – with royal patronage – mentioned in the 1086 Domesday book. The dedication, to Olav Haraldsson, King of Norway between 1015-28, later St Olav, caught the popular mood and several churches in London received the same dedication. The Warenne family – the freeholders – had first granted the Anglo-Saxon church to Lewes priory in Sussex. In 1327 a serious flood damaged the walls of the church and apparently carried away some of the bodies from the graveyard. At the Reformation the advowson was granted in fee to Thomas Lord Cromwell (1538) and when he fell from power, the church reverted to royal control.

Martha Carlin documented the presence, among its parishioners, of the 'Doche' (residents of German, Netherlandish and Northern French origins) residing in Southwark: in 1551 there were 188 such households, but only thirty-three in St Thomas's parish, twenty-eight in St Saviour's and twenty-five in St George's. John Stow confirms it presided over 'a far larger parish, especially of aliens or strangers, and poor people'. Carlin also added that St Olave's 'seems in fact to have been an exceptionally Catholic parish. It supported the largest number of guilds in Southwark' (five by 1533). Continues on p. 208. (Wyngaerde; Agas; Carlin, *VCH 4*)

(SB19) Prior of Lewes House: we know from John Stow that it was

opposite the church of St Olave in Tooley Street, i.e. on the south side of the street. It was a 'great house built of stone, with arched gates'. By 1600, however, it had become 'a common hostelry for travellers, and hath to sign the Walnut Tree'. In the early years of the nineteenth century Robert Wilkinson published what had survived from this ancient inn – the oratory – and what site it occupied under St Olave's Grammar School (top left).
(Stow)

(SB20) St Olave's Grammar School was founded in 1560, in 'Short Southwark' (now Tooley Street), south side, opposite St Olave's church, with money left by a brewer, Henry Leake, a 'stranger' from Flanders and the first in a dynasty of Henry Leakes involved in brewing in Southwark. In 1554 he was the owner of the inn and brewhouse known as the Dolphin and the Beare at the south western foot of London Bridge. His will of 1560 left £8 for the maintenance of a free school with a preference for St Olave's, provided the parish set up a school within two years of his death. It first operated from the local parish church, St Olave, before acquiring a school building on the south side of Tooley Street. The new school in fact occupied part of the site of the Prior of Lewes House, as was revealed in some detail at the beginning of the nineteenth century in Robert Wilkinson's *Londina Illustrata*.

One of the early Governors was Robert Harvard, church warden at St Saviour's church and father of John Harvard – though John was sent to St Saviour's School instead. St Olave's School received its charter in 1571 – its status being that of a grammar school called: 'The Free Grammar School of Queen Elizabeth of the Parishioners of the Parish of Saint Olave in the County of Surrey'. It was not affected by the 1676 fire but was extensively refurbished and extended at around that time.

The site of St Olave's first school and of the adjacent Flemish burial ground both lie under London Railway Bridge Station. Continues on p. 219.
(Wilkinson; *VCH 4*; Rendle & Norman)

(SB21) Abbot of St Augustine's House, east of St Olave's church, and its quay. In 1598 when John Stow was writing it was 'a great house of stone and timber, an ancient piece of work, and seemeth to be one of the first built houses on that side of the river'. A 1281 deed shows that the property was previously in the hands of the earls of Warenne and Surrey before it was 'granted in perpetual alms' to Nicholas, abbot of St. Augustine's of Canterbury, and the convent of the same, and their successors'. By the end of the sixteenth century, it was called Sentlegar House, after its occupant Sir Anthony Sentlegar, 'but divided into sundry tenements'.
(Stow)

(SB22) Bridge House, east from St Olave's was 'a storehouse for stone, timber, or whatsoever pertaining to the building or repairing of London Bridge', Stow tells us. He believed it dated from the building of London Bridge in the twelfth century but the earliest dated reference to it is a deed of c.1222–23 found by Martha Carlin while Tony Sharp believes that 'Peter de Colechurch [who oversaw the building of the stone London Bridge] and his associates probably took up residence … there after 1173'. This large compound of yards and buildings was also used for storing grain and, Stow tells us, for baking bread 'to the best advantage for relief of the poor citizens, when need should require'.

Bridge House in 1600 was the administrative heart of the Bridge House Estates (see below) – a repository of lands given to the City from 1189 onwards, the revenue of which was originally earmarked for the upkeep of Old London Bridge.

In 1522 or 1524, Alderman George Monnox (or Monoux) gave to the City a brewery called 'Goldings' which stood next to Bridge House. By the late sixteenth century according to John Stow, the old 'Goldings' brewery had been replaced by a new one; this brewery was mapped by Joseph Darvoll in 1653. The production of bread and beer had been made possible through City gifts.

The Bridge House Estates: the creation of the Bridge House Estates dates back to 1282, the year when five arches of London Bridge collapsed as a result of frost and poor maintenance. By then the bridge was in royal hands after having been the responsibility of the 'Brethren' (up to 1265) and St Katherine's monastery (1265–69). But after the 1282 disaster, Edward I placed the maintenance of the bridge under the control of the City who created the institution of the Bridge House Estates. Dorian Gerhold notes that London Bridge 'was the first in England to have a permanent endowment'. In 1592 the City Lands Committee of the Common Council was set up and became responsible for the Estates.
(Carlin; 'The origins of the Bridge-House Yard and the Bridge House Estates' by Tony Sharp – courtesy of Tower Bridge exhibition curators; Gerhold 2016, No 78; Stow)

(SB23) Abbot of Battle's Inn. Battle Abbey built a house on the bank of the Thames, between Bridge House and Battle Bridge – now the site of Hay's Wharf. It was there by 1230, accompanied by two tide mills. In 1576, Bridge House became the owner of this former monastic property.

(SB24) Battle Bridge at the Thames end of Mill Lane 'over a watercourse flowing out of Thames' is so called because it stood on ground which belonged to Battle Abbey in Sussex. According to Stow, it was built and maintained by Battle Abbey. A later seventeenth-century plan has survived which shows the exploitation of the site with a pair of tide mills –

This beautiful Delftware dish, dated 1659, has been ascribed to the Pickleherring Pottery and the scene it depicts identified as the parable of the Prodigal Son. Two narratives have been merged: 'And he would fain have filled his belly with husks that swine did eat' (from Luke 15:16); also 'And he arose, and came to his father' (Luke 15:20). This rural scene is typical of this corner of Southwark – farming, village church, thatched buildings as in the painting 'A Fete at Bermondsey' (p. 42).
(© The Trustees of of the British Museum)

Opposite:
Church of St Mary Magdalen of Bermondsey. This detail comes from the painting 'A Village Festival' by Marcus Gheeraerts, late sixteenth century (see p. 43 for the full picture).

the bridge being used as a landing stage. (Stow; Gerhold 2016 no 76)

(SB25) **The Maze**, sited on the south side of Tooley Street, opposite the Abbot of Battle's Inn, is another example of a grand mansion in Southwark/Bermondsey. Some of the earliest records mention that 'The manor of the Maze' was acquired by Sir William Burcestre in the mid–1380s. By the 1460s–1470s it was in the ownership of Roger Copley, citizen and mercer of London. It stayed in the hands of the Copley family until the mid-seventeenth century. In the 1550s 'the Maze' had seventeen small tenements and an alley. John Stow describes 'the walks and gardens … on the other side of the way before the gate of the said house'. In Stow's time it had become an ordinary inn called the Flower de Luce and surrounded by 'small tenements …

replenished with strangers and other, for the most part poor people'.
(Stow; Rendle; Carlin)

(SB26) **Fastolf Hall/'Beere House'**: this was at Horsleydown, the moated house of Sir John Fastolf (1380-1459), the probable inspiration for the character of Falstaff in Shakespeare's plays, who died in this house. He fought in the Hundred Years War and resided both at Caister Castle in Norfolk and at Southwark. Part of the Thames-side site was excavated by Museum of London archaeologists in the 1990s. Fastolf's 1440s property was developed from two moated enclosures – the first, on the west side was the residence of the Dunley family (Dunley Place), the second on the east side was the Rosary (also known as *la Rosere*), which had been built by Edward II in the 1320s and may have been left unfinished. Martha Carlin credits this royal connection as the reason for many grand houses in the neighbourhood.

There was a moat on the west side and a brewery existed on the east side by about 1425. In the 1480s this estate came to Magdalen College, Oxford, as part of the estate of Sir John; there is a 1521 inventory of the estate at the College. By the time the brewery site was leased to Alderman Edmund Lewin in 1667 and recorded by William Leybourn in 1684, several industries were sited there alongside brewing. William Rendle and Philip Norman may have been the first to suggest in *The Inns of Old Southwark* (1888) that the 'Beere Howse' featured on the Braun and Hogenberg map of 1572 probably showed the property which was built by Sir John Fastolf. 'The High Bere House' is also mentioned in Sir John Fastolfe's papers at Magdalen College, Oxford and in early Chancery proceedings as the 'High Bierehowse and gardeyn, lately known as ffastolfe's' (14 Edward IV, i.e. 1475).

Alongside the breweries found on Bankside, this area in Bermondsey was important for brewing. Towards the end of the sixteenth century, the Fastolf's site was occupied by brewer Henry Leake and from 1589 by Wessel Webling originating from Westphalia judging by his will. The Leakes and the Weblings were noted brewing families based in Southwark. Rendle and Norman noted 'how famous old Southwark was for its ales; many times Chaucer indicates their quality … the Flemings extended their breweries along the Bankside, from the Bridge Foot to Horselydown … They were said to have brought over with them great improvements in the trade, among other things the use of hops for beer, as distinct from ale, which continued for a time to be brewed in the old manner.'

By 1600, John Schofield explains, the former Fastolf mansion grounds had been divided into 'at least 103 separate household units'. Wessel Webling died in 1610, and left his Fastolf's property to cousin Nicholas Webling. To his wife he left his Essex property, Uphall. Charitable giving has a significant place in the will – discharging various people from debt, giving money to the poor of St Olave's, to Christ's Hospital and to the poor of Groten Recken in Westphalia. Schofield also points out that by the sixteenth century the parish of St Olave had largely become an industrial zone. A little later, the same parish became the home of another Southwark tin-glazed pottery – after Montague Close. It stood in the appropriately named 'Potter's Fields', close to the modern City Hall and was called the Pickleherring pottery which evokes the lost Pickleherring Stairs and Street along the Thames. The pottery was set up by Christian Wilhelm around 1618 and it lasted until 1723 (top left).

Also see The Boar's Head at SB15.
(Braun & Hogenberg; Rendle & Norman; Carlin; Schofield; MOLA 2009; Gerhold No 77)

(SB27) St Saviour's dock is close to the eastern edge of the area discussed in this book. It is believed to be the mouth of one of London's 'lost' rivers: the Neckinger. There are uncertainties and disagreements about the source and course of this river; it may have risen close to the site of the Imperial War Museum says historian Paul Talling now, while in the nineteenth century Walter Besant thought it was Newington Butts. In any case we know that the monks of Bermondsey Abbey used it for access to and from the Thames (it still bears the name of this abbey's dedication). The name Neckinger on the other hand apparently derives from the eighteenth-century Devol's Neckenger ('the devil's neckcloth'), the nickname given to the rope used to hang Thames pirates along the bank of the Thames – their bodies displayed there as a warning to others.
(Morgan; MOLA 2011)

(SB28) Bermondsey Cross/ Crucifix Lane Bermondsey Cross stood at the junction of Tooley and Bermondsey Streets, pointing the way to Bermondsey Abbey. William Rendle reminds us of their significance as in early deeds of grants of property

"The old cross " was often … a boundary or landmark of a township. Some of the crosses, even by the wayside, possessed a privilege of sanctuary — that is, a temporary refuge against vengeance and sudden and ill-weighted justice. They also served as stations for prayer, or even as guide-posts to some religious house near at hand. This cross was north on the way to the distinguished Abbey of Bermondsey, as another cross, south, was on the way from Kent Street to the same abbey.

(1542 map; Rendle 1878; Ellis)

(SB29) Church of St Mary Magdalen of Bermondsey, Bermondsey Street. The original medieval building, 'built by the priors of Bermondsey, serving for resort of the inhabitants … is called a parish church'. It was dilapidated by the seventeenth century and the church was rebuilt in 1675–79. It is sometimes stated that there are no images of this church prior to its rebuilding but this is incorrect as it is clearly featured on Richard Newcourt and William Faithorne's map of London, 1658. This is a generic picture rather than a portrait but it would still appear to confirm that the church illustrated on two late sixteenth-century paintings by Marcus Gheeraerts at Hatfield House is likely to be that of the medieval St Mary Magdalen, in approximately the correct location (see p. 43).
(1542 map; Stow; Carlin; VCH 4)

(SB30) Bermondsey Abbey The site's very first buildings date from late Saxon/early Norman times – during excavations in the 1980s –1990s, a latrine and chapel were recovered. The actual Cluniac priory was founded in the 1080s from La Charité-sur-Loire

in France; this was the second Cluniac foundation in this country after the foundation of Lewes Priory in Sussex. John Stow tells us: 'being a cell to that in France, was accounted a priory of Aliens'. No picture of the Priory has survived and for the reconstruction we have used recent plans prepared by archaeologists and drawn inspiration from Lewes Priory for the elevations.

The priory, perhaps consecrated in 1086 (Domesday Book), was dedicated to the Holy Saviour i.e. St Saviour's Bermondsey. The first monks at this priory arrived in 1089 and they followed the Benedictine rule. The building of the priory church was well advanced by the mid-twelfth century, and the second cloister (infirmary) by the first half of the thirteenth century. The Abbey was partially rebuilt and extended in the fourteenth century. Denization, the process by which an alien citizen or organisation acquired rights similar to those of a country's natives, came in 1380, when for the first time the priory was in the hands of an Englishman. At the insistence of the king its status changed from priory to abbey in 1399. At the dissolution of the monasteries, it was immediately surrendered to the Crown on 1 January 1538. The new owner was Robert Southwell (later Sir Robert) who immediately leased the property to Thomas Pope, Treasurer of the Court of Augmentations (later Sir Thomas); Pope bought the site in 1544. According to John Stow, it was Thomas Pope who pulled down the abbey; Pope's house, built around the main cloister, was presumably complete in 1555 when he reconveyed the property back to its original owner, Robert Southwell (right).

In the 1560s the Earl of Sussex (Thomas Radcliffe) became a tenant here and later became the owner of the house (see pp. 44–45). The Victoria County History states that at the death of the last known owner, Richard Croshawe in 1631, the property was split between his sister's three daughters, after which division 'the property ceased to be traceable'.

The remnants of the abbey – including the gate – were meticulously recorded by J C Buckler father and son at the beginning of the nineteenth century.

In the reconstruction, it is the powerful ghost of Bermondsey Abbey that is suggested (below). What came after this remarkable landmark is shown on the right and in the 1770 reconstruction. Continues on p. 211. (1542 map; Stow 380; MOLA 2011; *VCH 4*)

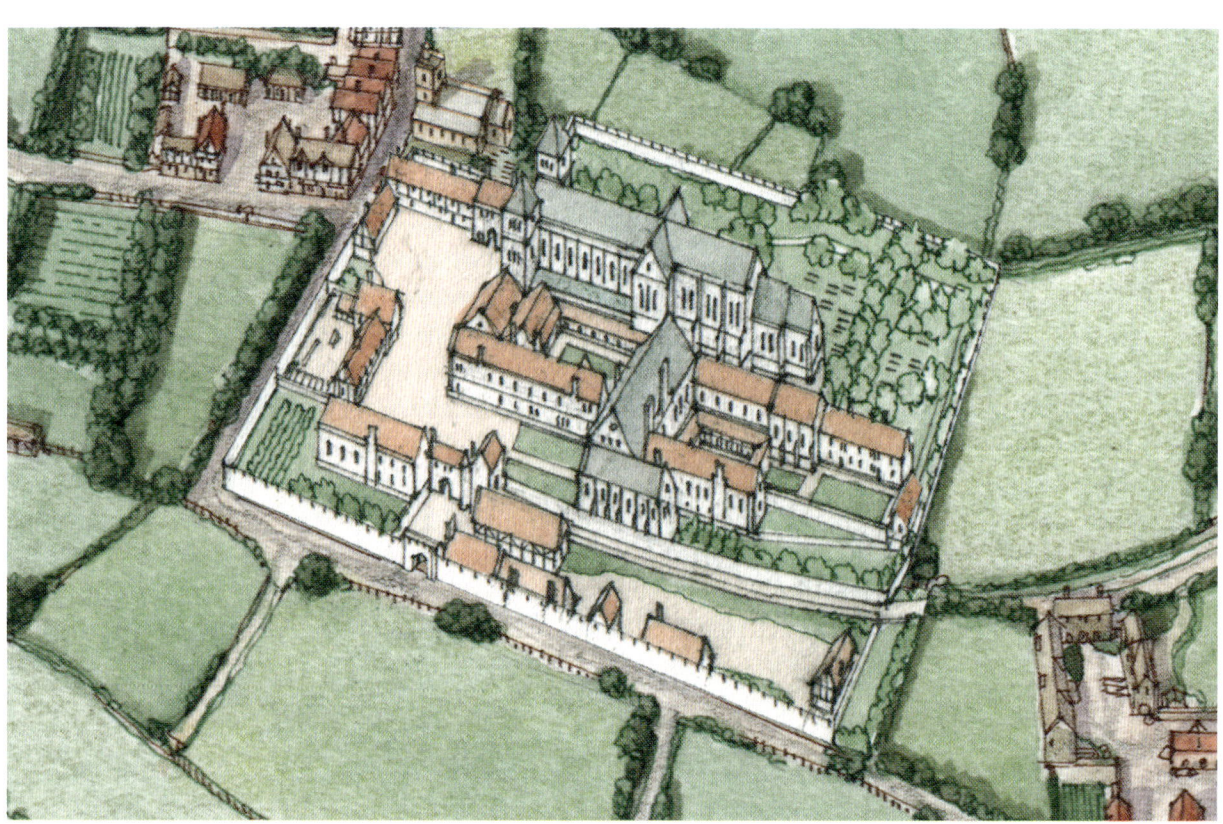

Above:
Thomas Pope's house was built on the site of Bermondsey Abbey. This reconstruction is based on William Faithorne's 1658 map of London
(© Stephen Conlin)

Left:
Detail from the main 1600 reconstruction: Bermondsey Abbey
© Stephen Conlin

THE SOUTH BANK AROUND 1770

Apart from romantic Southwark, the remainder of the southern bank was no more than one long stretch of wharves and occasional small factories, from Rotherhithe to Vauxhall. At their rear ran a long, more or less continuous road, like a backbone. Behind this ... [there were] meadows and marshes ... a few long roads to take wharf-goods by the shortest and straightest route to the higher and drier parts of Surrey. These roads across the lonely marshland were infested with highwaymen and footpads, who found this a most profitable thoroughfare ...

Hugh Phillips' *The Thames about 1750*, 1951

Hugh Phillips thus summed-up the essential geography of the South Bank in the eighteenth century. It provides a useful framework, though this sharp, simplified portrait may reflect the author's lack of enthusiasm for this part of London, often neglected in his otherwise remarkable book.

The most notable development in the eighteenth century is the industrialisation of the South Bank. It had started as early as the sixteenth century, accelerated in the seventeenth century but in the age of enlightenment it came to dominate the South Bank, eliminating all trace of royal or clerical living and housing. The extraordinary fact is that industry was able to take root in the empty shells of grand houses from the past – gun manufactory at Fox Hall or Fulke's Hall, a former Manor House; fire power was soon replaced by the manufacture of vinegar. At Carlisle House, the former home of the Bishop of Carlisle, a pottery developed. Another vinegar manufactory took over the popular Cuper's Garden, a large pleasure garden which had benefited from elite connections with Arundel House on the other side of the Thames. Glass found a home in the old Winchester Palace, a pottery appeared in the shadow of St Saviour's church, once a grand priory boasting wealth and comfort within its precinct. In Bermondsey, the extensive residence of Sir John Fastolf became slowly engulfed by the brewery which sat alongside his manor house. In Tooley Street, part of the vaulted basement of the former inn for the Priory of Lewes became a school while the early operators of Hay's Wharf used one of its vaults for wine storage.

1770 or thereabouts is a useful date to observe the changes that had occurred in the eighteenth century as a whole. For the reconstruction which opens this chapter, we were able to use the 1747 map by John Rocque alongside the late eighteenth-century map of London by Richard Horwood – and its 1813 edition, published by the London Topographical Society. Looking further back, the Restoration map by William Morgan proved useful to place developments in their right context.

Sources

Sources have been placed in brackets under each entry (full references in bibliography). Alongside the maps, contemporary sources have been used, such as the relevant volumes of the *Survey of London*, the publications of Dorian Gerhold, Graham Gibberd, Hugh Phillips, Warwick Wroth and others.

THE SOUTH BANK AROUND 1770 147

Antonio Canaletto, 'London seen through an Arch of Westminster Bridge', oil painting 1746–47.
(Collection of the Duke of Northumberland, Alnwick Castle. Image in the public domain; Wikimedia Commons)

VAUXHALL AND LAMBETH

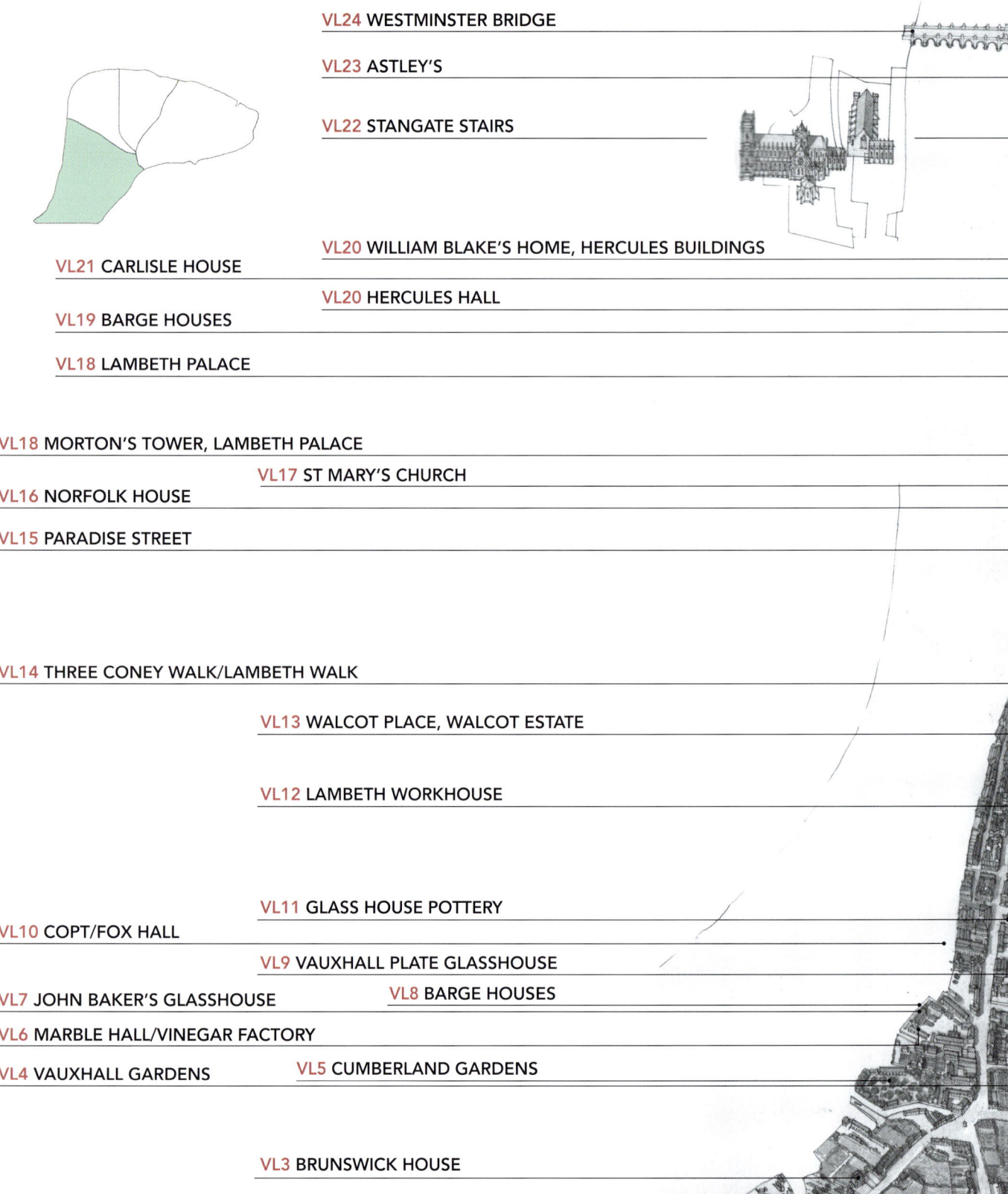

VL24 WESTMINSTER BRIDGE

VL23 ASTLEY'S

VL22 STANGATE STAIRS

VL20 WILLIAM BLAKE'S HOME, HERCULES BUILDINGS

VL21 CARLISLE HOUSE

VL20 HERCULES HALL

VL19 BARGE HOUSES

VL18 LAMBETH PALACE

VL18 MORTON'S TOWER, LAMBETH PALACE

VL17 ST MARY'S CHURCH

VL16 NORFOLK HOUSE

VL15 PARADISE STREET

VL14 THREE CONEY WALK/LAMBETH WALK

VL13 WALCOT PLACE, WALCOT ESTATE

VL12 LAMBETH WORKHOUSE

VL11 GLASS HOUSE POTTERY

VL10 COPT/FOX HALL

VL9 VAUXHALL PLATE GLASSHOUSE

VL7 JOHN BAKER'S GLASSHOUSE

VL8 BARGE HOUSES

VL6 MARBLE HALL/VINEGAR FACTORY

VL4 VAUXHALL GARDENS

VL5 CUMBERLAND GARDENS

VL3 BRUNSWICK HOUSE

VL1 TRADESCANT HOUSE
VL2 ASHMOLE HOUSE

This unusual oil painting set on the Thames outside Lambeth Palace is undated and anonymous. The luminous atmosphere, reminiscent of seventeenth-century Netherlandish paintings, became fashionable in the first two decades of the nineteenth century. The scene depicts a barge with tarpaulin over a temporary roof structure to protect bargemen and cargo from the rain. There is a cluster of tall mooring posts for barges and lighters. The close-up perspective invites us to read these posts as 'working towers' against a background of more architectural towers – of St Mary's church and Morton's Gate. (Yale Center for British Art; image in the public domain)

(VL1) **Tradescant House**, South Lambeth; continued from p. 95. In 1661 the lease of the 'Vauxhall Escheat' described it as: 'the moiety of a messuage, garden and orchard'. A year later, John Tradescant the Younger, the man who cared for garden and 'ark', died. Both Tradescants – father and son – are buried in the cemetery of the church of St Mary Lambeth (see pp. 363 & 368). At the death of Mrs Tradescant in 1678 the family collections went, controversially, to Elias Ashmole who later donated them to his university. They were lost to London but formed, alongside other collections, the basis of the new purpose-built Ashmolean Museum in Oxford, the first to open to the public in England in 1683, sixty-eight years before the British Museum. Also see pp. 387 ff.
(*Survey of London* 26; Gibberd; Potter)

(VL2) **Ashmole House**, attached to the Tradescants' House in South Lambeth Road. On 28 August 1675 the great collector and antiquary Elias Ashmole moved into the house with his wife. He purchased the house from a Mrs Blackamore or Bowyer (accounts vary). The move has been interpreted as rapacious and controlling, particularly in view of the fact that Ashmole did ultimately succeed in acquiring the collection of the Tradescants – the nucleus of the Ashmolean Museum. By the time he moved into this house both father and son Tradescant had died, and Hester, who survived her husband John the Younger, complained bitterly of Ashmole's interference. After her

death, Ashmole continued to acquire further plots in the Vauxhall Escheat. (Illustrated on p. 96)
(*Survey of London* 26; Gibberd; Potter).

(VL3) **Brunswick House** in Vauxhall, which still survives, was known as Belmont House in the eighteenth century. Some accounts have argued that the house's basement suggests a building date in the mid-seventeenth century. But the *Survey of London* is clear-cut: 'This house was built in 1758 on freehold land owned by the Dawson family, purchased by Richard Dawson in 1737 from Joseph Pratt.' Forty years later the property was described as a mansion house, with offices, coach-house, and stable, lately erected by John Dawson (nephew and heir). In 1791 it was divided into two parts, the southwest section being leased to David Hunter while William Anderson leased the rest of the house. The house changed name following the arrival in 1811 of Friedrich Wilhelm, Duke of Brunswick who purchased Anderson's part. He had fled to England after his defeat in battle against Napoleon. He was George III's nephew and the brother of Caroline, the estranged wife of the future George IV.

Today, the house has been restored and is the home of LASSCO, the London Architectural Salvage and Supply company; it has a rather spectacular suite of showrooms. The atmospheric basement is also accessible to visitors. The Brunswick restaurant is on the ground floor (Horwood 1813 (33); *Survey of London* 26)

(VL4) **Vauxhall Gardens**. See p. 372 ff

(VL5) **Cumberland Gardens** was immediately south of Marble Hall (see below). This pleasure garden appears in Richard Horwood's map and it is also well illustrated in one of the Museum of London's cuttings' books *South London Pleasure Gardens*. Originally known as Smith's Gardens, it opened before 1779 and had a local audience. On 25 May 1825, the tavern and adjoining ballroom were found to be on fire – despite valiant efforts to put out the fire, both were completely destroyed and the gardens damaged. (Horwood 1799; Horwood 1813; Wroth)

(VL6) **Marble Hall**, recorded on Rocque's map of 1747; this most evocative name described a pleasure garden which had opened in 1741. The licence appears to have been withdrawn after 1755 as in the following year, it opened merely as a coffee house and tavern. By the 1790s, however, a vinegar manufactory, recorded on Leigh's panorama, had set up shop on its doorstep, on the north side – it was the property of Messrs Fassett & Burnet, recorded on Horwood's map of 1799. On the 1813 edition, it was simply a 'Vinegar Manufactory' which had expanded to take over the site of Marble Hall, now a 'Vinegar Yard'. But unlike the manufactory, the vinegar yard may not have lasted very long because it was on the route of the forthcoming Vauxhall Bridge (1809-1816). Possibly this is where Sir Joseph Mawbey (1730-1798) of Kennington's 'Mawbey estate' was apprenticed to 'distiller' Joseph Pratt at Vauxhall. Also see John Baker's entry below. (Rocque 19; Horwood 1799; Horwood 1813; Leigh's Panorama; Wroth; *Survey of London* 26 for the Mawbey estate)

(VL7) **John Baker's glasshouse** at Vauxhall. This glasshouse does not feature on seventeenth- or eighteenth-century maps of London. The main reason being that it was short-lived, starting between 1663 and 1681, closing down by 1704 and demolished by 1706. It was one of England's many glasshouses at the end of the seventeenth century – of eighty-eight in 1696, sixty-one made flint, green and ordinary glass, and twenty-seven solely made crystal glass (according to John Houghton's 1696 list). Twenty-four were 'in and about London and Southwark', a buoyant industry regulated by the Glass Sellers Company established in 1664 (though Lambeth and Vauxhall were outside its jurisdiction).

This was the first of London's seventeenth-century glasshouses to be excavated and its archaeological report throws light on glasshouses in London including those on the South Bank. The excavation revealed that the main product was bottles, mostly green-glass wine bottles, which became the standard type in eighteenth-century London's inns and taverns. The best document to have survived for this glasshouse is Thomas Hill's 1681 map of the manor of Vauxhall (see p. 94). John Baker was the landlord but the man who was most likely running the glasshouse was John Bellingham, who, in the late 1660s, had worked in Amsterdam and Harlem, making mirrors. In the early 1670s he worked in the Duke of Buckingham's plate glasshouse, a stone's throw from the site under review – see VL9 below.

The furnace excavated here could work six crucibles at one time – up to 1800 wine bottles – though it is not known how often, if ever, the furnace worked to capacity. A complaint about the glasshouse, made in 1681, gives some idea of its impact on the immediate neighbourhood: Mr Foster deplored the 'constant fires' and wanted the glasshouse demolished. His complaint was not upheld.

After the death of John Bellingham in 1700 this property changed hands often, eventually falling into the ownership of Joseph and Richard Pratt, distillers, in 1743. The late eighteenth-century Horwood map shows the site occupied by Messrs Fassett & Burnet's Vinegar Manufactory.

The London market was dominated by the production of bottles, vessel glass and window glass, though by the second quarter of the eighteenth century, lead-crystal dominated the market. (Horwood 1799; Horwood 1813; MoLAs 2005; Harry J Powell, *Glassmaking in England*, 1923)

(VL8) Bargehouses at Vauxhall. Following the example which had been set by Henry VIII and other members of the royal family (see p. 107), ceremonial barges – for the City Mayor and City companies – appeared on the Thames around the middle of the seventeenth century. A 1654 plan survives which shows the arrangement of the Fishmongers', Mercers' and Clothworkers' bargehouses at Vauxhall. They predate the Skinners' bargehouse in Lambeth (see VL19) and do not show a separate dwelling house for the barge keepers. Accommodation for them was above the bargehouses. The common garden at the back was generous and shared between all three companies. The site for these was near the present Vauxhall Bridge (Gerhold specifies near the south west corner of MI6, which was excavated in 1989, see MoLAs 2005 in bibliography). Also see p. 172. (*Survey of London* 23; Gerhold 2016, No 121)

(VL9) Vauxhall Plate Glasshouse. This glasshouse, set up and owned by George Villiers, 2nd Duke of Buckingham, from 1663, appears on Rocque's map to be the largest glasshouse on the South Bank. It was very close to John Baker's glasshouse but it was established on much firmer ground for two reasons.

First there was a tradition of glassmaking on this site which went back to the early days of the glass industry in London – as far back as the 1590s, initially in the hands of aliens and their descendants. This site had been connected to glassmaking since at least 1613 when the royal courtier Sir Edward Zouch was running a glasshouse, securing a patent the following year, which covered the entire field of glassmaking. In 1615 the factory was taken over by Sir Robert Mansell, the Lord High Admiral who also secured a monopoly for glass-making in England.

Secondly, when George Villiers took over the site in 1663, he also obtained a monopoly: the manufacture of plate-glass for mirrors. The glasshouse manufactured looking-glass plates, flat glass and glass for coaches. It ceased trading in 1786 and by the time Richard Horwood produced his late eighteenth-century map, it had been redeveloped as a residential area around 'Vauxhall Square', the sole reminder of its previous incarnation being the presence of a 'Glasshouse Street'. (Rocque 19; Phillips; Eleanor S Godfrey, *The Development of English Glassmaking 1560–1640*, 1975)

(VL10) Fox Hall or Faux Hall/Fulke's Hall, Vauxhall riverside; continued from p. 96. By the mid-seventeenth century, Fox Hall was where the prolific inventor Edward Somerset, 2nd Marquess of Worcester, had a workshop, assisted by the Dutch engineer Caspar Kalthoff. It soon became a gun manufactory, alongside a residence for John Bishop, 'Engineer and Overseer of all the Instruments of Warre' – hence the name of nearby 'Gun-House Stairs' on Rocque's map. (Rocque 19; Horwood 1799; Horwood 1813; *Survey of London* 23)

(VL11) Lambeth potters. Most were found between Vauxhall and Lambeth Palace – the exception being Carlisle Pottery near Lambeth Marsh (see VL21). 'The late 18th-century Lambeth wares were mostly for use in taverns: ale mugs and jugs for spirits and beer. Other vessels included storage jars, sanitary wares and bottles', summarised the 2005 MoLAS publication on Doulton stoneware. The two best documented pot houses – because they have been excavated – were in Glasshouse Street and Norfolk House. Lambeth's first tin-glazed ware opened for business in 1676 at Copthall near Glasshouse Street; the pottery at Norfolk House followed in

Large drug jar of Lambeth Delftware for holding Mithridatum – a concoction made up of a great number of ingredients, believed to be effective against poison. (Wellcome Collection; image in the public domain)

1680 and three years later another at Vauxhall. The 2008 archaeological report concludes 'The London tin-glazed ware industry was ground-breaking, fuelled by foreign expertise and imports which could be copied'. Stoneware was first manufactured at the Carlisle House pothouse, Lambeth Marsh (c. 1704–1727), see VL21. From 1712 stoneware and tin-glazed ware were made at the Vauxhall pothouse. Porcelain came later, at the Glasshouse pothouse (c. 1751–1763) which otherwise produced mainly tin-glazed ware; though these dates contradict the 1710 account of the German scholar Conrad von Uffenbach who left a vivid description of a visit to an unnamed pot house in Vauxhall in 1710:

> On 21st July, Monday morning, we first went to see the porcelain sheds at Foxhall. The articles made here are very coarse and heavy, and not so fine as those from Frankfort or Hanau. The work is no different from what I saw in Berlin, except that clay is washed in great vats in the yard, dried in the sun, and prepared for manufacture.

It is likely to refer to the Vauxhall pothouse set up by John de Wilde from the Netherlands (as distinct from the Glasshouse Street pot house) which operated between 1683 and 1802.

The Glasshouse Street pottery was excavated on three separate occasions in the 1980s and the final report (MoLAS 2008) describes its three distinct phases: the business was started by John Sanders in 1743, producing tin-glazed ware until 1784, and also porcelain between 1751 and 1763; then stoneware was produced between 1784 and 1823. In its final phase (1823-46) the pottery returned to tin-glazed ware, 'the last of the English tin-glazed pothouses'.

The pot house which was based at Norfolk House operated between 1680 and the 1770s. It was started by James Barston who had been potting in Southwark before setting up in Lambeth. At his death his wife took over the business: 'a significant feature of this history is that the pothouse was run by women from 1693 to 1721' (MoLAS). The site was first excavated in the late 1960s when 'the foundations of one kiln and remains of a second were discovered' alongside 'delftware wasters'. The short report which was published in March 1969 noted: 'This is the first tinglazed earthenware kiln to have been excavated in England' (*Surrey Archaeological Society Bulletin*).

For a comprehensive list of potteries in Greater London, see Troy Dawson Chappell, *An English Pottery Heritage – A survey of Earthenware & Stoneware 1630–1800*, part 2, 2016 (Northern Ceramic Society – online) (Rocque 19; Phillips; Gibberd; MoLAS 2008; Reg Jackson's website www.bristolpottersandpotteries.org.uk; MoLAS 2005(B))

(VL12) Lambeth workhouse, Lambeth Butts (now Black Prince Road). When the mapmaker John Rocque published his great map of London in 1747, the Lambeth workhouse had been in operation for almost twenty years – it features on his map but is not named. According to a 1731 account it was 'a large new Brickhouse … built near Lambeth Butts … opened in 1726, for receiving all the Poor of the Parish that receive Alms; where there are now 60 Men, Women and Children'.

By the last decade of the eighteenth century, mapmaker Richard Horwood shows that the workhouse had doubled in size and had given its name to the street it was in – Workhouse Lane. If we now turn to the statistics prepared by Peter Higginbotham for his remarkable workhouse website, the capacity increased from sixty inmates in 1727 to 270 in 1777 and finally 1100 in 1866, indicating that by the 1790s the number of inmates had probably increased five times.

Every resident worked, including children – kitchen and laundry duties for women and spinning yarn for men and children. Children were taught to read but not write. Continues on p. 237.
(Rocque 19; Horwood 1813 (33); Higginbotham, Peter The workhouse www.workhouses.org.uk, information retrieved 29 September 2020)

(VL13) Walcot Place, Walcot estate, seventeen acres. The Lambeth part of the estate spread across both sides of Kennington Road, formerly named Walcot Place. In his will of 21 January 1667 (i.e., 1668) Edmund Walcot left his estate to the poor of the parishes of Lambeth and Southwark, administered by St Mary's and St Olave's churches. The land was mainly in Lambeth but Edmund's life had been mostly spent in Southwark, living and trading from his father's premises on London Bridge – on the south east side, very close to Traitor's Gate, overlooking St Olave's where Edmund was buried. Both parishes only came into possession of the land around 1700.

The New (Kennington) Road, made in 1750–51, is labelled Walcot Place on Horwood's plan, indicating that it was, in part, carved out of the Walcot estate. This opened up the way to building development. Robert Hardcastle was the first to erect houses in Walnut Tree Walk on the basis of a building lease dated 1755. Progress continued which can be measured on Horwood's 1799 map. The shape and extent of the Lambeth estate may be ascertained from later estate maps: two triangular plots on the west side of Kennington Road, one at Walnut Tree Walk and the other a little further north; the rest on the east side of Kennington Road – Walcot Square and St Mary's Gardens and the corresponding section edging Kennington Road.

Issues regarding the legal status of the Walcot estate and the partitioning

This watercolour by Paul Sandby shows the so-called drug mill of the Apothecaries Company near Lambeth Walk. It was used to grind and prepare medicinal remedies and this landscape is a good example of the rural sights that could be afforded in Lambeth around 1780.
© London Metropolitan Archives (City of London)

of land between Southwark and Lambeth kept on surfacing and the matter was not fully resolved until the 1828 Act of Parliament which also settled the status of the adjoining Hayle's estate, on the east side, also set up in the seventeenth century (1671) to benefit the poor people of St Mary's parish in Lambeth. The two estates were eventually amalgamated and still exist under the name 'Walcot Foundation'.
(Horwood 1813; Lambeth archives; *Survey of London* 23; Gerhold 2019)

(VL14) **Lambeth Walk** was a rural path in the eighteenth century known as Three Coney Walk. Mapmaker John Rocque recorded a round structure in its vicinity, on the site of modern Juxon Street – the 'drug mill of the Apothecaries Company' according to Edward Walford (*Old and New London*), but the editors of The *Survey of London* point out: 'nothing has been found in the records of the company to confirm this'. The site has also been described as Gray's Walk which ran between Lambeth Walk and Princes Road. By the time Horwood published his 1799 map, the path had changed its name to Lambeth Walk.
(Rocque 19; Horwood 1813 (33); *Survey of London* 23)

(VL15) **Paradise Row (later Street)** running between Lambeth High Street and Lambeth Walk. The street was formed at the end of the seventeenth century on land which had belonged to Norfolk House. Bishop Tenison bought this land and stipulated in his will that the revenue of the houses at Nos 2–18 should be used towards the running of Lambeth School. These houses have disappeared.
(Rocque; Horwood 1813; *Survey of London* 23)

(VL16) **Norfolk House and Lambeth School**, Lambeth High Street; continued from p. 97. Much of the remaining land on which

stood Norfolk House was eventually purchased by Archbishop Thomas Tenison (1636–1715) and 'enclosed with a Brick-wall'. Richard Walcot (d. 1654) had purchased acres in 'Cottmansfield' immediately east of Tenison's, crossed by Three Coney Walk – the future Lambeth Walk and the origins of the Walcot estate. Tenison's will of 1715 spelt out in detail what his intentions were as he assigned the land to named Trustees 'for the only Use and Benefit of the Parishioners of Lambeth'. He went on to stipulate that it meant 'an Additional Burial-place for the same Parish' also clarifying arrangements for the school he had erected 'at the West End of the said Church-yard for the Education of Twelve Poor-Girls of the said Parish of Lambeth'. (also see Paradise Row above). For Norfolk House pottery, see VL11.
(Rocque; *Survey of London* 23; Tenison's *Memoirs*)

(VL17) **Church of St Mary, Lambeth**; continued from p. 97. The churchwarden accounts record the mid-seventeenth century shift towards puritanism with the removal of the screen separating nave from chancel and the sale of the steeple cross as old iron. The church expanded at the end of the seventeenth century and in the early years of the next. A gallery at the west end was erected in 1699, and the south gallery was built in 1708.

Further improvements came in the 1770s: first the insecure foundation of a column close to the pulpit had to be fixed after tomb digging carried out too close to its base resulted in a state of suspension rather than solid support; next came 'a handsome Gothic portal', in 1778, put up at the west end of the church 'for the convenience of those parishioners who kept carriages'; finally, charity children were provided with a gallery of their own. There were two noteworthy tombs in the churchyard – that of the Tradescant family is discussed on p. 368. The second belongs to Vice-Admiral William Bligh (1754–1817), one-time colonial administrator but better known as the unfortunate master and commander during the Mutiny of the Bounty (1789). Continues on p. 239
(Horwood 1813; *Survey of London* 23)

(VL18) **Lambeth Palace**; continued from p. 157. It is in the eighteenth century that Lambeth House started being called Lambeth Palace. For the Commonwealth years the *Survey of London* describes the 'long series of entries in the burial register [which] give melancholy proof of the number of royalist prisoners who died during their incarceration in Lambeth Palace'. The Great Hall, largely demolished, was rebuilt by Archbishop William Juxon (1582–1663), sometime after 1660. The Archbishop chose to have it rebuilt in the Gothic style, a decision which sought to avoid a harsh visual break with its medieval predecessor, though certain more contemporary details such as classical pediments and a frieze of carved swags and masks, could not be resisted. The diarist Samuel Pepys thus commented in his diary for 22 July 1665: 'viewed the new hall, a new old-fashioned hall as much as possible'. It is remarkable for its overwhelming use of the blackamoor motif which formed part of the arms of Archbishop Juxon.
(Rocque; Horwood 1813; *Survey of London* 23; Tatton-Brown)

(VL19): **Bargehouses close to Lambeth Palace**. A late seventeenth-century plan of the Skinners' bargehouse in Lambeth sheds light on the site labelled 'the barge houses' on Rocque's 1747 map (just above Lambeth Palace, next to the Archbishop's garden). The narrow sloping strips of land which accommodated some of these ceremonial barges were made up of a barge house (nearest to the Thames), then a dwelling for the keeper of the site, a small garden and

Interior of the Great Hall (1660s) at Lambeth Palace: The oak hammerbeam roof draws inspiration from Gothic art, by then regarded as old-fashioned. The motif of the blackamoor is abundantly used throughout the hall as it formed part of Archbishop Juxon's coat of arms, the man responsible for rebuilding the hall. It was converted into a library in the nineteenth century.
(© The author, 2016)

Astley's amphitheatre near Westminster Bridge before the existence of its permanent building. In captioning these images, the artist explained: 'The representation of horses, &c. seen on the top of the building were painted and cut out to the form required … The ground of the Amphitheatre was on the original soil … the performances were only by day-light'. Engravings after drawings by William Capon made in July and September 1777.

(From Charles John Smith's *Historical and Literary Curiosities*, 1875)

a yard. Following the Restoration, the Archbishop of Canterbury renewed the lease in 1661, after church property was recovered.
(Rocque 19; *Survey of London* 23; Gibberd; Gerhold 2016 No 122)

(VL20) Hercules Hall and Buildings. Hercules Hall was the home of the equestrian performer/entrepreneur Philip Astley – from 1788 until at least 1804; it sat alongside the southern side of the triangular site which was developed in the 1780s – this particular plot of land was owned by the City of London. By 1831 the hall was in the hands of a zinc manufacturer, Thomas Barton Lawrence. It was demolished in 1841 (see p. 378).

On the northern side of the triangle stood 'Hercules Buildings', a row of three-storey terraced houses which hemmed in Hercules Hall, shielding it from the street also called Hercules Buildings. The terraced houses were photographed in the early twentieth century shortly before they were demolished in 1915. The 'William Blake estate' which has now replaced the Georgian terrace was built by and currently maintained by the Corporation of London; they are responsible for the pale blue plaque marking the spot where stood the house which William and Mary Blake occupied between February 1791 and 1800 (see p. 378).
(Horwood 1813; *Survey of London* 23)

(VL21) Carlisle House in Carlisle Lane; continued from p. 100. Part of the house was used as a pottery from 1690 but in 1721 a pottery lease was agreed with the Archbishop of Canterbury, which stipulated that all salt glazing should take place at night time; it was insured as a pottery in 1723. By 1730, however, it had become a tavern. It finally settled as the home of the Carlisle Academy for Young Gentlemen from 1739 until 1827 when being 'very ancient and much out of repair' it was demolished. This followed the granting of an Act which permitted the Bishop of Carlisle to issue building leases. Two local builders, one residing at Hercules Buildings, the other at Crozier Street developed the site but the development fell victim to railway expansion. Virtually all of it was destroyed except for a short terrace of houses – numbers 28 to 38 Hercules Road (between Centaur and Virgil Streets).
(Horwood 1813, labelled

'Carlisle School'; *Survey of London* 23; Gibberd)

(VL22) Stangate, now the site of St Thomas' Hospital; continued from p. 101. The arrival of Westminster Bridge in 1750 disrupted the many ferrymen who could be found at this ancient Thames crossing. Stangate Stairs, clearly marked on Morgan's 1682 map and Rocque's 1747 map, disappeared. This stretch of the river (on either side of Westminster Bridge) was an important centre for boat building (for instance Searle's), timber yards and bargehouses (see above, VL8). The road associated with this neighbourhood, the continuation of Narrow Wall, was named 'Stangate' in Rocque, 'Bishop's Walk' in Horwood 1799 and back to Stangate in Horwood's 1813 edition. Stangate Street was formed in the second half of the eighteenth century, and the houses were built on either side between 1761 and 1788.
(Rocque; Horwood 1799; Horwood 1813; *Survey of London* 23)

(VL23) Astley's Amphitheatre, close to Westminster Bridge. Philip Astley (1742–1814), the 'father of modern circus', made his humble debut in the performing arts on the South Bank in the late 1760s (after a false start in Islington where daring horsemanship was all the rage). He opened a riding school in a field called 'Halfpenny Hatch', between the New Cut and the Thames. The son of a struggling Staffordshire cabinet-maker, Astley had enrolled in the army in the 15th Light Dragoons cavalry regiment at the age of seventeen. There he became an excellent horseman, taking part in the Seven Years War (1756–63), generally distinguishing himself and becoming a Sergeant-Major; he was honourably discharged in 1768 and given a white horse. He made enough money at Halfpenny Hatch to purchase a better site, a former timber merchant plot at the bridge end of Westminster Bridge Road (1769). He named his new establishment the British School of Riding. It would, in due course, become Astley's Amphitheatre (left).

In the book *Pleasures of London*, Barker & Jackson recount Astley's lucky break in 1771. On Westminster Bridge George III lost control of his horse which had taken fright at cheering crowds; Astley witnessed the incident, confidently stepped forward, grabbed the horse and calmed him down. Astley then introduced himself as 'late of Your Majesty's 15th Light Dragoons'. Accounts vary regarding his reward: some that the grateful King rewarded Astley with a licence, others that he was asked to perform for the King – in any case a gesture likely to have brought him some fame and more customers.

By 1779 Astley had made enough money to be able to erect a partially roofed Riding House. He could then devise more ambitious shows involving horses but also other acts, including 'Chinese shadows' which, from March 1779 remained a standard feature of the bill for ten years. Also on the bill in these early days were: a conjuring horse, a human conjuror and a Signor Rossignol 'who played a concert on a stringless violin and imitated bird songs'; fireworks were an added attraction. In 1783 Astley added a stage, described in 1826 as 'probably the largest and most convenient in London' while the circus ground was 'covered with pulverized saw-dust'. From then on, the programme would also feature drama … alongside equestrian feats.

This building burnt down in 1794, was rebuilt, renamed the 'Amphitheatre of the Arts' and patronised by the Prince of Wales. Astley, father and son, ran the new facility. That, too, burnt down in 1803 and was rebuilt in 1804 after a design by Astley. On both occasions the horses were saved by Mr Searle, the boat builder of Stangate. The new facilities had a clear dual purpose: a circus ring and a stage with the orchestra pit between the two.
(Horwood 1813; Barker & Jackson 2008; Altick)

(VL24) Westminster Bridge. Building a crossing here had been first discussed after the Restoration, but the opposition of the City and the watermen had resulted in no action being taken. The project was revisited in 1721 when the growth of Westminster justified the financial and logistical upheaval. Several designs were submitted, including some by respected architects such as Colen Campbell and Nicholas Hawksmoor but all were rejected. In 1736 an Act of Parliament authorised the project but the man in charge – the Swiss-born engineer Charles Labelye – was only appointed in May 1738. Compensation of £25,000 was paid to the watermen, while the Archbishop of Canterbury, who owned the Horseferry, received £21,000.

For the first time in England the technique of 'caissons' was used for the foundations – watertight timber structures that were sunk into the ground. Three lotteries raised a considerable amount of funds enabling the bridge to open toll-free. It was ready at the end of 1746 but disaster struck soon after when one of the piers collapsed (Canaletto recorded the affected pier being repaired (see overleaf). The architect and his supporters received heavy criticism but after the bridge opened to traffic on 18 November 1750, it was regarded as an object of wonder: 'a very great ornament to our metropolis, and will be looked on with pleasure or envy by all foreigners' wrote the *Gentleman's Magazine*.
(Rocque; Horwood 1813; *Survey of London* 23; R J B Walker, *Old Westminster Bridge – The Bridge of Fools*, 1979; Labelye in *Dictionary of National Biography*, accessed 28 January 2021)

(VL25) The 'Asylum for Female Orphans' or 'House of Refuge', (overleaf) was set up in 1758 on the

Above:
Antonio Canaletto, Westminster Bridge being repaired, oil on canvas, c. 1747. The view is taken from the north, with a good view of the Lambeth waterfront.
(Private collection; Image in the public domain, Wikimedia Commons)

Opposite top:
The Dining Hall of the Female Orphan Asylum in Westminster Bridge Road. The text which accompanies this print mentions 'the good order … the sweet innocence of the children, and the benevolence of the guardians'. The dining hall is top-lit, which limits the presence of windows; the walls are bare, the fire roaring, and the children are being fed. The agitated little girl dressed in yellow in the middle of the room is accompanied by her parents who are no doubt supporters of the institution. She contrasts with the sober attire and 'good order' of the orphan girls.
(Rudolph Ackermann, *Microcosm of London*, with plates by Augustus Pugin and Thomas Rowlandson, 1808-10, Vol. I)

site of the former Hercules Inn and Gardens, in Westminster Bridge Road. It was established by magistrate Sir John Fielding 'for the reception of orphaned, friendless or deserted girls' between the ages of nine and twelve. Two hundred 'are daily sheltered and protected from vice and want, supplied with food and raiment, and taught whatever can render them useful in their situation, or comfortable and happy in themselves' records *The Microcosm of London* (1808–1810). This publication uses interchangeably the words 'girls', 'children', 'females', emphasising their vulnerable status and the dangers of being exposed 'to the solicitations of the vicious, and the consequent misery of early seduction'.

They were taught the 'principles of religion', 'reading, writing, needlework, and household business' along with 'the first four rules of arithmetic'. 'At the age of fifteen, or sooner', they would be placed 'as domestic servants to reputable families of Great Britain'.
(Horwood 1813; Pugin & Rowlandson; *Survey of London* 23)

(VL26) Dog and Duck and St George's Spa in Lambeth Road, (right) on the site of the Imperial War Museum for the Dog and Duck and a little further west for the Spa. There was a tavern here since at least 1642 but the Spa was discovered much later. The waters were being sold from 1695 although the site was only fully exploited from 1731. The Spa acquired a Long Room in the 1750s and between 1754 and 1770 the place was reputable – Dr Johnson even recommending the waters to his beloved Mrs Thrale of Bankside and Streatham Place. From the 1770s the owner, the energetic Mrs Hedger, who had good business acumen, improved the facilities, turning tavern

Left:
'Saturday evening scene at the Dog and Duck': this anonymous etching, dated 1785, displays the characteristics of the eighteenth-century pleasure garden – supper boxes in the background, walking and flirting, with people in groups (in the supper boxes), couples and also single people.
© London Metropolitan Archives (City of London)

Church of St Mary Newington before and after 1789 when it was rebuilt – not for the first time. Both views are taken from the south west – on the left an engraving after J B C Chatelain (1750) and on the right an anonymous watercolour dated 1798.
© London Metropolitan Archives (City of London)

and Spa into a desirable destination. Her son inherited the family business; its reputation slipped under his management as he seemed more interested in building development than in his Spa or garden (see below and p. 199). By the late 1790s this property was labelled 'Public Kitchen' on Horwood's map of London; by the 1813 edition of this map the new Bethlem Hospital was on the site.
(Rocque; Horwood 1799; *Survey of London* 25)

(VL27) West Square. Colonel Temple West owned a substantial estate in St George's Fields at his death in 1784; he left it to his wife Jane, and after her death to his son Temple. The estate could issue 99-year leases and the first of these, in West Square, dated from 1791. The plot was developed by Thomas Kendall and James Hedger (from the Dog and Duck). By 1794, the north, east and west sides of the square were ready and the three-storey terraced houses tenanted, including No 14 where panoramist Robert Barker lived (see pp. 56–57).
(Rhinebeck; Horwood 1813; *Survey of London* 25)

(VL28) Fishmongers' Almshouses, also known as St Peter's Hospital, Newington Butts. They were made up of two blocks, one built in 1618 'at the expense of several members of the Company' which catered for twenty-two tenants; and the other in 1719, within the same enclosure but south of the above; this was founded by James Hulbert, from the Fishmongers' Company and catered for forty-nine men and women. There was a garden and a chapel. The layout is very clear on the Rocque and Horwood maps. The almshouses stayed on this site, practically unaltered, until 1851 when they moved to Wandsworth.

The buildings were demolished and this was recorded in watercolour by James Findlay. (London Metropolitan Archives).
(Rocque; Horwood 1799; Manning & Bray; *Survey of London* 25)

(VL29) Church of St Mary Newington, Newington Butts. Continued from p. 94. In 1714, in the middle of Sunday service, 'there happened a sudden Rupture in the Wall' and everyone fearing the worst, rushed out of the church in such haste that several people were trampled and wounded. The church, on the west side of Newington Butts, was found in such poor condition that it was completely rebuilt and extended to the west. By the end of the eighteenth century its physical state had deteriorated again and it was rebuilt for a second time (1789). Its position right against the road remained problematic and led to its demolition in the Victorian period. Continues on p. 244.
(Rocque; Horwood 1813; *Survey of London* 25)

(VL30) Kennington Oval. See p. 380

WATERLOO

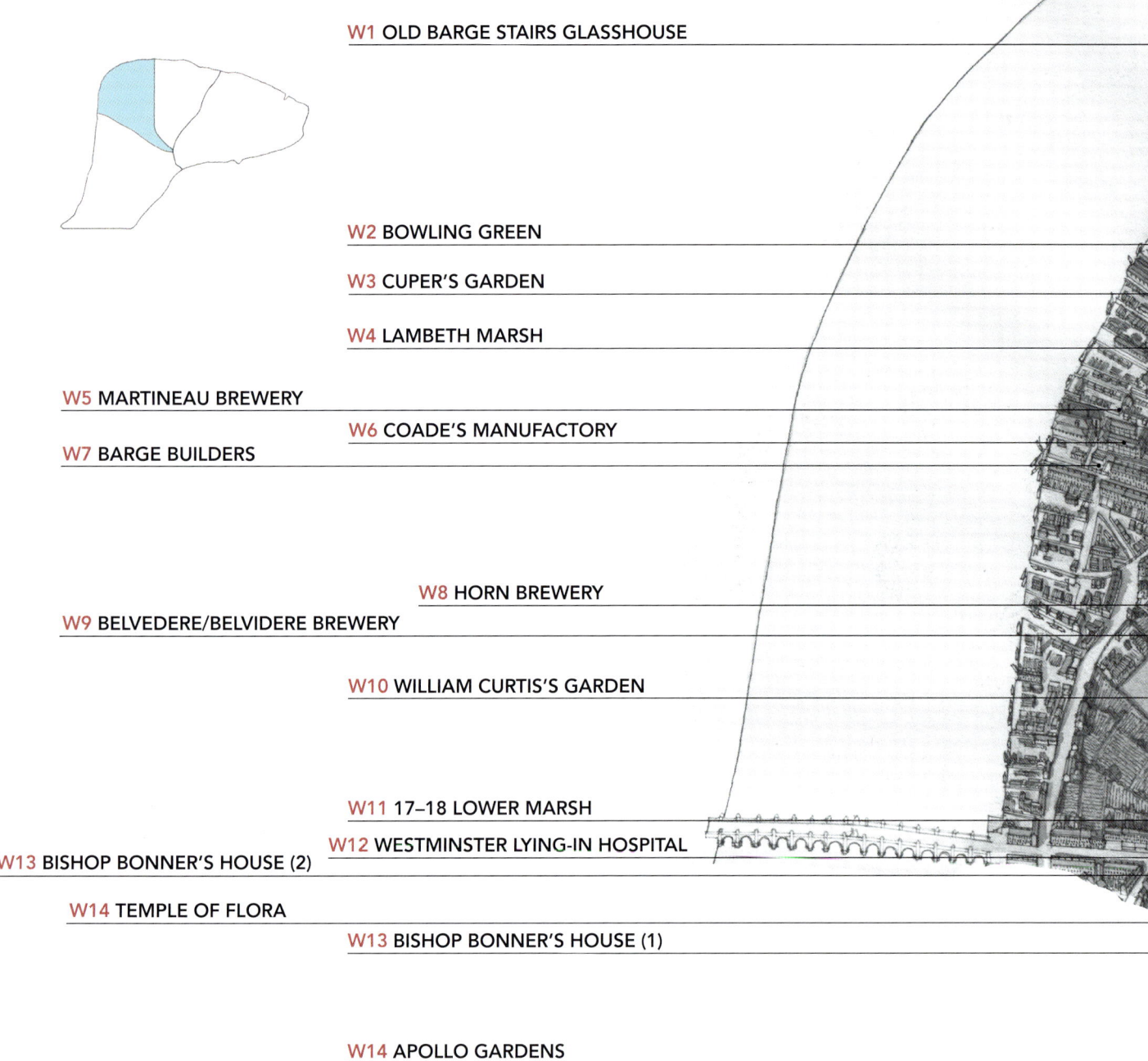

W1 OLD BARGE STAIRS GLASSHOUSE

W2 BOWLING GREEN

W3 CUPER'S GARDEN

W4 LAMBETH MARSH

W5 MARTINEAU BREWERY

W6 COADE'S MANUFACTORY

W7 BARGE BUILDERS

W8 HORN BREWERY

W9 BELVEDERE/BELVIDERE BREWERY

W10 WILLIAM CURTIS'S GARDEN

W11 17–18 LOWER MARSH

W12 WESTMINSTER LYING-IN HOSPITAL

W13 BISHOP BONNER'S HOUSE (2)

W14 TEMPLE OF FLORA

W13 BISHOP BONNER'S HOUSE (1)

W14 APOLLO GARDENS

This remarkable watercolour brings home the size of the thriving timber trade on the riverbank at Waterloo. The presence of the square shot tower makes its Waterloo location clear but also helps date the watercolour to after 1789. The two men carrying wood are porters, recognisable by their characteristic headgear.
© London Metropolitan Archives (City of London)

(W) **Timber Yards**, north of Westminster Bridge, all along the river bank. There are ten timber yards, clearly marked on Rocque's 1747 map, and about the same number on Horwood in 1799; this is a considerable number (more in the next section – Bankside and Borough). It was clearly the dominant occupation on this stretch of the Thames, bar a stone wharf and a whitening wharf (Rocque only). The timber yards already featured on William Morgan's 1682 map. The owners of these different trades are named in Strype's 1755 edition of John Stow's *Survey of London* (Vol II): Mr Hooper, Mr Malthors, Mr Moore, Sir Peter Rich, Mr English – the latter, one of the occupants of Belvidere House. (Rocque; Horwood 1799; Horwood 1813; Phillips)

(W1) **Old Barge Stairs Glasshouse**, east of Cuper's Garden: the glass house operated between 1730 and *c.* 1776 when it was run by John Matthews and Co. It specialised in green glass and is clearly depicted in Thomas Sandby's panorama of the south bank (British Museum number 1952,0403.1).

A German visitor, Conrad von Uffenbach visited a Southwark glasshouse in 1710, possibly not this one, and recorded: 'Next day we drove to see the small glass furnace there, but found that of little note. The people allowed us to take tubes into our own hands and blow. It is amazing how one can blow glass if one perseveres'.
(Rocque; Phillips)

(W2) **Bowling green**. Waterloo and Borough had two bowling greens – shown on Rocque's map and the only ones on the South Bank. According to sports historian Simon Inglis the game of bowls has formed part of everyday life since at least Shakespeare's time – with several references to the sport in his plays. He also points out that bowling greens were amongst the earliest sportscapes in London to be identified on maps. These two bowling greens were not recorded in 1682 when William Morgan published his London map. Their presence on the South Bank reinforces two of this area's strong themes: gardens and entertainment. The Waterloo bowling green was split into two by 'Commercial Road' (now Upper Ground). This is made clear on a map by Robert Wilkinson which accompanied the engraved 'View in Cuper's Garden'. By the late eighteenth century, both bowling

greens had disappeared.
(Rocque; Inglis; *Survey of London* 26)

(W3) Cuper's Garden and Messrs Beaufoy vinegar manufactory. The garden stretched from the church of St John all the way to Narrow Wall (later Belvedere Road). It drew its name from mid-seventeenth century owner, Abraham Boydell Cuper, a local man who had been employed at Arundel House, on the north bank, just across the Thames from Cuper's Garden. Mr Cuper's son opened the garden to the public in 1678, the year when Arundel House was demolished. The garden closed in 1760 and two years later the vinegar merchant Mark Beaufoy (1718–1782) purchased a twenty-year lease of the Cuper's Garden site with permission to demolish the house and re-use its materials. A number of prints and drawings show the almost harmonious blend of structures belonging to the site's former garden with new industrial apparatus. Thomas Pennant described the premises in *Some Account of London* (1791 edition): 'On first entering the yard, two [vessels] rise before you, covered at the top with a thatched dome; between them is a circular turret, including a winding staircase, which brings you to their summits, which are above twenty-four feet in diameter. One of these conservatories is full of sweet wine, and contains fifty-eight thousand one hundred and nine gallons … Its superb associate is full of vinegar'.

The manufactory, which produced wine and vinegar, was successful but Beaufoy encountered problems with the lease and in 1810 moved his factory to South Lambeth (see p. 246). The site was soon purchased by the Strand Bridge Company in charge of building the future Waterloo Bridge. (Rocque; Horwood 1799; Horwood 1813; *Survey of London* 23 & 24; Wroth; Phillips; Gibberd; Martin Adams & Tim R Smith, 'Vinegar: its manufacture and history in London', in *Journal of London's Industrial Archaeology* 10, 2012)

(W4) Lambeth Marsh area: At the end of the seventeenth century Lambeth Marsh was charted in some detail on William Morgan's 1682 map – an empty space criss-crossed by water channels, except for some development along the street called Lambeth Marsh, which had doubled in size since 1600. By the time Rocque published his detailed survey in 1747, the area was clearly shown as market gardens. The next development is described in vivid terms by Graham Gibberd:

> For centuries the marsh ensured the rural existence of a green and pleasant oasis close to London's centre, but then suddenly within a single life span it all changed. Between 1780 and 1820 Lambeth Marsh turned into the scourge of civilised society to be written about by each new generation, such as Dickens, Mayhew and Booth, as an example of the worst

Detail from Canaletto's 'View of the Thames from the house of the Duke of Richmond', 1746, with from left to right: Cuper's Gardens (the white cupola beneath St Paul's Cathedral), and most of the low sheds roofed with red tiles belong to the timber yards which lined this stretch of the river. This painting offers a rare and sustained view of the South Bank (also see p. 54 for the full picture).

(Goodwood House. Image in the public domain, Wikimedia Commons).

A view of Beaufoy Vinegar works after they took over the site of Cuper's Garden. The artist Charles Tomkins has captured the attractive blend of industry and greenery in his 1798 watercolour – though the arrangement did not last; Beaufoy relocated at South Lambeth with the arrival of Waterloo Bridge.
(© Trustees of the British Museum)

poverty and deprivation that man could produce.
See illustrations on pp. 403-403.

The graphic artist Louis Philippe Boitard (*fl.* 1733–1767) who made a valuable contribution to images of London, lived at the Westminster Bridge Road end of Lambeth Marsh in a house called 'The White Gates' according to Hugh Phillips. Paul Sandby provides one of the liveliest records of the street Lambeth Marsh (see p. 173).
(Morgan 1682; Rocque 1747; Rhinebeck; Horwood; Phillips; Gibberd)

(W5) Martineau Brewery, north of King's Arms stairs, on land which was owned by Jesus College, Cambridge. Founded by David Martineau in 1784, the enterprise was purchased by Whitbread brewery in 1812 and was in operation until 1842. This is the site of the future East India Military Stores or India Depot Store.
(Horwood 1813; *Survey of London* 23)

(W6) Coade's artificial stone manufactory, next to Martineau's brewery in Narrow Wall (later Belvedere Road). Long before the arrival of the Coade family, Richard Holt had set up an artificial stone business, obtaining two patents in 1722 (one with Thomas Ripley, the other with Samuel London). He first advertised his products in 1730, warning his readers against 'a certain pretending Architect' (the garden designer-architect Batty Langley) who was trying to steal his thunder. Holt opened premises at King's Arms Stairs, overlooking the Thames but probably went out of business in the 1730s. Daniel Pincot was also established in that neighbourhood by about 1767. The Coades set up a manufactory of artificial stone in 1769 … a little further inland but a stone's throw from Richard Holt. That year, George Coade, the head of the family, had gone bankrupt in Exeter and died.

The Lambeth Coade factory was run by Eleanor Coade Junior (1733–1821), an established City merchant, and her mother, also Eleanor (1707–1796). It was *Miss* rather than Mrs Coade who ran the business; there has been some confusion about this as both women were called Eleanor and known as Mrs Coade, despite Eleanor junior remaining unmarried; but Alison Kelly in her excellent book on Mrs Coade disentangled the tangled strands, adding that the Coade precursors 'all … had one thing in common – failure'.

In 1771, two years after their arrival, Mrs Coade Jnr dismissed the man who had become head of her factory, the now disgraced Daniel Pincot, replacing him by the sculptor John Bacon (see pp. 519 ff) – an inspired appointment. She also went into partnership with her nephew Edward Sealey (died 1813). By the time the Coades started trading in Lambeth, the Rococo style was waning and the neo-classical style of the Adam brothers was all the rage. In Alison Kelly's words: 'from the beginning she [Mrs Coade] copied the well-known festoons of husks, the oval paterae, the plaques with classical figures in low relief, which were the hallmarks of the Adam style'.

In 1798, Eleanor Jnr bought a building lease of the site between New Inn and Pedlar's Acre (Narrow Wall, later Belvedere Road), on the north side of Westminster Bridge Road. Coade's Row was built there, and one of its houses was subsequently used as a gallery. Alison Kelly explained that Mrs Coade 'opened her exhibition gallery in 1799 because visitors had had so much difficulty in finding the factory'.

From 1814 the firm was run by William Croggon (d. 1835), a cousin of Eleanor by marriage, who was

These two watercolours show the arrangement of Coade's Artificial Stone Manufactory – one shows the outside of the family house doubling as office and showroom, with a yard and workshop at the back (anonymous, dated *c.* 1800); the road running alongside it is Narrow Wall. The other watercolour, by George Shepherd and of a similar date, focuses on the working quarters with John Bacon's famous 'River God' costing £105. The other landmark sculpture was the Lion Brewery lion which has survived (southern end of Westminster Bridge) in almost mint condition.

(© London Metropolitan Archives (City of London); © The author, 2018)

succeeded by his son. But in 1837 the artificial stone manufactory permanently closed its doors and the secret formula of the successful 'stone' was lost for many years. This is the date of the magnificent lion of the Red Lion Brewery (see previous). Although the brewery was demolished, the lion was saved and now graces the southern approach to Westminster Bridge.

Thomas Routledge and John Danforth Greenwood, later Routledge & Co acquired the site and ran a business centred on terracotta and scagliola work.
(Rocque; Horwood 1799; Horwood 1813; *Survey of London* 23; Gibberd 31 & 59; Kelly)

(W7) Barge builders. On a site opposite Whitehall Palace, the shipwright John Hall built a most spectacular barge in 1731-32. This was Prince Frederick's barge, now in the collection of the National Maritime Museum, designed by William Kent with decorative carvings by James Richards. After Frederick's death in 1751 it was used by various members of the Royal Household until 1849.
(Horwood 1799 labelled 'Messrs Peach & Larkin'; Horwood 1813 labelled 'Barge builders'; Leigh; K N Palmer's *Ceremonial Barges on the River Thames*)

(W8) Horn Brewery, The Cut. The brewery had its own windmill, hence the name Windmill Street off The Cut. It also had its own tap house which has survived as the Windmill pub. The windmill and brewery were operating in 1799.
(Horwood 1813; Gibberd)

(W9) Belvidere (or Belvedere) Brewery and Dr James's medicinal garden, Vine Street, now under Waterloo Station. There is little information about this brewery which is often confused with the (later) Lion Brewery in Belvedere Road. Research by Richard Woollard into the life of Dr Robert James (1705–1776) casts indirect light onto the brewery's site which was on the doorstep of Dr James's property in Vine Street. This property was threatened with various road building schemes and is unusually well documented as Dr James campaigned hard against these, publishing his own plan of his house and neighbourhood around 1770. In his large garden, ornamented by a long lake, he grew and prepared herbs and medicinal plants to make the pills and powders for which he was famous.

Dr James is first recorded at that address in 1745. He died in 1776 after which date the Lambeth premises stopped being occupied. This led Woollard to conclude: 'it was presumably then, in 1776, that they were taken over by the Belvedere Brewery.' Gibberd on the other hand gives slightly different dates for the brewery: 1799–1819. The Brewery is described in 1826 as belonging to Mrs Edwards. Its water supply came from a pond (shown in Horwood) and a stream.
(Horwood 1799; Horwood 1813; Gibberd)

(W10) William Curtis' London Botanic Garden. Curtis moved his botanic garden from Bermondsey, off Willow Walk, to near Lambeth Marsh – off Webber Street, roughly between Mitre Road and Ufford Street. He opened his botanic garden to the public in 1779. By 1789 the garden contained 6000 different plant species, named according to Linnaeus's classification system, published in 1735; this was the first example of its systematic use in this country. After a decade or so, the looming menace of the arrival of The Cut, air pollution ('the smoke of London, which, except when the wind blew from the South, constantly enveloped my plants') and draining ditches turning into open sewers, encouraged Curtis to move away from Lambeth to Fulham where he set up his new garden.

Curtis was a friend of the White brothers – Thomas and Benjamin – also Lambeth residents. Benjamin, the wealthiest of the brothers was a pioneering bookseller and publisher of natural history books in the Strand, though he died long before his more famous brother, the naturalist Gilbert White (1720–1793) was published. The latter's journal mentions frequent visits to the Lambeth countryside. (see p. 377). All three brothers were keen Curtis' supporters and Curtis paid tribute to Thomas' patronage in his *Botanic Garden Catalogue*.

Curtis's contribution to the world of publishing was remarkable: in 1787 he started *The Botanical Magazine* which flourished under this title for almost 200 years until someone changed it to *The Kew Magazine*. Curtis's equally beautiful *Flora Londiniensis* came out in seventy-two parts between 1775 and 1798, drawing attention to the 'many plants which formerly grew plentifully around us' but were becoming rare thanks to the 'rage for building … in the environs of London'.
(Rocque; *Survey of London* 23; Gibberd)

(W11) The oldest houses in North Lambeth, now 17–18 Lower Marsh dating from the early eighteenth century: the street frontages have been refaced but the back view confirms that they are authentic historic houses (best viewed from the first floor access balcony of Monro House). Local resident architect Richard Woollard attempted to have these houses listed and submitted a case to Historic England, which sadly, was rejected (pictured overleaf).

Woollard noted that these houses 'were documented by the Royal Commission on Historic Monuments in their recent survey of London's Smaller Eighteenth Century Houses where they were given the designation Monument No 1361665'. Their description in that survey reads:

> Nos 17 and 18 Lower Marsh are two early-eighteenth-century

brick houses, among the last early survivals from the marginal hamlet that was Lambeth Marsh. No. 17 is a large three-storey three-bay fronted building with a rear-staircase plan, its front rebuilt in the 19th century. No 18 is narrower and had a central-staircase layout before its front parts were rebuilt, also in the 19th century.

In 2020, the houses were redeveloped – enlarged, then rebuilt to look like their former selves. (Gibberd; Peter Guillery, *The small house in eighteenth century London – a social and architectural history*, 2004)

(W12) (Westminster) New Lying-in Hospital, on the north side of Westminster Bridge Road. This hospital sought to bring relief to pregnant women from poor backgrounds; it was one of the first maternity hospitals in Britain. It was the brainchild of Dr John Leake (1729–1792), who trained in Rheims, France and was the hospital's first physician. First proposed in 1765, it opened its doors in April 1767. Continues on p. 252.
(Horwood 1813 captioned 'Lying in Hospital'; *Survey of London* 23)

(W13) Bishop Bonner's House. See p. 106.

(W14) Pleasure Gardens: (a) Temple of Flora, (b) Apollo Gardens, (c) Flora Tea Gardens, Westminster Bridge Road. After the closure of Cuper's garden in 1760 (see W3 above), the neighbourhood had no pleasure gardens, but in 1786,

Paul Sandby's watercolour of Lambeth Marsh, now Lower Marsh, 1770. The view is taken from the south west looking down Lambeth Marsh towards the City, with the Monument clearly recognisable with its flame topping and on its right the steeple of St Margaret Pattens. With the rapid change of scale in our own times, the relationship between Lower Marsh and the City has miraculously survived, unobstructed, with the Leadenhall building on the right and the Heron Tower on the left.. The pub on the left has been identified as The Artichoke while the house on the right is likely to be that (wrongly) associated with Bishop Bonner (W13).
(Lambeth Archives)

the Temple of Flora opened just off Lambeth Marsh. The owner Mr Harvey attempted to promote his 'British Elysium', the elaborate display he had engineered for a 'Grand Gala' at Ranelagh Gardens in Chelsea. The new resort had a summer garden, a winter garden, an orange grove, a hothouse with a statue of Pomona, a Chinese Pagoda, goldfish ponds and a grotto, complete with the indispensable hermit. This auction advertisement dated December 1791 illustrates one of their activities: 'the largest and most beautiful collection of ARTIFICIAL FLOWERS, Ever seen in this Kingdom (made for the supply of the Nobility & Gentry to decorate

The backs of 17–18 Lower Marsh before and after 'redevelopment' (© The author, 2019 and 2022)

their festive apartments)'. However, the garden's early success and air of respectability were short-lived (1788–91); by 1796 the place was the 'haunt of profligate characters and young apprentices'.

Two years after the opening of the Temple of Flora, the Apollo Gardens opened, round the corner from the Temple of Flora. The owner, Walter Glagget, was the former lessee of the Pantheon (Oxford Street).

Both the Temple of Flora and the Apollo Gardens presented concerts alongside horticultural displays. At the Apollo they also had paintings and transparencies (large trompe l'oeil pictures placed at strategic places in the gardens). Like the Temple of Flora, the Apollo only lasted a few years and was shut by magistrates in 1793.

Finally in 1796 Flora Tea Gardens (or Mount gardens) opened opposite the Temple of Flora, but they barely lasted a couple of years. (Wroth; *Pleasure Gardens of South London*; *Survey of London* 23)

(W15) St Georges's Circus see St George's Fields on p. 197.

(W16) The Royal Circus, St George's Circus. This place of entertainment opened on 4 November 1782 and after some difficulty with the Surrey authorities, was eventually licensed as 'an Exhibition of Horsemanship, Ballets and Pantomimes'. It stood on the west side of Blackfriars Road close to the obelisk. It was a joint venture between Charles Hughes, a riding master and 'strong man' who had worked for Astley's, and Charles

Dibdin, the composer and singer. There were equestrian feats but also canine actors, their handlers earning the title of 'dog-stars'. The partners fell out, leading to the closure of their establishment 'for several years'. It reopened in 1798, under the new management and proprietorship of Messrs Jones, Cross and Hodson. It burnt down on 11 August 1805, was remodelled as an elegant, classical building designed by Rudolph Cabanel, the architect of the Royal Coburg theatre in Waterloo, and renamed the Surrey Theatre. Continues on p. 260.
(Horwood 1813; *Survey of London* 25; Barker & Jackson 2008; Altick)

(W17) The Magdalen Hospital, Great Surrey Street (now Blackfriars Road). It was founded by a group of philanthropists, including Robert Dingley and Jonas Hanway. This House, 'for the reception of penitent prostitutes', was first discussed in 1758 and had been in operation for fourteen years when it moved to St George's Fields from a site in Prescot Street, Whitechapel. In their first year in the East End (August 1758 to July 1759) they received 144 applications and took in 116 girls to live in a 'safe and quiet retreat in this abode of peace and reflection'; one in seven had not reached the age of fifteen. The new building was designed by Joel Johnson, landowner, and carpenter-architect based in Whitechapel (he also designed the London Hospital).

Admission day was on the first Thursday of every month and the most 'deserving' cases were sought out. We are told 'they are instructed in the principles of religion, in reading … and the various branches of household employment'. After varying lengths of stay, the women were either returned to their family or placed with employers. 'We hail … an institution calculated to restore the miserable victims of seduction to a life of virtue and industrious comfort'.

Dr William Dodd championed the institution from the start and continued to preach at the House after it moved to St George's Fields. The Octagonal Chapel, sited in one corner of the House's quadrangle was open to public worship, attracting a sizeable audience drawn to the passionate sermons given by William Dodd – nicknamed the 'macaroni parson' in reference to his fashionable and profligate life-style. But he was soon attracting the wrong kind of attention, leading on 5 February 1777 to his arrest for forgery – the signature of the Earl of Chesterfield no less. Despite returning the stolen money and having the support of the formidable Dr Johnson, he was sentenced to death and executed – the last man to be hanged at Tyburn.
(Rhinebeck; Horwood 1813; Pugin & Rowlandson; *Survey of London* 25 and their blog of 21 October 2016 for Joel Johnson)

(W18) Wesleyan meeting house, Lambeth Marsh (overleaf). This modest building was erected in 1778 by a Methodist lay preacher, John Edwards; the congregation must have been thrilled when John Wesley paid a visit the following year on 7 January, though personal visits were in keeping with the usual methods of the charismatic but autocratic religious leader. Methodism emerged in the 1730s and Michael Mullett described the highly structured Wesleyan Methodist organisation as pyramidical with the specific society at its base (for instance the building under review), each society subdivided into bands and classes, with societies grouped into 'circuits' required to meet quarterly from 1748. The precise whereabouts of the chapel in Lambeth Marsh is not known.
(Mullett; Lambeth Archives)

(W19) Christchurch workhouse. See St Saviour's Workhouse at p. 189.

(W20) Christ Church. Established in 1671 thirty years after John Marshall left money for its construction, it immediately became the parish church for the manor of Paris Garden. The spire was completed in 1695. Its foundations, laid on marshy ground, were apparently very weak when it was surveyed in 1721 and the whole church was eventually rebuilt, in brick, between 1738 and 1741. Continues on p. 259.
(Rocque; Rhinebeck; Horwood 1813, *Survey of London* 22)

(W21) Tenter grounds. Tenter grounds were a familiar feature on the South Bank in the seventeenth and eighteenth centuries. For many years the area provided the two vital ingredients for this activity – open flat ground and clean water. Gibberd explains: 'Tentering was a cloth-milling process that … had to be carried out in open ditches running with clean water. The cloth was unrolled to its full length into the ditch, soaked and then stretched out to dry in the open on wooden frames held there by hooks, the 'tenterhooks' (also see the related and well documented whitening process in Bermondsey at p. XX).

However, by the end of the eighteenth century the tenter grounds which had flourished fifty years before had all but disappeared. Messrs Stonard & Watson's Starch Manufactory, which features on Horwood's map of 1799 has become a Mustard Manufactory on the 1813 edition just over ten years later, no doubt reflecting changes in the area, away from marshland and tenter grounds.

The arrival of glasshouses was clearly a contributing factor as is shown by the petition made to the King on 12 August 1688:
one John Straw and others are erecting glass houses in the middle of the parish to the utter ruin of many of the inhabitants whose livelihood depends upon washing and to the annoyance of several gentlemen who have paid out large sums of money

The 'First Home of Wesleyans in Lambeth' was to be found at Lower Marsh though its precise location is unknown. Anonymous engraving of c. 1730 published in the Jubilee brochure of Francis & Son Department Store in 1887.
(Lambeth Archives)

Opposite:
The Rotunda, 3 Great Surrey Street, near Blackfriars Bridge: 'A Perspective View of the Grand Saloon and Gallery at the Museum, late Sir Ashton Lever's, Surrey end of Blackfriars Bridge', engraving by William Skelton after a drawing by Miss [Sarah] Stone and Charles Reuben Ryley, c.1790.
© London Metropolitan Archives (City of London)

upon their gardens for health and recreation, and praying his Majesty to put a stop to the erection of such glass houses till they be heard.
(Rocque; Horwood 1799 and 1813; Rhinebeck; Horwood 1813; Gibberd; Colin and Sue Brain, *Pioneering Glass* website at www.cbrain.mistral.co.uk accessed in December 2020)

(W22) The Leverian Museum, the collection of Sir Ashton Lever, initially known as the 'Holophusikon', moved from Leicester Square to the Rotunda in Great Surrey Street around 1790 (Blackfriars Road, west side, close to the bridge). It happened when its new owner, James Parkinson, realised that the Leicester House galleries were far too expensive to rent. Sir Ashton Lever (1729–1788) had started his collection at Alkington Hall near Manchester and moved it to London in 1776. The Holophusikon was immediately the talk of the town and there are many visitors' accounts which bring to life the sort of institution it was (right): 'The birds of paradise, and the humming birds, were I think among the most beautiful … a young crocodile – a room full of monkeys … Lizards, bats, toads, frogs, scorpions and other filthy creatures in abundance …' recounts Susan Burney. For 'the room full of monkeys', we have the testimony of the American scientist Benjamin Silliman in 1805 or 1806: 'the artist has employed them as busied about various human employments. The Taylor monkey … The house-carpenter monkey … The clerk of the monkey room sits writing at a desk. The shaver has one of his own species seated in a chair …'.

But sooner or later, successful showmanship loses its appeal and … its visitors! The £13,000 ticket receipts between 1775 and 1784 were concentrated in the early years. As early as 1781 Lever had tried twice to sell his collection valued at £50,000, without success. His marketing was not modest: 'The first Museum experience in the Universe'. In 1783 he tried to sell it to the British Museum, at a much-reduced price but this, too, failed. By an Act of Parliament in 1784 he was able to hold a lottery offering 36,000 tickets for sale, the winner taking the collection; but fewer than 8000 tickets were sold. After a considerable delay James Parkinson, law stationer and estate agent, claimed the prize when he came across the ticket his wife had bought some time before she died. Parkinson tried, unsuccessfully, to sell the collection abroad. He then decided to move the museum to a cheaper location. He commissioned the gifted builder-developer James Burton to build the new venue – the Rotunda – at 3 Great Surrey Street, a four storeyed terraced house, just across the road from the famous Albion Mills. Parkinson seemed determined to give the museum a second lease of life and he also commissioned a detailed Guide. But Parkinson's efforts could not revive the fortunes of the Leverian Museum and make it commercially viable. Soon, Parkinson was looking for buyers: the British Museum again – this time they were ready to pay £20,000 for the collection but a last-minute consultation with one of their trustees proved fatal to the deal – Sir Joseph Banks who was supposed to 'hate' Lever, and therefore his collection, perhaps secretly resentful that Lever should have so many artefacts from Captain Cook's voyages, when Banks himself had taken part in Cook's first voyage.

Finally, in 1806, Parkinson resorted to the auction house and sold as much of the collection as he could. William Bullock, the antiquarian showman who created the Egyptian Hall in Piccadilly was amongst the bidders; another bidder, Leopold von Fichtel, bought on behalf of the Imperial Collection at Vienna: '82 mammals, more than 200 birds, 60 reptiles, 73 fishes, and other objects of various classes of the animal kingdom'. Richard Altick recounts a less glorious end to the part of the collection which remained unsold: 'as late as 1829 a portion of the Leverian collection was exhibited at Camberwell Fair by an agent for a "Society of Gentlemen", which probably means a cut-price syndicate of speculators … "Several commodious caravans" were advertised as holding 1,600

cases of stuffed birds alone, as well as twenty five serpents … and the heads of two chieftain warriors from the South Pacific.'

After the 1806 auction and the departure of the Leverian Museum it was the **Surrey Institution** (overleaf) which occupied the Rotunda; subscription closed at the end of December 1807 and the building opened to the public on 1 May 1808. Richard Altick described it as 'the South Bank counterpart of the Royal Institution', the latter set up in 1799. This is acknowledged in the appropriate entry of *The Microcosm of London*. 'the extent of the Metropolis was a sufficient reason for the formation of another, in a more central and populous situation'. The institution offered 'a series of lectures, an extensive library [overlooking the garden and with more than 5000 volumes by 1810] and reading rooms'; also 'a chemical laboratory and philosophical apparatus'. The Surrey Institution was short-lived: it closed its doors in 1820.

The theatre of the Surrey Institution is described in the text it accompanies as 'one of the most elegant rooms in the Metropolis'. The lecture in progress is that of Frederic Accum, professor of chemistry and mineralogy. This was arguably the South Bank Centre of its day, combining museum, library and lecture hall.
(From Rudolph Ackermann, *Microcosm of London*, with plates by Augustus Pugin and Thomas Rowlandson, 1808–10, Vol. III)

When Volume 22 of the *Survey of London* was published in 1950 the building was still there, described as: 'At the rear of No. 3 [Blackfriars Road] are the much-mutilated remains of the Rotunda or Surrey Institution'. (*Survey of London* 22; Altick)

(W23) Albion Place and Great Surrey Street, known now as Blackfriars Road. Albion Place was immediately at the southern end of Blackfriars Bridge while Great Surrey Street ran from Albion Place to St George's Circus. The 1756 Blackfriars Bridge Act made provision for a bridge approach but this was found to be inadequate and a new Act was secured in 1768 to form a road running south from Blackfriars Bridge. Albion Mills was on the east side of Albion Place and the west side was occupied by two blocks of elegant terraced houses (also see the Leverian Museum entry, above). The houses in Great Surrey Street were built between 1765 and 1790 on land which mostly belonged to the 'Barons', the descendants of the Lords of the Manor. Great Surrey Street became Blackfriars Road in 1829. Continues on p. 270.
(Horwood 1813; *Survey of London 22*; Pragnell)

BOROUGH AND BANKSIDE

BB2 BLACKFRIARS BRIDGE

BB3 ALBION MILLS

BB1 SURREY CHAPEL

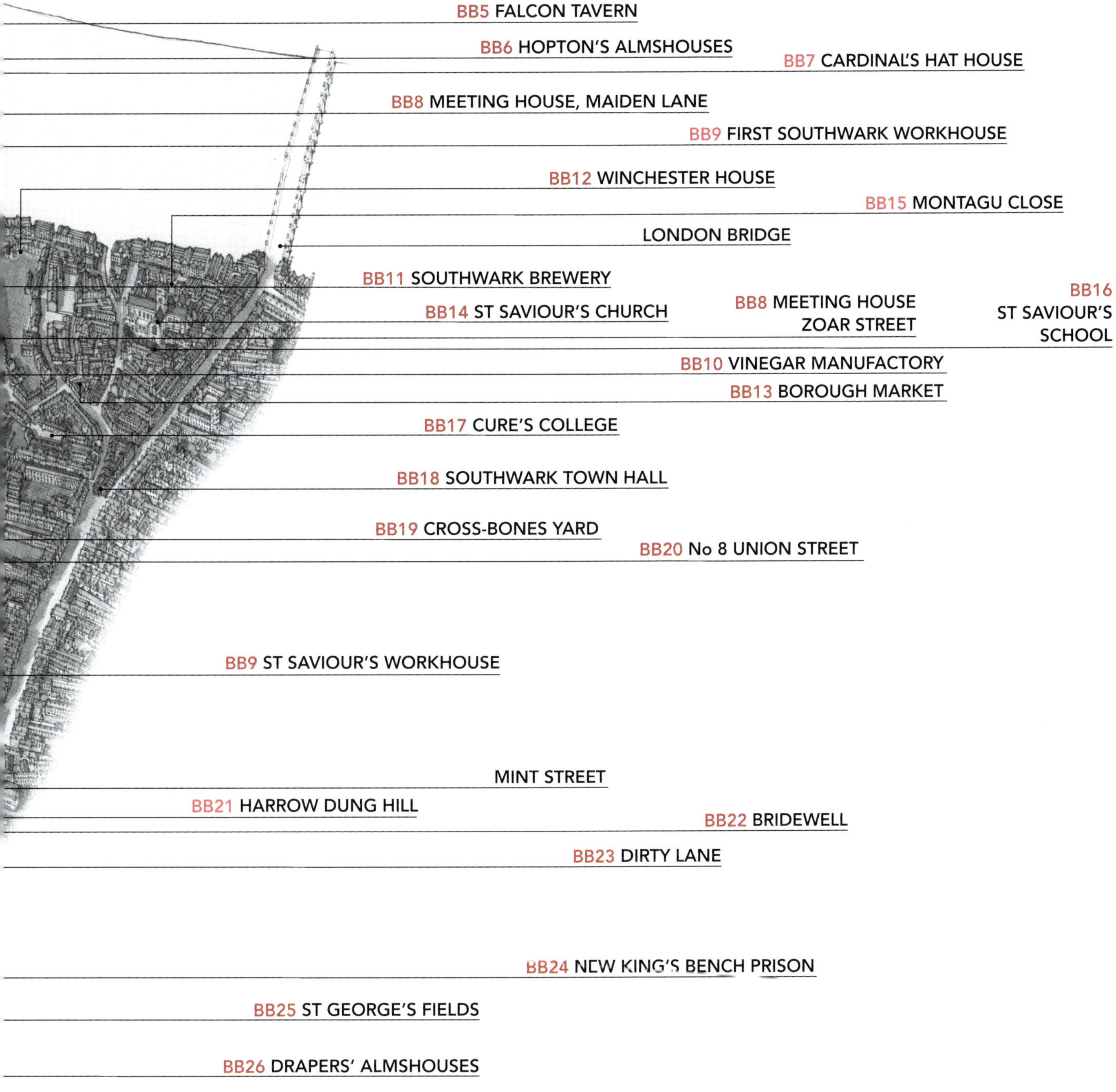

BB4 FALCON GLASSWORKS
BB5 FALCON TAVERN
BB6 HOPTON'S ALMSHOUSES
BB7 CARDINAL'S HAT HOUSE
BB8 MEETING HOUSE, MAIDEN LANE
BB9 FIRST SOUTHWARK WORKHOUSE
BB12 WINCHESTER HOUSE
BB15 MONTAGU CLOSE
LONDON BRIDGE
BB11 SOUTHWARK BREWERY
BB14 ST SAVIOUR'S CHURCH
BB8 MEETING HOUSE ZOAR STREET
BB16 ST SAVIOUR'S SCHOOL
BB10 VINEGAR MANUFACTORY
BB13 BOROUGH MARKET
BB17 CURE'S COLLEGE
BB18 SOUTHWARK TOWN HALL
BB19 CROSS-BONES YARD
BB20 No 8 UNION STREET
BB9 ST SAVIOUR'S WORKHOUSE
MINT STREET
BB21 HARROW DUNG HILL
BB22 BRIDEWELL
BB23 DIRTY LANE
BB24 NEW KING'S BENCH PRISON
BB25 ST GEORGE'S FIELDS
BB26 DRAPERS' ALMSHOUSES

(BB) **Paris Garden**; continued from p. 109. In 1655 William Angell purchased Paris Garden from Thomas and Mary Browker. He built some houses and made Angell Street – now Broad Wall, recently truncated, which ran from the Old Barge House to Melancholy Walk, now Surrey Row. In 1660 Angell sold the notorious 'Holland's Leaguer', still 'incompassed with a moat', to Hugh Jermyne, a woollen draper; it was used as bleaching ground and Jermyne increased his holdings with more acreage of whitening ground. Angell sold very advantageously other parts of his estate, finally mortgaging the manor in 1677 to George Baron and others. The Baron family owned the manor throughout the eighteenth century and into the nineteenth century. When descendants died out the manor went to the Lethbridge family into which the last Baron had married. Parts of the manor were still in their hands in 1950.
(Rocque; *Survey of London* 22)

(BB1) **Surrey Chapel**, also known as Rowland Hill's Chapel, Blackfriars Road. Rowland Hill (1744–1833), the charismatic preacher whose sermons consistently attracted massive crowds, was a singularly unfortunate man. When at university (he graduated in 1769, from St John's College, Cambridge), he had come under the influence of the Methodists and was drawn to preaching in the open air. This led to serious difficulties with the religious authorities and when he attempted to take orders, he was refused by six different bishops. He was finally ordained deacon of the church of Kingston, Somerset but since he continued his evangelical tours, he was refused priesthood. For twelve years, without renouncing his orders, he continued to tour and preach when and where opportunities arose. Finally inheriting money at his father's death, and receiving additional help from some of his followers – for instance Lord George Gordon of Gordon riots fame and Selina Hastings, Countess of Huntingdon – he was able to build the Surrey Chapel, perhaps inspired by the Revd Whitefield's Tabernacle near Tottenham Court Road. It opened its doors in 1783 and its open-door policy turned it into a busy, thriving centre of nonconformity. Rowland Hill himself had leanings towards Calvinistic Methodism but his Chapel remained firmly independent.

Hill was the preacher at Surrey Chapel until his death in 1833 – he died at his home at nearby 45 Charlotte Street, now Union Street; but he never abandoned itinerant teaching and also contributed to some of the great religious and philanthropic movements of his age as chairman of the Religious Tract Society, a supporter of the British and Foreign Land Bible Society, as well as the London Missionary Society. Perhaps surprisingly, he was an active advocate of vaccination against smallpox, claiming towards the end of his life that he had vaccinated some 9000 people. The Surrey Chapel was one of the earliest to introduce

Interior of the Surrey Chapel during a packed service. Aquatint after John Flowerdew, c. 1820.
© London Metropolitan Archives (City of London)

Sunday school in this country (1786). (left) Continues on p. 274 (Rhinebeck; Horwood 1813; *Survey of London* 22; Mullett)

(BB2) Blackfriars Bridge. In 1756 the City obtained an Act of Parliament to build a new bridge across the Thames – the third, after London Bridge (twelfth century) and Westminster Bridge (1750). Surprisingly, the young and unknown Scottish architect Robert Mylne won the competition. The work took almost ten years (1760–69) but finished under budget. In his superb and efficient stride, Mylne also designed St George's Circus (see BB25) and a house for himself on the east side of Great Surrey Street (as Blackfriars Road was then named). Blackfriars Bridge was a toll bridge until 1785. (Rhinebeck; Horwood 1813; *Survey of London* 22; Tames)

(BB3) The Albion Flour Mills stood on the south east side of Blackfriars Bridge; they were probably the poet William Blake's 'dark Satanic mills' mentioned in his poem *Albion*, 1804. At a planning symposium in 2001, architectural historian Andrew Saint argued that they symbolised 'the arrival on the South Bank … of large-scale industry, housed in works and warehouses of a size which the North

The destruction by fire of the Albion Flour Mills on 3 March 1791, etching and aquatint, 1808. The text which accompanies this picture explains that this image was chosen not only because fires are a common occurrence in the capital but also this 'representation afforded an opportunity of more picturesque effect; the termination of the bridge, the extensive area in front, and St Paul's in the back ground, contribute so many interesting parts to a representation which is altogether great and awful'. This quote is in full harmony with the late eighteenth century taste for the sublime. There were 4000 sacks of corn in the premises and only thirty were recovered.
(Rudolph Ackermann, *Microcosm of London*, with plates by Augustus Pugin and Thomas Rowlandson, 1808-10, Vol. II)

Bank on the whole missed out on'.

Albion Mills took three years to build and opened its doors in 1786, attracting London tourists, who flocked to its site as they had to the Barclay Perkins brewery – another 'Industrial wonder'; instantly antagonising locals and labourers. Just as the ferrymen feared for their jobs with the arrival of bridges, millers feared for theirs with the arrival of vast, highly productive steam-powered flour mills.

London's first great factory brought together the expertise of three men: Matthew Boulton, James Watt and John Rennie. After Boulton and Watt formed a partnership, Boulton's aim was to awe Londoners with the first factory to be entirely steam-powered. A born entrepreneur, he was wealthy, presiding over a coterie of Birmingham luminaries and after being involved in Sheffield plate, silverware and ormolu (powder gold or gold-like), he had purchased a share in James Watt's steam-engine patent. Albion Mills was a huge advertisement for steam power and despite serious difficulties, Boulton succeeded in finding a site and raising the finance. Two of the shareholders were brothers of the successful architect James Wyatt and included Samuel, also an architect. The brothers pursued the development of a new square – Albion Place – incorporating the Mills into this elegant new Georgian quarter. Thomas Jefferson, future American president (1801–1809) but at that time first American ambassador to France, visited the scheme. The third man, John Rennie (1761–1821), was in his early twenties when he met James Watt and so impressed him that he was commissioned to design the machinery for the flour mills.

On 2 March 1791, the Industrial Wonder went up in flames. Historian Timothy Shaw tells us that 'within half an hour the interior of the mill was utterly destroyed'. He also recounts a story of sixth sense in such vivid terms that it seems worth reproducing here:

> [The architect John] Rennie, whose house was only a short distance away from the mill, had gone to bed early the night before, but was unable to sleep. An uncanny premonition of great catastrophe hung over him. He tossed and dosed fitfully but suddenly woke up in cold terror, having had a nightmare that the Albion Mills were on fire. Still half asleep, he got out of bed and reassured himself by looking out of the window down the long street towards the river and the dark mass of the mill. All was

A Glasshouse, etching by Charles Grignion published in the *Universal Magazine* in 1747. This print is likely to show a glass house in Southwark as it accompanied an article on the art of glass making 'by a Southwark correspondent'. Perhaps the Falcon glasshouse or the Old Barge Stairs glasshouse?

(© The Trustees of the British Museum)

well. There was no fire, and at last Rennie fell into a deep and peaceful sleep.

But at six o'clock in the morning a fire … did in fact break out somewhere in the mill.

For Rennie, it was literally a baptism of fire: he had just moved his home and civil engineering business to Blackfriars where he would remain until his death. The fire burnt for three days but the Mills seemed to attract even more visitors after its destruction than before (previous page). The damage to the outside of the building was minimal compared to the devastation inside. Millers rejoiced, dancing on Blackfriars Bridge. Sales of the steam-engine were unaffected, thriving even. The remains were finally pulled down in 1809. (Horwood 1799; Horwood 1813; Timothy Shaw, 'A Blaze for the London Mob – The Burning of the Albion Mills' in *Country Life*, 29 December 1966)

(BB4) Falcon Glassworks, Bankside. These consisted of three glasshouses – two in the parish of St Saviour's which later amalgamated and another further west, closer to the Falcon Tavern; no doubt these glasshouses were amongst the four recorded by mapmaker John Rocque in 1747, but not named. They were set up by Francis Jackson and John Straw and were first mentioned in the *London Gazette* of 27 February 1693/4. Jackson and Straw advertised their 'Glasshouses near the Faulkon in Southwark and at Lynn in Norfolk', claiming to make 'the best and finest drinking glasses'. In the eighteenth century there were many glasshouses along this stretch of Bankside.

The number of coal wharves along the river bank was significant. Coal was introduced to the glass industry in the first half of the seventeenth century. One of these glasshouses developed into the famous nineteenth-century Falcon Glassworks of Messrs Pellatt and Green, later simply Apsley Pellatt. Continues on p. 270.

(Rocque; Horwood 1813; *Survey of London 22*; Eleanor S Godfrey, *The Development of English Glassmaking 1560–1640*, 1975; Colin and Sue Brain, Pioneering Glass website at www.cbrain.mistral.co.uk, accessed in December 2020)

(BB5) The Falcon tavern, Bankside, was on church property; it was first mentioned in a 1541 deed and changed hands many times post-Reformation, but when it was sold in 1647 there is a detailed description of this establishment:

> all that tenement or inn with the appurtenances known by the name of the Faulcon, part and parcel of the possessions of the late Bishoprick of Winchester, consisting of 29 rooms, 3 cellars, 1 stable, with hayloft yard, and a wharf with a pair of stairs to land at from the river Thames.

This substantial inn was leased to John Hayward and his son in the last quarter of the seventeenth century; they rebuilt

The Falcon tavern was sited just across the road from Falcon's glassworks. This large inn was the subject of many prints and drawings.
(Engraving published in Robert Wilkinson in *Londina Illustrata*, 1819 and 1829 – 2 volumes)

Above:
This print, published by Robert Wilkinson in 1813, shows what happened to 'the late Revd. Charles Skelton's Meeting House adjacent to the site of the Globe Theatre' in Maiden Lane and close to the Zoar Street chapel. Its fate was similar to that of its neighbour since it was converted into 'A Mill, erected some Years sinse [sic], on the Basement of the Meeting House'.
(Engraving published in Robert Wilkinson in *Londina Illustrata*, 1819 and 1829 – 2 volumes)

Opposite top:
The interior of the Zoar Street meeting house – John Bunyan's – is barely recognisable in this watercolour by Robert B Schnebbelie, dated 1822. By that date the building had long been converted into a workshop, the upper galleries being used for storage.
© London Metropolitan Archives (City of London)

Opposite bottom:
The caption for this view reads: 'An Interior View of the school connected with and under a part of the Meeting House'. This establishment is often described as 'Bunyan's meeting house' Movingly, the actual pulpit, illustrated here, has survived and is in the collection of the John Bunyan Museum in Bedford. Published by Robert Wilkinson in 1822.
© London Metropolitan Archives (City of London)

the inn around 1690 with a house alongside it. This is the establishment which was published by Robert Wilkinson in 1811 (previous page).
(Rendle & Norman; *Survey of London* 22)

(BB6) Hopton's Almshouses, Hopton Street. Charles Hopton (c. 1654–1731), a fishmonger and Westminster resident, owned property in the parish of Christ Church; unmarried, he left some of that property to his sister during her lifetime. At her death in 1739, trustees took over the land to establish the almshouses, as prescribed in Charles' will. From John Morgan they purchased the following:

> 'All Those five Messuages . . . with the Outhouses, Yards, Gardens and Peice of Ground . . . near the Green Walk in the Upper Ground . . . and all that peice of Ground called the Back Orchard and also all Those Eight Messuages . . . Scituate . . . on the Eastward Side of the Green Walk . . .'

All the buildings were pulled down and the almshouses erected at a cost of £2700. They were ready in 1752 and the trustees chose twenty-six poor persons. Almsmen could marry. The size of the alsmhouses was increased in 1825 with the addition of two more units. The almshouses have survived and now bear witness to the extraordinary change of scale in London in the twenty-first century.
(Rocque; Horwood 1813; *Survey of London* 22)

(BB7) Cardinal's Hat House and Alley, at No 49 Bankside; continued from p. 120. This house dates from around 1710, built on the site of a former inn. It was not built in isolation but as part of a terrace of houses, which have not survived but have been reconstructed by Gillian Tindall in her book *The House by the Thames*. Numbers 50, 51, 52 Bankside are early eighteenth-century houses – there used to be 'a lead rain-water head on the front bearing a crown and inscribed "B.H.S. 1712.".'
(*Survey of London* 22; Tindall)

(BB8) Meeting Houses. By the end of the eighteenth century the **Maiden Lane meeting house** recorded on Rocque's 1747 map appeared to have been swallowed up in the development of the Southwark brewery. It was also featured by Robert Wilkinson in his *Londina Illustrata* as the 'View of the Late Revd Charles Skelton's Meeting House adjacent to the site of the Globe Theatre, Maid Lane, Southwark' (1813) (above). Wilkinson charts its history in some detail – dating from around 1672 'when Charles II granted indulgence in favour of religious profession' he described the structure as 'capacious, though built of wood, and it contained three galleries'. The Presbyterian church was dissolved in 1752 and a new 'Congregation of Dissenters denominated Independents took over the building'. The last and principal minister was Charles Skelton who resigned in 1776 when the congregation had declined considerably. Wilkinson concludes: 'it was converted to various secular purposes, and was successively a place for warehousing goods; afterwards a mill was erected here to grind bones; and it is at present [1813] appropriated for the purpose of grinding stones, and similar materials'.

The Zoar Street chapel, close to Maiden Lane, also features in *Londina Illustrata* but it has been more widely illustrated because of its association with John Bunyan who is reputed to have preached there in 1688, the year of his death. The meeting house is not labelled on Rocque's map though Zoar Street is named; Zoar meaning 'refuge, sanctuary' is the name of a biblical city, one of the fives which God had earmarked for destruction – the city was spared when Lot and his daughters took refuge there. The chapel housed a school (bottom right) – the earliest documented non-conformist school in London – and three account books have survived for the period 1687–1745. One of the exhibits of John Bunyan's Museum in Bedford, is the pulpit from this chapel; it was a gift, in 1927, from the National Sunday School Union. The *Survey of London* has summed up the fate of this modest street: 'Zoar Street was rebuilt early in the 19th century. It was a typical narrow Southwark alley of that period with central gulley, and with little in the way of lighting or other amenities … The whole of it was demolished during the war by enemy action.'
(Rocque; Horwood 1813; Wilkinson; *Survey of London* 22)

(BB9) St Saviour's and Christchurch Workhouses, various addresses. With the help of Peter Higginbotham's detailed website, it is possible to reconstruct Bankside and Borough's string of workhouses, starting in 1728 with a workhouse at Maid Lane (now Sumner Street) which is not named on Rocque's map, followed in 1777 by a workhouse in Pepper Street (Horwood 1813, just east of Nelson Square). In the same year Christ Church acquired its own workhouse for up to 150 inmates in

Marlborough Street (Horwood 1813, the street is not named but it is the southern continuation of Broad Wall, W19 in the Waterloo section of this chapter). In 1814 came the short-lived workhouse built in wood at the corner of New Kent Road and Newington Road. It was destroyed by fire three years later.

The very first workhouse, in Maid Lane, was built for seventy adults and fifty children: 'they are employed in carding and spinning wool for Mopp Yarn, and for Worsted, and knitting', it was reported in *An Account of several work houses* in 1732.

Overall, there are few visual records of South London's workhouses. A rare example is the workhouse in Mint Street which was set up by the parish of St George-the-Martyr (the church itself is in the Southwark and Bermondsey section of this book). Also see p. 274.

While the Lambeth workhouse eventually changed location to grow in size and complexity, Southwark adopted a different approach, in response to the 1782 Gilbert's Act, encouraging relief on a county-wide basis and the creation of unions of parishes. Gilbert Unions were set up and administered by a Board of Guardians, one per parish. Historian Peter Higginbotham points out that their 'elections by ratepayers and appointment by local magistrates … represented a major shift in power from the parish to the landed gentry'. In 1836 the administration of the Poor Law changed, encouraging parishes to pool their resources together. Continues on p. 258.
(Horwood 1813; Peter Higginbotham 'The workhouse' http://www.workhouses.org.uk, information retrieved 21 October 2020)

(BB10) Vinegar manufactory: Mr [Samuel] Rushe's Vinegar Yard on Rocque's 1747 map was a substantial operation which had started on a modest scale as far back as 1641. Its operation was described by Martin Adams and Tim R Smith as 'the first commercial vinegar maker'. In 1790 John Pott was the new owner; he had been making vinegar in Whitechapel since around 1766 prior to his

Messrs Pott's Vinegar Manufactory near Bankside. This anonymous watercolour dates from the early years of the nineteenth century. It captures well the substantial size of Pott's manufactory next to Barclay Perkins' Brewery but also the contrast between the 'working' industrial South Bank bristling with tall chimneys and landmark London on the other side of the river.
(© Museum of London)

Southwark move. Under his direction the company became 'the largest producer of vinegar in Britain'. It was located immediately to the west of the Barclay Perkins' Brewery. The Pott family and vinegar making continued on the site and the Museum of London has an excellent watercolour of the manufactory around 1840 when it was in the ownership of C A & W Pott, then the third largest vinegar brewers (left). The firm subsequently declined and was acquired by Beaufoy's in 1902.

(Rocque; Horwood 1813; Martin Adams & Tim R Smith, 'Vinegar: its manufacture and history in London', in *Journal of London's Industrial Archaeology* 10, 2012)

(BB11) Southwark brewery: William Rendle and Philip Norman's book on the inns of Southwark acknowledged the importance of the Anchor brewery in Bankside, adding that 'In fact the brewhouses about here were thick as hops'.

Brewing became an important industry in Southwark and Bermondsey when hop growing was introduced in Kent in the fifteenth century – the Brewers' Company's first charter dates from 1437. The first brewhouse on this site was set up by James Monger around 1616. In 1710 the Southwark brewery was in the hands of Edmund Halsey. His hardworking nephew Ralph Thrale was able to purchase the brewery at the death of his uncle. When Ralph himself died in 1758, his son Henry took over the business. This was the Henry Thrale who married Hester – the soon famous Mrs Thrale gathered in her Streatham Library a coterie of luminaries, including Dr Johnson; these were the 'Streatham Worthies' (described in Your London Publishing's *The Streatham Sketchbook*).

Henry Thrale (1728?–1781) was a brewer and Member of Parliament for Southwark between 1765-80. He divided his time between Bankside and Streatham Place. At Bankside,

the four-storeyed house stood at the entrance gate to the brewery's cobbled yard in Deadman's Place; the house is visible on Horwood's map. At Thrale's death, the executors, including Dr Johnson, sold the business to Quaker Robert Barclay – a member of the banking family; Barclay paid the impressive sum of £135,000 and soon invited the brewery's manager, John Perkins, to become a partner. A comparison between the maps of Rocque (1747) and Horwood (1799) shows the considerable expansion of the brewery – not named on Rocque. Continues on p. 272.

(Horwood 1799, labelled Messrs Barclay, Perkins & Co; Horwood 1813 (25), labelled Anchor Brewery; *Survey of London* 22; Rendle & Norman)

(BB12) Winchester House; continued from p. 119. Lancelot Andrews is believed to have been the last Bishop of Winchester to use the House and he died there in 1626. It had tenants for a few years prior to

The multiplication of tenants and the presence of industry in and around Winchester Palace certainly contributed to an increase in fire risk. At the end of the eighteenth century a large section of the premises was occupied by a mustard manufactory owned by Messrs Lingard and Sadler (later Messrs Wardale), mustard makers. On 28 August 1814, a fire devastated the premises of Messrs Wardale but revealed the palace's original hall with its striking rose window as shown in this 1815 print.

(Engraving published by Robert Wilkinson in *Londina Illustrata*, 1819 and 1829 – 2 volumes)

this event (fifteen names recorded in 1614) but from 1642 it became a prison – continuing to 'host' such illustrious names as Sir Kenelm Digby, Sir Francis Williamson and Sir William Brockman. In 1649 the whole property was sold for over £4000 to Thomas Walker of Camberwell – the large estate included Rochester House, which had been leased to the Bishop of Rochester since 1604/5. Walker financed the making of Stoney Street, linking Deadman's Place and Church Street to Clink Street. Buildings were divided into tenements rather than pulled down. At the Restoration in 1660 all was restituted to the Bishops of Winchester (Palace and land) and two years later the Bishop sought to lease tenements by private Act of Parliament.

From the mid-seventeenth century onwards, various crafts operated from Winchester Palace: glassmaking, briefly, in the early 1660s, carpentry, a charitable training scheme for apprentices, and finally in the late eighteenth century, a large part of the property was acquired by mustard makers, Messrs Lingard and Sadler, followed by Messrs Wardale. On Sunday 28 August 1814 a fire broke out which destroyed the factory, but revealed the old medieval hall, its splendid rose window and some of the ancient neighbouring buildings (previous page).

Clink prison, Winchester Palace; continued from p. 119. It had probably fallen into disuse after Winchester House was sold in 1649. In 1761 R & J Dodsley described it in their book *London and its environs* as 'a very dismal hole, where debtors are sometimes confined, but little used.' The Gordon rioters burnt down the prison in 1780 and it was never rebuilt. ('Winchester Yard' on both Rocque and Horwood 1813; *Survey of London* 22)

(BB13) Borough Market; continued from p. 130 (Southwark Market). In 1663 the City confirmed the right to hold a market in Southwark. Both the market and Southwark Fair were held in Borough High Street, causing a great deal of traffic and confusion. Between 1672 and 1692 there was a proposal to move the market to St Margaret's Hill (left). A lively print depicts it at the new site; but it stopped being held in

that restrictive location before 1754, when the market authorities secured permission, by Act of Parliament (1755), to hold the market in Rochester Yard, the former site of Rochester House, and the origins of the present Borough Market. The site was known as the 'Triangle'.
(Horwood 1813; *Survey of London* 22)

(BB14) St Saviour's church; continued from p. 117. In 1614 the Vestry had purchased the church from James I and VI. In 1703 the Great Screen of St Saviour's was concealed by a painted wooden screen on which were inscribed the Lord's Prayer, Creed, the Ten Commandments, with the image of a dove descending amidst a group of cherubs' heads topped with flaming urns – this concealment would not be lifted until 1833. The church slowly deteriorated throughout the eighteenth century but restoration only came in 1818, lasting twelve years in the hands of local architect George Gwilt the Younger, a passionate advocate of medieval architecture. Continues on p. 274.
(*Survey of London* 22 – Introduction)

(BB15) Montague Close; continued from p. 117. In the seventeenth century industry and cheap dwellings had gradually occupied the site of the gardens of the Priory House north of St Saviour's but from 1625 the new owner of Montague Close sought to replace degradation with respectability. By 1775 'there were sixty messuages and four wharves in the close'; also, eight almshouses erected by Mrs Alice Shaw Overman in 1771. This area became progressively neglected (above) and finally disappeared when London Bridge had to be replaced in the 1830s.
(Rocque; Rhinebeck; Horwood 1813; *Survey of London* 22)

(BB16) St Saviour's grammar school; continued from p. 118. There are conflicting accounts about whether or not this school burnt in the great fire of 1676. R C Carrington, who has researched the school's archives, is unequivocal: 'There is a gap in the minutes and signs of some confusion, and when they resume, it is to mention the paying of the bills for rebuilding the school.' It was rebuilt on the same site and has been widely illustrated (overleaf).
(Rocque, labelled 'Fre[e] sc[hool]'; Horwood 1813; Rendle 1878; R C Carrington, *Two Schools*, 1962)

(BB17) Cure's College, Park Street; continued from p. 118. This institution is simply labelled 'Almshouses' on Horwood 1799 and described as St Saviour's Alsmhouses in the 1813 edition. The observant eye might revel in the graphic naming of a nearby street on Rocque's map: 'Whores nest', a tiny alleyway just north of the College. Ten of the almshouses were rebuilt in 1820. The cemetery would become the second most used parish

This etching captures well the sense of dereliction from which St Saviour's church and its surroundings suffered prior to its restoration. This image dates from 1815 and was engraved for the *Antiquarian Itinerary* by Thomas Higham after a drawing by William Deeble.
© London Metropolitan Archives (City of London)

Opposite:

This rare view of Southwark market was created after the market moved away from the east side of Borough High Street, where it obstructed traffic, to Margaret's Hill where it was tucked away next to the Town Hall – seen on the right-hand side – and before it moved again to its current location. This engraving by R Sheppard may be dated to the 1730s but is somewhat misleading for it shows the church of St George (rebuilt in 1733) in the background, when the view is in fact looking north towards London Bridge.
© London Metropolitan Archives (City of London)

Cure's College almshouses in Park Street, overlooking the burial ground. A grave digger is at work on the right hand side. Undated watercolour by George Gwilt, around 1800.
© London Metropolitan Archives (City of London)

burial ground after the parish churchyard south of St Saviour's parish church.
(Rocque labelled 'College Yard'; Horwood 1799; Horwood 1813; *Survey of London* 22; MoLAS 1999)

(BB18) Sessions House/Town Hall; continued from Southwark Compter and Sessions House on p. 120.

The arrangement described on p. 120 was destroyed in the great Southwark fire of 1676. The site was left derelict for several years until local residents petitioned the Court of Aldermen in 1682. In 1685 a new Sessions House was finally built, paid by the City of London and embellished with a statue of Charles II (partially seen on p. 192). A plan of the building, dated 1686, is in the Metropolitan Archives, showing a series of tradesmen's premises on the east side along Borough High Street – mostly metal workers, and the Compter or prison at the northern end. The Courtroom/Sessions House was upstairs; sandwiched between the two was a pub, the King's Arms. As with King's Bench prison, the Compter had a Common Side and a Master's side – here labelled 'Counter kitchen' and 'Parlour'. This plan bears the arms of the city and the symbol of Bridge House to show that north and south banks had vested interests in these premises – both under the jurisdiction of the City. Continues on p. 274.

The Compter moved to Tooley Street in 1717. Publisher Robert Wilkinson issued a print of the Sessions House just before it was demolished in 1793. It was replaced by a new town hall and the statue of Charles II was removed to Three Crown Court east of Borough Market. (Rocque – the triangular site is labelled 'St Margaret's Hill' and the street running on the east side 'Compter Street'; Horwood 1813; Rendle & Norman; *Survey of London* 22; Gerhold 2016 No 113)

(BB19) Cross-Bones burial ground at the corner of Redcross and Union Streets; continued from p. 115.

There has been disagreement about the date when Cross-Bones Yard became one of St Saviour's burying grounds. The 1999 MoLAS publication makes clear that in 1852 no one knew – Dr Sutherland, commissioned by the Secretary of State, submitted his report to the Burial Board stating that the ground 'had been in use for above 100 years but the exact date of its opening is stated not to be known'. By 1883 a 22 December letter from Lord Brabazon to *The Times* where he complained of the cavalier treatment of the dead at that site, stated that 'the first lease of this ground [to the parish], dated about 1708'. While in 1950 the *Survey of London* favoured a 1673 date when 'the newe Church yarde in the Parke' was mentioned in the vestry minutes.

We learn from the Museum of London site panel at Cross-Bones

THE SOUTH BANK AROUND 1770: BOROUGH AND BANKSIDE 195

yard (post 2015) that in 1791 locals objected, in vain, to plans to build a Boys Charity School on the site. They were apparently concerned that 'the remains of their friends and family will be disturbed'. In 1819, a 'twin' National Free School for Girls opened at Cross-Bones alongside the Boys School on the south side of the burial ground (above). Also see 'Graveyard schools' p. 461.
(Rocque 13, labelled 'St Saviour's Burying Ground'; Horwood 1813 labelled 'St Saviour's School and Burial Ground'; Survey of London 22; MoLAS 1999)

(BB20) 8 Union Street (later 18 Union Street) (overleaf). This four-storey house with basement formed part of a terrace at the eastern end of Union street, north side; the street was laid out for a new workhouse after a 1774 Act was passed. The street was ready by 1781 and the architect George Gwilt the elder (1746–1807) built the terrace on the north side around 1789. No 8 is the house the architect took for himself. His two sons were born there and George the younger (1775-1856) continued to live there after the death of his father. He had a passion for antiquities and archaeology and set up his own museum by converting the stables at the back of the house. Local historian William Rendle described the 'charming museum' in great detail in 1888:

> At the end of the interior stood a classical figure with the light reflected upon it. Around on pedestals were busts of Roman emperors. The floor was paved with genuine tesserae, and in the windows stained glass, old and new. Antique remains, mostly

The south side of Cross-Bones burial ground became used as a site for two schools. This undesirable juxtaposition started in 1791 when a charity school for boys was built on the corner of Red Cross and Union Streets. It was followed in 1819 by 'St Savio[u]r's National School for Girls' with its main entrance on Union Street. Both establishments followed the same design. Watercolour by G Yates, 1825.
© London Metropolitan Archives (City of London)

This late Victorian watercolour by J Appleton records the appearance of the late Georgian house of architect George Gwilt the elder. The building, at 8 Union Street, stood next to Cross-Bones Yard which this architect's son would later survey in 1821 (see p. 456).

© London Metropolitan Archives (City of London)

Roman, were, as they came to hand from below-ground in Southwark, deposited in the passage and offices. When I saw the place after his death, it was in a state of deplorable neglect. (*The Antiquary*, volume 17, p. 241) The house was demolished at the close of the nineteenth century. (Horwood 1813; *Survey of London* 22)

(BB21) Harrow Dung Hill in Harrow Street, almost opposite St George's church. In 1733 the Scottish Physician George Cheyne, appalled by the polluted air of the capital wrote in his book *The English Malady*: 'the crouded *Churches, Church Yards and Burying places*, with the putrefying *Bodies*, the *Sinks, Butchers Houses, Stables, Dunghills* etc, and the necessary Stagnation, Fermentation … more than sufficient to putrefy, poison and infect the Air for Twenty Miles around it'. The famous panorama of London by the Buck Brothers dated 1749 depicts two such 'dung hills' or 'laystalls' of human waste – one at Whitefriars and another close to St Paul's Cathedral (right) but both on the North Bank. By the end of the eighteenth century and the beginning of the nineteenth, the place-name 'Harrow Dung Hill' still featured on Horwood maps. More houses had been built on the stinking 'piazza' perhaps suggesting the actual dung hill had gone. (Rocque; Horwood 1799; Horwood 1813; Ralph Hyde, *A Prospect of Britain – The Town Panoramas of Samuel & Nathaniel Buck*, 1994)

(BB22) Bridewell or the House of Correction in St George's Fields. This was a purpose-built prison which was designed by John Millner and opened in 1773. It offered improved facilities, as prescribed by the 1772 Act which gave this project the go ahead; it had 'separate wards for men, women, and apprentices, … two bathing tubs and a sick room'. But this did not alleviate the miserable life of prisoners who suffered from cold and hunger with little to eat and little to do, reported William Smith in his 1776 *State of the Gaols* publication. The existence of this House of Correction, however, was short-lived; in 1798 its inmates were transferred to Horsemonger Lane prison and by 1813 when Horwood's map was re-issued, the facility had become a 'Soap Manufactory'. (Horwood 1799; Horwood 1813; *Survey of London* 25)

(BB23) Dirty Lane which later ran into **Gravel Lane**, started life as a path from the north east side of St George's Fields and the Bishop of Winchester's park to the riverside near Paris Garden. It had been the focus of a dispute in 1618 – between the actor/entrepreneur Edward Alleyn and the innkeepers of Borough High Street who felt by-passed and deprived of potential custom. This convenient shortcut remained, known as Dirty Lane, no doubt because of the general swampy character of St George's Fields. It was

later widened and renamed Great Suffolk Street.
(Rocque; Horwood 1813; *Survey of London* 25)

(BB24) The [new] King's Bench Prison, Borough Road (at the junction with Blackman Street e.g. Borough High Street); continued from p. 132. The old King's Bench prison, in Borough High Street, having been judged 'unsafe for the custody, and dangerous to the health of the prisoners', a new Act was passed in 1754 and the new prison, built in St George's Fields on land which belonged to Catherine West, was ready in 1758. Prisoners, however, were unable to benefit from its semi-rural setting according to the Dodsley brothers writing in 1761: 'all prospect of the fields, even from the uppermost windows, is excluded by the height of the walls with which it is surrounded.' There was only one prisoner per room, but the rooms were very small.

If debtors could afford the fee, they were free to leave the prison provided they stayed within 'the Rules' – the Rules was a substantial area centred on St George's Circus (overleaf). When the great prison reformer John Howard visited the King's Bench in 1776, he found it totally overcrowded with many lying in the chapel; the total number was around 1400 with two thirds sleeping inside the prison and a third outside, within the Rules. This is because the parole system was widely abused as reported by William Smith also in 1776: 'Many prisoners ... occupy rooms, keep shops, enjoy places of profit, or live on the rent of their rooms a life of idleness; and being indulged with the use of the key, go out when they please, and thereby convert a prison ... into an alms-house for their support.' All in great contrast with the situation described for 1600 (see p. 132).

During the Gordon riots (1780), part of the prison burnt down but was subsequently repaired. The prison

shut its doors for the last time in 1869 when imprisonment for debt was abolished; the site was cleared ten years later. Continues on p. 276.
(Horwood 1799, labelled 'New Bridewell'; Rhinebeck; Horwood 1813; *Survey of London* 25)

(BB25) St George's Fields; continued from p. 115. In 1789 a journalist, noting the success of the Royal Circus establishment at St George's Circus (see W16 on p. 174), remarked on how well connected the site was to other parts of London:

> The rage for building in St George's Fields is now so great, that London has joined the Royal Circus from London, Blackfriars and Westminster Bridges, on both sides of the road, and the lamps being remarkably well lighted and pretty numerous, and the footpaths so clean and so well-paved, that it is the pleasantest part of London to walk at night-time.
> (*Pleasure Gardens of South London*, see bibliography)

With the building of Westminster and Blackfriars Bridges (1750 and 1769) roadwork development gathered momentum but it still took many years before the landowners, the Bridge House Estates, were able to redevelop this area comprehensively. Two Acts

This rare depiction of a 'dung hill' or 'laystall' was recorded by the Buck brothers on the north bank of the Thames in their 1749 panorama of London. But this is presumably what the 'Harrow dung hill' opposite St George's church would have looked like.
© London Metropolitan Archives (City of London)

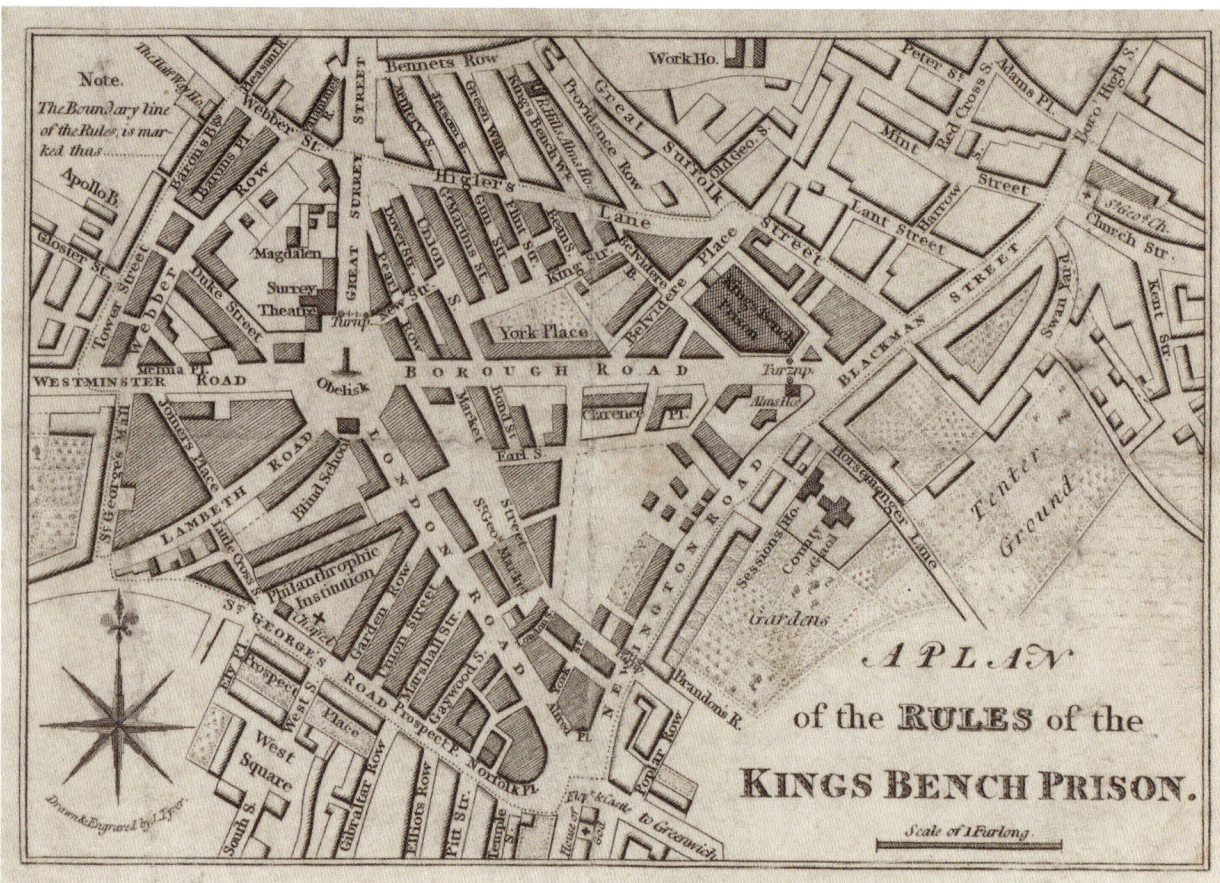

The shaded parts of this plan show how far prisoner-debtors could roam outside the new King's Bench prison in Borough Road, provided they paid the authorities the appropriate fee. A detail is reproduced on the opposite page: St George's Circus. Engraving by James Tyrer, 1813.
© London Metropolitan Archives (City of London)

of Parliament, in 1719 and 1751, authorised the formation of Borough Road (continuation of Borough High Street) and New Kent Road (from Newington Butts to Old Kent Road). Early schemes for Blackfriars Road advocated a junction close to Blackfriars Bridge but in the end, it was more practical to move the junction further south which was not so built-up, i.e., St George's Circus. After the opening of Robert Mylne's Blackfriars Bridge, this engineer also designed and project managed the approach to the bridge and the new road network was in place by 1770. This was done at record speed, within a year. In 1771, the newly formed St George's Circus acquired an obelisk in its centre (overleaf).

Concern about the land at St George's Fields had been voiced in earnest in 1746 when complaints, from principal tenant Revd Thomas Clarke and others, reached the Bridge House Estates: there was no fencing and the land was regularly abused by a range of different people including those encroaching or looking for shortcuts when travelling. The complaints were upheld but action was slow to follow. George Dance, the City Surveyor, was ordered to survey the land in the early 1770s and short-term leases were issued while waiting for the outcome of discussions.

The level of 'abuse' or simple trespassing was in evidence when two artists captured major events held there – first, the Gordon riots in 1780 with the massing of troops around the commanding figure of Lord George

THE SOUTH BANK AROUND 1770: BOROUGH AND BANKSIDE 199

 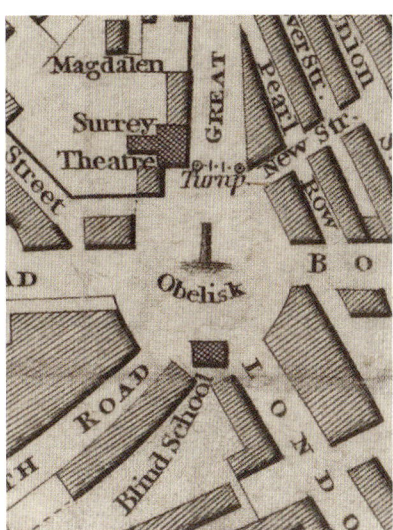

Gordon (right). Five years later, the famous ascent of Lunardi's balloon (overleaf) was also set by the obelisk in St George's Fields.

Between 1780 and 1800, two of the site's major tenants, the Hedger family who owned the famous Dog and Duck pub (see p. 160) and the West family started to develop areas which were still technically common land.
(Rocque; *Survey of London* 25; Galinou & Hayes No 46)

(BB26) Drapers' Almshouses, Newington Butts. The land 'att the entrance into St. George's fields' in the parish of St George the Martyr, was granted by the City Corporation and the money came from John Walter, Clerk of the Drapers' Company; the site would be close to modern day Borough Station. The almshouses for sixteen residents were ready by the late 1640s and in the early 1650s, a chapel and a room for the trustees were added. They were rebuilt in the mid-eighteenth century, further back from the main road; when the road was widened, it absorbed the original site of the first almshouses. Continues on p. 275
(Rocque 20; *Survey of London* 25)

Top left:

Lord George Gordon (1751–1793), president of the Protestant Association is portrayed at St George's Fields on 2 June 1780. Gordon organised a petition for the repeal of the Catholic Relief Act which he would only deliver to the House of Commons if he was backed up by at least 20,000 men. Members were asked to gather at the Obelisk – hidden behind the figure of Gordon. They were organised into four 'divisions': Southwark (A), London (B), Westminster (C) and the Scotch (D); they marched to Parliament carrying the petition shown under Gordon's foot, which in reality was so heavy it could barely be lifted. Etching published by John Harris on 4 August 1780 and 'drawn from life' by R Bran.
(Image in the public domain, Wikimedia Commons)

Top right:

Detail from the map opposite: St George's Circus.

While the picture of Lord George Gordon emphasises the calculated design of the new St George's Circus, the painting by Julius Caesar Ibbetson shows just how much of St George's Fields was actually fields in the late eighteenth century, and not urban development. The circular arena and accompanying contraption concerned 'The Ascent of Lunardi's Balloon from St George's Fields', the title of the painting. The crowds have gathered in an essentially rural spot. This painting has been dated 1788–90, almost ten years after the Gordon Riots scene (previous page).
(© Museum of London)

SOUTHWARK AND BERMONDSEY

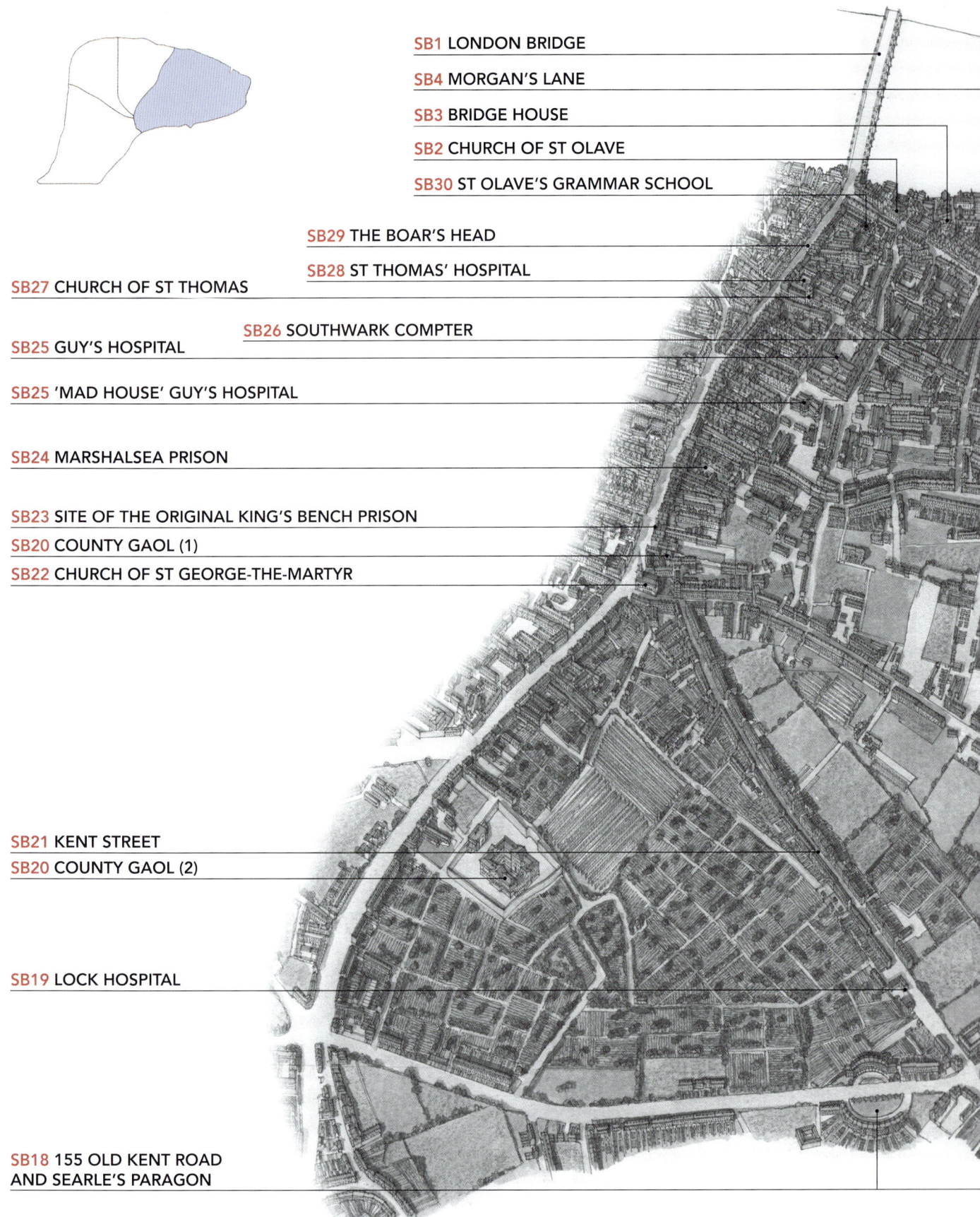

- **SB1** LONDON BRIDGE
- **SB4** MORGAN'S LANE
- **SB3** BRIDGE HOUSE
- **SB2** CHURCH OF ST OLAVE
- **SB30** ST OLAVE'S GRAMMAR SCHOOL
- **SB29** THE BOAR'S HEAD
- **SB28** ST THOMAS' HOSPITAL
- **SB27** CHURCH OF ST THOMAS
- **SB26** SOUTHWARK COMPTER
- **SB25** GUY'S HOSPITAL
- **SB25** 'MAD HOUSE' GUY'S HOSPITAL
- **SB24** MARSHALSEA PRISON
- **SB23** SITE OF THE ORIGINAL KING'S BENCH PRISON
- **SB20** COUNTY GAOL (1)
- **SB22** CHURCH OF ST GEORGE-THE-MARTYR
- **SB21** KENT STREET
- **SB20** COUNTY GAOL (2)
- **SB19** LOCK HOSPITAL
- **SB18** 155 OLD KENT ROAD AND SEARLE'S PARAGON

to the 'Comon Sewer'. The smelliest operations were carried out in the 'Beam House' as far away from the house as was possible. The plans also record a 'Buttery', 'oven', 'Shedd', 'pump', 'Stable', 'Bark house', 'The old mill house and kill house' with newer premises in the opposite corner, and a 'Tann pitt house'. The house was given a new roof in 1737 while one of the adjoining houses needed rebuilding.

Leather manufacture was the second largest industry in the seventeenth century after wool production and it was concentrated in Southwark and Bermondsey which were well supplied with water and had about eighty tanneries in the seventeenth century. This community of tanners which started in the fifteenth century was still thriving in the late eighteenth century – with the presence of associated trades such as a 'Glue Manufactory' in Upper Russell Street or detectable in place names such as 'Old Packthread Ground'; there was basic housing for the workers such as 'Wilds Rents' or 'Wittals Rents', while more comfortable accommodation could be had in Grange Walk, judging by the survival of fine late seventeenth/early eighteenth-century houses which were once part of the Abbey's gate (e.g. the Grade II properties at 6 and 7 Grange Walk). In this community there were pubs; a parish church (St Mary Magdalen) and also a school (named on Rocque only). Should workers be more inclined to attend a meeting house, there was one on Five Foot Lane, later Russell Street, now Tanner Street and close to St Saviour's Dock (named on Rocque only).

One of the industry's most high-profile companies is that of Barrow Hepburn and Gale of Government despatch boxes fame – the ministerial red boxes Hepburn & Sons started in Bermondsey in 1760, merging first with the Gales, then the Barrows. It is rewarding to look them up in Horwood's 1799 map which names so many of the businesses it features: 'Mr Hepburn's Tan Yard' is in Long Lane immediately opposite the Quakers' burial ground. Continues on p. 286.

(Rocque; Horwood 1813; Gerhold 2016, No 83 and 144)

(SB16) **Bermondsey Spa**. The site of this small pleasure garden in Grange Road was particularly rural as is shown on Horwood's map. The proprietor, Thomas Keyse, took over the Waterman's Arms tavern at that site and opened the pleasure garden in 1765. A Spa was discovered in 1770, in 1774 the venue obtained a music licence and from 1782 outdoor spectacles were added such as 'the Battle of Gibraltar' or a huge model of the Rock of Gibraltar (1786). Eventually the venue had a Spa, pump room, tea room and a picture gallery exhibiting the work of Keyse, a gifted self-taught painter. He died in 1800 and the gardens closed around 1804. (Horwood 1813; *Pleasure Gardens of South London*)

(SB17) **Asylum for the Deaf and Dumb**, on the west side of Kent Street (now Old Kent Road) was 'one of the earliest institutions in this country for the education of deaf children' points out the *Survey of London*. It was founded in 1792 by a priest, the Rev. J. Townsend of Jamaica Road, Bermondsey; an MP for Southwark, Henry Thornton; and the Rev. H Cox Mason, Rector of Bermondsey. It was enlarged in 1819.
(Horwood 1813; *Survey of London* 25)

(SB18) **155 Old Kent Road**, the house of the architect Michael Searles (1751–1813), set within the Rolls estate (Searles was its surveyor) and dating from 1800. Searles is described as follows in Cherry & Pevsner: 'he could be described as the first local architect to make a genuinely original contribution to the architecture of South London. His buildings are of great elegance, but, alas, he cannot have been a good businessman, for almost all belong to uncompleted schemes'. He is best known for his highly original 'Paragon' at Blackheath (which has survived) but his lost '**Paragon**' in the New Kent Road came first, in 1789–90, and not very far from

to give an obeliscal silhouette. Mr [Kerry] Downes seems to divide the blame between James and Hawksmoor.
(Horwood 1799; Horwood 1813; Summerson as cited; *The Commissions for Building Fifty New Churches: The Minute Books, 1711–27, A Calendar*, London Record Society, 1986)

(SB12) Bermondsey workhouse, first established in Salisbury Street (now Wilson Grove) in 1729; four years later, records show it sheltered forty-seven adults and eleven children; by 1777 it numbered 291 inmates but is not shown on Rocque's map. In 1791 it moved to a brand-new building in Russell Street (now Tanner Street). This is the establishment we are showing in our reconstruction.
(Horwood 1813; Higginbotham 2019)

(SB13) Church of St Mary Magdalen, Bermondsey Street; continued from p. 139. At the end of the seventeenth century the church was so dilapidated that it was rebuilt in 1675–79; it retained the lower part of its fifteenth-century square tower. William Morgan's 1682 map records its appearance soon after rebuilding but our reconstruction is based on eighteenth century images. *Victoria County History* records that the eighteenth-century galleries (1793) 'are good examples of woodwork of that period'.
(Morgan 1682; Rocque; Horwood 1813; VCH 4; Weinreb & Hibbert)

(SB14) Site of Bermondsey Abbey, Bermondsey Street; continued from pp. 139–140. The rise of antiquarianism in the late eighteenth century accounts for some of the best images of the abbey and its successors. The monastery's heart had been King John's Court, which, at the end of the eighteenth century, had become 'Bermondsey Square' – the site of the Abbey's Inner Court, west of the cloister. A house in Grange Walk marked 'Gate House' indicates its closeness to the Abbey gates. Cherry & Pevsner tell us that Abbey Street, made in 1820, lay over the Abbey's nave; the church's crossing was probably near the junction with Tower Bridge Road. Continues on p. 289.
(Rocque; Horwood 1813; MOLA 2011; Cherry & Pevsner)

(SB15) The Grange and tanneries: The most ancient streets are those which led from Southwark to Bermondsey Abbey e.g., Long Lane and Bermondsey Street. The area called The Grange, east of the Abbey is so called because it was the site of the Abbey's grange – where no doubt the tithe barn would have been sited. By the seventeenth and eighteenth centuries, the area was teeming with tanners – in Long Lane and its continuation. One of these tanneries, run by Elizabeth Smith in Grange Road, on land belonging to St Thomas' Hospital, was recorded in two separate plans at the end of the seventeenth-century, showing a simple two and a half storeys 'dwelling house' with a long, thin piece of ground running at the back all the way

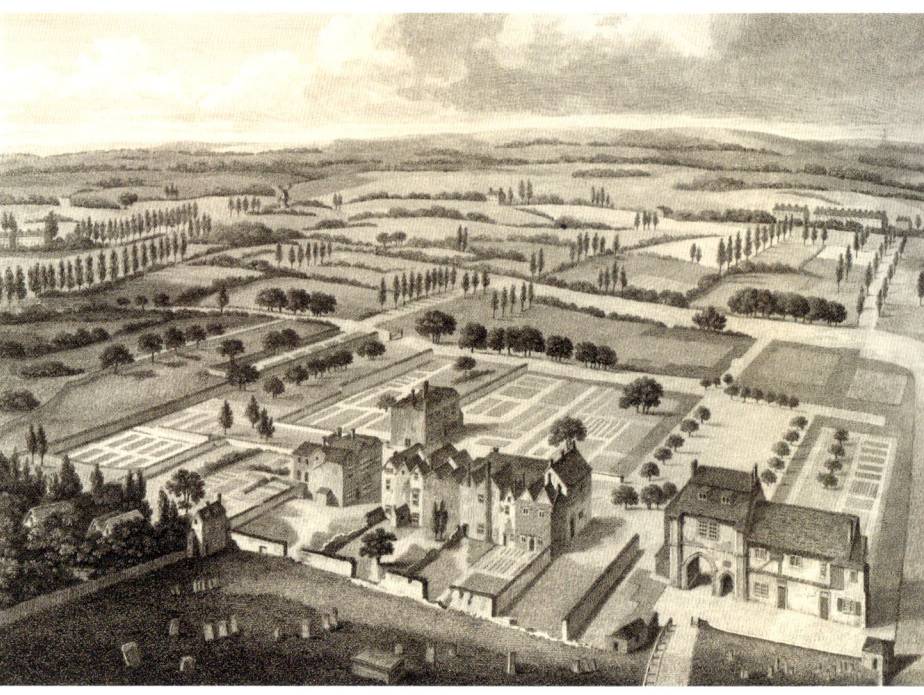

'A General View of the Remains of Bermondsey Abby, Surry As it appeared in the Year 1805 with the adjacent Country. 'Taken from the Steeple of the Church of St. Mary Magdalen', reads the caption for this engraving. The abbey itself had long disappeared but the entrance gate and adjoining building had survived and may be glimpsed on the far right. What is more puzzling is 'the adjacent country' as Horwood's plan makes clear the area was fairly built up by that date. Engraving published by Robert Wilkinson in *Londina Illustrata*, 1819 and 1829 – 2 volumes.
(© Trustees of the British Museum)

Church of St John Horsleydown, described by Charles Clarke as 'a handsome stone structure' with 'neat ornaments'. This etching, after G Shepherd was first published in 1814.
(From Charles Clarke's *Architectura Ecclesiastica Londini*, 1820)

seventeenth century.

Much later, Tower Bridge was built at the junction between Shad Thames and Pickle Herring Street. It is at that junction, too, that John Courage ran his brewery from 1787. This was the site of Fastolf's manor house in the fifteenth century, which turned into a 'beere house' in Braun and Hogenberg's 1572 map, and was in the hands of brewer Wessell Webling in the early seventeenth century (see p. 138). **John Courage's brewery** must have been a fairly modest operation as it does not feature on Horwood's 1799 or 1813 maps. Courage died unexpectedly in 1793, so his wife took over the management of the business, but she, too, died a few years later in 1797.

From 1800 and for the next fifty years the brewery was known as Courage & Donaldson as John Donaldson, the brewery clerk, was then running the business. Also see pp. 512–513.
(Morgan 1682; Rocque; Horwood 1813; *Old and New London*; John Pudney, *A Draught of Contentment – The Story of the Courage Group*, 1971)

(SB7) Flockton's Turpentine Factory, between Potter's Fields and Freeman's Lane. Turpentine was a solvent which was made from pine timber, little used for making furniture but needed in shipbuilding (masts) and useful for its resin which yielded turpentine, tar and varnish (1754 patent), and was also used for medicinal purposes. After 1700 when the normal supply from Scotland was drying up, pine timber was imported from the Baltic or the Americas.

The factory was still around in 1857 when Loveday produced his survey. It was at Hartley's Wharf, in the occupation of wharfinger William Parker who specialised in 'tar, turpentine, rosin, oil &c.'.
(Horwood 1799; Horwood 1813 without naming the owner; Trades; Loveday)

(SB9) Crucifix Lane. Some historians believe that Crucifix Lane, lying between modern Shand and Barham Streets, was so-named because of the Bermondsey cross (see p. 139). Others think it is a corruption of the name Christopher. The lane, on land belonging to Christ's Hospital, was developed by Robert Burt a carpenter of St Olave's in Tooley Street (and a citizen and cordwainer of London). The redevelopment lasted until about 1810 when it was redeveloped again.
(1542 map; Gerhold 2016 No 174–75)

(SB10) St Olave's workhouse, Parish Street, west of the church of St John Horsleydown. This workhouse was set up by the parish of St Olave in 1729 when it sheltered fifty adults and seventy children, the latter being taught to read but not write and also receiving a basic religious education. St John Horsleydown became a parish in 1733 and this workhouse became theirs – St Olave's had its own with 250 inmates. The workhouse was rebuilt in 1831.
(Rocque; Horwood 1813; Higginbotham 2019)

(SB11) Church of St John Horsleydown. With St Luke's Old Street, both churches were designed by Nicholas Hawksmoor and John James, and built between 1727 and 1733; they were the last two erected by the Commissioners for building Fifty New Churches. Only twelve out of the fifty were fully financed by the Commissioners and Nicholas Hawksmoor was involved in eight out of the twelve. A further five were subsidised and two more were bought. John Summerson poured a little vitriol over this enterprise in his *Georgian London* book:

> to James is sometimes attributed the incredibly philistine church of St John, Horsleydown (burnt in the war and now demolished), with its spire consisting of an ionic column grotesquely distorted

show that the medieval church was repaired and improved throughout the seventeenth and early eighteenth century but by 1737 part of the church had collapsed and the rest was nearly derelict. An Act of Parliament enabled its rebuilding and it was completed by 1740. Built of Portland stone in a classical style, it had a small chancel, a nave with two aisles, and a tower. The upper part of this tower survives in Tanner Street Gardens (below). The church was designed by Henry Flitcroft who also built St Giles in the Fields. Continues on p. 283
(Rocque; Horwood; *VCH 4*)

(SB3) **Bridge House**, Tooley Street (east of St Olave's church); continued from p. 137. For the Bridge House in the eighteenth century, John Rocque's 1747 map of London is the most detailed document, naming: 'Bridge Yard', 'Bridge House', 'Stone Yard' and 'Timber Yard'. The large brewery belonging to the Bridge House Estates (on the site of Hay's Wharf) was still operating in 1803.
(Rocque; Horwood 1813 but not named)

(SB4) **Morgan's Lane** – this name comes from Edmund Morgan of Lambeth who, in 1638, leased the property from Magdalen College, Oxford. The site was part of Sir John Fastolf's estate and was bequeathed to the College at his death in 1459. At that point the property consisted of the High Brewhouse (west), two water mills known as Pickleherring Mill, wharves and watercourses. The brewery existed by 1425; the water mills were pulled down shortly after 1667 to make room for a wharf. The lease holder who took this action was Alderman Edmund Lewin and his tenant Thomas Franklin, a miller, thereby antagonising the neighbourhood whose livelihood depended on the water. The removal of the mills was followed by the driving of piles in the stream to build a house over it. The millstream is still shown on Rocque's 1747 map but had disappeared by the end of the century.
(Rocque; Horwood 1813; Gerhold 2016, No 77)

(SB5) **Stoney Lane brewery** (north of Tooley Street). It is labelled 'Brew House' on Rocque, 'Clowes & Co Brewery' on Horwood's 1799 map and 'Phoenix Brewery' on Horwood's 1813 edition. Its history is that of Clowes & Western – the brewery of James Myatt in 1783, followed by that of Clowes, Maddox & Newberry until 1813. After that date, it was John Clowes and James Western until 1821 when it was taken over by Henry Meux & Co. In 1830 Meux sold the brewery to Barclay, Perkins & Co. Ltd who kept it until 1890.
(Rocque; Horwood 1799; Horwood 1813; breweryhistory.com; accessed on 30 October 2020)

(SB6/SB8) **Shad Thames & Pickle Herring Street** ran westwards from St Saviour's Dockhead, parallel with the Thames. These old and narrow streets are clearly glimpsed on Morgan's 1682 map where both are featured but only Shad Thames is named; both are missing from William Faithorne's 1658 map; they could therefore be dated to the last quarter of the

This picture of the church of St Olave in Tooley Street may be slightly later than the period under review but it is a rare depiction from the river. It shows the church which was rebuilt in 1740 with its burial ground; note the intriguing pyramidal monument. This etching, after G Shepherd was first published in 1814.
(From Charles Clarke's *Architectura Ecclesiastica Londini*, 1820)

Previous:

Detail from the Rhinebeck Panorama, watercolour in four sections, dating from around 1810 – here we reproduce the left hand-side only, in two sections; the inclusion of a fire and a funeral cast a sombre note over Southwark, likely to be 'generic' rather than a reference to specific events. The two events have been linked visually by the otherwise inexplicable long shadow running from the fire to the funeral. The fire is being tackled by invisible firemen with water sprouting upwards from the streets below; while a funeral takes place in the burial ground of St John's Horsleydown. The panorama is remarkably detailed and accurate and references to it are made throughout the gazetteer.
(© Museum of London)

Right:

Shooting the arches of London Bridge when the tide was changing; the exercise was so dangerous that 'only the most foolhardy watermen attempted it, and many who did so were drowned' wrote Peter Jackson, the London historian who drew this reconstruction for his book *London Bridge – A Visual history* (1971).
(Look and Learn / Peter Jackson Collection)

Opposite:

The small turret which stood on top of St Olave's tower miraculously survived two deaths – that of the main body of its church in 1926 and two years later that of the tower itself which was pulled down to allow redevelopment of the area. At the heated debate in the House of Commons a pledge was made that some of the money would be used to create a local community garden – Tanner Street Gardens, the current home of the turret turned fountain from St Olave's. It is Grade II listed.
(© The author, 2021)

(SB1) London Bridge; continued from p. 126. The disastrous fire of 1725 started in Tooley Street and spread to the bridge, destroying all the houses up to the stone gate which was also damaged. Out of the fifteen which burnt down, eleven were rebuilt and the Bridge House Estates also took the opportunity to widen the stone gate since it needed to be repaired. Nonsuch House survived. Concerns about the state of London Bridge were formally recorded in 1746 when the Lord Mayor Sir Richard Hoare set up a court of enquiry; but it came to a dead end when the City realised that the proposed solution – removing the buildings and widening the arches of the bridge – wouldn't work. If they attempted to curb the treacherous waters around the bridge – which had led to countless drownings, this would adversely affect the City's water supply. London historian Hugh Phillips commented: 'Incredible as it may seem to-day, 1750 Londoners drank the Thames'.

Most of the leases fell in in the 1740s and the City architect George Dance prepared a scheme for rebuilding the houses and reducing their number, but the scheme found no takers. Bridge House Estates went ahead ordering ten new houses to replace the most ruinous buildings on the bridge. However, a slump in the property market resulted in only four being taken. Public opinion about inhabited bridges was also changing: 'nothing can be more ridiculous than [a bridge] encumber'd with houses from end to end', grumbled James Ralph, in complete contrast to his sixteenth-century antecedents. The houses, including the old gates, were finally removed in 1755-56. A wooden footbridge was erected for the use of pedestrians during the demolition of the houses, which caught fire. The last of the houses came down in 1762. Sir John Fielding, the magistrate and social reformer, voiced his opinion some twenty years

later: 'London Bridge is now rescued from the hideous deformity of old ruinous houses that so long rendered it a disgrace to the City, and a horror to the eyes of all curious spectators' (*A Brief Description of the Cities of London and Westminster*, 1776). But other problems remained: the foundations were slowly becoming unsound, aggravated by the widening of the central arch when the houses were removed from the bridge; and every year about fifty watermen lost their lives 'shooting the rapids created by the small arches' (above). Continues on p. 282.
(Phillips; Gerhold 2019; Barker & Jackson 1974)

(SB2) Church of St Olave, Tooley Street; continued from p. 136. Records

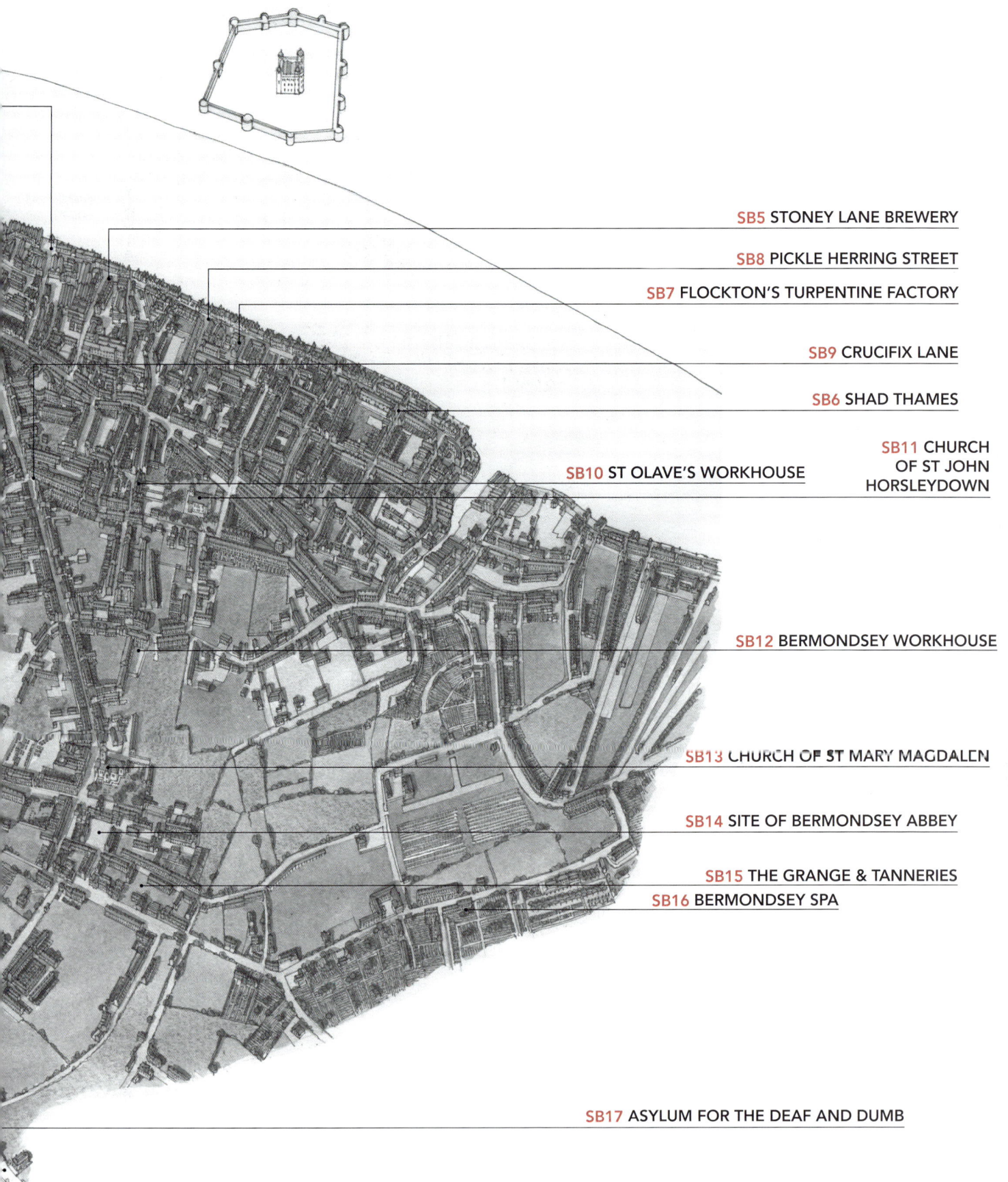

the house under review. (*Survey of London* 25; Cherry & Pevsner)

(SB19) Lock Hospital and Portland Place (now known as 1–19 Bartholomew Street); continued from p. 130. When leprosy, the original purpose of the Lock Hospital, had waned, the Hospital was used as a centre for venereal diseases in the eighteenth century. By 1754, it was felt that both this institution and its companion in Kingsland Road should be abolished. It took a few more years but in 1760, both were closed. The buildings at the Lock were leased to William Hale in 1764, who restored them. The chapel and parlour survived into the early years of the nineteenth century. The freeholder – the Trustees of St Bartholomew's Hospital – decided to develop the land after the formation of Great Dover Street in 1814. It gave rise to Portland Place (on the site of Lock Hospital) and the Paragon.

After the creation of Great Dover Street and the closure of Lock Hospital, the Trustees of St Bartholomew's Hospital, the freeholders, decided to develop further this part of their estate. They formed a diagonal road running from Great Dover Street to the New Kent Road and had agreements with two developers for the building plots on either side of the road. Portland Terrace was built in 1818-19. Five houses with storage vaults, were erected on the south eastern side of the street – only two of them survive. (Rocque; Horwood 1813; *Survey of London* 25)

(SB20) County Gaol (2), Horsemonger Lane – see below

County Gaol (1) and House of Correction, Borough High Street stood next to Old King's Bench prison; since at least 1635 there had been regular complaints about the poor state of these facilities when they were based at the old White Lyon Inn (below and p. 131). But a brand-new gaol was completed in 1724 next to the Marshalsea, after a delay of around seventy years. Built by Edward Olliver of Newington, carpenter, it was ordered that two wells should be sunk in the yards. Throughout the eighteenth century it was known as the 'New Gaol' populated mostly by felons with a small number of debtors. The site was extremely cramped and when the House of Correction needed repairing in 1772 it was decided to erect a new one on a different site – close to the second King's Bench Prison in Great Suffolk Street

The White House, at 155 Old Kent Road, the house and office of the architect Michael Searles
(© The author, 2023)

Opposite:
Another charitable landmark for the South Bank: The Asylum for the Deaf and Dumb in the Old Kent Road. This 1813 print depicts another grand scheme which addresses society's under-privileged.
© London Metropolitan Archives (City of London)

Interior of the White Lyon prison in Borough High Street, watercolour. The artist, John Crowther, must have gained access to these disused rooms in 1887, when he recorded the prison room and another adjoining it.
© London Metropolitan Archives (City of London)

County Gaol in Horsemonger Lane, watercolour by T King, 1802. William Wynn Ryland was the last man to be executed at Tyburn in 1788 and John Badger of Camberwell Green the last man to be hanged at Kennington gallows. But public executions did not stop – they took place in prisons, Newgate for the north bank and Horsemonger Lane for the south. County Gaol had a 'spacious lead-flat' roof which lent itself to a sense of spectacle when the Surrey felons were hanged there.
(© London Metropolitan Archives (City of London)

(see p. 197). A 1791 Act enabled the County Justices to build a new County Gaol in Horsemonger Lane (County Gaol (2)) while the old building was sold to the Marshalsea who used it as an annex until it was abolished in 1842. When the Horsemonger Lane gaol was ready, prisoners were moved to the new prison from the House of Correction. The Horsemonger Lane prison (now Harper Road) was designed by George Gwilt the elder. See p. 288 for execution witnessed by Charles Dickens and Henry Mayhew's description of this prison in 1862.

(Rocque, labelled 'New Gaol'; Horwood 1799 – first site, labelled 'Borough Gaol'; Horwood 1813 – second site labelled 'Soap Manufactory'; *Survey of London* 25; Newman)

(SB21) Kent Street (now Tabard Street and the Old Kent Road); continued from p. 130. The paving of Kent Street up to Lock Hospital (1565) encouraged development along both sides of the road. John Strype's negative comments, in 1720 when he updated John Stow's *Survey of London*, described the street as 'ill Built, chiefly Inhabited by *Broom Men*, and *Mumpers*.' Soon, Strype's 'old sorry Timber Houses' turned into ghastly rookeries. After 1814, bypassing the problem, through-traffic was redirected to Great Dover Street. The section of road beyond the Lock Hospital started being known as Old Kent Road from the early years of the nineteenth century, soon after the arrival of New Kent Road – built under the Act of 1751. Continues on p. 289.
(Rocque; Horwood 1813; *Survey of London 25*)

(SB22) Church of St George-the-Martyr, Southwark; continued from p. 130. The church was enlarged in 1629 but by 1732 the building's poor condition, had been found 'dangerous for the Inhabitants of the Parish to attend the Worship of God therein'; so, a petition to allocate £6,000 from the funds of the Commissioners for the Building of Fifty New Churches, was authorized by Act of Parliament. The rebuilding of St George's was 'with Brick' and Portland stone after designs by John Price (1734–36). The clock in the steeple followed two years later, painted 'in as good and handsome a manner as the Clock at Greenwich Church'. It was made by George Clarke of Whitechapel for £90 in 1738.

Throughout the rest of the century, the impoverished rector, without a parsonage, was struggling to make ends meet, with frequent stays in the King's Bench prison for debts. An adequate salary did not materialise until 1809 when the next rector obtained an Act of Parliament which increased the amount from £125 to £400. Continues on p. 284. (Rocque; Horwood 1813; *Survey of London* 25)

(SB23) The old King's Bench Prison, Borough High Street; continued from p. 132. A plan in the National Archives, dated around 1660, was drawn up when the prison was run as a private concern by Sir John Lenthall between 1633 and 1668. By then it was one of the largest debtors' prisons with 393 inmates in 1653. The prison was based on a two-tier system, as was clear from the façade which had two entries: one labelled 'Commonside dore' for ordinary prisoners, the other 'Dore into the Lodge' or 'Master side' for prisoners who could afford to pay for privacy and comfort. The eastern side is labelled 'New Brick buildings with the Chappell'. The north range of houses had to be rebuilt after the 1689 fire. The arrangement prevailed until 1758 when the prison was moved to a new site in St George's Fields (see p. 276) and the old building demolished in 1761, therefore it is not shown in our reconstruction.
(Rocque; *Survey of London* 25;

Gerhold 2016 No 112)

(SB24) Marshalsea Prison, Borough High Street; continued from p. 132. The two-tier system favoured in the eighteenth century (see old King's Bench above) was also in evidence at Marshalsea, with its 'Master's side' and 'Common side'. The prison reformer John Howard in his ground-breaking book *The State of the Prisons in England and Wales* (1777) gave a vivid account of his visit there:

This prison is an old, irregular building (rather several buildings)

Church of St George-the-Martyr, Borough High Street. This etching, after G Shepherd, was first published in 1814.

(From Charles Clarke's *Architectura Ecclesiastica Londini*, 1820)

Portrait of Thomas Guy (1644–1724) by John Vanderbank. This oil painting was probably executed shortly before the sitter's death.
(Art Renewal Centre. Image in the public domain; Wikimedia Commons)

St Thomas' Hospital with its chapel. This early eighteenth-century print shows the layout of buildings around courts with the chapel on the right-hand side with its distinctive tower (still in existence).
(Wellcome Library no. 39271i.
© The Wellcome Library, London)

in a spacious yard. There are in the whole nearly sixty rooms, and yet only six of them now left for Common-side Debtors. Of the other rooms, – Five are let to a man who is not a prisoner: in one of them he keeps a chandler's shop; in two he lives with his family: the other two he lets to Prisoners. Four rooms, the *Oaks*, are for women. They are too few for the number; and the more modest women complain of the bad company, in which they are confined. There are above forty rooms for men on the Master's-side, in which are about sixty beds; yet many Prisoners have no beds or any place to sleep in other than the Chapel, or the Tap-room. The prison is too small and greatly out of repair. Little regard is shown to the late Act for white-washing and cleaning the rooms. No Infirmary. The yard is well supplied with water. In it the prisoners play at rackets, mississipi &c; and in a little back court, the Park, at skittles.

The Tap is let to a Prisoner in the Rules of the King's Bench Prison, this Prison being just within those Rules …

Mr Alnutt who was many years since a Prisoner here; had during his confinement, a large estate bequeathed to him. He learned sympathy by his sufferings; and left a £100 a year to release poor Debtors from hence. Many are cleared by it every year.

This account exemplifies the corruption of the prison system alongside the suffering of prisoners and the importance of philanthropy. But what sealed the fate of the first Marshalsea was its state of disrepair in 1799, duly acknowledged by the Government. It was decided to rebuild it a little further to the south, on the site of the White Lyon prison or Borough Gaol. The new prison opened in 1811 catering for two classes of prisoners – court martial Admiralty prisoners and debtors. This new facility proved relatively short-lived: it was abolished in 1842, by Act of Parliament. The Rocque and Horwood maps show the original site only.
(Rocque; Horwood 1813; *Survey of London* 25; John Howard, as cited)

(SB25) Guy's Hospital, St Thomas Street. Unlike St Thomas' Hospital which was a medieval religious foundation, the arrival of Guy's Hospital in Southwark marked a very different age. The population of London had nearly doubled in the eighteenth century and premature death had been ever present with various epidemics, but the State did not regard medical services as its responsibility. The names of new hospitals bear witness to new attitudes – while medieval foundations were named after saints (St Thomas, St Bartholomew) later foundations reflected the backing of individuals, singly or in groups. Guy's Hospital was named after Sir Thomas Guy (1644–1724). He had been a Governor and supporter of St Thomas' Hospital, and had observed the growing number of patients described as 'incurables' who were turned away from the busy hospital. He wished to set up an annexe nearby which would help the patients St Thomas's could not accommodate.

Thomas Guy was a successful publisher and bookseller based in the heart of the City, close to Mansion House. He lived frugally and while countless investors found themselves completely ruined by the so-called 'South Sea bubble', Guy was one of its rare winners, realising a profit of over £200,000. Work on the new hospital started in 1721 but Guy died four months prior to the opening of his hospital in 1725 (left).

Guy had purchased the leases of various plots within the hospital's 'close'; he eventually obtained a 1000 year lease from the Hospital Governors for land south of St Thomas' Hospital, at a yearly rent of £30. The entrance to the new hospital was not in St Thomas' Street but in Collingwood Street, the south side of the original block. The Hospital could cater for 400 patients and above, spread across twelve wards with wooden cubicles, cared for by two physicians, two surgeons, a chaplain, a matron and eleven nurses; there was also a bug catcher and from 1799, a dental surgeon. The design followed the internal courtyard layout found at St Thomas'. Just over twelve years later the trustees needed additional space and land was acquired on the north side up to St Thomas Street; the east wing which housed a committee room was built to a design by James Steer, the hospital surveyor, who also laid out the familiar courtyard. On completion of this work, the statue of Thomas Guy by Peter Scheemakers was moved from the internal courtyard to the middle of the new courtyard in 1739. The west wing was built between 1774 and 1780, designed by Richard Jupp.

Accommodation for the insane was planned from the start. A temporary structure was ready in 1728 but the hospital waited almost seventy years for a permanent building, designed by James Bevans and completed in 1797:

> The Guy's Lunatic House was the first hospital building in the British Isles, and possibly in the world, to follow the principle of the panopticon as proposed by the philosopher Jeremy Bentham in 1787. (R H S Mindham)

For hospitals, prisons, schools and factories Bentham proposed grouping buildings around an 'observation tower' which would enable wardens to observe without being observed.

The hospital acquired further land on the south side in the first decades of the nineteenth century, principally the Maze Pond estate in 1806. The hospital chapel, in the middle of the west wing, contains four important tombs in the crypt: those of Thomas Guy (for the monument in the chapel, installed in 1779, see pp. 519 ff); Charles Joye (died 1739), the treasurer of St Thomas and Guy's Hospitals; William Hunt from Petersham, a particularly generous benefactor (died 1829); Sir Astley Paston Cooper (died 1841), surgeon at Guy's from 1800. Continues on p. 288.
(Rocque; Horwood 1799; Horwood 1813, the 'Mad House' is labelled; *Survey of London* 22; Richard H S Mondham, 'The Lunatic House, Guy's Hospital, London, of 1797' in *British Journal of Psychiatry*, Vol. 211, Issue 1, July 2017)

(SB26) Southwark Compter, west of Mill Lane, moved from the High Street to Tooley Street in 1717. John Howard's book *The State of the Prisons in England and Wales* (1777) provides a description:

> This prison, in Tooley Street, … has, for Master's side Debtors – seven rooms. – For Common-side Debtors, a Room on the ground floor, for which Felons &c. are with them night and day; a long room upstairs, the *Rookery*; and a room over it, useless, because not secure. – The Women are in the Stone Kitchen, now divided into two rooms. Three of the Common-side rooms have barrack beds. Among the Debtors are many poor creatures from the Court of Conscience who lie there till their debts are paid. — There is a small court-yard; and a Chapel, but no Chaplain is appointed.
> The whole Prison is much out of repair, and ruinous. No Infirmary. No bedding or straw.

(Rocque, not labelled; Horwood 1813, labelled 'Borough Clink'; *Survey of London* 25; John Howard, as cited)

(SB27) Church of St Thomas, St Thomas Street; continued from p. 135. In 1697 the fabric of the church was in such poor condition that people were apparently afraid to go inside, so it was rebuilt between 1698 and 1702, after designs by Thomas Cartwright – Christopher Wren's master mason. At that time Wren was one of the Hospital's Governors and supporters, so he may have been consulted about this design. Cartwright had worked on three of Wren's City churches as well as the Royal Exchange. The houses on the east side of the church were built shortly after completing the church in the early years of the eighteenth century; they were for hospital staff and the church Minister. Continues on p. 288.
(Rocque; Horwood 1813; *VCH* 4; The Old Operating Theatre Museum guide)

(SB28) St Thomas' Hospital, Borough High Street; continued from p. 135. Sir Robert Clayton (1629–1707), a rich City merchant and President of the Hospital, conducted a campaign to rebuild these premises which were much decayed. By the early eighteenth century the Hospital had been transformed into an elegant and well-articulated complex of buildings and courtyards with men's wards on

218 LONDON'S SOUTH BANK

'Blue Boar Court formerly an Inn on the East side of the High Street' is how the artist, J C Buckler, described his wash drawing in 1827. Southwark's back alleys were intricate and their layout positively medieval – this has been identified as 'Boar's Head Place'. The historians Rendle and Norman explain: 'In 1720 the Boar's Head [inn] had dwindled into a court, 'but small', says Strype … The final clearance took place in 1830'.
© London Metropolitan Archives (City of London)

Opposite:
St Olave's School – with the Flemish burial ground in the foreground. This 1815 watercolour by R B Schnebbelie includes the square tower of St Olave's church in Tooley Street, with the Shot Tower which stood nearby. For schools overlooking burial grounds, see p. 461.
© London Metropolitan Archives (City of London)

the north side and women's wards on the south side. The entrance was on the High Street and St Thomas church straddled across St Thomas' Street and the hospital's second courtyard. Continues on p. 288.
(Rocque; Horwood 1813; *Survey of London* 23)

(SB29) **The Boar's Head**, on the east side of Borough High Street, the former property of Sir John Fastolf; continued from p. 134. Seventeenth-century leases and a plan dated 1684 show clearly that the two tenements with shops which made up the façade on Borough High Street were separate from the inn which was at the back and not visible from the street. The stable and stabling were arranged on the three sides of a courtyard. The room labelled 'kitchen' was probably the tap room. Next to it, a 'warehouse' had been used by 'market ffolkes … to lay baskets and other things in'. The inn was renovated after 1684 and the street facade changed. It would appear that the inn escaped the 1676 fire which destroyed so many inns in the High Street. By 1721 the inn had been divided into tenements. The building was pulled down when the old medieval bridge was pulled down and replaced by a new bridge in 1830.
(1542 map; Gerhold 2016, No 98)

(SB30) **St Olave's grammar school**, Tooley Street (south side); continued from p. 135. The school received a second royal charter from Charles II in 1676 which widened its remit to parish duties, including the relief of the poor, alongside those of an educational nature. R C Carrington, the school's historian noted:

> The social provisions of the second charter were almost unparalleled among grammar schools and were finally abolished as an anomaly in the second half of the 19th century.

Fees at St Olave's were abolished in 1757 and after 1798, only students living in the parish could attend. The school was based at Tooley Street until 1831 when it was demolished. Continues on p. 285.
(Horwood 1813 shows burial ground and adjacent school, unnamed; *VCH* 4; Rendle 1878; Carrington)

THE SOUTH BANK AROUND 1845

'THE HORROR AND THE ECSTASY'

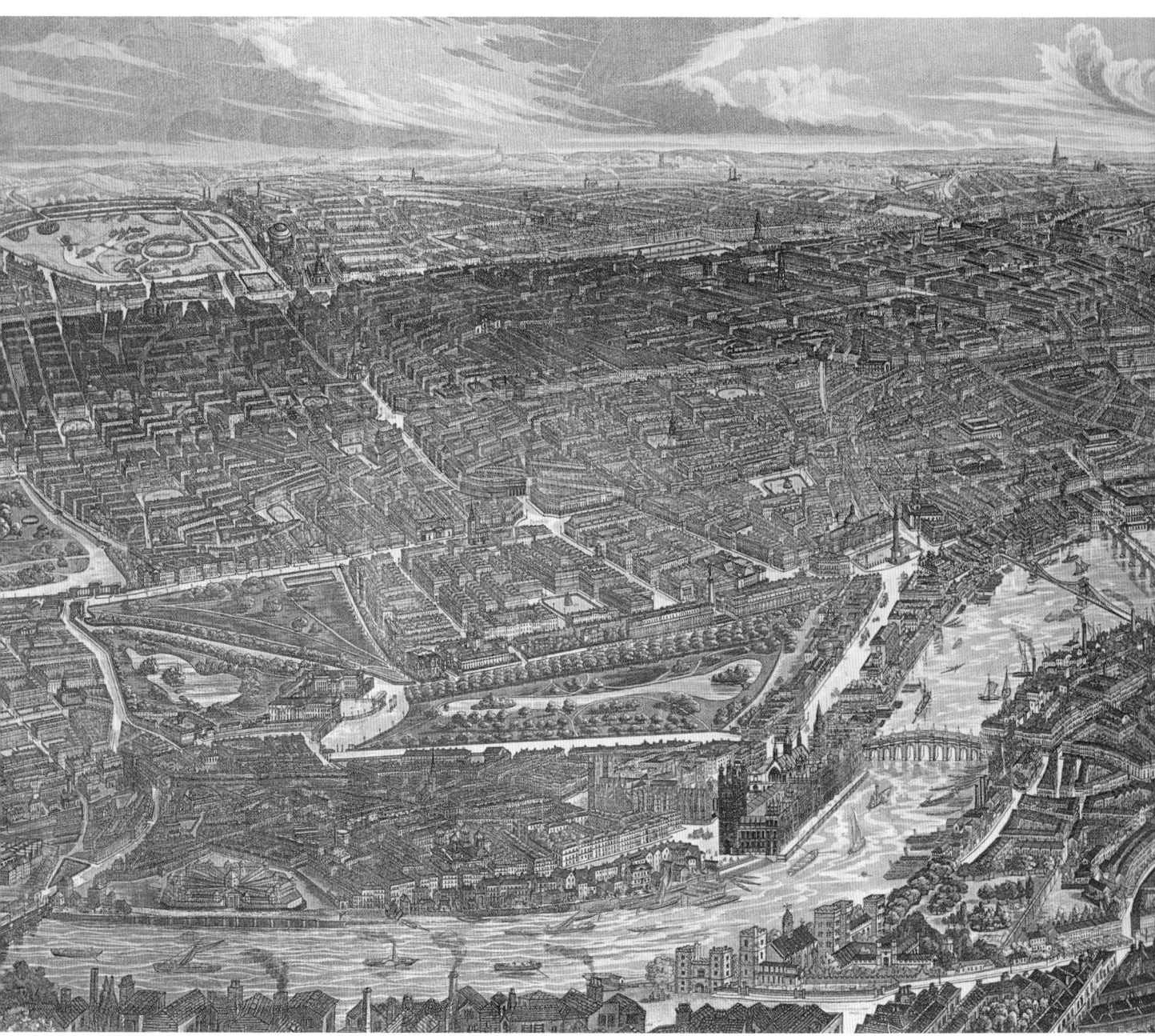

This detailed Victorian aquatint by J H Banks was first published in 1843 under the title 'A Cosmoramic View of London'. The version reproduced here dates from 1845 when the title had been changed to 'A Panoramic View of London'. It is exceptional for its rendition of the South Bank, though the late Ralph Hyde, the panorama expert, pointed out that the unusual technique, etching and aquatint on steel (rather than copper) may account for a 'not entirely successful' outcome.
© London Metropolitan Archives (City of London)

THE SOUTH BANK AROUND 1845

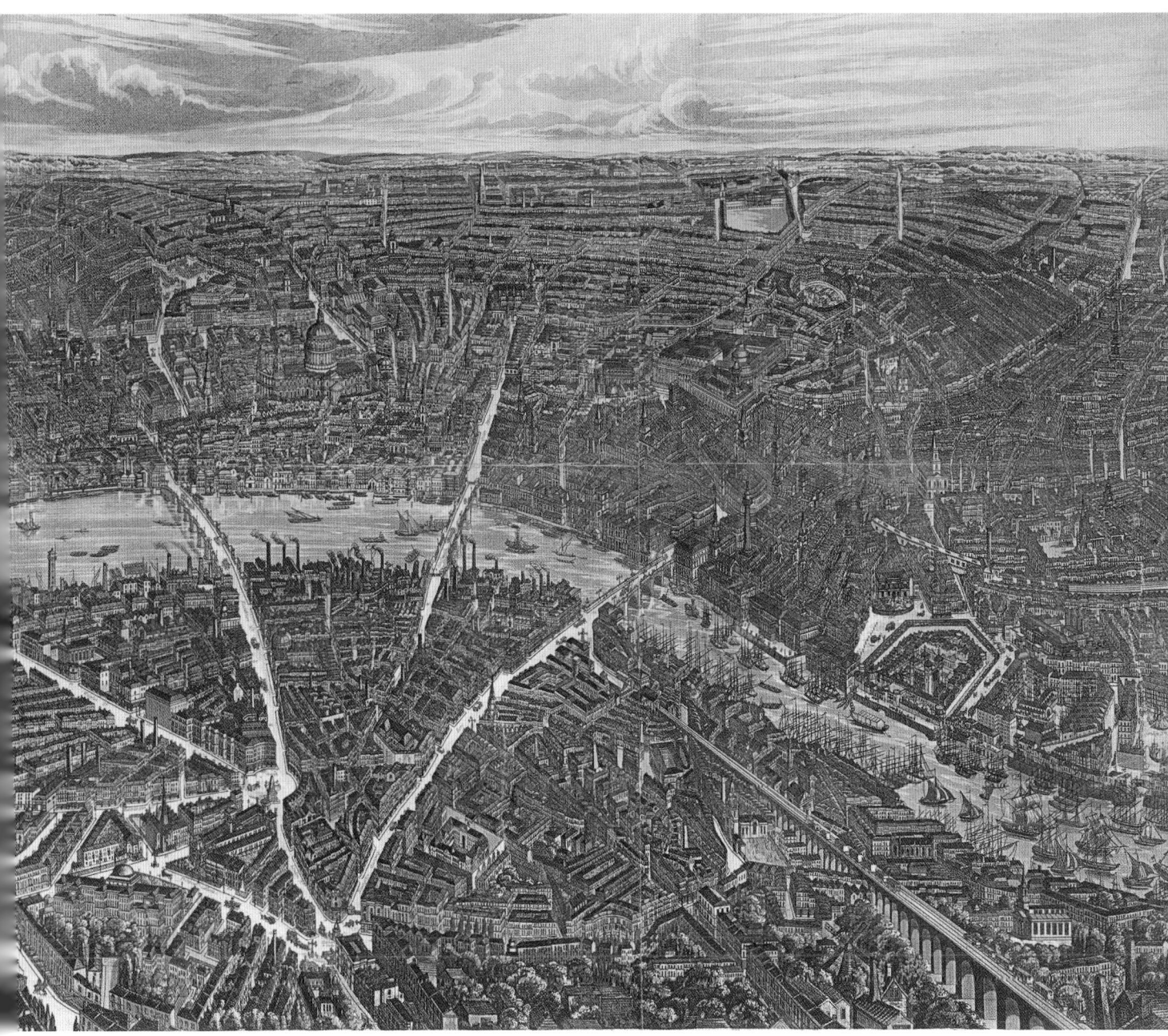

Jules Arnout, Panorama of London taken from the south bank and looking north showing the South Bank between Westminster Bridge and Waterloo Bridge. The limited view of the south bank shows it to be heavily industrialised, particularly when compared to the north bank, with Waterloo Bridge framed by two shot towers. There is an abundance of black smoke spewing out of tall chimneys. Lithograph published by Ernest Gambart between 1845 and 1850.

(© The Trustees of the British Museum)

We have seen something of the horror of nineteenth-century London and there is more to come. But we need to counterbalance starvation and ignorance and violence and filth with the boundless fun and ready laughter to be had in London's streets and parks, and the ecstasy derived from a whole world of entertainment in shows and exhibitions and on the stage. In some degree the horror and the ecstasy were inseparable bedfellows.

Jerry White, *London in the nineteenth century*, 2007

The 'horror and the ecstasy' are strange bedfellows – you may experience the latter from the height of a balloon or even the top of a building. The horror on the other hand belongs to street level and this chapter considers both viewpoints.

The Banks panorama

John Henry Banks's great panoramic view of the South Bank, published in 1845, is our primary guide. The viewpoint, high in the sky above the Elephant & Castle, allows a rare glimpse of the Victorian South Bank before the arrival of its two great centres of activity: Waterloo and

London Bridge Stations (though the London to Greenwich Railway was already in operation). This panorama is rarely reproduced – historians tend to favour the better known 'A Balloon View of London', taken from Hampstead, which shows the north bank in great detail and was published six years later, in 1851. The comparison between these two views is discussed in the last chapter.

Little is known about John Henry Banks (1816–1879). Born in Marylebone, he married Eliza Charlotte Jewell in 1837 and they had eleven children. He is known to have died in Battersea; these details come from the British Museum website (accessed on 17 November 2021). At exactly the same time, a French artist was also producing balloon views, not simply of London but of other European cities. His name was Jules Arnout (1814–1868?) and his panorama of London is reproduced here. Some of his prints were published by the great French art dealer Ernest Gambart (1814–1902) who lived in St John's Wood between the late 1850s and 1882. It seems a strange coincidence that both artists were publishing balloon views of London at around the same time. Might they have been sharing a balloon? Unfortunately, information about Jules Arnout is equally scarce, but he trained under his father Jean Baptiste who specialised in views of Paris; Jules would have been around twenty when he was working in London. Much later, in 1861, he contributed four lithographs to the glossy publication *Paris dans sa splendeur*, all aerial views.

The panorama is associated with a useful key which gives us a glimpse of what early Victorians regarded as significant landmarks. There are just over 400 entries for the whole of London and fifty-two for the South Bank. Some highlight extremely recent developments such as the appearance near Bethlehem Hospital of Southwark Cathedral or the

Above left:
This detail from 'Jacob's Island, Bermondsey' blends 'ecstasy and horror'. At first sight the drawing appears to be picturesque before slowly turning horrific as the viewer realises that the walls and the timber work are patched up, derelict and the water ghastly and polluted. Watercolour by James Lawson Stewart, 1887 – the full picture is reproduced on pp. 292–293.
(© Museum of London)

Above right:
Ewer Street, in the Mint slum district. The seventeenth-century timber houses once adorned a neighbourhood of fields and tenter-grounds, but by the mid nineteenth-century the houses were seriously dilapidated and overcrowded. The large building in the middle was a lodging house sheltering forty-three people. Watercolour by T H Shepherd, 1852
© London Metropolitan Archives
(City of London)

Leathermarket in Bermondsey. Others flag ancient structures such as the church of St Saviour or Lambeth Palace. Each landmark discreetly carries a number, reproduced in this text; *these entries are in red* to enable the reader to note which are contemporary with the panorama and which have been added for this book.

Major changes, rising concerns

Since 1770, the date of the previous bird's eye view reconstruction, four more bridges have been built – Southwark, Waterloo (originally called Strand Bridge), Hungerford Bridge and Vauxhall Bridge; even London Bridge is no longer 'Old London bridge' as it was replaced by a brand-new bridge in 1831. For each new bridge new roads had to be made. The proliferation of bridges was a sign that the city was becoming denser but also the sign of an age ready for major improvements. Bridge-building in the first half of the nineteenth century was eye-wateringly expensive, and bridge commissioners, despite the adoption of new cheaper materials had to be seriously very wealthy to become involved in these enterprises, as is shown by what happened with Vauxhall Bridge. John Rennie's estimate for a stone bridge had been £269,000. Eventually the commissioners felt they would not be able to afford such a high target. A new Act of Parliament enabled them to use different – cheaper – materials; they also changed the design and the designer. Superficially, contracts seemed to be considerably lower – £70,000/£80,000. But many years later, in 1878, an accountant of the Metropolitan Board of Works pored over the Company's books and worked out that the overall cost had in fact come to just under £300,000 – £175,432 for the bridge, £38,925 for approach roads, the rest spent on professional and legal fees alongside compensation money to the Battersea Bridge Company. Bridge companies remained responsible for the upkeep of bridges and approach roads until 1858 when local authorities took over responsibility. In 1877 The Metropolitan Board of Works bought Vauxhall Bridge and abolished tolls on bridges with compensation money going to the bridge companies.

Other major infrastructure improvements included the development of the docks, after decades of intolerable congestion in the Port, and the arrival of the railways – the very first one, the London and Greenwich railway was built on the South Bank. The presence of steam boats (since 1815) and omnibuses (since 1829) meant that the city was teeming with activity on land and water.

The population of Bermondsey and Southwark almost doubled between 1801 and 1841 – from 109,000 to 203,000. Alas, the explosion of population also led to the explosion of slums in Lambeth and Southwark – the most notorious were those of the Mint in Southwark, Jacob's Island in Bermondsey (previous page) and a little later Waterloo Station – from the 1850s. In 1842, three years before this panorama was published Edwin Chadwick (1800–1890) published his Report on the *Sanitary Conditions of the Labouring Classes*, while influential authors such as the architect George Godwin (1813–1888) described the physical reality of the slums in the popular magazine *The Builder*, which he edited between 1844 and 1883, and books such as *London Shadows* (1854). A much more recent contributor, the London historian JFC Phillips explored Ewer Street, when researching his *Shepherd's London* book (previous page), citing a Victorian newspaper article:

Ewer Street, during the intense hot weather of the last summer, presented at night a sickening and humiliating spectacle. The houses … are literally *alive with vermin*, and the wretched occupiers were actually driven out of doors … and at nightfall, for weeks and months, were to be seen sleeping huddled together on the doorsteps, and on the footways …

The voices of Chadwick, Godwin and Thomas Southwood Smith (1788–1861), a medical man and friend of Chadwick were not heard. The sanitation and health issues which appalled them would only be partially solved with the creation of the Metropolitan Board of Works in 1855. It was given enough power to make a difference and, after the disastrous 'Great Stink' of the Thames in 1858, it appointed Joseph William Bazalgette (1819–1891) to design and build a modern sewerage system. Its infrastructure is underground but its immediate effect was 'the transformation of the muddy and smelly river banks into the Embankments which provided foundations for the proud riverside architecture of the later C 19' according to Pevsner – Albert Embankment on the south side (1869) and Victoria Embankment on the north bank (1872).

The panorama predates all this and hides in its dense folds, the structural problems which troubled so many. The slums and housing problems were long lasting. 'Prince Albert's Model Lodge' – four cottage flats – presented by the Society for Improving the Condition of the Labouring Classes at the Great Exhibition of 1851 were designed by Henry Roberts and afterwards moved to the northern edge of Kennington Park where they still stand today. The Society had been funded by Prince Albert. Many argued that these homes could never be afforded by the very poorest. Yet the designs were later used in Stepney (Cowley Gardens), in Kensington (Fenelon Place) and in Hertford outside London. In the 1860s, key organisations were formed and provided partial improvements – the General Society for Improving the Dwellings of the Working Classes (1852), the Peabody Trust (1862) and Sydney Waterlow's Improved Industrial Dwellings Company (1863).

Please note:

- **In red:** these landmarks feature on the 'Key of Reference' to the panoramic view under the titles given. The numbers in brackets refer to the Key. Occasionally the same number has been used for two different landmarks, but this is pointed out in the text.
- St George's Fields and St George's Circus will be found under 'Bankside & Borough'. These are ordinarily split across the four divisions but have been placed there to assist the reader.

Sources

These have been placed in brackets under each entry (full references in bibliography). Alongside the maps, contemporary sources are used such as the relevant volumes of the *Survey of London*, the publications of Gibberd, Pevsner & Cherry, Hyde 1985, including websites:
database.theatrestrust.org.uk/resources/theatres/show/3182
www.arthurlloyd.co.uk

VAUXHALL AND LAMBETH

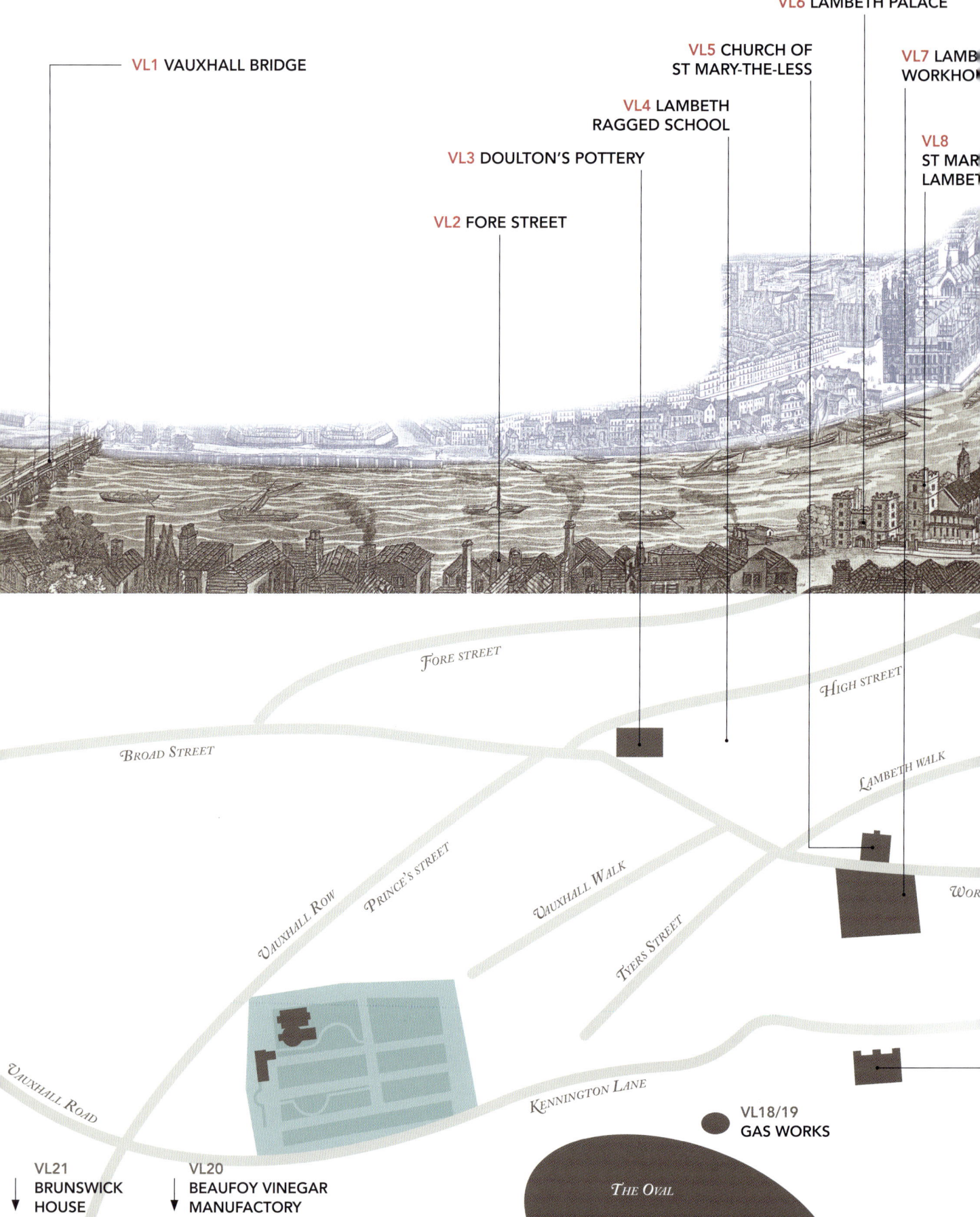

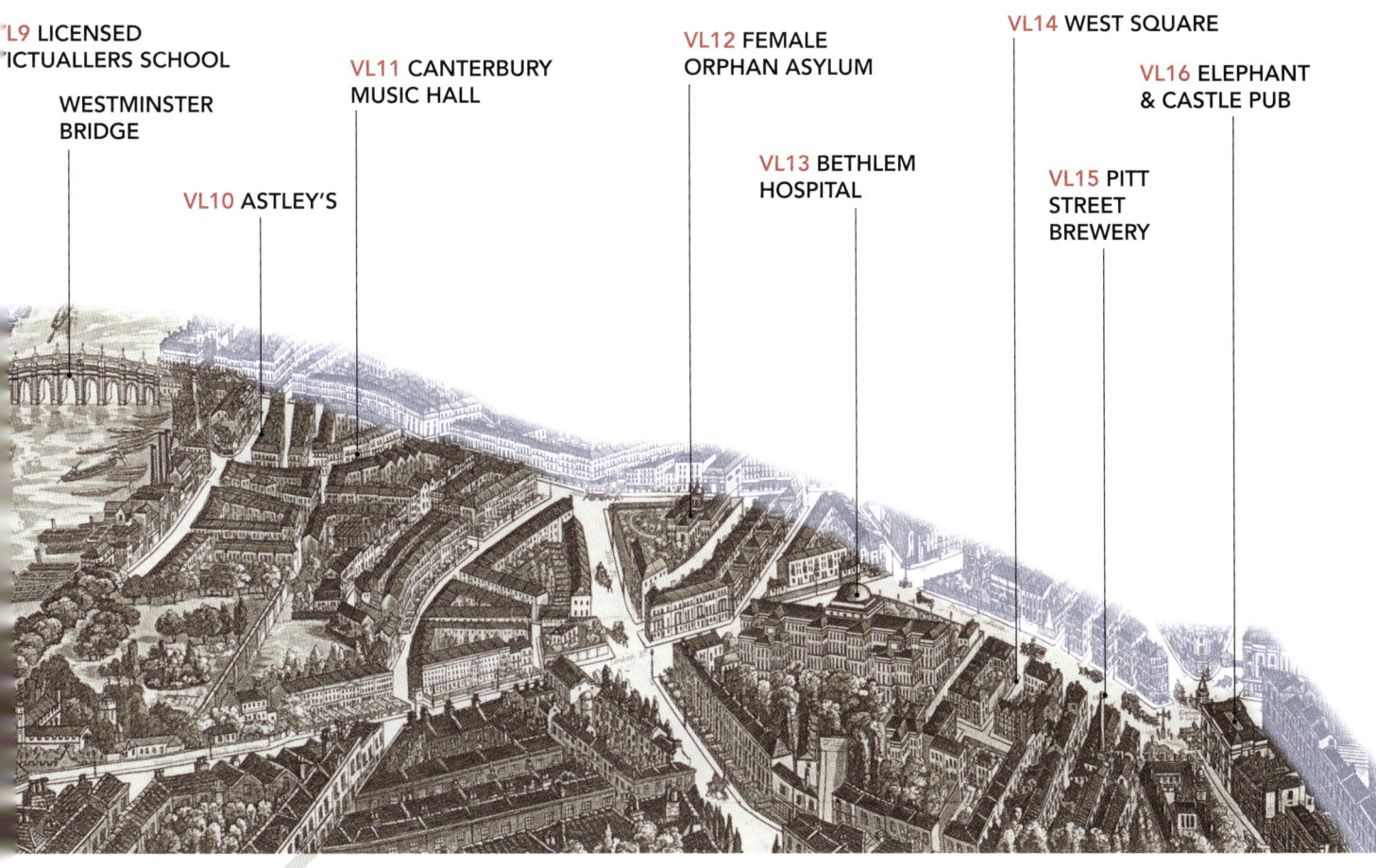

Fore Street disappeared with the building of the Albert Embankment in the late 1860s. This lithograph by Giles Firman Phillips was published around the time of Banks's mid-nineteenth-century Panorama.
©London Metropolitan Archive (City of London)

(VL1) 'Vauxhall Bridge and Road' (UV301), originally known as Regent's Bridge, 1816. There was no bridge crossing the Thames between Westminster Bridge (1745) and Battersea Bridge (1771), and this despite the cross-roads of major routes at Vauxhall, e.g. Kingston Road, South Lambeth Road, Kennington Lane and Prince's Street. Early plans envisaged a stone bridge and John Rennie provided a design with eleven arches. As had happened in Battersea, which downgraded from stone to wood for reasons of cost, Vauxhall had to downgrade from stone to iron.

The bridge was first discussed in 1806, an Act of Parliament was secured in 1809 and the foundation stone laid on 9 May 1811. At this point the Company realised that Rennie's estimate was almost certainly beyond its means and quickly obtained a new Act of Parliament (1812) to authorize the use of different building materials. By November of that year, a new design was ready, prepared by a naval architect and experienced engineer Sir Samuel Bentham. Doubts about the bridge's foundations led to Bentham's dismissal, and a new design, closely following Bentham's, was prepared by James Walker. The nine-arch toll bridge opened in the summer of 1816. It did not immediately bring prosperity to the bridge commissioners, as development was slow to follow. The bridge lasted until 1898 when it was demolished and eventually replaced by the present bridge in 1906, designed by Sir Alexander Binnie, the Council's Chief Engineer and ornamented with large scale statues by Alfred Drury (four on the east side) and Frederick Pomeroy (four on the west side).
(Bacon 1888; *Survey of London* 26)

(VL2) 'Fore Street, Lambeth' (F109). Fore Street and neighbouring courts and alleys were swept away with the building of the Albert Embankment (1866-70). This old, picturesque street ran parallel with the river south of Lambeth Palace. It stood in the heart of the area called Water Lambeth which was subject to flooding whenever there was a particularly high tide. It was also where many of the crafts and industries of Lambeth had been sited prior to the nineteenth century – in particular potteries and glass (left).
(Horwood 1813; *Survey of London* 23)

(VL3) Doulton's pottery, Lambeth.

In 1845, 'Doulton & Watts, potters and filter ma[nufacturers]' were based at 28 High Street, Lambeth, on the corner with William Street.

The pioneering pottery of John Dwight (c. 1637–1703), 'the father of English pottery', was originally set up in Fulham in the 1670s; in 1672 he obtained a fourteen-year patent for the manufacture of 'stone ware, vulgarly called Cologne ware'. Fulham-born John Doulton (1793–1873) did his apprenticeship there and became a very gifted thrower. Most of the Fulham production was utilitarian – blacking, beer and ink bottles, chemical vessels, spirit jars etc., with a sprinkle of relief jugs, sometimes called 'Toby' ware. Doulton left Fulham in 1812 to work at the small Union pottery at 14 Vauxhall Walk, almost opposite the entrance to Vauxhall Gardens. It was run by Martha Jones, widow, assisted by John Watts. Three years later John Doulton and John Watts, had become partners in Mrs Jones's business, producing utilitarian stoneware similar to that of the Fulham pottery. Mrs Jones withdrew from the partnership in 1820 and by 1826 Doulton & Watts were ready for larger premises – in Lambeth High Street, taking over an old pottery with a large garden. By the time the Banks panorama was made, they had built two new kilns, enlarged them twice, and acquired seven properties close to their premises. The company changed its name to Doulton & Co when Watts retired in 1853. By 1854 the pottery occupied the full length of Lambeth High Street on the east side, they employed 100 staff and used 1500 tons of coal and 1000 tons of clay a year.

'Stoneware was the mainstay product in the early 19th century, just as it had been in the late 17th century' sums up the 2005 MoLAS publication on Doulton. But in the 1830s Doulton & Watts had started manufacturing terracotta figures, as garden ornament, and in 1840 a new kiln was built dedicated to this work.

John Doulton's son, Henry (1820–1897), was keen to learn pottery and joined his father's firm at the tender age of fifteen (1835). He, too, was a gifted potter and a creative businessman who would later introduce many improvements: steam to drive the potters' wheels – well ahead of the competition –, the manufactory of terracotta for architecture and crucially, mastering the production of industrial ceramics. In 1846 he opened Henry Doulton & Co, a separate business on the west side of the High Street, which manufactured sanitary wares, drainpipes, insulators for the

The printed letter head of this invoice shows the exterior of Doulton & Watts pottery in Lambeth High Street in 1847. (Lambeth Archives)

This wood engraving comes from the celebrated *London A Pilgrimage* illustrated by Gustave Doré in 1872. The text which accompanied this image, by Blanchard Jerrold, is somewhat dismissive, encouraging visitors on their way to Vauxhall, 'to hasten' past the 'coarse Lambeth potteries on the Surrey side' – where Doulton and Watts and many others were based.
(Lambeth Archives)

telegraph and electrical industries and acid-resistant vessels for the chemical industry. James Stiff, at 39 Lambeth High Street on a two-acre site, was the only competition, with fourteen kilns and 200 staff.

Alongside industrial ware, which firmly underpinned Doulton's success, the firm produced decorative sculptural pieces though Doulton's artistic output developed later, from the 1860s and 1870s, when they collaborated with Lambeth School of Art (overleaf).
(Bacon 1888; *The Doulton Lambeth Wares*, Desmond Eyles, 2002; MoLAS 2005(B))

(VL4) Lambeth Ragged Schools in Newport Street. One of the best contemporary accounts of the origins of the schools comes from John Transwell's *Antiquities of Lambeth* published in 1858.: 'Mr Frederic Doulton, the honorary secretary to the committee, gave a sketch of the origin of the school' at its inauguration on 5 March 1851:

In 1845, a few of the destitute and degraded children of Lambeth were accustomed to assemble for instruction on sabbath evenings in a school-room in Palace-yard, near the Palace. In the following year, a committee was formed, at the instance of Lord Ashley [Earl of Shaftesbury], by some gentlemen in the neighbourhood, for affording the children instruction during the week. The school was shortly removed to one of the arches of the South-Western Railway Company, kindly granted for the purpose, and about that time excited the sympathy and support of the late Mrs Beaufoy; and on her death, her husband intimated his intention of perpetuating her memory, and fulfilling her benevolent wishes, by founding these schools. The building cost £10,000 and the munificent donor further set apart £4000 for the permanent

maintenance of the building. The schools accommodate about 800 children. There are two large classrooms, one for boys, and one for girls, there are also two reception-rooms for the training of the children on their first admission, and there are four smaller classrooms where young persons who show more than usual diligence, are taught in the higher branches of education.

The early school documents, kept at Lambeth Archives, show that Henry Beaufoy (1785–1851) started receiving contributions towards the project from John Doulton as early as 2 February 1847–.

Amongst Henry Beaufoy's papers at Lambeth Archives may be found a small selection of extraordinary drawings recording the site before and after the building of the school (overleaf).

Two-thirds of the school were demolished for improvements to the railway. What was left of the building has now become an art gallery – Beaconsfield Contemporary Arts. (Bacon 1888; *Survey of London 23*; Lambeth Archives; Tanswell)

(VL5) The Church of St Mary-the-Less on the north side of Prince's Road (now Black Prince Road) opened in 1828 when it was consecrated as a parochial chapel, attached to St Mary's Lambeth. It was designed by Francis Bedford (1784–1858), the architect of St John's Waterloo and three other South London churches, all in a Greek revival style. Unlike Bedford's other churches, St Mary-the-Less was in

William Strudwick (1834–1910) photographed Fore Street around 1866. The scene includes Doulton's Drainpipe Wharf, with Lambeth Bridge framing the composition on the left. Construction of the Albert Embankment is in progress in the foreground. The large, dark house next to Doulton's is Diamond Hall, the former home of the Bishop of Hereford.
(Lambeth Archives)

Overleaf:

These illustrations show the progress from an improvised Sunday school in one of the rooms of a dilapidated cottage to the brand new and elegant Ragged School which opened in Newport Street in 1851.

Above and right:

The small wood engraving comes from John Tanswell's *History of Lambeth*, and the other pictures from the Beaufoy papers at Lambeth Archives. Henry Beaufoy (1785–1851), the vinegar distiller based at Caron Place in South Lambeth, financed the building of a Ragged School in Newport Street (above); he commissioned the watercolours from the artist James Digman Wingfield – the photograph of the sepia drawing which shows the completed school is anonymous. The watercolours are exceptional in recording a totally non-picturesque London neighbourhood and carry the following caption:

> Site proposed for building the new Ragged School. N.E. view taken from the back of the houses in Broad Street Lambeth, showing on the left the Dust heap and sheds in the occupation of John Wright [nightman] with the three untenanted houses … on the right are the cottages and sheds from Adams' Row to Doughty Street. Drawn on the spot, July 3rd 1848 by J. D. Wingfield.

(Lambeth Archives)

a Gothic style, 'built in grey brick with stone dressings. It has a stone octagonal spirelet mounted on an open arcaded stage over the south gable. The interior … is simple in detail and presents a cheerful appearance following the recent redecorations'. The church was granted its own parish in 1842 and there, in 1854, started the future City and Guilds of London Art School. (*Survey of London* 23)

The Lambeth School of Art was founded at St Mary-the-Less in 1854. Churches have always encouraged the arts through special commissions: from stained glass to sculpted decoration, mural and panel paintings, mosaic, silver and more. But the small church of St Mary-the-Less did better than that: it set up an evening art class which grew, flourished and became Lambeth School of Art. This was done under the guidance of Robert Gregory, vicar there between 1846 and 1874. But the real impetus came from Brixton-born John C L Sparkes (1833–1907) who joined the school in 1857, fresh from graduation at the 'Normal Training School of Art' – the

Ancient Houses in Palace Yard.

future Royal College of Art. He was an outstanding educator and given the post of Principal the following year (later also becoming Principal of the future Royal College of Art). It was Sparkes who suggested a collaboration, technical and creative, with the neighbouring Doulton's pottery and also Farmer and Brindley, the stone masons in Westminster Bridge Road. Soon Henry Doulton became one the school's keenest supporters.

By 1860 the school had outgrown its premises and it was agreed that it could move next to St Peter's church In Vauxhall which was being planned by the architect John L Pearson as an ambitious complex of church, vicarage, school and orphanage. This development included the new art school, still standing in Oswald's Place but now converted into residential quarters. A small side door marked 'art school' is still in situ – a touching memento (overleaf).

Some of the greatest names in Victorian art trained there, e.g. George Frampton of 'Peter Pan' fame in Kensington Gardens, W Goscombe John whose slightly melodramatic memorial to Arthur Sullivan stands in Albert Embankment Gardens, Arthur Rackham, famous for his book illustrations, and the sculptor George Tinworth (see pp. 386–387).

(Bacon 1888; *Survey of London* 23; David Beevers, 'St Peter's Church, Vauxhall: A History – The Rev Robert Gregory the Parish Schools and the origin of St Peter's Church', 1991 published by St Peter's Heritage Centre and the Vauxhall Society https://vauxhallhistory.org/st-peters-vauxhall/)

(VL6) Lambeth Palace (L164) and **Lambeth Road (L165)**; continued from p. 157. It would be easy to assume, at a glance, that nothing had changed at the Palace. The overall medieval looking outline has remained, hiding in its midst new buildings in a medieval/Tudor style. The kitchen and stable blocks visible in Hollar's 'Prospect of London and Westminster taken from Lambeth' (p. 392) have been demolished to make way for a new structure designed by the architect Edward Blore. This was completed in 1833.

In January 1829 Archbishop William Howley had appointed Blore to survey the Palace and his report could not have been more damning – 'I find in almost every respect Lambeth Palace to be miserably deficient'. Blore proposed to demolish a large number of buildings, including the picturesque manor house, the cloister, the kitchens and old stable block which he replaced by a residential block and new services described

by Sir Walter Scott as 'in the best Gothic style'. Blore recorded in watercolour all the historic buildings he demolished and also moved the library into the Great Hall (overleaf).

Lambeth Palace suffered bomb damage in the Second World War but was gradually brought back to life through careful restoration, not completed until 1955.
(Horwood 1813; Bacon 1888; *Survey of London* 23; Huelin; Tatton-Brown)

(VL7) Lambeth workhouse, Workhouse Lane, now Black Prince Road; continued from p. 155.

Right:
Church of St Mary-the-Less in Prince's Road (now Black Prince Road). It stood opposite the workhouse and was remarkable for starting evening art classes, which soon gave birth to the Lambeth School of Art. Engraving after Robert Schnebbelie, published in the *Gentleman's Magazine* in 1831
© London Metropolitan Archives (City of London)

Below:
The new buildings for the Lambeth School of Art which had outgrown its original premises at the church of St Mary-the-Less in Prince's Road; they have survived, including the charming entrance to the art school in St Oswald's Place (bottom)..
Lithograph published in *The Illustrated London News*, 1861.
(© London Metropolitan Archives (City of London); © The author, 2023)

'The workhouse buildings form a long rectangle, divided into two completely enclosed squares, which contain the male and female departments respectively. On the whole, the situation might be called tolerably open, since there are streets on three sides of it … cottage gardens on the fourth, and on the south side an extensive view of the country over the tops of some low houses' (*The Lancet*, 4 November 1865).

The workings of the Lambeth workhouse came twice under scrutiny in the 1860s – first on 4 November 1865 when *The Lancet* visited this workhouse as part of a series of reports on London Workhouse Infirmaries; also in January 1866 when James Greenwood (1832–1927), a journalist at the *Pall Mall Gazette* and a pioneer of investigative journalism, created a stir by publishing 'A Night at the Workhouse'. He was the first to go under cover in pursuit of a reportage – pioneering the work of George Orwell's classic book *Down and Out in Paris and London*.

The reportage of James Greenwood, meticulous in detail, was in turn colourful, repelling and movingly compassionate: 'the little heaps of outcast humanity strewn about the floor'. He only spent one night at the workhouse, arriving around 9.00 p.m. and leaving the following morning shortly before 11.00 a.m., after the obligatory labour shift in exchange for shelter. The inmates spent the evening story-telling, song-singing, and playing games, including the 'swearing club'. Time seemed to go very slowly for the intrepid journalist:

> The church chimes audibly tolled 12. After this the noise gradually subsided, and it seemed as though everybody was going to sleep at last … In a little while all was quiet save for the flapping of the canvas curtain in the night breeze, the snoring, and the horrible, indescribable sound of impatient hands scratching skins that itched …'

The last person to join the workhouse was a man who had just attended (and enjoyed) a pantomime at the [Old] Vic: 'As the night wore on the silence was more and more irritated by the sound of coughing. This was one of the most distressing things in the whole adventure'. Recalling how he had fared so far James Greenwood continued:

> The conversation was horrible, the tales that were told more horrible still, and worse than either … was

that song, with its bestial chorus shouted from a dozen throats … while as for the coughing, to lie on the flagstones in what was nothing better than an open shed, and listen to that, hour after hour, chilled one's very heart with pity … coughing from vast hollow chests, coughing from little narrow ones … Though the youngest, the boys like Kay, were unquestionably amongst the most infamous of my comrades, to hear what cold and hunger and vice had done for them at 15 was almost enough to make a man cry.

The shed served the triple purpose of bed-chamber, workroom and breakfast-room. After breakfast everyone was expected to work a 'crank' shift, turning shafts to grind flour for the baker next door. A final comment from Greenwood: 'My companions had a discussion during the night as to the respective merits of the various workhouses, and the general verdict was that those of Tottenham and Poplar were the worst in London'.
(Bacon 1888, Higginbotham, Peter The workhouse http://www.workhouses.org.uk information retrieved 29 September 2020)

(VL8) 'St Mary's Lambeth' (S165); continued from p.157. What happened to Lambeth Palace also happened to the adjoining church of St Mary-at-Lambeth, around fifteen years after this panorama was published. The main body of the church was completely demolished and rebuilt; only the fourteenth century tower remained. The man in charge in 1851–52 was the architect Philip Charles Hardwick (1822–1892). He designed a number of large offices for the City of London; Hardwick went on to design the church of St John at Deptford in a gothic style (1854). At St Mary's the new nave and aisles needed to harmonise with the sixteenth-century tower, which set the tone for Hardwick's design. The *Survey of London* is of the opinion that 'little of the 14th century church can have survived in 1851, when the whole building, except the tower, was pulled down and the present church erected'. The church became redundant in 1972 and plans were afoot to demolish it. It was rescued by the Nicholsons and became the Garden Museum (see pp. 387 ff).
(Horwood 1813; Bacon 1888; *Survey of London* 23)

Before embarking on his large-scale demolition programme at Lambeth Palace, the architect Edward Blore recorded in meticulous detail all the buildings he planned to pull down – this is the South Front before and after Blore's work.
(Images courtesy of Lambeth Palace Archives)

Exterior view of the Licensed Victuallers School in Kennington Lane. Engraving by R Matthews, 1830s.
© London Metropolitan Archives (City of London)

Right:
Canterbury Music Hall, Upper Marsh, wood engraving published in *The Illustrated London News*, 1856
(Lambeth Archives)

(VL9) Licensed Victuallers School, Kennington Lane. The Society of Licensed Victuallers is the oldest charity for the drinking trade. It was set up in 1793 to help members of the trade in poverty or old age. Seven trustees representing the Friendly Society of Licensed Victuallers leased (1802), then purchased (1807), a large Georgian House, 'Kennington House', opposite Devonshire Street, from Sir Joseph Mawbey Junior (died 1817). They established a charity school which opened in January 1803, it flourished and was expanded – two adjoining houses were acquired.

These three Georgian houses acquired for the school at the beginning of the nineteenth century, must have proved unsuitable because the Society decided to demolish them to erect a brand-new school, designed by Henry Rose (above); its 1836 foundation stone specified 'for the Education, Clothing and Maintenance of the Orphans and other Destitute Children of Members of the Friendly Society of Licensed Victuallers'. There were 142 pupils in 1844.

The Licensed Victuallers' School held an annual outdoor fete at various venues, including Vauxhall Gardens in the 1840s. But on 24 June 1830, it was held in the grounds of the Eyre Arms in St John's Wood and duly recorded by E F Lambert in a highly detailed painting now in the collection of the Museum of London. It depicts the children in uniform and may portray a number of the supporters and administrators of this society.

This imposing building has survived and was recently converted into flats.
(Horwood 1813, labelled 'United Publicans Charity School'; Bacon 1888; *Survey of London 26*; Galinou & Hayes, Cat. No 74)

(VL10) 'Astley's Amphitheatre, Stangate Street, Westminster Bridge' (A & S23), continued from p. 159. Philip Astley, who had widened his interests to several European cities, had been replaced in Lambeth by Andrew Ducrow (1793–1842). Astley's Amphitheatre continued to flourish under Ducrow and his sons. It was loved by Charles Dickens who declared it to be 'delightful, splendid and surprising'. As with regular theatres, Astley's setbacks had been the result of several fires – two in the previous entry and again in 1841. This led to the breakdown and early death of Ducrow. The owner of another circus, William Batty (1801–1868), purchased the site and in 1843 opened the New Royal Amphitheatre of Arts. Ten years later it was let to William Cooke, who, like Batty, kept Londoners interested in its programmes. But when his departure in 1860 led to a downward trend, it was rescued by George Sanger in 1871 who purchased the site from Batty's widow and carried out considerable improvements. It lasted another twenty years but the embattled Sanger was having to fight both the LCC, a demanding licensing authority, and the ecclesiastical authorities who owned the land. He gave up in 1893 and the Amphitheatre (right) was immediately demolished. (Horwood 1813; Bacon 1888; Pugin & Rowlandson; *Survey of London* 23)

(VL11) The Canterbury Music Hall, which opened in Upper Marsh in 1852, had started life in the 'Canterbury Arms'. It acquired its hall in 1852 – 'the first specifically built for variety shows'. It could seat 700 and its manager, Charles Morton, would later be nicknamed 'the Father of the Halls'. This building is regarded by most music hall historians as the first purpose-built music-hall in London. According to William Walford (*Old and New London*, 1878) the 'singsong' had started in a room above the bar. This new hall barely lasted two years. Its success was such that Morton planned a bigger building, designed by Samuel Field; to save time and money, it was erected around the original hall, was partly opened in October 1854, fully opened the following January and further extended to include vestibule, grand staircase, smaller supper room and art gallery by 1858, the latter soon attracting the title of 'The Royal Academy over the water' (Walford). The model for the first Canterbury Hall (below) was Evans's famous supper rooms in Covent Garden – an exclusively male establishment offering traditional fare and music.

It later became a theatre, then a cinema, before it was destroyed in the Second World War.
(Barker & Jackson 2008, p. 133; William Walford, *Old and New London*, 1878; http://www.arthurlloyd.co.uk/canterbury.htm, accessed on 7 April 2022, Bomb Damage Maps)

(VL12) 'Female Orphan Asylum, Westminster Road' (F103) or 'Asylum for Female Orphans' or 'House of Refuge'; continued from p. 159. The 1758 institution was rebuilt in 1824 after designs prepared by L W Lloyd. The new building received an enthusiastic response from James Elmes in his *Metropolitan*

Improvements: or London in the Nineteenth Century (1827): 'one of the prettiest productions … choice example of the purest Grecian elegance'. This institution moved out of London in 1866 and the site was re-developed in two parts: in 1873 a manufactory of emery paper called Wellington Mills, was established, run by J Oakey & Sons. The rest of the site went in 1876 to the Surrey

'Astley's Amphitheatre'. The text which accompanies this aquatint is euphorically positive: 'The present theatre is … in some respects the most beautiful of any in this great metropolis … the stage … the largest in England … and extremely well adapted to the purpose for which it was built … grand spectacles and pantomines'.
(Rudolph Ackermann, *Microcosm of London*, with plates by Augustus Pugin and Thomas Rowlandson, 1808–10, Vol. I)

Chapel Centenary Fund, set up to commemorate the birth centenary of Rowland Hill, the first pastor of the Surrey Chapel in Blackfriars Road (see p. 184). They built Hawkstone Hall to replace the one they lost in Waterloo Road, compulsorily purchased by the Charing Cross Railway in 1867. They also built a chapel and other buildings.
(Horwood 1813; *Survey of London* 23; Pugin & Rowlandson)

(VL13) Bethlem Hospital (B31), Lambeth Road, was England's first mental institution and 'the oldest psychiatric hospital in Europe to be still in use', according to historian Patricia Allderidge. It was founded as a priory outside the City walls (ward of Bishopsgate without) in 1247 by Alderman and Sheriff Simon FitzMary. FitzMary had 'a special and single-minded devotion to the church of the glorious Virgin Mary at Bethlehem' (these words come from the original charter). The land at Bishopsgate, including all its buildings, was handed over to the Bishop of Bethlehem and his descendants 'to have and to hold in free, pure and perpetual alms'.

Bethlem or Bedlam as the institution became known, was therefore founded as a daughter house of the Church of the Nativity in Bethlehem.

The first reference to the priory as a 'hospital' dates from 1329. A few years later, in 1346, the master called on the City for help and it received it. The first evidence that the hospital catered for insane patients dates from the Royal Visitation of 1403, set up to investigate the institution's scandals and malpractices when it was in the hands of the porter Peter Taverner. This is confirmed a few decades later in a commonplace book compiled by William Gregory (Lord Mayor in 1451): 'And yn that place ben founde many men that ben fallyn owte of hyr wytte'. At the Reformation in 1547, Henry VIII granted the government of Bethlem to the City. A list of patients survives for the year 1598. The twenty patients are referred to as 'prisoners' reflecting the hospital's association with Bridewell – a workhouse turned prison.

In 1674 the hospital was described as 'old weake & ruinous'; it was also overcrowded. A new building was commissioned from Robert Hooke and the first custom-built hospital for the insane in England was ready in 1676 and was able to cater for 120 patients. Its enormously long and elegant façade was finely decorated and the landscaped Moorfields on its doorstep considerably enhanced the appearance of the whole. It soon became one of London's sights.

In 1799 a detailed survey of the building revealed its problematic condition – sinking in the absence of foundations and use of poor construction materials. By 1805 the east wing had had to be demolished and the search for a new site accelerated. In 1810 James Lewis won the competition for the design of the new hospital which would be sited in the now largely developed St George's Fields – a haven for 'hospitals' and other charitable institutions.

The design of 'New Bethlem' was strongly reminiscent of its predecessor, but was very austere; the facility opened in August 1815 and could accommodate 200 patients. It also now catered for the criminally

insane in two separate blocks at the back of the principal building: the State Criminal Lunatic Asylum, funded, maintained and controlled by the Home Office. It was replaced by Broadmoor in Berkshire in 1864, and these blocks demolished. Three patients in the criminal department shared the unusual desire to advance their delusional goals by making attempts on the life of George III: Margaret Nicholson in 1786 (forty-two years at Bedlam), John Frith in 1790 and James Hadfield in 1800 (above, forty-one years at Bedlam).

Barely fifteen years had passed when the hospital planned extensions and improvements which were carried out by Sydney Smirke, who became the hospital's architect. In 1845 he replaced James Lewis' flattened rotunda dome by one which made more of a statement. Patricia Allderidge was blunt when she described the mid-nineteenth century hospital as a 'bleak and comfortless place' despite the improvements.

The years of major reform came in the 1850s when the hospital was under the enlightened management of Dr Charles Hood (1852–62) and his steward G H Haydon (1853–89). Attention was paid to gardens, interior decoration and a variety of activities for patients.

The patient who clearly benefited from these developments was another would-be royal assassin: Edward Oxford who attempted to assassinate Queen Victoria in 1840, at the young age of eighteen. While incarcerated in the criminal unit he learnt several languages, the violin, chess, house painting, wood graining and knitting. He was transferred to Broadmoor in 1864 and freed in 1867 on the condition that he would emigrate. He changed his name to John Freeman and thrived in Melbourne. There was also the sad tale of A W Pugin, the architect of nearby Southwark Cathedral who suffered a serious mental breakdown in February 1852. He spent a short time at Bethlem

On 23 July 1826 James Hadfield, one of the criminally insane inmates, was so distressed at the accidental death of one of his pets, a squirrel named Jack, that he wrote an epitaph to Jack, beneath his illustration. This is a detail which includes a bird cage, unconnected to the story – perhaps its author's way of representing Bethlem as his home-cage. Hadfield was imprisoned in the State Criminal Lunatic Asylum at the back of the Bethlehem Hospital between 1814 and his death in 1841 – his punishment for attempting to assassinate George III at Drury Lane theatre in 1800.
(Bethlem Museum of the Mind)

Opposite:

When it first opened in 1815, the new Bethlehem Hospital was an austere building which imposed through its size rather than its minimal decoration: 'a small pumpkin-shaped cupola was all that crowned the squat central lantern' wrote the hospital's historian. This shows the 1848 design by Sydney Smirke, the hospital's architect in the 1840s – he replaced the small dome by a grander structure.
© London Metropolitan Archives (City of London)

Hospital before moving to a private facility. Unfortunately, he never recovered and died in September of that year, at the age of forty. But perhaps the most famous criminal inmate was the artist Richard Dadd who was committed for life after killing his father. His 'fairies' compositions filled with extraordinary detail, have become very familiar; he never stopped being an artist.

Bethlem slowly switched from a charitable hospital for the poor to an institution of middle class respectability, particularly after 1882 when a handful of paying patients were admitted, a move which signified a change of direction. (Horwood 1813; Bacon 1888; Allderidge)

(VL14) 'Telegraph, West Square, near Prospect Place' (T55*).
*This number has also been allocated to the Castle Brewery in nearby Pitt Street

In 1812 the Admiralty erected a telegraph tower at No 36 on the east side of West Square (above). The *Survey of London* explains: 'the shutter telegraph apparatus used to convey messages between Whitehall and New Cross, and thence to and from Chatham and Sheerness'. Banks' tower shows in fact the Castle Brewery in Pitt Street.
(*Survey of London* 25)

(VL15) 'Castle brewery, Pitt Street, Lambeth Road' (C55*).
*This number has also been allocated to the Telegraph Tower in nearby West Square

(VL16) 'Elephant and Castle, Newington' (E95). This is the pub which gave its name to the whole neighbourhood. According to Rendle and Norman, the ground on which it stood was, in 1658:

> a piece of waste, and granted for building purposes. It was indeed a charitable donation to the poor of Newington parish. The grant was renewed and confirmed in 1673, the premises and appurtenances being then described as lately built.

The lease was regularly renewed, including in 1797; the land acquired the name 'Elephant and Castle' in the second half of the eighteenth century – it is so named on Horwood's map of 1799. At the expiry of the 1797 lease in 1818, it was put up for auction of four lots and the pub clearly identified: 'the house called the Elephant and Castle, used as a public house, fell to Jane Fisher, for a term of 31 years, at an annual rent of £405 and an immediate outlay of £1200, the whole estate realising £623 a year'. The picture reproduced here (right) still carries the name of Jane Fisher across the outside of the famous coaching inn. (Rendle and Norman; Weinreb and Hibbert)

(VL17) **Church of St Mary Newington**, Newington Butts; continued from p. 163. The church's site was far from ideal, right against the road thus restricting the width of Newington Butts (later Kennington Park Road). In 1876 it was demolished to widen the road and a year later a clock tower was erected to mark the site of the demolished church. The old burial ground remained in situ. James Fowler's replacement church was built further south, on the east side of Kennington Park Road, outside the area under review.
(*Survey of London* 25)

(VL18) **South London Waterworks** at the Oval. The London Metropolitan Archive holds two fascinating documents in their picture collection: an early proposal by Ralph Dodd dated 1804 with a different arrangement to the one which was adopted – two reservoirs, one labelled 'Tide', the other 'Summit', were placed on either side of the Oval. The Tide reservoir was surrounded by a circle of semi-detached houses overlooking the water (see p. 381). The company was incorporated in 1805 and drew its water from the Effra at Vauxhall Creek which eventually turned out to be an unsatisfactory solution for the 'purity' of the water.

In 1827 the company built a new pumping station by Vauxhall bridge and these works were connected to the Kennington installation by a four-foot tunnel in 1832. The Company became Vauxhall Water Works in 1834. For a decade or so there was futile competition between this company

and the Southwark and Lambeth companies which was resolved when they were amalgamated in 1845. The Kennington works were dismantled and the site acquired by the Phoenix Gas Company in 1847.
(Horwood 1813; *The Water Supply of London* by the Metropolitan Water Board, 1961)

(VL19) The site occupied by the Gasholder Station at the Oval from 1847 had once been portrayed as a rural idyll when it was occupied by one of London's Waterworks Companies (see p. 382). By 1845 the former South London Waterworks Company, renamed the Vauxhall Waterworks Company (1834), had merged with the Southwark and Lambeth companies. The original site, no longer needed, was dismantled and sold to the Phoenix Gas Company.

The Waterworks moved to Hampton and Kennington acquired its first gasometer in 1847 – it was rebuilt in 1877–79 by Corbet Woodall and its capacity increased by Frank and George Livesey in 1891-2. Gasometer 1 is Grade II listed – 'the world's largest gasholder when built' in the words of Historic England. Four smaller gasometers joined the main structure in subsequent decades – No 3 was demolished around 1975 but Nos 2, 4 and 5 have survived and are listed locally. The station was decommissioned in 2014 and the site is being developed by Berkeley Homes, in collaboration with the Peabody Trust, into 'A Vibrant New Community with Apartments and Tesco Supermarket' said the sign when I photographed it in 2021 – 'Oval Village'. Gasometer 1 has been

This lively print focuses on the Elephant and Castle pub which gave its name to the neighbourhood. By 1826 when it was published, the place was already a great hub of communication. The viewpoint is St George's Road looking east towards New Kent Road with its soft line of trees; various horse drawn vehicles may be observed and the scene enlivened by street sellers with an oyster stall on the right. Aquatint by George Hunt after S J E Jones.
© London Metropolitan Archives (City of London)

Opposite:

Telegraph Tower at West Square in Southwark. Wash drawing by J C Buckler dated 1827.
© London Metropolitan Archives (City of London)

Right:

Map showing the location of Beaufoy Vinegar manufactory, south of Carroun House – the successor of Caron House and the estate on which part of Vauxhall Park and Fentiman Road are now sited – with The Lawn, which will later become Vauxhall Park.

(*Survey of London* 26/redrawn by Stephen Conlin)

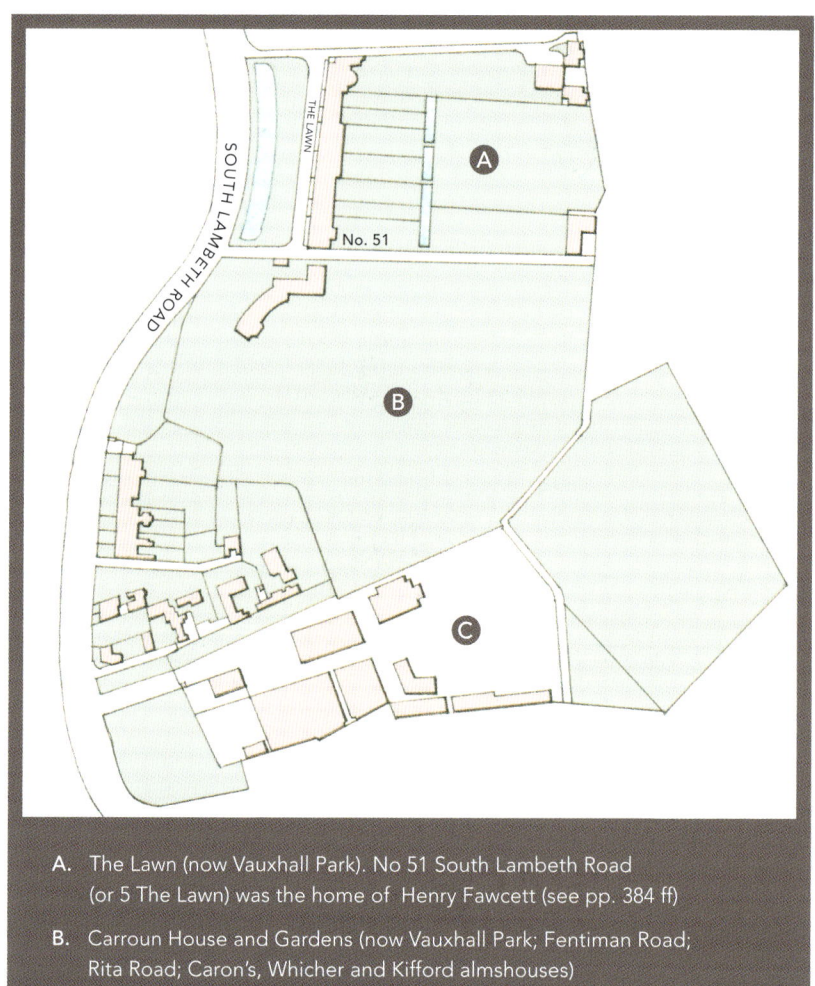

A. The Lawn (now Vauxhall Park). No 51 South Lambeth Road (or 5 The Lawn) was the home of Henry Fawcett (see pp. 384 ff)

B. Carroun House and Gardens (now Vauxhall Park; Fentiman Road; Rita Road; Caron's, Whicher and Kifford almshouses)

C. Beaufoy's Vinegar Works

Interior of Beaufoy's vinegar manufactory at South Lambeth where John Hanbury Beaufoy relocated his Waterloo operations. This wood engraving shows the sending-out warehouse and was published in the *Penny Magazine* in 1842.

(From George Dodd, *Days at the Factories*, 1843)

converted into flats.
(Bacon 1888; *Survey of London* 26; https://historicengland.org.uk/listing/the-list/list-entry/1427396?section=official-list-entry accessed 4 April 2022)

(VL20) Messrs Beaufoy vinegar manufactory; continued from p. 169. The Waterloo factory moved to 87 South Lambeth Road (Tradescant/Ashmole neighbourhood) from their site at Cuper's Garden, Waterloo, in 1810. The move was organised by John Hanbury Beaufoy after negotiations with the Duchy of Cornwall. The site of the new manufactory was on the former Caron estate; soon after the death of Sir Noel Caron, the House had reverted back to the Duchy of Cornwall and was demolished in 1683-84. The manufactory was ready in 1812, abandoning wine making to concentrate on the production of vinegar.
(LTS 1987; *Survey of London* 23; Gibberd)

(VL21) Brunswick House, 30 Wandsworth Road, Vauxhall; continued from p. 153. This large, three-storied Georgian house which had been split into two halves at the

end of the eighteenth century was primarily residential until 1845 when one half of it was acquired by the Western Gas Company which sold it to the London and South Western Railway Company in 1854. The second half followed the same pattern at later dates. The two halves were reunited by the railway company and became known as Brunswick House. The building was used as offices, with an institute and club for railway workers upstairs.

In 1994 the railway company sold the building to its association of workers who in turn sold it on in 2004. The new owner, Ferrous Augur, revitalised the dilapidated building which had also been used by squatters for a few years prior to its sale. He has turned it into the flagship store for his architectural salvage company LASSCO, furnishing it with a mass of fascinating historical objects which are for sale, and has turned the mansion into a venue for unusual, extravagant parties also including an interesting tenant – a foodie restaurant.
The building above is Grade II listed.
(*Survey of London* 26)

The eighteenth-century Brunswick House switched from residential to commercial premises in the Victorian period; it has survived to this day.
(© The author, 2022)

WATERLOO

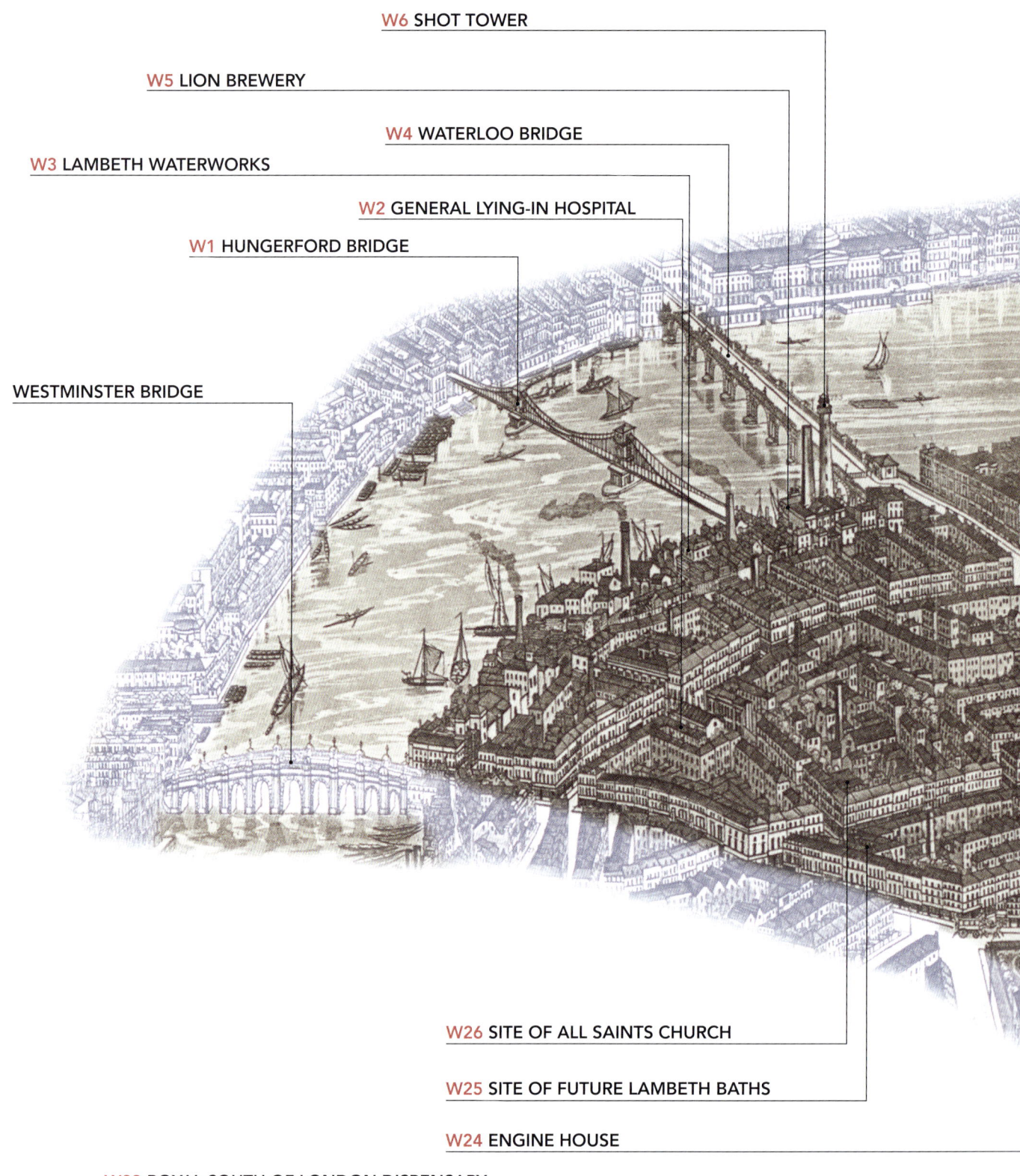

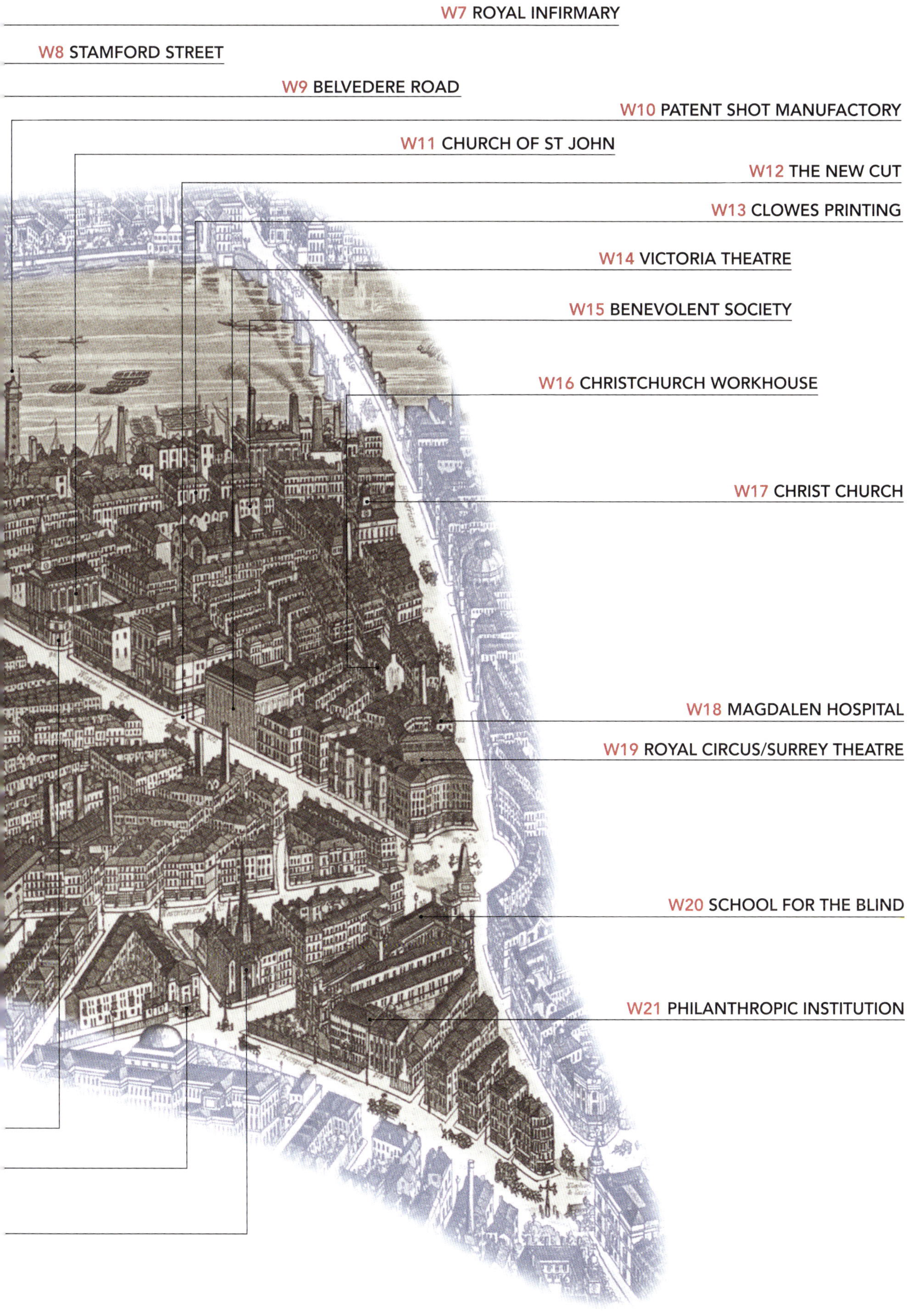

W7 ROYAL INFIRMARY
W8 STAMFORD STREET
W9 BELVEDERE ROAD
W10 PATENT SHOT MANUFACTORY
W11 CHURCH OF ST JOHN
W12 THE NEW CUT
W13 CLOWES PRINTING
W14 VICTORIA THEATRE
W15 BENEVOLENT SOCIETY
W16 CHRISTCHURCH WORKHOUSE
W17 CHRIST CHURCH
W18 MAGDALEN HOSPITAL
W19 ROYAL CIRCUS/SURREY THEATRE
W20 SCHOOL FOR THE BLIND
W21 PHILANTHROPIC INSTITUTION

(W1) 'Hungerford Market [on the north bank] and Foot-bridge' (H151). The market was an old institution but the footbridge – a suspension bridge designed by Sir Isambard Kingdom Brunel and called Hungerford or Charing Cross Bridge – was completed in 1845, the year of the panorama.

The market had been in existence since 1682, the brainchild of the last of the Hungerfords – Sir Edward, who had quickly acquired a reputation for extravagant spending and was hoping to emulate the success of Covent Garden market. It did not achieve the result he had hoped for and the site was sold three years later to Sir Christopher Wren and Sir Stephen Fox, who did not succeed in turning the market's fortune around. It was subsequently sold to the royal gardener Henry Wise (1718) and stayed in the Wise family until 1830 when it was acquired by the Hungerford Market Company. Determined to make their venture a success, they commissioned a new market building, designed by Charles Fowler, which opened in 1833. Despite fitting the new facility with many improvements, the market remained a commercial failure, even after the building of Hungerford Foot Bridge. The bridge's existence was secured by two Acts of Parliament, in 1836 and 1843 'with the intention of bringing more custom to the newly rebuilt Hungerford Market' the *Survey of London* explains. It was demolished in 1859, barely fourteen years into its life, as a result of the passing of the Charing Cross Railway Act, authorizing the construction of a railway link between Charing Cross, Waterloo and London Bridge (see pp. 414 ff). The chains and ironwork of the bridge sold for £5,000 and were used in the building of Clifton Suspension Bridge in Bristol. The new railway bridge which opened in 1864 included pedestrian access.
(*Survey of London* 23)

(W2) General Lying-in Hospital, York Road (G117); continues from p. 173. By the early 1820s the lease of the premises in Westminster Bridge Road had to be renewed but as the facilities probably needed improvements, the decision was taken to move the hospital to York Road. The new building, in an elegant classical style, was designed by Henry Harrison and opened in September 1828; the word 'Westminster' was dropped from its name. It has survived to this day – currently as an Ibis hotel.

An account book for 1800 was photographed by the LCC in 1951 (see London Picture Library).
(Horwood 23, *Survey of London* 23)

(W3) Lambeth Waterworks in Belvedere Road, on Waterloo riverfront next to the Lion Brewery. The Lambeth Water Works Company had been incorporated by Act of Parliament in 1785. The company installed their waterworks on part of the gardens of Belvidere (or Belvedere) House, a Queen Anne building which had briefly opened as an inn with pleasure garden between 1781 and 1785; not during the reign of Queen Anne as is sometimes stated. They were taken over by Lambeth waterworks.

Water was taken directly from the Thames to be supplied to local residents. Complaints about the quality of the water led to pumping from the middle of the Thames, not a long-term solution with heavily polluted water. In 1847 when pollution reached unacceptable levels, the company promoted a Bill in Parliament to enable them to build new facilities at Long Ditton, Surrey. The works were finally moved to Surbiton and Whitton in 1853.
(Horwood 1813; *Survey of London* 23; Wroth; Leigh; *The Water Supply of London* by the Metropolitan Water Board, 1961)

(W4) Waterloo Bridge was the fourth bridge to be erected in London after London Bridge, Westminster Bridge and Blackfriars Bridge. Unlike its predecessors, it was developed as a commercial venture and therefore became a toll bridge – its checkpoint is clearly visible on the panorama. Its promoters obtained an Act of Parliament as early as 1809 and John Rennie was appointed engineer. It took a further eight years before the bridge was officially opened (also see p. 413). The first stone was laid down on 11 October 1811 when the bridge had started life under a different name – Strand Bridge. Another Act of Parliament was obtained in 1816 to change its name to Waterloo Bridge, in honour of the great British victory against Napoleon – 'a lasting Record of the brilliant and decisive Victory achieved by His Majesty's Forces in conjunction with those of His Allies, on the Eighteenth Day of *June* One thousand eight hundred and fifteen'. The bridge opened on 18 June 1817 (illustrated p. 413).

The approaches to Waterloo Bridge, built on brick arches, were made between 1813 and 1816. Ten years later, Narrow Wall was widened and straightened and changed its name to Belvedere Road (1824–29).

To avoid the toll, many made the detour over either Westminster or Blackfriars Bridges. As a commercial venture the bridge lasted until 1877 when it was acquired by the Metropolitan Board of Works and freed from toll. It was demolished in 1936, amongst protests, and the present bridge erected between 1937 and 1942.
(*Survey of London* 23, Weinreb and Hibbert)

(W5) The Lion Brewery, Belvedere Road. In the mid-1830s, John Kershaw obtained a building lease from the Archbishop of Canterbury, the freeholder, which he assigned to James Goding who erected the Lion Brewery in 1836-7 (see p. 407 for picture). Designed by Francis Edwards, it was the first in a long line of hefty utilitarian buildings along

Waterloo Bridge, engraving by George Cooke after Edward Blore, 1829
© London Metropolitan Archives (City of London)

the riverfront, which would eventually disappear when the site was chosen for County Hall. Its famous lion, perched on top of the multi-storey building (riverside) has survived and has guarded the eastern entrance to Westminster Bridge since 1960. The lion was made in the workshop of Mrs Coade's Artificial Stone Manufactory (see p. 171). In 1853 the site of Belvedere House nearby was added to that of Goding's brewery and then renamed 'Lion Brewery'. With the benefit of hindsight Gibberd wrote: 'the most famous brewery [in Lambeth] was the [Red] Lion Brewery' but in 1845 when this panorama was made, the brewery which was singled out was the Castle brewery in Pitt Street between West Square and the Elephant & Castle (see below). Nowadays the Belvidere Brewery is frequently confused with the Lion Brewery (see p. 172 for the Belvidere brewery in Viner Street).

(Survey of London 23; Gibberd)

(W6) Shot Works (New), Waterloo Bridge (S253). This circular Shot Tower, at 63 Belvedere Road, was built for Thomas Maltby & Sons in 1826. In 1839, it was taken over by Walkers, Parker & Co who operated the other (square) Shot Tower east of Waterloo Bridge (see W10). They continued to operate it until 1949. Two years later, it was used as a landmark exhibit in the 1951 Festival of Britain. Hugh Casson who was Director of the Festival's architecture section described the process of shot towers in a 1991 recording, in most vivid terms: 'It's a factory chimney, with a staircase inside it, and you take hot lead up to the top, and you drop it down, in drops, and the drops don't make tears as you'd expect … they're absolutely perfect globes, and they're tiny … they're absolutely wee, like the shot you get inside a cartridge' (Sound Archive, British Library). The tower was finally

Royal Infirmary for Children. Engraving by Robert Grave after David Laing, 1823.
© London Metropolitan Archives (City of London)

89 and 91 Stamford Street on the corner of Coin Street – two early nineteenth-century houses, one with three storeys (partly hidden by the tree) the other, on the street corner, has four; these are amongst the earliest late Georgian buildings to have survived to this day.
(© The author, 2022)

pulled down in 1962 to make way for the Queen Elizabeth Hall.
(*Survey of London* 23)

(W7) 'Royal Infirmary, Waterloo Road' (R244) on the corner with Stamford Street (above). The Royal Universal Infirmary for Children was one of the earliest buildings in Waterloo Road, the successor of the Universal Dispensary for Sick and Indigent Children set up by Dr J Bunnell Davis in the City of London in 1816. This charitable organisation 'supported by voluntary subscription', was for women and children and moved to Lambeth from the City in 1823.

The charity was known to be chronically short of funds but they succeeded in opening a surgical ward in 1851. The charitable Hayles estate which would later merge with the Walcott estate, organised referrals of poor women. This establishment was almost entirely rebuilt in 1903–5 to designs by Messrs Waring and Nicholson, who were also responsible for the adjoining nurses' home which was ready in 1927. The glazed ceramics of the entrance porch were a gift from H Lewis Doulton in 1905.

Waterloo may have been associated with prostitution but within a stone's throw of each other two charitable institutions were set up to address the health of struggling women and children – the other, in York Road was the General Lying-in Hospital (see below).
(*Survey of London* 23)

(W8) 'Stamford Street' (S29) runs between Blackfriars Bridge Road and Waterloo Road. This road was built in stages – the eastern section, around 1790, while the western section or Upper Stamford Street was made in 1803. The road was finally connected to Waterloo Road in 1815. No 18 – formerly 27 and later 52 – was the house where the architect engineer John Rennie lived between 1794 and 1821 (see BB3, p. 185). His son, Sir John Rennie, was born there. It was demolished, along with other houses, in 1923 . The best survival of original late Georgian houses may be found at numbers 28–40 of similar date to Rennie's building but three storeys rather than four (right).

The Greek façade of the Unitarian Chapel in Upper Stamford Street was a striking landmark when it was first built in the 1820s and it continues to attract attention, with its projecting portico in the Doric style. It was built to accommodate two separate Unitarian congregations – those of Westminster and Southwark when both lost their buildings, the first one sold to finance the next move, the second because its lease ran out. However, after its flamboyant start the chapel's fortunes declined and in 1859 the congregation was so thin that closure was discussed. The arrival of the Rev. Robert Spears two years later changed everything and the building received a new lease of life, with extensions in 1882 and 1897. The site was acquired by the Nautical School in 1965 when the main body of the chapel was demolished to create a playground for the school children. The façade of the chapel was restored by the GLC and has survived, now lodged into an eight-storey

residential block (2010s) by Stafford-based architects Horsley Huber Architects Ltd.

The chapel, then and now, adjoined a school building originally built for 400 poor Irish children (Benevolent Society of St Patrick, founded in 1784), which was also erected in the 1820s. The LCC bought the building in 1921, to use it as the Central Building School – the future London School of Printing and Graphic Arts. Many alterations followed. The Nautical School – the current freeholders – was set up back in 1915 following the disaster of the Titanic (1912). Originally based at Rotherhithe, it moved several times but eventually purchased the site of school and chapel in 1965.
(Horwood 1813, unfinished; C & J Greenwood map of 1828; *Survey of London* 22 & 23; the London Nautical School website accessed on 15 May 2022)

(W9) Belvedere Road was created between 1824 and 1829 by widening and straightening the appropriate section of 'Narrow Wall' – the coastal road which is recorded on Rocque's mid-eighteenth-century map of London. New houses were built alongside this improved axis of circulation and the houses in College Street and Belvedere Crescent (the former Ragged Row) were built or rebuilt at this time. (Gibberd; *Survey of London* 23)

(W10) Patent Shot Manufactory. The square shot tower, the first known in Lambeth, was located on the east side of the (future) Waterloo Bridge (see p. 168 for picture); it was built around 1789 by Messrs Watts – William Watts invented the process in 1782 and built his first shot tower in Bristol in the same year. In his 1791 *Picturesque Views on the River Thames*, Samuel Ireland described it as 'a new structure … [which] cost near six thousand pounds, but cannot be considered as an object ornamental to the river Thames.' It was part of the Lambeth riverbank for almost a hundred and fifty years – between 1789 and 1937. Shortly after it was built, Ireland noted that the top was destroyed by fire but was repaired and put back into use. A second fire, in 1826, was recorded pictorially (overleaf). It was later joined by a second shot tower, on the west side of Waterloo bridge (see W6). In the Victorian period both towers came to be operated by Walkers, Parker & Company. This Shot Tower was in use until the last decade of the nineteenth century and was finally demolished in 1934.
(Horwood 1799; Rhinebeck; Horwood 1813; *Survey of London* 23)

(W11) 'St John's, Waterloo Road' (S96). To celebrate the end of the Napoleonic Wars, and also address the massive growth of the population, Parliament passed the Act for Building New Churches in 1818; it allocated a sum not exceeding one million pounds to build new churches throughout the country but 'more particularly in the Metropolis and its Vicinity'. The initial financial arrangement turned out to be insufficient – in 1822 the parish of Lambeth alone secured £64,000 to meet the cost of its four 'Waterloo churches': St Matthew's in Brixton, St Mark's in Kennington, St John's near Waterloo Bridge, and St Luke 's in West Norwood. All four churches were built between 1822 and 1824 each dedicated to one of the four Evangelists. Soon, a New Act was needed to expand the scheme and it was secured in 1824. This group of churches built between 1818 and 1856 are sometimes called Commissioners' churches or 'Waterloo churches' or 'Million Act churches'.

The land was purchased from the Archbishop of Canterbury and the building designed in a Greek revival style by Francis Bedford (encountered in the previous section, at the church of St Mary-the-Less). The exceptionally swampy conditions of the plot led to the involvement of John Rennie the Younger who recommended that the most appropriate type of foundation in this case would be oak piling under all the walls – the vast crypt being the fruit of this decision. The crypt is now impressive, cleared of all its coffins in a post-war restoration and after a complete facelift in 2021.

The church is a Grade II listed building. It was praised by James Elmes in his *Metropolitan Improvements* volume (1827) which described it as having 'some faults and many beauties'. He hated the steeple which he felt was 'the ugliest perhaps in London' – though others have praised it.
(*Survey of London* 23; Cherry & Pevsner)

(W12) The New Cut ran between Waterloo and Blackfriars Roads. Although The *Survey of London* states it was built around 1820, it must date from the late eighteenth century as it is shown – though not named – on

Fire at Messrs Watts' Shot Tower in Waterloo. Lithograph by William Day, 1826.
© London Metropolitan Archives (City of London)

Horwood's 1799 map and labelled 'The New Cut' on the 1813 updated version of this map. Graham Gibberd, who has looked into this in great detail, has dated it c. 1797. In volume six of his *Old and New London* (1878), Edward Walford describes the New Cut as being 'chiefly remarkable for the number of its brokers' shops, which line both sides of the way. The thoroughfare, on Sunday mornings, has somewhat the character of its rival near Aldgate, formerly called Petticoat Lane; and it provided a rich source of inspiration to Henry Mayhew for his sketches of *London Labour and the*

London Poor (above).'

The area north of the New Cut was developed by John Roupell while the south side was in the hands of Samuel Short.

A review of the Old Vic which appeared in the *Pall Mall Gazette* in May 1888 described the New Cut's context in these terms:

> The very road, wide and well-paved, forms a striking contrast to the small and narrow houses most of whose windows are brown and dull with a thick coat of dust. And high above all other houses, a very giant among pigmies, rises the 'Vic', its front windows lit up with many lights, its side walls gloomy and ugly as those of some strong old prison. But round no prison gates – except perhaps when the Bastille was stormed – have ever yet been seen such eager crowds, clamouring for admission' (cited in Coleman)

(Horwood 1799; Horwood 1813; *Survey of London* 23; Gibberd; Coleman)

(W13) William Clowes & Sons – 'the country's largest printing works for over a hundred years' wrote Graham Hibberd in 1992. William Clowes (1779–1847), who founded and developed this firm, was dead by the time Banks' panorama was made, but his sons had taken over the running of the large printing works off Stamford Street in Duke Street – where Coin Street housing now stands. The firm's first incarnation, a printing establishment at 20 Villiers Street on the north Bank was started by William Clowes in 1803. The workshop grew relatively quickly, moving to nearby Northumberland Court in 1807. There in 1824 Clowes installed the first steam-powered press for book printing in London. The landowner, the Duke of Northumberland, found the noise level unacceptable, took Clowes to court and won – though he had to pay compensation for Clowes's move to the south bank. The factory was bombed in 1940.

Clowes & Sons printed George Dodd's *Days at the Factories*, published in 1843. The present book makes several references to Dodd's volume (overleaf).
(*Survey of London* 23; Gibberd; Renier; W B Clownes, *Family Business*, 'Sunday June 5 12, a.m. The New Cut Lambeth'. The New Cut was the continuation of Lower Marsh east of Waterloo Road, both sections occupied by a thriving market; this led many to think of the New Cut 'as the line of communication or "cut" from Blackfriars to Westminster-road' explained *The Illustrated London News* (7 March 1846). The church's entrance on the left is that of All Saints (p. 264) which, according to *Kelly's 1859 Post Office Directory*, was next to a potato salesman, a butcher, a cooper, a grocer, the Artichoke pub, and a cheese monger, all technically in Lower Marsh. This print after Percy Cruikshank captures a lively population made up of members of the lower classes and the poor – for instance the woman and her children on the left with a porter (see headgear) to her right. *The Illustrated London News* came to the conclusion that it was 'a district of spiritual destitution if we may judge by the great extent of its Sunday trading'.
(Private Collection)

This engraving, from George Dodd's *Days at the Factories*, 1843, bears witness to the giant footsteps made in the world of printing in the first half of the nineteenth century. Simply described 'printing machine'. This is a detail from the print sprawled over two pages; it was meant to impress.

1803–1953, published by the firm in 1953)

(W14) 'Victoria Theatre, Waterloo Road' (UV202). The future Old Vic, which started as the Royal Coburg was renamed the Victoria Theatre in 1833 – 'one of the oldest theatres in London'. By the mid-nineteenth century this theatre had been in existence since 1816 when the three lessees – James Jones, James Dunn and J L Serres – had commissioned German architect Rudolph Cabanel to build a new theatre in the Cut, long before it had a railway station. However, crucially, the neighbourhood was about to be transformed by the arrival of Waterloo Bridge. Many theatre owners came and went, each struggling to settle and strike a balance between popular offerings and ones likely to attract a new and more discerning public. Between 1841 and 1856, the Victoria theatre was in the hands of the actor David W Osbaldiston and his glamorous partner, the much-loved actress Eliza Vincent. Osbaldiston had managed her career since 1834, the year he scandalised many by leaving job, wife and family to be with Eliza – a local girl who had found success at the Coburg theatre as a child actor. Osbaldiston had made his name at the Surrey Theatre which he left for the Coburg after he fell in love with Eliza. Although the pair managed to revive the fortunes of the Victoria which had been declining since 1835, their contribution was judged harshly as they bore the brunt of the commentators' scorn for instance in this extract from *Alton Locke* by Charles Kingsley:

> We were passing by the door of the Victoria Theatre … and the beggary and rascality of London were pouring in to hear their low amusement, from the neighbouring gin palaces and thieves' cellars. (cited in Rowell) Also see pp. 424–429).

(*Survey of London* 23; Rowell)

(W15) Benevolent Society, Stamford Street (B29). (right) The Benevolent Society of St Patrick was established in 1784 for educating and clothing children born of Irish parents, in or near London. Also see W8.
(*Survey of London* 23)

(W16) Christchurch workhouse, Marlborough Street; continued from p. 189. In 1834, just as the New Poor Law was coming into force, the workhouse on this site was rebuilt after designs by George Allen and it became the workhouse for the new St Saviour's union (though it continued to be called Christchurch workhouse). In 1834 the 'union' joined the parishes of Christchurch and St Saviour's. For a while there must have been two workhouses – Marlborough Street west of Blackfriars Road and St Saviour's east of Blackfriars Road (in Pepper Street, beyond Nelson Square) and both feature on Horwood's 1813 map. Before the 1860s, the Pepper Street workhouse had become a 'Hat and Cap Manufactory' and later still,

Benevolent Society, Stamford Street, watercolour by G Yates, 1825. This view also includes the portico of the Unitarian chapel on the left at the back
© London Metropolitan Archives (City of London)

the Headquarters of the London Fire Brigade; the former Christchurch workhouse was renamed 'St Saviour's Union Workhouse'.

In 1869, the parishes of Southwark, St George the Martyr and Newington St Mary were added to the St Saviour's Union, renamed Southwark Union in 1901. They took over the workhouse on Mint Street and Newington's workhouse on Westmoreland Road and redistributed inmates across the new network: Marlborough was for the infirm, Southwark site (Mint Street?) was for able-bodied men, the Newington site for able-bodied women. The detached infirmary at Newington was enlarged but by 1881 it must have been found inadequate and ground in East Dulwich was purchased to erect a new, larger infirmary: Southwark Union Infirmary in East Dulwich Grove which opened in April 1887.
(1872 Ordnance & Survey map; Bacon 1888 (23) where it is named 'St Saviour's'; Higginbotham, Peter The workhouse http://www.workhouses.org.uk information retrieved 29 September 2020)

(W17) 'Christ Church, Surrey Road' (C65); continued from p. 175. In 1816 and 1817 when the church sought to consolidate its finances and enlarge its churchyard through Acts of Parliament, this revealed some of the problems it was facing:

> there is a public Footway over and through the said Church Yard, leading from *Great Surrey Street* [Blackfriars Road] … to the South End of *Bennet Street*, and over the Graves in the said Church Yard, whereby … [it] is exposed to Inroads and Depredations, and the Graves therein routed up, trampled upon, and injured by idle and disorderly Persons, and by Dogs and Swine.

In 1819 the church, which up until that point had been reached via Bennet Street (= Rennie Street) on its north side, became directly connected to Blackfriars Road. The densely packed neighbourhood depicted on the panorama is misleading as there was and still is today a great deal of burial ground/open space around this church, which was destroyed in the last war and rebuilt in 1958. It is now Grade II listed, mainly due to its remarkable stained glass (by Frederick Walter Cole). Also see p. 328 for the substantial development which is currently being planned.
(Horwood 1813, *Survey of London* 22; Historic England listing website).

(W18) 'Magdalen Hospital, near the Obelisk' (M182); continued from p. 175. It opened in St George's Fields in 1772 where it raised considerable funds thanks to the excellent attendance at the Chapel services and the money collected. In Janet Weeks's booklet *Refuge for Fallen Women*, she observed the subsequent deterioration of the neighbourhood – factories and tenements – followed by a 'sharp drop in chapel collections'. In 1805 they had totalled £1984 but in 1857 the total was a mere £73. The Hospital moved to Streatham in 1868 and the site sold to Peabody estates who built 'Peabody Square' there.
(Janet Weeks, *Refuge for Fallen Women – A Brief History of the Magdalen Hospital at Streatham*, Streatham Society, undated)

(W19) The Surrey Theatre, St George's Circus; continued from p. 174. It opened in 1810 – part restoration of the burnt-out Royal Circus and part rebuilding. It opened with 'The Beggar's Opera', presumably John Gay's, described as a melodrama in three parts 'carefully compressed' with Act II, 'A Grand Masquerade', involving singing and dancing. The evening concluded with a new pantomime 'Q in the corner or Harlequin Schoolboy'. Doors opened at 5.30 p.m. and the show started at 6.30 p.m. The transformation of the Royal Circus into a theatre had been achieved by the actor-manager William Robert Elliston (1774–1831).

In 1806 Elliston had become the lessee, 'retiring' in 1814 but returning in 1827. One of his most memorable achievements was putting on a play by Douglas Jerrold (1803–1857), this writer's first success – *Black-eyed Susan* – premiered at the Surrey Theatre on 8 June 1829, the year Jerrold had quarrelled with and left the Royal Coburg theatre – the future Old Vic. The show ran for 150 performances and was also performed at Covent Garden.

The Surrey Theatre (right) was the first theatre to open on the South Bank since the golden years of Elizabethan theatre. Throughout its existence it was in competition with its Waterloo rival – the Royal Coburg, later the Royal Victoria Palace, renamed the Old Vic – sometimes swapping managers (e.g. George Davidge) or writers (e.g. Douglas Jerrold).

On 30 January 1865 a fire broke out in the ceiling during a performance. The audience were asked to leave quietly which they did and there was no loss of life; but the building burned to the ground. It was immediately rebuilt after designs by John Ellis and opened on Boxing Day 1865. It thrived under the ownership of George Conquest but lost its appeal after his death in 1901, was remodelled as a music hall, then a cinema (1920) before it finally closed in 1924 and was demolished ten years later.
(Rhinebeck; Horwood 1813 (24); *Survey of London* 25; http://www.arthurlloyd.co.uk/surrey.htm)

(W20) Blind School, Lambeth Road. The School for the Indigent Blind stood on the south east side of St George' Circus overlooking Mylne's obelisk. The first institution of its kind in London and one of four created in Britain on the model of a Parisian institution. It was started in 1800 in the Long Room of the Dog and Duck in Lambeth Road with just fifteen pupils. In 1801 the school took over the tea gardens' lease – building and gardens – soon teaching fifty two children (thirty five male and seventeen female). When the lease was near expiry the school took a lease from the City Corporation for a plot just north of the Philanthropic Society. A new school was erected to the design of George Tappen in 1811–12. As the building was found to encroach on the Circus, it was very nearly demolished until a compromise was reached. The school bought the freehold of the plot in 1832. As the school kept on growing (112 pupils in 1833) it became necessary to expand plot and building – a new piece of land was leased from the City Corporation and a new wing added to designs by Jon Newman in 1835-38. The Banks panorama shows the school in its extended form. The teaching focused on crafts such as mat and basket making, knitting. The site was compulsorily purchased by the Baker Street and Waterloo Railway and the school moved to Leatherhead in Surrey in 1901.
(*Survey of London* 25)

(W21) Philanthropic Institution, Chapel and School, Lambeth Road (P219). This Society was incorporated by Act of Parliament in 1806 'to give a good education, with the means of acquiring an honest livelihood, to

When the Royal Circus burnt down in 1810, it was replaced by the Surrey theatre, here both recorded in watercolour. The first, anonymous, must predate 1810, the other by T H Shepherd dates from around 1835.
© London Metropolitan Archives (City of London)

some, who must otherwise set out in life under circumstances of peculiar disadvantage'.

The children taken under the care of this society are either the offspring of convicted felons or such as have themselves been engaged in criminal practices … They are seldom taken younger than eight or nine, or older than twelve … The Society has, for the children under its care, an House at Bermondsey called The Reform, and a manufactory in St George's Fields for the boys; and a spacious building, adjoining to the manufactory, for the girls … all intercourse between them and the

Philanthropic School at St George's Circus: 'Manufactory for Bookbinders, Tailors, Shoemakers &c.' and 'Shoemakers School in the Philanthropic Society's Manufactory'. Watercolours by G Yates, dated 1825.
© London Metropolitan Archives (City of London)

boys is effectually prevented by a wall of considerable height.

The Society had started in 1788, in a small house at Cambridge Heath on the north side of the river. In 1793 the lease of a piece of land in St George's Fields was obtained and there they built workshops and houses; additional leases followed in 1805 and 1811 before the land was finally purchased. The large manufactory in St George's Fields could accommodate 122 boys; there many trades could be learnt (printing, copper-plate printing, shoe-making, tailor's work, rope-making, twine-spinning), with another building next to it for forty-nine girls who were expected to make their and the boys' clothes, and also wash and mend for the manufactory. The large chapel with its entrance on St George's Road, opened in 1806 – its collections providing a welcome source of funds alongside membership fees, donations and money from the sale of the children's work.

Around the time the Banks panorama was made, in 1848, the Society was struggling financially and it obtained parliamentary permission to sell or rent their premises to move out of London – to Redhill in Surrey where it set up a farm school. (Horwood 1813; *Survey of London* 25; Pugin and Rowlandson)

(W22) Catholic New Church, St George's Fields (C56). Sited across the road from the Bethlehem Hospital, St George's Cathedral was designed by A W Pugin, who in 1834 converted to Roman Catholicism; it is around that time that the project of a large Catholic church was mooted by Father Doyle whose congregation at the London Road chapel had completely outgrown the 1793 building. Pugin had made his name working alongside Charles Barry at the Palace of Westminster. He was also regarded as the most prominent expert in Gothic architecture after the publication of his book *Contrasts* in 1836.

Pugin's design for a church and other facilities was chosen at the 1839 Competition – the church to seat 2500 on the ground floor, plus a house for the clergy, a school for boys (300) and girls (200) would all be 'in the style of of the time of Edward III'. Pugin's design for the church was based on that of the church of St Austin Friars near Old Broad Street. By 1843, the church was well advanced, but completion of the ensemble delayed through lack of funds. It was not formally opened until 4 July

1848 when public feeling towards Catholicism was still antagonistic as was clear from *The Times*'s account of the consecration:

> The elevation of the pointed Gothic arches on which the roof rests seems too low for a sublime effect and too high for elegance of detail. The side windows, which are six in number on each side, have not yet been filled with stained glass and their blank and cheerless appearance no doubt added to the naked and hungry aspect of the aisles.

The *Survey of London*'s summary of the project is worth quoting:

> It is now generally agreed that St George's was not one of the best products of Pugin's restless genius, but in view of its size, the limitations imposed by the site and the small funds available, it was a remarkable achievement.

Pugin celebrated this 'achievement' by being the first to be married there (to his third wife) in 1848. The church suffered devastating damage during the Second World War but was sensitively reconstructed.
(*Survey of London* 25)

(W23) 'Royal South of London Dispensary [sic], Lambeth Road' (R245). This purpose-built dispensary which was ready in 1841, has survived to this day. It provided valuable services during the Victorian period but ran out of funds in 1917 and had to close. Bethlem Hospital, just across the road, acquired the building and it became the Hospital for Nervous Diseases until 1927 when funds ran out once again forcing it to close down. It became Elizabeth Baxter Hostel for Distressed Women and Girls from 1930. In its latest incarnation it is the School of Historical Dress, set up in 2012 and located on this site since 2016. It was responsible for the sensitive restoration of the building and for revealing the name in relief at the top of the façade.
(https://livinglondonhistory.com/52-lambeth-road-a-hidden-gem-with-an-amazing-story/)

(W24) Engine House, Waterloo Road (E96). This is a mysterious entry. The number has been placed next to a small building which is normally identified as the watch house – a small lodge in the south west corner of St John's burial ground. Why it was described as an 'Engine House' in this panorama is possibly a mistake. The watch house was erected in 1824 and finally demolished in 1932.
(*Survey of London* 23)

(W25) Lambeth Baths appeared a few years after this panorama was made. They opened in 1853, in response to developments in the previous decade. The Committee for Erecting and Promoting the Establishment of Baths and Wash Houses for the Labouring Classes was set up in October 1844 – this initiative of the Bishop of London and the Governor of the Bank of England was supported by 230 businessmen, philanthropists and churchmen. Only one 'Model Baths' made up of slipper baths and wash house was completed, in Whitechapel.

But a parallel scheme, led by the vicar at St Martin-in-the-Fields resulted in the Baths and Wash Houses Act of 1846 which empowered local authorities to borrow money to build affordable public baths with three levels of service: washhouses (laundering of cloth and linen); slipper baths (with clean towel included); open bathing baths (communal baths). The latter turned out to be unexpectedly popular, despite the potential difficulty of keeping the water clean.

Lambeth Baths (1853), designed by A H Ashpitel and John Whichcord, was built with private capital supplemented by charitable donations and was a very influential model, demonstrating the potential of large-scale pools and the popularity of swimming as a sport. Historian Simon Inglis explains: 'Lambeth had first

All Saints Church in Lower Marsh is thus described in *The Illustrated London News*: 'it is a neat design, in the Anglo-Norman style, with a Tower and Spire rising 160 feet and upwards of 100 feet from the body of the Church … the Tower and Spire being thus in line with the New Cut … It will accommodate 1200 persons; the seats in the main body of the Church being free, and those in the gallery are to be let.
(*The Illustrated London News*, 7 March 1846)

and second class pools measuring 122' and 133' respectively, and as a result became the capital's new hub of competitive swimming'. Lambeth pioneered the closing of pools during the cold months (November to March), hiring out the empty pools for sports and events: 'the public baths took their first steps on the road to becoming what we now call 'leisure centres'.
(Inglis).

(W26) Site of the Church of All Saints, off Lower Marsh. The church was designed by William Rogers and opened in 1846, seemingly too late to be included in the Banks' panorama; the parish of All Saints was formed a year later out of that of St John the Evangelist. The church was unusual with its tower standing apart from the main body of the church but linked to it via a colonnade or 'cloister'. It attracted praise from *The Builder* Magazine but scorn from *The Ecclesiologist* magazine which found it 'contemptible'. The tower was declared unsafe in 1878 and taken down. The whole was demolished in 1901 when Waterloo Station expanded once again. It had the dubious role of serving the Granby Street community – notorious for all manners of vice, including prostitution.

By the 1870s a school for boys and girls operated alongside the church of All Saints. When the church was demolished, the parish merged

with that of St Andrew (church by S S Teulon, built 1855). The latter's site was sold in 1956 and a new church erected – the church of Waterloo St Andrew with St Thomas in Short Street (rebuilt 2005).

The All Saints neighbourhood features in the novel by Michael Sadleir – *Forlorn Sunset* (discussed on p. 409) – who described the way in which the church was likely to operate within its vice-ridden context. A group of wealthy people living in well-appointed houses across the water in places such as Belgravia were only too aware of the massive gap between their situation and that of slum-dwellers over in south London.

So 'they would select a vicar in some poor district, make a pet of him and provide him with funds – often very large funds – for the alleviation of distress.' The use of funds was rarely supervised turning the vicarage into 'a Mecca for vagabonds' and the vicar into 'a doleful distributor'. All Saints church, alas, was a notorious case in point: 'its reputation for bread, circuses and ceremonial invited exploitation by wastrels from miles around'.
(O/S map 1872; Bacon 1888; *VCH 4*; *Survey of London* 23; Sadleir; Vauxhall History website, accessed on 3 October 2022)

Detail from 'London from the South Side of the Thames' by Thomas Sulman who specialized in balloon views; wood engraving, 1861. Eighteen years separate this view from the Banks' panorama we have discussed in this chapter. Waterloo Bridge is top right with Hungerford Bridge to its left.
(From Supplement to the *Illustrated London News* of 9 February 1861)

From the same panorama, the detail on the far left shows Doulton's Lambeth pottery on Lambeth High Street.

BOROUGH AND BANKSIDE

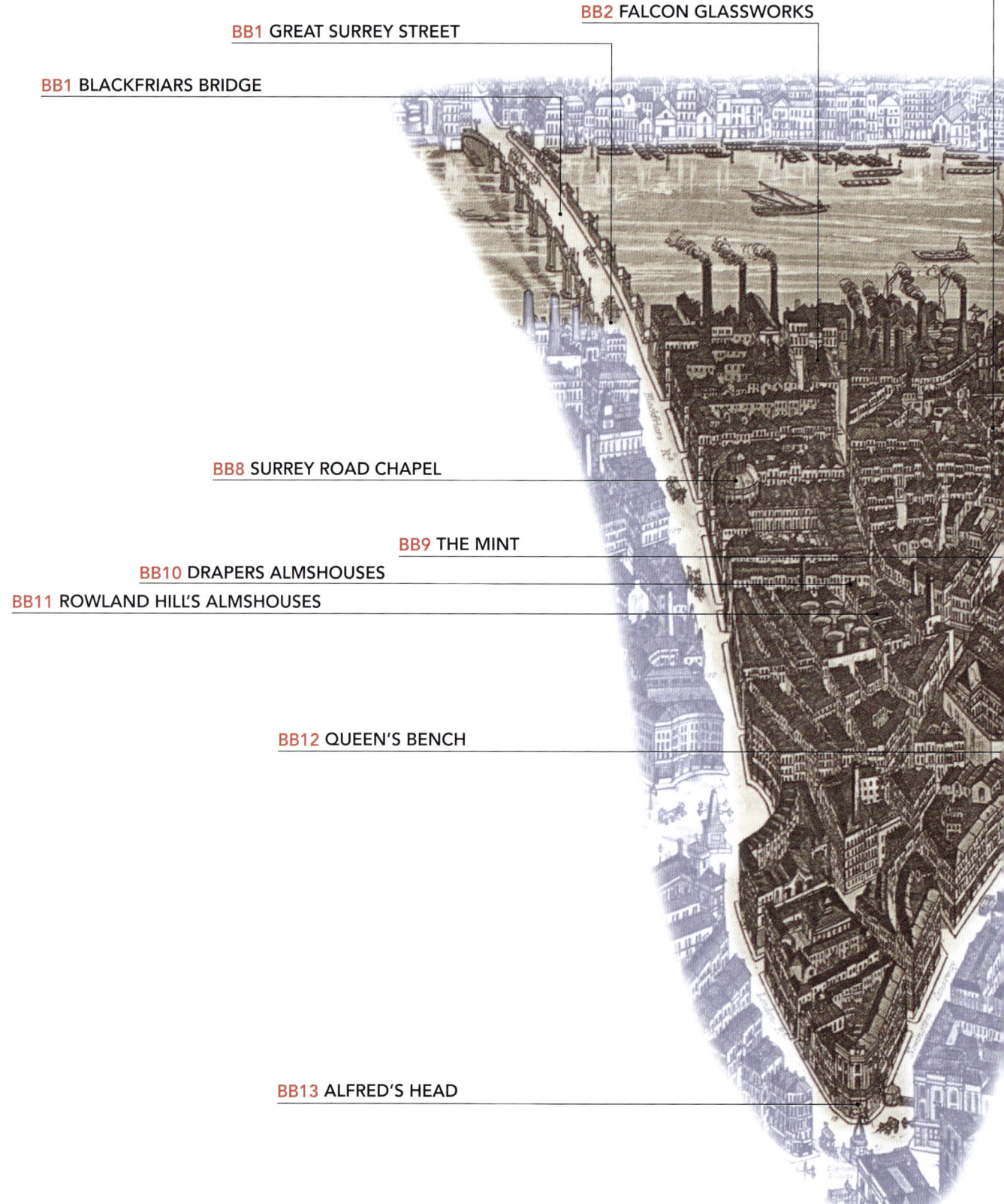

BB4 BARCLAY PERKINS BREWERY

BB5 SOUTHWARK BRIDGE

BB6 ST SAVIOUR'S CHURCH

BB7 TOWN HALL

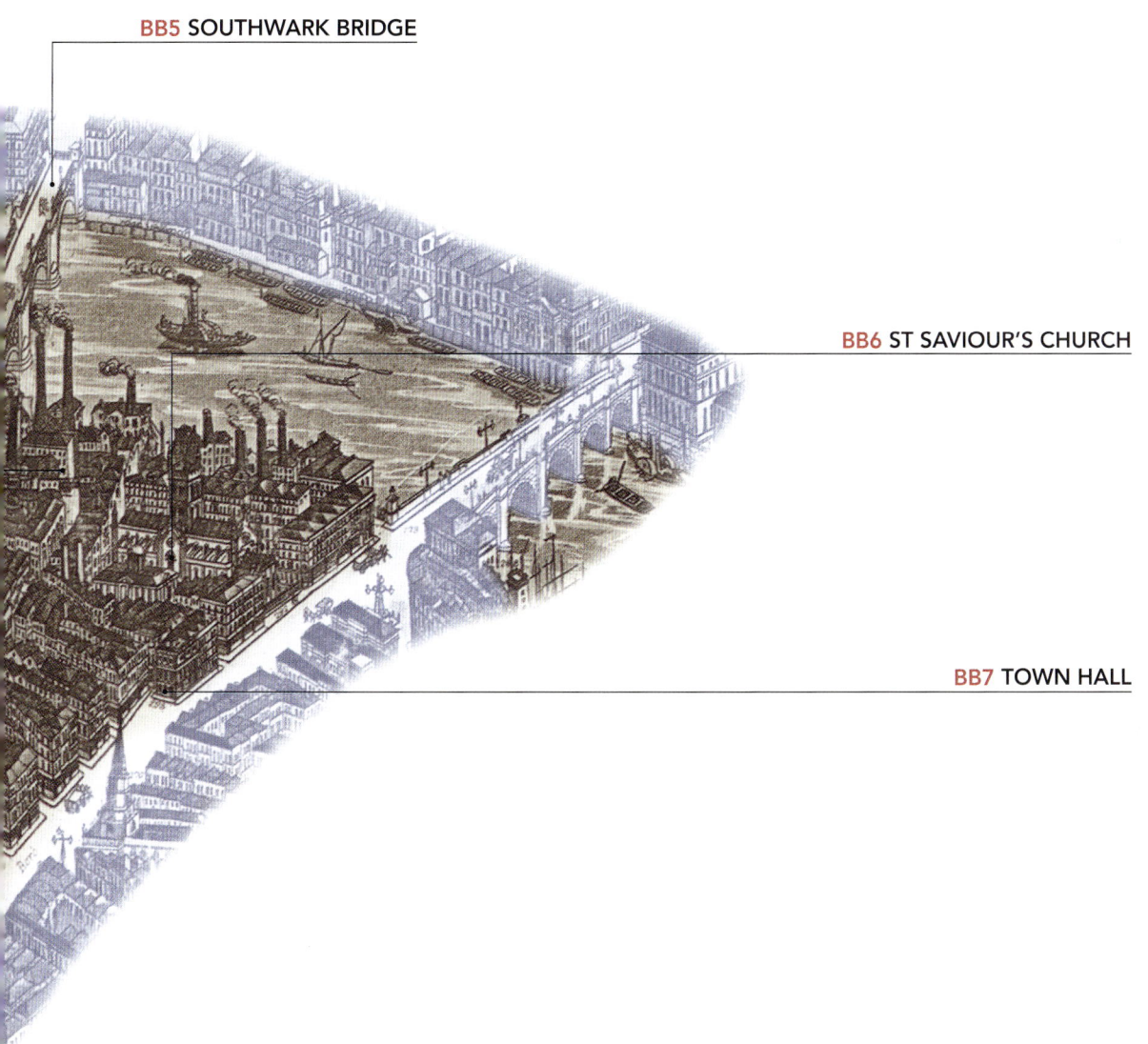

The premises of 'White, Greenwell and Company, Linen Drapers, Silk Mercers &c. 53, 54 & 55 Blackfriars Road, London'. The shop stood on the west side of Blackfriars Road, close to the Surrey Chapel.

(From John Tallis's *London Street Views* 1838-40)

Opposite:
Church of St Peter in Sumner Street with St Saviour's Grammar School alongside it at the far end. Wood engraving, 1839.
© London Metropolitan Archives
(City of London)

(BB1) Blackfriars Bridge and 'Great Surrey Street, Blackfriars Road' (G127); continued from p. 185. Robert Mylne's Blackfriars Bridge lasted about 100 years; until showing signs of decay it was demolished in 1860 and a new bridge by Joseph Cubitt was opened by Queen Victoria in 1869. Although Great Surrey Street had become Blackfriars Road in 1829, the individual who prepared the key for the Banks panorama could not relinquish the earlier name of 'Great Surrey Street'. By the mid-nineteenth century, Blackfriars Road was a lively mix of residential and shops as may be judged from the *Survey* carried out by John Tallis in 1838-40. Most of the residential blocks lining up both sides of the road were fitted with shops/workshops on the ground floor sometimes advertising their services across the whole façade, an advertising privilege which had to be paid for, for instance: 'Shaw Wholesale Ironmonger and Manufacturer' at No 253, 'Chequer Sadler & Harness Manufacturer' at No 248, 'Tilley Fire Engine Maker Improved Leather Pipes &c.' at No 245, 'Hammond Guestonian Medicines for Gout &c,' at No 244, 'Groves Sadler & Harness Manufacturer' at No 243, 'King Chemist & Druggist' at No 232 or 'Johnson Tea Dealer and Grocer' at No 152 to name those closest to Blackfriars Bridge (left).
(Survey of London 22; Tallis)

(BB2) Falcon Glassworks, Holland Street, close to Blackfriars Road; continued from p. 187. The glasshouse was rebuilt around 1820 and was the largest glassworks in London in the first half of the nineteenth century. In the late eighteenth century, Apsley Pellatt Senior (1763–1826) had purchased the establishment, in association with Mr Green and together they also ran their splendid glass showroom at St Paul's Churchyard, City of London; Apsley's son, another Apsley (1791-1863) joined the family business in 1811.

The Museum of London owns an anonymous painting of around 1840 which shows the interior of the glassworks giving a vivid rendering of all the different stages in glassmaking (right).

The workforce was male including child labour. The melting furnace is in the middle of the composition, which also shows the annealing oven on the right, and the pot room may be glimpsed up above on its left – George Dodd compared it to Ali Baba's cave filled with oil jars and thieves! The glassblowers are not using moulds but are shaping claret jugs requiring greater skills. The artist has included a break for refreshments on the left of the painting.
(Ordnance Survey 1873; Bacon 1888; Dodd; Galinou & Hayes Cat No. 115)

(BB3a) 'St Peter's Sumner Street, Southwark Bridge' (S41). This church and the street in which it stood, were contemporary with the Banks panorama. Sumner Street was formed in 1839 to connect Southwark Bridge Road with Great Guildford Street; it was macadamised the following year. It was named after Charles Sumner, Bishop of Winchester between 1827 and 1869. Both the street and the church stood on ground which had been leased to Messrs Potts, the vinegar manufacturers, by the Bishop

of Winchester. The land for the street was purchased while the land for the church was a gift from Messrs Potts. The ground for the church was consecrated on 7 November 1839. The design, in the Gothic style, came from the surveyor to the Clink Paving Commissioners, Christopher Edmonds. It was judged 'handsome' but 'not very richly adorned'. It was completely destroyed in the Second World War. (right)
(*Survey of London* 22)

(BB3b) St Saviour's Grammar School, Sumner Street; continued from p. 193. This sixteenth-century school remained near Green Dragon Court on the south side of St Saviour's church until 1838 when an Act was secured to enable the school to sell its premises (the site was needed for the extension of Borough Market) and build a new school elsewhere. It did not move far and purchased land on the north side of Sumner Street from the Bishop of Winchester. The new school abutted the newly built church of St Peter (1839). The smart appearance of this group of buildings lasted a few decades after which, the *Survey of London* informs us, the school 'had fallen on evil days by the end of the [nineteenth] century. It was hemmed in by factories and warehouses and its numbers had dropped to twenty-three'. The 1873 Ordnance Survey map shows the situation very well: Anchor Brewery/Boiler Works/Vinegar Distillery and Iron foundry on the east side, Engineering works, Phoenix Gas Works, Glassworks, sealskin works and numerous other

Falcon Glassworks, Holland Street, anonymous painting, c. 1840. This is the earliest known detailed painting of the interior of a London glasshouse.
(© Museum of London)

NEW CHURCH OF ST. PETER, AND GRAMMAR-SCHOOL, SOUTHWARK.

Barclay Perkins brewery
(© Museum of London)

smaller operations on the west side. In 1899 the school merged with St Olave's school – from then on its Sumner Street premises were used for Sunday school by St Peter's church. (O/S 1873 Bankside; *Survey of London* 22)

(BB4) Barclay Perkins Brewery; continued from p. 191. Also known as the Anchor brewery. Peter Cunningham's *Handbook of London* lavished massive praise on its operations in 1850:

> The establishment in Park-street is now the largest of its kind in the world. The buildings extend over ten acres and the machinery includes two steam-engines. The store-cellars contain 126 vats, varying in their contents from 4,000 barrels down to 500. About 160 horses are employed in conveying beer to different parts of London.

The Museum of London painting reproduced above dates from 1835–40 and shows the brewery's main entrance in Deadman's Place. However, it arguably fails to convey the spectacular statistics above and the true size of this brewery's operations. The anonymous artist has included a picturesque baked potato stall in the right foreground. The painting is an earlier and much more satisfactory rendering of a similar scene in George Dodd's *Days at the*

Factories (1843): 'Entrance to Barclay's Brewery'.
(Quote cited in Tames; Galinou & Hayes)

(BB5) 'Southwark Bridge' (S 258) and 'Bridge Street Southwark' (B41), the future Southwark Bridge Road. An 1811 Act of Parliament empowered the company formed in the same year to build a new bridge across the Thames, London's fifth, and also to build an approach to the bridge. Designed by the Scot John Rennie, it went up between 1814 and 1819. The *Survey of London* is unequivocal: it was 'generally regarded as having been unsurpassed as an example of the use of cast iron in bridge building', Richard Tames specifying it was the largest ever to be built of cast-iron and it bankrupted the Rotherham firm which produced its ironwork. But the panorama makes clear that unlike its neighbours London Bridge and Blackfriars Bridge, Southwark Bridge was a toll bridge; it was only freed from toll in 1864. The City of London Corporation rented the bridge until 1868 when they purchased it.

We encountered John Rennie at Albion Mills; Rennie was an adopted South Londoner – his home was at Stamford Street, Waterloo and his workshop at Holland Street near Blackfriars Road.

The brewers Barclay, Perkins & Co had always supported the Southwark Bridge project and they acquired land on the east side of the Bridge approach to build Anchor Terrace (1834), now a Grade II listed building. In 1989 archaeologists discovered the 'real' site of the Globe theatre – underneath Anchor Terrace. A small dig of a section of the car park was all that could be investigated, but it confirmed the findings of Dr William Martin in 1909 (see p. 303).

The present bridge was begun in 1912 but, delayed by World War II, did not open until 1921 (designed by Sir Ernest George and Alfred Bowman Yeates). (*Survey of London* 22; Tames)

View of Southwark Bridge taken from Bankside; engraving by William Wallis, after T H Shepherd, 1827.
© London Metropolitan Archives (City of London)

Pot or 'copper' from the Mint workhouse, dating from around 1910 – a gift to the Cuming Museum from 1921 by the Workhouse Board of Guardians. This is how it is described on Southwark Heritage blog: 'It stood in the corner of the large stone hall at the workhouse and the broth or gruel was ladled out to hungry inmates' (accessed on 19 September 2022).

(Cuming bequest collection/Heritage team/Southwark Council)

(BB6) 'St Saviour's [church] Southwark' (S292*); continued from p. 193. The *Survey of London* points out that only 'minor alterations were made to the interior of the church in the 18th century but by the beginning of the 19th century the fabric was so greatly decayed that a proposal was made for the destruction of the entire building except the tower'. George Gwilt the Younger (1775–1856) may have made his name designing the vast warehouses at West India Docks (1801), but his heart was in history and archaeology and his proudest moment, the 'restoration' of the tower and choir of St Saviour's (1822-25). He was an active member of the Society of Antiquaries and turned part of his Southwark home into a museum of local antiquities (see p. 195). He combined a deep interest in understanding medieval architecture with what we would now regard as dubious practices; for instance, he inserted his own designs when there was insufficient archaeological evidence for returning St Saviour's east windows to their thirteenth century appearance.
*This number has also been allocated to St Thomas' Hospital.
(*Survey of London* 22)

(BB7) 'Town Hall, Southwark' (T298); continued from p. 194. A new Town Hall was erected in 1793 but it was relatively short-lived, the *Survey of London* noting: 'By the middle of the 19th century the jurisdiction of the Court of Aldermen in Southwark had been reduced to a formality and the Town Hall had fallen into decay.' In the mid-nineteenth century demolition followed lack of use and decay.
(*Survey of London* 22)

(BB8) 'Surrey Road Chapel' (R240 but numbered 199 for nearby Nelson Square); continued from p. 184. In 1845 this chapel had another three decades of life before, in 1876, the congregation moved to Christ Church in Westminster Bridge Road and the Old Chapel was finally closed as a place of worship in 1881. The building survived until the Second World War, most memorably used as a boxing venue, 'The Ring'. It was badly damaged during that war and was demolished. Its memory as a boxing ring is preserved in the pub named 'The Ring' at the junction of The Cut and Blackfriars Road (south west corner) where boxing memorabilia is on display.
(*Survey of London* 22)

(BB9) **The Mint**, neighbourhood based around Mint Street, and sited across the road from St George's church; its local 'landmark' was the workhouse (left). There is irony in the name whose origins were the mint set up by Henry VIII at Suffolk Place. The 1600 chapter records that the mint was discontinued, ownership of the land switched from King to Church; the building deteriorated considerably, was demolished and replaced by cheap housing. In the eighteenth century, it was a sanctuary for debtors and thieves – highwaymen Jack Shepperd and Jonathan Wild took refuge there. In the Victorian period it was one of the poorest neighbourhoods in south London – a rookery which respectable people and the authorities feared to enter. Also see pp. 226–227.

The Victorian author George Godwin was appalled when he visited the district in the mid-1850s: 'Its evil character has not departed from it. With a gin-shop at the High-street end, and St. George's Workhouse at the other, it has on either side of it con genes [sic] of filthy courts unfit for habitation. The houses are tumbling down, the approaches in a miserable condition'. Various attempts at cleaning up the district in Victorian times came to nothing. It was only the building of Marshalsea Road in 1888 which finally proved to be a turning point.
(George Godwin, *London Shadows*, 1854; *Survey of London* 25)

The Drapers' Almshouses in Hill Street (now Glasshill Street) which have survived to this day. The Drapers' and Rowland Hill's Almshouses are two out of around seventy the artist T H Shepherd recorded in London in the 1850s, many of his drawings acquired by Frederick Crace, the great collector of London images. Watercolour by T H Shepherd, 1842.
© London Metropolitan Archives (City of London)

Exterior view of Rowland Hill's Almshouses in Hill (later Glasshill) Street, watercolour by T H Shepherd, 1832–37
© London Metropolitan Archives (City of London)

(BB10) **Drapers' Almshouses**, Hill Street (now Glasshill Street); continued from p. 199. These almshouses were moved a third time, in 1820, when they were rebuilt on their present site next to the Rowland Hill's almshouses. Again, the City Corporation provided the land and £1200 towards the cost of rebuilding.
(Rocque 20; Ordnance Survey map 1872; Bacon 1888; *Survey of London* 25)

(BB11) **Rowland Hill's Almshouses**, Hill Street (now Glasshill Street). These were set up in 1812 by the famous preacher Rowland Hill to house

Right:
'Chapel and School of the Revd Rowland Hills Almshouses', watercolour by G. Yates, 1825.
© London Metropolitan Archives (City of London)

The Alfred's Head pub at the junction of London Road and Newington Causeway at the Elephant and Castle. Etching published by M Skelt around 1830.
© London Metropolitan Archives (City of London)

twenty-four poor widows, members of the Surrey Chapel – hence also known as Surrey Almshouses. At the beginning of the twentieth century, they moved to new accommodation in Ashford in Middlesex and the organisation merged with The Vaughan Charity, originally founded in the parish of Christ Church in 1863 and which had moved to Ashford in the late Victorian period.
(Ordnance & Survey map 1872; Bacon 1888; Edward Walford, *Old and New London*, Volume 6, 1878; Rowland Hill Almshouses website, accessed 30 September 2022)

(BB12) 'Queen's Bench Prison in Southwark Bridge Road' (Q228). In 1837, when Queen Victoria acceded to the throne, King's Bench Prison would have become Queen's Bench prison. In 1842 an Act of Parliament abolished the Fleet prison on the north bank and the Marshalsea in Southwark; the name of Queen's Bench prison was also changed to Queen's Prison – Londoners may at first have struggled to remember the correct name, as did the person who compiled the key to the Banks Panorama. The Queen's Prison became the sole prison for debtors and bankrupts. Fees and privileges were abolished. Imprisonment for debt only came to an end in 1869 when the Queen's Prison closed. It was demolished and replaced by the prison-like Queen's Buildings in the early 1880s (now demolished).
(Horwood 1813, *Survey of London* 25)

(BB13) The Alfred's Head (A19) public house at 140 Newington Causeway opened around 1803, run by William Secker. It seems that at his death the establishment was run by his wife Mary (?) – the Secker family having had the longest run as landlords. Between 1803 and the 1840s the pub changed hands ten times. The former owner was the brewery Coombe & Co, which at the end of the nineteenth century became Watney, Coombe, Reid, & Co. Might there be some connection between the name of this pub and the statue of King Alfred which turns up in Trinity Square around 1830?
(pubwiki and pubology websites, accessed on 3 November 2021)

(BB) The Cross-Bones burial ground in Red Cross Street – not visible on this panorama; continued from p. 194. Although it cannot really be picked out from this crowded panorama, we know that around this time, it was literally bursting at the seams. See pp. 456–457.

In the 1990s the Museum of London's archaeological unit excavated the site ahead of work for the Jubilee Line. The burial ground was estimated to hold some 15,000 bodies – men, women and children from a humble background. 148 skeletons were removed.
(Horwood 1813 labelled 'St Saviour's School and Burial Ground'; *Survey of London* 22; MoLAS 1999)

SOUTHWARK AND BERMONDSEY

SB1 LONDON BRIDGE
SB2 SHOT TOWER
SB3 ST OLAVE'S CHURCH
SB4 TOOLEY STREET
SB5 LONDON BRIDGE STATION
SB6 ST GEORGE'S CHURCH
SB7 ST OLAVE'S SCHOOL
SB8 LEATHER MARKET
SB9 CHURCH OF ST JOHN HORSLEYDOWN
SB10 TRINITY CHURCH SQUARE
SB11 HORSEMONGER LANE PRISON
SB18 ROCKINGHAM ARMS
SB19 PARAGON
SB20 BRICKLAYERS ARMS
SB21 CHURCH OF ST MARY MAGDALEN
SB22 OLD KENT ROAD

SB12 ST THOMAS' HOSPITAL
SB13 CHURCH OF ST THOMAS
SB14 GUY'S HOSPITAL
SB15 BARCLAY'S BREWERY
SB16 ANCHOR BREWERY
SB17 CHURCH OF ST JAMES ROTHERHITHE
SB24 GREENWICH RAILWAY
ST SAVIOUR'S DOCK
SB23 BERMONDSEY SQUARE

Borough High Street during the construction of New London Bridge. The panoramic view is framed by Southwark Cathedral on the right and the shot tower off Tooley Street on the left. Lithograph by George Scharf, July 1830.
© London Metropolitan Archives (City of London)

(SB1) London Bridge (L173); continued from p. 208. The previous reconstruction (1770) showed the old bridge shorn of its houses. But in the 1820s they did away with the medieval bridge altogether – it had lasted over six centuries. The Banks panorama therefore presents a completely new structure.

Parliament decided Old London Bridge had to be replaced in 1821, and the designs submitted by John Rennie senior (1761–1821) – who had designed Waterloo, Southwark and Vauxhall bridges – were accepted. Rennie the Elder died soon after securing the commission, but when construction started in 1824 his son John (1794–1874) took over the operational lead; the bridge opened in 1831 – on a slightly different site: the new Bridge stood 100 feet to the west of the old. This had significant consequences for Southwark. Borough High Street had to be considerably widened close to the bridge. The new bridge was also wider and had five arches only, instead of nineteen. The Old Bridge was only demolished in 1832 once the new bridge was fully operational. The rebuilding of London Bridge by John Rennie Junior

(1794–1866) was rewarded with a knighthood. An unnamed grave came to light during the demolition of the bridge
(*Survey of London* 22; Barker & Jackson 1974; Tames)

(SB2) Shot Tower, on the riverfront, next to the church of St Olave. At the beginning of the nineteenth century, the site was taken over by the Admiralty to be used as an Ordnance depot. They built a shot Tower for the production of gun shot. It was destroyed in the 1843 fire at Topping's Wharf, but immediately rebuilt under the direction of George Allen. It is included in various pictures of the river bank, including the Rhinebeck Panorama – see p. 206. (Ellis)

(SB3) 'St Olave's [church], Tooley Street, London Bridge' (S288); continued from p. 209. Building maintenance, the remuneration of the rector and the inadequate rectory house were placed at the top of this church's agenda in 1817. An Act of Parliament was obtained which stated that some of the trustees will need to pay the rector £600 instead of tithes, which had proved an insufficient source of funds. Extra funds would no

Detail from 'The Demolition of the Old London Bridge', 1832. The view is taken from the South Bank looking towards the Monument and the church of St Magnus; the new bridge is on the left. Oil painting signed JWS.
(Guildhall Art Gallery, London, Acc. No 515. Image in the public domain; Wikimedia Commons)

Opposite:
This engraving for Brailey's History of Surrey (1841) shows St Olave's school premises between 1835 and 1849 when the institution was forced to move away from their ancient site in Tooley Street to new premises in Bermondsey Street.
© London Metropolitan Archives (City of London)

doubt have been needed after the church was damaged by fire in 1843. The church closed its doors for the last time in 1926, the nave was demolished in 1928 and the tower a little later when the site was redeveloped as Olaf House (see p. 510).
(*VCH* 4)

(SB4) **'Tooley Street' (T288)**; continued from p.129 [1600]. Barely legible on the Banks's panorama, this ancient street ran along the back of the busy wharves east of London Bridge. It was a lively thoroughfare, particularly constricted near the junction with Borough High Street. This may be clearly observed in George Scharf's lithograph reproduced on the previous page, in striking contrast with the widened High Street with the arrival of New London Bridge.
(Horwood 1799 and 1813; O/S map 1893–96)

(SB5) **London Bridge Station and hotel** are not highlighted in the key to this panorama. The station had been built between 1843 and 1844, shortly before the panorama was published – partly rebuilt in 1847 and subsequently enlarged. Banks's later panorama (1851) includes an excellent vignette showing station and hotel (see p. 558).
(*Survey of London* 22)

(SB6) **'St George's High Street, Borough' (S270)**; continued from p. 214. In 1807-8, the sum of £9400 was spent on repairing and 'beautifying' this church, as opposed to the original estimate of a £2000 restoration. The building needed new foundations, so the pews were removed and replaced by single pews 'so that the people could all face the minister'; the ceiling was replaced and the slates on the roof renewed. Small galleries were

Exterior of St Olave's Free School, Southwark

Interior of St Olave's Free School, Southwark

added above the west gallery, on either side of the organ, stairs were moved or repaired to accommodate charity children and the pulpit was placed in the middle of the nave facing the congregation. Finally, the 1737 clock which featured in Hogarth's painting reproduced on p. 487, was replaced.

In Victorian times this church had strong associations with Charles Dickens since it was the scene of Little Dorrit's christening and marriage. The novel was published in serial form between 1850 and 1857 and used the image of the sun streaming in through the stained glass of the east window – this detail did not exist in 1820s when the story was set. In his life of Dickens, Peter Ackroyd notes that in his novels 'churches themselves tend to be portrayed as dusty places of empty forms and rituals ... he was a man of religious sensibility, but his beliefs were determined by his own vision of the world rather than by any inherited or specific creed'. However, it is Dickens' knowledge and sensitivity to this appalling part of London which has fired up and opened our minds to this neighbourhood's heavy past – slum and prison life as background to the remarkable story of Little Dorrit. Writing in 1948, J Pinder recounted an anecdote about the 'Dorrit vestry'; this is where Little Dorrit slept after being accidentally locked out of the Marshalsea prison where she lived with her father, and this is also where she signed the register on her wedding day:

> Visitors frequently ask to see the actual entry and are disappointed when told that Little Dorrit was a character of fiction and that, while Dickens knew the church very well indeed, there is no entry for his well known character.

(John Pinder, *St George the Martyr Church Southwark – A Short History*, 1948)

(SB7) St Olave's school, Bermondsey Street and Tooley

Street; continued from p. 219. In 1823 the school was completely reorganised and the Madras system introduced – 'based on the principle that masters were to be reduced in number, that senior boys were to be put to teach junior boys, and, in short, that the whole system was to be organised along factory lines for mass production' explains R C Carrington. This system, generally regarded as a disastrous move, would only be abolished in 1855.

With the arrival of London Bridge Station in 1839 the site of the school was requisitioned and it moved to Bermondsey Street (previous page). This would have been its address in 1845 but was relatively short-lived as the new site was again needed for widening the railway in 1855. The school moved to Queen Elizabeth Street in Horsleydown. The substantial institution is featured on the London Bridge Station Ordnance Survey map of 1872–93, named 'Queen Elizabeth's Grammar School'. It had an English School, a Commercial School, a Dining Room, a covered area, a library and a playground. As with its original site opposite the church of St Olave, it abutted a burial ground (see p. 219). The school amalgamated with St Saviour's grammar school in 1896. This school eventually moved to Orpington in 1968 and its former home, designed by Edward William Mountford, ready by 1893, has become a hotel.
(Ordnance Survey map 1872–93; Carrington; *VCH 4*)

(SB8) 'New leather warehouses, Bermondsey' (N203). This is the Leather (or Skin) Market which the principal tanners of Bermondsey erected in 1832 in Weston Street. Up until then, the fourteenth-century Leadenhall market in the City had been at the centre of the trade – originally a food market which had diversified to sell leather, wool and raw hides, but which had also outgrown its size. The Bermondsey property was on the tanners' doorstep and of a generous size.

Charles Dickens Junior in his *Dictionary of London* (1879) thus described its atmosphere:

There is no noise or bustle, and but a few people about. There are no retail purchasers, the sales being almost entirely made to the great tanners in the neighbourhood. The warehouses round are all full of tanned hides; the yards behind the high walls are all tanneries, with their tens of thousands of hides soaking in the pits.

Dickens also mentioned the 'horrible smells which pervade the whole neighbourhood'. The journalist James Greenwood dwelt at length on the two distinct parts of the market: leather and skins. In agreement with Dickens, he explained there was little happening on the leather side but the situation was very different when he switched to the skin market – carts, horses, 'a swarm of busy-men-buyers and sellers, and blue-smocked porters' contrasted greatly with the 'listless' individuals encountered in the leather market or 'the flatness of the leather trade'.

Henry Mayhew described another aspect of this massive operation – the preparation and sale of trotters or lamb's feet. From the market they are taken to a fellmonger with extensive premises 'situated, as are nearly all branches of the great trade connected with hides and skins, in Bermondsey … Thus there are, weekly, "cooking" in one form or other, the feet of 20,000 sheep [80,000 feet] for the consumption of the poorer classes'. Mayhew specified that 'the trotter business is kept distinct from the general fellmongering'. Distribution was entirely in the hands of street sellers. Once again, the image of the market is considerably squeezed in the Banks 1845 panorama but the 1851 version, reproduced on p. 558 does greater justice to the tall buildings.

Tanning was one of a number of anti-social trades which thrived in the suburbs of London. It is difficult nowadays to have a proper idea of the levels of pollution for those passing through or living in these neighbourhoods. There are two excellent reconstructions in Mira Nair's 2020 BBC series 'A Suitable Boy', which deal with the preparation of leather and the transformation of the product into articles for sale (episode 3 for the tanning process and 4 for shoemaking).

(*VCH 4*; Charles Dickens, as quoted on the website 'Dictionary of Victorian London'; James Greenwood, *Unsentimental Journeys or Byways of the Modern Babylon*; 1867; Henry Mayhew *London Labour and the London Poor*, Vol. 1)

(SB9) 'St John, Horsleydown' (S273*); continued from p. 210. This church in Fair Street, at the junction with Tower Bridge Road, dated from the early eighteenth century. The church's burial ground ceased to be used in 1853. The church was severely bomb damaged during the Second World War and not rebuilt. The church's foundations were retained and the site redeveloped to become an office block, Nasmyth House, designed by John D. Ainsworth & Associates for the London City Mission (1972-76).
*This number has also been allocated to the church of St Mary Bermondsey. (*VCH 4*)

(SB10) 'Trinity church, Horsemonger Lane' (T146). Holy Trinity Church in the middle of Trinity Square is the centre piece of the Trinity House Estate in the parish of St Mary's Newington, formerly in the Manor of Walworth. The estate belongs to the Corporation of the Trinity House and was a gift in 1661 from Christopher Merrick, in trust 'for Releiving comforting Easing & Maintaining of the poor Aged Sick Maimed Weak and decayed Seamen

Holy Trinity Church in the centre of Trinity Square; the statue of King Alfred is clearly visible which means it was in place by 1829, when this picture was engraved for Allen's *History of Surrey and Sussex*.
© London Metropolitan Archives (City of London)

and Mariners of this Kingdom, their Wives children and Widowes where most need was'. The land is framed by Borough High Street on the west side, Great Dover Street on the north side, Falmouth Street on the east side and Horsemonger Lane (now Harper Road) on the south side. The land, used for garden ground, market gardening, tenter-ground and grazing remained largely unbuilt until the making of Great Suffolk Street East (now Trinity Street) in 1813–14. Although the road was not completed until 1830 when it was taken over by the Commissioners of Roads, this encouraged development; this was without a masterplan and in the hands of several speculative builders. The Corporation required approval for all schemes by checking all plans and elevations prior to building – a method almost identical to that pursued by the Eyre brothers on their St John's Wood estate.

In spite of wars and the ravages of time most of the Trinity House property remains in external appearance substantially as it was built and the estate as a whole forms an interesting example of early to mid-nineteenth century residential building development (*Survey of London*).

The site for the church was previously occupied by a tenter-ground, clearly shown on the Rhinebeck panorama. Holy Trinity Church was built following an Act of 1820 which authorized the erection of a church on the Trinity estate in the parish of St Peter's Walworth. The Trinity estate appointed the architect Francis Bedford 'of whom we know little, except that he travelled to Greece, corresponded with Cockerell on the subject of Greek architecture, and that he was one of the runners-up in the competition for St Pancras' noted John Summerson in his *Georgian London*. Bedford designed St John's Waterloo, another austere rectangular box with bare walls, the decoration of both churches inspired by the classical world. Holy Trinity church was consecrated on 16 December 1824 and the garden, laid out by William Chadwick, lost most of its railings in the Second World War. It is enlivened by the presence of a fascinating statue said to be of King Alfred (see p. 543).

The development of Trinity Square, now Trinity Church Square, was approved in 1824 when William Chadwick, mason, obtained a building lease; he was 'responsible for the development of part of the Trinity House estate'; the square was finally completed in 1832. Swan and Cole Streets were laid out in the 1820s.
(*Survey of London* 25)

(SB11) 'Horsemonger Lane Prison Newington Causeway' (H146); continued from p. 213. The genesis of this prison was presented in the previous chapter. Here are Victorian descriptions by two important witnesses. Charles Dickens' account of an execution held there, was published in a letter to *The Times* on 14 November 1849. Dickens arrived at around midnight the day before and spent the night waiting amongst the assembled crowd. He set out his intention clearly: 'I went there with the intention of observing the crowd gathered to behold it, and I had excellent opportunities of doing so'. Then came the awful realisation that:

> The horrors of the gibbet and the crime which brought the wretched murderers to it, faded in my mind before the atrocious bearing, looks and language, of the assembled spectators ... When the sun rose brightly – as it did – it gilded thousands upon thousands of upturned faces, so inexpressively odious in their brutal mirth or callousness, that a man had cause to feel ashamed of the shape he wore, and to shrink from himself, as fashioned in the image of the Devil. When the two miserable creatures who attracted all this ghastly night about them were turned quivering into the air, there was no more emotion, no more pity, no more thought that two immortal souls had gone to judgment, no more restraint in any of the previous obscenities, than if the name of Christ had never been heard in this world, and there were no belief among men but that they perished like the beasts.

Dickens concluded his piece by asking *The Times*' readers to consider 'the moral evils of the land' and 'whether it is not a time to think of this one, and to root it out'. The *Survey of London* judged this to mark the beginning of 'the agitation against public executions which culminated in their abolition in 1868'.

Henry Mayhew on the other hand noted in his 1862 publication *The Criminal Prisons of London and Scenes of London Life*, that Horsemonger Lane was 'the only Common Jail in London i.e., the only place where debtors are still confined under the same roof as felons'.

The prison shut its doors in August 1878 and in 1884 Mrs Gladstone opened part of the site as a children's playground. It was finally demolished in 1892 when T Blashill designed a weights and measures office for the LCC on part of the site.
(*Survey of London* 25; Mayhew and Dickens as cited)

(SB12) 'St Thomas' Hospital, London Bridge' (S292*); continues from p. 217. This is almost a last glimpse of the hospital prior to its move away from the area. Part of the hospital was in the line of railway development when in 1859 an Act of Parliament authorised the building of the Charing Cross railway from London Bridge to Waterloo and Hungerford Bridge (see p. 414). The governors tried in vain to oppose the bill, finally agreeing to sell their site to the railways; all the buildings were destroyed except for St Thomas' church, the adjacent treasurer's house and the south side of the outer court. The hospital relocated to a temporary site in Surrey Gardens until 1863 when negotiations started with the Metropolitan Board of Works for the current site on the Albert Embankment. The new hospital was designed by Henry Currey, the hospital's architect, and it was ready in 1871. The *Survey of London* noted that 'Florence Nightingale was consulted both on the original move from Southwark and on the design of the new building. Its erection in separate blocks rather than in one large building is probably due to her influence.'
*This number has also been allocated to St Saviour's church.
(Horwood 1813; *Survey of London* 23; *VCH* 4)

(SB13) 'St Thomas, Southwark' (S292bis); continued from p. 217. This church, at the heart of the eponymous hospital complex, survived the demolition of most of the hospital buildings around 1860 after the move of the hospital from this site to Lambeth. It is the oldest surviving part of the hospital and houses the remarkable Old Operating Theatre Museum and Herb Garret..
(Horwood 1799 and 1813; *VCH* 4)

(SB14) 'Guy's Hospital, near London Bridge' (G133); continued from p. 216. The hospital consolidated its position and status through bequests and donations (notably William Hunt's), acquisition of land around the hospital (in 1816 and 1833) and building expansion – most notably Hunt's House in 1853, designed by Rhode Hawkins (the north wing came later, in 1871).
(Horwood 1799 and 1813; *Survey of London* 22)

(SB15) Barclays Brewery in Stanton's Wharf, on the corner of Stoney and Pickle-Herring Streets; continued from p. 209. It was so

named after being purchased by Southwark's Barclay Perkins brewery in 1830. It is unclear why the brewery which features on Loveday, was not fully surveyed.
(Loveday)

(SB16) Anchor Brewery, Liddard's Wharf, corner of Shad Thames and Horsleydown Lane; continued from p. 209. The Courage brewery was so modest at the end of the eighteenth century that it did not feature on the main maps for the period. Unlike the Stoney Street brewery (above), it is not labelled on Greenwood's 1828 map of London either. But by 1857 when *Loveday's London Waterside Surveys* is published, the brewery does at last come into its own – it lies at Liddard's Wharf, next to Hartley's Wharf and is thus described: 'Messrs Courage & Co's "Anchor Brewery" and Granaries adjoining'. The three granaries and a warehouse were occupied by other wharfingers but Courage occupied the rest of the site – its four-storey brewhouse overlooking the Thames, with the vat rooms, store rooms, stables, a dwelling house and a public house on the south side of Shad Thames, all forming part of the Anchor Brewery. A third vat room was sited on Hartley's Wharf close to the painters' and carpenters' shops. All the buildings were brick and timber built.
(Loveday)

(SB17) New church, Rotherhithe (N204). It is the church of St James Bermondsey, designed in a neo-classical style by James Savage, and completed in 1829, hence the use of the word 'New'. It is one of the so-called 'Waterloo churches' (see p. 255 St John's).

(SB18) 'Rockingham Arms, Newington Causeway' (R239), 175 Newington Causeway. This was one of a trio of imposing pubs at this major south London junction, the other two being The Alfred's Head and the Elephant and Castle inn. The present Rockingham Arms dates from the 1960s but is approximately on the same site.

(SB19) 'Paragon, Kent Road' (P216). See p. 212

(SB20 and SB22) Kent Road (K158); continued from p. 214. The western section of Kent Street was renamed Tabard Street in 1877. The key to the 1845 panorama flags the **'Bricklayer's Arms, Kent Road' (B43)**, which, in the 1799 Horwood map, stood in splendid isolation; but not in this panorama. The pub was at 37-39 Old Kent Road, opened by 1791 and demolished in the 1960s. This is a visual record of its early incarnation (it was rebuilt around 1881). It is on the same horizontal line as the Paragon and its reference number, 43, is found on the white side wall of this building.

The South Eastern railway and the London & Greenwich railway were responsible for building a station at Bricklayers' Arms as an alternative to the overcrowded London Bridge terminus. It opened in 1844, but there is no sign of it in the panorama.

(*A to Z Victorian London*; *Survey of London* 25; https://www.pubology.co.uk/pubs/4734.html; https://www.pubwiki.co.uk/LondonPubs/SouthwarkStGeorgeMartyr/BricklayersArms.shtml, both accessed on 3 November 2021)

(SB21) 'St Mary Bermondsey' (S273*); continued from p. 211. In the Banks' panorama, the church of St Mary Magdalen in Bermondsey Street, is almost squeezed out of existence by the London to Greenwich railway line – one of the compromises the ballooning artist had to make to try and fit in all the different landmarks in his challenging composition. The church was restored in 1830 – the west front remodelled in a gothic style, refaced with stucco and the upper part of the tower rebuilt. There were two further restorations in the nineteenth century.
**This number has also been allocated to the church of St John's Horsleydown.*

(Weinreb & Hibbert)

(SB23) 'Bermondsey Square, new Greenwich Railway' (B27); continued from p. 211. This entry is addressing two separate sites – Bermondsey Square, which stands on the former Bermondsey Abbey, and the elevated tracks of the London to Greenwich Railway, showing a train heading towards London Bridge.

While Bermondsey Square is the top layer of centuries of history, the London and Greenwich Railway (LGR) was a brand-new landmark, not only for the South Bank but the whole of London as it was London's first suburban passenger railway. The idea came from General George Thomas Landmann (1779–1854) and was originally discussed in 1831, followed by an Act of Parliament in 1833. The line opened in stages between 1836 and 1838. It was the first railway line in London and the first to be built on a viaduct (878 arches). The railway line rapidly turned into a leisure attraction, in the same way that Barclay Perkins brewery and Albion Mills had. But apart from the LGR being an object of contemplation, it was also primarily used as an excursion railway line (overleaf).

In 1835 *The Gentleman's Magazine* described it as 'the most extraordinary work of the kind in our age' and the viaduct was frequently compared to an ancient Roman aqueduct. Historian Alex Werner remarks: 'comparing London's new structures to the ancient world was not uncommon as commentators found it difficult to find anything comparable in size and extent in the modern world … Charles Dupin, the French engineer, described Waterloo Bridge as 'worthy' of 'the Caesars". The company created a walkway on the south side of the railway which was accessed on payment of a small fee.

Land acquisition and compensation monies meant that the line was very costly to build and to recoup some of the money, the

company pursued a conversion scheme to turn the arches into shops and dwelling-houses. The project attracted no takers: 'apart from the noise, the main problem was the damp caused by rainwater seeping through the bricks' Alex Werner explained. Though this was good enough for London's homeless poor who, at night, took shelter under the arches as they did, later, at Waterloo (see p. 416). The railway line also set the scene for the no-compensation approach to the thousands of people whose homes would disappear overnight – property owners were compensated, not their tenants.

The line carried nearly 5.8 million passengers in the first four years, learning valuable lessons from the other railways, in particular the Liverpool and Manchester Railway; but the journeys were very short, the line never made real profits and it struggled with 'problematic narratives' which were associated with its arches sheltering the homeless of the city and its tree-lined walkway being vandalised. The carriages of the LGR mirrored the busy street and pavements of the city. The rail service had to confront overcrowding, disturbances, drunkenness and defacement of its property. The urban railway had been born.

The line closed in 1923.

The steep perspective makes it difficult to see Bermondsey square at the bottom of this detail. We know that it was already formed by 1799 when it is clearly featured on Horwood's great map. A later lithograph by Henry Lavelock Phillips, dated 1866, is rather more revealing about the Victorian appearance of the square and its relationship with the past (above).

This useful picture is reproduced here and part of its caption, which informs us that looking straight ahead on the left you could see:

> At the opening to the Square between the Kings John's Head Public House and the Oilshop stood the North or great Gatehouse of the Abbey, demolished about 1807. At the back of the houses on the left, in a Builders Yard, Remains of Old Walls are to be seen. On the far corner to the right is seen the entrance to the Long Walk, here in excavating for a sewer, a few years since, was discovered a stone coffin, still to be seen in the vaults of the Parish Church. Midway between the entrance to the Long Walk, and the Salt Warehouse [right foreground], stood the Mansion House, which old Stowe tells us "was a goodly house builded of wood and stone, the materials for which being taken from the Abbey". Turning round by the Salt warehouse, we reach the Grange Walk, here even at the present time is to be seen the East Gate House, together with the hinges upon which the gates hung, this with a few old houses in Bear Yard are the only remains now to be seen of this once famous Abbey.

(R HG Thomas, *London's First Railway – the London & Greenwich*, 1972; Alex Werner, unpublished paper)

(SB) Jacob's Island, east of St Saviour's dock (overleaf). This is on the edge of the area under review in this book, but its notoriety was such in the nineteenth century that it would be strange to omit it. It is Dickens who put this grim neighbourhood on our mental maps. In *Oliver Twist*, published in 1838, the infamous Bill Sikes, robber, murderer and member of Fagin's gang lived there; there he died too, miserably. Back in the seventeenth century the area may have looked idyllic with its surrounding 'canals' of water fed by the Neckinger river – Jacob Street and Water Lane crossing the island which had been formed in this way. Even then, the area had long lost its sixteenth-century appeal to become industrial and poor.

This is how Henry Mayhew found it in 1849-50 in an article entitled 'A Visit to the Cholera District of Bermondsey'. He starts with a blanket comment about the South Bank when looking for 'the plague-spots of London' –

> for as truly as the West-end rejoices in the title of Belgravia, might the southern shores of the Thames be christened Pestilentia … Out of the 12,800 deaths which, within the last three months, have arisen from cholera, 6,500 have occurred on the southern shores of the Thames; and to this awful number no localities have contributed so largely as Lambeth, Southwark and Bermondsey.

The section dealing with Jacob's Island describes scene after scene of filth and disgust:

> But now the running brook is changed into a tidal sewer … where the ancient summer-houses stood, nothing but hovels, sties, and muck-heaps are now to be seen … The striking peculiarity of Jacob's Island consists in the wooden galleries and sleeping rooms at the back of the houses which overhang the dark flood, and are built upon piles, so that the place has positively the air of a Flemish street, flanking a sewer instead of a canal; while the little rickety bridges that span the ditches and connect court with court, give it the appearance of the Venice of drains.

(Horwood 26; Victorian London website)

Bermondsey Square, lithograph by Henry Lavelock Phillips, 1866.
© London Metropolitan Archives (City of London)

Spa Road Station, Bermondsey, watercolour by Robert Schnebbelie, 1836. This is the earliest known depiction of a London railway station. The first section of the London and Greenwich Railway was built between Spa Road and Deptford. When the line reached London Bridge in December 1836, Spa Road ceased to be used.
(© Museum of London)

Overleaf:

James Lawson Stewart, Jacob's Island, Bermondsey, watercolour, 1886 (also see p. 225).
(© Museum of London)

THE SOUTH BANK NOW

If the great spate of new buildings in London has any theme it is that the city is moving from imperial grandeur and industry to a lighter, more fluid future, a city which lives on its communications, tourism and its culture and wits. The wheel [London Eye] is entirely open and democratic, lighter and airier than any other structure in the land.

Andrew Marr, *The Observer*, October 1999

Previous page:
This image was captured in an aerial survey on 14 June 2021, at ten-centimetre resolution. From this perspective, the area's high-rise buildings become invisible, bar the long shadows they project on the ground.
(Photo: Getmapping)

'Bank Holiday Weekend', this watercolour, gouache and acrylic picture of the London Eye by Robert Soden vibrates with light and airiness, against one of the artist's famous skies. The wheel appears to vibrate in the wind in defiance of its massive, solid infrastructure.
(© The artist, 2004)

The content of this chapter covers the 1950s to 2022, i.e., roughly the last seventy years (with occasional exceptions). It is not comprehensive but will give the reader a taste of how things are and may develop.

It is not easy to capture in our own times the nature of what is new and so speedily assimilated before it has even been properly assessed. In contrast to, and in contradiction with, this chapter's opening statement about transparency and access to all, we should mention the worrying concept of 'pseudo-public spaces' thus described by *Guardian* journalist Jack Shenker:

> Although they are seemingly accessible to members of the public and have the look and feel of public land, these sites – also known as privately owned public spaces or "Pops" – are not subject to ordinary local authority bylaws but rather governed by restrictions drawn up [by] the landowner and usually enforced by private security companies …
> Under existing laws, public access to pseudo-public spaces remains at the discretion of landowners who are allowed to draw

up their own rules for "acceptable behaviour" on their sites and alter them at will. They are not obliged to make these rules public …
Nearly all of the city's ongoing major redevelopment projects, from the mammoth Nine Elms neighbourhood … to new construction in Elephant and Castle and at Shoreditch's Bishopsgate Goods Yard, is set to include new pseudo-public space, but details of what rights Londoners will enjoy there – or the ways in which they can expect to be policed – remain a mystery. (*The Guardian*, 24 July 2017)

And to the transparency evoked by Andrew Marr in the chapter's opening quote – which does exist – we must evoke the total lack of transparency which governs neighbourhoods such as the More London estate off Tooley Street. Security guards immediately intervened when Jack Shenker attempted to interview members of the public, escorting him to the security office where he was told 'that unsanctioned journalistic activity is banned on the site'. This was deplored by another *Guardian* journalist, Oliver Wainwright, also writing about the More London estate:

Owned by the sovereign wealth fund of Kuwait and patrolled by private security guards, it is a damning symptom of the capital's thrall to foreign investment that journalists must seek permission to conduct interviews outside its own seat of democracy. (*The Guardian*, 20 June 2018)

City Hall, now defunct, does indeed stand on More London's private enclave. *Guardian Cities*, also sadly defunct, carried out a fairly comprehensive investigation of pseudo-public spaces in London mapping many of its principal sites. For the South Bank the list includes the More London estate, Tabard Square, Bankside, Neo-Bankside and … the London Eye! Not so 'open and democratic', as Andrew Marr claimed in the London Eye quote.

Millennium fever

In 1997, to celebrate the coming of the new millennium, the Lothbury Gallery in the Bank branch of Natwest, presented an exhibition called 'The New Millennium', curated by the modelmakers Pipers International. Visitors could walk around a huge model of London which included over thirty 'Millennium projects'. The *Architect's Journal* published the accompanying booklet and it is quite instructive to revisit its ideas. Paul Finch wrote in the Introduction that the exhibition was 'a lively indication of the adrenalin which is flowing through the construction industry in relation to the capital, encouraging many of our best architects to produce work for which they will be long remembered. Long may this spirit last'. (This model survives in the New Architecture Gallery at the Building Centre in Store Street, though it does not get updated often enough).

In 1997, these were the projects which were selected for the South Bank and regarded as outstanding:

- Jubilee Line: six stations south of the Thames, three of them in the area under review.

Robert Soden, Southwark tube station during construction, watercolour, 1997. The artist was commissioned by London Transport to record the building of the Jubilee line. From the artist's diary: 'While I was working at Southwark I was the beneficiary of a can of beer and ten pence given by a homeless man who thought I was a pavement artist, Refusal might have offended, so I accepted with thanks. He subsequently proceeded to defend me at what he thought was unjust criticism of my painting by a passer-by'.
(Image supplied by London Transport Museum © The artist)

Waterloo was designed by JLE Architects, Southwark by McCormac Jameson Prichard, and London Bridge by JLE Architects & Weston Williamson.

- Refurbishment of the South Bank Centre – Richard Rogers' scheme went head-to-head with that of Allies and Morrison. Richard Rogers was chosen but the scheme would eventually be dropped; Allies and Morrison were subsequently appointed (see pp. 542–543).
- Tate Modern by Herzog & de Meuron opened to great acclaim in 2000 (see pp. 473 ff).
- Imperial War Museum refurbishment (Holocaust display). This display was recently updated.
- Vinopolis: the venue permanently closed its doors in 1999.
- The Millennium Bridge, by Norman Foster, recovered from its wobble to become a major pedestrian point of entry to the South Bank.
- Hungerford Bridge – or the Golden Jubilee Bridges which flank both sides of 'Hungerford [railway] Bridge' – pedestrian walkways. Completed in 2002 (see below).

What was not known was that the Millennium projects were not the culmination of a trend but the beginning of a frenzy of new developments which have totally transformed London's cityscape, its scale and even its way of life.

After the 1968 Ronan Point disaster in Canning Town– a gas explosion which made one side of a council tower block collapse – there was general agreement that high rise buildings were bad and should be avoided, particularly for residential housing. This is forgotten now and developers and architects are competing with one another on the number of storeys and most elegant high-rise designs.

In April 2022, New London Architecture published their annual 'London Tall Buildings Survey' (buildings over six storeys), developed with research partner Knight Frank. The 'On London' website noted that the data was contradictory, with the *Financial Times* asserting developers were scaling back 'tower block' projects while the *Construction Enquirer* described the trend as reaching 'record levels'. Other salient points were thus summarized: 'The overall tall building pipeline contains 583 projects … of which 70% are residential … Tower Hamlets, home of Canary Wharf, still leads the way with 95 in its pipeline, followed by Southwark with 60, then Greenwich with 50.'

But the projects they did not see coming have had a powerful impact on the South Bank – the Shard at the entrance of London Bridge – its success followed by the sudden rush to erect buildings at bridge heads, e.g., Blackfriars, Waterloo and Vauxhall. London's development is driven by the London Plan which was published in March 2016 and will remain in force until 2036. It has identified 'Opportunity Areas' (OAs) in London – virtually the whole of the area under review in this book contains OAs which were identified back in 2004:

- London Bridge, Borough and Bankside: 'potential for 4,000 new homes and 5,500 jobs by 2041'
- Waterloo: 'potential for 1,500 new homes and 6,000 new jobs by 2041'
- Vauxhall, Nine Elms, Battersea: 'with potential for 18,500 new homes and 18,500 new jobs by 2041'
- Elephant & Castle: 'with potential for 5,000 new homes and 10,000 new jobs by 2041'

The thriving development work flourishing on the South Bank has severe critics whose aggressive viewpoints constitute many salutary warnings. Here is Simon Jenkins, rightly appalled at Lambeth Council's decision to grant planning permission to the 'Slab', 'London's latest eyesore' in Waterloo (to replace LWT tower):

> As for their utility, the towers are overwhelmingly empty investments. At the Tower at St George Wharf in Vauxhall, at 184 of the 214 flats over 50 storeys, no one was registered to vote in 2016. The idea that these buildings answer London's "housing crisis" is sick; most are international bank balances in the sky. (*The Guardian*, 6 May 2022)

Projects for our times

The development scene on the South Bank is more thriving than ever but perhaps two regeneration projects stand out for their size and the impact they are likely to have on their neighbourhoods: Vauxhall/Nine Elms (Boroughs of Lambeth and Wandsworth) and Elephant and Castle (Borough of Southwark). They are both creating spiky clusters of very tall towers. You gain a sense of the capital's new scale at the Elephant, where, for now, the Draper estate survives. When it was built in the 1960s the twenty-five storey Draper Tower was the tallest block of flats in London; designed by Hubert Bennett and Kenneth J. Campbell, the topping out ceremony took place in December 1963. When the Strata building came onto the scene (2007–2010) it became the tallest residential building in London – forty-three storeys (147 m). 'One the Elephant' (2016) looks dizzyingly high because of its slender proportions but with its thirty-seven storeys, it only reaches 124 m.

At the Elephant there are twenty-five projects in the regeneration programme, but the two main developments are Elephant Park on the site of the Heygate estate – 3000 new homes, fifty shops and 'a major central park' to be completed in 2025; also the new 'town centre' on the site of the now demolished shopping centre – 'to create a transformed environment for shoppers, retailers and residents', 1000 homes, a new campus for UAL's London College of Communication and a revamped tube station.

The ghost from the past is still haunting the present

Several recent developments have turned Bankside into a major venue for Shakespearean theatre – the extraordinary discovery of the Rose theatre in 1989 with its high-profile excavation; the discovery of the actual site of the Globe Theatre in Park Street, also in 1989; the brilliant obstinacy of an American actor, Sam Wanamaker (1919–1993), to recreate the Globe Theatre on Bankside, and his success in doing so, much to everyone's surprise given the long list of obstacles to overcome. The popular film made by John Madden, *Shakespeare in Love*, released in 1999 plausibly recreated the life of theatres on Bankside. It brought back to mind and life, the continuing appeal of the Bard and his contemporaries.

The original site of the Globe theatre was discovered nineteen years after Sam Wanamaker first set up his Shakespeare Globe Trust. A bronze relief and information panel mark the site (opposite). However, for decades the Globe project, despite its many supporters and devoted volunteers, seemed unable to take off since so much money was needed to realise the original vision. But it did take off eventually, later benefiting from the input of contemporary architects – Allies and Morrison – to deliver its most vivid recreation, the Sam Wanamaker playhouse, as rustic as the Globe when it comes to seating, but with the enchantment of candlelit performances (see p. 482).

At the time of the Festival of Britain, the urge to destroy – mainly old Victorian architecture – was strong; by contrast Herzog and de Meuron were regarded as heroes for so cleverly rehabilitating the derelict Bankside power station, without taking it down. And the South Bank, in spite of some of its showy developments, also found room for restoring, recycling, breathing new life into forgotten landmarks from the past, for instance, in addition to the Tate, the revamp of Oxo Tower, the Leather Market west of Bermondsey

This remarkable plaque was erected in October 1909 by the Shakespeare Reading Society of London and by Subscribers in the United Kingdom and India. At that time, it was embedded into the outside wall of the Barclay Perkins brewery, later destroyed while safeguarding the plaque. It is signed bottom right: 'W MARTIN MA LLD FSA designer ED LANTERI', the latter being the French sculptor Edouard Lanteri (1848-1917). A year later, *The Mercury* newspaper published an article carrying 'sensational' news: 'Dr [William] Martin believes he has actually discovered evidence of the existence of the stage of the Globe Theatre so recently as 1891'. This evidence, substantiated in the *Mercury* article, was challenged by Martin's contemporaries but in 1989 when the car park which now occupies the site of the brewery was excavated, the site of the Globe was confirmed.
(© The author, 2022)

Street, the Maltings or Sarson's vinegar factory off Tower Bridge Road to name just a few examples.

Oliver Wainwright, *The Guardian*'s architectural and design critic, does not mince his words: 'The construction industry … is a greedy, profligate, and polluting monster, gobbling up resources and spitting out the remains in intractable lumps' (*The Guardian*, 3 January 2020). On 12 September 2019, *The Architect's Journal* launched its Retrofirst Campaign 'urging architects to prioritise refurbishment over demolition and new build'. The new approach is also imbedded in Ruth Lang's book *Building for Change* (2022): 'Demolishing is a decision of easiness and short term. It is a waste of many things – a waste of energy, a waste of material and a waste of history. Moreover, it has a very negative social impact. For us, it is an act of violence' (quoted by Oliver Wainwright in his review of the book (*The Guardian*, 12 September 2019). This approach is new and not yet on general release. No-one overturned the demolition of the Heygate estate (2011–14), the Elephant and Castle shopping centre (2021), or most of the Shell estate in Waterloo.

Housing

Given that the South Bank is now regarded as part of Central London, it is fascinating that it has retained such a strong public housing component. This extraordinary heritage must be flagged as a significant feature; and this despite local authorities being quick to press the sales or demolition button – see for instance what happened at the Ethelred estate for partial demolition or the Heygate estate for total obliteration. In terms of residential towers, both Southwark and Bermondsey featured high in the

The 'modern' architect was seduced by the ideas of Le Corbusier here expressed in Kennington's Brandon estate (top). Below, Octavia Hill's sweet cottages in Redcross Way (Southwark) were no longer fashionable or sustainable.
(© The author, 2020 and 2018)

league table of 'Housing Completions' between 1945 and 1964 – on the eve of the reconfiguration of London's boroughs. Lambeth had completed 4920 units while Southwark's figure was at 2220. For the period 1965-68, the figures are reversed – Southwark heading the league table at 2443 with 3973 under construction while Lambeth was at 861 with 1155 under construction (figures: Glendinning & Muthesius).

'The prime need after the war was to provide more houses' wrote Bridget Cherry when reviewing public housing in Lambeth and Southwark. Professor Steve Schifferes calculated that in Great Britain 20,000 to 30,000 homes were built before the First World War, which rose to one million in the twenty years following this war and then five million after that; with the most high-rise flats built between 1966 and 1971 found in London by a long margin: 47% against 19% in Scotland and 21 % in the Northwest. At the 1951 elections, the Conservatives pledged to build 300,000 homes per year and they exceeded that target by 1954 under the Housing Minister Harold Macmillan. But this was partly achieved by lowering standards and relaxing rationing and building controls, which led to a boom in private housing. From a stylistic point of view, Bridget Cherry made these points:

> For those who believed in the Modern Movement … the most radical were beguiled by the powerful images of Le Corbusier's towers in parkland [Edward Hollamby's Brandon estate in Kennington]; others looked to the tall flats built in Scandinavia. The garden city image was no longer acceptable [Octavia Hill's cottages in Redcross Street].

The new agenda gained impetus when the LCC's Architect's Department was reorganised in 1950, taking over housing from the Valuer's Department. The 1970s introduced a new approach to public housing 'which has done more than any other type of building to alter the face of the inner suburbs in the last fifty years' noted Bridget Cherry. The move away from the Modern Movement style to embrace a revival of traditional forms and materials – for instance the 1970–76 Wellington Mills by GLC architect Barbara Bienias – did not help the public housing cause. Cherry again: 'Neo-vernacular forms, however attractive, were not enough to make the concept of the council estate widely acceptable, despite the example of some imaginatively planned schemes …'.

As early as 1946, Anthony Eden had proclaimed: 'We, of the Conservative Party must maintain that the ownership of property is not a crime or a sin, but a reward, a right, and a responsibility that must be shared as equitably as possible among all our citizens'. This was more aspirational than a reflection on reality as there was nothing on offer to follow through. But presumably it foreshadowed the 'Right to Buy' first embedded in the Housing Act of 1980 – usually associated with Margaret Thatcher in the minds of all, though its architect was Michael Heseltine.

Steve Schifferes concluded: 'Britain's story of public housing is unique. No major developed country built more council housing as proportion of its total housing stock in the fifty years to 1971. But no country dismantled its system of public housing so quickly and drastically as Britain in the 1980s.'

Hotelmania

Writing for the *New York Post* on 2 October 2014, Jennifer Ceaser shone a light on hotel building in London when reviewing five large and luxurious new hotels which appeared on the scene that year – two of them on the South Bank: the 'Shangri-La' at the Shard and 'Mondrian London' at Sea Containers UK. These are some of the more glamorous examples, but so many more have been built – no less than four for the Plaza Group, all close to one another near the Lambeth waterfront; six Premier Inn; three Hilton; three Novotel; three Marriott (if you count the two 'Autograph Collection' in Southwark) and many more, the long list crowned by the amazing Shangri-La in the Shard. The historian Jon Newman described how these hotels, too, are contributing to London's change of scale:

> Between Royal Street and the foot of Westminster Bridge the triumvirate of Becket House (12 storeys), DLD College (18 storeys) and the Park Plaza Westminster Bridge (12 storeys) suggests the future of Royal Street and a new template for Lambeth … The four Lambeth hotels of the Park Plaza group … tower over our shoulders … Are these [William Blake's] *new-chartr'd streets*? The objections to loss of office space, to saturation and to the impact of tall buildings have been overruled and former government buildings, charities and industrial spaces have been stripped out for 'upper upscale' hotel rooms with 'stunning river views' – and the illusion [in Lambeth] to be in Westminster.

Londoners can be blind to hotelscape as their buildings are often regarded as places for tourists, and non-essential or not relevant to the local population. But they should not be overlooked as they clearly form an important part of London's fabric and economy.

Sources have been placed in brackets under each entry (full references in bibliography).

Edmund Bird and Fiona Price, *Lambeth Architecture 1965–99*, 2015; *The Art of the Jubilee Line – Constructing the Extension*, 1999, London Transport/Museum of London; Marshall; Miles Glendinning and Stephan Muthesius, *Tower Block: Modern Public Housing in England, Scotland, Wales and Northern Ireland*, 1994; *The Guardian*, as cited;

VAUXHALL AND LAMBETH

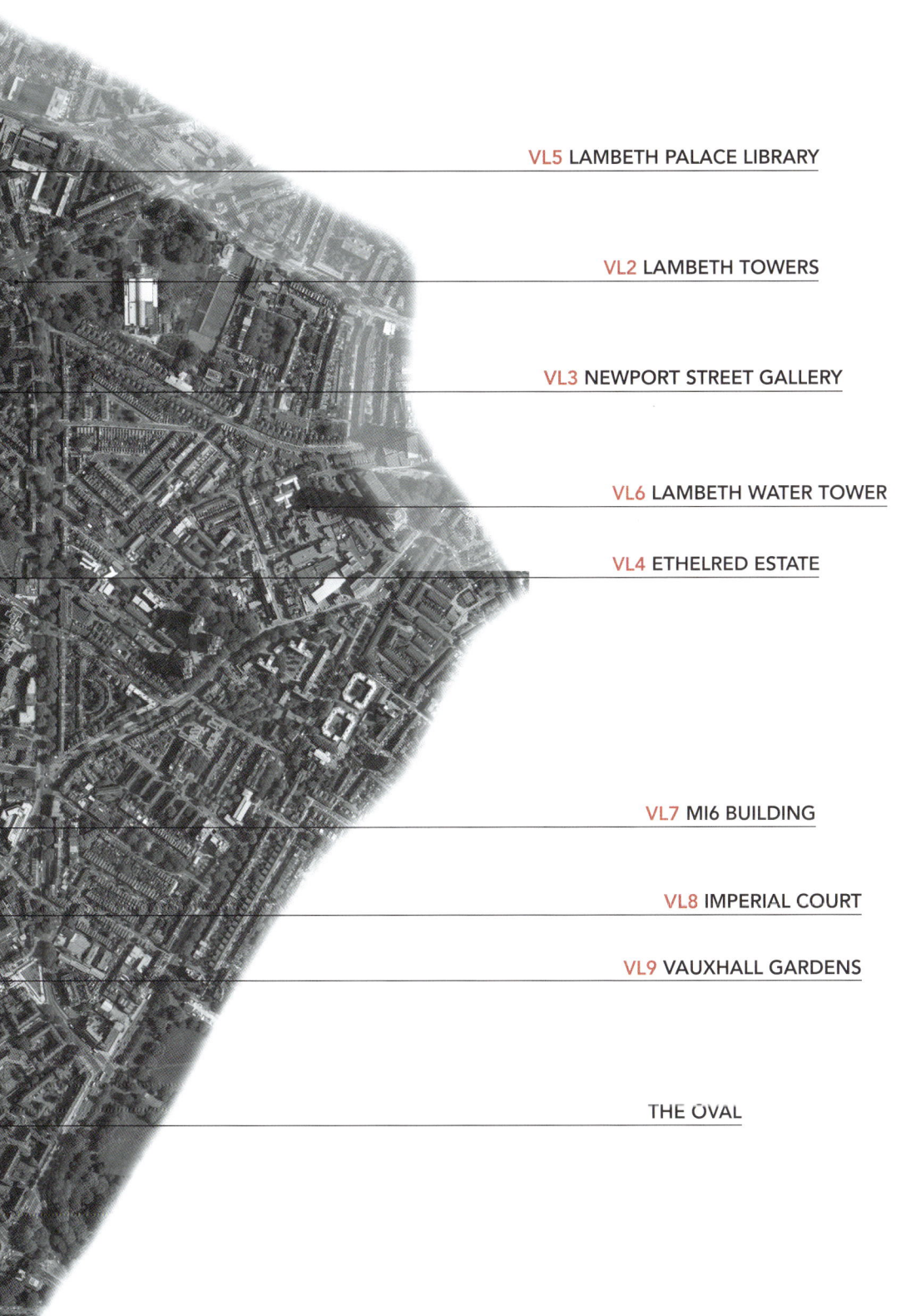

VL1 WESTMINSTER BRIDGE
VL5 LAMBETH PALACE LIBRARY
VL2 LAMBETH TOWERS
VL3 NEWPORT STREET GALLERY
VL6 LAMBETH WATER TOWER
VL4 ETHELRED ESTATE
VL7 MI6 BUILDING
VL8 IMPERIAL COURT
VL9 VAUXHALL GARDENS
THE OVAL

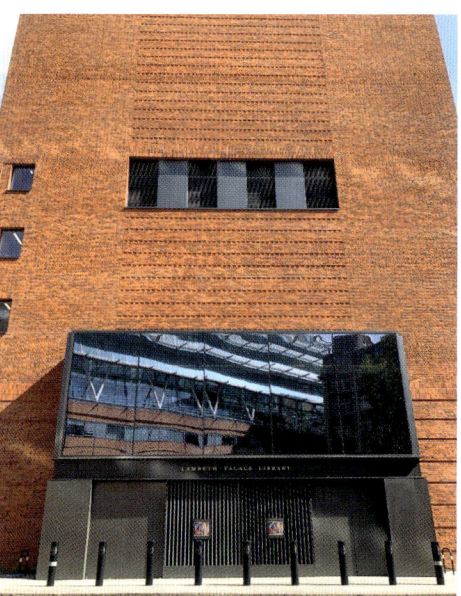

Lambeth Palace Library, Lambeth Palace Road, is sited at the far northern extremity of Lambeth Palace Gardens which it overlooks.
(© The author, 2022)

Above & opposite:
Damien Hirst's Newport Street Gallery just south of Lambeth Palace boasts enormous galleries carved out of this former theatre scenery studios. The staircases (opposite) are pure poetry.
(© The author, 2023)

(VL1) Westminster Bridge; continued from p. 159. Thomas Page's cast-iron bridge replaced the eighteenth-century bridge and opened in 1862. It was Grade II listed in 1970 (amendment in 1981).

Westminster Bridge, painted green, and Lambeth Bridge, painted red apparently take their cue from the colours of the seats in the Houses of Parliament – red for the House of Lords and green for the House of Commons. The Gothic decoration was designed by Charles Barry the elder. (Historic England listed buildings)

(VL2) Lambeth Palace Library at the northern end of the Palace's gardens in Lambeth Palace Road, provided yet another tower for Lambeth Palace, this time to house the Church of England's archives and library. Designed by Wright and Wright, it opened its doors in spring 2021. The landscape designer Dan Pearson was commissioned to deal with the building's garden side. From the architects' website: 'The contemporary redbrick building has four and five-storey wings, rising to a nine-storey central tower, crowned by a viewing platform that will be periodically open to the public'. Oliver Wainwright reviewed this new London venue for *The Guardian* in an article headed: 'Guarding the apocalypse: inside the fortress of the new Lambeth Palace Library' where he explains:

> Wright & Wright, won the project in an invited competition, beating major international names including Zaha Hadid and Herzog & de Meuron, in part because they were the only firm to push the building right to the edge of the site in order to occupy less of the garden.

Of the magnificent collections the new building houses, Wainwright writes:

> For centuries, this precious hoard has been kept in a series of leaky, draughty rooms in the palace, gradually filling up every cramped corner. Now, after 400 years, it finally has a purpose-built home – and it's safe to say that, if the apocalypse ever comes to south London, this fortified building will probably survive it.

(*The Guardian*, 22 December 2020)

(VL3) Newport Street Gallery by Caruso St John Architects, 2004-15. The gallery takes up most of the east side of Newport Street. It is made up of five buildings: industrial buildings in the centre, framed by contemporary buildings at either end.

The industrial buildings at 1–7 Newport Street were Grade II listed by English Heritage (1991). 'Mara's scene painting shop' was a theatre carpentry workshop at Nos 1 and 3 while Nos 5 and 7 housed the painted scenery shop. What made it remarkable was 'the facility to design an entire theatrical set … Only 4 early theatrical painting workshops are known to exist', English Heritage pointed out, but 'although the other 3 are 10 years earlier this is the only one with the facility to design and build an extra set'.

In 2016 the conversion and expansion project won the prestigious Stirling Prize for the UK best building,

the gallery being thus described:
> the conversion of almost an entire street of listed industrial buildings … into a free public gallery for artist Damien Hirst's private art collection by Caruso St John Architects … This is a very bold and confident project wherein old and new are seamlessly joined and reinterpreted to create superb gallery spaces in a building with a very significant civic presence … The gallery is set to have an important beneficial impact on the larger surrounding community.

(RIBA website, accessed November 2022; Historic England listed buildings website)

(VL4) Ethelred estate, 1969–87, Black Prince Road, was designed by the Architects Co-Partnership and built in six phases. It was originally composed of four tower blocks, medium-rise blocks and the Beaufoy School (now Lilian Baylis, listed and converted to housing). Cherry and Pevsner found the estate 'grim'. On 26 June 1997, the twenty-two-storey Kerrin tower was rocked by an enormous explosion, caused by the communal boiler at the base of the tower; followed injuries for eleven out of the eighty-six residents, and also homelessness though luckily, no one died. Two years later Lambeth Council who pleaded guilty to health and safety failures – the result of a botched refurbishment – were fined. The tower was demolished in 1999 in pursuit of regeneration plans which did not materialise; after five years in limbo the Council sold the site to Barratt homes: their development of 214 new homes across five medium-sized blocks, renamed Kennington Park Square, was ready in 2009, and thus judged by the *Inside Housing* magazine: 'Kennington Park Square sits rather incongruously in the middle of a post-war council estate, like a shiny new car in a line of old ones'.

After Grenfell, London's own 'towering inferno', everything changed: every tower block in England has been scrutinised for defects and Kennington Park Square failed the test, leading to the damning headline: 'They have swapped one unsafe building for another'. Public or private, it seems no scheme is immune and Lambeth Council is no longer running the estate which has been offloaded to the housing association Watmos.
(Bird & Price, 2015, p. 68; Cherry & Pevsner; "They have swapped one unsafe building for another': the story of Kennington Park Square' by Peter Apps in *Inside Housing*, 10 June 2021, accessed 31 October 2022)

(VL5) Lambeth Towers, 1964–71, at the junction of Lambeth and Kennington Roads, was designed by George Finch (1930-2013), assisted by engineer Ted Happold. The quirky design was published in 1965 and the building opened in 1972. It is tempting to compare it with its namesake in Southwark, erected three years later in 1975, near London Bridge; though this is an unfair comparison between a housing block and an office tower, it also exemplifies the considerable gap between the two boroughs. Southwark was influenced by its proximity to the City, erecting large housing estates for the masses (Aylesbury, Heygate) while Lambeth pursued a socialist, people-centred programme through figures such as George Finch and Ted Hollamby (1921-1999), a life-long devotee of the great socialist and founder of the Arts & Crafts movement – William Morris (1834–1896).

Elaine Harwood in her *Guardian* obituary for Finch on 27 February 2013, wrote:
> Finch's masterpiece was Lambeth Towers, a one-off design opposite the Imperial War Museum, 10 storeys of flats set over a luncheon club and doctor's surgery, inspired by the work of Moshe Safdie and built at the same time as Safdie's Habitat blocks for the

George Finch's Lambeth Towers at the corner of Kennington and Lambeth Roads, photographed in 2012.
(Photo: Sean Macintosh. Image in the public domain, Wikimedia Commons)

Montreal Expo of 1967. Each flat was individually articulated within a cranked concrete frame that maximised the tight site, creating a strong, square patterning that evoked Piet Mondrian's paintings (left). (Bird & Price, 2015, p. 93; Cherry & Pevsner)

(VL6) Lambeth Water Tower, Renfrew Road, near the Elephant and Castle; continued from pp. 237–239. This water tower was once part of a vast Victorian establishment – the Lambeth workhouse and infirmary, famous for its association with Charlie Chaplin, however brief the actor's sojourn there actually was – weeks rather than years. Renfrew Road was designated a conservation area on 28 October 1985 as it is the home of several important civic buildings including a fire station (1868) and a courthouse, with prison cells (1869) alongside the workhouse for 820 inmates (1871–3) and the Infirmary (1877, later Lambeth Hospital). Much has been destroyed but Historic England have Grade II listed what survives: the Magistrates' Court (1993, now the Jam Yang Buddhist Centre), the former Fire Station at 46 Renfrew Road (2000), the former workhouse's administrative building in Dugard Way (2008) which houses the cinema museum and the Water Tower (2008). The latter was recognised as being 'of special architectural interest as an imposing and distinctive water tower in the Venetian Gothic style, constituting a rare feature in inner London'. It was built in 1877, designed by Fowler and Hill.

In 2010, Leigh Osbourne and Graham Voce, based at the nearby Strata tower were so interested in the derelict Water Tower, that they bought it for £380,000. The full restoration and extension of this landmark was the object of a Channel 4 'Grand Designs' programme (aired on 17 October 2012). The owners appointed Acanthus WSM Architects and spent almost 2 million bringing it back to life – an extraordinary luxury 'house' in a ten-storey tower with two new extensions – one for the lift and one for the kitchen-dining-living spaces on four storeys. Its crowning glory at the top of the tower – the prospect room – nesting in the original water tank which was 'retained and holes were cut into the one-inch-thick cast iron structure to create windows'. The 'house' was first put on the market in 2018, originally priced at 3.6 million; it eventually sold in 2021 for around 2.75 million. It was bought by Jamie Hamer, a London-based commercial director.
(Historic England's Listed Buildings website; the Architects' website has Karen Stylianides' article on the Tower published in *Grand Designs* Magazine, 28 February 2017; *Evening Standard*, 29 June 2021)

(VL7) **MI6 building**, 85 Albert Embankment, Vauxhall Cross, was designed by Sir Terry Farrell and the site developed by Regalian properties Plc; construction of the ten-storey building began in 1990 and it was opened by Queen Elizabeth II in 1994. Its real name is the SIS building for Secret Intelligence Service. Built by Laing Management Contracting for Regalian Properties and then purchased by the Government. It is made of reinforced concrete, clad with concrete panels. Described by Edmund Bird as 'one of the best examples in England of the post-modern style which reigned supreme in the 1980s'; its monumental outline recalls that of a truncated pyramid and the choice of green and off-white colour scheme is particularly resonant with the presence of Vauxhall Gardens on the east side and the building's original use of trees on the river facade.
(Bird & Price, 2015, p. 25; Historic England – images and books)

(VL8) **Imperial Court**, 225 Kennington Lane; continued from p. 240. The grand premises of the former School of Licensed Victuallers were taken over by the Navy, Army and Air Forces Institutes (NAAFI) between 1921 and 1992, after which it was reconverted into private apartments. The building had been Grade II listed in 1981. To account for the magnificence of its architecture Cherry and Pevsner wrote: 'a school would never have been so ambitious in its architecture before the C19, when higher education for the middle class became important enough to call for the monumental'.
(Bacon 23; *Survey of London* 26; Cherry and Pevsner)

(VL9) **Vauxhall Gardens**. For the history of these gardens,

This is what the 'Hawk's Tower' looks like now, known as the Lambeth Water Tower.
(© The author, 2023)

Opposite:

David Hepher, The Hawk's Tower (Elephant and Castle), 1986-7, oil on canvas. This is the world of David Hepher, filled with solid walls and lofty structures – the water tower (left) and the infirmary (right) were both part of the massive Lambeth workhouse which stood on that site. The artist turns the hawk, a symbol of wild life, into the star of the painting; the human figures along the bottom pay homage to L S Lowry. This evocation of Lambeth in the 1980s could not be more at odds with the 2020s neighbourhood above: the water tower, restored and expanded, has become a luxurious residence, the hospital demolished and replaced by housing towering over streets of Victorian housing.
(Photo: Flowers Gallery © The artist)

see pp. 327 ff. The famous pleasure gardens were demolished in 1859. On 27 June 1860, the Prince of Wales laid the first stone of the Schools of St Mary-the-Less which relocated to the southern edge of Vauxhall Gardens and still exist, now converted to a residential development. The area then was described in *The Builder* as 'a very poor district' adding 'Vauxhall Gardens are now being built over, so that in a short time the population will be most materially increased' (quoted in *The Illustrated London News*, 23 March 1861). The church of St Peter next to the school was built in 1863–4, its altar standing on the site of Vauxhall Gardens' firework tower; both the school and church were designed by the Victorian architect John Loughborough Pearson. The rest of the gardens were completely built over. The development lasted until the 1970s when the dilapidated, sometimes bomb-damaged houses which had become slums were demolished and replaced by a park which opened to the public on 9 October 1976 – Spring Gardens, renamed Vauxhall Pleasure Gardens in 2012.

('David Beevers, 'St Peter's Church, Vauxhall – a History' published on https://vauxhallhistory.org/st-peters-vauxhall/; http://www.vauxhallgardens.com/vauxhall_gardens_briefhistory_page.html#VauxhallToday)

(VL10) The Vauxhall/Nine Elms redevelopment, one of the largest regeneration areas in London – stretching from Lambeth Bridge to Battersea Power Station (227 hectares across Lambeth and Wandsworth Councils). Regeneration has been guided by three major documents:

• The Mayor of London's 2012 Opportunity Area Planning Framework (OAPF)
• The 2013 Vauxhall Supplementary Planning Document (SPD) by Lambeth Council
• The 'Visioning Vauxhall' document prepared by Allies and Morrison, Urban Practitioners and Lambeth Council, May 2016: '3,500 new homes and 8,000 jobs will be created in Vauxhall'.

All were online and in addition, Transport for London prepared proposals for removing the one-way system and improving the transport interchange.

(VL10a) Keybridge, Vauxhall, by Allies and Morrison for BT Property,

Far left and left:

Keybridge, this Allies and Morrison's model is described as a 'massing model'. With its sliding height levels, from St Anne and All Saints church to the Tower, the architect sought to accommodate the two extreme scales at work on this site.

(Allies and Morrison)

Mount Anvil. This development replaces a 1970s building, called Keybridge House, a large concrete podium and tower, designed by G W Mills & Associates for the Post Office Telecommunications as their telex centre. This is how the new scheme is described on Allies and Morrison's Instagram post of 21 November 2019: 'Keybridge is a hybrid housing scheme incorporating multiple typologies, mansion blocks, towers, terraces, maisonettes, a school and even 'houses on roof tops'.'

This multiplicity of building types on varying scales has been given a name, 'urban picturesque', by the lead Allies and Morrison architect: Alfredo Caraballo (Instagram post 7 April 2019). Keybridge's predecessor was an austere 'forbiddingly huge' building with 'a crushing effect' on the church of St Anne. The new tower with its thirty-five floors, is no different but the scheme gives each of its components breathing space and variety of form. The design seeks to relate to two contrasting scales: that of the past – the church, the pub – and that of the present – the cluster of towers which has lately sprung up in Vauxhall. The development is 'permeable', one of this firm's tenets, and includes several pockets of open space.

Allies and Morrison considered converting the old Keybridge House but were defeated by 'the almost 5m-high floor to ceiling heights in the tower, specifically constructed for their original telephone exchange function'.

The first residents moved in in spring 2020 and the scheme was complete in 2021.
(Cherry & Pevsner; Bird & Price, 2015, p. 161; Allies and Morrison's website)

(VL10b) The 'Atlas' building at Vauxhall was designed by Fielden Clegg Bradley on a restricted triangular site for student accommodation (553 rooms, with roof gardens, with a gym and pool in the basement). Illustrated overleaf.

(VL11) St George Wharf and tower, Vauxhall Cross by Broadway Malyan architects, 2001–2010. This development, which at dusk on the river glitters like the emerald city of Oz – without the yellow brick road – has both been successful and widely criticised. It was shortlisted for the Carbuncle Cup in 2006. The forty-nine-storey tower is 181 metres high, one of the tallest residential buildings in London and it was the last to be built (2012). It is a mixed-use development with 1400 apartments,

David Hepher, 'Birth', 2021, exhibited in 'Concrete Skies: the Vauxhall series' (2002) based around the early stage of construction of the thirty-two storey Atlas building. But the artist is not interested in the final product, focusing instead on the construction of the austere lift/service shaft rising to the sky, 'fed' by the umbilical cord like structure – the crane sitting alongside it. In keeping with Hepher's methods, the painting is created on a layer of concrete; human presence is only suggested through graffiti – a realistic touch when dealing with aging housing estates but a paradox on a building which has not yet been built.

(Photo: Flowers © David Hepher)

The Atlas building at Vauxhall, completed. © The author, 2022

offices, retail space and restaurants. The London Borough of Lambeth had such reservations about the tower ('too tall', 'harmful to the views of the Palace') that they felt it should not be built. As with the Shard, the decision was left in the hands of John Prescott. Conservative Kenneth Baker made a passionate plea against building the tower, comparing it to Aldous Huxley's *Brave New World*, a tower for the 'toffs':

> So we have a Labour deputy prime minister, a man who I think would describe himself as a good-old socialist, giving approval for a tower for the toffs. The other irony is that half of those flats, which will sell upwards of £1 m – probably the higher one goes, more than £5m – will be bought by foreigners.

St George Wharf development with tower, Vauxhall Cross, photographed from the north bank in 2014.

(Photo: Jamesbeard. Image in the public domain, Wikimedia Commons)

Prescott approved the scheme saying it was 'a first-class design', but Lord Baker had a point, as demonstrated by journalist Robert Booth in his piece for *The Guardian*: 'The clocks over the concierge desk show the time in Hong Kong, Abu Dhabi and Moscow – leaving visitors in little doubt who owns homes in the Tower.'
(Robert Booth, 'Tower for the toffs': UK's tallest skyscraper and playground of the rich, *The Guardian*, 24 May 2016)

   (VL12) Vauxhall Bridge. See p. 232

   (VL13) US Embassy – see pp. 396 ff

   (VL14) Albert Embankment: several developments of luxury apartments and penthouses, squeezed between the Albert Embankment and the railway line. The site was developed by the St James Group, one of the property subsidiaries of the Berkeley Group and comprises: Riverbank Park Plaza at No 18; The Corniche by Foster & Partners; the Dumont by David Walker architects, 180 apartments, completed in 2020; and Rogers Stirk Harbour's (RSHP) Merano building. Simon Elmer from Architects for Social Housing used The Corniche and Merano as examples of his 'Architecture of Death' exposing the way in which such high-flying developments sometimes hide corrupt practices and questionable outcomes. When considering early apartment sales, both The Corniche and Merano attracted 100% of overseas investors. This figure would have certainly dropped a little as more flats were sold, though Market Towers at one Nine Elms was still at 97.8% after the sale of 141 apartments. Two of these developments have been selected here:

   (VL14a) The Corniche, 23–24 Albert Embankment, is by

Right:

Vauxhall is rapidly becoming a neighbourhood of two halves – life at the top in a contemporary tower or at the bottom in the sweet old-fashioned Victorian houses which have survived redevelopment.

(© The author, 2021)

Below:

The rapid development of Albert Embankment near Vauxhall is best viewed from the north bank.

(© The author, 2021)

Foster + Partners (RSHP), 2012-19, and thus described on the architects' website:

> The Corniche is a mixed-use development of three landmark towers along the Albert Embankment on the south bank of the River Thames, opposite the Houses of Parliament. The buildings range from 15 to 27 storeys in height and provide 253 apartments, including affordable homes for senior living, along with offices, restaurants and a residents' bar, gym, pool and spa. They contribute to the wider regeneration of the Nine Elms development zone, a 195-hectare development between Lambeth Bridge and Chelsea Bridge of 16,000 new homes, which represents the largest urban initiative of its kind in Europe. (Accessed November 2022)

The affordable housing element is squeezed at the back of the de Luxe towers, overlooking the railway line: 'Bankhouse' was developed by One Housing Group Housing Association.

(VL14b) RSHP's Merano building, 2011–18, twenty-eight floors at 30-34 Albert Embankment. From the architects' website:

> The structure of the building is a simple concrete frame

with steel bracing used to provide stability. This allows for the east and west façades to be primarily glass, creating a lightweight, transparent envelope ... Balconies and winter gardens are formed of a lightweight steel structure with colour applied to the soffits and flank walls, which brighten the exterior in contrast to the building's monochromatic surroundings. (Accessed 25 November 2022).

Judged by RIBA Journal to be 'of the highest architectural quality using prefabricated elements', this award-winning scheme was designed by Graham Stirk from Rogers Stirk Harbour and Partners (RSHP). (https://architectsforsocialhousing.co.uk/2018/10/07/the-architecture-of-death/; architects' website as cited; *London Se1 community website*, 15 August 2012 for Merano, 19 March 2013 for The Corniche and 11 March 2015)

(VL15) **Lambeth Bridge**, 1929–32, 'a five-span steel arch structure carried on granite-faced reinforced concrete piers and abutments'. The first bridge, designed by Peter W Barlow, opened in 1862 on a site which had long been associated with the Horseferry running between Westminster and the south bank.

> It was of stiffened suspension type, 252.4m long, divided into three spans, each 81.7m wide, by piers carrying the towers which supported the suspension cables. Tolls were abolished in 1879 but by this time the iron structure had begun to rust severely and major repairs had to be carried out in 1887. Despite this, the state of the bridge continued to deteriorate and in 1910 it had to be closed to vehicular traffic.

The First World War delayed rebuilding and the next bridge opened in 1932, designed by engineer Sir George Humphreys and architects Sir Reginald Bloomfield and G Topham Forrest. The bridge blends seamlessly red cast iron decorations with stone and steel. The Bridge was Grade II listed in 2008 with 'attached parapets, light standards, associated walls to approaches and obelisks'. It is easily recognisable with its obelisks and quirky lamp posts. (Historic England Listed buildings, accessed 5 December 2022)

WATERLOO

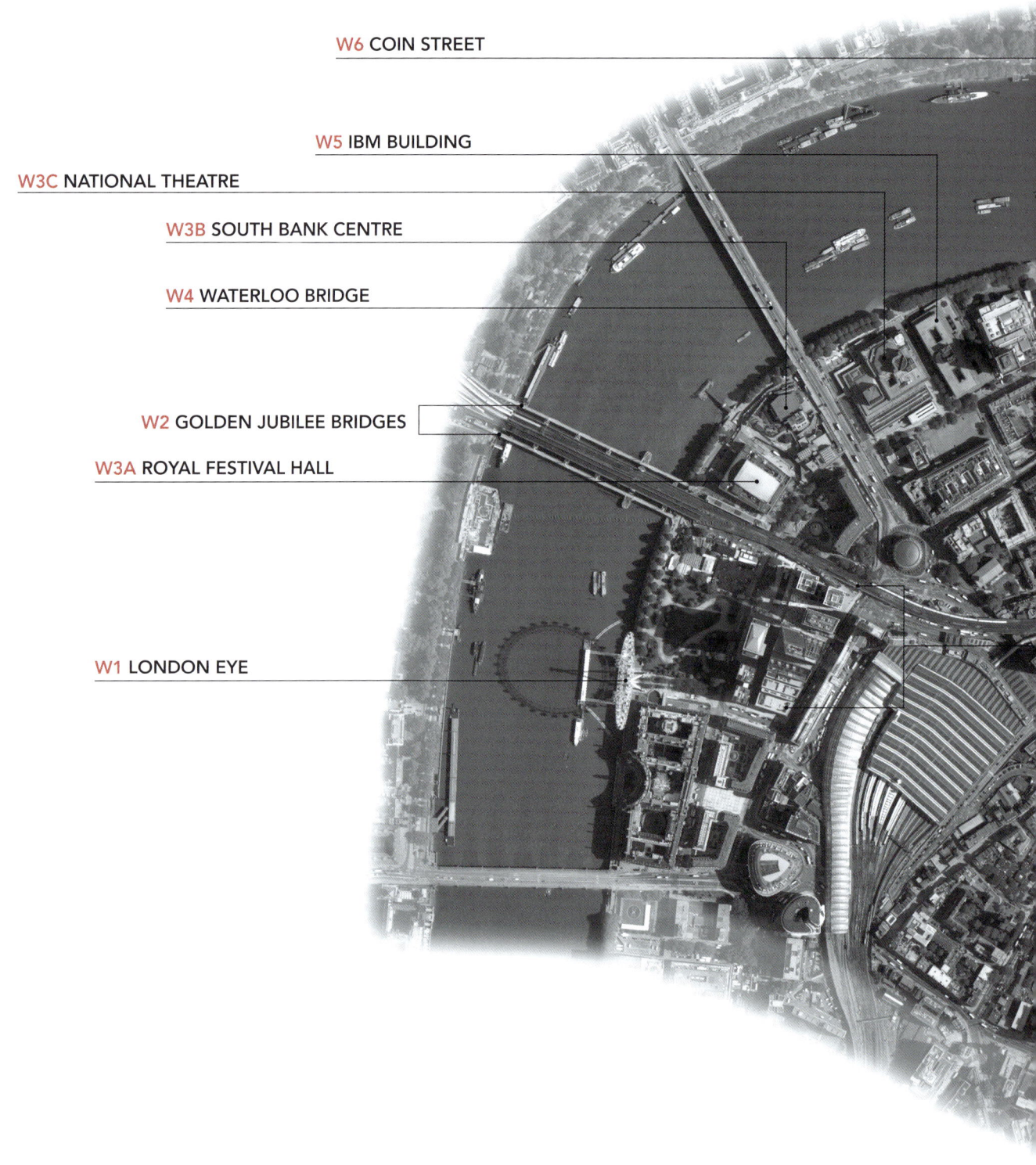

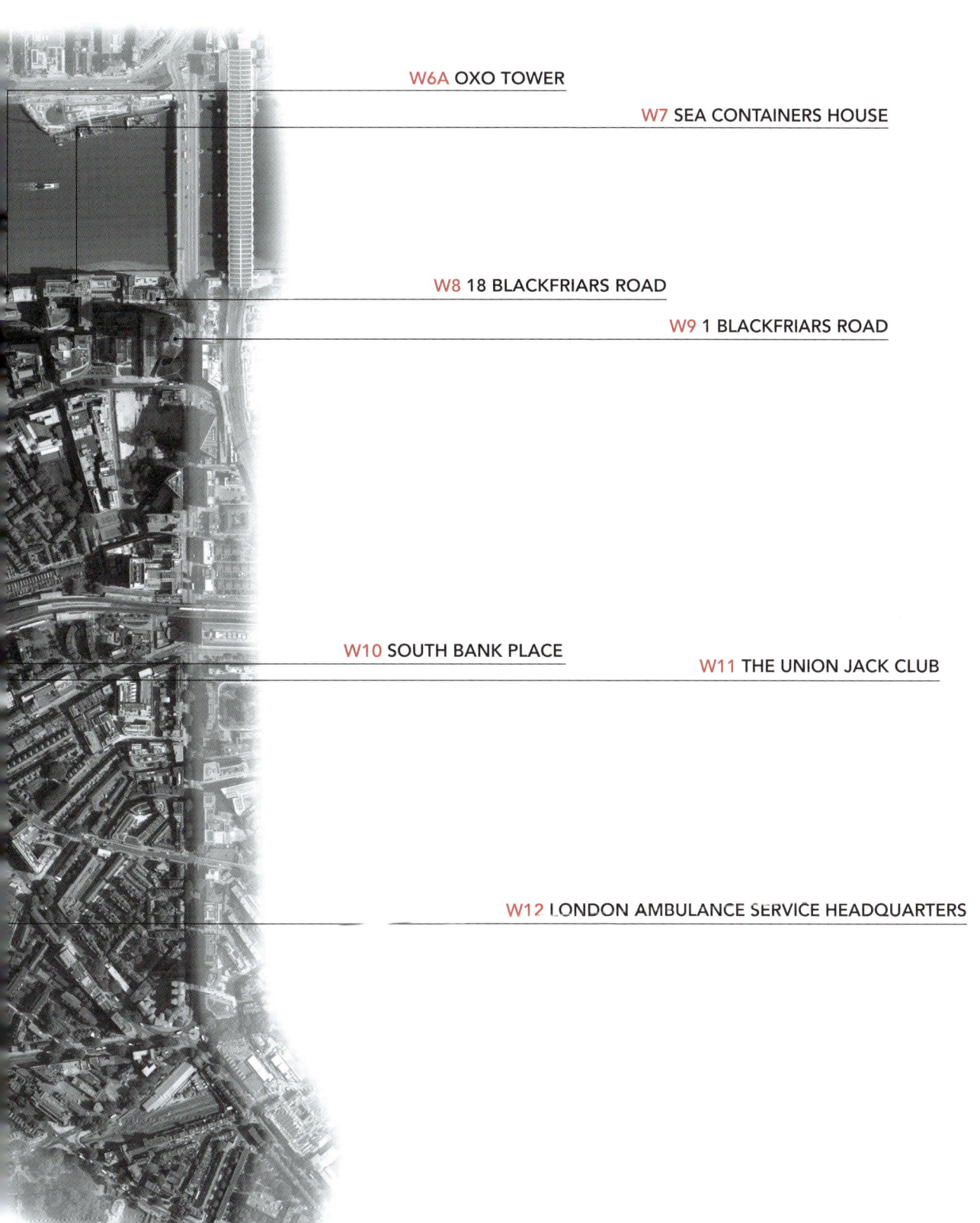

(W1) The London Eye, originally conceived and designed by Marks Barfield Architects, opened to the public in 2000. See p. 298 for picture.

'Our house and our livelihoods were on the line. Then – in front of the world's media – it didn't lift up' architect David Marks recalled. There were indeed plenty of set-backs but the wheel has triumphed over the odds. The story is briskly told in a frank *Guardian* interview. Husband and wife team David Marks (DM) and Julia Barfield (JB), entered a competition in 1993 for a landmark to commemorate the new millennium; they were attracted by the prospect of the designs being published in the *Sunday Times*. DM came up with the idea of the wheel and JB with the site on the South Bank. Alas, nobody won that competition as the judges felt none of the entries were good enough. But Marks Barfield firmly believed they had had a great idea and after endless consultation, a planning application was submitted.

'The Eye was meant to be bigger – 500 ft high with 60 pods holding 16 people' explained DM but

> we realised that, if you had fewer pods, there'd be more space between them and therefore better views. So we reduced the number to 32.

And the height was reduced to 443 ft (135m) for budgetary reasons. It was the biggest Ferris wheel in the world when it was first erected – so called after George Washington Ferris's first wheel at the 1893 World's Columbian Exposition in Chicago; its correct description should be 'a cantilevered observation wheel', and as such, it still is the world's tallest.

It was built as a temporary structure with a five-year lease but in July 2002 Lambeth granted it permanent status. The original owners were Marks Barfield, the Tussauds Group and British Airways, but Tussauds bought British Airways' share in 2005 and then Marks Barfield's in 2006. It now belongs to Merlin Entertainments. Julia Barfield proudly recalled: 'The thing we're most proud of is that, when we negotiated the long-term plan in 2006, we ensured the Eye contributed 1% of ticket revenues in perpetuity to the local community'.

There were of course a number of requests for repeating this feat elsewhere but MB explained some of the reasons why the project could not readily be duplicated:

> It was very much designed for London, for the circumstance in which it is: for three or four million visitors a year, for a location that was highly accessible, with fantastic views. And if you want to do a similar kind of project in another location, it may not have the visitor numbers, it may not have the views, it may not have the revenues or the funds available to build or operate it. The London Eye employs about 300 people. It's a very expensive operation … there are only a handful of places in the world where you could do a similar project. (*The Guardian*, 27 March 2006)

One of the most exciting aspects of this project was described in a *Civil Engineering Journal* article:

> The project was truly European with major components coming from six countries [much coming by water]:
> - steel – supplied from the UK and fabricated in Holland
> - cables – came from Italy
> - bearings – came from Germany
> - spindle and hub – cast in the Czech Republic
> - capsules came from France (and the glass for these came from Italy)
> - electrical components and civils work – all UK based

The article also bears witness to the astonishing success of the London Eye: public demand for 'flights' was almost overwhelming in the year of opening: 3.2 million visitors, well over the original forecast of 2.2 million. ('Towering ambition' by Steve Rose in *The Guardian*, 27 March 2006; 'Architects David Marks and Julia Barfield – How we made the London Eye' in *The Guardian*, 20 February 2015; 'Building the British Airways London Eye' by A P Mann, N Thompson and M Smits in *Civil Engineering*, May 2001, Volume 144, Issue 2)

(W2) The Golden Jubilee Bridges, by architects Lifschutz Davidson Sandilands, were ready in 2002. They are two pedestrian bridges framing Charing Cross (railway) bridge which many Londoners still call Hungerford Bridge. The new bridges share the foundations of the railway crossing. From the architects' website (accessed 17 November 2022): 'Their true success was confirmed in 2014, when it was revealed that 8.4million pedestrians use them each year, making them the most-used pedestrian crossings over the Thames.'

These architects have been involved with several landmark projects on the South Bank. They realised several schemes for Coin Street Community Builders in the 1990s (see W6) and in Bermondsey, they delivered the Jacob's Island residential project of 200 apartments (1996) on the site of the famous rookery illustrated on p. 292. In 2001, commissioned by the South Bank Employers' Group, they prepared the South Bank Urban Design Strategy. More recently, they designed the Hoxton Hotel near Christ Church (2019) and also designed and coordinated 'illuminated river' – the lighting of nine bridges, from London Bridge to Lambeth Bridge (2021) which had first been suggested by Marks Barfield in 2006 (Steve Rose's 'Towering Ambition' in *The Guardian*, 27 March 2006).

(W3) The South Bank

What so many Londoners casually designate as the South Bank can best be described as the Cultural Quarter of the South Bank. It is massed along the Thames at Waterloo and consists of three distinct clusters which, in chronological order, are:

(W3a) The Royal Festival Hall, Grade I listed building (in 1988), designed by Leslie Martin and Peter Moro, for the 1951 Festival of Britain. In a terrific 2007 article Jonathan Glancey wrote for *The Guardian*, he described the building as

> some giant postwar oceanliner berthed on London's South Bank ... the fundamental design of the building remains an intellectual and structural joy ... The architecture was ... inspired by a symphony of ideas drawn from sources as diverse as revolutionary Soviet constructivism, Le Corbusier, politely democratic Scandinavian modernism and, of course, ships and the sea.

Allies and Morrison were appointed in 1992 as 'house architects' and carried out a major restoration between 1999 and 2007: a programme of 'pure restoration', 'discrete new additions' and reversing the 'gradual incursion of service accommodation into the foyers' after the arrival of Greater London Government offices in 1986. Jonathan Glancey again: 'the building has been brought back to life in a way wholly recognisable to those who first came to listen to concerts here ... Equally, the RFH looks wonderfully fresh and new'. Also see p. 541.

The Festival Hall is the home of the Poetry Library 'housing the largest public collection of modern poetry in the world' specifies the South Bank website (accessed 3 December 2022). Founded in 1953, it moved to the Festival Hall in 1988. The current poet in residence, Simon Armitage, found suitable words to describe its soul: 'The National Poetry Library is Britain's poetic brain'.

(W3b) The South Bank Centre, 1963–68, is made up of The Hayward Gallery, the Queen Elizabeth Hall (1106 seats) and Purcell Room (372 seats) – an art gallery and two music venues, all examples of Brutalist architecture, a style widely adopted in the 1960s-70s and widely criticised and destroyed later on, many complaining of its austere, unfriendly aesthetics. The LCC/GLC's Architects' Department was responsible for this cluster of buildings linked to one another, by elevated walkways, not all on the same level: 'it is a thrilling experience, if the weather is fine and you are at leisure', wrote Bridget Cherry, 'But what if it rains, what if you are late, what if you

'Approaching storm', acrylic on paper by Gethin Evans, 2015. The artist is particularly sensitive to the quality of light on the South Bank. The view is taken from the north west corner of the Royal Festival Hall, looking east in the direction of Waterloo Bridge. The artist is partial to the play of horizontal and vertical lines enhanced during the refurbishment of the concert hall by Allies and Morrison, completed in 2007.
(© The artist)

find steps a strain?' she added, and went on to compare the contraption to the nightmarish prisons (*Carceri*) dreamt up by the eighteenth-century artist Piranesi.
(W3c) The National Theatre, 1961–76, was designed by Sir Denys Lasdun & Partners, using grey concrete with shuttering marks, and raking struts on the east side. The square building holds three theatres: the Olivier (1160 seats), the Lyttelton (890 seats) and the Dorfman (former Cottesloe, up to 400 seats, depending on layout). The fly-towers of the Olivier and Lyttelton theatres project boldly upwards, as do the entrance turrets but all verticals are firmly counterbalanced by strong horizontal lines. Also see pp. 437–439.
(Jonathan Glancey, 'Pomp and circumstance', *The Guardian*, 30 May 2007; *Allies and Morrison*, ed. by Ian Latham, 2019; Bird & Price, 2015, pp. 32 ff; Cherry & Pevsner)

(W4) Waterloo Bridge, 1937–42; continued from p. 252. The current bridge, the second on the site, was planned in the 1930s with a design by Sir Giles Gilbert Scott, assisted by engineers from Rendell Palmer & Tritton. The Second World War delayed its construction. This bridge became known as the 'ladies' bridge' because the war considerably depleted the workforce available and women were drafted in to help. This has been established through research by Dr Christine Wall, making a mockery of Sir Herbert Morrison's rousing words at the opening ceremony on 10 December 1945:

> the men who built Waterloo Bridge are fortunate men. They know that, although their names may be forgotten, their work will be a pride and use to London for many generations to come. To the hundreds of workers in stone, in steel, in timber, in concrete the new bridge is a monument to their skill and craftsmanship.

This bridge was first listed in 1981 (amended 2015).
(Historic England Listed Buildings)

(W5) IBM Marketing Centre, 76–78 Upper Ground, was designed by Sir Denys Lasdun & Partners shortly after the National Theatre (NT) to accommodate offices for 1000 staff. It was Lasdun's last major work. This five-storey building, 1979-83, stands next to the NT on the Thames waterfront. Edmund Bird observes 'it has a particularly successful relationship' with it. This was analysed by The Twentieth Century Society when it defended the IBM building against the proposed invasive extension of 2020: 'The IBM building was deliberately designed as a low key neighbour to the NT, and in C20's view the proposed increase in size would destroy the subservience the IBM building displays towards the adjacent NT'. The Society, alarmed by the plans of Allford Hall Monaghan Morris architects, had taken immediate steps to have the building listed and were successful. This led to the headline in *SE1 online magazine* of 22 June 2020: 'Plans to alter the IBM building on the South Bank have been thrown into doubt after the Government listed the building at grade II'. The planning application was withdrawn; but a revised scheme has now been granted planning permission. The architects had been commissioned by the Dubai-based owner – prior to this, it belonged to Lord Sugar's Amsprop firm. Historic England's entry on this building reveals:

> The NT objected to the designs of the new IBM building, but Lasdun argued that the NT would benefit from an amplified setting, in which the NT would remain the dominant element, and the pair would be able to hold their own better against the new developments coming to the area.

The project had its detractors, Deyan Sudjic in *Blueprint* (October 1984) wrote that it is: 'not the kind of building that is immediately appealing. It is grey, made up of a series of slabs piled one on top of each other, and it is conspicuously lacking in decoration'. Though the critic admitted there was much to admire in the building's detail.
(Cherry & Pevsner; Bird & Price, 2015, p. 161; Historic England's Listed Buildings website; SE1 Community News website)

(W6) Coin Street, Waterloo. In the run up to the new millennium, Coin Street Community Builders seemed to go from strength to strength after acquiring industrial land from the GLC in 1984. Their ethos was to build affordable housing for local people and they first delivered Mulberry Housing Cooperative on the north side of Stamford Street, completed in 1988, before turning their attention to another plot, on Broadwall, overlooking Bernie Spain Gardens – the Palm Housing Cooperative, designed by Lifschutz Davidson (1994). 'This award-winning scheme is one of the most highly acclaimed housing developments in London to be built in the 1990s', wrote Edmund Bird. Finally, the Iroko Housing Co-op for large family homes was designed by Haworth Tompkins and completed in 2001 (fifty nine homes). However, the land was purchased almost forty years ago, and the last housing scheme they delivered is over twenty years old. What has been happening at Coin Street since? A well-informed local resident, who wishes to remain anonymous, commented:

> It seems quite scandalous that some of the land bought cheaply in 1984 with the aim of providing social housing is still undeveloped. And however laudable the institution, it seems wrong to have provided a site for the Rambert Dance Company on this land and also to envisage the construction of a skyscraper of private flats in Doon Street even if it subsidises a swimming pool. The director of Coin Street Community Builders was instrumental in thwarting

the office development originally proposed but he now seems to run this organisation as a personal project in a rather unhurried manner, with no accountability and no pressure to get things done. The Coin Street Community Builders developed a good working relationship with Lifschutz Davidson architects who devised several highly successful schemes for them. After the Broadwall housing scheme came the complex refurbishment of Oxo Tower Wharf (1996) – transforming the former 1900 power station, turned warehouse in 1928–30 for its Oxo owners, into a mixed-use scheme (**W6a**): designer studios and shops on the ground floor, five floors of housing and two large restaurants on the top floor.

They also upgraded and redesigned the Riverside Walkway between Tate Modern and the London Eye to make it a highly popular destination (1996). Also see p. xx
(Lifschutz Davidson website; Coin Street website; Cherry & Pevsner; Bird & Price, 2015, p. 142)

(**W7**) **Sea Containers House**, 20 Upper Ground, overlooking the Thames. The enormous Sea Containers building was originally designed by Warren Platner as a hotel but changed direction half way through construction to become office accommodation instead, ready in 1978. The name is that of one of its long-term tenants, a shipping company. The building roughly looks like a cruise liner moored to the bank of the Thames. Between 2011 and 2014, the building was completely refurbished and the marine theme was relentlessly pursued throughout the striking Mondrian Hotel (designer Tom Dixon). *Time out* listed this hotel as amongst the best in London: 'There's no shortage of wow factor, starting with a copper-clad hull crashing through the lobby, but if you by any chance tire of the maritime interiors, most rooms offer great views of the Thames'.

The tri-partite arrangement of the river facade reflects the current partitioning of the building – the central bloc occupied by a hotel (Mondrian at first, but Sea Containers

The copper clad hull/reception desk at the Mondrian Hotel, photographed in 2017. It has since become the Sea Containers Hotel.
(© The author, 2017)

Above:
Number One Blackfriars is seen from the river with the smaller and former IPC tower to its right (see p. 497)
(© The author, 2018)

Right:
Southbank Place in Waterloo, photographed in 2020.
(© The author)

since January 2019) framed on either side by two blocks of offices. (Wikipedia, retrieved 26 November 2022)

(W8) **18 Blackfriars Road**, Foster + Partners, on a site vacant since 2016. This project has a chequered history, well summarised by *The Architects Journal*:

> The consortium [who purchased the site in 2021] inherited a consented proposal for a Wilkinson Eyre-designed scheme dominated by two towers – a 53-storey residential tower and an office tower of 34 storeys – but opted to replace the architects, appointing Fosters to develop new plans.
> The revised proposals, which have now gone out to public consultation, are comprised of three brick-clad towers clustered round a central plaza which connects to the Christ Church Garden.
> The tallest of the towers, which all feature green terraces and roofs, will be a 210m office building, followed by the 160m Stamford Building, a residential block, and a third high-rise, the Paris Building, which will contain affordable housing and be no taller than 100m.

(Daniel Gayne 'Fosters' plans for a £1bn Blackfriars tower cluster given public airing' in *The Architects' Journal*, 12 August 2022; Aaron Morby, 'Designs revealed for £1bn London Blackfriars tower blocks' in *Construction Inquirer*, August 2022)

(W9) **One Blackfriars** (bottom left), nicknamed the Boomerang or the Vase (2013-18), fifty storeys (170m), was designed by Simpson Haugh and partners. It contains residential flats, a hotel on the ground floor and retail accommodation. The original brief was for sixty-eight storeys (225m) and the design switched from a hotel to luxury residential accommodation, with 'winter gardens' rather than balconies as with 251 Blackfriars Road. Reif Larsen described it as: 'the pregnant monolith of One Blackfriars, a 50-story mixed-used building, looms over the Thames like an alien mother ship'. (*New York Times*, 18 July 2017)

The developers, St George, part of the Berkeley Group, settled for a cash payment to Southwark Council rather than incorporate affordable housing within the design under review – a move which was criticised at the planning committee meeting of October 2012, as reported in SE1 Community website: 'Looking at the public gallery at Tuesday's meeting Cllr Adele Morris added: "I am very conscious that this room is full of consultants and developers … a room full of people here thinking 'They have got away with this; we are all going to get away with it too'."'

By contrast, 18 Blackfriars Road (left), incorporates its element of affordable housing on the same site. (*SE1 Community News Website*, 10 October 2012, https://www.london-se1.co.uk/news/view/6351)

(W10) **South Bank Place**, York Road, see p. 436

(W11) **The Union Jack Club** in Waterloo Road replaces its 1907 red brick antecedent by Harry Bell Measures – a residential club for members and ex-members of the British armed services. The Edwardian building was demolished in 1970 and replaced by the present design, made up of three distinct towers of differing heights rising from a brick podium (80 metres, then 69 and 35). It was designed by Fitzroy Robinson & Partners and ready in 1976. The armed forces club is housed in the tallest fully glazed tower, with 'over 300 bedrooms and club facilities'.
(Cherry & Pevsner; Bird & Price, 2015, p. 24; Edmund Bird and Fiona Price, *Lambeth's Edwardian Splendours*, first publ. 2010)

(W12) **The London Ambulance Service headquarters**, 220 Waterloo Road. The GLC Architects' Department designed this building which opened in 1973, while its former home – the LCC Waterloo Road Fire Station (1910) – has now become a bar and restaurant. The building, found clumsy by some, has also been described as 'an austere essay in pre-cast concrete – one of the last examples of the 1960's Brutalist style'. The author of this comment, Edmund Bird also points out that 'the Brutalist style [was] beloved by the LCC in its last years' citing the example of the 1965 Oval Ambulance Station.
(Bird & Price, 2015, p. 18; Cherry & Pevsner)

Pearman Street, which runs along one side of the Ambulance Headquarters (left), is clearly the ambulance street, often spilling out beyond its 'natural habitat'.
(© The author, 2021)

BOROUGH AND BANKSIDE

BB1 BLACKFRIARS BRIDGE

BB4 MILLENNIUM BRIDGE

BB3 TATE MODERN

BB2A 89 SOUTHWARK STREET

BB2B 85 SOUTHWARK STREET

BB5 THE GLOBE

BB6 SOUTHWARK BRIDGE

BB8 NEO-BANKSIDE

BB7 BANKSIDE 1, 2, 3

BB10 BOROUGH MARKET

BB9 BLACKFRIARS CIRCUS DEVELOPMENT

One of the interiors of 89 Southwark Street which Allies and Morrison architects bought and beautifully restored, and used as an extension to their studios at No 85. They later sold the building.
© The author, 2015

(BB1) **Blackfriars Bridge**; continued from p. 270. This bridge was designed by Joseph Cubitt and opened by Queen Victoria on 6 November 1869. The bridge was widened on the west side in 1907–10 – from 70 to 105 ft. It famously hit the newspaper headlines in June 1982 when the body of Italian banker Roberto Calvi was found hanging – a Mafia assassination as it subsequently turned out.
(Weinreb and Hibbert)

(BB2a/b) **85 and 89 Southwark Street**, Allies and Morrison Studios, 1999-2003 for No 85 and 2009–12 for no 89. Also see p. 474 for No 85. The restaurant 'The Table', linked to No 85, was established by Allies and Morrison in 2005. They explain: 'When it was first opened The Table was the only restaurant in the immediate vicinity, and its launch was symptomatic of the practice's faith in the potential regeneration of this part of Southwark'.

As for No 89 (left), originally an extension to the architects' offices, no longer in their ownership, they 'sought to reinstate the original massing of the building. The post-war mansard roof was replaced with a simpler pitched roof, an awkward rear extension was removed, and the top of the façade was extended to align with the original parapet'.
(*Allies and Morrison, Projects 2003–12,* 2019)

(BB3) **Tate Modern**, see pp. 473, 476–481.

(BB4) **Millennium Bridge**. This pedestrian suspended bridge links the City and St Paul's Cathedral to Tate Modern and Bankside. The bridge opened on 10 June 2000 and was immediately tried by around

100,000 people in the first weekend. It became even more famous when it experienced what the architects' website describes as 'greater than expected lateral movement' and what everybody else has described as the 'wobbly bridge'. It closed two days after its opening and only re-opened in February 2002 after the 'wobble' had been fixed.

A competition, organised in 1996 by RIBA and Southwark Council, yielded a winning design which was the outcome of a collaboration between architects Foster + Partners, sculptor Sir Antony Caro and structural engineers Arup Group. Construction started in late 1998. The elegant design won the heart of many Londoners. (left)

(BB5) The Globe theatre and the Sam Wanamaker playhouse, see the introduction to this chapter and pp. 452 and 482.

(BB6) Southwark Bridge; continued from p. XX. The bridge replaced Rennie's ground-breaking iron bridge which had been purchased by the City Corporation in 1868. In 1912 it was replaced by the present structure designed by Sir Ernest George and Sir Basil Mott.

(BB7) Bankside 123, Southwark Street, Allies and Morrison, 2000-2011. Three large office buildings have been placed at different angles in relation to Southwark Street. They have replaced the austere St Christopher's House – 'a singular, unloved 1960s linear building that contributed neither permeability nor activity to the street' – which, when it was built in 1959, was described as 'the largest office block under one roof in Europe'. It was pulled down in 2003.

Bankside 1, the largest structure with thirteen storeys, is the Blue Finn building: 'the syncopated arrangement of vertical blue louvres' are the 'Blue Fins'. They provide shade to this fully glazed building. Externally, the ground floor is entirely occupied by shops; the interior courtyard is traversed by suspended bridges linking opposite sides of the building in the upper storeys. The architects thus describe the project:

> This development is an early example of the regenerative effect of the opening in 2000 of both the Tate Modern art gallery in the former Bankside Power Station and the pedestrian Millennium Bridge … With its new landscape of granite paving, trees, lighting and benches, the development proved instrumental in the subsequent regeneration of the Bankside district.

Also see pp. 474–475.
(Allies and Morrison, *Projects 2003–12*, 2019; Cherry and Pevsner)

(BB8) Neo Bankside, 60 Holland Street, by RSHP (Richard Rogers & Partners), 217 residential units across three towers, 2009–12. When the development was listed for the Stirling prize, many greeted the news with surprise, leading to a string of negative comments, amongst these: 'It looks like something churned out by his [Richard Rogers] office's B-team, generic glass silos wrapped up in the trademark steel bracing, destined for a corner of the world where critics hopefully wouldn't notice' wrote Oliver Wainwright in *The Guardian* (21 July 2015). But the greater problem, setting a dangerous precedent was thus summed up: 'developers failed to live up to its original affordable housing claims' – the affordable housing being moved elsewhere in the borough.

The *Architects' Journal* was rather more positive: 'Neo-Bankside ticks all the boxes: brownfield, dense, permeable, mixed use, near the riverfront and transport nodes, and built to very high standards. Yet recognising these qualities can be difficult when so much of the project's focus is branding' (17 March 2011).

But controversy and difficulties never seem far away from this project. The residents lodged a complaint with

Opposite:
'Misty Millennium Bridge'; This photograph by John Chase pays tribute to the structure's grace and the ease with which a contemporary work blends with a cathedral dating back to the seventeenth century.
(© John Chase Photography, 2013)

Above:
142 Blackfriars Road, photographed in 2019.
(© The author)

Above right:
The residents of Neo-Bankside took Tate Modern to court after objecting to their lack of privacy, with visitors peering into their flats from the Tate's Blavatnik Gallery. Was anyone fighting the corner of the charming Hopton Street almshouses (foreground) when they were completely dwarfed by the new development?
(© The author, 2018)

Tate Modern about the way in which the viewing gallery of the Blavatnik tower seriously compromised their privacy. When Tate Modern refused to shut the offending section of the 360 degrees gallery the residents instructed their lawyers. In 2021 the matter was referred to the Supreme Court and won in early 2023. In the meantime, a tragic event led to the temporary closure of the offending gallery – the fall in August 2019 of a six-year-old French boy from that same gallery, pushed over by a deranged youth who was jailed for it. (*The Architect's Journal* and *The Guardian*, as quoted)

(BB9) Blackfriars Circus development, 142 Blackfriars Road, a Barratt development of 336 homes, including fifty-six 'rented properties for Southwark Council'. Designed by Maccreanor Lavington, the buildings – five blocks including a tower – are organised around two new squares and have been praised for their highly creative use of brick. This multi-award development is thus described on the RIBA website after it won both its National and London Regional awards in 2021:

> Challenged with a brief to rejuvenate a semi-derelict brownfield site, the architect

responded by creating a sustainable new neighbourhood. The scheme comprises several blocks with attractive roof gardens and a 28-storey tower. It restores the urban grain and creates new public realm and welcome breathing space, repairing a large portion of the street and revitalising the St George's Circus area generally.
(The websites of RIBA and Maccreanor Lavington, accessed on 28 November 2022)

(BB10) Borough Market

After years of decline the Trustees decided, in the early 1990s, to launch a specialist food market which would not only attract customers but also new stall holders and businesses. They also commissioned Greig & Stephenson Architects to refurbish, expand and regenerate the market buildings, without any interruption to trading. These architects specialise in market redevelopments at home and abroad and are 'passionate about the wider social and economic regeneration qualities of markets'. They embarked on 'a comprehensive, 20 year, 15£m project to regenerate Borough Market and the surrounding area'; they started in 1995, completing the work in 2015. They restored the cast-iron Victorian market, created the Jubilee market close to the cathedral, designed the Fish! restaurant, and demolished a 1950s concrete building to replace it with a new building fronted with one of the redundant porticos of Covent Garden Floral Hall. Many more people flocked to this enticing market which had grown from two days a week to seven-day trading.

The spectacular success of this regeneration programme acted as a magnet for other projects. Network Rail commissioned the architects Jestico + Whiles to handle the challenging project of inserting a 400 m long viaduct, 'vital to the Thameslink route' within a conservation area, whilst preserving the Grade II listed public house The Globe. A brand-new market building was also built at Borough viaduct – glazed screens on a steel frame.

The latest addition, by MARC, a private development, is the exciting Borough Yards. They combine a hint of medieval topography – 'Dirty Lane', small courts and alleyways, alongside the restored Victorian arches. Trevor Morriss, the lead architect from SPPARC was interviewed by the *Architects' Journal*: 'part of the challenge was how to embrace and use the Victorian viaducts on the site. This constraint became a virtue, carving new openings to aid pedestrian movement … creating new monumental spaces under the arches for shopping experiences.'
(Greig & Stephenson's website accessed 17 February 2023; Architects' Journal (AJ), 16 October 2012 for Jestico + Whiles and their website; Architects' Journal (AJ), 9 December 2021, SPPARC interview by Rob Wilson)

ELEPHANT AND CASTLE

'the Piccadilly Circus of the South'

EC9 251 SOUTHWARK BRIDGE ROAD

EC8 PERRONET HOUSE

EC7 SHOPPING CENTRE VERSUS TOWN CENTRE

EC6 DRAPER ESTATE

EC5 HIGHPOINT

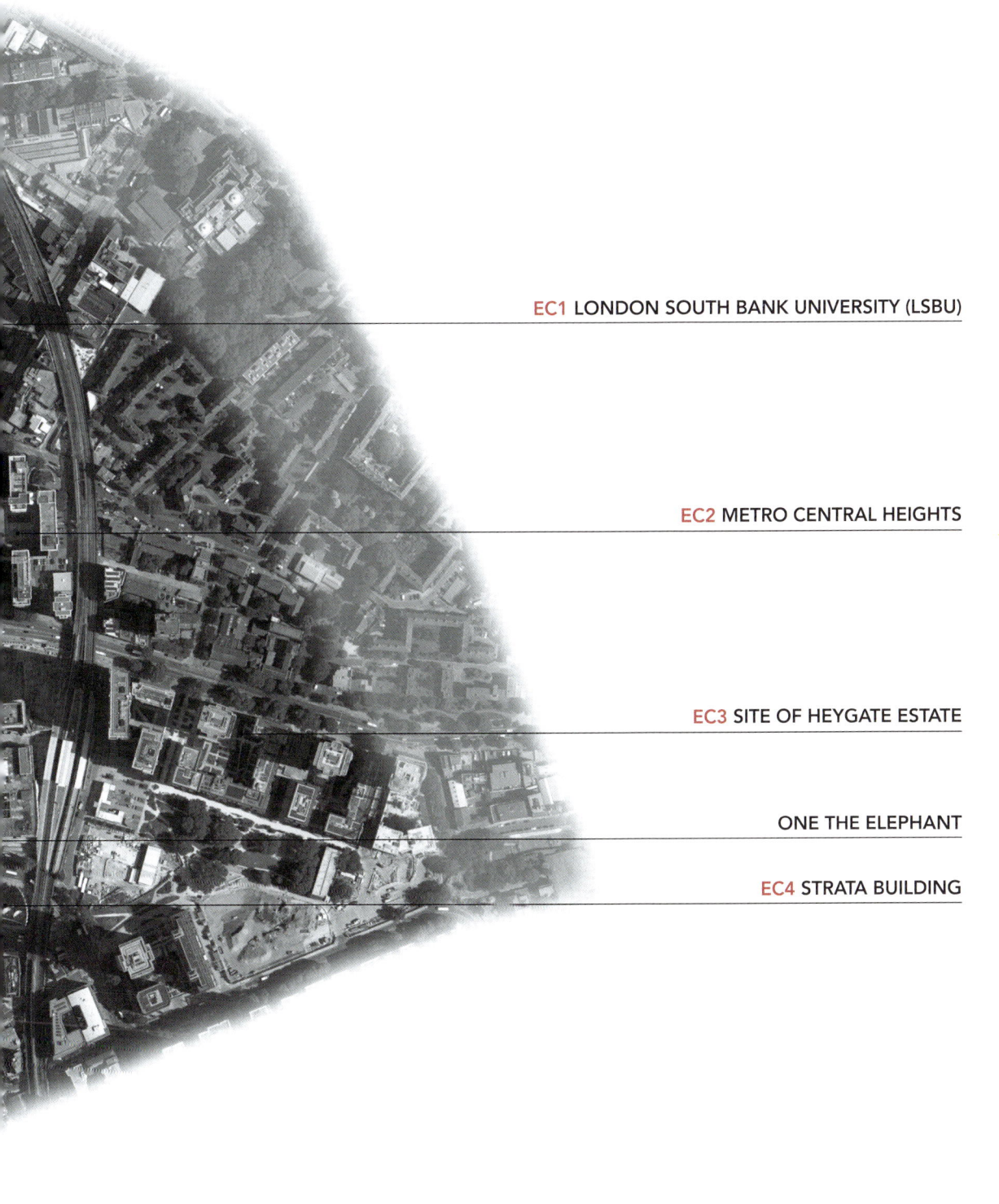

EC1 LONDON SOUTH BANK UNIVERSITY (LSBU)

EC2 METRO CENTRAL HEIGHTS

EC3 SITE OF HEYGATE ESTATE

ONE THE ELEPHANT

EC4 STRATA BUILDING

History

Stephen Humphrey, the author of *Elephant and Castle, A History*, points out that his 'book could have been called *Newington: A History*, for that was clearly the name of the district for hundreds of years'. Humphrey reckons that the area's heyday was between the 1840s and the beginning of the Blitz: 'large stores, countless smaller shops, pubs, restaurants, places of entertainment and good transport connections were the life blood of the old Elephant'. At the heart of the neighbourhood were two 'islands' or 'wastes' (leftovers), created when the road junction was formed. These two islands, probably the so-called 'Butts of Newington', have been swallowed up in today's twin roundabouts.

There are arguably three main periods to the history of this neighbourhood:

- **Rural days:** a farrier's workshop at the sign of the White Horse appeared in 1641 at the now famous cross-roads with nearby village which had long been known as Newington.
- **From country district to suburb:** the opening of Westminster Bridge in the 1750s and the making of New Kent Road, and soon the farrier's workshop was replaced by a pub, probably in existence in the 1750s but licensed to George Frost in 1765. It was named the Elephant and Castle, an ancient symbol which 'had become a common heraldic badge centuries before it arrived at our junction' concluded Stephen Humphrey. This pub was rebuilt twice, in 1818 (see p. 245) and in 1898. Whereas the late seventeenth-century rent of £6.00 a year had lasted until the 1750s, in 1776 it went up to £100, then £194 in 1797, £736 in 1849 and £850 in 1870. The site became freehold in the 1890s which also saw the arrival of the Elephant and Castle station and the pub was rebuilt in grand style in 1898, after a design by John Farrer. The neighbourhood was thriving, many of its shops and Department stores (Tarn's and Hurlock's) attracting customers from beyond this locality. The Elephant and Castle pub was the largest, but one of many (see Banks panorama, Chapter 3.4).
- **Regeneration:** the war created havoc in this lively area, leading to the infamous post-war re-development, harshly judged by Stephen Humphrey:

    > When the present dismal development had been put in place by the 1960s, the vital spark had been extinguished … What is less well-known is that much nevertheless remained, and could have been added to instead of being razed and squashed by the megalomaniac redevelopment of the late 1950s and early 1960s.

    We are now on the threshold of a dramatic new redevelopment which, like the previous one, appears to be led by destruction – the shopping centre, the Heygate estate and the London College of Communication. Will it be more of the same mistakes or a breakthrough? Time will tell. There are two major massive developments redefining this neighbourhood: the Town Centre on the enlarged site of the old Shopping Centre and The Elephant Park on the site of the Heygate estate.

(EC1) The London South Bank University (LSBU) 103 Borough Road. This Victorian institution appears in this section because of its rebranding and terrific expansion in the last fifty years.

In 2022, LSBU celebrated its 130th anniversary as an institution and its thirtieth birthday as a university. In 2016, it was named 'Entrepreneurial University of the Year' at the *Times Higher Education* Awards, though in truth, the dynamism which was celebrated then, had been the hallmark of this institution's existence from the very beginning, in 1892, when it was named the Borough Polytechnic Institute. By 2016 however, 'the University without Ivory Towers' – their slogan since 1992 – had opened two major new buildings: the Keyworth Centre in 2003, designed by BDP Architects and the K2 in 2009, designed by Grimshaw Architects for the School of Health and Social Care and also the Centre for Efficient and Remarkable Energy. They had opened too, the Borough Road Gallery and a new Student Centre in 2012 (designed by Hawkins/Brown), an Enterprise Centre in 2013, and they had sponsored the opening of University Academy of Engineering South Bank in 2014. Finally, they had opened Elephant Studios, their new Media Centre in 2016. In this phase of expansion, they have maximised cooperation with other institutions at home and abroad.

The growth of this institution has been fed by regular mergers with other institutions, for instance the Brixton School of Building and the City of Westminster College in 1970, the Battersea College of Education in 1976 and the Central Catering College in 1991. Barely four years later it was the turn of the Redwood College of Health Studies and Great Ormond Street School of Nursing. The original aims of this polytechnic had been 'the promotion of the industrial skills, general knowledge, health and well-being of young men and women' and at the opening gala, Lord Rosebery had exclaimed: 'the Polytechnic would do its share towards perfecting a valuable gem found in the slums of London'. The slums may have gone but it is remarkable that 70% of UK students at LSBU are Londoners and that they

primarily come from South London boroughs. It is also remarkable to read on the University website: 'Our roots are in the real world. We offer industry-relevant degrees that mean you can become the best version of yourself … We put wellbeing at the heart of everything we do, from helping local businesses to supporting your personal growth'. (Accessed 14 December 2022). In summary, though this institution has diversified and expanded beyond recognition, it has succeeded in maintaining a sense of continuity. The university is now organised in seven Schools: Applied Science, Arts and Creative Industries, Built Environment and Architecture, Business, Engineering, Health and Social Care, Law and Social Sciences. (LSBU website; Wikipedia entry, accessed December 2022)

(EC2) Metro Central Heights (formerly Alexander Fleming House) was designed by Hungarian-born Erno Goldfinger (1902-1987) – 'a major exponent of the European Modern Movement in Britain and an architect of international standing' wrote English Heritage (Historic England), which listed the building in 2013. Goldfinger was very influenced by French architects Auguste Perret and Le Corbusier along with Russian constructivism; he regarded Alexander Fleming House as his major work. The vast group of five blocks was built in two phases between 1959 and 1967;

'Bathing' (detail) by Duncan Grant formed part of the mural decoration of Room No 9 – a student dining room at the Borough Polytechnic, now London South Bank University. The scheme was co-ordinated by Roger Fry; the murals, on the theme of 'London on Holiday', are art-historically important because 'Mr Fry's enterprise was the earliest of this revival of mural decoration in the 20th Century and I think the set should be preserved and kept together' wrote Charles Aitken, the Director of the National Gallery They purchased the works in 1930 which transferred to the Tate Gallery in 1955.
(© Tate, Photo: Tate)

it received a bronze medal from RIBA in 1964 and was used for the offices of the Ministry of Health up until 1989. The complex remained vacant for many years and was finally refurbished as a residential estate in 2002; it was then renamed Metro Central Heights. (Historic England listed buildings)

(EC3) Heygate estate – life and death of a 'utopian' council estate. The estate, designed by Jim Tinker, was completed in 1974. It did not make it to its fortieth anniversary as partial demolition started in 2011, completed in 2014, after years of the estate being neglected and run down. The demolition was controversial as many disagreed with the received idea that the place was not fit for purpose. Here is how, Jerry Flynn, a former resident summarised the situation:

> Up until 1999, it did not have a reputation for being a bad place to live. But as regeneration progressed, the estate's reputation dropped.
> Almost overnight we woke up to be told we were living on one of the worst estates in Britain. It was a combination of laziness on the part of journalists, and public policy that decided estates such as the Heygate bred antisocial behaviour and crime, and needed to be broken down. (Stephen Moss for *The Guardian*, 4 March 2022)

Tenants were advised as early as 1997 that they would have to leave their flats by 2000, putting an immediate stop to any improvements they might have had in mind. The state of uncertainty in fact continued for ten years; tenants only started being 'decanted' from the estate in 2007 – with 'difficult' temporary tenants moving in. By 2010 only twenty die-hard permanent tenants remained. Their flats would be compulsorily purchased.

A September 2013 London Assembly report had found the estate to be structurally sound and recommended refurbishment. The Design Council, The Twentieth Century Society and even the estate's architect all felt Heygate 'could have enjoyed a second life' (in the words of the Design Council). So its demolition was truly controversial and Southwark Council was on very thin ice, when the economics of the operation were revealed in 2013; it was bluntly interpreted in a recent article by Damien Gale:

> critics of the regeneration say that the plans for the area are simply pushing out the working-class community it has long served and housed. When it emerged that the local council, Southwark, had sold the land on which the 1,200-home Heygate estate sat, for £50m, but paid more than that to remove and rehouse its residents and demolish the site, it was accused not just of gentrification, but social cleansing.
> (*The Guardian*, 24 September 2020)

Stephen Moss interviewed Ann Power, professor of social policy at the London School of Economics:

> If you think low income is vanishing, then it makes sense to reduce the amount of social housing that you've got. If you think low income isn't vanishing – and all the evidence would suggest it's not – then it makes no sense to get rid of social housing unless you've got an alternative for low-income people … What are you going to do about low-cost housing in a city that relies entirely on low-paid, low-skilled jobs for almost everything that its rich clientele depends on? Its hotels, its restaurants, its nurseries, its transport system, its street cleaning, everything depends on low-paid workers, and we are going to create one hell of a terrible society if we don't recognise that. (*The Guardian*, 4 March 2011)

The site is now being developed for housing and retail space, renamed Elephant Park.
(Stephen Moss, 'The Death of a Housing Ideal' in *The Guardian*, 4 March 2011; 'Larry and Janet move out – a documentary about the Heygate estate' by David Reeve and Patrick Steel, 2014, with interview of the architect Tim Tinker at https://www.youtube.com/watch?v=MvSmC7susNI)

(EC4) Strata Building, designed by BFLS (formerly Hamiltons Architects) and completed in 2010. It won a string of awards, including the unfortunate Carbuncle Cup of the year 2010 – the ugliest new building in Britain, an annual award run by Building Design between 2006 and 2018. They had this to say about the building:

> The building's grim stridency is exacerbated by its sporty livery of alternating black and white stripes, configured, needless to say, in voguish barcode distribution. And to literally cap it all off there are the three gargantuan wind turbines at the top. The architect has trumpeted that these could supply 8% of the building's energy requirements, which seems nothing much to shout about given the enormous expenditure in carbon that has been required to engineer such a baroque arrangement and the fact that this is a part of London that has absolutely no need for the creation of a 147m-tall tower.

The 'baroque arrangement' soon stopped working, partly because there were complaints of noise, but also because the contraption, regardless of the noise issue, never worked properly. The building was judged far less harshly by the savvy former architectural editor of *The Guardian*, Jonathan Glancey:

> The views are spectacular. Most front doors open directly onto gaping vistas of London, framed by giant windows … [the lead architect, Ian Bogle, adding] 'You

certainly feel as if you own the entire city from up here'… Strata is the first building in the world to incorporate wind turbines into its structure … whether its turbines will set a precedent for future British towers is less clear: this rooftop was exceedingly hard to construct, almost prohibitively so, every part of it having to be hauled up … 'You've got to take your hat off to the design team for delivering a building that captures the imagination,' says Paul King, head of the UK Green Building Council. 'I doubt wind power will become a common feature in high-rise inner city projects, but without this type of bold innovation, how would we ever know?'
(*Building Design*, 12 August 2010; Jonathan Glancey, 'Spin-city: London's Strata Tower', *The Guardian*, 18 July 2010)

(EC5) Highpoint (also known as UNCLE, the name of its Canadian management company, and 360 Tower), RSHP (formerly Richard Rogers architects, then Rogers, Stirk, Harbour & Partners), 9 Churchyard Row, 2006-2017. The development consists of two residential buildings – a forty-five-storey tower with sky garden for residents (142 m) and a seven-floor timber building with a planted roof. The scheme includes a theatre, community open space, cycle storage and recycling facilities at basement level.
(RSHP website)

(EC6) Draper estate, see p. 302 and picture above

(EC7) Shopping Centre versus Town Centre at the Elephant & Castle
On Friday 25 September 2020, a day after the permanent closure of the pioneering 1960s Shopping Centre at the Elephant, *SE1 Community News* mourned the imminent disappearance of the familiar landmark, the first one of its type in this country:

It's a building that some love to hate, but many locals have learned

Mike O'Dwyer's photograph is taken from the west and focuses on the brand-new cluster of towers at the Elephant: Highpoint in the centre with Strata to its right, and One the Elephant to its left. The inclusion of the Draper estate at the foot of the Strata building gives a sense of the new building scale. The Draper's residential tower was the highest in this country when it was built in the 1960s and now it barely reaches the half point of the Strata building.
(© Mike O'Dwyer, 2018)

This photograph was taken by Mike Seaborne in 1996 and shot from a balcony on a housing block on the south side of the Heygate estate that fronted the Walworth Road, near its junction with Newington Butts. The Draper estate is on the left and the low pink block in the centre is the Elephant and Castle Shopping Centre.
(© Mike Seaborne, www.mikeseaborne.co.uk/)

to love. The Elephant & Castle Shopping Centre closed its doors on Thursday, after 55 years at the heart of the community.

The centre's closure has been foretold so many times that some doubted it would ever happen. It's more than 30 years since the first public meeting to discuss the regeneration of the Elephant, and there have been many false starts along the way.

The current owners of the centre – led by Delancey – had their redevelopment plans approved by the Deputy Mayor of London in December 2018 after receiving Southwark Council's backing in July that year.

For its redevelopment the site has been merged with that of the London College of Communication. The expanded footprint gives considerable scope for a complete re-think, now described as a town centre, with Allies and Morrison in charge of its delivery:

[It] offers the opportunity to correct post-war urban challenges that have long afflicted one of south London's busiest junctions. Anchored by a new outwardly facing LCC [London College of Communication], this is a remarkably hybrid scheme which will have many rich ingredients, from Britain's largest purpose built build-to-rent housing project to incubator workspace for recent grads and a new home for the [College's] Stanley Kubrick Archive - all integrated with one of London's best connected transport hubs.

Allies and Morrison also remind us that 'over the last twenty years, five different masterplans attempted to make sense of this challenging site. None of them had worked'. The College will now replace the Shopping Centre moving across the former Roman road. The completion date is the 2020s. (*SE1 Community News* and Allies and Morrison websites, both accessed on 28 November 2022)

(EC8) Perronet House, 44 Princess Street (overlooking the northern roundabout at the Elephant and Castle). Designed by Sir Roger Walters, architect to the GLC, it was completed in 1970. A year later it received a commendation at the Good Design in Housing Awards. This is how it was judged:

> This very high density scheme, on a site with considerable problems of traffic noise and access, is designed with a boldness and conviction which is impressive. The committee ... also found some arbitrary and unnecessary additions to the facades which added nothing in protection of the dwellings against traffic noise.

This ten-floor block was built for Southwark Council. It is a building much loved by architects for its subtlety and ingenuity and by specialised estate agents such as the Modern House, based at nearby King's Bench Street, who thus described an apartment close to the top floor:

> But our real highlight is the configuration of the space. The split-level apartment is built to a clever upside-down, with the bedrooms on the building's eighth floor, and the living space upstairs on the tenth. (It's also somewhat scissor-shaped – the intervening ninth floor is a staircase.)

(http://www.perronethouse.com/wp-content/uploads/2012/12/PerronetHouseGoodDesignAll.jpg; https://www.themodernhouse.com/journal/listing-of-the-week-upside-down-apartment-perronet-house/ accessed November 2022)

(EC9) Two Fifty One, 251 Southwark Bridge Road by Allies and Morrison. The forty-storey residential tower and the adjacent seven-storey commercial building were completed in 2017. A public landscaped garden was part of the package of this luxury development fitted with a cinema, residents' gym, meeting room and access to 24hr concierge services. (Allies and Morrison website)

This model of the Elephant and Castle new Town Centre has yet to take shape on the ground now that the Shopping Centre has been demolished. The height and density of the new buildings contrast greatly with the previous arrangement. (Model and photo: Allies and Morrison)

SOUTHWARK AND BERMONDSEY

SB1 LONDON BRIDGE CITY

SB9 LONDON BRIDGE

SB7 HAY'S WHARF

SB8 SHARD & SHARD QUARTER

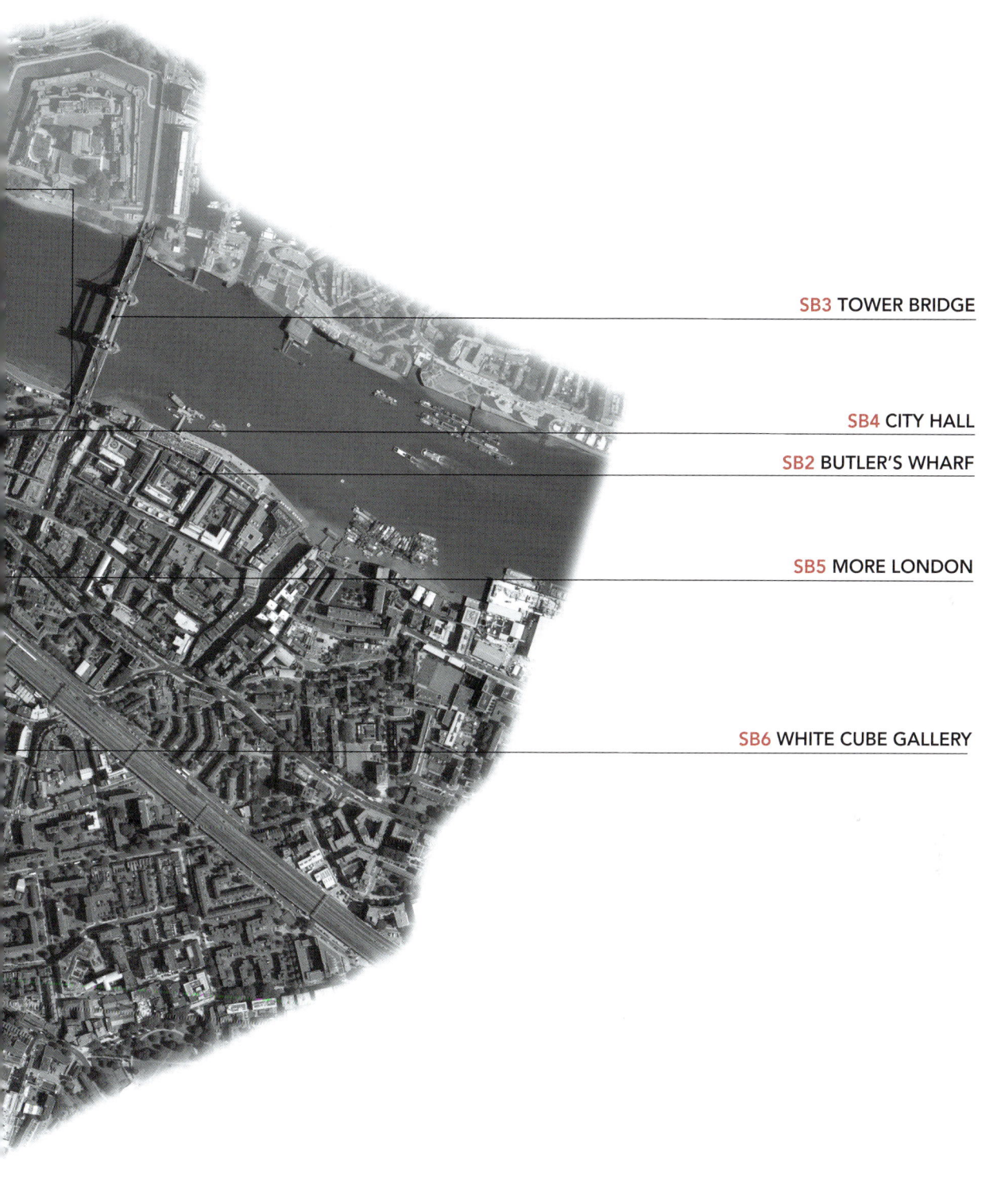

This bronze monument stands at the Tooley Street entrance to More London. The numbers on the roofs correspond to the buildings' postal address.
(Photo: The author, 2022)

(SB1) **London Bridge City**; the name, a recent 'creation', surfaced when the area was being redeveloped in the 1980s. The former string of 'sufferance wharves' (see p. 505 ff) became 'London Bridge City'. The London Hospital was ready in 1983, No 1 London Bridge and the Cottons Centre in 1986, Hay's Galleria in 1987, the More London estate was developed from 1998, City Hall was ready in 2002 and the whole development completed in 2010 with 7 More London for PricewaterhouseCoopers, the last building to arrive on the scene. It's a developers' paradise which reads like a who's who of the world of development in the late twentieth-early twenty-first centuries: John S. Bonnington Partnership for No 1 London Bridge, Llewelyn Davies, the heavy weight of hospital architecture at London Bridge Hospital (also involved with Guy's and St Thomas' Hospitals); Laing Management (1985-88) at the Cottons Centre. But the real piece de resistance in this mosaic of old and new – historic St Olaf's House and Hay's Wharf are listed buildings – must be the elegant, though abundantly challenged More London (SB5).
(London Bridge City website)

(SB2) **Butler's Wharf, Shad Thames**, restoration and development 1980s–90s; see pp. 504-510 for history. The warehouses were Grade II listed in 1982 (under Shad Thames). Historic England's website brings to our attention that: 'It remains the largest surviving range of a dockland 'canyon' in its bridged relationship with the warehouse on the south side of the road'. (left)

Terence Conran (1931–2020) is arguably best remembered for creating the store Habitat, but as the *SE1 Community News website* points out:

> Locally he will be best remembered for leading the 1980s redevelopment of Butler's Wharf on Shad Thames, creating a 'gastrodome' centred on restaurants such as Le Pont de la

Tour [opened 1991] and Cantina del Ponte and bringing the Design Museum to Southwark. In 2010 he told the *Telegraph* 'it was one of the great moments of my life, realising I could afford to buy 13 acres on this bank of the river in the early eighties'. … Until the first decade of this century his London residence was on Shad Thames, on the upper floors of the building recently vacated by the Conran & Partners architecture practice.

His impact was such that his generation would often refer to the area as 'Conran land'.
(*SE1 Community News website*, 14 September 2020)

(SB3) Tower Bridge, 1886–94: A new bridge was needed to relieve congestion on the other bridges. Sir Joseph Bazalgette's early design for this bridge – a single arch road bridge – was rejected for insufficient headroom. The solution was a bascule bridge designed by Sir Horace Jones with John Wolfe-Barry as engineer: 'Two bascules, each weighing over a thousand tons, are lifted by hydraulic machinery housed in the flanking towers. It was hoped that the Gothic design would blend in with the nearby tower'. (Barker & Jackson) (Weinreb and Hibbert; Barker & Jackson 1974)

(SB4) City Hall, Foster + Partners, completed in 2002 (above). From the architects' website (accessed 3 December 2022):

One of the capital's most symbolically important new projects, City Hall advances themes explored in the Reichstag [Berlin], expressing the transparency and accessibility of the democratic process and demonstrating the potential for a sustainable, virtually non-polluting public building. Designed using advanced computer-modelling techniques the building represents a radical rethink of architectural form. Its shape achieves optimum energy performance by maximising shading and minimising the surface area exposed to direct sunlight. Offices are naturally ventilated, photovoltaics provide power and the building's cooling system utilises ground water pumped up via boreholes. Overall, City Hall uses only a quarter of the energy consumed by a typical air-conditioned London office building.

This eulogy is partially undermined by the building's location (see pp. 298–299). Also, in 2020 Sadiq Khan announced the move of the London Assembly to the Crystal in East London. The move was complete by March 2022.

(SB5) More London, 1998–2003, is a private estate which forms part of London Bridge City (top left and overleaf). One of the most surprising but excellent pieces of writing about this development sprang up from the filling-in of the seductive water feature which up until 2018, divided this private estate into two dynamic halves; it included a surprise vista of Tower Bridge, in searing contrast with the mass of dark corporate architecture at that site.

The former London City Hall is located within the private estate of More London, on the riverfront.
(© The author, 2016)

Opposite:

Shad Thames: in the 1980s when this street looked abandoned and derelict, it was still possible to smell the spices which had once been stored in the neighbourhood. Terence Conran bought this forgotten part of Docklands, restored the warehouses and injected new life into Butler's Wharf and Shad Thames by turning them into a desirable residential area with restaurants and the Design Museum.
(© The author, 2022)

More London: these photographs are taken from this private estate's principal entrance off Tooley Street. It is marked by the positioning high above eye level of a sculpted man and woman looking in the direction of the Shard (they are by the contemporary German artist Stephan Balkenhol). Nearby is a bronze model of the More estate (p. 352). The other striking feature at that site is the stream, now filled in, which ran in a diagonal from Tooley Street to 'The Scoop' – a sunken open-air amphitheatre next to City Hall.
© The author, 2013, 2022

No ball games, no busking, no protests – and now no stream. The More London estate, which covers 13 acres of the south bank of the Thames, providing a home for City Hall, has always been an apt symbol of the London's creeping privatisation.

The Rill, as the water feature was known,

was no work of genius, but the little trickle added interest and an unlikely frisson of danger as you walked the tedious gauntlet of M&S and Jamie's Italian, towards the spiky Mordor-like entrance of PricewaterhouseCoopers.

This gave Oliver Wainwright the opportunity to raise the issue of public/private space in cities and state the threat that London is slowly slipping down the slope of 'privatised public space'. For the clash between private estates and public space, see this chapter's introduction.

Foster & Partners, of wobbly bridge fame, masterminded the whole site. In 2007, the project was one of six designs shortlisted for the infamous Carbuncle Cup (see p. 344), by Edwin Heathcote, architecture critic on the *Financial Times*. They did not win. But the scheme won four awards including RIBA's in 2013.
(Oliver Wainwright, 'Smartphone use blamed as water feature is bricked up' in *The Guardian*, 20 June 2018; Foster + Partners website)

(SB6) White Cube Gallery, Bermondsey Street, opened in October 2011; it demonstrates the astonishing success of its owner, Jay Jopling, who, back in 1993,

The Anselm Kiefer exhibition held at Bermondsey White Cube in 2019: room after room was filled with some of the largest paintings to which the artist has accustomed his public.
(© The author, 2019)

seemed to defy the long-established cluster of Old-Masters galleries in St James's by opening a small avant-garde gallery in their midst in Duke Street. He set up another gallery in Shoreditch's Hoxton Square before expanding his operations to the South Bank and abroad. He established his new, enormous gallery in Bermondsey by commissioning the German architects Casper Mueller Kneer to renovate and redesign the 1970s industrial building he had purchased in 2010 – the former Recall warehouse – initially for storage; but its potential as gallery space soon became apparent. The architects won the Stirling Prize in 2012.

One of the most memorable exhibitions shown there was devoted to the German artist Anselm Kiefer 'the largest presentation of Anselm Kiefer works ever staged in London'; it was breath-taking. At the artist's request all of the walls were covered with lead; *The Art Newspaper* interviewed the artistic director, Susan May: 'We pretty much cleaned out every lead merchant in Europe, certainly in the UK. Apparently the price of lead fluctuated as a result'. (Gallery's website; *The Art Newspaper*, 5 July 2018; *SE1 Community News website*, 10 December 2010)

(SB7) Hay's Wharf; see pp. 504-510 for its history. The Hay's Wharf Company recovered from the devastation of the Second World War but the arrival of containerisation and a bitter labour dispute led to its relocation at Dagenham and they announced the closure of the South Bank wharves in 1969. St Martin's Property Group, owned by the sovereign state wealth fund of Kuwait, purchased the land in the early 1980s and redeveloped it. Hay's Wharf was Grade II listed in 1980 (listing amended in 1998). The listed warehouses were restored mixing residential formula (upper floors) with commercial (ground floor). Glazing was introduced between two of the warehouses – 'the Galleria'. (Historic England Listed Buildings website; https://portoflondonstudy.wordpress.com/; Marshall)

(SB8) Shard and Shard Quarter. See Chapter 4.4

(SB9) London Bridge, 1967–72, designed by Lord Holford with engineers Mott, Hay and Anderson; continued from pp. 282–284. Rennie's bridge was sold, dismantled stone by stone, and re-erected at Lake Havasu City, Arizona. Its replacement, built on the same site as Rennie's bridge, of concrete and steel, has simply three arches of 'pre-stressed concrete box girders'. It is in the ownership of the Bridge House Estates which entirely financed the project.

THE QUEST

Above:
Jiro Osuga, 'Walker', 2021, oil on canvas.
The artist is both a flâneur and a quester, and his muse is almost always London.
(Flowers/© The artist)

Opposite:
Jiro Osuga, 'The Road less travelled' 2010, oil on canvas.
The Quester should be ready for obstacles.
(Flowers/© The artist)

Previous page:
Mattheus van Helmont, The Alchemist, mid seventeenth century, oil on canvas
(Science History Institute, Philadelphia, US/Photo: Chemical Heritage Foundation. Image in the public domain, Wikimedia Commons)

The lover of universal life enters into the crowd as though it were an immense reservoir of electrical energy. Or we might liken him to a mirror as vast as the crowd itself; or to a kaleidoscope gifted with consciousness, responding to each one of its movements and reproducing the multiplicity of life and the flickering grace of all the elements of life.

Charles Baudelaire, *The Painter of Modern Life*, 1863

Charles Baudelaire's crowd was in his home city of Paris, but his observations could easily transfer to other cities, including London. He used the noun 'flâneur' to describe the activity of walking the streets of Paris to take in the spectacle of urban life. To describe his flâneur as a huge 'mirror' reflecting what is in front of him or as a conscious 'kaleidoscope' strongly recalls the experiment of the looking glass curtain at the Royal Coburg theatre in Waterloo (see p. 422), borrowed from a Parisian theatre in around 1820 – a seated theatrical crowd reflected to themselves by a stage curtain made up of many small mirrors. Nowadays we would probably say 'I am the city', based on the angry cry which took social media by storm in 2015 after the terrorist attack on the French magazine *Charlie Hebdo*.

It is clear that 'I am Charlie' described a process of identification which was pro-active, defiant and almost the opposite of Baudelaire's flâneur, a passive exercise, often played in slow motion, even when caught in the midst of a large crowd. Flâner, the verb, is a non-judgemental and serene state of mind, soaking in life and energy without ever questioning.

The purpose of this book is dynamic. Parts of it rely on walking and absorbing the random, never-ending manifestations of the city; but the 'search' engine is turned on, which means looking for meaning and seeking to uncover significant clues. This is the story of the South Bank, THE original suburb, as close to central London as it is possible to be since it actually holds its geographic centre (see p. 19) – a good place for setting up a full-scale investigation. There will be plenty of challenges in this quest since, as announced in the Prologue, it is an ambitious one: the search for London's soul. Will the South Bank turn out to hide/host London's spiritual heart?

Is the south bank a mere reflection of what happens on the north bank? Is it doomed to remain a convenient place for rejects from the north bank? But it could also be a place where compassion and healing thrive given its long list of established vital services

– hospitals, ambulance services, charities, genuinely affordable housing, pioneering fire service. It is also a place for vibrant creativity which saw the birth of the theatre, circus and music halls, all within proximity of fabulous gardens.

Fast forward to our own times: we know that the arrival of computers has revolutionised the planning and meaning of cities. Long before the actual birth of a new London neighbourhood, architects and developers have made its virtual existence appear entirely realistic. Historians too, have reconstructed, with the help of computers, whole buildings, neighbourhoods and indeed cities.

The preceding chapters have attempted to chart the past through a series of maps which, imperfect and incomplete as they are, give you glimpses, snapshots of the South Bank in history. But it is the shell of the past rather than its beating heart that we most often capture. At the risk of being mocked by all the sceptics in a sceptical age, I will make a determined attempt to find the city's soul.

The aim of 'The Quest' is to pull significant themes for the South Bank, out of the mass of available data. Each of the four areas under review has a distinctive personality, perhaps the sum of the important events which shook or inspired its inhabitants. The continuing magic of the gardens of Vauxhall and Lambeth; the creativity which was deployed at Waterloo to fight against deprivation and sin; while at Bankside and Borough, the arts have rescued the area from its early reputation for low life and industry; Southwark's Shard triumphs over the austerity of a landscape which had long been shaped by commercial productivity and docks – with little attention paid to aesthetics.

Here you will find the building blocks upon which the final interpretation of the South Bank will rest … to be revealed in the final chapter.

VAUXHALL AND LAMBETH
Paradise regained

Recreating the original garden	**363**
The Tradescants	363
Paradise on earth?	363
Death in the garden	366
The Ark	369
Vauxhall Gardens: 'Garden of Earthly Delights'	**372**
A London nature diary	**375**
William Blake	**377**
The Oval: town planning centred on open space	**380**
Vauxhall Park	**382**
Legacy:	**387**
The Garden Museum	387
The Garden of Lambeth Palace	391
Bonnington Square and Harleyford Road Community Gardens	391
Garden of the US Embassy	396

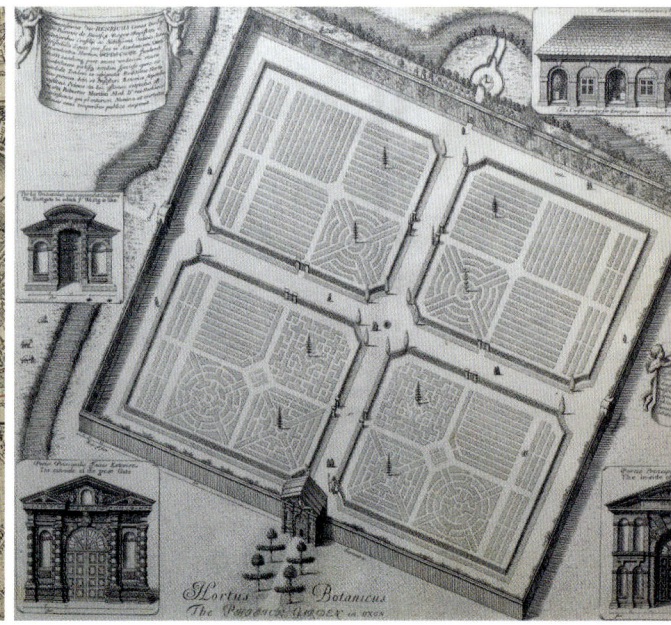

Previous:

Detail from a painting on oak panel by Jan Brueghel the Elder (1568–1625) which dates from around 1600. 'The Temptation in the Garden of Eden' illustrates the transition from a literal interpretation of the biblical Garden of Eden (see p. 366), to one which depicts a lush and inviting environment where the inconvenient original sin committed by Adam and Eve is relegated to the barely visible back of the painting – the glory of the garden or nature takes over from original sin; though not without a hint at the Ark with its paired animals, almost ready to go on board.
(© Victoria and Albert Museum, London)

Above left:

This detail from Rocque's 1747 map of London shows areas of market gardening in Lambeth and Vauxhall.
© London Metropolitan Archives (City of London)

During the seventeenth century, Protestant theologians encouraged people to read the Bible literally and as a coherent historical narrative. In this narrative, the events which took place in the garden of Eden defined the rest of the course of human history … Although the basic narrative was easy to establish, the meaning of the events which had taken place in the Garden was often the subject of debate.

Jim Bennett and Scott Mandelbrote,
The Garden, the Ark, the Tower, the Temple, 1998

In the beginning was the garden, and these words are especially fitting at Vauxhall, South Lambeth. This may surprise readers as the place nowadays is criss-crossed by large traffic arteries, more evocative of spaghetti junction than of peaceful cultivated havens. But in the seventeenth and eighteenth centuries it was the gardens which attracted many visitors to this part of London: their reputation reached far and wide, including abroad. Two gardens in particular were very influential: the Tradescants' in South Lambeth and Vauxhall Gardens.

However, gardening was simply not there to benefit the well-off. In her chapter on 'feeding the city' for the book *London's Pride*, Rosemary Weinstein summarized:

The cultivation of vegetables, especially lettuce and other salad plants, had been a highly developed industry in the Low Countries since the fourteenth century. The market gardens outside Amsterdam were well known by the fifteenth century. This system of food production spread to England and was particularly encouraged by the arrival of Dutch refugees from 1567 onwards … by the late sixteenth century areas around London were developing market gardens.

Netherlandish gardeners came to Surrey about 1600 and intensive market gardening spread to many areas, including Lambeth. By the mid-eighteenth century the outcome of their exertions can be seen through the eyes of mapmaker John Rocque (far left) – all manners of well-ordered plantations organised in rectangular plots dotted with trees. Here and there the trees' density thickens, possibly orchards or remains of former woods, planted or otherwise. When the trees follow the lines of paths this indicates deliberate planting at a time when avenues of trees denoted pride in property ownership.

Recreating the original garden

The Tradescants

One of the most important gardeners of seventeenth-century England 'landed' in South Lambeth Road in 1628 or 1629: John Tradescant the Elder (1570–1638), the creator of a remarkable botanical garden and of 'the Ark'. The Ark was this country's very first museum to open to the public. And next door to the Ark, a rich and exotic garden thrived with the many plants which the Tradescants, father and son, collected, remarkable for new plant introductions and its rare specimens. In the early days of this golden age of the garden, the idea of recreating paradise on earth was never far from the idea of gardening. So, the Ark was established to collect and save important inanimate natural objects while the role of the garden-paradise was to preserve live plants from around the world: all the natural world in a corner of Lambeth.

Paradise on earth?

> 'God Almighty first planted a garden: and, indeed, it is the purest of human pleasures'.
> Francis Bacon, *Of Gardens*, 1625

John Tradescant the Elder is also firmly linked to England's first full-scale botanic garden – in Oxford, not London. The five-acre site near Magdalen College in Oxford had been provided by the earl of Danby in 1621, to create a physic garden for the use of the Faculty of Medicine. Tradescant was approached in 1636 to supervise the planting of this garden. He held the post for just over a year when death put an abrupt end

The artist Wenceslaus Hollar, a friend of the Tradescants, incorporated the portraits of father and son into his picture of their tomb at Lambeth church. The original etching dates from around 1670. This print, based on Hollar, was re-published in 1793 by Nathaniel Smith.
(National Portrait Gallery. Image in the public domain; Wikimedia Commons)

Opposite right:

Could the original layout of the Oxford Physic Garden mirror Tradescant's own South Lambeth garden in some significant way? Recent scholarship suggests that Tradescant would have had the opportunity to start planting the Oxford garden before he died in 1638. Would he have scaled up his own Lambeth garden to fit the Oxford site? One important distinguishing feature is the shape of the two gardens – square in Oxford but long and narrow in South Lambeth.
(From *Oxonia Illustrata*. Science Museum, London. Attribution 4.0 International (CC BY 4.0) [Free use]. Wikimedia Commons)

to this project. Jacob Bobart father and son followed Tradescant, and history granted them recognition for making this particular garden thrive. More recently, Jennifer Potter found evidence that John Tradescant the Elder may have lived just long enough to have made a good start on the garden. As a mark of commitment, he employed his own manservant in Oxford and had: 'at least one full growing season to begin planting the garden, which by [David] Loggan's plan of 1675 was laid out in four quarters' (previous page).

In the seventeenth century a botanic garden was regarded as an encyclopaedia. 'Contemporaries interpreted the foundation of these encyclopaedic Gardens in a context of the re-creation of the earthly Paradise, or Garden of Eden' explains John Prest in his book *The Garden of Eden*. But it is fair to say that early on, any type of garden, not simply botanical gardens, traced its origins to the Garden of Eden. Sir Hugh Plat (1552–1608), inventor, distiller and plant grower published a book in 1608 entitled *Floraes Paradise* which was re-issued in 1653 as *The Garden of Eden*. For all the flourish of its title, it is described by Scott Mandelbrote simply as 'an analysis of the different sorts of fruit, flowers, herbs, and trees which may be grown by the assiduous gardener'.

By 1634 when the elder Tradescant published his plant list, his garden contained more than 770 separate varieties 'which would almost certainly have been laid out in order beds according to plant families, as in the botanic gardens he had admired in Europe' commented Jennifer Potter. It was rich in flowering bulbs, had twenty-seven different varieties of rose, and contained 170 different varieties in the orchard. By 1656 when the younger Tradescant published a second list of plants, the number had more than doubled in size to a vast 1701 varieties.

The garden's first recorded visitor, in 1632, three or four years after the older Tradescant settled at his South Lambeth address, was Thomas Johnson, the man who courageously undertook the massive task of updating and revising John Gerard's famous *Herball* of 1597. The new edition was published a year later in 1633, containing many references to Tradescant's plants, including the extraordinary story of how Gerard and Tradescant acquired, probably from the same source, the *Epimedium* plant: 'This rare and strange plant was sent to me from the French Kings Herbarist, *Robinus*, dwelling in Paris at the signe of the blacke head, in the street called Du bout du Monde, in English, The end of the world'. The translation is perhaps misleading – suggesting the end of the world as in the Apocalypse when it may have simply indicated a geographical position – [at] the [other] end of the world. However, this may also reveal the preoccupations of the religious Londoner in the early years of the seventeenth century.

Surprisingly, Johnson made no mention of Tradescant's orchard, despite the fact that it would later become very well known, its reputation resting on having some of the best fruit and varieties in the country, as was made clear by the great English botanist John Parkinson (1567–1650) in his book *Paradisi in Sole Paradisus Terrestris* (1629):

> my very good friend Master John Tradescante, who hath wonderfully laboured to obtain all the rarest fruits he can hear off in any place of Christendome, Turky, yea or the whole world.

Perhaps his orchard was not sufficiently established by 1632? But Jennifer Potter emphasized Tradescant's 'overriding passion' for fruit adding that 'many of Tradescant's fruits were indeed extremely rare'.

In an age of political and religious turmoil when many sought spiritual answers, the Oxford nurseryman Ralph Austen, a contemporary of John the Younger and the author of an important treatise on fruit trees, blended spiritual thinking based on trees with practical advice on how to grow them. In the section dealing with tree grafts, he reflected that the lack of success of certain types of grafts was comparable to a marriage based on worldly advantage rather than true compatibility. Bennett and Mandelbrote saw Austen's *The Spiritual Use, of an Orchard …* (1653) as giving 'the husbandman in his orchard … constant opportunity to meditate on the Fall and on original sin' before concluding that in Austen's writings:

> the teachings of the book of nature … and the book of scripture are shown to be in close harmony. Biblical history is deployed to justify a particular approach to improvement, and to suggest that bodies and souls, as well as material conditions, can be returned to a paradisial state through prudent and devout activity.

Plant introductions did not necessarily require the travels of gardeners or nurserymen – it was enough to have contacts with plant hunters, merchants or other purveyors of exotic goods. However, both Tradescants were great travellers and visited many countries, not always for botanical reasons, but almost always leading to botanical ends: France, the Netherlands, North Africa and Russia for John the Elder; while his son went to north America, at least twice, bringing back in 1638 '200 plants until now unseen in our part of the world' recorded John Morris, son of Peter, of London Bridge waterworks fame and fortune. John the Elder himself never crossed the Atlantic but he was involved with the Virginia Company and knew many people who could have provided him with those special plants the Tradescant garden became so famous for. For instance, the blue Spiderwort of Virginia which was later named after the old Tradescant – *Tradescantia virginiana*; John the Elder introduced it without going to Virginia since John Gerard's 1633 edition of the *Herball* explained: 'M. John Tradescant first procured it from Virginia'. John the Elder was also a friend of the colourful soldier-adventurer Captain John Smith (1580–1631), who made his name, perhaps most memorably, for his vital input in the running and survival of England's first American colony – Jamestown, Virginia – mapping vast tracts of surrounding land in the process, to the benefit of future arrivals. The friendship between the two men appears to have been close since Smith included John the Elder in his will.

The Tradescant garden was regularly mentioned by visitors as an object of admiration but by the mid-eighteenth-century William Watson's description in the *Royal Society Journal* of 1 January 1750, struck a very melancholic note. His visit took place on 21 May 1749:

> This Garden was … probably the first botanical Garden in *England*. Mr Tradescant's Garden has now been many years totally neglected, and the House belonging to it empty and ruin'd; and though the Garden is quite cover'd with Weeds, there remain among them manifest Footsteps of its Founder … There are yet remaining two Trees of the Arbutus, the largest I have

This traditional representation of the Garden of Eden comes from a fifteenth-century French manuscript which recounts the history of the world. The garden is planted with 'every tree that is pleasant to the sight, and good for food' and also includes the source of the four rivers which marked the site of the Garden of Eden, often depicted running out of a fountain in medieval imagery. The main protagonists God, Adam and Eve are prominently placed in the foreground which contrasts greatly with later interpretations of the same theme (see p. 360).
© British Library Board. All Rights Reserved/Bridgeman Images)

seen; which, from their being so long used to our Winters, did not suffer by the severe Colds of 1729 and 1740, when most of their kind were kill'd throughout *England*.

Death in the garden

The Tradescants' garden at South Lambeth Road would certainly have been created with the powerful motive of emulating the Garden of Eden. This idea is alluded to in the final verse of the inscription found on the Tradescants' tomb in the churchyard of St Mary's Lambeth (now the Garden Museum).

> Know, stranger, ere thou pass, beneath this stone
> Lie John Tradescant, grandsire, father, son
> The last dy'd in his spring, the other two,
> Liv'd till they had travelled Art and Nature through,
> As by their choice Collections may appear,
> Of what is rare in land, in sea, in air,
> Whilst they (as Homer's Iliad in a nut)
> A world of wonders in one closet shut,
> These famous Antiquarians that had been
> Both Gardeners to the Rose and Lily Queen,
> Transplanted now themselves, sleep here & when
> Angels shall with their trumpets waken men,
> And fire shall purge the world, these three shall rise
> And change this Garden then for Paradise.

As well as evoking the prospect of Paradise for those buried within, the text alludes to The Tradescants' Ark as 'A world of wonders in one closet shut' and also finally, to the Last Judgement – 'Angels shall with their trumpets waken men, And fire shall purge the world'. Therefore this text confirms the importance of the two Old Testament stories which underpinned the world of the Tradescants at Lambeth: the Ark and the Garden of Eden.

The fusion of these two separate Bible episodes may also be observed in seventeenth-century paintings, for instance 'Adam and Eve in the Garden of Eden' (1617), by Jan Brueghel (1568–1625), this chapter's opening picture. The figures of Adam and Eve and the Tree of Knowledge have been relegated to the background and the Garden of Eden is inhabited by all manner of animals, in pairs, ready, almost, to board the Ark. Previous artistic interpretations of the Garden of Eden had closely followed the description offered in Genesis (left): the Tree of Life or the Tree of Knowledge, the four rivers and above all Adam and Eve, central to the composition.

But the other theme to emerge from the fascinating inscription on the roof of the Tradescants' tomb is the end of the world, and Last Judgment: 'Angels shall with their trumpets waken men', i.e., the dead will emerge from their tombs to be judged, and 'fire shall purge the world'. Destruction and retribution should be expected with the fire standing for hell and we should therefore expect the reliefs which adorn the tomb to echo some of these ideas.

One of the difficulties in interpreting the tomb's imagery is that it has been restored on a number of occasions; and clearly some of the detail has changed. However, it is a monument much recorded in drawings and prints, and examination of the earliest drawings prior to the monument's first restoration in 1773 should be useful. The earliest images were those commissioned by Samuel Pepys (1633–1703). They are not completely satisfactory because they are not drawn very precisely. The landscapes as they stand now, appear to show destruction on one side of the tomb while the other side gives a more pristine rendering of buildings in a landscape, with the foreground forming a frieze of objects, all drawn from the natural world such as different types of shells, also a crocodile, possibly Egyptian and popular in contemporary cabinets of curiosities. (Overleaf)

The person responsible for commissioning the tomb was neither John Tradescant the Elder nor his son John the Younger. It was the latter's second wife, Hester Tradescant, née Pookes, who had probably met her husband when, in his father's footsteps, he became keeper of the royal gardens, based at Oatlands Palace. There he would have come into contact with artists in the king's service, in particular Cornelius de Neve and John de Critz the Elder, both related to Sarah Pookes, a 'cousin' of Hester. When Hester set about commissioning the family tomb after her husband's death on 22 April 1662, she presumably called on the large network of artists in her family to produce a design for the tomb. Jennifer Potter commented: 'The tomb she commissioned was strikingly original'. Little is known about the genesis of this fascinating monument though by November 1662 Hester had the agreement of St Mary's, after donating £50 – a large sum 'for ye Use of ye Poor of ye Parish'.

Hester's ancestry has not been entirely elucidated but her 'cousins' were certainly connected to the great John de Critz family of artists – John de Critz the Elder having secured the major post of Serjeant-Painter in 1603, and whose large workshop connected him to many Netherlandish artists, including Marcus Gheeraerts the Younger (his father is on pp. 41 ff), the famous miniature painter Isaac Oliver, and Robert Peake to name the most well-known. The Elder Critz had three sons – also named John –

Detail from the Tradescants' tomb. The landscapes contain exotic elements with fragments of columns and demolished buildings - a scene of destruction which recalls those found in prints of Roman ruins or the destruction of cities such as Jericho by the Flemish artist Maarten van Heemskerk (1498–1574). Except that Heemskerk's engravings feature many figures and these landscapes have none.
(© The author, 2020)

who all followed in their father's footsteps. The number of portraits of the Tradescant family which have survived is remarkable and bears witness to their easy access to this prolific circle of artists. (Left)

When she died in April 1678, Hester was buried in the tomb she had commissioned for three generations of Tradescant gardeners. The details of her sad death, in her garden, have come down to us, penned by Elias Ashmole – the erudite collector who became her nemesis, as we shall soon discover.

The paradox with the Tradescants is that deliberately or not, they are connected with many important historic artefacts which have given them considerable visibility – the large number of portraits, a relatively grand tomb, a *Florilegium* to show off their most eye-catching plant introductions, two published lists of what they were growing in the garden, a list of all the exhibits in the Ark-museum. And yet we still have no idea of what either the garden or the Museum looked like, we barely know what made them collect things or the circumstances of collecting and we know nothing about their domestic quarters. Father, son and grandson were gardeners

The Tradescants' Chest tomb at St Mary's Lambeth (now the Garden Museum) – Who is buried within? And other facts

- 1 June 1635: burial of Jane Hurte, first wife of John Tradescant the Younger and the first Tradescant to be buried at Lambeth.
- April 1638: death of John Tradescant the Elder while his son was in Virginia.
- 11 September 1652: death of John Tradescant III, at the tender age of eighteen, son of John Tradescant the Younger (portrait above)
- 11 April 1662: death of John Tradescant the Younger at the age of fifty-three.
- November 1662 Hester Tradescant, wife of the late John Tradescant the Younger obtained permission to erect the chest tomb from St Mary's parish.
- 1662–1677: Samuel Pepys commissioned drawn records of the Tradescant tomb. These will be engraved by Hollar.

- 4 April 1678: death of Hester Tradescant (née Pookes), second wife of John Tradescant the Younger. Although suicide may have been in the minds of her contemporaries, she was interred two days later 'in a Vault in Lambeth Church yard, where her husband & his son John had been formerly layd' recorded Elias Ashmole.
- 1773: tomb badly decayed – first restoration, based on Pepys' drawings. The lid was replaced (the original lid is in the Garden Museum).
- 1793: the tomb was recorded for J T Smith's *Antiquities of London*, reproducing Hollar's portraits of the Tradescants above it (see p. 363).
- 1853: second restoration was carried out by G P White from Vauxhall Bridge Road.

Photos: three sides of the Tradescants' tomb at Lambeth church, now the Garden Museum. Could the seven-headed monster, be the seven-headed beast of the Book of Revelation in the Bible? And the fallen buildings symbolical of the destruction of Babylon, the sinful city? The pyramid and crocodile (of Egypt?) are certainly evocative of the Middle East. (© The author, 2020)

but horticulturists rather than scientists, practical artisans rather than scholars or archivists. That has left a substantial gap in the overall picture which is difficult to fill. Will the Ark, their most enduring legacy, throw further light onto this conundrum?

The Ark

Above:

Title page of Ole Worm's book *Museum Wormianum, seu historia rerum rariorum*, Leiden, 1655. Historian Jennifer Potter has likened the Tradescant's Ark to the museum of this Danish collector and professor of medicine, Ole Worm, adding that 'Tradescant's collection was more of a jumble … and to make any sense of it you would have needed the services of its keeper, whose dramatic delivery was legendary'.

(Wellcome images. Image in the public domain; Wikimedia Commons)

> Although London had fewer individual collectors than any comparable European capital or seat of learning, by the middle of the [seventeenth] century it possessed what was widely regarded as the finest and largest natural history museum anywhere. This was the famed "Tradescant's Ark", whose founder John Tradescant, was a professional gardener successively in the employment of Lord Salisbury, Lord Wotton and the Duke of Buckingham.
>
> Richard Altick, *The Shows of London* (1978)

Where the original Ark in the Tradescants' South Lambeth home was located is something of a mystery. The whole Tradescant residence became known as the Ark over the years when their museum was open to the public – for a charge of sixpence per person. The thorough, determined research of Jennifer Potter only delivered the following conclusion: 'No detailed description has come to us of how the rarities were displayed … On balance, a … case can be made for locating the rarities in an upper room of the house itself, which was certainly large enough to accommodate the collection.' Hester Tradescant was recorded 'to have "fetched downe" a Queen Elizabeth milled shilling from the "Clossitt of rarityes" that Tradescant had "kept in a room in his house in South Lambeth"'. The overall appearance of the room in the early 1660s was described by the artist Willem Shellinks (1623–1678) – 'one can see in a large long room a collection of rare antique curiosities, costumes of various nationals and strange weapons, also fishes, plants, horns, shells.'

The Tradescants employed a keeper for their collection which was regarded as a serious educational tool by schoolmaster Charles Hoole in 1660, arguing that London 'is best for the full improvement of children in their education, because of the variety of objects which daily present themselves to them, or may easily be seen once a year, by walking to Mr John Tradescant' (cited by Leith-Ross).

Contemporary documents to help historians assess John the Elder's 'collecting policy' for the Ark, are almost non-existent though Jennifer

Opposite top:

This oil portrait of Hester Tradescant and her stepson John, is dated 1645 and attributed to Thomas de Critz (1607–1653). Hester was married to John Tradescant the Younger and inherited the 'Ark', having survived her husband and the stepson depicted in this painting.

(Ashmolean Museum. Image in the public domain; Wikimedia Commons)

Potter has done a fine job of recovering this gardener's collecting impulse … by proxy! She summed it up in one short phrase 'A Passion for Strangeness', and it was revealed after scrutinising a letter from John the Elder written on behalf of the Duke of Buckingham, his employer. It is addressed to Edward Nicholas, Secretary to the Navy and dated 31 July 1625; the letter is accompanied by a detailed list of potential artefacts. It is reproduced in full in Leith-Ross's biography but here I choose to reproduce Jennifer Potter's analysis after she introduced the reader to who the ultimate recipients of the request were: 'All Marchants from All Places But Espetially the Virginie & Bermewde & Newfound Land'. She concludes that:

> John Tradescant's European journeyings had clearly stirred his curiosity about the natural world … Buckingham's wealth and natural acquisitiveness would enable him [Tradescant] to turn curiosity into collecting, ostensibly for his master but almost certainly on his own account, too.
> Letter and list give us a fascinating insight into Tradescant as a collector: size and strangeness are his chief criteria. Like a tourist describing the marvels he wishes to see, everything must be 'the Bigest that canbe Gotten'.
> Tradescant's sense of wonder is compressed into his final request for 'any thing that is strang'.
> The records are strangely silent on whether Buckingham's collection ever had a separate existence, or whether he simply allowed Tradescant to use his name … It is tempting to think that many of the strange beasts and birds sent to Buckingham found their way to Tradescant's own collection at South Lambeth.

A 1669 visitor to the Ark – which he called 'India House' – gave a detailed description of some of the exhibits, including that of a truly monstrous fish:

> Equal in size to a sea-calf, without scales, but covered with a rough and uneven skin, and having a long and deformed head, with a horrid-looking mouth, in which are two rows of teeth, both upper and under, in shape like those of a saw.

This account was written by Count Lorenzo Magalotti, who accompanied Cosmo III, Grand Duke of Tuscany, on a Vauxhall tour which had started with the 'hydraulic machine' at the Marquess of Worcester's Vauxhall works.

One of Tradescant's most stunning exhibits fits perfectly the criteria of 'size and strangeness' but is also the least understood object in the collection: 'Powhatan's Mantle', from Virginia in the United States (right). Because 'it is unique with no known parallels' it is even more difficult to interpret. 'Its original purpose is unknown and despite being called "mantle", "habit" and "robe" in the 1600s, it was probably always meant for display rather than worn as a garment', reads the Ashmolean Museum caption. Powhattan, the overall Indian chief when Captain Smith was running the Virginia colony, is best remembered as the father of Princess Pocahontas. In the words of Jennifer Potter, his 'cloak' is 'one of the most iconic native American artefacts outside North America'. It was first described in 1638 as 'the robe of the king of Virginia', the connection with Powhattan being made later. Although it is just feasible that this item was brought back by John the Younger on his first voyage to Virginia, it was perhaps more likely to have been brought back by the leading Indian trader, William Claiborne, according to Jennifer Potter.

The arrival of Elias Ashmole (1617–1692) into the life of John the Younger was described as 'A snake in Eden' by Jennifer Potter and 'Enter Ashmole' in Prudence Leith-Ross's biography. Even the less charged 'Enter Ashmole' is filled with self-assured poise: forging ahead when others might recoil. The two men met on 15 June 1650, in the words of Ashmole: 'My selfe, wife & Dr: Wharton, went to visit Mr: John Tradescant at South Lambeth'. Ashmole had become interested in botany in 1648 when he first started 'simpling' (gathering medicinal herbs or other simples) and visiting gardens.

From humble beginnings, Ashmole, the son of a Lichfield saddler, trained as a lawyer and became extremely well connected and wealthy. He claimed to have developed a passion for Oxford when he studied natural Philosophy, mathematics, astronomy and astrology there – he was particularly partial to alchemy and astrology. But Oxford was the headquarters of the King and this may have exerted a significant influence on our Royalist social climber.

Hester, the wife of John Tradescant the Younger seemed to have developed a close friendship with Mary, Ashmole's wife; while the men – Ashmole and his friend Dr Wharton – were quick to offer their assistance to John Tradescant to catalogue his museum collection. This was done by listing objects of nature separately from art objects. The publication was much delayed but eventually came out in 1656, Ashmole meeting its cost. 'As he [Tradescant] must have been well able to have stood the cost himself, it is difficult to imagine the reasons that persuaded him to accept this offer', wrote Prudence Leith-Ross. This placed the gardener in Ashmole's debt, possibly preparing the ground for the future controversial 'Deed of Gift'.

'The Deed of Gift', claimed Ashmole, was prepared at the behest of Tradescant on 14 December 1659 and it was signed by the same and by his wife Hester. The Tradescants' intentions had been

> to leave the rarities to Ashmole *in trust* [my italics] for a university as they both recognized the importance of saving the collection for future generations and had agreed it should not be left in private hands.
> When they carefully read through the deed they found that, contrary to their intentions, the collection was to go to Ashmole without restriction.

wrote Prudence Leith-Ross. The Tradescants tried in vain to annul the dangerous deed by cutting off the seal and obscuring the signatures; they even considered burning it (they did not, to keep it as proof). John also prepared a will which made his final wishes clear:

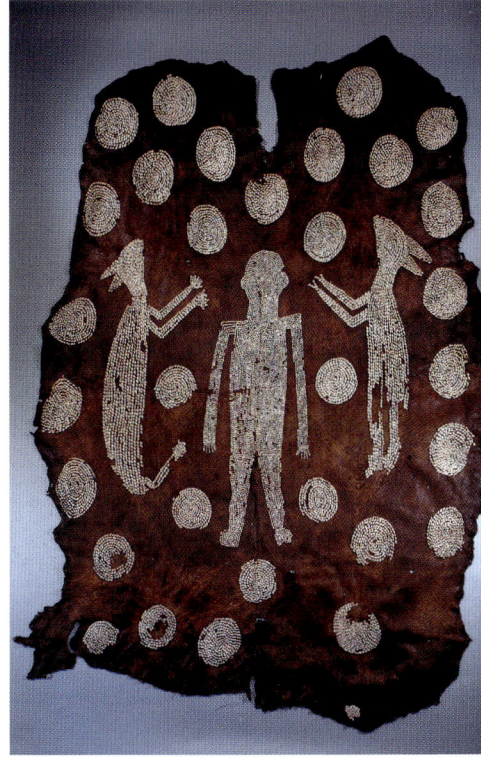

Powhatan's Mantle, one of the Ashmolean Museum's rarest exhibits, was once in the Ark at John Tradescant's house in Lambeth. (© Ashmolean Museum, University of Oxford)

I give, devize and bequeath my Closet of Rarities to my dearly beloved wife Hester during her natural Life, and after decease I give and bequeath the same to the Universities of Oxford and Cambridge, to which of them shee shall think fit at her decease.

But no amount of effort to undo the wretched deed could overturn its content. There was a court case after the death of John the Younger and Ashmole won with ease. Hester tried to argue that on the night when the deed was signed, her husband had come home 'distempered' (drunk) accompanied by four strangers who produced the deed which they both unadvisedly signed, without reading it, when it was produced.

After losing the long-term ownership of the Ark, Hester continued to open her house to the public, including schools; but when Ashmole purchased the property next door to her own (with adjoining walls) and she was also served a writ of execution regarding the outcome of the court case, she must have hated Ashmole with a vengeance. He moved in on 2 October 1674 and recorded the time: '11H. 30. A. M. … I & my wife first entred my House at South Lambeth'. By 1 December the main bulk of the collection had been transferred to the attic of his house next door. Hester was made to sign a humiliating declaration: 'I have very much wronged Elias Ashmole … by several fals scandalous & defamatory Speeches Reports …'.

'Whatever his legal rights, Ashmole's persecution of the ageing widow is one of the shabbiest chapters in the Tradescant story' concluded Jennifer Potter. By a strange twist of fate, the details of Hester's death came from Ashmole himself. He recorded it on 4 April 1678 "11H:30' A.M. my wife told me Mrs Tredescant: was found drowned in her Pond. She was drowned the day before about noone as appeared by some Circumstances'. Suicide or symbolic death? It may have been both.

For Ashmole the astrologer, the accurate recording of time and date would have been important. Would he have drawn any conclusion from the timing involved: 11.00 a.m. when he first moved into the house and 11.30 a.m. when he discovered Hester's death, four and a half years after his arrival at South Lambeth? Historian Prudence Leith-Ross pointed out there was nothing known about the pond since the garden was never systematically recorded. The image of a cursed and dispossessed woman drowning in a pond in the 'Garden of Eden' is sad and shocking.

Shortly after Hester's death Ashmole purchased the Tradescant property. He died at South Lambeth in 1692 and he, too, was buried at St Mary's Lambeth close to the Tradescants – a strange thought, though his coffin has disappeared, presumed lost during the Victorian rebuilding of the church. Ashmole may have been 'the snake in the garden' but he ensured the long-term legacy of the Tradescants' Ark as we will see later on in this chapter.

Vauxhall Gardens – 'Garden of Earthly Delights'

When in 1729 the enterprising Jonathan Tyers took over these gardens – then named the New Spring Gardens – the move heralded a new era; this venue's reputation would soon travel far and wide to become a source of inspiration for many gardens across London, Britain and indeed Europe.

Vauxhall Gardens was the archetypal eighteenth-century pleasure garden. In the absence of a Royal Academy – founded in 1768 – , Vauxhall Gardens was the earliest public arena for artists in this country. Smaller pleasure gardens would follow suit and include paintings as part of their attractions (see pp. 173–174).

The gardens' origins lay on the north bank, squeezed between Whitehall and St James's Park. They are depicted in William Morgan's 1682 map and were first mentioned by name, 'Spring Gardens', in 1610; they had probably become public by the mid-1630s. After an unsettled period when they closed and reopened several times, the site was built over after the Restoration (1660) and the gardens moved to Vauxhall, hence the name 'New Spring Gardens' as illustrated on Thomas Hill's map of the Manor of Vauxhall (see p. 94). Perhaps the decision to move to Vauxhall was connected to the area's rural appearance with previously noteworthy gardens: Tradescant's and Caron House? This secluded and attractive piece of countryside may well have prompted the artist William Hogarth and his new bride to take lodgings in this area shortly after they were married, away from Central London and their frayed relationship with the bride's father,

This watercolour of Vauxhall Gardens by Thomas Rowlandson was painted around 1784 and is one of the best-known images of the famous pleasure garden. Up in the orchestra Mrs Weichsell is singing – the 'gothic' orchestra building was completed in 1758. Other contemporary celebrities include Dr Johnson and the Prince of Wales. On the left-hand side is a close-up detail of one of the supper boxes with a large man perhaps getting tucked into the notoriously thin slices of ham, the rest of the company simply drinking. On the right the artist has captured well the familiar gesture of a waiter opening a bottle. He is at the table of Mrs Barry – 'The Old Baud of Sutton Street'.
(Yale Center for British Art. Image in the public domain; Wikimedia Commons)

The artist Francis Hayman (1708–1776) made his name at Vauxhall Gardens – opposite; he painted this family portrait for garden proprietor Jonathan Tyers (1702–1767) in 1740, around the time when he was commissioned to paint Vauxhall's supper boxes. The Tyers lived on site at Vauxhall Gardens and Jonathan, seated left, died there. He is depicted with his wife Elizabeth (née Fermor) and his four children. His sons Jonathan and Thomas inherited the gardens at their father's death. The relief over the chimney piece is that of the Prince of Wales, the site's freeholder. (National Portrait Gallery. Image in the public domain, Wikimedia Commons)

the artist Sir James Thornhill, who disapproved of their union?

The first sign of the gardens' transformation under Tyers' management came in 1732:

> We hear that several Painters, and Artificers are employed to finish the Temples, Obelisks, Triumphal Arches, Grotto Rooms, etc. for the Ridotto Al' Fresco, commanded for the 7th June, at Spring Gardens

So David Coke tells us in his published writings on Vauxhall Gardens. This public entertainment made up of music and dancing was a great success and seemed to have sealed the fame of the gardens early on. But Jonathan Tyers (below). was also a fine marketing man – the term may not have existed then but the ideas were the same. The land belonged to the Prince of Wales, so the prince was given his own spacious pavilion, perhaps built by his favourite architect William Kent (bottom left) Tyers also sought 'the publicity that controversial art inevitably attracts' (David Coke). There was a substantial amount of commissioned site-specific art if you include first, the paintings which decorated the backs of every arbour or supper box, altogether fifty-three! Francis Hayman having designed the majority of them (right), except four by Peter Monamy, two by Hubert Gravelot and two by Hogarth; second, the artistic illumination of the gardens, including large scale 'transparencies' to close some of the vistas, and finally, the extraordinary statue of 'Mr Handel' by Roubiliac which greeted visitors near the gardens' entrance. The 'Turkish Tent', erected in 1744 as a shelter for diners, perhaps by William Kent, and the Gothic Orchestra building (1758) encapsulated the spirit of Vauxhall: 'of such contrivance and Form, as a Painter of Genius and Judgment would chuse to adorn his landscape with'.

The making of Vauxhall Gardens was not an overnight affair, unfolding new delights every season or so – a season lasted from April/May to October weather permitting. 1758 marked the end of significant additions; it was also the year when Tyers purchased the estate.

The earliest illustration of the gardens dates from 1736 – an etching on the so-called 'Vauxhall Fan' (British Museum). But the set of pictures which are most detailed about the gardens' atmosphere and its main landmarks are the paintings and engravings

produced by and after Antonio Canaletto and Samuel Wale around 1750. The reconstruction at the beginning of this section is based on the engraving by Johann Sebastian Muller after Samuel Wale with, from right to left: the Grand Vista punctuated by arches with a set of supper boxes near the entrance, the Orchestra building in the middle, and the Supper Boxes on the left hand side. (Overleaf)

Each of the fifty supper boxes at Vauxhall Gardens was decorated with specially commissioned paintings. The artist Francis Hayman, a friend and protégé of the gardens' proprietor, was responsible for almost all of the paintings. With its rural theme 'Bird nesting', dated 1741–2, was in perfect harmony with the spirit of the place.
(© Victoria and Albert Museum, London)

A London nature diary

'The green wood-pecker laughs in the fields of Vauxhall. Owl hoots at Vauxhall', 14 March 1778,

Gilbert White's *Journal*

Should we be surprised to discover that England's first ecologist, the Hampshire parson-naturalist Gilbert White (1720–1793) had close links with South Lambeth? Some regard his magnus opus, *The Natural History and Antiquities of Selborne*, published in 1789, as pioneering in its use of fieldwork and the close observation of nature, laying the ground for the future success of great natural scientists such as Charles Darwin. Much of Gilbert's work was based on Selborne but two things drove the inveterate naturalist to London: family ties and institutions such as the Royal Society and the Society of Antiquaries.

Opposite:
This 1859 watercolour by J Findlay depicts the pavilion and gallery erected by the proprietor of Vauxhall Gardens for the Prince of Wales – a generous and clever gesture on the part of Jonathan Tyers who thus honoured the Prince, who was the owner of the land at Vauxhall Gardens. Although in Tyers' day, the Prince paid his own entrance fee!
© London Metropolitan Archives
(City of London)

'A General Prospect of Vaux Hall Gardens': this useful engraving by John S Muller, after the original painting by Samuel Wale, gives a good idea of the overall layout of the gardens in 1751. The orchestra, in the middle of the central square, was framed on either side by the supper boxes, arranged in semi-circular structures.
© London Metropolitan Archives (City of London)

Gilbert White's *Journal* bears witness to his London visits – the 1982 editor, Walter Johnson, helpfully placed in square brackets the geographical areas of 'London' for Central London and 'Lambeth' or 'South Lambeth' and 'Vauxhall' for the suburbs. White's younger brother by four years, Thomas, was a merchant who had retired to South Lambeth, at the 'Vauxhall Escheat' which included the Tradescant enclave on the former estate of Noel Caron. A second brother, Benjamin, younger still, was a bookseller in Fleet Street – he was responsible for purchasing the lease for Thomas's farm and later moved to this neighbourhood. At his death in 1794 the estate was placed in trust until 1820. Both brothers, like Gilbert, were fascinated by nature – Thomas was interested in trees, and Benjamin published books on birds and animal life.

Touchingly, Gilbert's own powers of observation took an unexpected turn when confronted with the urban environment. Editor Walter Johnson, made the point that 'he inspects the markets and fishmongers' shops to become acquainted with new kinds of game or fish'.

The Lambeth entries cover the period 1774 to 1793. On 28 January 1776 Gilbert recorded 'Fierce frost: ice under people's beds, & cutting winds' and on 26 April 1778, he mentioned a visit to Ashton Lever's Museum in the (future) Blackfriars Road (see p. 176). But for the year 1780, which witnessed the murderous Gordon riots, there are vivid entries which give a strong sense of the passing seasons:

> **February 29.** [South Lambeth] Remarkable vivid Aurora borealis.
> **March 6.** [London] Sky-larks mount and sing.
> **June 6.** […] Terrible riots in London: & unprecedented burnings, & devastations by the mob.
> **June 19.** [South Lambeth] Dust well-laid on the road. Barley in ear on the sands. Much Upland-hay mowed near London.
> **June 20.** Early pease abound. Strawberries, & cherries ill-ripened, & very small. Roses blow. Much wall-fruit.
> **June 22.** Gloomy and moist, rain. Sold my Saffron the 13th crop. Lighted a fire in the dining room. Rain at St Lambeth 32 [hundredths of an inch].
> **June 27.** Swallows feed their young on the ground in Mr Curtis's botanic garden in George's Fields.
> **December 12.** […] The Barometer at South Lambeth was this day at 30-6-10: a sure token that South Lambeth is much Lower than Selbourne [Selbourne 10-1-10.]

William Blake

At the end of the little garden in Hercules Buildings there was a summer house. Mr Butts calling one day found Mr. and Mrs. Blake sitting in this summer-house, freed from "those troublesome disguises" which have prevailed since the Fall. "Come in!" cried Blake; "it's only Adam and Eve, you know!" Husband and wife had been reciting passages from [Milton's] *Paradise Lost*, in character, and the garden of Hercules Buildings had to represent the Garden of Eden; a little to the scandal of wondering neighbours, on more than one occasion.

Cited in Peter Ackroyd's *Blake*, published by Vintage (1999)

'Mr and Mrs Blake in their Garden'. This delightful scene showing the artist William Blake (1757–1827) and his wife's gambols in their Lambeth garden – in the nude, as Adam and Eve – is clearly not contemporary with the life of the great poet. It was imagined and executed with great vividness by painter Michael Johnson in 2017 – a Blake devotee who draws constant inspiration from the garden of nature.
(© The artist)

So now we know the Garden of Eden could also be found in Hercules Buildings in the closing years of the eighteenth century! William and Catherine Blake moved from 28 Broad Street, just south of the British Museum, to Lambeth in February 1791. There they could afford to live in a modest three-storey terraced-house at 13 Hercules Buildings with a precious back garden (above). The kitchen was in the basement and there were two rooms per floor. William's rolling press was accommodated in the ground floor room, street-side, and the second room, overlooking the

13 Hercules Buildings (now Hercules Road), is where William Blake and his wife Catherine spent ten happy years. The house was demolished around 1917-18 and the Corporation of the City of London, who owns the site, built the William Blake estate which replaced the Georgian terraced houses Blake knew.
(Lambeth Archives)

garden was also his studio. Philip Astley (see p. 159) was a neighbour in the triangular plot bordered by Hercules Buildings (now Hercules Road) and York Place (now Kennington Road). There in the middle of the plot, 'terraced-locked' was Astley's very own 'Hercules Hall'. (Below)

William Blake's search for redemption and infinity was sometimes on a collision course with the sacred relationship the artist had with his city. Blake's vision was filled with cities; and Los, one of the four 'living creatures' peopling his imagination, is firmly linked to the (imaginary) city of Golgonooza. Los represents the creative impulse which, to the eyes of Blake, was Fallen Man's escape route to redemption. The image of an old man led through city streets by a little boy turns up twice in Blake's oeuvre: to illustrate his 'London' poem (right) and also in his long poem 'Jerusalem':

> I see London, blind and age bent begging thro the streets
> Of Babylon, led by a child. His tears run down his beard

Yes, London is old, over 2000 years, and it is creaking like an old man overburdened with experience, a fallen man wandering the streets of Babylon – the fallen city. He is assisted, led by a child: experience and innocence in one single eloquent picture.

Those cultural commentators who do not overlook the bond of the poet with London, and Lambeth in particular, are those already mindful of the city's transformative powers. London-inspired author Peter Ackroyd is clear: 'Blake was the poet of eternity, but he was also the poet of late eighteenth-century London'. Focusing on Lambeth, he asserts that Blake 'refers to it more often than to any other London region: "From Lambeth/ We began our Foundations; lovely Lambeth"'. But the ties between the artist and his Lambeth muse are more deeply analysed in Jon Newman's wonderful booklet *Lovely Lambeth* which takes the shape of a walk:

Hercules Hall stood on the south east side of the triangle formed by Hercules Buildings and Kennington Road. It was the home of Philip Astley (1742-1814), founder of Astley's amphitheatre which stood close to the southern end of Westminster Bridge. The hall was at the back of William Blake's house. This watercolour, by an unknown artist (initials GPH), appears to have been made prior to its demolition in 1841.
© London Metropolitan Archives
(City of London)

> The poem 'London' was not only conceived and written in Lambeth but was also, arguably, imaginatively located within that place ... In it a host of familiars – the poor, the disenfranchised, the damaged, the sick at heart and the exploited – are encountered wandering the streets of the city.

London

I wander thro' each charter'd street,
Near where the charter'd Thames does flow.
And mark in every face I meet
Marks of weakness, marks of woe.

In every cry of every Man,
In every Infants cry of fear,
In every voice: in every ban,
The mind forg'd manacles I hear

How the Chimney-sweepers cry
Every blackning Church appals,
And the hapless Soldiers sigh
Runs in blood down Palace walls

But most thro' midnight streets I hear
How the youthful Harlots curse
Blasts the new-born Infants tear
And blights with plagues the Marriage hearse

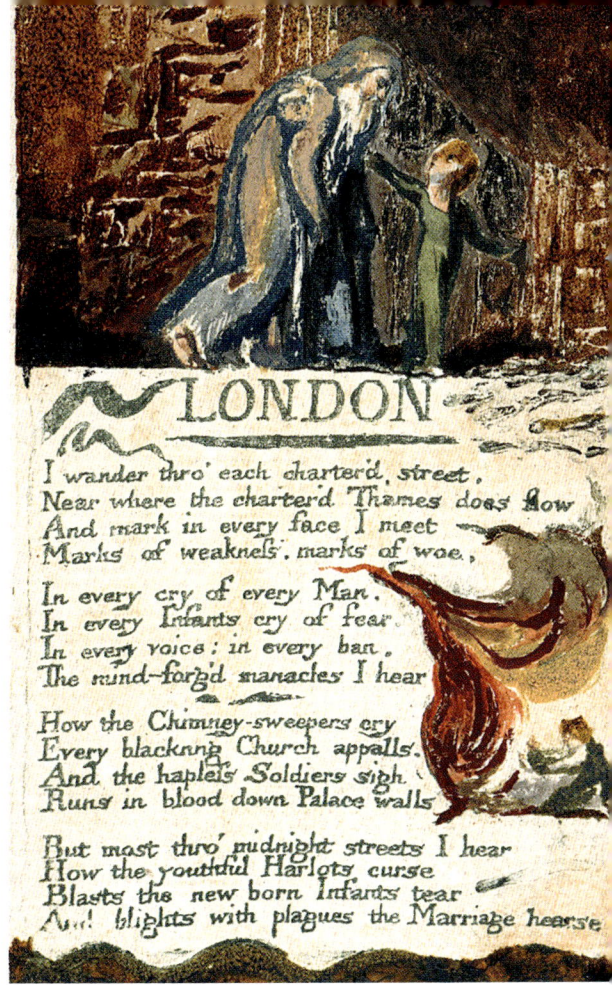

William Blake has drawn a small child guiding the steps of a blind old man through the derelict streets of London to illustrate his poem 'London', written when Blake lived in Hercules Buildings in Lambeth. This moving depiction of old age, poverty and decay draws strength from the innocent willingness and energy of the young child. From *Songs of Experience*, London 1794
(Yale Center for British Art. Image in the public domain. Wikimedia Commons)

This is the antithesis of the Garden of Eden. This is the fallen city groaning with the cries of its enslaved dwellers.

Jon Newman is persuasive when he brings our attention to the proximity of the Thames from Hercules Buildings and the plausible 'charter'd streets', perhaps those of Water Lambeth, he suggests; also pointing out that the three institutions within a stone's throw of Blake's house 'each of them a response to the different casualties of London Street prostitution', the curse of the poem's last quatrain – the Westminster Lying-in Hospital, the Asylum for Female Orphans and the Magdalen Hospital for Penitent Prostitutes.

The poem 'London' is embedded in Blake's *Songs of Experience* which were written and published in Lambeth; these contrast deeply with his *Songs of Innocence* written in Westminster, north of the river; the contrast is made deliberately explicit in two poems bearing the same title: 'Holy Thursday'. There Blake juxtaposed the innocence and joy of charity children glimpsed at St Paul's Cathedral with the desperately sad counter-version he crafted, and no doubt witnessed, south of the river. So, at the same time as Blake felt at home in his own Lambeth 'Garden of Eden', it is also in Lambeth that he revealed the sins committed against children, poverty and the 'eternal winter' of the poor in the city.

Blake identified with Lambeth in a most unusual manner. He devised new techniques to enable him to combine poetry and engraving, thus taking control of the means of production. When in 1794 he published his 'Songs of Innocence' and 'Songs of Experience', the imprint stated 'The Author and Printer W Blake'. Jon Newman noted: 'After that date every book produced at Hercules Buildings would carry the place of production 'LAMBETH'. A unique detail amongst publishers recording the city of publication, not obscure South London suburbs!

I also encountered Blake when researching St John's Wood – which formed part of his vision of a new Jerusalem – 'fields … built over with pillars of gold'. Lambeth is a more muddled picture – domestic bliss and 'Garden of Eden' mixed with the pain of witnessing tortured humanity on stepping outside his front door. The great art critic John Ruskin memorably described this clash between inside and outside realities:

> A great part of the Virtue of Home is actually dependent on narrowness of thought. To be quite comfortable in your nest, you must not care too much about what is going on outside.
>
> **(quoted in Celina Fox's** *Londoners***)**

But Blake did care about what was going on outside and there is no better proof than the poem 'London'. Blake's experience in Lambeth appears to have revolved around two opposite poles: blissful contentment in the 'Nest', fallen humanity when stepping out of the front door, though tampered by the hope of finding infinity.

> There is a Grain of Sand in Lambeth that Satan cannot find
> Nor can his Watch Fiends find it: tis translucent & has many Angles
> But he who finds it will find Oothoon's palace*, for within
> Opening into Beulah*, every angle is a lovely heaven.
>
> *Oothoon is a proponent of free love in the poem 'Jerusalem'.
> *Beulah: feminine, a gentle place of refuge from harsh reality. Marriage.

Might these verses echo the Lambeth idyll of the Blakes at home? The lines come from Blake's great poem 'Jerusalem' which was written long after the couple had left Lambeth. Jon Newman wrote perceptively about this too, the moment when Lambeth became a memory rather than everyday life: 'a highly personal Lambeth of the imagination began to emerge, which continued to resound mysteriously through the poetry of his final books'.

The Oval

Walking around the Oval now will not reconnect you with the area when it was first laid out as a *green* oval site. The open land has been replaced by a large accumulation of buildings and grass pitch, an important cricket club, but fenced off and resolutely closed to the street. The semi-detached villas which once graced the outer side of the curvilinear street have been replaced by a jumble of residential blocks – some no doubt with a view over the cricket pitch; exciting for some, but a minority advantage.

The original (and unusual) layout – green oval with villas facing it, dates back to the late eighteenth century when the land was in the hands of Sir William Clayton (1762–1834), 4th Baronet of Harleyford Manor, Buckinghamshire (hence the naming of Clayton and Harleyford Streets) and MP for Great Marlow (1783–90). On 1 July 1789, Clayton entered into an agreement with plasterers John Harwood and Thomas Dickinson, brickmaker Isaac

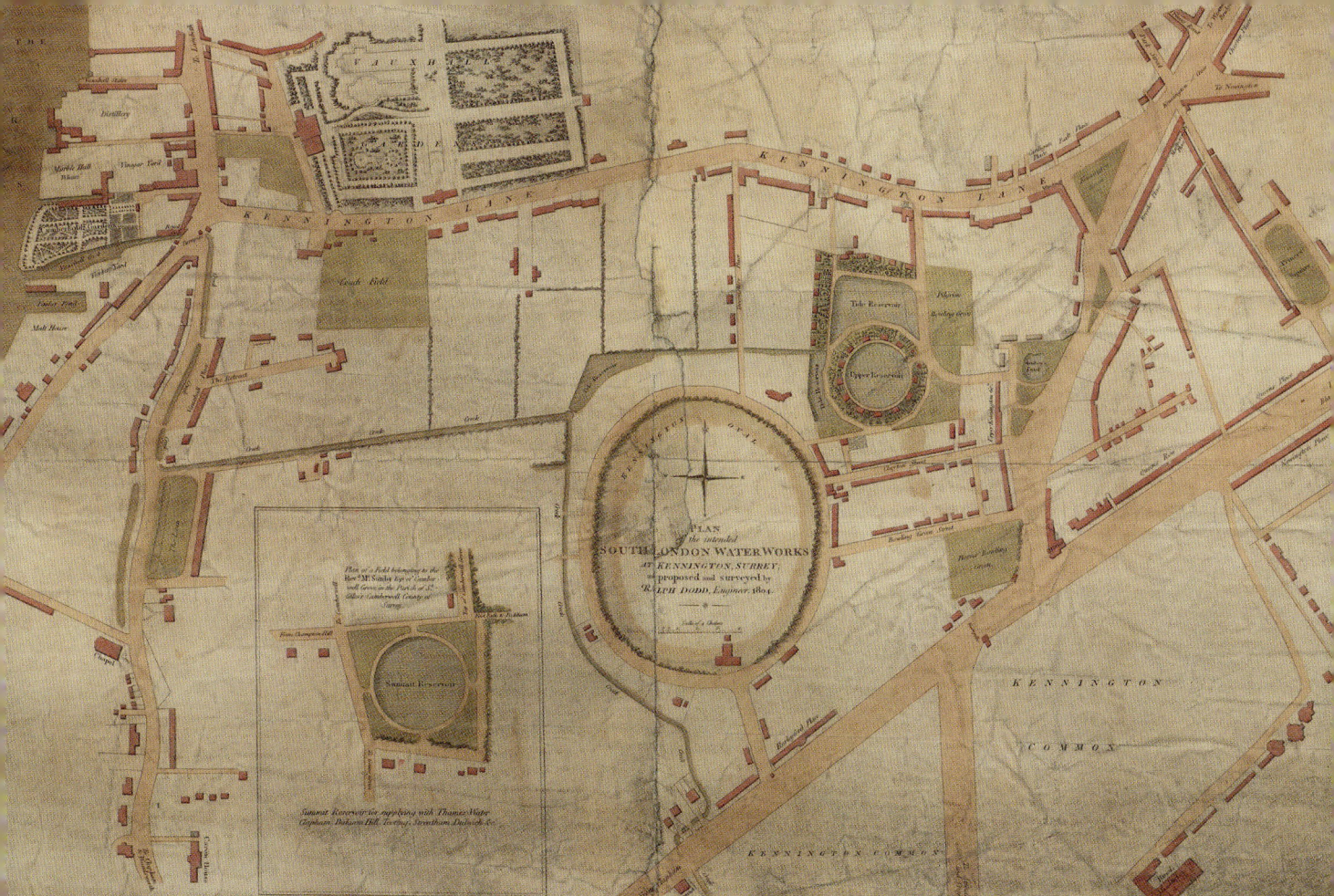

Bates and surveyor Richard Wooding, for the development of this land and the agreement stipulated at least 110 houses. But in 1790 the lease of the Oval was granted to a market gardener. By 1799 Clayton Street had been made and some terrace housing built but the villas overlooking the Oval had not yet appeared on Horwood's map. In William Faden's updated 1813 edition of the same map, terrace housing in Clayton Street had been completed and some of the villas had been built.

There is arguably nothing particularly unusual about delays and stoppages in urban development, however, this becomes a significant project when it is placed within the context of other contemporary developments. The fashion for circuses and crescents which appeared in London in the second half of the eighteenth century, was clearly a response to the work of John Wood (father and son) at Bath. There, a new model for town planning was born which combined harmoniously square (1729–39), circus (1754–67) and crescent (1767–74). It inspired several schemes in London – the earliest was George Dance's late 1760s Minories development at Tower Hill (destroyed in the Second World War); the second was also by George Dance, a plan for Camden Town from around 1790, which made use of the circus and a split oval which is named 'Camden Coliseum' (never built, the plan is in the collection of the Sir John Soane Museum); the third

This detailed plan, dated 1804, is informative on two counts: it shows how the two proposed water reservoirs would be placed on either side of the Oval. It also shows how many gardens there were in that part of South Lambeth – Cumberland Gardens (top left) facing Vauxhall Gardens; going down South Lambeth Road, the rectangular patch of grass is 'The Lawn', on the future site of Vauxhall Park; while the cluster of round and oval shapes are almost treated as park/garden features, with the upper reservoir surrounded by garden villas very close in concept to the 'British Circus' proposed but never built at St John's Wood.

© London Metropolitan Archives (City of London)

was the never implemented master plan drawn up for the St John's Wood estate in 1794. The Tower Hill scheme was very urban with no room for gardens or plants but the other schemes included individual gardens and open space, particularly so with the St John's Wood estate – the very first garden suburb in this country. It was developed by the Eyre brothers who, well into the 1820s, held out hope they could create their beloved 'British Circus' with a double row of villas placed around a central green area.

The Oval at Kennington – the only such green development to have been created in London – was certainly close to what the Eyre brothers had in mind for St John's Wood but its shape echoed George Dance's scheme at Camden Town. The Oval project was thus described in the 1830s: 'the advantage of a large, open space, for the free circulation of air; but also a pleasant and agreeable object … to look upon'. This was the assessment of the Duchy of Cornwall's surveyor when a development scheme threatened to disturb the peace of the Oval.

The cricket ground came to occupy the Oval much later, in the spring of 1845. The unpleasant smell of 'decayed vegetables' and the general 'ruinous condition' of this open space was thus remedied: ten thousand turves from Tooting Common were laid and permission was granted to cut down some of the trees. A cricket ground was clearly more profitable to the leaseholders, the descendants/trustees of the Rev William Otter, minister of St Mark's church, than market gardening. By the late nineteenth century Kennington's idyllic, rural setting had suffered setbacks: the intrusion of the Phoenix gas light and coke Company in 1845 replaced the more idyllic waterworks but also the slow replacement of villas by denser terraces.

Vauxhall Park

Our tour of Lambeth gardens has, so far, focused on private gardens. However, after the 1833 Select Committee on Public Walks, and the realisation then that a substantial amount of open space had been lost, with unhappy consequences for the poorer classes, the authorities understood they had to be pro-active: 'the parks were the lungs of London … so necessary to the ventilation of the city' according to Mr Wyndham, a member of this committee. New parks and gardens were created, starting in the East End, which was particularly deprived and poor. The arrival of council parks such as Victoria Park (1845), Crystal Palace Park (1854), Battersea Park (1858), Alexandra Park (1875), and Brockwell Park (1892) were the outcome of this new awareness.

This visualisation of the Vauxhall reservoirs in an early nineteenth-century lithograph by Ingrey and Madeley, confirms the deliberate intention to create a rural idyll. But by then, around 1807, the reservoirs had been built and the inscription reads: 'The Directors [of the South London Waterworks] having established New Works on the South Bank of the Thames, are now able to take the supply of water from that part of the river Thames which is on a line with the third Arch of Vauxhall Bridge, where the water has long been remarked for its undisturbed state and brilliant appearance'.

© London Metropolitan Archives (City of London)

Brockwell Park marked a turning point. It was the first project of the London County Council (LCC) Parks Department, created in 1892 – four years after the establishment of the LCC (which replaced the Metropolitan Board of Works). It is also entirely typical of the fundraising for open spaces at the turn of the twentieth century: a joint effort between local authorities, private estates, with the input of small but determined campaigning organisations such as the Metropolitan Public Gardens Association (founded in 1880), and influential individuals such as the housing reformer Octavia Hill. Also, crucially in the case of Vauxhall Park, the involvement of the Kyrle Society – the brainchild of Miranda Hill, Octavia's sister (see pp. 467 & 470) though it should be made clear that Octavia Hill was closely involved with the Society's Open Spaces Branch, as was Robert Hunter – both later founders of the National Trust.

The best account of this park's history is Robert Whelan's who also researched in great depth the history of the Kyrle Society (see bibliography). The formation of Vauxhall Park pre-dated the formation of the Parks Department at the LCC; so, it may have been one of the first to embrace the purchase model which would later prevail at Brockwell and Ruskin Parks. The land was acquired by the Lambeth Vestry in 1889 with contributions from the LCC, the Charity Commissioners and local distiller and philanthropist Mark Beaufoy. High profile champions for the green cause were also needed and they came in the guise of the Hill sisters, and in the memory of Henry Fawcett (1833–1884), the blind postmaster general and MP who had lived on the site at 51 South Lambeth Road (5 The Lawn, see map on p. 381), when attending parliamentary sessions (1874–84), dying unexpectedly at the age of fifty-one. He was a long-term supporter of women's rights and married Millicent Garrett, the sister of the famous physician suffragist Elizabeth Garrett Anderson (Henry's first choice for marriage but she turned him down).

Left:

This recent photograph of Vauxhall Park was taken after extensive re-designing and re-planting on the part of Lambeth Council. The beds of lavender in the background replaced the giant lavender plants so familiar to the locals and which were ritually harvested every year. It will be a while before the new planting regains the established look of its predecessor. However, the planting of the flower garden has been a success almost from the very start – here a tempting display of 'Silver Queen' (*pittosporum*), wormwood (*artemisia absinthium*), with two varieties of salvia (*officinalis purpurascens and yangii*).
(© The author, 2021)

Above:

This photograph, taken in 2019, shows the established and very tall lavender plants (*Lavandula intermedia Grosso*), which have now been replaced by new beds mixing *Lavandula intermedia Grosso* with *Lavandula Angustifolia*.
(© The author)

This page from the *Illustrated London News* was published on 12 January 1889. The caption indicates that the Vauxhall Park project has only just been formulated: 'Vauxhall Park, South Lambeth – Proposed purchase of ground'. A layout is proposed (bottom left) and overall, the picture focuses on the association with Henry Fawcett – showing his mulberry tree and the view from his house at the front (top left) and back (top middle). The house at the bottom right corner is the second Caron or 'Carroun' House on which estate Vauxhall Park was sited.

Fawcett was a well-respected member of the community and his biographer, Stephen Leslie, gives us a vivid, though not entirely positive description of Vauxhall in 1885:

The last house, with which his friends especially associate his memory, is in a region not very attractive at first sight. It is within hearing of the ceaseless roar of trains at Vauxhall Station, within the smoky and grimy neighbourhood which welcomes the astonished stranger on entering London by the South-Western Railway. But it had the great recommendation that it was within an easy walk, chiefly along the Embankment, of Westminster Bridge and the Houses of Parliament. The inferiority of the district in a social sense, implied cheapness and therefore enabled him to have a strip of garden, about three-quarters of an acre in extent, in which he could at any moment enjoy a stroll. It included a couple of small greenhouses, in which he could raise flowers, and it was his special pride to send presents of asparagus and sea-kale to his parents to show the superiority of the London climate for the growth of vegetables. The house itself was small, but a very pretty old-fashioned residence, suitably adorned by the taste of his wife.

'The Lawn' where stood the Fawcett house was built in the early years of the nineteenth century (see Horwood 1813 map). This description is interesting for the way in which the garden is presented as one of the redeeming features of this address. It is often stated that Vauxhall Park was the wish of Henry Fawcett; this is what *The Illustrated London News* asserted when they published the proposed plan for Vauxhall Park on 12 January 1889 'to promote the health, and happiness and social welfare of the working classes in one of the most crowded and neediest parts of London'. The article added that this wish was 'actively' pursued by his loyal wife Millicent. Henry Fawcett was an ardent campaigner for the Commons Preservation Society, founded by Octavia Hill, Robert Hunter and others (now called the Open Spaces Society). The MP's biographer, Leslie Stephen, recorded that 'he more than once remarked to me that there was no part of his political career upon which he could look back with unalloyed satisfaction. An open space, as he pointed out, once destroyed is destroyed for ever.' However, I could find no evidence of Fawcett's 'wish' in relation to Vauxhall Park, either in Henry's biography or Millicent's autobiography (*What I remember*, 1924). But when the campaign initiated by Octavia Hill was in full swing, Millicent Fawcett, probably at the invitation of Octavia, was present at a meeting held at Willis's Rooms on 21 January 1889. At that meeting a letter from the Archbishop of Canterbury was read out, supporting the campaign

This 1887 watercolour by 'Thompson' records the home of the popular and blind MP Henry Fawcett at 51 South Lambeth Road. After Fawcett's death, the house survived the demolition of its terrace, standing in the middle of Vauxhall Park as a symbol of the silent support of a neighbourhood for this much-loved MP, but the house did not fully integrate into its new context and was demolished in 1891.
(Lambeth Archives)

> to save The Lawn and Carroun House from the builder [because it] would greatly enhance the health of the neighbourhood, and secure to future generations of children a reasonable chance of growing up under favourable conditions of existence.

The popular figure of Fawcett so closely associated with the site was bound to have a positive impact on the campaign – a fact Octavia Hill would have known and one that she may have engineered. Initially all The Lawn houses were demolished except his, but as there were no clear idea about its function within the park, the Kyrle Society tentatively suggested that 'it should be the home of a small museum or art collection', but this was not followed up and the Lambeth vestry had it demolished in 1891.

The site chosen for Vauxhall Park was formerly part of the Caron estate which, by the 1880s, contained the Lawn, so called since the houses, very much set back from the road benefitted from a substantial lawn at the front; and Carroun House, one of the two nineteenth-century houses which were built on the estate after the original Caron House was demolished. The other, Caron Place, was on the site of the local Beaufoy distillery. This site, threatened with development, was secured in August 1888 by an Act of Parliament: 'An Act to authorize the acquisition of the Lawn and Carroun House Lambeth and its utilization for public purposes'. Also see p. 246.

Top:
A very large sculpture of Henry Fawcett was placed on the site of his former residence – fittingly, a central position in Vauxhall Park, at the intersection of the gardens' two main paths (see the 1897 Ordnance Survey map). It was designed by George Tinworth. The memorial was demolished by the Council in the early 1960s.
(Lambeth Archives)

The Kyrle Society contributed to the purchase price of the land – as did Henry Tate and the Duke of Bedford amongst others. But the society's main outlay was the design and planting of the park, in the hands of the society's own landscape designer – Fanny Wilkinson. This is the version of events in volume 26 of *The Survey of London*, apparently based on two articles published in *The Times* (7 and 8 of July 1890). On close inspection, however, different versions emerge. *The Times* of 7 July reads: 'A very charming garden has been laid out from the designs of Miss Wilkinson and Mr Harrison Townsend' while on 5 July the *South London Press* reported that the plan it reproduced 'has been kindly sketched for us by Mr. C. Harrison Townsend, the architect and surveyor to the Kyrle Society, who has prepared the plans for Vauxhall Park'. This plan differed from the one published when Octavia Hill and the Kyrle Society were fundraising for this project. The final plan, as shown on Ordnance Survey maps dated between 1893–6, is that reproduced in the *South London Press*. It seems likely that either Wilkinson was responsible for the early design (on previous page) or that both designers worked together on developing the layout. The Ordnance Survey map of 1893-6 confirms that the layout adopted was that published in the *South London Press*.

As the Vestry was seriously concerned about maintenance costs, local philanthropist Mark Beaufoy stepped in to guarantee such costs for the first three years and also interest accrued for the purchase of the land. Historian Robert Whelan comments that without the generosity of Mark Beaufoy 'the project would probably have failed, but the society took the view that Vauxhall Park should be passed from the vestry to the LCC as soon as possible to release Beaufoy from his "exceptional expenses"'.

The park was formally opened by the Prince of Wales on 7 July 1890. One of Octavia Hill's letters pinpoints precisely what she felt was such a special moment: 'it was to me a very solemn scene, because all classes were so entirely gathered in, each to do what in them lay to accomplish the good work'. This is quoted by Robert Whelan who added:

> In retrospect, the laying out of Vauxhall Park can be seen as the high-water mark of the Society. Although other organisations had been involved, the society had been the main driver throughout and its behind-the-scenes liaison among groups, funders, public bodies and commercial interests was critical to the success of the project.

The model village at Vauxhall Park, made in the 1930s, has survived to this day but in a much-reduced form, with just nine buildings left. It was created by Edgar Wilson, a Norwood resident with a passion for model villages. He also made model villages for Brockwell Park and Finsbury Park. This photograph by Bill Beck dates from around 1950.
(Lambeth Archives)

Opposite below:

The sculptor George Tinworth (1843–1913), a South London man brought up in poverty, made a name for himself after attending the Lambeth School of Art. He was commissioned by Henry Doulton to design the Henry Fawcett monument. Here photographed by F E Edwards in 1897.
(From The British Workman, 1897)

Charles Harrison Townsend also designed the gates and railings which have mostly disappeared and when Fawcett's house was demolished in 1891 Henry Doulton stepped in and donated the enormous statue of Henry Fawcett designed by George Tinworth, one of Lambeth School of Art's star pupils (opposite). It was an ambitious and elaborate piece which has not survived. The park is much loved and used by locals and visitors alike and is often the site of new initiatives. Did you know that the park had an outdoor children's theatre in the 1940s? and that the small group of miniature houses close to the children's playground is but a small relic of the full-scale model village created by Edgar Wilson in the 1930s (above) – one of three he created for South London parks? Henry Doulton also provided a fountain at the same time as the Fawcett statue was erected – long gone, but replaced in our own times by a less elaborate specimen. Polly Freeman has uploaded her useful talk on Vauxhall Park onto the Friends of Vauxhall Park website. She is one of the trustees, knowledgeable about both old and new developments.

Legacy

The Garden Museum

Oxford University had planned, built and opened its Ashmolean Museum by May 1683 – they now like to 'boast that it is the world's first purpose-built public museum' (2015 Museum Guide). The varied components of the original Tradescant's Ark were eventually distributed to several recipients: the Museum of Natural History (zoological specimens, including the sad remains of the dodo, head and left foot); the Bodleian Library (books and manuscripts); the Pitt Rivers Museum (ethnological material); the Ashmolean Museum (paintings and antiquities); and finally, the Garden Museum whose 'Ark' display is only made possible by the long-term loans secured from the Ashmolean Museum.

The ancient church of St Mary-at-Lambeth, the current home of the

The designing and planting of St Mary's Gardens, outside the Garden Museum was the work of Stephen Crisp (see p. 396). The project was initiated by the Friends of the Archbishop's Garden and completed in 2008.
(© The author, 2021)

Garden Museum, suffered in the second half of the twentieth century. Dwindling congregations and dilapidation meant that services were discontinued and the church made redundant in 1972, followed by further dereliction and the threat of demolition. These events, paradoxically, were taking place just a few years after the Borough of Lambeth had designated the area around Lambeth Palace as a 'conservation area', one of their first (1969). Rosemary and John Nicholson were determined to save the church and the extraordinary chest tomb of the Tradescants in the churchyard. They established the Tradescant Trust, received a 99-year lease from the Diocese of Southwark and reopened the church as the Museum of Garden History in 1977. There were no collections for this museum, but from that time onwards gifts of historic artefacts came streaming in. The charming knot garden designed by Lady Salisbury, the Trust's first president, was ready in 1980. After fixing the roof and taking care of other essential repairs, the museum's first exhibition, in 1981, was on Captain Smith.

The arrival of a new director, Christopher Woodward, marked a new phase in the life of this museum. He introduced professional standards into the struggling project by creating galleries where there were none: in 2008 Dow Jones Architects won the contract for this work. This was soon followed by an ambitious full-scale redevelopment plan using the same architects and set in train in 2011. The Museum was successful in securing a substantial grant from the Heritage Lottery Fund and closed for eighteen months between 2015 and 2017. It reopened with considerable improvements: exhibition space, special gallery for the 'Ark' display (opposite top), redesign of the garden/churchyard (Dan Pearson), education galleries, restaurant – not obvious within the shell of a former church. In August 2020, I visited their wonderful Derek Jarman exhibition (right) and also savoured another viewing of the dark and mysterious room dedicated to the Ark – far more atmospheric to my eyes than the 'grand manner' approach to the same theme at the Ashmolean Museum.

The Tradescant 'Gift' at the Ashmolean Museum is regularly reinterpreted and redisplayed. The latest offering conjures up a vision of rational collecting in a classical building – the backdrop is made up of a huge blow-up of the first Ashmolean Museum building (overleaf). This seems very far from the original idea of the dense 'Clossitt of Rarityes'.

The 'Ark' at the Garden Museum: this atmospheric display has been created in the chancel of the former church of St Mary. It has subdued lighting and an air of mystery totally suited to the once famous collection of curiosities of John Tradescant, father and son.
(© The author, 2020)

These two photographs were taken at the 2020 Derek Jarman exhibition at the Garden Museum. The stage designer Jeremy Herbert explained: 'I wasn't so much trying to recreate the cottage as evoke its relationship with the landscape – the sense of looking out and looking in'. Exceptionally evocative, the show won the 2021 Exhibition of the Year Award, the judging panel commenting: 'At any time it would have been remarkable but in this particular venue, during a pandemic, it was all the more so. An incredibly accurate representation of the original, it was atmospheric, poignant and moving.'
(Photos: © The author)

The latest display at the Garden Museum is set within the context of a former medieval church, old stones and side chapels; it is arguably a more conducive environment to recreate the magical Ark. All the objects are on loan from the Ashmolean. The subdued lighting and darkened walls are more evocative of a cabinet of curiosities, but which would speak to you the most?

The two displays, in Oxford and on the South Bank, are also

The 'Ark' at the Ashmolean Museum greatly contrasts with the parallel display at the Garden Museum. The classical building erected by Elias Ashmole (1617-1692) to house the Tradescant collection set a very different visual agenda.
(© The author, 2021)

complementary, each reflecting the culture and personality of very different men – the Tradescants steeped in the world of 'strange curiosities', and Ashmole interested in the curiosities, alchemy and astrology but striding towards the light of baroque architecture and the 'enlightenment' age.

In Lambeth the Ark is housed in the most sacred part of the church, the chancel, made even more special now that recent development work unearthed a secret vault below the chancel with a hoard of up to thirty coffins (below):

> This is a vault for high status burials … including up to five Archbishops of Canterbury, including Archbishop Bancroft, who died in 1610, having overseen for the newly-crowned King James I the translation of the Holy Bible which we call 'The King James Bible'. (Garden Museum website, accessed 28 May 2021)

The Heritage Lottery Fund provided a further grant to carry out a full archaeological investigation. This should yield fascinating new information.

And yet, I am not entirely convinced that this institution succeeds in doing justice to its dual function of church heritage and garden history flagship institution. The 'world's first garden history museum' is restricted by its local envelope and its limited collections. This site has yielded great heritage stories but they have all come to the museum from its neighbourhood: the tomb of Elias Ashmole –

even though it can no longer be found; the amazing Tradescants' tomb; the proximity of Lambeth Palace and the church's symbiotic relationship with this great landmark.

The Garden of Lambeth Palace

I sometimes wish the artist Wenceslaus Hollar (1607–1677) could have found a slightly higher viewpoint for his impressive 'Prospect of London and Westminster taken from Lambeth' published in 1647 (overleaf).. His accurate pencil would have then been able to render more precisely the contents of the kitchen and decorative planted parts of the garden at Lambeth Palace, close to the buildings. His etching may have been mostly drawn from the tower of the church of St Mary-at-Lambeth before he repositioned his viewpoint within the completed picture, as artists would commonly adopt this small cheat. It certainly shows the considerable extent of the garden which in medieval times covered eight hectares.

We could turn to William Faithorne's 1658 map for an interpretation of the planted garden, though, alas, he is not as accurate as Hollar. The history of this ancient garden has received insufficient attention, but then as now, it would thrive in leaps and bounds as and when its owners showed interest, for instance Matthew Parker and his wife in the sixteenth century (see p. 99) or more recently, Rosalind Runcie in the 1980s.

Bonnington Square and Harleyford Road Community Gardens

These two wonderful community gardens – some of the best in London – belong to the Bonnington Square Garden Association and the Harleyford Road Community Gardens; they are linked to two distinct residential estates. The first, the 'Pleasure Garden' was developed on a Second World War bombsite (the imprint of six houses), briefly fitted as a children's playground, which was not alas properly maintained and fell into disrepair. The site panel at Bonnington Square pays tribute to the strong local garden tradition: 'The garden is partly homage to the Vauxhall Pleasure Gardens which existed 100 m to the north of here.'

The Bonnington Square Garden Association was set up in the early 1990s at the peak of the area's transformation from a derelict, abandoned group of Victorian houses awaiting demolition, into a thriving community of squatters – many coming from abroad (in particular New Zealand) and welcoming the challenge of making things work again. The documentary which was shot in 2010 by Acacia Films (directed by Alistair Oldham) charts in detail the experience these early squatters had – some still living in Bonnington Square to this day. Jenny for instance, paints a passionate picture of the London context at that time:

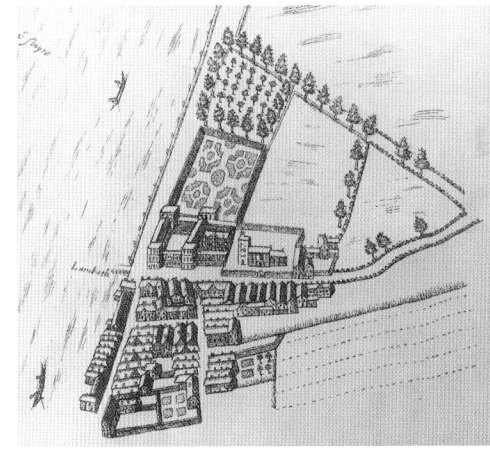

Above:

Lambeth Palace and Gardens. Detail from William Faithorne and Richard Newcourt's map of London, 1658; republished in 1905 by the London Topographical Society.

Opposite:

While the Garden Museum was being extended and refurbished in 2018, the workers came across a most extraordinary and unexpected discovery in the chancel. The 'Ark' photograph on p. 389 shows the glazed, square opening in the floor which leads to a hoard of around thirty lead coffins filled with the remains of archbishops and other high-ranking officials. An Archbishop's mitre had been placed on top of one of the coffins. The cramped underground vault has been filmed, remotely, but not yet fully investigated.

(Garden Museum, London. Photo: Craig Dick)

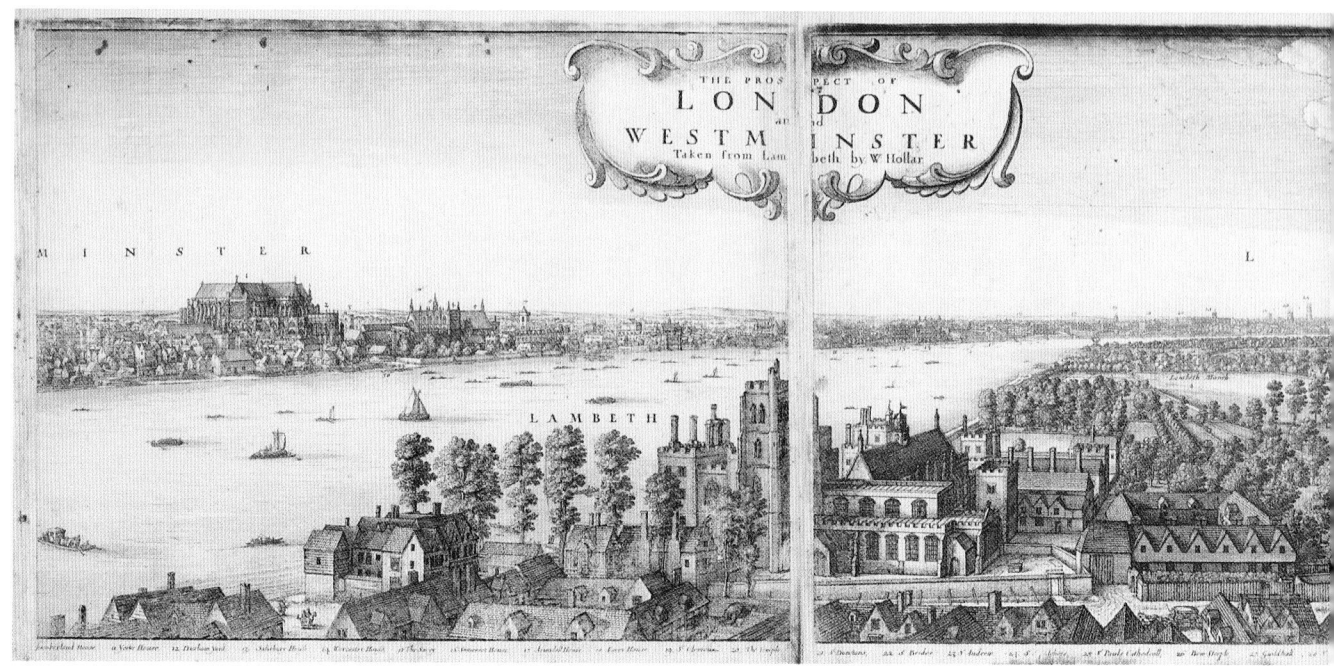

Wenceslaus Hollar's 'The Prospect of London and Westminster taken from Lambeth', 1647, comes from the etching's first state, a unique impression showing St Paul's Cathedral as a medieval building. This print shows Lambeth Palace and its gardens in great detail, also Lambeth Marsh.
(© The Trustees of the British Museum)

Opposite:
These photographs of Bonnington Square Gardens and Harleyford Gardens were taken in 2020. Some of the plants have since disappeared (the climbing rose bush for instance), but this miraculous green-fingered heaven continues to charm residents and visitors alike – a healthy counterpoint to the dizzy towers which are being built around Vauxhall station.
(© The author, 2020)

Squatting was not just a matter of finding somewhere to live. It was also a political act, because London was just full of empty houses at that time and there were so many people looking for places to live and you just saw everywhere rotting houses just falling to pieces and it just seemed criminal, really criminal to have all these houses wasted in the middle of London.

The hardworking squatters fixed the houses and started organising themselves. As soon as the essential work had been carried out, they turned their attention to community assets – a centre for culture, gardens, trees. The trees came first. There were all sorts of grants available for improving the streetscape and the new residents were ready to liaise and collaborate with the authorities – the ILEA (Inner London Education Authority), the Council and other essential bodies. The garden was started in August 1994, 'transforming the land into a little slice of paradise' the site panel tells the visitor. The famous garden designer Dan Pearson lived there between 1993 and 1997. His website documents the small but enchanting roof garden he developed at Bonnington Gardens – quite apart from his involvement with the local community garden (overleaf). Paul Wood, the author of *London's Street Trees*, describes Bonnington Square gardens as 'an oasis of New Zealand in Vauxhall'. Some of the original squatters were antipodean and left a trail of unusual trees such as the New Zealand Lacebank, the Cabbage Tree and the Lancewood. The Café, which so suddenly closed down in 2020, has a Judas Tree close to its entrance.

VAUXHALL AND LAMBETH – PARADISE REGAINED

It is both fitting and paradoxical that Bonnington Square should have been taken over by trees, plants and gardens. Before it was built in the late 1870s/1880s the site had been used as a nursery, a worthy ancestor. But when they built the houses there was not a sliver of green to be seen. Worse still, the 'square' of Bonnington Square was completely built over with no front or back gardens for any of the houses. The buildings, too, were misleading; their elegant facades hid their true status – not houses at all, but tenement flats. Visually, the houses are very similar to those built in Pearman Street, Waterloo. Architect Richard Woollard has researched the history of Pearman Street, named after John Pearman, its developer. The houses are later than Bonnington Square since they date from around 1884 when John Pearman registered the name of the street with the authorities. Woollard has established that the 1881 census which misspelt 'Boddington' Square documents the development as it was being built.

By contrast with Bonnington Square, the Harleyford Road Community Garden is actually set on former gardens – the roomy back gardens of Regency houses built overlooking Harleyford Road after it was formed under the Act of 1818. The houses were built by 1828 when they are shown on the C & J Greenwood map of that date. They were demolished in the 1970s, releasing the gardens to the use of the community. This community garden is considerably larger than the Bonnington Square garden and connected to it by a 'secret passage' in the north east corner of the square. It has a children's play area, a pond and a picnic area. As with Bonnington garden, it has been designed and maintained by local residents – only the

mature sycamores date from the site's former incarnation The garden association was created in 1984, a little earlier than that of Bonnington Square. The site panel points out that 'it is the only accessible wild life site in the neighbourhood giving refuge to many species.' The nearest such creation is in the Bishop's Park which adjoins Lambeth Palace.

Dan Pearson and the South Bank

Dan Pearson's sensitive approach to garden design, is described on his practice's website – Dan Pearson Studio:

> Every decision we make is grounded in an acute sense of place and a deep understanding of how natural environments affect human emotions.
>
> **(retrieved 25 May 2021)**

1964	Born in Windsor
1989	Starts practising as a garden designer
1993–97	Dan Pearson lived at Bonnington Square where he created a small roof garden (left) and also helped to create Bonnington Square Garden
2005	Roof terrace for the new Evelina Children's Hospital next to St Thomas' Hospital
2009	Dan Pearson studio is set up at the Nursery, 50 Westminster Bridge Road
2013	Dan was the planting designer for Thomas Heatherwick's Garden Bridge (unrealised)
2013	'Green Fuse: The Work of Dan Pearson', an exhibition at The Garden Museum
2015–17	Redesign of the Garden Museum churchyard and entrance garden
2015	Wins the competition with Wright and Wright for the landscaping of Lambeth Palace's new library tower – 'to form a rich wildlife setting'
2018	Urban greening strategy for Lambeth Garden, with Publica. Design for a Lambeth village green, sited outside the Garden Museum; also establishing a continuing green axis along Lambeth High Street to join up with Old Paradise Gardens. Based on an idea from the Garden Museum
2021	Mary Duggan Architects selected for the pavilion of Lambeth village green (above)

Opposite:

Dan Pearson's garden at Bonnington Square was a mere twelve square metres on a top floor-flat. He used plant species 'suited to this exposed and windy environment … The planting was all chosen to be drought and wind tolerant and included a lavender hedge, numerous Mediterranean herbs and grasses as well as a number of coastal species including broom, tamarisk, kniphofia and coyote willow.' He enjoyed this garden between the years 1993 and 1997.

© Andrew Lawson

The spiky cube of the new American embassy at Vauxhall may invite awe, but not rest while the gardens and 'moat' which surround it do. They have been designed by Stephen Crisp, the Head of Landscape at the American Ambassador's residence in Regent's Park and its new Embassy.
(© The author, 2019)

The Garden of the U S Embassy

There is little doubt that the discovery of the New World turned the old one inside out, eventually freeing the Western imagination from the straitjacket of scholastic thought laid down by ancient Greek and Roman authorities.

Jennifer Potter, *Strange Blooms*, 2007

So, it is fitting that the U S Embassy should have relocated so close to the Tradescants' Lambeth garden, which was filled with plants from Virginia alongside those from other parts of the world. We should simply dismiss

President Trump's capricious (and political) sulk published in *The Evening Standard* of 12 January 2018 as 'Donald won't go South of the River'!

The Embassy relocated from Grosvenor Square in the West End to Vauxhall, south London in 2017. Since the violent anti-Vietnam demonstrations outside the Embassy in 1968, there had been a number of serious security issues at the Grosvenor site and relations between the U S and London government must have been tense. But perhaps the introduction of the congestion charge in February 2003, the unpopular traffic-calming measure which the U S diplomats (and others too) had hoped to bypass, was the last straw. On 17 August 2009, *The Independent* newspaper reported that the Embassy owed 3.5M which the newly appointed ambassador still refused to pay. By February 2020, according to the BBC, the figure was standing at 12.5M, covering the period 2003-2018, the highest of all the London embassies – the overall bill from unpaid charges by the diplomatic contingent was over 116M at the beginning of 2020.

The move to south London took almost ten years – choosing a site in 2008, buying the land, having the architect approved by the White House – Kieran Timberlake in 2010 since it has by law to be an American firm with substantial experience in security; finally, construction started in 2013 and was completed four years later.

The embassy staff moved to their new premises in 2017. They had been used to a large green open space in the West End, overlooking the Duke of Westminster's Georgian square, the centre piece to the Duke's Mayfair estate – it was the green, green grass of England with large, mature trees. In Vauxhall it was replaced by a pampas-style garden with a 'moat', the word picked by *The Times* suggests a deep tie to English traditions! The site panel describes it as 'the pond' … as in 'across the pond'? The official description on the site panel addresses instead current ecological concerns:

> the embassy's holistic water system which aims to retain all the rain water that falls on the site … This rainwater is either absorbed by the earth or filtered through drainage bioswales and planting trays before being stored in the pond.

More prosaically the water feature could also be described as fully 'modern urban' in its design and function (for instance what has been created at Canary Wharf near the tube station) – blending the refreshing sound of falling water with the soothing sight of reflections. The planting is thus described on the site panel:

> The embassy's plant palette has its foundations in the shared history of ecological exploration, discovery and exchange between the United States and the United Kingdom. Planted with tall grasses and wild flowers, the embassy landscape is reminiscent of both the expansive American rolling prairies and the site's early history as a river Thames wetland. These plants not only create a diverse, colorful meadow, but also enrich the soil and require little maintenance as they regenerate each spring.

John Harvard and his descendants created a shrine to American achievements in education at Southwark Cathedral, the other end of the South Bank. It is good to know that Vauxhall holds another, more up to date, manifestation of the 'special relationship'.

Opposite:

With the alarming development of Vauxhall into dizzying towers, residents and visitors will benefit from the gentle and calming effect of this neighbourhood's green oases – Vauxhall from Westminster Bridge (top); In Vauxhall Park (bottom).

(© The author, 2021 and 2019)

If I were a planner … or a politician …

I would endeavour to capitalise on Lambeth's long-standing gardening tradition. Apart from the major or simply delightful gardens which have been highlighted in this chapter, we should add a couple more gems to the emerald crown, as for instance the surprising return of Vauxhall Gardens in 1976. It had disappeared after 1859 when the gardens were dismantled and the ground was covered with low quality housing. By the end of the Second World War the houses were very dilapidated, so they were demolished and the neighbourhood restored to parkland. But the largest garden of them all was that of Lambeth Palace which after 1660 expanded with the acquisition of the estate of the Bishop of Carlisle next door. It is the oldest surviving garden on the South Bank and there are very early references to its care (see p. 99). In 1869, Archbishop Tait, who was particularly concerned about poverty, opened up the Carlisle side of the garden to the poor and it became known as the Lambeth Palace Field. Later the Metropolitan Gardens Association campaigned for its retention as a public park – Archbishop's Park was redesigned and formally opened to the public in 1901.

The idea of the Garden Bridge project, abused by so many, was beautiful to me. I have long known – since 1990 when I curated the exhibition 'London's Pride, the Capital's Gardens' at the Museum of London - that gardens were one of this country's most perfect forms of artistic expression and that projects dedicated to their flourishing could be truly blessed. It is true that the section of London between Westminster and Tower Bridges is already very congested. But Lambeth, with its green agenda and formidable legacy? and the host of 'the world's first garden history museum'?

Sources (full references for abbreviated entries in bibliography)

Horwood 1799; Horwood 1813; *Survey of London 26*; Gibberd; Potter; Leith-Ross; Galinou 2010; James Prest, *The Garden of Eden*, 1981; Bennett & Mandelbrote; Coke & Borg; Michael Snodin (ed), *Rococo – Art and Design in Hogarth's England*, 1984; www.vauxhallgardens.com/vauxhall_gardens_briefhistory_page.html#VauxhallToday (accessed on 4 June 2021; particularly useful for Vauxhall's more recent history); *Journals of Gilbert White*, edited by Walter Johnson, 1982; Galinou 1990; Newman; Andrew Solomon, *William Blake's Great Task – The Purpose of Jerusalem*, 2000; Peter Ackroyd, *Blake*, 1995; Stephen Leslie, *Life of Henry Fawcett*, 1885; Millicent Fawcett, *What I Remember*, 1924; Whelan; www.vauxhallpark.org.uk/2020/11/16/vauxhalls-park-for-the-people-a-historical-tour/ (accessed on 2 June 2021); 'Holy orders: Garden Museum extension, London, UK by Dow Jones Architects', by Rob Bevan, *Architectural Review*, 21 February 2021.

WATERLOO
Fall and redemption

In The Footsteps of William Blake — 403

The Fall — 404
    Fallen woman: Found drowned — 405
    Fallen man: Lambeth Tragedy — 406
    Fallen neighbourhood: Lust, Greed and Sloth — 409

The Beating Heart of Waterloo Station — 412

Railways – The Culprit? Adventure, gluttony and envy — 414

Regeneration Story – 'a penny' for the arts Temperance, Chastity and Fortitude — 418
    Music Hall — 418
    Resurgence of theatres on the South Bank — 421
    The Old Vic — 424
    Spreading the love: Education, Education, Education — 429
    Morley College — 429

Resurrection — 430
    The Festival of Britain — 431
    The Shell development — 435
    Southbank Place — 436
    The Jewel in the Crown: culture along the South Bank — 437

Previous page and below:
The detail from Charles Deane's oil painting of 'Waterloo Bridge and the Lambeth Waterfront from Westminster Stairs', was taken from a viewpoint very close to that of Canaletto's Richmond House (see pp. 54 and 168). Sixty-five years separate the two works. Canaletto's viewpoint is higher than that adopted by Charles Deane. But the most noticeable differences are the disappearance of greenery, reasonably abundant in 1746, totally gone by 1821, and the considerable change of scale – the mostly 'bungalows' in Canaletto with occasional taller structures are replaced by taller buildings in the Deane painting, alongside towers such as those of shot towers or churches, this time fully integrated to the cityscape rather than forming a detached fringe on the horizon.

(© Museum of London)

This picturesque image of rural life above may well have been how all suburbs started in the vicinity of London, but at Waterloo the contrast between rustic idyll and dense urban development happened almost without warning and within just one generation.

John Roupell (1761–1835) made his money in lead-smelting at his workshop turned factory in Bear Lane in Southwark. He lived in great simplicity close to work but he was an inveterate investor in property – near his workshop, near the future Waterloo Bridge, and in Brixton and Streatham too. He acquired the land where the future Roupell Street

would be built in 1796 – the 'street' then being a path through marshy land. By 1810, he was giving his address as Cuper's Bridge near the future St John's church Waterloo. Development of Roupell Street started in 1824. Judy Harris, who has researched the Roupells in great detail writes: 'small, closely packed terrace houses, dwellings for workers, rapidly appeared … by 1829 the Roupell buildings were listed as twenty-seven houses and thirty-five buildings'. By 1835 when John died, there were seventy-three houses and by 1839 eighty-two. In 1834 Roupell's 'workshop' in Bear Lane was described as Lead-works and an Iron Foundry.

There are around thirty-five years between Capon's watercolour above and the development of the Roupell estate. The utter transformation of the area from an airy and charming garden suburb to stretches of dark urban terraced houses for the working classes could not embody a greater contrast.

In the footsteps of William Blake

It is surprisingly easy to interpret modern history, including our own godless times, through the filter of Christianity. The fall, redemption, virtues and vices, paradise and hell – these great narratives work as successfully today as they did when they were first recorded. They certainly guided the

Opposite top:

William Capon's watercolour, 'A View from a Gentleman's seat in Lambeth Marsh', is evocative of a garden suburb. It is dated 1804, the year the Eyre brothers began to create this country's first garden suburb in St John's Wood. But in Lambeth there was a major difference – public pleasure gardens had multiplied and thrived in the eighteenth century. An inscription on the back of this drawing identifies the main topographical landmarks though not the old-style brick house in the middle of the painting. According to Graham Gibberd it was the home of John Cooke, Esq., a local landowner.

© London Metropolitan Archives (City of London)

Above:

Jonathan Pike, 'Rooftops', 1983 is one of several paintings this artist devoted to the subject of the Roupell estate in Waterloo. In the 1980s, he was based in Deptford and often travelled on the train to Waterloo East, drawing inspiration from the picturesque rooftops. He let his imagination wander and even included a figure straight out of Gustave Courbet's famous 1854-55 painting 'L'atelier du peintre' (The Artist's Studio).

© Guildhall Art Gallery, City of London Corporation; Image © Jonathan Pike

author William Blake (1757–1827) in his poetic explorations of the world and of Lambeth in particular.

As a Lambeth resident for almost ten years (1791–1800), Blake holds an important place in the previous chapter and two of his great epic poems, 'Jerusalem' and 'Milton', give Lambeth a prominent place. The latter is generally recognised as being closely based on the poet's daily life experiences:

> The Surrey hills glow like the clinkers of the furnace: Lambeth's Vale
> Where Jerusalem's foundations began; where they were laid in ruins,
> Where they were laid in ruins from every Nation & Oak Groves rooted,
> Dark gleams before the Furnace-mouth a heap of burning ashes.
> When shall Jerusalem return & overspread all the Nations?
> Return, return to Lambeth's Vale, O building of human souls!
> … And you shall Reap the whole Earth from Pole to Pole: from Sea to Sea: Beginning at
> Jerusalem's Inner Court, Lambeth ruin'd and given
> To the detestable Gods of Priam, to Apollo: and at the Asylum
> Given to Hercules, who labour in Tirzah's Looms for bread…
> Lambeth mourns calling Jerusalem: she weeps & looks abroad
> For the Lord's coming, that Jerusalem may overspread all Nations.

Although he would not have known this at the time, Blake lived in Waterloo. Apart from identifying Lambeth with the ruined Jerusalem, the poet uses local landmarks in drawing up his picture of a fallen city: very close to his house stood *Apollo* Gardens – one of a number of small pleasure gardens which had sprouted in this part of Lambeth in response to the success of Vauxhall Gardens. It opened in 1788 but was shut by magistrates five years later. The *Asylum* was clearly a reference to the Asylum for Orphan Girls, also a stone's throw from Blake's house (see p. 159). And Hercules is a reference to Blake's own address at Hercules Buildings.

So, was William Blake the only one to experience the biblical Fall?

The Fall

Prostitution seems always to have existed but in London its rise in the popular imagination is arguably a Victorian phenomenon, perhaps because our nineteenth-century forefathers tried so hard to eliminate it. Waterloo, as we shall see, was unquestionably a haven for prostitution in Victorian times but I was fascinated to read that as far back as 1710, the distinguished German visitor Zacharias Conrad van Uffenbach (1683–1734) described a visit to Cuper's Gardens, formerly on the site of modern day Imax Cinema in front of Waterloo Station: 'Afterwards we rowed to "Cupid's Gardens" since countless whores are to be found here, and there are disgraceful goings on … Near it is a tavern where men drink and find occasion for the devil's own work'.

Sometimes the past seems to cast an impossibly long shadow on this nineteenth-century neighbourhood. When abusers and abused revel in a vicious circle, what can be done? Help the victims? Punish the perpetrators? Let's explore Victorian sin; there was plenty of it in Waterloo and here are two tales which show both sides of the same problematic coin.

Above:
George Frederick Watts, 'Found Drowned', 1849–50, oil on canvas. This very large painting, over two metres long, depicts the death of a desperate young woman who has thrown herself into the Thames at Waterloo Bridge.
(Watts Gallery. Image in the public domain, Wikimedia Commons)

Fallen woman: 'Found drowned'

The author and poet Thomas Hood (1799–1845) was mostly noted for his contribution to comic literature during his lifetime, but he is now best remembered for two poems dwelling on the harsh conditions faced by poor women in Victorian London. The first one, 'The Song of the Shirt' (1843) described the backbreaking, mind-numbing work of a seamstress killing herself at a task which barely brought her a living. A year later, in 1844, Hood published 'The Bridge of Sighs' which is set under one of the arches of Waterloo Bridge, the 'suicide bridge' as it came to be known.

Thomas Hood, was in poor health for most of his life but, despite his debts, lived in the comfort of a St John's Wood's home when he wrote the Bridge poem. His starting point had not been Waterloo Bridge at all but the notorious suicide attempt of seamstress Mary Furley, a forty-year-old single mother who set out to drown her children and herself rather than return to the Bethnal Green workhouse. Her plan failed but she was given the death penalty for drowning one of her children; however, she had the sympathy of the public and obtained a reduced sentence – transportation for seven years. In the end, Hood transferred this real-life story to the more central location of Waterloo Bridge, and with a younger victim of unrequited love, abandonment?

> Near a whole city full
> Home she had none

The poet laments, adding:

> Anywhere, anywhere
> Out of the world!

Was she, like Susan in John Stafford's play *Love's Frailties, or Passion and Repentance* (1835) lured to London by her seducer? Michael Booth in 'The Metropolis on Stage' explains: 'Maddened by guilt and horror, she throws herself into the Serpentine, but is rescued by her brother, who has come to London to look for her'. Moncrieff's *The Scamps of London* (1843) has a scene at Waterloo Bridge by moonlight, 'with the homeless settling down for the night under the dry arches; in a few moments the heroine throws herself off the bridge and is saved by a boat putting off below'. But the heroine is not saved in 'Found Drowned'.

Artists responded enthusiastically to Hood's heart-wrenching verses; drama, graphic and painted interpretations of the poem increased their public appeal. 'Found drowned' is the title George Frederic Watts gave to his painting dating from the late 1840s. It is also the legal term used in a coroner's inquest, its neutral tone clashing with the tragic, emotionally charged outcome of a life of unbearable distress. Like Hood, Watts did not normally depict the world of social realism but both men found themselves utterly moved by the plight of poor and desperate female Londoners. Watts painted another three paintings of 'hard times' alongside 'Found Drowned'. He never sold these paintings.

In 2015 the Foundling Museum put on an exhibition called 'The Fallen Woman'. 'Found Drowned' was chosen as this exhibition's lead image 'because it perfectly encapsulates the way art mythologized the idea of the "fallen woman", and the social and moral debates contained within the fallen woman narrative, including desire, illegitimacy, religion and the dangers of the city', explained the Director Caro Howell.

But in this chapter's next section we are confronted with 'Fallen Man', one who had enjoyed a reasonably privileged life – wealthy and well educated.

Fallen Man: Lambeth tragedy

> 'a Heinous Crime, a Terrible Event, an Atrocious Occurrence, a Vile Murder'

Incarcerated at Broadmoor for murdering a Lambeth man, ex U.S. Military man becomes a key contributor to the Oxford English Dictionary

This is more or less the newspaper headline which broke this true story to America in 1915. More recently the story has been told with great eloquence by Simon Winchester in *The Surgeon of Crowthorne* (1998).

The victim was George Merrett, a 34-year-old stoker at the Red Lion Brewery, at the Surrey end of Westminster Bridge. He resided with his family (six children between the ages of one and twelve plus wife Eliza, pregnant with a seventh child) at 24 Cornwall Cottages, Cornwall Road. He was walking to work on the morning of 17 February 1872 when, for no apparent reason, a man coming out of Tenison Street, a complete stranger, started shouting at him. Merrett who had almost reached the brewery, decided to run when the stranger fired three or four shots, the last one hitting Merrett on the neck made him collapse. In his book the author Simon Winchester observes: 'even in a place as louche and notoriously crime-ridden as the Lambeth Marsh, the sound of gun-shots was a rare event indeed'. Almost immediately three police constables coming from different directions were on the scene: the victim was taken to St Thomas' Hospital, which had moved from Southwark and re-opened in Lambeth the previous year. The assailant was arrested and taken to Horsemonger Lane Gaol in Southwark.

Nothing could be done about poor George Merrett. Police interrogation revealed that this seemingly straight forward case would prove complicated: the murderer, Dr William Chester Minor, 37, was a qualified surgeon, a former army officer, and a US citizen from New Haven, Connecticut. This meant that the US minister in London would have to be notified. Minor, who lived alone in an upstairs room at 41 Tenison Street, was described as having 'a prodigious sexual appetite'; he had had a long history of sexual promiscuity and was suffering from gonorrhoea at the time of his arrest. He was a well-educated man but probably chose to settle near Waterloo Station because it had a reputation for rampant prostitution. Minor had only been living in Lambeth for a couple of months when the murder occurred. He had been retired from the US army on grounds of ill health and had spent time in an American asylum.

But the full extent of Minor's troubled life was only revealed during his murder trial in April 1872. The police admitted that Minor was known to them: he had made various allegations against men coming to his room at night, trying to poison him. Williamson, the Scotland Yard detective who looked into Minor's allegations, reached the conclusion the man was insane and no action was taken. Other people testified about his strange habits and behaviour. On 6 April 1872, 'Minor was found legally innocent of a murder that everyone including him knew he had committed', the Judge summing up: 'You will be detained in safe custody, Dr Minor, until Her Majesty's Pleasure be known'.

There had been a time when 'safe custody' could have been secured at Bethlem Hospital just down the road from where the crime had been committed; it housed the State Criminal Asylum in two blocks at the back of the main hospital from 1815. But in 1864 this asylum was moved to Broadmoor in the town of Crowthorne, Berkshire. So Minor was sent there.

During his time in Broadmoor two significant meetings would bring meaning to his confinement. The first, the meeting with his victim's wife, came about when Minor, increasingly filled with remorse, wrote to her, care

Above:
The general appearance of the Lion Brewery and its immediate neighbourhood would have changed little between 1872 – when Dr Minor committed his crime – and 1939 when this photograph was taken by the LCC. The view is taken from Hungerford Bridge looking east.
© London Metropolitan Archives (City of London)

of the American Embassy. He apologised and offered money to alleviate the family hardship he had caused. She accepted and even suggested a visit. A supervised visit was granted in 1879 and a relationship of sorts developed. Minor, who was collecting books and slowly building up a library, must have asked Eliza whether she would be willing to collect and bring the books he had ordered from various antiquarian dealers in London. The arrangement lasted only a few months because Eliza apparently took to drink and lost interest in this likeable murderer.

Above:
Portrait of Dr W C Minor at Broadmoor Asylum for the criminally insane, c. 1900, anonymous photographer.
(Image in the public domain – Wikimedia Commons)

The next serendipitous event occurred around 1880 when Minor stumbled across an appeal for volunteers, perhaps in one of the book packages brought to Broadmoor by Eliza. What sort of enterprise would be recruiting an army of volunteers, very unusual at that time? It was the writing of a state-of-the-art English Dictionary. The project had been proposed by the Dean of Westminster Richard Chevenix Trench, as he was delivering a lecture on the subject of dictionaries at the London Library on 5 November 1857. It needed 'the combined action of many' (not unlike our modern Wikipedia) and it was Trench who proposed to recruit hundreds and hundreds of unpaid volunteers. The energetic James Murray (1837–1915) rescued the almost moribund project when he became its editor in 1879. Two years later a circular was printed and distributed via bookshops and libraries. Minor saw it and soon became one of the Dictionaries' most loyal and reliable contributors. James Murray, as chief editor, failed to register the full implications of a Broadmoor address and retrospectively stated: 'I never gave a thought to who Minor might be. I thought he was either a practising medical man of literary tastes with a good deal of leisure, or perhaps a retired medical man or surgeon who had no other work'. Murray was totally unaware of Minor's 'predicament' until the late 1880s, almost ten years after Minor first wrote to him to offer his assistance.

The two men finally met in January 1891 and became friends. As time passed and his circumstances changed, the mental and physical health of the prisoner of Cell Block 2 deteriorated and, in his desperate but resolute attempt to rid himself of his demons he castrated himself. He was eventually discharged on 16 April 1910, after spending thirty-eight years at Broadmoor. Fully escorted, he returned to his country and finished his days in two American asylums, dying on 26 March 1920. *The New English Dictionary* was finally completed in 1928. It became known as *The Oxford*

English Dictionary when a supplement was published in 1933.

On his way back to America Dr Minor paid a last visit to Waterloo: 'Spanholtz [the escort] and Minor were at the mighty vaulting cathedral of Waterloo Station – a much larger station now than it had been when, no more than a few hundred yards away, the murder that began this story had been committed on that Saturday night in 1872'.

Fallen neighbourhood: Lust, Greed and Sloth

The tragic suicide of a young woman found drowned represents the harshest possible message to all fallen women of the Victorian era, but there is a sense of transcendence in Thomas Hood's poem which invited his readers to respond in a compassionate way to the plight of women ostracised by all. Equally, although Dr Minor cuts a tragic figure, there are redemptory aspects in his life.

By some fascinating coincidence, another book – unconnected to the above – has charted in some detail the very neighbourhood where the 'heinous crime' was committed, at the time it was committed – the 1870s – , offering reasons why Dr Minor, a military man, was attracted to these streets of shame, prostitution, drink and sexual depravity.

The author, the English publisher Michael Sadleir (1888–1957), had a passion for collecting books and he explained: 'Among the headings into which my book collection falls is "London Underworld"; and I have for years sought out and gathered books, pamphlets, and periodicals which describe those departments of London life during the nineteenth century which the polite literature of the day preferred to ignore'. This collection is now at the University of California, but Sadleir's novels bear witness to the questionable activities going on behind the grim facades of London's slums (Waterloo) or even those of London's more respectable quarters (St John's Wood). In his 1947 novel *Forlorn Sunset* both are documented through the character of Lottie Heape – the little girl who was saved from the slums of Waterloo and ended up in St John's Wood, one of this neighbourhood's infamous mistresses. Commenting on the book and his better-known earlier work, *Fanny by Gaslight* (1940), Sadleir wrote: 'Again the seventies [1870s] … an attempt to reconstruct the kind of life which was being led behind the dun-coloured facades of mouldering terraces, and in melancholy little squares through which no traffic ran'.

The area of Waterloo which Dr Minor would undoubtedly have frequented in the early 1870s, was immediately south of Waterloo Station:

'Upon my soul, Gladwin, you must be off the hooks altogether to want to go trapesing about Whoreterloo' (such in current slang was the district's name) 'in the middle of the afternoon!' …

You went under an archway into Granby Street, which led at right angles off Waterloo Road …

When Paul and Matt stopped on the pavement of Waterloo Road and looked through the archway, Granby Street was empty. In the sunshine it looked dingy and sour … Outside in the main road the noise of wheels and hoofs and the raucous cries of street-arabs and hawkers had been incessant. Here in Granby Street was silence. It was an uneasy silence – the silence which in any large city is characteristic of a bad area.

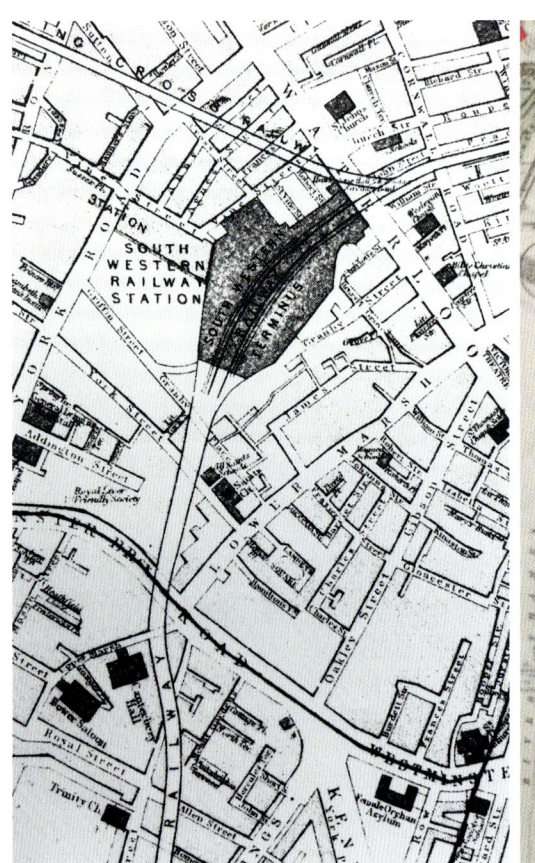 

Above:

The map on the left was used by Michael Sadleir's in his novel *Forlorn Sunset* (1946). It shows Waterloo around 1868 and the site of its notorious slum, south of the station: 'by the end of 1847 the Granby Street area was built to the last yard, and began a career of brazen and crapulous infamy without parallel in the history of nineteenth century London. It was a career of no more than thirty years.'

(Lambeth Archives)

The detail on the right comes from Charles Booth's colour-coded poverty map, 1898-99. Even though Granby Street had been demolished for about twenty years there is still a strip south of the station coloured dark blue ('Very poor, casual. Chronic want') and black ('Lowest class. Vicious, semi-criminal').

(London School of Economics/Image in the public domain)

No children played or screamed; no slatternly women shouted at one another through lines of drying clothes; no cheerful errand-boy whistled along the street …

They had gone about twenty yards when a man turned the corner of Henry Place and came towards them. He was a small pale man, with a broken nose and the eyes of a rat, and as he approached he gave them a keen look from under the peak of his cap. As they came abreast, he stopped … and muttered in the ingratiating undertone of the professional tout: "Beg pardon, gents, but there's nice fresh greens far end of Grove Place. Last door but one on left. Ask for Daisy. Not many of 'em work in this time o' day, but Daisy's the ticket. Tell 'er Slippy sent ye, and I wager ye won't regret it."

… Henry Place was an exact replica of Granby Street but had a shade more animation. Two doors beyond the public-house, a fat girl sitting at an open window caught at Paul's arm as he passed. She was dirty, uncombed, and rather drunk, and appeared to be wearing nothing but a chemise.

"Cub od, dearie", she said. "Cub ud 'ave a bulls-vorth of tick-tack."
"Sorry, honeypot" Paul replied with some presence of mind.

"Promised to Daisy. Another day if you are free."

The two protagonists ended up running 'like hell' out of the grim streets into lively Lower Marsh, clutching the hand of a small girl, Lottie Heape, who had come out screaming from one of the houses in Grove Place, begging the men to save her from the violent woman who was chasing her.

The archetype of the little girl growing up in a tough neighbourhood and becoming a beautiful woman is a powerful vehicle in the world of novels. Somerset Maugham, too, focused on this very theme for his first novel *Liza of Lambeth* (1897). In a later preface to the book, he explained that he wrote it while studying medicine at St Thomas' Hospital:

> I think I must have been in my fourth year. I had spent the usual time in the out-patients departments … then I did the obstetric work. In order to obtain the necessary certificate the student had to attend twenty confinements … you were appointed obstetric clerk for a period of three weeks during which you had to be on hand day and night … The messenger led you through the dark and silent streets of Lambeth, up stinking alleys and into sinister courts where the police hesitated to penetrate, but where your black bag protected you from harm … I attended sixty-three confinements in three weeks. This was the material I used for this book.

Maugham insisted: 'I exercised little invention. I put down what I had seen and heard as plainly as possible … I was forced to stick to the facts by the miserable poverty of my imagination'.

Much of the action in *Liza of Lambeth* takes place in Vere Street, Maugham's invented name for a small street off Westminster Bridge Road. The novel describes thriving lives lived on the street and this is confirmed in the *Notebooks* for Charles Booth's famous poverty maps: 'Men, women and children seem to live in the street more than they do North of the Thames' (District 31 – Lambeth and St Saviour's Southwark, p. 25). One of the novel's scenes takes place at Waterloo Station:

> One evening they [Liza and her doomed lover Jim] had been sitting at Waterloo station; it was foggy outside – a thick yellow November fog, which filled the waiting-room, entering the lungs, and making the mouth taste nasty and the eyes smart. It was about half past eleven, and the station was unusually quiet; a few passengers, in wraps and overcoats, were walking to and fro, waiting for the last train, and one or two porters were standing about yawning.

The almost empty and melancholic station stood for the rolling dark clouds over their heads: 'Liza and Jim had remained for an hour in perfect silence, filled with gloomy unhappiness, as of a great weight on their brains.'

Liza of Lambeth was well received and led to Somerset Maugham's abandonment of his medical studies in favour of becoming a writer.

Above:
This was published in *The Illustrated London News* in 1848, shortly after the station at Waterloo was completed – a relatively humble structure since at that stage no one envisaged it would become a terminus. It was simply a stop on the line which had been projected between Nine Elms and the City of London.
(*The Illustrated London News* of 1 July 1848)

Above:
The offices of the Necropolis Company were first established in York Road after obtaining parliamentary consent to remove South London's dead to Brookwood cemetery in 1852. In 1902 they moved to new premises at 115–123 Westminster Bridge Road which have survived to this day.
(© The author)

The Beating Heart of Waterloo Station

The location which the author Somerset Maugham chose for the ending of the affair between Liza and Jim was the almost empty maze of Waterloo Station. By 1899, two years after his novel had been published, it had sixteen platforms but only ten numbers, so some of them repeated; the station spread over different levels and was the home of several railway companies, each pursuing their own schedules, with no overall plan.

Waterloo station is the vast terminus station which was not planned as a terminus, but simply as one of the stops on the extension by the London and South Western Railway linking Nine Elms to the City. Even though most of the Nine Elms/Waterloo section was built on a viaduct to minimise disruption on the ground, the company still had to demolish 700 houses. The station opened on 11 July 1848. There were four tracks in the hope that other companies might follow suit and also use the line; as indeed was the case with the London Necropolis and National Mausoleum Company in 1854, when they started rolling their dead cargo to Brookwood Cemetery (below).

William Tite (1798–1873), whose main claim to fame is his design of the third and current Royal Exchange, was the architect of the London and South Western Railway and responsible for the first Waterloo station (he also designed Nine Elms station). The station was successful and as traffic increased, it was enlarged several times, always as a 'temporary' measure, since all expected the line to be taken to London Bridge and the City. This made the navigation of the station increasingly difficult, platform one becoming inexplicably stranded in the middle of the station. This confusing, dysfunctional maze was growing like a cancer, almost out of control.

By the last decade of the nineteenth century, it was clear that Waterloo would remain a Terminus Station. In 1893 an Act was passed to provide a Tube Railway link to the City; the Waterloo and City Line ('the Drain') which opened five years later, the final solution to a scheme which had first been envisaged in the 1840s. It was time to plan 'The Great Transformation'. This took over twenty years with staged-openings to reorganise and rebuild Waterloo Station (including the years of the first World War); two architects and a railway engineer were involved. First J W Jacomb-Hood, then the engineer Alfred Weeks Sczlumper and finally James Robb Scott who designed the Victory Arch at the station's main entrance as well as the range of offices. Land had been cleared by 1903, the principal booking hall had opened by 1911 and the main station had its grand

Previous page top:
Arturo Di Stefano, 'Waterloo Station' (detail), 1994–95, oil on linen. This painting shows platforms 1 and 2 at the (former) Eurostar end of the station. The artist captured this uncharacteristic ghostly view on the day of a national railway strike. This vision of light, airiness and emptiness is in complete contrast with the early interpretation of the station as being in the heart of a sinful place.
(Private collection © The artist)

Previous page bottom:
John Constable 'The opening of Waterloo Bridge ('Whitehall Stairs, June 18th, 1817')' (detail), oil on canvas, first exhibited in 1832. John Constable moved from Suffolk to London in the year that Waterloo Bridge opened, so presumably, he was an eye-witness to the opening ceremony depicted here. But it took two more years before he made a start on this enormous painting – one of Constable's largest. Thirteen years in the making, it also commemorates the second anniversary of the Battle of Waterloo.
(© Tate, Photo: Tate)

opening, with Queen Mary, on 21 March 1922. Order had been achieved.

Nowadays Waterloo Station is the largest and busiest station in the country. It also has the greatest number of platforms: twenty-four. Were the somewhat disorderly origins and growth of Waterloo Station responsible for the historic fall of this neighbourhood?

Railways – the culprit? Adventure, gluttony and envy

Waterloo's reputation was very poor indeed, and the journalist and author George Augustus Sala did not mince his words:

> I wish that I had a more savoury locality to take you to than the New Cut. I acknowledge frankly that I don't like it …. It isn't picturesque, it isn't quaint, it isn't curious. It has not even the questionable merit of being old. It is simply Low. It is sordid, squalid, and, the truth must out, disreputable …. It is horrible, dreadful, we know, to have such a place: but then, consider – the population of London is fast advancing towards three millions, and the wicked people must live somewhere …

From *Twice Round the Clock*, 1858

How did Waterloo run into difficulties so soon after being created, and despite major investment in its infrastructure? Such as a bridge in 1817 (previous page), Waterloo Road soon after, connecting to the southern end of Westminster Bridge Road, from there to St George's Circus and Blackfriars Road and Bridge; the railway station in 1848, and a second railway line in the 1860s.

In urban areas everywhere, there are countless examples of the slow deterioration of buildings which make up a neighbourhood – slipping from new bright streets, full of promise, to lost, forlorn arteries of shame. This theme was powerfully anatomised by playwright Paul Mercier in Dublin (see p. 63). Here in Waterloo, it was investigated in 1967 by an American urban historian, Henry C Binford, for his MA thesis at Sussex University, which was later revised and published in an academic journal.

The author considered the area immediately north of Waterloo station as it underwent a transformation after railway 'interference'.

> In the nineteenth century, the evolution of North Lambeth was considered a classic example of the process of railway blight.

Henry C Binford, February 1974

The 1859 Charing Cross and Railway Act gave a green light to the building of a station at Charing Cross and to the linking of this new terminus to Waterloo and London Bridge stations. This involved a bridge across the

Thames and a line of track to and from Waterloo station, altogether just over two miles. The company acquired hundreds of houses along the route and it followed that thousands of people would be displaced. At the time it was considered 'a great improvement' and 'essential to the orderly growth of London'. It also created a big, indiscriminate tear in the fabric of South London. Parliament had long resisted the presence of railway termini in the centre of London while also showing concern about the general increase in traffic. It finally authorised the building of a station at Charing Cross and four others – Victoria in 1858, Farringdon Street in 1860, Liverpool Street in 1864 and St Pancras also in 1864.

Below:
This terrace development at 80-86 Waterloo Road is a good example of the work of L N Cottingham in the neighbourhood. It is where the architect lived, at No 86, and developed his museum of architecture – here are two of seven photographs recording its holdings. The LCC photographs were taken between 1949 (right) and 1961 (middle).
© London Metropolitan Archives (City of London)

L N COTTINGHAM's house and museum.

The architect Lewis Nockalls Cottingham lived and worked in Waterloo from the 1820s – at 4 Bazing Place, Waterloo Road, later known as No 86 Waterloo Road. No 77, on the corner with Exton Street, is the only surviving Cottingham building with similar details to his own house.

Cottingham was more than an architect. His obituary in the *Gentleman's Magazine* (XXVIII) states that about the year 1825 Mr Cottingham undertook the management and arrangement of the very extensive estate belonging to the late John Field, esq., of Tooting, on the Surrey side of Waterloo Bridge, and thereon erected the principal portion of the houses forming the large parish of St John's Lambeth, immediately surrounding his own residence. This also he built, and provided with large suites of rooms attached, for the purpose of depositing the valuable works of art and the library, which he had, with the true earnest zeal of an artist devoted to his profession, spared neither trouble nor expense to acquire.

After Cottingham's death in 1847, his son, Nockalls Johnson Cottingham, lived at No 86 until 1851, presumably taking care of his father's collection, which was catalogued by Henry Shaw and published in 1850 under the title *Catalogue of the Museum of Mediaeval Art*. By some remarkable occurrence, some of the rooms of Cottingham's 'museum of architecture' were photographed by the London County Council. This is the second 'museum of architecture' on the South Bank – the first was established by George Gwilt the Younger (1775–1856) in Southwark (see p. 195, BB20).

Below:
Mint Street, opposite St George's church was found in the notorious 'Borough Mint' slum in Southwark, once the site of the grand and wealthy Suffolk Place. The author Michael Sadleir believed that Waterloo's fall was in part due to the poisonous influence of the Borough slums.
(From George Godwin, *London Shadows*, 1854)

Henry Binford examined 'the impact of the Charing Cross railway on the inhabitants of North Lambeth, an area acquired and partially cleared by the railway between 1860 and the taking of the census on 31 March 1861 … at the time of the preliminary survey in 1858, there were 269 houses, 221 of which fell within the limits of deviation'. This area was where Dr Minor chose to live at the end of 1871.

The area was developed by two 'teams': the northern half in the 1820s by Henry Warburton MP (formerly in the timber trade) with Alexander Tillett (former saltpetre merchant); whereas the southern half, south of York Road and closest to the station, was developed by John Field and Agnes Bazing in the 1830s. John Field, a wax chandler, was the proprietor of a candle works factory in Upper Marsh and used the services of the prominent architect Lewis Nockalls Cottingham (1787–1847).

Binford noted that after the first round of railway development in the 1840s, vagrants and derelicts began to appear in the arches under its viaduct. By the 1850s, cheap music halls were common in Waterloo Road and a slum appeared along the railway to the south, and the area just south of Waterloo station was one of London's most notorious centres of prostitution (in and around Granby Street).

Unfortunately, Binford does not dwell on the impact of the first 1840s railway development (Waterloo station) on its neighbourhood and in the end, he is not able to link the relatively gentle deterioration of North Lambeth to the second railway construction of the 1860s. He was forced to conclude: 'the degree of railway influence cannot be precisely determined on the basis of the present evidence. The impact may have provoked some residents to flee; it may have accelerated an ongoing process of decline; but long-term processes of evolution were also at work.' The decline was certainly clear to the social investigators who walked those streets, between Belvedere and York Roads, in the last years of the nineteenth century, gathering information for Charles Booth's Poverty Maps:

> All these streets are alike p[in]k to purple in character: 6 roomed houses letting at 12/- & 14/- per week: & sublet: streets themselves badly kept & want mending … turning W[est] at the York Public house: 'Poverty junction & out at Elbows Corner' the corner where the poorer music hall artists loaf in hope of a job: York Road itself is full of variety agents: 'the demand for 'pros' increases every year.

By contrast with Binford, the conclusions of historian and novelist, Michael Sadleir, are far more assertive and pertinent. He evoked the turmoil, amongst developers, caused by the arrival of a railway station (1848) which deepened when it was followed by a financial crisis. Finally, he mentioned the infiltration, from around 1845, of rough characters from the Borough, describing the 'Southwark Mint' 'as evil a patch, of villainous courts and thieves' kitchens as the south side could boast'. A well-researched portrait of the birth, life and death of a London slum, can be found in the riveting and meticulous work of Sarah Wise, who chronicled the anatomy of a London slum in her book on East London's 'Old Nichol' – *The Blackest Streets*.

Railway mania fuelled the unstoppable growth of what the railway companies would soon optimistically describe as 'a public service'; but the vast amount of destruction of mostly working class housing, never ceased to generate debate, even after the railwaymen tried to argue their works were 'objects of civil pride and not of suspicion'; or that the occupants of houses moved to better tenements in the suburbs; or that they were performing much needed slum clearance: in the words of T Hammond in 1835 'the nurseries of vice, the nuclei of filth and disease' (Dyos and Wolff).

The urban historian H J Dyos placed these figures in a wider London context, with shocking statistics. He established that for the 680,000 workers who depended on casual labour in Central London, 'distant lodgings would have been a crippling handicap'. He also pointed out 'There were in all sixty-nine separate [railway] schemes, involving the displacement of 76,000 persons between 1853 and 1901. Fifty-one of these schemes, affecting 56,000 persons occurred in the period before 1885, during which no provision was made for re-housing those displaced … The period of most intense activity was, in fact, a comparatively short one, for nearly 37,000 displacements occurred in the period from 1859 to 1867 alone.'

In 1874 the Council of the Charity Organisation Society set up a committee of MPs and others, chaired by the Lord Mayor Sir Sydney Waterlow, to force railway companies to give displaced inhabitants eight weeks' notice and to provide alternative accommodation. These guidelines were embodied in several Acts but railway companies were able to ignore them for a further nine years. Even after 1885, when these requirements were strictly enforced, 'the invariable time-lag between demolition and the provision of alternative accommodation ensured that its ultimate occupants were seldom, if ever, the same persons as those originally displaced.'

But the Wheel of Fortune often ensures that what goes up will

Below:
This wood engraving of the Royal Victoria Palace and Music Hall illustrates three different parts of the future Old Vic: the pit and galleries (top left), the stalls and boxes (top right) and the cafe below. To the surprise of Emma Cons's detractors, the coffee room (part of Romaine Delatorre's grand 1871 refurbishment of the Royal Victoria) was successful, run by John Pearce so was the programme of concerts (unlike the variety shows).
(From *The Graphic*, 20 August 1881)

eventually come down and what has deteriorated can also be reborn. The Granby Street slum disappeared, swallowed up by the relentless growth of Waterloo station.

Regeneration story – 'a penny' for the arts: temperance, charity and fortitude

> The idea of service was often the way in which Victorian women philanthropists expressed their religious impulses, rather than in more contemplative or purely doctrinal fashion. Miranda [Hill] observed that in [her sister] Octavia's case, 'all the depth and ardour of her nature were called out by her faith which was ever the underlying motive and guide of her whole life'.
>
> From *Octavia Hill – Social reformer and founder of the National Trust* by Gillian Darley (1990)

This also describes the passionate nature of the extraordinary women who performed so many regenerative feats in Victorian London. They worked within specific geographical areas but also set up supportive networks as well as being excellent fundraisers. So, for the South Bank, Emma Cons (1838–1912) worked in Waterloo/Lambeth, Octavia Hill (1838–1912) in Southwark and, a little later, Ada Salter (1866–1942) in Bermondsey. We will explore their legacies but Emma Cons's heart most definitely 'belonged' to Waterloo/Lambeth. Historian Gillian Darley, recounts a significant anecdote (narrated by Sophie Lonsdale) which also bears witness to the primary role played by Emma's religion:

> Miss Cons' courage and spirit and hopefulness never left her. I remember walking across Lambeth Bridge with her one day and we stopped in the middle to look down the river. She said to me: 'When one thinks of all the sin and misery there is in London, what's to prevent one's throwing oneself over there, except one's faith'.

The methods used by all of them were similar and involved tackling basic human needs (shelter, health) and also operating a purpose-built base for educational and cultural programmes: the Old Vic for Emma, the Public Hall attached to Octavia's model housing in Red Cross Street, or, further afield, Whitechapel's Toynbee Hall set up by Henrietta and Samuel Barnett. Later came the realisation that open space was of paramount importance; this required campaigning for open space, public and private gardens, and the setting up of ambitious projects such as the National Trust (Octavia Hill) or Hampstead Garden Suburb (Henrietta Barnett). The drive and the energy were phenomenal.

Music hall

Music hall, even at the height of its glorious years (1880–1920), was often interpreted as a sign of struggling or disreputable neighbourhoods as is clear from *The Notebooks* for Charles Booth's 'Poverty Maps', commenting on York Road: 'variety agents [=music hall agents]: warehouses: hotels: prostitutes: many hotels little else than brothels: Girls live

Above:
Walter H Lambert: 'Popularity or the Stars of the Edwardian Music Hall', 1901-3. This extremely large painting depicts the junction of Waterloo Road and the Cut, looking up towards Waterloo Bridge with the Old Vic behind the artist's right shoulder.
(© Museum of London)

there and bring men home: some servants …'. Although cheap theatres are not mentioned here they could just as easily have followed in the same breath. George Augustus Sala, whose dislike of the New Cut was palpable, had this to say on the subject of cheap and popular shows:

> These poor people … have not been to the university of Cambridge … they can't afford to purchase a 'Shilling handbook of etiquette'. Which is best … that they should lie in wait in doorways and blind alleys to rob and murder, or they should pay their threepence for admission into the gallery at the 'Vic' … If we want genteel improprieties, sparkling immoral repartees, decorously scandalous intrigues … we must cross the bridges and visit the high priced theatres of the West End. (1858)

For those who loved the music hall, Waterloo and Lambeth were the Holy Grail and there is no louder celebratory proof of this than the painting by Walter C. Lambert, music hall artiste, impersonator of 'Lydia Dreams' and 'amateur' painter, though he did attend Harrogate School of Art. His enormous painting 'Popularity – the Stars of the Edwardian Music Hall' (above) shows a scene at the junction of Waterloo Road and the New Cut, looking north: 'one of the places known as 'Poverty Corner' where the unemployed pro's met to swap stories and to see their agents, whose offices were in or near the Waterloo Road' wrote Harry Powell Lloyd (Arthur Lloyd website). Lambert's painting, dated 1901–1903, comes at the height of music hall's popularity though its end is in sight after decades of growth and success. What was the reason for its amazing success?

It is arguably possible to see a link between today's enthusiasm for karaoke and the rise for music hall entertainment in Victorian London. At the origin of both is the singing instinct, though in our times it is also backed by the desire to become a centre of attention and to identify with the charismatic, successful singers of the day. Back in Victorian times, attention was definitely focused on the music hall stars who led the joyful jamborees – from the tiny but well-proportioned 'Little Tich', to heart-throb Dan Leno, via impersonator 'Lydia Dreams' – the Dame Edna of his time, and the author of the 'Popularity' painting. It all started simply enough, as chronicled in Barker and Jackson's *Pleasures of London*: 'In the crowded bar of a public house there is a bang on a table and a call for silence. The pianist takes a quick gulp of beer and strikes a chord. To scattered applause a singer embarks on a raucous song. Customers join in the chorus. This is music hall in its earliest and most basic form sometimes in the 1830s'. Edward Walford, writing in 1878, called it a 'singsong' or 'harmonic meeting'.

When London's entrepreneurs realised that these impromptu variety shows in public houses were loved by the public, they orchestrated the transition to purpose-built music halls. There are several possible contenders for the very first music hall but historians favour the Canterbury in Lambeth over and above the Great Harmonic Hall, also on the South Bank, later the Surrey Music Hall. Before abandoning the Surrey shores in pursuit of glittering West End prizes, Charles Morton (1819–1904), the impresario behind the Canterbury established two important guiding principles – encouraging women in the audience, as well as free entry in the early days prior to building a hall, which was followed by an advantageous pricing system upon the arrival of a proper hall: 'Three pence per head for any part of the house!' states Morton's partial (and posthumous) autobiography (1905).

Charles Morton attempted to present 'theatrical sketches' at the Canterbury but was fined on several occasions for infringement of the 'Theatres Act 1843'. Spoken drama could only be performed in 'patent theatres' – and originally there were only three in London, the Theatre Royal at Drury Lane, the Theatre Royal at Covent Garden and the Theatre Royal at Haymarket. All the other theatres fell into the category of 'minor theatres', their status limiting their repertoire, but encouraging innovation. The 1843 Theatres Act broke the monopoly of the patent theatres. However, both theatres and new plays could only operate or be performed after obtaining licences, initially from the Lord Chamberlain who could ban anything without proper justification but increasingly, after 1843, by local authorities. It was sometimes possible to obtain temporary licences and there were other ways of cheating the system. Victorian 'melodramas', comedy and dance all escaped the

Below:
Gustave Doré, A Penny Gaff, the cheapest form of theatre, popular among the labouring classes.
(*From London A Pilgrimage*, by Gustave Doré and Blanchard Jerrold, 1872)

rules, either because there was no spoken word or because it was not continuous spoken word – melodramas using music and action scenes, comedy even, alongside limited dialogue. This Act was only repealed in 1968.

In his novel, *Liza of Lambeth*, Somerset Maugham described in vivid language an evening at an un-named local theatre which presented a 'New and Sensational Drama'. This may have been a 'penny-gaff', a mid-nineteenth century form of entertainment for popular classes, mixing drama and comedy and throwing in dance and music too, all for the price of one penny. Penny-gaffs were first mentioned by Henry Mayhew in his celebrated *London Labour and the London Poor* (three volumes published in 1851, a fourth one in 1861). Unlike Mayhew who was very judgmental – 'the stage … is turned into a platform to teach the cruellest debauchery', Maugham candidly records the impact a show had on his characters: 'I've never see sich a good ply in my life. Lor'! Why, it mikes yer blood run cold; they 'ang a man on the stige; oh, it mide me creep all over!'; the author further clarifying: 'the blood and thunder, the shooting, the railway train, the murder, the bomb, the hero, the funny man – jumbling everything up in her excitement, repeating little scraps of dialogue – all wrong – gesticulating, getting excited and red in the face at the recollections'.

The word 'penny' was key to mobilising the labour classes and penny readings, like penny gaffs, also began in the mid-nineteenth century, first outside of London. The concept was adopted and reinterpreted at the Old Vic by its late nineteenth-century owner, Emma Cons in her great mission of driving the poor from their misery into the world of 'improving' entertainments.

A further example is Lambeth School of Art (see p. 236) which deliberately and systematically sought to improve the unfulfilled lives of those too poor to redress their own struggling human condition. Could education and the arts alleviate the ills of fallen neighbourhoods?

Resurgence of theatres on the South Bank

Just as animal baiting predated the arrival of Elizabethan theatres on the South Bank, animal-based shows in late eighteenth and early nineteenth-century Lambeth, also predated the rise of popular theatre. They constituted the earliest form of what would soon be called 'circus'. Philip Astley (1742–1814), horse rider extraordinaire, won over the approval of crowds when he finally settled at his 'Amphitheatre' in Westminster Bridge Road (see p. 159).

In *The Pleasures of London*, Barker and Jackson, described the central role of theatre in London at the end of the nineteenth century:

> Between 1880 and 1910 twenty-six theatres opened in London – nearly one a year – seven of them in the newly created Shaftesbury Avenue … It has been described as the 'Renaissance of the English Theatre' and, with sixty central and suburban playhouses, London became – and has remained – the theatrical capital of the world.

But there is a major problem with this punchy statement; it was largely focused on what happened in the West End. Even the useful Arthur Lloyd [theatre] website concentrates its attention on the West End in its section on 'Theatreland Maps'. Without

taking any of the credit away from the West End, it is important to examine the unique development taking place on the South Bank before and during that time. The Old Vic may have become one of the oldest theatre buildings in London but it was not the first to appear on the South Bank; it was the Surrey Theatre, a venue on Blackfriars Road at the St George's Circus end, which had started life as a 'circus' set up by a former employee at Astley's.

The time has come to consider the extraordinary 'Looking Glass' curtain (overleaf), unveiled at the Royal Coburg Theatre, the future Old Vic, on Boxing Night 1821. It is a useful and memorable manifestation of the bond between a theatre and its audience. It was introduced by the theatre's first manager, Joseph Glossop, who had copied the idea from a Paris theatre:

> The first night it was lowered there was great applause at its audacity, but after three or four minutes a voice from the gallery called out: 'That's all very well. Now show us summut else'.

This anecdote comes from the dramatist and polymath James Robinson Planché (1796–1880) in his *Recollections*. This very special 'curtain' was made up of sixty-three mirrors assembled in a gilt frame, weighing around five tons. The frame was suspended from the roof, endangering the whole structure of the theatre. It was both a gimmick and a deeply revealing symbol. This mirror-curtain embodied the intimate relationship which existed between stage and audience: we put you, the spectator, on stage, echoing Shakespeare's lines: 'All the world's a stage/And all the men and women, merely players', the opening lines of *As You Like It*. More recently, Sally Greene, another established figure in the world of theatre, also set out to exploit this special relationship when trying to seduce potential board members to the Old Vic at a time (2000) when its very existence was once more threatened.

> I put a dining table on the stage … and those I really wanted to seduce would be looking out towards the auditorium, because it's beautiful. All the lights up, and flowers, and sweets on the table …

Who came to dinner? Elton John and Michael Bloomberg, others too, of course. The imaginative event paid off.

But at the same time that the theatre holds up a mirror to its audience, signalling a meaningful transaction, it also has to deal with its audience's fickle ways, only spending the price of a ticket if programming titillated their dreams and desires, as far away from the real world as it is possible to be. What's next … what's next which is going to be new and

Opposite:
The famous 'looking-glass curtain' at the Royal Coburg Theatre (the future Old Vic): 'Theatrical reflection – or a Peep at the Looking Glass Curtain at the Royal Coburg Theatre', 1822. It may look as if the artist has positioned himself on the stage to draw the audience on a packed performance. Not so. The artist is amongst the spectators, looking into the famous Curtain which reflected the image of the entire audience to themselves. This special 'curtain', made up of sixty three mirrors, was dangerously heavy, and there were fears that it might pull the ceiling down. (Image in the public domain, Wikimedia Commons)

exciting? Begging for the comfort of tradition and illusion while also craving the shock of the new? On the night that the 'Looking Glass Curtain' was unveiled for the first time the show was 'The Temple of Death' described in Clarkson Stanfield's catalogue as

> a fine example of the horrors of 'transpontine melodrama' used here as Christmas entertainment.

The Old Vic

Things had started promisingly enough at the Old Vic, or rather the Royal Coburg Theatre. Two of the original trio of lessees, James Jones and his creditor James Dunn, had been forced to abandon their previous home, the Surrey Theatre, when the landowner Colonel Templeton West (the developer of nearby West Square) had put up the rent from £220 to £4200. They felt their money would be better spent in a new venture, found an additional lessee in the much-respected marine painter John Thomas Serres, marine artist to the King. It was almost certainly Serres who was able to secure the new theatre its 'Royal' title, commemorating the 1816 marriage of Princess Charlotte, the Prince Regent's daughter, to Prince Leopold of Saxe-Coburg (the future Leopold I King of the Belgians). The young couple had been the first subscribers to the theatre's building fund. The theatre, designed by Rudolph Cabanel, a German architect, opened on 11 May 1818.

From the outset the Royal Coburg sought to indulge its audience with the thrill of the spectacular – the memorable stage sets of the early days: waterfalls and horses on stage, a ship making its way through a sea of ice, a little later the mirror curtain and also the performing of the great and famous like the actor Edmund Kean in 1831. On arrival, the audience was also greeted by the exuberant talent of the 'resident' painter: J T Serres.

John Thomas Serres (1759–1825) lived and worked at a time when panoramas were all the rage, sweeping Londoners off their feet in 'Panoramania' fever. Richard Altick quotes in his outstanding book *The Shows of London* the 1805 journal of Benjamin Sillivan: 'I am fond of panoramas, especially of battles. Their magnitude, the circular position of the canvas … give one the strongest impression of the reality of the scene'. Panoramas of places and events 'became the newsreels of the Napoleonic era'. Robert Barker – a South London resident – dominated the scene but there were others including Serres himself, who in 1805 had exhibited a 150 ft canvas of Boulogne at the height of the scare of Napoleon's invasion ('Boney is Coming!'). During the opening preparations at the Royal Coburg Theatre, he created a marine saloon which included a panoramic view of the Royal Navy's bombardment of Algiers in 1816 and a view of Venice with a 'cast' of around 500 figures. For the theatre's second season he added a view of Moscow before the 1812 fire which destroyed the city, ahead of the arrival of Napoleon's troops. Richard Altick summarised: 'what the first panoramists did, in effect, was to bring this kind of instant-history painting to a somewhat broader public – … [it] had the forthright appeal of topicality realistically and dramatically presented'.

Current events and topics painted on an awe-inspiring scale also made their way on stage via the medium of moving panoramas. In 1819 the scenery painter Clarkson Stanfield, engaged both at the Coburg (under Serres) and Astley's, produced a moving panorama of York for Astley's 'Richard Turpin'. Two of Astley's most spectacular shows

Design by Waterloo-based Walter Hann, scenery painter operating from Murphy Street. The stage setting was for a production of 'Junius' by Edward Bulwer-Lytton. Pen and ink, watercolour with Chinese white, 1885.
(© Victoria and Albert Museum, London)

'The Battle of Waterloo' and 'The Burning of Moscow' brought dramatic episodes of contemporary history straight to the London stage, the Moscow show echoing Serres's own painting at the Coburg.

The first lessees at the Royal Coburg were well aware of the importance of Waterloo Bridge – making the West End suddenly easy to reach. Of course everyone hoped it would work the other way around too and attract an audience used to West End theatres alongside the local audience of the South Bank. There were occasional London-wide successes but this was not the regular pattern which consisted mainly of a local audience. The theatre was also struck a blow when, after securing its royal patronage, and before its official opening, the shocking death of Princess Charlotte in childbirth weakened the raison d'être of its name. Also, the theatre had needed extra funds from the very beginning, which were not forthcoming until the involvement of Francis Glossop father and son. Francis was a wealthy tallow chandler based in Soho where he had supplied lighting for theatres and was a supporter of the Drury Lane theatre; and Joseph his youngest son, who would get closely involved with several theatres in his lifetime. With the backing of Francis, Joseph became the Royal Coburg's first manager soon purchasing the interests of Jones, Dunn, and Serres (by 1818). He was already involved with the Royalty Theatre near the Tower of London, and transferred several of their staff to the Royal Coburg, including the young scenic artist Clarkson Stanfield (1793–1867). Stanfield was at the Coburg in 1818 and also between 1821 and 1823; he transferred to the Drury Lane Theatre in 1823, which was also patronised by the Glossops. He was the first scenery painter to be elected to the Royal

Above:
Portrait of Emma Cons (1838–1912), photograph published in *The Idler: an illustrated monthly magazine*, January 1897 (Image in the public domain, Wikimedia Commons)

Academy. The authors of the excellent 1979 Clarkson Stanfield catalogue believed that 'Stanfield's influence on the scenery of the theatre … was lasting and painting standards at the Coburg remained notably good.'

Much later in 1899 the researchers for Booth's Poverty Maps recorded 'the great theatrical scene painters studio' of Walter Hann (1838–1922) on the west side of Murphy Street, very close to the Old Vic. At that date there were seventeen names listed under 'Scene Painters' in London's Post Office Directory – one in the north, one in the south west, five in the West End and eleven in the south east (Lambeth). The preponderance of scene painters in Lambeth evolved slowly; back in 1879 only three names were listed, two of them in SE and in 1887 the eight names were distributed between Central London (three) and Lambeth (five). Who would have thought Lambeth was harbouring the greatest number of scene painters in London? They were surely capitalising on cheap rents and proximity to theatreland.

Returning to the Coburg, in November 1822, Joseph Glossop fled to the Continent to avoid being arrested for debts. There, he became involved with Italy's two greatest opera houses: La Scala in Milan and the San Carlo in Naples, and eventually, in 1833, came back to London, where he was finally declared bankrupt. Despite this, he succeeded in being reinstated at 'the Royal Victoria' – the Royal Coburg's new name after the visit of Princess Victoria on 28 November 1833.

Having failed to attract West End patrons, and having exhausted the enthusiastic energy of the Glossops, the theatre had, by 1840, settled for a quick turnover of popular melodramas and animal shows leading the journalist Frederick Tomlins to write:

> It has been everything by turns but nothing long – ever aiming at novelty but never pursuing any course sufficiently steadily to raise a character or secure a continuous and respectable audience. Situated in one of the worst neighbourhoods, its audiences are of the lowest kind.

Given the theatre's precarious finances, it could be argued that its main stroke of luck was not to have burnt down – the recurrent misfortune of most theatres in London in the nineteenth century. Historian Terry Coleman thinks that 'Lilian Baylis's long rule was of course the greatest good fortune … Without her saintly monomania, the theatre would have come to nothing, and monomania is rare and lucky'. Arguably the most extraordinary period in the history of the Old Vic is that during the ownership of Emma Cons (1838–1912) followed by her niece Lilian Baylis (1874–1937).

There were two things which might have stopped Emma Cons from getting involved with the Old Vic: first, she was not interested in theatre and secondly, she was passionate about temperance. So why on earth did she buy the Old Vic in 1880? Terry Coleman laboured the point: 'Miss Cons had no interest in the theatre and in all her time there never even asked for a theatre licence'. However, she was already working in the neighbourhood having set up the South London Dwellings Company the previous year, to channel funds towards her Surrey Lodge housing project. She had also set up the Coffee Music Hall Company 'to provide for the working and lower middle classes recreation such as the music hall offers, without the existing attendant moral and social disadvantages.'

Emma Cons's devotion to the struggling classes was noticed by Beatrice Webb when she visited Emma's Surrey Buildings in 1885: 'Absolute absorption in work; strong religious feeling, very little culture or interest in things outside the sphere of her own action … but devotes much time to other work in connection with amusement and instruction of the people. A calm enthusiasm in her face, giving her all to others …'. She excellently sums up Emma's work and designs in Waterloo:

Above:
Portrait of Lilian Baylis wearing the Master's cap and gown she received for her Oxford honorary MA degree. She was immensely proud of the honour which had been conferred upon her and always wore this 'uniform' on special occasions. Photograph around 1925.
(Image in the public domain, Wikimedia Commons)

> … one of the most saintly as well as the most far-sighted of Victorian women philanthropists, deserves to be more widely known … became an independent manager of working class dwellings on the Surrey side. Realizing that what was needed, even more than sanitary but dismal homes, was the organization of the pleasures of the poor in great cities, she, in 1880, took over the management of the Victoria music hall, at that time a disreputable centre for all that was bad … and ran it as a place of popular musical entertainment, free from vice, and unsubsidized by the sale of alcoholic drink. Supported by Samuel Morley [the MP], Miss Martineau and Lord Mount Temple, Miss Cons kept this enterprise going until her death in 1912, when she was succeeded by her niece, Miss Lilian Baylis who had been assisting her …

It was her work in housing management for and with her oldest friend and mentor, Octavia Hill, which had persuaded her of the evils of drink. She had surprised Octavia back in the 70s when she successfully persuaded the band of musicians she had set up at one of Octavia's Marylebone housing schemes to become teetotal. She had not bought a theatre but a building. In his history of the Old Vic, Terry Coleman quotes her writing in 1902: 'The work of the Hall is primarily Temperance work … The workers at this Hall have been labouring for 23 years to provide such a "people's palace" – one that should furnish only innocent amusement …'. A journalist from the *Birmingham Daily Post* described it as 'the civilization of the roughs' adding that 'Emma Cons has found the way to console and pacify the troubled soul'.

Emma Cons may not have had the theatrical bug but she pushed for

Above:
The Yorkshire Society's School in Westminster Bridge Road, was founded in 1912 for the education and maintenance of boys born in Yorkshire or of Yorkshire parents. It was the second home of Morley College (the first was the back of the Old Vic), where it gained independence. The school closed in 1917, was briefly occupied by the Britannia Club for Soldiers and Sailors before becoming Morley College in 1923. It was destroyed in the Second World War.
© London Metropolitan Archives (City of London)

a community agenda with all her might. Theatre and culture enthusiasts were not always impressed, for instance the social reformer Beatrice Webb (1858–1943):

> Went with two fellow-workers to the Vic[toria Theatre]; managed by that grand woman Miss Cons. To me a dreary performance, sinking to the level of the audience, while omitting the dash of coarseness, irreverence and low humour which give the spice and the reality to such entertainments. To my mind the devil is preferable, and in every way more wholesome, than a shapeless mediocrity.

November 1885, Beatrice Webb *My Apprenticeship*, first published 1926

On the one occasion that Emma attempted to put on a pantomime at the Vic in 1886, she was dragged in front of the magistrates by a former stage manager and lessee of the Old Vic, J Arnold Cave (by then working at the Elephant & Castle theatre). He argued that the pantomime was really a play, for which the Vic had no licence. Miss Cons, who had everyone's sympathy for the work she was doing at the Old Vic, was very reluctantly fined half a crown.

Emma's temperance and 'improvement' agenda also came under criticism, summarised much later, in 1926, by her niece Lilian Baylis:

> It must not be imagined that the movement to 'elevate the masses' met with immediate success; on the contrary, the masses showed plainly enough that they did not much want to be elevated. (Cited in George Rowell)

However, the person who replaced Emma at the helm of the Vic did have the theatre bug. It was Lilian Baylis (1874–1937), Emma's niece. She came from a musical household – both her parents were musicians and the trio had gone on a nine-month tour of South Africa, performing in major and minor urban centres. Lilian arrived in England in 1897, to recuperate from a kidney operation, but she very quickly found her feet at the Old Vic, taking responsibility for implementing the new London County Council fire safety recommendations; then introducing the highly successful 'animated pictures' in 1901, which by 1905 had solidified into 'film night' on Mondays. She also tried, in vain, to persuade her aunt and her management committee to apply for a theatre licence. However, two months after Emma's death in July 1912, she had secured a theatre licence from the Lord Chamberlain and that spelt the end of variety shows at the Old Vic, ending a thirty-two-year tradition.

Programming changed, with the Old Vic soon championing operas (Lilian's love) and Shakespeare, the idea of Rosina Lippi who was promoting a 'People's Theatre' based on Shakespeare's plays. Her company was granted two nights a week but Rosina and Lilian really were reluctant collaborators, so Rosina had to leave though Shakespeare stayed. His presence at the Old Vic was consolidated by the experienced Ben Greet who, after four years of successful productions, had turned the great playwright into an Old Vic tradition.

Spreading the love: education, education, education

The legacy of the Old Vic is extraordinary and it is surely the combination of community work (Emma) and theatrical excellence (Lilian) which was responsible for the enormous influence it has had on London's culture. Not only did the Old Vic survive but it thrived and spread its magic to the far corners of London and indeed the world. Who could have predicted that from the backstage activities of the late nineteenth century a fully-fledged adult education college would be born – Morley College, in honour of Samuel Morley, the unfailing supporter of the work of Emma Cons? Terry Coleman noted: 'The Victoria was the only music hall ever to give birth to a college' And who would have thought that Lilian Baylis would also, based at the Old Vic, save, nurture and run Sadler's Wells theatre which would become one of the world's centres for ballet and modern dance? Later the Old Vic sheltered one of the most important post-war cultural developments in England: the birth of its National Theatre.

Above:
In 1928 Edward Bawden and Eric Ravilious were paid £1 a day to decorate Morley College's refreshment room in its first independent home. The acclaimed artwork based on Shakespeare and other Elizabethan playwrights, was lost during the war. Bawden agreed to paint new murals for the new refectory (1958-61).
(*Evening Standard* 3 February 1930; photo courtesy of Morley College)

Morley College

The early lantern lectures proving of interest, Emma followed suit with her 'penny lectures', in association with the scientific journal *Nature*. These, held on Tuesday night, were introduced in 1882 (the penny fee was for the gallery, the pit and balcony were slightly more expensive). They became popular with the locals and other people too, attracting an audience of up to 700 or 800 per night. In 1884 two clerks, regular fans, but a little frustrated by the fragmented approach to science, their favourite subject, asked Emma Cons whether she could introduce regular scientific classes in the evenings. Five years later Morley Memorial College for Working Men and Women had been established while the penny lectures carried on, broadening out their repertoire to include geography, history, literature and practical topics such as gardening and animal husbandry.

Just as J L Sparkes had ensured the future of Lambeth School of Art by joining forces with the City and Guilds of London Institute in 1878 (see p. 236), Emma wanted to secure the future of her own enterprises – the Vic and the nascent college. She had persuaded her old supporter Samuel Morley that the freehold of the Old Vic should be purchased and that the 'college' should become his legacy. Samuel Morley died in 1886, the freehold was purchased in 1888 and the Morley Memorial College came into being in 1889.

The college which had grown at the back of the Old Vic was open to both male and female workers; the teaching was voluntary but the roll-call of extraordinarily distinguished men and women who taught there included Virginia Woolf (Stephen in her pre-married days), the great historian G M Trevelyan, the philosopher G E Moore, Ralph Vaughan Williams and Gustav Holst for music and more recently the author Margaret Drabble and the artist Maggi Hambling. In the early 1920s the philosopher Bertrand Russell was teaching a psychology class. Eventually the college was forced to acquire independent premises on Westminster Bridge Road when the LCC requested alterations to the Old Vic, including the removal of the College from the theatre. This happened in 1924, with the financial help of Sir George Dance. The college moved to an eighteenth-century house which, between 1812 and 1917, had been the Yorkshire Society's School 'for educating, boarding, and clothing boys born in Yorkshire, or one of whose parents was born there, and whose parents were in a respectable line of life, and are either reduced by misfortune or dead' (see p. 428). When the school closed down, the building was briefly used by the Britannia Club for Soldiers and Sailors.

The 1930s were full of exciting developments – the decoration of the great hall and refreshment room by Edward Bawden, Eric Ravilious and Cyril Mahoney; a project inspired by Rex Whistler's murals in the Tate restaurant. The much-lauded project was also the focus of a visit from Queen Mary. In 1932, the first day-time classes for the unemployed began and five years later there was an extension to the College, including the remarkable Holst Room; by 1938 the student roll was 3000.

During the Second World War, the Holst Room stood as a symbol for resilience and creativity. Having survived the bomb of 15 October 1940 which destroyed Morley's main building, it was turned into a temporary mortuary three weeks later when the hostel for homeless men across the road collapsed, killing seventy-one of its occupants. Michael Tippett (1905–1998) was appointed Director of Music soon after these events and by organising concerts, reviving the choir and orchestra, he brought human warmth and a sense of community to Morley College. The counter-tenor Alfred Deller recalls:

> … to have made the "black-out" journey, often punctuated by sirens and bombs, and then enter the Holst Room at Morley to a hubbub of voices with Michael in the centre shaking with laughter, was an assurance that all was right with the world – the true world of the spirit.

Resurrection After The Fall

The South Bank Centre sits on a piece of land which is unusually well documented from the seventeenth-century onwards. Using the *Survey of London* and the *Victoria History of the County of Oxford*, the evolution of the site may be charted through its

Above:
This striking bird's eye view of the 1951 Festival of Britain was prepared by John Dean Monroe Harvey (1895-1978), a trained architect turned draughtsman of architectural perspectives.
(The National Archives (UK), ref. WORK25/64/25)

tenants but also in terms of value. At the death of Sir Leoline Jenkins (1623–1685), a long-term benefactor of Jesus College in Oxford, the struggling College received a substantial amount of land, in London and elsewhere, including two pieces of land in Lambeth – one would achieve notoriety as Cuper's Garden, the other further south along the river bank was known as The Hopes and centred around College Street.

After the arrival of Waterloo Bridge in 1817 the section of land between Waterloo and Westminster Bridges soon acquired more substantial buildings than the timber yards and wharves of the eighteenth century, particularly after Belvedere Road was created in the 1820s. The area slowly became punctuated by increasingly monumental landmarks: a Shot Tower (1826), the Lion Brewery (1836–7), Hungerford Bridge (1845), India Stores Depot (1861), Crosse & Blackwell Jam and Pickle factory (1882–3), London County Hall which was developed from 1922 onwards while the 1785 Lambeth Waterworks continued to serve the local area.

The Festival of Britain

The Festival of Britain of 1951 has been regarded as a success – despite its modest budget and inevitable shortcomings – it, too, was affected by the doom mongers and those indifferent to the project. The

Above:

'The Englishman's Home' by John Piper was placed in the Homes and Gardens Pavilion, parallel with Waterloo Bridge: this huge mural on forty two panels (477 x 1547 cm overall size) was painted in the artist's Oxfordshire garden in 1950. When the Festival ended the mural went to Harlow. It was purchased by the Rothschild Foundation in 2022 for the collection of Waddesdon Manor (National Trust).

The two buildings framing this architectural landscape have not been identified; against a dramatic and romantic sky, the landmarks include buildings from Brighton, Epsom, Yeovil, the dome of Castle Howard and Owlpen Manor.

(Photo: Liss Llewellyn Gallery, London. © The Piper Estate/DACS, 2021)

suggestion originally came from the Royal Society of Arts in 1943 – who thought a celebration of the 100th anniversary of the pioneering Great Exhibition of 1851 would be worthwhile. The idea was followed up by Gerald Barry, editor of the *News Chronicle*, who was lobbying for an international exhibition. The project languished with the Board of Trade for a while and was eventually scaled down to a national rather than an international event, costing about one sixth of the original idea with a budget of 12 million pounds. In 1947 the project landed on the desk of the British Labour politician Herbert Morrison (1888–1965), a South Londoner by birth and conviction. Morrison pushed the project through the House of Commons on 7 December: 'a national display illustrating the British contribution to civilisation past, present and future, in arts, in science and technology, and in industrial design'. The Festival was made up of three elements – the main event which was held on the river front between Westminster and Waterloo bridges, a site chosen in 1949; a funfair at Battersea Park; and smaller festivals throughout the country.

The preparation of the site required the demolition of a great many houses, including those designed by L N Cottingham (see p. 415). Local architect Richard Woollard noted that there was still some resentment about this among older residents when he started living in Waterloo in 1978.

Bevis Hillier, co-editor with Mary Banham of 'A Tonic to the Nation' – The Festival of Britain 1951 wrote, with the benefit of hindsight in a book published to accompany a 1976 exhibition at the Victoria and Albert Museum:

> I'm sure a trip in a time machine to 1951 would re-awaken a hatred for the over-dressed pretensions of Victoriana. To it, and the rat-infested ruins created by the war, the clarity of the South Bank in '51 came like a bite of lemon at half time.

A particularly appropriate way of describing a project which was being 'marketed' (before the word had really come into its own) as 'A Tonic to the Nation' – not surprisingly coined by newspaper man, Gerald Barry. The art critic Edward Lucie-Smith indirectly concurred in his highly entertaining 1976 contribution 'On not visiting the Festival of Britain':

> I was eighteen, and at eighteen one is suspicious of all forms of innovation. Though the Festival made play with the idea of 'tradition', I was right in thinking that it was in essence innovative…

Lucie-Smith who settled in London in 1946 after growing up in the West Indies also 'felt, at some deep level, that I might be presented with more excitement, more ideas, than I could comfortably absorb'. As further reasons for not going to the Festival, he invoked the 'air of enforced jollity' and 'the hypocrisy of a second-class power still masquerading as a first-class one' but finally admitted:

> I looked at the site from across the river, Skylon piercing the air, and kept resolving to make my way there. I even went to the funfair at Battersea Park, as a way of getting up my courage for the real thing, and attended the old-fashioned music hall, which I enjoyed whole-heartedly. But still I didn't go.

For the Battersea funfair we have the relaxed and candid testimony of the painter John Piper (1903–1992) who, in collaboration with another artist, Osbert Lancaster, created a fun streetscape with structures inspired by some of the extravagant architecture painted by the seventeenth-century artist Monsu Desiderio (his real name was François de Nomé). His employer was James Gardner: 'It was dotty, really, working for Gardner. We never met each other at all, or hardly ever … and there was some other overlord over both of us. I've forgotten the names but the whole thing was wonderfully and adorably vague, you know!' Doubtful that the creative process would ever lead to anything concrete, Piper was amazed when completion day came: 'it was realised astonishingly well, I thought it was fantastically good. Exactly what one hoped it would look like. He went on:

> I thought that the Festival Gardens in this Desiderio-ish folly kind of design was an enrichment which might even – in one's rather pretentious way – affect the development of modern architecture'.

And when asked whether it did:

> No, not in the slightest … In fact as I was telling you, it was very cold-shouldered by all the critics. I don't think it was even noticed in the *Architectural Review* [AR]. If you go through the pages of the *AR* you won't get a smell of it.

As with the Millennium Dome more recently, all the great and the good of the creative world seemed to have been contributing: the Arts Council commissioned sixty painters and twelve sculptors, and a panel of judges selected five paintings for the Arts Council to buy. Jane Drew, in charge of the Riverside Restaurant next to Waterloo Bridge, adding that 'One of the things that we, in common with many an architect, were anxious to do was to use our sculptor and painter friends. In the Riverside Restaurant we used Barbara Hepworth, Ben Nicholson and Eduardo Paolozzi'. Ben Nicholson contributed a curved mural which was subsequently purchased by Frederick Gibberd to hang in the VIP lounge at Heathrow airport. The Festival played a vital role in establishing state support for the arts. The smarter Regatta Restaurant against Hungerford Bridge was chosen for the Festival's launch party: there 'everything is made with atoms', explained Basil Taylor in the Festival's Official Guide.

There were over twenty architects, three main contractors and seventeen display contractors and they had sixteen months to build the Festival of Britain. The futuristic

Skylon (Powell and Moya architects), a 'vertical feature' hovering above ground, ensured the Wow factor along with the dazzling Dome of Discovery (Ralph Tubbs). But sometimes the simplest things bring the greatest delight and the architectural journalist Hugh Pearman recounts in an exhibition pamphlet (May–June 1994) the following anecdote:

> I had been to a lecture by Sir Hugh Casson architect-planner of the 1951 exhibition and he had told us that people visiting the South Bank during those few months ... used to dance in the rain in their hats and overcoats. Was this true I asked my mother? Yes, it was she confirmed. People danced in the rain to jazz orchestras of the kind they were used to hearing on the Light Programme.

At the end of the film '84 Charing Cross Road' (1987), directed by David Jones, there is just such a scene, shot at night time. Mrs Pearman also commented that everything on the South Bank seemed bright and lively while the rest of the country appeared to sit in darkness.

The Shell development

The simplicity of the architecture of the Shell Centre certainly embodies 'the clarity' Bevis Hillier claimed for the South Bank during the Festival of Britain ... though many people argued that the architecture was just rather dull. The enormous size of the development and the resolute adoption of window uniformity partially accounted for its monotony. It was made up of the 'Upstream Building' which comprised a single 26-storey

Above:

The Shell Centre on the former site of the 1951 Festival of Britain was designed by Sir Howard Robertson and built by Sir Robert McAlpine between 1957–62. The large development was awkwardly situated on either side of Hungerford (railway) Bridge: the 'Downstream Building' was sandwiched between Hungerford and Waterloo Bridges while the Upstream building (with the tower) was on the west side of the development.
(Opringle at English Wikipedia, in the public domain)

The other photograph shows what has survived of the Shell estate west of Hungerford Bridge.
(© The author, 2020)

Above:
The building of Southbank Place – site visit as part of Open House, September 2018.
(© The author)

tower – the highest in London before it was overtaken barely a year later by the Millbank tower – and three horizontal units; the 'Downstream Building', on the east side and separated from the main complex by the Charing Cross railway bridge was the first element of the composition to be sold; it is now called the White House and was transformed into a residential block in the 1990s – round about the time that Shell also sold its previous headquarters across the river, at Shell-Mex House. The *Survey of London* points out that while several architects had worked on a masterplan for the South Bank, including the much-respected Charles Holden, in the end 'Shell redeveloped their own land without much relation to the rest of the area'.

The site for the Shell Centre formed part of that used by the Festival of Britain and it was Shell's new headquarters in this country, formerly sited on the north bank at Shell Mex House. The presence of Jubilee Gardens, which has considerably softened the very harsh landscape around the Shell complex, is linked to a covenant which protects the land between tower and Thames from development. The complex was designed by Sir Howard Robertson and built by Sir Robert McAlpine between 1957 and 1962. Robertson was close to seventy and the end of his career when he received the commission.

While the proportions of these different blocks may have made them look overbearing and austere, the materials used – entirely clad in Portland stone – and the interiors were distinctly luxurious. Co-ordinated by Lady Casson, several designers were used including the flamboyant Italian Ernesto Nathan Rogers. The Shell complex started life with a full-size swimming pool, a gymnasium, a theatre designed by Cecil Beaton, but gone after 1998, two restaurants, a rifle range, snooker room, a staff supermarket; but little remains.

Southbank Place

In July 2011, a joint venture between Canary Wharf and Qatari Diar was announced. They had bought a 999-year lease of the Shell Centre, explaining that they would keep the tower but redevelop the rest of the site. From 2016 onwards anyone driving south along Waterloo Bridge could not fail to notice the large building site which soon bristled with gigantic cranes. On 22 September 2018 I joined a group of about twenty people for a tour of Southbank Place. Construction had started about a couple of years before and although we were moving around a building site, wearing high visibility jackets and helmets, the site had already taken shape. We all trooped into the safe but incredibly rickety lift going up outside 30 Casson Square. The views at the top were breath-taking despite the wind and the rain. This was part of Open House weekend and although the weather was truly abysmal it was a privilege to be there. The well-organised event started with a visual presentation shown in one of the slightly rough but warm temporary offices – these are some of the statistics which were rolled out on the day: the largest structural steel beam weighs forty tonnes and is twenty-five metres long; at its peak the site had sixteen cranes, twenty-six hoists and 1900 people!

The new development is made up of seven towers clustered around the 1950s Shell Tower which switched from being an office block to being residential. It was masterminded by Squire and Partners who were working alongside Stanton Williams, GRID, Patel Taylor and Townshend Landscape Architects. The final result is a pleasant mix of high and low levels: giddiness when you look up but the public spaces at ground level have been sensitively handled to provide greenery, roofed areas, public sculpture and shops. From the pedestrian point of view it feels more integrated and fluid than the Shard Quarter where you are encouraged to look up and admire the architecture, losing your sense of human scale in the process.

The jewel in the crown: culture along the South Bank

'We're the largest arts centre in the UK and one of the nation's top five visitor attractions' asserts the South Bank Centre on its website (2020). It did not happen straight away. Slowly, but surely, the South Bank Centre has been instrumental in resurrecting the fortunes of this stretch of the Thames. After the excitement of the Festival of Britain came its dismantling – except for the Festival Hall, the concert hall the LCC had financed in a bid to make up for the destruction of the Langham Place Queen's Hall by German bombing on 10 May 1941.

The general mood turned its back on Victorian warehouses, in fact to anything Victorian. Behind the scenes, the mood had also turned away from industry and even housing after Herbert Morrison showed no enthusiasm for proposed residential blocks in one of the (unrealised) South Bank's schemes.

The South Bank Centre

Calls for a National Theatre had been distinctly heard ever since an anonymous critic using the pseudonym Dramaticus published a pamphlet in 1847 called 'the stage as it is'; but a viable proposal only came in the late 1940s – the LCC offered land on the site of the Festival of Britain in 1948 and the National Theatre Act was passed in 1949 offering some financial support. A foundation stone was laid in 1951 but ten years later the government backtracked arguing the country could not afford a National Theatre. Strapped for cash, the government later tried to force the amalgamation of the following companies: the Royal Shakespeare Company, the Old Vic and Sadler's Wells (despite the LCC bending over backwards to lighten the load and support the National Theatre project). Progress came in July 1962 when two boards were set up – one to overlook construction, the other to run a National Theatre company. In the end it fell to Laurence Olivier to form the latter and while waiting for their building to be constructed they were based at the Old Vic – between 1962 and 1977.

When examining the forces that shaped this stretch of the south bank at a 2001 conference, the architectural historian Andrew Saint felt that:

Culture was a late-comer in thinking about the South Bank; the prime mover was traffic, and the problems with river-crossings and north-south communication in London.

The traffic-issues Andrew Saint is referring to were the 'battle of the bridges', Hungerford and Waterloo and the south bank tram, bought and electrified by the LCC, but never connected to its north bank counterpart. These issues may have been all-consuming in the short term but are less convincing when taking the long view. The context evoked by Andrew Saint was the river bank between 1945 and 1950, and, wary of straying from his brief should he dwell too long on the distant past, started his 'modern history' in 1786 with the arrival of Albion Mills and 'large scale industry'. But the 1780s was also the decade which witnessed the rebirth and growth of show-business on the South Bank. As in the sixteenth century, animal-focused shows came first with Astley's horses and the Royal Circus; then came the opening of small pleasure gardens, quickly followed by theatres – the Surrey first, and its great rival the Royal Coburg, the future Old Vic.

Culture, and in particular culture for the people, was a highly significant presence on the South Bank throughout the nineteenth century. Industry may have fed its workers but culture helped them bear the daily grind. Industry had wealth, while culture, always up against it, had none at all. Creative solutions meant survival – so the students of Lambeth Art School found renewed prospects in their collaboration with local businesses Doulton or Farmer & Brindley, while the Old Vic, working for 'its people', staff and audience, went from strength to strength, led by strong, hard working women.

The idea of the South Bank taking on the role of cultural centre was a natural outcome borne from decades of local cultural endeavours. But it was only properly voiced in the 1943 *County of London Plan prepared for the London County Council* by J H Forshaw and Patrick Abercrombie, generally known as the Abercrombie plan. The plan recognised that the South Bank needed regenerating as far down as the Elephant and Castle, but as it concentrated on 'monumental central London' it stated it was

> chiefly concerned with the strip between the County Hall and London Bridge, with a depth back to York Road, Stamford Street and Southwark Street. Here in succession could be planned a riverside embankment, a series of buildings of varying character, starting, perhaps, with a great cultural centre, followed by theatres, concert halls and assembly halls; with offices at the new Waterloo Bridge head, terminating at the eastern extremity in commercial and other buildings, with Southwark Cathedral in a worthy setting as the completion of the scheme.

We learn from Andrew Saint that this 'germ of the idea for a cultural centre … comes neither from the LCC, nor from Abercrombie, but from the Shakespeare Memorial National Theatre Committee' – formed in 1908 from the merger of the campaigns to found a national theatre and to erect a memorial to William Shakespeare in London. 'Desperate to escape from a site that has proved too constricted for them opposite the V&A … the theatre people, with Bernard Shaw in tow, came cap in hand to the LCC in June 1942'.

They were offered a site between Waterloo and Hungerford Bridges but although Andrew Saint's argument of extensive 'planning improvisation' convinces, this did not come completely out of the blue. As George Rowell points out in his history of the Old

Vic: 'important negotiations had taken place between the Governors [of the Old Vic] and the Shakespeare Memorial National Theatre Committee' and these were minuted by the Governors as early as 1939 (10 March) at a time when the Old Vic was threatened with demolition during the 'Battle of Bridges'.

If the National Theatre authorities would accept the Old Vic Company as their planners and the Old Vic could accept the National Theatre as their building when the Old Vic was demolished, these two could become one.

Which of course they did when the National Theatre was waiting for their building and was based at the Old Vic.

If I were a planner … or a politician

The opinionated author G A Sala (1828–1895) despised the New Cut in Waterloo (see p. 414); yet he vigorously defended the Old Vic's 'blood-and-murder' pieces. In these dramas, he believed:

> for all the jargon, silliness and buffoonery, the immutable principles of right and justice are asserted; in which virtue in the end, is always triumphant, and vice is punished; in which cowardice and falsehood are hissed, and bravery and integrity applauded; in which were we to sift away the bad grammar, and the extravagant action, we should find the dictates of the purest and highest morality.

Published in 1859 in *Twice Round the Clock*, this was followed by an era of the highest respectability when the Old Vic was in the hands of Emma Cons and her disciples – they banished alcoholic drinks and set out to educate and civilise. They won: the Old Vic is still a major theatre, and Morley College, born in its back rooms, has turned into an impressive educational institution. These remarkable women created a new species of Londoners – cultivated paupers and cultured labouring classes. They have not left the area to try and do better elsewhere and they have not lost their raw attributes and their no-nonsense attitude but they are now wiser, more knowledgeable and experienced; they will have no hesitation in entering the development 'arena' and confronts Goliath. Remember, remember their Coin Street victory. Listen to them and empower them – they have achieved quite extraordinary things for the community.

Sources

(Full references for abbreviated entries in bibliography)

Harris; Winchester; Sadleir; Maugham; Dyos; Dyos & Wolff; Gibberd; Darley; Barker & Jackson 2008; Galinou & Hayes; Coleman; Rowell; *Survey of London* 23; Sacks. Also: Henry C Binford, 'Land Tenure, Social Structure, and Railway Impact in North Lambeth 1830–61' in *The Journal of Transport History*, Vol. II No 3, February 1974; *Clarkson Stanfield* 1793–1867, exhibition catalogue, Tyne and Wear County Council Museums, 1979; www.arthurlloyd.

co.uk/; Dyos; Dyos & Wolff; Woolf; Beatrice Webb, *My Apprenticeship*, 1926; Banham & Hillier; Graham Gibberd on William Capon's Lambeth watercolour in the *Newsletter of the Southwark & Lambeth Archaeological Society*, June 1984

Disclaimer: dividing the South Bank into neighbourhoods for organisational purposes has created some awkward splits. For ease of discussion several forms of entertainment crossing the Westminster Bridge Road 'frontier' have been drawn together. The entries on individual venues have remained in their 'correct' topographical arrangement.

Jeffery Camp's dream-like images taken from the South Bank, are not easy to integrate into a book devoted to factual history. Camp was drawn to water and 'naked vulnerability'. 'Plunge' (1987) has heroic undertones – it blends human nakedness and night time with the dark, dangerous waters of the Thames. It is dynamic and explosive with the act of plunging set off against the fiery red-yellow lights of the north bank constantly reflected in the water. It is a plunge into the depths of the city, scary and beautiful – just as the city itself.
(Photo courtesy of Art Space Gallery)

BOROUGH AND BANKSIDE
Sinners and saints, life and death

Memory and Sin — 444
    Cities, like people, have short term and long-term memory — 444
    Capital sins – Southwark's first recorded prostitute — 445
    Of prostitutes and the city — 445

Theatres — 448
    Chronology — 449
    Shakespeare & Company — 450
    An alternative to John Stow's vision of London — 453
    Society revealed through London comedies — 454

Dark shadows – death and burials — 454
    Cemetery heritage — 454
    Cholera — 458
    In our own times — 458
    Graveyard schools — 461

Burning to heaven — 462
    Southwark fires — 463
    And then there was Alice's fire … pray for her soul — 464
    The Art of Fire — 467
    Postscript — 471

Reconstructive surgery: — 471
    Tate Gallery — 473
    Allies & Morrison — 474
    Long after Shakespeare's days but before Bankside returned to culture — 478
    When the present embraces the past — 478

Previous:

John Bryce, 'Thames Arachnid', engraving, 2009. Before the sculpture 'Maman' was placed on Tate Modern's Thames terrace, it had loomed over the massive Turbine Hall, when the gallery first opened its doors in 2000. The gigantic spider was created by Louise Bourgeois (1911–2010) in 1999 for the grand opening of the Tate the following year, setting the tone for the gallery's ongoing programme of thought-provoking installations in the Turbine Hall. 'Maman' was subsequently moved outside where it created stunning vistas; it was acquired by Tate for its permanent collections in 2008. This is the largest of all Bourgeois' spiders – an autobiographical piece which casts a gloomy light on Bankside, merging the personal with the local and perhaps making Londoners shudder, still, at this formerly cursed part of London.

(© The artist)

Memory and sin

Cities, like people, have short-term and long-term memory

Long-term memory will be considered in the final chapter, but J J Magenis understood London's short-term memory very well. When in 1929 the *South London Press* published an article about the discovery of human bones on a site in Union Street, he wrote: 'any stranger would conclude that this discovery was a revelation and that the disturbance of the dead was an accident'. The site in question was Cross-Bones burial ground (now known as Cross-Bones Yard) and Mr Magenis, of 59 Nelson Square, remembered it was used as a fair ground when he was a teenager in the 1890s. When it was closed down following noise complaints, the *South London Press*, Mr Magenis recalled, specified that the plot could not be built upon because it was a disused burial ground – at the junction of Union and Redcross Streets.

> Since then the land has been ingeniously concealed … and now that the public memory has failed and its conscience stifled, building excavations are permitted, and local officials express surprise that human remains are recovered … Where are the champions of open spaces? They have permitted a known disused burial ground to be built upon and exhumation permitted without a Home Office order.

(From a press cutting in Southwark Archives)

In fact, Magenis himself had fallen victim to urban short-memory syndrome! In November and December 1883, Lord Brabazon, chairman of the Metropolitan Public Gardens, Boulevards and Playground Association had fought that very same battle in the pages of *The Times*, at a time when Cross-Bones Yard was used as a builder's yard.

> This ground is now being offered to the public, on lease as an "eligible building site" [for a block of industrial dwellings]. It is with a view to save this ground from such desecration, and to retain it as an open space for the use and enjoyment of the people that I now address you. The land is vested in the wardens of St Saviour's … I think your readers will regret to hear that such desecration of an ancient burial place is actually authorised by Act of Parliament, and I trust that it may not be long before such a scandal may become impossible through the passing of a short Act making it illegal to build over ground which has once been used for burial.

The irony is that in Roman times, extensive tracts of Southwark, were used as cemeteries, well separated, by the Thames, from the walled city (see p. 455). The Romans strongly believed in the physical separation of the dead and the living and *in-muro* burials were not permitted. A few centuries later Southwark is almost completely built over.

Cross-Bones Yard has become a *cause célèbre* in recent times – a development which hinges on the belief that this burial ground, on unconsecrated land, was used for the burial of prostitutes in the sixteenth century. (see p. 115)

Capital sins – Southwark's first recorded prostitute

Historian Martha Carlin may have found the earliest record for the Borough's first prostitute, a woman called 'Cristina la Frowe'. The Bishop of Winchester's Pipe Rolls (1299 to 1300–1) record that she was fined. 'Froes of Flanders', mentioned by John Stow, were notorious as Bankside prostitutes and Cristina may have been an early example of one of these. The term implies that they were 'alien' prostitutes, from Flanders. Records also suggest there were a substantial number of Flemish prostitutes – a claim which found echo in Henry VIII's 1546 edict when he declared prostitutes should depart by Easter 'to their natural countries with their bags and baggages'.

The assimilation of aliens into the life and fabric of London was a major theme in sixteenth and seventeenth centuries plays about the Royal Exchange since it was a place for foreign merchants to gather – and also St Paul's Cathedral, see p. 492. Within the context of the whorehouse, which harboured a significant number of aliens, the same principle was at work, demonstrated for instance by the main character of the 1632 play *Holland's Leaguer* based on the real-life character of Susan or Elizabeth Holland who ran an upmarket brothel in the former Manor House of Paris Garden. She turned into a local celebrity when she successfully evaded being seized and imprisoned soon after the authorities raided her establishment (see p. 109). She was the perfect example of the clever, emancipated business woman who could hold her own in the face of adversity. And it is worth remembering that this true story has lived on thanks to a play. In John Marston's *The Dutch Courtesan* (1605) the flesh trade signalled just another form of legitimate business and was described as 'the most worshipful of all the twelve companies' – referring to London's top twelve city guilds.

Of prostitutes and the city

From at least the mid-fourteenth century until the middle of the sixteenth century, Bankside was principally known for its taverns and its

This wall of bones, uncovered during the 1993 excavation of Cross-Bones Yard may have been formed at the end of the nineteenth century when warehouses were erected on the site. Disturbed bones were not removed but packed into the foundations of new buildings, within the construction trenches of the walls.
(Photo: Maggie Cox/MOLA)

Jan Steen, 'The Wench', c.1660–62, oil on canvas. Prostitution was a popular subject for Netherlandish painters; there was clearly a market for these works which could be found in respectable homes. The presence of a 'procuress' in the background removes any doubt as to the type of encounter we are viewing. As with cityscapes, Flemish painters led the way but much later, this work would be echoed in Hogarth's 'the Harlot's Progress' (scene 2, 1731).
(Musée de l'Hotel Sandelin, Saint-Omer. Image in the public domain; Wikimedia Commons)

'stews' or stewhouses, eighteen until 1506, when the number was reduced to twelve, according to John Stow.

The 'stews' – the name probably derives from the stew ponds which were prevalent in the neighbourhood – were 'a sequence of tenements and cottages, fronting on Bankside and backing onto gardens' which bordered Maiden Lane. We learn from John Stow and others that to attract custom from the north bank, the river facades of these houses 'were whitewashed … and their emblems were painted on the white walls rather than on hanging signs'. By 1608, Thomas Dekker gave a far more daring account of whorehouses in *Lantern and Candlelight*, though not necessarily in Southwark: 'the doors of notorious carted bawds like hell-gates stand night and day wide open, with a pair of harlots in taffeta-gowns, like two painted posts, garnishing out those doors, being better to the house than a double sign'.

Bankside brothels were regulated by a series of ordinances dating back to the twelfth century. They were under the direct control of the Bishop of Winchester who owned and profited from their trade, hence the term 'Winchester geese' to describe the prostitutes. This particular community has been well documented thanks to a fifteenth-century 'customary' which has survived (discussed in Martha Carlin's PhD thesis). The book of rules sought to protect the bawds from possible abuse from the stew-holders. The prostitutes themselves were not allowed to own premises. The stew keepers were often notorious while the prostitutes tended to be more shadowy figures – 'many of them seem to have come from the Low Countries'.

There had long been tolerance towards prostitution *per se* but it was the disorder which accompanied these establishments which was regarded as deeply problematic and in need of attention. Carlin recounts the grim tale of prostitute 'Founsing Besse' in 1548, and her fate reveals just how intolerant things had become. She had been 'banished out of divers wardes of this cittie', and when she was caught pleasuring one of the King's trumpeters in a garden of Finsbury Court, she was sent to one of the city's counters or prisons, then to the Standard in Cheapside:

> and their sett on the pillorie, her heare [hair] cut of by the eares and a paper sett on her breast declaring her vicious living, and so stoode from tenne of the clocke till eleven, which punishment hath bene an old auncient lawe in this citie of long tyme and now putt it vse againe.

This new form of cruelty towards prostitutes was indirectly created by Henry VIII in April 1546 when he ordered the closure of whorehouses in London. This immediately led to a two-tier system in prostitution: the 'common' whore operating in a licensed establishment which despite the royal edict failed to disappear, and the 'private' whore, freelance, entrepreneurial, clever and also mobile, for her own survival. Until 1546, London's red-light district was effectively on the south bank; Cock Lane in Smithfield was the only permitted site north of the river. Henry VIII's edict banished prostitution from Bankside, though only temporarily as it turned out. The royal move created in fact an explosion of new venues on sites scattered all around the City. According to theatre historian Jean Howard:

> Bawdy houses cluster at predictable places outside the city walls: Whitefriars in the west, Clerkenwell and Long Lane on the northwest, Whitecross Street in the north, Shoreditch in the northeast, Aldgate, East Smithfield, and St Katherine's to the east. In effect, the walled city was ringed by the equivalent of modern red light districts.

The brothel, far from providing 'a site for stories of women's social death and abjection' triggered 'narratives that attempt to come to terms with the entrepreneurial and multinational place that London was fast becoming'. Henry VIII's banishing edict led to emancipation for some women while encouraging episodes of horrible repression for others. Overall, however, Jean Howard concluded: 'Collectively, whore plays negotiate the changing place of women and strangers in the city'.

Bankside was London's pleasure district and the arrival of bear baiting arenas in the mid-1550s, soon highly popular, simply confirmed this identity. The Hope theatre, erected in 1613 as a joint enterprise between Edward Alleyn, by then fully retired from acting, and his father-in-law Philip Henslowe, even attempted to combine bear baiting and theatre. The venture was unsuccessful – the actors eventually rebelled against the unsatisfactory dual purpose of the venue and they left the Hope in 1617. It closed down in 1653, was demolished three years later but the saddest tale of all, recounts Julian Bowsher, was what happened to the seven remaining bears – they were 'shot to death … by a Company of Souldiers'.

Theatres

> [Elizabethan and Jacobean] London was not necessarily transparent to those who lived there. Demographic growth, physical expansion, high death rates, and high in-migration meant that the city was opaque and unfamiliar to many of its inhabitants. The theatre helped to make sense of city life. In play after play foreigners and strangers intermingled with London-born citizens … [The] stories … interpreted, hierarchized, and distinguished the incompetent from the boorish, the insider from the pariah, in the process of figuring new social relations … and new solutions to pressing urban problems.
>
> **Jean Howard,** *Theater of a City – the Places of London Comedy 1598–1642*, **2009**

Not only were bawdy houses suddenly ubiquitous around London and within the City, but they were also 'ubiquitous in early modern London comedies' observed Jean Howard. Life and theatre walking hand in hand was of course memorably expressed by Shakespeare when Jaques, in *As You Like It* (1599), uttered: 'All the world's a stage/And all the men and women merely players'. But Howard focused on less familiar territory, away from the well-known plays of William Shakespeare, or Christopher Marlowe examining the work of Thomas Dekker, Thomas Heywood, William Haughton, Shackerley Marmion and others. Before considering this less trodden path, we should evoke the popular and now almost mythical appeal of Elizabethan and Jacobean theatre on Bankside. It was magnificently captured by the film *Shakespeare in Love*.

Chronology of playhouses & other forms of entertainment on Bankside

Sources:
The Rose – Bankside's first theatre. Text by Elizabeth Gurr, 2009, Rose Theatre Trust
Jan Piggott, *Dulwich College – A History 1616–2008*, 2008
Julian Bowsher, *Shakespeare's London Theatreland*, 2012

1526	The **Bear Garden**, a 'Game place', was used as an animal house, from that date.
1572	The 'Act for the punishment of vagabonds' required all actors to be in permanent repertory companies with aristocratic patrons. Re-issued in 1604.
1576	James Burbage built London's first enduring theatre: **'The Theatre'** at Shoreditch. The company based there became known as **Lord Strange's Men**.
1576	James Savage built a new playhouse at **Newington Butts**; but there is very little documentation to judge its significance.
1577	Opening of **The Curtain**, close to The Theatre, Shoreditch, which would later be operated by James Burbage: 'the largest and longest standing of the early Elizabethan playhouses', and able to hold up to 1400 people. Archaeologists established that its stage 'was 14 metres from stage left to stage right, running across the width of the playhouse ... ideal for hosting ... sensational dynamic scenes' (MOLA blog, 30 January 2018).
1579	Sir John Tylney (d. 1610) was appointed Master of Revels (a post established in 1545).
1580s-90s	Successive Lord Mayors tried to ban plays, so the playing companies worked outside the City.
1583	The third Bear Garden on Bankside collapsed in January with great loss of life.
1587	Fifth custom-built playhouse built: Philip Henslowe's **the Rose**, the first successful playhouse on Bankside. The site of the Rose was leased to Philip Henslowe (1555/6-1616), a property entrepreneur, as early as 1584.
1592	Edward Alleyn (1566-1626) fell out with James Burbage in 1591 and switched to the Rose Theatre in February, taking with him a number of Lord Strange's Men. Alleyn was the greatest actor of the period and the Queen's favourite. He made the roles of Tamburlaine (*Tamburlaine the Great*), Faustus (*Doctor Faustus*) and Barabas (*The Jew of Malta*) famous.
1592	Shakespeare arrived in London. His 'lost years' were between 1585 when he was in Stratford and 1592. The playwright (1564-1616) must have done much of his early theatregoing at the Rose, seeing and learning his craft from plays by Christopher Marlowe, Robert Greene, Thomas Lodge and Thomas Kyd. Shakespeare will always be strongly associated with the Globe where the Chamberlain's Men were based.
1592	Philip Henslowe enlarged the Rose. The playhouse worked throughout the year, six afternoons a week. This enlarged second Rose lasted six months before being closed along with all London's playhouses due to the plague.
1592	In October Alleyn married Henslowe's stepdaughter – Joan Woodward – and began a partnership with Henslowe which lasted until the latter's death in 1616.
1594	London's theatres reopened. The Lord Chamberlain licensed two new companies drawing the best players from several companies to form the **Chamberlain's Men** (The Theatre) and the **Admiral's Men** (The Rose): they had protection and status.
1594	Henslowe purchased the lease of the **Bear Garden** where they baited bears and bulls.

1595	Bankside's second theatre, the **Swan**, opened its doors with an 'illegal' company (i.e. not licensed by the Crown): **Pembroke's Men**.
1597	In Shoreditch The Theatre's ground lease ran out: when the landlord refused to renew the lease, the company transported the playhouse timbers across the Thames and re-erected the same on Bankside. It was renamed **The Globe** and could accommodate 3000 people.
1599	Opening of the Globe on Bankside. The Rose and the Globe, were now side by side, run by London's only two licensed companies, though by that date the Rose, which had always been a small theatre, was an ageing building.
1603	At the death of Queen Elizabeth, King James became patron of the Lord Chamberlain's Company of actors, renamed the **King's Men**.
1604	Shakespeare moved to North London.
1606	By January 1606, Henslowe had clearly abandoned the Rose which had a new owner; the Rose was subsequently demolished and stripped to its foundations. Archaeological findings indicate that it was 'more likely to have been carefully dismantled, rather than wantonly demolished'.
1606	The carpenter Peter Street, who built the Fortune theatre for Henslowe in Cripplegate, rebuilt the Bear Garden and its stables.
1613	Henslowe & Alleyn pulled down the Bear Garden and on the same site built a unique multi-purpose playhouse and baiting-arena, naming it the **Hope**.
1613	The Globe burnt down – a spark ignited the thatched roof. It reopened the following year with a tiled roof on the same foundations.
1613	Shakespeare finally left London to return to Stratford.
1616	Death of Shakespeare; death of Henslowe (Alleyn inherited most of their joint properties).
1626	Death of Edward Alleyn.
1642	Closure of the theatres.
1644	After that date the demolition of the Globe was ordered by order of Parliament under the Puritans. The site at the eastern foot of Blackfriars Bridge is commemorated by a plaque put up by 'Shakespeare Reading Society of London and subscribers in the UK and India' (see p. 303).

Shakespeare and Company

Allow me to explain about the theatre business. The natural condition is one of insurmountable obstacles on the road to disaster.

Lines spoken by the owner of the Rose playhouse in the film 'Shakespeare in Love'

Could anyone bring to life the companies of men who swarmed London's first theatres more vividly than 'Shakespeare in Love', directed by John Madden and released in 1998? The theatrical world at the onset of the seventeenth century was extremely complicated. Theatres appeared, disappeared – burned down, collapsed, and were rebuilt, or changed location. Companies similarly moved around and changed their names; actors

switched allegiance or fled the plague – a feared sickness that shut theatres and led to the introduction of new venues; with *playhouses* open to the sky and *theatres* in comfortable interiors, while crueller activities were found in bear gardens. The competition between all of these was fierce in its pursuit of profits, success, or mere survival.

The script of *Shakespeare in Love* by Marc Norman and Tom Stoppard conjures up London in 1593, exploring the triangular arrangement upon which this world depended. Royalty and aristocrats could be found in one camp, a company of actors based on the north bank in another camp (the Chamberlain's Men at The Theatre, Shoreditch) and a rival theatre company based on the south bank (the Admiral's Men at the Rose theatre), all scheming and working alongside two silent and disapproving partners: the City of London and the Church.

This book focuses on what was happening on the south bank but the dialogue between the two banks was a vital component of that understanding … until the men on the north bank became those on the south bank! The first two 'proper' London theatres appeared in 1576 – James Burbage built The Theatre in Shoreditch while James

Playwrights John Fletcher (1579–1625) on the right and Francis Beaumont (1584–1616) on the left collaborated on a number of Jacobean plays. We know from John Aubrey's *Lives* that 'they lived together on the Bankside, not far from the playhouse, both bachelors; lay together (from Sir James Hales) etc; had one wench in the house between them, which they did so admire; the same clothes and cloak, etc'. Both works, by unknown artists, are in the National Portrait Gallery – oil on oak for Fletcher (c. 1620) and mezzotint for Beaumont (1740s).

(© National Portrait Gallery, London)

An audience in the Globe Theatre, 2019 the public was allowed to choose which play, out of three on offer, would be performed on that particular summer day, an exciting but uncommon event.
(Photo: Pete Le May)

Savage built a barely documented theatre at Newington Butts (Elephant and Castle). The latter may have failed, hence the sparsity of evidence, but Burbage's establishment in Shoreditch flourished, soon attracting competition in the shape of 'The Curtain' theatre a year later.

Professional acting had started in the late 1530s and was established in London by the 1540s when actors were performing at inns or hiring large halls to put on shows. So, what drove the building of expensive theatres when the infrastructure of halls and inns seemed adequate? It was the threat of the 1572 'Act for the Punishment of Vagabonds', introduced by Elizabeth I and re-issued in 1604. A theatre company with no fixed abode and no permission to exercise their trade would no longer be tolerated – the Act required actors to be in permanent repertory companies, patronised by the aristocracy who would be held responsible for them.

Philip Henslowe's Rose was London's fifth purpose-built playhouse, when it opened its doors in 1587. It was Bankside's first successful playhouse – for a few years Christopher Marlowe was its star writer and from 1591, the great actor Edward Alleyn, having fallen out with James Burbage, switched from The Theatre in Shoreditch to the Rose, becoming its star actor and strengthening his ties to owner Philip Henslowe by marrying his stepdaughter, Joan Woodward.

In 'Shakespeare in Love', the competition between the Curtain and the Rose shadowed that of The Theatre and the Rose in real life. Side by side competition followed ten years later, in 1597, when The Theatre, unable to renew its lease at Shoreditch, opted for a suitably dramatic solution: the Burbage brothers (father James had recently died) decided to dismantle their playhouse in secret, in the dead of night, to move it to Bankside. Historians Barker and Jackson attempted to reconstruct this spectacular flight in *The Pleasures of London*. The route probably avoided the City where the authorities might have created difficulties, therefore doubling the length of the final journey. Next, they pitched on Bankside and rebuilt The Theatre next to the Rose; it was renamed The Globe – Richard Burbage (son of James) was its star actor and William Shakespeare its star playwright. In the words of Barker and Jackson:

> The stages were now set for the battle of the two supreme actor-managers of the day: Burbage at the Globe with Shakespeare as his resident playwright and Alleyn at the Rose occasionally reviving Christopher Marlowe, the author with whom he had made his name as an actor.

An alternative to John Stow's vision of London

Jean Howard casts a perceptive light on two opposed trends in Elizabethan London. She describes the work of historian John Stow as that of someone who regarded change as a sign of:

> decline and decay and often wrote with nostalgia about what he felt to be a vanishing city … For him, the important places of London were its guildhalls, churches, and public endowments such as hospitals.

Howard contrasts Stow's nostalgic text where contemporary developments such as the birth of the theatre are barely mentioned, with the approach of his contemporary, Thomas Dekker (c.1572–1632), focusing on his 1609 prose satirical pamphlet – *The Gull's Hornbook* (a basic guide for gullible fools) and explaining:

> If, for example, in Stow's city the highest virtue is charity, in the London of Dekker's pamphlet it is fashionability. All advice to the gull rests on the premise that making a good appearance is in every instance of the utmost importance. That means being seen at the right places in the right clothes and saying the right things … But in doing so it strikingly calls attention to a cityscape defined less by churches and guildhalls than by places of consumption and pleasure and it points to the new practices they encourage.

At this point we might reasonably expect the author to home in on Bankside. It was clearly London's most famous leisure district, duly acknowledged by its many visitors. But Howard does so, indirectly only, when she brings to the fore the work of Thomas Heywood (1575–1641), 'that naïve and often-scorned champion of the city … who recognized the special nature of the link between London and its theaters'. In his *An Apology for Actors* (1612) Heywood writes: 'Playing is an ornament to the Citty, which strangers of all Nations … report of in their Countries'; also inviting us to share his vision of London as offering world-class theatre, for instance through this comparison with Rome:

in the midst of the river Tyber, standing on pillars and arches, the foundation wrought under water like London-bridge, the Nobles and ladyes in their Barges and Gondelayes, landed at the very stayres of the galleryes. After these they composed others [theatres], but differing in forme …and every such was called Circus, the frame Globe-like, & merely round.

This surprising juxtaposition between the theatres of Rome and London evokes the ancient London Bridge and the crossing of the Thames in ferry-boats for those going to the theatre, circular-shaped structures in both cities: 'One can read, as in a watery mirror, the lineaments of one city in the features of the other'. Heywood ranked London theatre on a par with that of Ancient Greece and Rome describing London's contribution to the art as being of international stature.

Society revealed through London comedies

In the film 'Shakespeare in Love' there is a delightful sequence set at the Whitehall theatre when Elizabeth I (Judi Dench) gives in to hysterical laughter at the sight of a small dog causing mischief in the middle of a scene. A few minutes later she is filmed nodding off while watching a poetic and deeply serious declaration of love to Sylvia in the play *The Two Gentlemen of Verona*. The scene makes a memorable point since the universal appeal of comedy is established using the country's highest symbol of power – its sovereign.

Comedy and satire are excellent tools for imagining and interpreting life in the city, for acting out its problems and introducing possible solutions. Howard interrogated Elizabethan and Jacobean plays on four themes. First, commercial London, which is represented by the newly acquired Royal Exchange (1571); next, law and order, using London's prisons – in particular the counters which dealt with debtors (south London prisons, so numerous, are mentioned but under investigated); third, social order or disorder, through the presence, even abundance of 'Bawdy Houses' often featured as 'generic' places in many plays; finally, London's West End is examined through the prism of 'Ballrooms and Academies'. Unsurprisingly, Southwark took the lion's share when it came to prisons and bawdy houses.

Dark shadows – death and burials

Cemetery heritage

This book's first chapter introduced the idea of Southwark as a City of the Dead. This neighbourhood was conveniently located outside the city walls and since the Romans did not believe in mixing the dead with the living, Southwark – and other suburbs – had the grim task of assuming the role of valley of tears. Not that the Romans were as sentimental about

---

Cross-Bones Yard

Archaeology and human remains

All work at the Cross-Bones Yard, including the removal of bodies,

was carried out using a small team of five, all of whom had several years of human burial excavation experience … under the auspices of a Licence for the Removal of Human Remains, issued by the Home Office on 16 November 1992.

This lays out the conditions which have to be observed, the relevant one being that:

"the removal must be carried out with due care and attention to decency; the ground shall be screened from public view while the work is in progress and the remains shall be examined under the arrangements of The Museum of London".

(From MoLAS 1999 – see Bibliography)

BOROUGH AND BANKSIDE – SINNERS AND SAINTS, LIFE AND DEATH

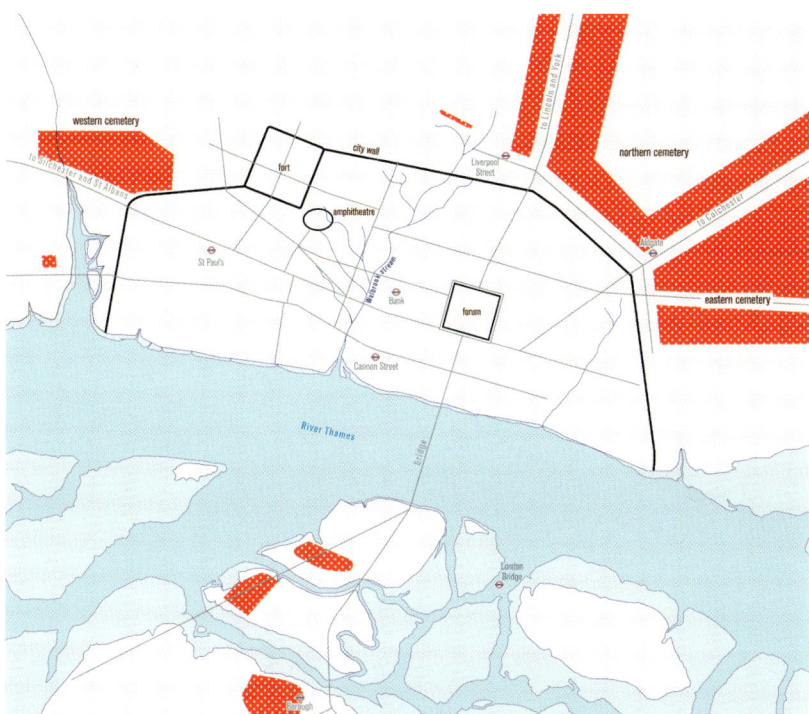

These generalised maps show Southwark's close association with death in Roman times and also how the whole of the South Bank was engulfed in the 1849 cholera pandemic – the second in London, with the greatest number of casualties.

This map was created in 2018 to contextualise the Museum of London exhibition 'The Roman Dead' presented at their Docklands Museum. The string of cemeteries in a Southwark made up of islands and streams, shows the large percentage of land used for the dead, the curator admitting that 'archaeologists have only found a tiny portion of the Roman burials in London'.

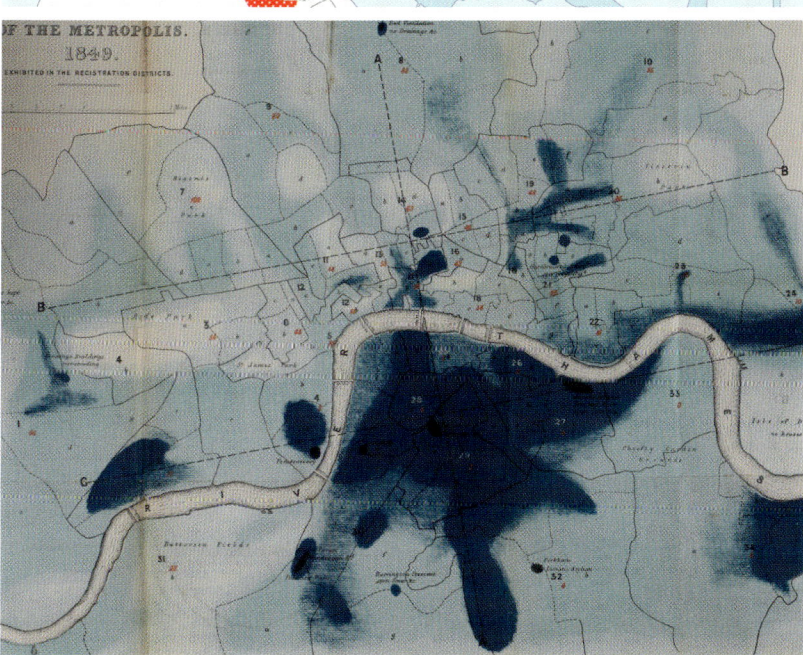

The cholera map carries a Reference section which gives mortality figures for each parish: St Saviour's (331), St Olave's (364), Bermondsey (670), St George Southwark (563), Newington (486), Lambeth (959, this figure includes Brixton). The mapmaker has drawn an 'axis of evil' which cuts through the South Bank horizontally, linking three notorious danger zones, shown in black. From east to west: 'Jacob's Island Poisoned Water open Ditches' – one of London's worst slums; then close to the Elephant and Castle 'Defective Sewerage &c.'; finally 'Lambeth Workhouse'.

(MOLA for the mapping of Roman cemeteries and Wellcome Collection for the Cholera map, the latter in the public domain, Wikimedia Commons)

death as we are. They 'knew' the dead continued to live, in the underworld. However, while the rules for juxtaposing cemeteries and the living have since changed, the instinctive revulsion at the physical blend of the two has not gone away; it is very much alive and manifests itself through increased respect for human bones (see text in box) and a determination

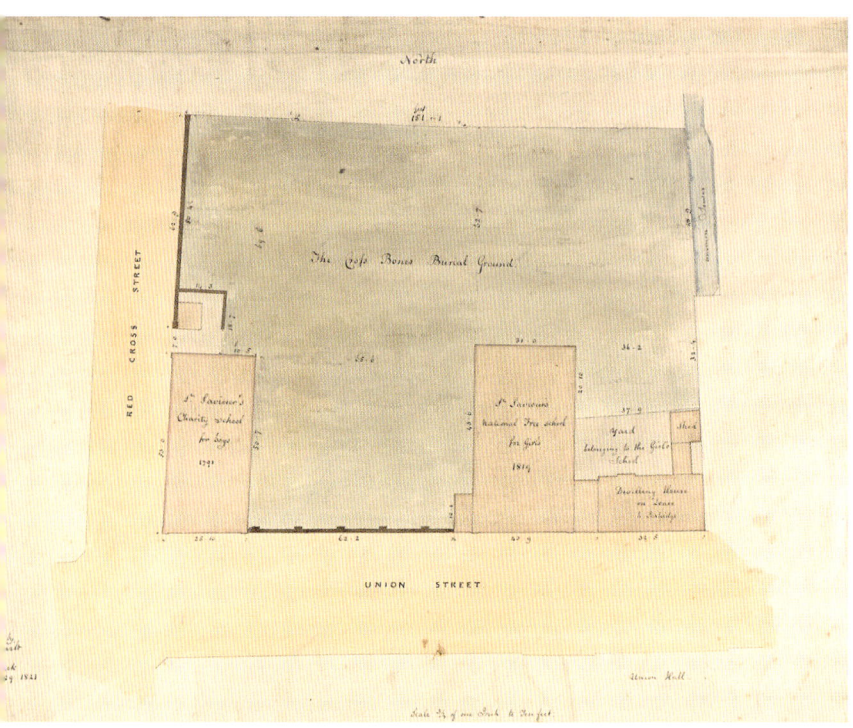

St Saviour's vestry commissioned the architect George Gwilt to survey the Cross-Bones burial ground in 1821. This plan shows its position at the corner of Union and Red Cross Streets. The architect's own house, not shown in this plan, is immediately to the right of the 'Dwelling House'. Twenty-eight years after this drawing was made, the Gwilt family was still occupying the house and battling the vestry for rectifying the atrocious side-effects of living next to Cross-Bones Yard. Also see p. 195 for street elevation.
© London Metropolitan Archives (City of London)

to treat burial grounds as sacred, in the sometimes futile belief that this is possible. In Roman days *Londinium* was encircled by cemeteries in what was the outskirts of the city but now very much part of London. City dwellers are living on a carpet of bones, some deeply buried others resting in shallow graves.

The uncomfortable juxtaposition of the dead with the living was documented in graphic detail in Borough in the eighteenth and nineteenth centuries. The sequence of events has been reconstructed by archaeologists. Slowly but surely, the disposal of the dead in the parish of St Saviour's, a growing and never-ending task in an expanding city, overwhelmed the parish authorities. They had three burial grounds at their disposal: St Saviour's churchyard, the almshouses' College ground in Park Street and the Cross-Bones burial ground – the last was reserved for the burial of the poor and was the first to show early signs of misuse. Early concerns were addressed in 1831: a committee for improving Cross-Bones yard was set up, the authorities noting 'with apprehension the reported progress of that awful malady the Cholera Morbus'. The minutes of 15 November 1831 recorded that it was 'necessary immediately to adopt the measures recommended by Government for cleaning the streets, courts and alleys, and the houses of the poor of this parish'. Little did they know the infection was water-borne, rather than air-borne. It soon became clear that 'the ground was nearly full of coffins, and but little, if any, room can be found for further burials in consequence of the irregular manner of burial heretofore'. It was closed the following year (1832), but reopened on 22 March 1833. A few years later the author of *Gatherings from Graveyards* (1839), George A Walker, provided an explanation. It seemed that the reopening had been partial:

> the greater portion of this ground has not been opened for some time past, in consequence of its very crowded state; the remaining part, however, is still used for interments, many of the poor Irish are buried in it.

Walker's text made it clear that the state of all burial grounds in the parish was appalling, one of the grave diggers confessing the lack of 'sufficient depth' and having to give just 'a covering to the body'. In a footnote he recounted how, despite all this, the vestry meeting of 20 February 1839 'was holden "for the purpose of considering the propriety of re-opening the Cross-Bones burying ground"'. The arguments he recorded describe the difficulties of this issue:

> The ground had been closed about two years (*the time generally allowed for the destruction of bodies!*) and it was moved that it be re-opened; the mover of the resolution stating, that in consequence of the aversion generally manifested to bury in what is named the "Irish corner", many bodies were taken out of the parish to be buried. This corner, however, had been cleared, and room made for about a thousand bodies. One gentleman argued that "if the graves had been made deeper, hundreds more corpses might have been buried there". Another admitted that it really was too bad to bury within eighteen inches of the surface, in such a crowded neighbourhood, and it was even hinted that "the clearing", viz. the digging up and removal of the decayed fragments of flesh and bones, with the pieces of coffin, etc. would be the best course, were it not for the additional expense.
> The funds of the vestry and the health of the living were here placed in opposite scales – the former had its preponderance.

In a letter of August 1849 Mrs Gwilt who lived next door to the Cross-Bones ground, described the situation in graphic words:

> we have all this sickly Summer almost daily witnessed the most distressing sights: our remonstrances are vain – in the bone house with its open grating which is not more than eight or ten yards from five of our windows we have during these last fatal six weeks had sometimes as many as from three to nine bodies lying in their shells [shrouds?] at a time for days (as many as ten days) in the aforesaid Bone house close under our windows – One of these shells contained the body of a woman who was brought here supposed dead from Cholera, but actually broke a blood vessel, trying to get out, whilst being carried along she not being dead then –

Mrs Gwilt was a respected member of the community, wife of George Gwilt Junior (1775–1856), the architect often employed by the parish, who notably restored St Saviour's church and set up a museum of antiquities at his home in Union Street – the home which the architect's father, George Gwilt the elder, had built (see p. 195). Having turned a blind eye to the problem for almost twenty years, the parish refuted most of the points raised by Mrs Gwilt, later describing them as 'false and exaggerated statements'. The Board of Health, on Mrs Gwilt's side, tried and failed to close the ground. The matter only came to a head three years and more complaints later when another damning report from Dr Sutherland on 25 November 1852 concluded: 'the Burial Ground accommodation for St Saviour's parish' was 'entirely inadequate to the wants of the population'. Of Cross-Bones yard he wrote: 'It is crowded with dead and many fragments of undecayed bones, some even entire are mixed up with the earth of the mounds over the graves.'

The burial ground was finally closed on 24 October 1853. The solution to the seemingly insoluble problem of caring for the dead came in the form of private cemetery companies and suburban burial grounds on an industrial scale. For the South Bank it was Brookwood Cemetery near Woking, founded by Act of Parliament in 1852 by the London Necropolis and National Mausoleum Company. The southern half of the ground, designated Anglican, was consecrated on 7 November 1854 and opened to the public a few days later. Access to the cemetery was by train from a dedicated platform at Waterloo station operated by the London Necropolis Company. The company relocated from York Street to Westminster Bridge Road in 1902; this second main entrance survives to this day (see p. 412). Brookwood is the largest cemetery in England, Grade 1 listed, and described on Historic England's website as follows: 'to house London's dead'.

Cholera

The arrival of Brookwood cemetery came after two Asiatic cholera pandemics which reached London, one in 1831–32 – the Board of Health was set up in 1832 – the other in 1848–49 (with further repercussions in 1854). These, on top of the population increase, must have placed serious pressure on burial grounds. We have seen how the first pandemic was mentioned in connection with Cross-Bones Yard; 6536 lives were lost in London in 1831–32.

The second outbreak in 1848–49 was mapped showing the disproportionate toll which was paid by south London (see p. 455); this time 14137 lives were lost in London. Yet the most talked about outbreak was that which affected Soho in 1854 because it was only then that Dr John Snow's theory of water-borne illness, first published in 1849 but refined by his experiment in Soho, was accepted by the authorities (Snow observed the spread of cholera around the contaminated water pump in Broad Street). 10738 lives were lost in London during that outbreak.

In our own times

In the 1990s Cross-Bones Yard received a new 'lease of life'.

> Those buried in the Cross Bones ground were the poorest members of a poor community. Many were unable to afford their own funerals and had to rely on the parish to cover the costs. Around 18% of those buried in the ground came from the parish workhouse, where many people were recorded as 'not able bodied' and a significant number had suffered accidents. The state of the burial ground, as recorded in the letters of complaint received by the vestry, shows the lack of care with which the dead poor were treated.

From MoLAS 1999 in bibliography

This account is not simply that of someone feeling the wretchedness of the human condition or of someone's call for arms to implement social reform, but from someone who confronted, physically, the plight of the poor

BOROUGH AND BANKSIDE – SINNERS AND SAINTS, LIFE AND DEATH   459

In its latest incarnation, Cross-Bones Yard has become a memorial to the outcast, under the protection of the Virgin Mary (opposite). The moving tributes people pay to their loved ones are plastered across the iron gates of the former burial ground which has now become a garden of remembrance.
(© The author, 2018 and 2021)

in Victorian London. The statement comes from the archaeologist(s) who, in the 1990s, excavated a small section of Cross-Bones burial ground.

Archaeologists became involved with the site when a series of evaluations, excavations and watching briefs were carried out by the Museum of London between 1992 and 1997 as a result of the Jubilee line being given a green light in 1989. The site of Cross-Bones Yard was chosen to house a new electricity sub-station, so the work undertaken was within the footprint of this sub-station. The results were published in 1999. The Crossbones website takes up the story:

> In 1996, the writer John Constable had a vision in which 'The Goose' revealed to 'John Crow' [John Constable] the secret history of Crossbones. This was the inspiration for *The Southwark Mysteries* – the epic cycle of poems, plays and esoteric lore performed in the Globe and the Cathedral – and informed the magical works at Crossbones: the creation of a shrine at the red iron gates in Redcross Way, dedicated to 'the outcast dead', and now a garden of remembrance.

The 'Goose' was one of the 'Winchester geese' as Bankside prostitutes were known in the sixteenth century and 'John Crow' was local writer and spiritual guide John Constable. This vision harked back to the unconsecrated 'single woman's churchyard' mentioned by John Stow in 1598 though this author provided no geographical location for it. In her PhD thesis Martha Carlin observed that 'the story is supported by the parish register, which carefully notes the burials of prostitutes as e.g., 'Alys a senglewoman' or 'Margaret Savage common woman' while taking only rare note of the occupations of others buried'. Carlin was also able to trace the association of the Cross-Bones site with Stow's women's burial ground to the *Victorian* historians William Rendell and Philip Norman (see bibliography).

True or not, this new urban myth has taken hold. Crime writer Kate Rhodes chose the site for her novel *Crossbones Yard* published in 2012. In the novel, the murdered body of a woman was not immediately visible behind 'the two ironwork gates … with dozens of ribbons and tags of paper hanging from the railings … A second look confirmed that my eyes were telling the truth. A hand was lying on the pavement besides my foot'. Little more is said about Cross-Bones Yard but the heroine – a psychologist at Guy's Hospital includes other fascinating (and morbid) details from the neighbourhood:

> There are two mortuaries at Guy's. The first is for people who die under normal circumstances. Their bodies are kept cool, between 2°C and 4°C for a week or two, before being taken away for burial or cremation. The second is the cold room, where the temperature stays below freezing point, between -15°C and -25°C. Bodies spend months or even years there, while forensic work is done, or the unidentified wait to be claimed. Roman Catholics would describe it as a particularly chilly version of limbo.

Elsewhere Sondra Hausner, currently Professor of Anthropology of Religion at Oxford University, has explored the way in which the new spiritual movement to emerge from Cross-Bones Yard, is commemorating 'the souls of medieval prostitutes believed to

View of St Saviour's (free) grammar school overlooking the churchyard of St Saviour's parish church (south side); this engraving has been dated c. 1815.
© London Metropolitan Archives (City of London)

be buried there', under the guidance of John Constable. These words come from the back cover of her book *The Spirits of Crossbones Graveyard – Time, Ritual and Sexual Commerce in London*, published in 2016.

Graveyard schools

Cemeteries and cholera have cast their respective shadows on this chapter but there is another intriguing development to come out of this gloomy survey – it was the parish's decision in 1791 to build a Boys' school on part of Cross-Bones Yard in the south west corner. This was followed by a Girls' school in 1819 in the south east corner; both entrances were in Union Street with the back of the buildings overlooking the cemetery or what was left of it. This group of buildings would later be known as St Saviour's Charity School – sometimes confused with St Saviour's Grammar School. When you consider the distressing scenes described by Mrs Gwilt a few decades later (see above), this makes one wonder whether such a thing could ever be desirable? The juxtaposition was no doubt driven by financial factors and made more acceptable by the more casual relationship people had with death at that time.

However, the study of historic maps and images makes it clear that the association of schools and churchyards at Cross-Bones was by no means exceptional. St Saviour's grammar school overlooked St Saviour's churchyard on the south side of what is now a pleasant green space south of Southwark Cathedral; while St Olave's grammar school in Tooley Street overlooked the Flemish burial ground (see p. 219). In neighbouring Lambeth parish, a school for girls was also built overlooking the churchyard in Lambeth High Street – the land for both having been donated by

Archbishop Thomas Tenison in 1715 who specified what its use should be.

Burning to heaven

The association between children and death may have seemed quite normal to Victorian Londoners. But Cross-Bones Yard was on a site which seemed to have thrived around this particular connection. Apart from the charity school for boys and girls which was built over the southern end of the graveyard (still there in 1950 according to the *Survey of London*), a Catholic church sprang up across the road, on the east side of Redcross Street, soon followed by a school. As if that was not enough, a Ragged School appeared opposite in 1907, on the south west corner of Redcross and Union Streets – a third school within a stone's throw of the other two.

Poverty allied to the presence of all these children led to the founding in the nearby Mint district of the Evelina Children's Hospital. It was sparked by a personal tragedy which was gently coaxed towards a much-needed facility for the Borough. When on 4 December 1866, Baron Ferdinand de Rothschild (1839–1898) suffered the agony of a still-born baby and later that day also lost Evelina, the young wife he had married the previous year, he became determined to create a memorial in her name. His first thoughts were for a Lying-in hospital, but his friend and adviser Dr Andrew Farre, the obstetrician who had attended Evelina's confinement and birth, suggested a children's hospital. As a young child Evelina had visited the Southwark slums with her mother and Rothschild purchased the site of South Sea Court for his new hospital, in the notorious Mint district

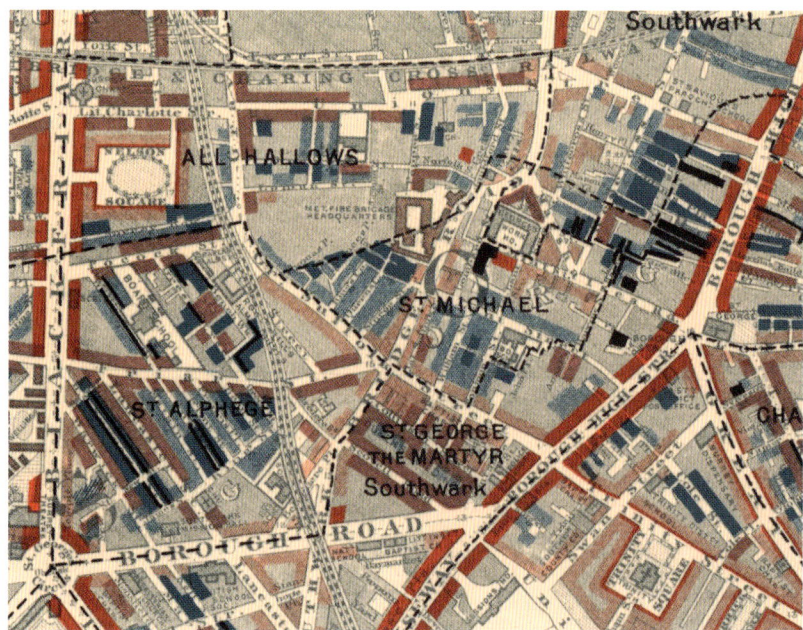

This detail from Charles Booth's 1898–1899 poverty map highlights the Borough's worst slums – the Mint, across the road from St George's Church and the parish of St Alphege, east of Blackfriars Road. According to Booth's key, the areas filled in with black ink denote 'Lowest class. Vicious, semi-criminal'; those in dark blue 'Very poor, casual. Chronic want'; and those in paler blue, 'Poor. 18s. to 21s. a week for a moderate family'.
(London School of Economics. Image in the public domain)

and just across the road from the London Fire Brigade headquarters at 94 Southwark Bridge Road.

Child mortality figures were high, particularly in the Borough where two substantial clusters of extremely poor housing spread across the southern half of the neighbourhood: the large Mint district west of Borough High Street, where St George's Workhouse stood, but also the parish of St Alphege east of Blackfriars Road, which, despite the presence of a church, a Board School and two almshouses (in Hill Street) descended into a slum.

However, it was the death of two children, their parents and their carer in a house fire in 1885 that sent waves of compassion throughout this neighbourhood, the South Bank and the whole of London. Like the dead of Cross-Bones Yard, their memory lives on across the years.

Southwark fires

> The conflagration had burned for two days and consumed over three hundred yards of wharf and warehouse, damage unequalled since the Great Fire of 1666, damage not to be seen again until the Blitz.
>
> There had been other fires, of course: the Mustard Mills in 1814, Topping's Wharf in 1843, Bankside in 1855; it seemed to him that fire was as necessary to Southwark as birth and death, that it provided an essential means of growth and regeneration.
>
> Deborah Crombie, *In a Dark House*, 2005 (the Tooley Street Fire of 1861)

There had been many other significant fires across the centuries … The 1212 fire destroyed the unfinished St Mary Overie's Priory – the future Southwark Cathedral – along with the first incarnation of St Thomas' Hospital. The Globe theatre burnt down in 1613, only taking a couple of hours after its thatched roof caught fire. Then came the fire which broke out on London Bridge in 1632/3, destroying countless houses. One of Southwark's major fires took place in 1676, ten years after the Great Fire of London, starting 'att one Mr. Welsh, an oilman, neer St. Margaret Hill, betwixt the George and Talbot Innes' and 500 houses were lost at the northern end of Southwark. Barely thirteen years later, the 1689 fire which started in a stationer's shop on Borough High Street burnt down another 180 houses. In 1725 a fire which had begun in Tooley Street spread to London Bridge. King's Bench prison burnt down twice, in 1780 and 1799, while the Clink went up in flames in 1780 and was not rebuilt. The vast Albion Mills went up in smoke in 1791 and the Royal Circus, at the other end of Great Surrey Street, burnt down in 1805. It was the turn of the Mustard Mills in Bankside in 1814 and then Barclay Perkins Brewery in 1832. The 1843 fire at Topping's Wharf virtually destroyed St Olave's church in Tooley Street while Bankside fell to the flames in 1855, but the most spectacular fire of them all, the largest since the Great Fire of London, contemporaries claimed, was the 1861 Tooley Street fire which burnt for two weeks, causing a massive £2,000,000 of damages and taking the life of local hero James Braidwood, commander of the London Fire Brigade (see p. 507).

Samuel Pepys, the great chronicler of London life and the author of one of the best eye witness accounts of the Great Fire of London – took to the river and then to Bankside to describe its awe-inspiring spectacle. On Sunday 2 September 1666, he wrote:

> All over the Thames, with one's face in the wind, you were almost burned with a shower of firedrops … When we could endure no more upon the water; we [went] to a little ale-house on the Bankside, over against the Three Cranes, and there staid till it was dark almost, and saw the fire grow; and, as it grew darker, appeared more and more, and in corners and upon steeples, and between churches and houses, as far as we could see up the hill of the City, in a most horrid malicious bloody flame, not like the fine flame of an ordinary fire … We staid till, it being darkish, we saw the fire as only one entire arch of fire from this to the other side the bridge, and in a bow up the hill for an arch of above a mile long: it made me weep to see it. The churches, houses, and all on fire and flaming at once; and a horrid noise the flames made, and the cracking of houses at their ruins.

And then there was Alice's fire … pray for her soul …

When: the night of 23 April 1885

The Street: Union Street which had once been associated with royalty. In 1682 it ran in two sections between Gravel Lane (now Great Suffolk Street) and Redcross Street – the western section was named Duke Street and the eastern section Queen Street. This was until 1781 when Queen Street was extended east to Borough High Street. The extension soon acquired a Hall (Union Hall) and the Surrey Dispensary next door. This stretch of road was renamed Union Street in 1813. The Horwood map shows that at that date, the continuation of Union Street across the High Street was a new street named King Street – Union Street effectively linking Queen Street and King Street. Eventually the name 'Union Street' prevailed and now the street runs between Blackfriars Bridge Road and Borough High Street – King Street having been renamed Newcomen Street.

During Alice's short life the major cultural landmark in Union Street was the Raglan Music Hall at No 172. This venue had several incarnations/names but had livened up the street since the 1840s. It was in business until 1892, but twice succumbed to flames – the first time in 1871 and the second time in 1883, each time it was rebuilt. So fire was no stranger on this street.

The House was at 194 Union Street, a few doors up from the Raglan

This map detail is based on G W Bacon's 1888 map of London. The sites of Alice's fire (1) and of White Cross Street (2) which was renamed Ayres Street in her honour have been highlighted. The village-type hall, designed by E Hoole for Octavia Hill (3), was embellished with murals of every day heroes.

(© Stephen Conlin)

TERRIBLE FIRE IN THE BORO'–LOSS OF FIVE LIVES

'Alice's fire' at 194 Union Street, started in the early hours of the morning when everyone was asleep.
(From *The Illustrated Police News* of 2 May 1885; British Library, London, UK)

Music Hall, on the same side of the road. Neither building has survived but you can still see nearby examples of the stereotypical three storey house with a shop on the ground floor– for instance at No 35, but also 37 or 61.

The Shop – an oilshop which, according to Trade Directories, had been in the ownership of John Chubb between 1875 and 1885. But clearly Mr Chubb was not operating the business himself: his lessee, Henry Chandler, had been there since 1881 or 1882 having previously run a similar business in Clerkenwell (oil, paint and paraffin).

The Family: Henry Chandler had married Mary Ann Ayres from Isleworth in 1877. Their first child was born in 1879 and three more came in rapid succession. Mary Ann, who had had poor health prior to being married, needed help with the children and her young sister Alice offered to move in in April 1885. Both sisters came from a large family of ten children.

The Event: the fire broke out at night in the early hours of Friday 24 April following a 'fearful explosion'. Henry Chandler, his wife and six-year-old son Henry were sleeping in one bedroom while Alice slept in a bedroom across the landing with the other three children aged five, four and three.

The Heroine: The best account is found in John Price's fascinating book – *Heroes of Postman's Park – Heroic self-sacrifice in Victorian London*.

Alice Ayres' grave, with obelisk, at Isleworth cemetery.
(© The author)

Witnesses to the terrible fire that engulfed the shop premises and house of the Chandler family, at 194 Union Street, Borough, in April 1885 spoke of how a young female figure, clad only in her nightdress and carrying a small, crying child, appeared suddenly at an upper-storey window. Having successfully thrown a feather bed out of the window to help cushion the fall, the young woman carefully dropped the small child down to the waiting crowd, who then implored her to save herself. When she disappeared back into the smoke, the crowd presumably feared the worse, but the girl appeared with a second child, whom she also deposited into the waiting arms of the crowd. Once more she disappeared and once again reappeared clutching yet another child, whom she also dropped from the window to the crowd below. This time she heeded the calls to save herself, but apparently overcome by smoke and exhaustion, she fell limply from the window and, striking part of the shopfront in her fall, hit the pavement below. Conveyed to Guy's Hospital with severe spinal injuries, the young woman's condition deteriorated and two days later she died.

Alice's dying words were reported to have been: 'I tried my best and could try no more'. She was twenty-six.

The Victims: The fire cost the lives of five of the seven people living in the house. Rescuers found the charred body of Mary Ann with her son dead by her side upstairs by a window, and the badly burnt body of Mr Chandler, clutching a money box, was recovered on the staircase. The youngest child, baby Elizabeth aged three, died of her injuries in hospital, as did Alice. The survivors were two out of the three children Alice had attempted to save: Edith, aged five and Ellen, aged four. Funds were raised to enable them to go to Alexandra Orphanage in Hornsey.

R.I.P.: The public response to the heroism of Alice Ayres was extraordinary. Her sister and family were quietly buried at Lambeth cemetery in Tooting on 30 April but Alice herself was buried near the family home in Isleworth on 4 May, with massive crowds lining up the one-mile route from Magdala Road to the cemetery. Her 'coffin was carried by sixteen firemen in full-dress uniform, who worked in shifts of four along the route'.

The press had announced a subscription fund which would enable the erection of a monument and people had to be turned away from the memorial service at the lofty St Saviour's church (Southwark Cathedral). Funds came pouring in with many working-class families chipping in and the organising committee settled on a 'needle monument' inspired by Cleopatra's Needle which had been gracing the north bank of the Thames for the last seven years, since 1878. This miniature version, in red granite, was duly erected 'to commemorate a noble act of unselfish courage' says the inscription on her grave – still seen in Isleworth cemetery today (left).

Poets paid tribute to little Alice, such as Sir Francis Doyle in the *Pall Mall Gazette* (31 October 1887); this is an extract from 'The story of a modern heroine':

> A small mean house burst forth in flame,
> Within crash down the burning stairs;
> And, like a picture in her frame,
> Stands at the window, Alice Ayres.

The art of fire

Two years after the tragedy, on 5 September 1887, the distinguished artist G F Watts had a letter published in *The Times*. He attempted to sway public opinion or at least the country's intelligentsia to back a scheme which would 'surely be of national interest': 'to collect a complete record of the stories of heroism in every-day life … The roll would be a long one, but I would cite as an example the name of Alice Ayres … at an oilmonger's in Gravel Lane, in April, 1885, who lost her life in saving those of her master's children'. This was Queen Victoria's Jubilee Year and his letter was entitled 'Another Jubilee Suggestion'. He described Alice's cruel fate, concluding that 'the history of her Majesty's reign would gain a lustre were the nation to erect a monument, say, here in London, to record the names of these likely-to-be-forgotten heroes'.

There was no immediate response but eleven years later, in 1898, the vicar of St Botolph's church, Aldersgate, suggested the adjacent and newly planned Postman's Park site to Watts, due to open in 1900. Alice's tablet, made by the artist William de Morgan, was installed on 4 May 1902. The memorial may still be seen in Postman's Park today, next to the Museum of London roundabout in the City. However, the idea of commemorating the poor's heroic deeds was seized upon straightaway by the Hill sisters – Octavia, the housing philanthropist and Miranda, the founder of the Kyrle Society, 'a little society for the purpose of helping this great work of

General view of Postman's Park 'monument to heroic self-sacrifice', City of London; with Alice's tablet (top). The latest attempt to add a plaque to this Victorian monument was in 2021 to honour the memory of Jimi Olubunmi-Adewole, 20, who died trying to rescue a drowning woman from the Thames at London Bridge. He jumped in with Joaquin Garcia; the latter was able to save the woman's life without endangering his own, but Jimi's body was only recovered the following day. A petition to the Lord Mayor had over 160,000 signatures.

(© The author)

Evolution of the Alice Ayres' mural for Red Cross Hall – from newspaper cutting (Southwark Archives) to finished painting, via preparatory studies. (From *The English Illustrated Magazine*, Vol. X, June 1893).

None of these images is true to the actual events as they were reported at the time but the newspaper illustration (top left) is the most straight-forward and the mural the most idealised (bottom right). The artist's sketch partially relies on the newspaper illustration (above, middle) but is also looking for ways of ennobling the heroine (top right). The final version is as far away from reality as was possible (bottom right).

Walter Crane's *Reminiscences* published in 1907, are informative about the scheme; he describes the circumstances in the year 1890–92:

> I drew up a scheme of decoration to scale for the Red Cross Hall, consisting of a series of mural designs in colour, treated as large panels along each side of the Hall, embodying various deeds of heroism, particulars of which were supplied to me … The first panel, showing the rescue of children from a fire at an oil-shop … by … Alice Ayres, who lost her life in consequence … was duly designed and painted. I made a quarter-size cartoon in pastel of the subject from my small scale sketch, and this Mrs Barrington enlarged on to the full-sized fibrous plaster panel, which was sent to her studio … and the painting was started by Mrs Barrington (in oil on the plaster ground), and I added finishing touches. A second panel (they were 11 feet 6 inches by 6 feet in size) I painted in my own studio afterwards – an incident on the railway near Paisley, when two platelayers sacrificed themselves to save the train.
>
> These two panels were placed in the Hall, and duly inaugurated at a meeting there. A third panel – a rescue of a child from a well – I also painted, after an interval, and there are now three panels in the Hall. The work had to be largely a labour of love, as very little money was available for such a purpose, and as other work had to be attended to, and the busy years roll on, the scheme is still incomplete. The Hall however, is not all one could wish for such a work, and I fear the use of gas has injured the paintings.

Opposite:

The projected appearance of the Red Cross Hall with its proposed murals to the unknown heroes who sacrificed their lives to save that of others. Only three murals were completed.

(From *The Builder magazine*, 9 November 1889)

making beautiful places for the poor' (1876). Octavia Hill had been working in Southwark for the Ecclesiastical Commissioners since 1884 and in 1888 she coordinated the building of the much-praised Red Cross Cottages – six cottages, a Hall and a garden – followed by Whitecross Cottages at the back.

The hall was always meant as a focus for the whole neighbourhood, and its decoration mattered. The acclaimed artist Walter Crane (1845–1915) was a friend of Octavia and a committee member of the Kyrle Society. He designed a decorative scheme along the lines suggested by Watts – the 'heroic deeds of the poor' comprising nine large scale murals (previous page). The first one to be completed, in 1890, dealt with Alice Ayres. Mrs Russell Barrington, one of the scheme's supporters, published an article about the murals in *The English Illustrated Magazine* (June 1893). This article provides information on the house at the corner of Union Street and Gravel Lane – the site of the tragedy. In 1890, five years after the event, she returned to the scene after attending the inauguration of Walter Crane's painting of Alice Ayres (see previous page):

> On leaving the [Redcross] Hall I went round by Gravel Lane to find the exact spot which was the scene of the fire. Nothing had been touched or changed since the night in April, 1885, when the oil-shop had been burnt to the ground. A hoarding had been placed round the heap of ruins, otherwise it was left as the flames had left it. Coming straight from the crowded, bright lighted hall, resounding with music and gay with flowers, and standing before it in the dark solitary stillness of that Sunday evening, the lonely squalid little ruin seemed to have something strangely pathetic about it; left, as it were, out in the cold like a neglected grave.

The inauguration of the painting was attended by Walter Crane and Octavia Hill 'the good Squiress of the great village'. Mrs Barrington wrote: 'More than half of those who were present in the Hall that Sunday afternoon had witnessed the real fire. All spoke of Alice Ayres as the central point of interest in the event'. What did the witnesses make of the reinterpretation or artistic licence which drove the composition? We will never know but Mrs Barrington recorded her own thoughts: 'art … will be a lasting testimony to the heroism of English men and women, who … have displayed very typical English virtues – courage, fortitude, and an unquestioning sense of duty.' Adding later: 'the idea of memorialising the heroic deeds of the poor, carries us much further into the hearts of the poor than could any scheme for merely beautifying, however artistically, any of their dwellings or public rooms'. But she struck a deep chord when she wrote:

> No one has ever worked successfully among the poor, or really come into true touch with them …. who has not realised that what is really highest in human nature is found alike in the poor and the rich.

A second mural was inaugurated in December 1892 which commemorated two navvies working upon the railway line between Glasgow and Paisley. They gave their lives to fix a loose sleeper which would have derailed the express train hurtling towards them and a lofty viaduct. The overall painted scheme remained unfinished and was subsequently destroyed – when this happened is not known – though the hall still stands. So, despite Mrs Barrington's hopes, the art was not 'a lasting testimony'.

Postscript

In 1936 the London Borough of Southwark sought to remember and mark the event in a more permanent way – Whitecross Street was renamed Ayres Street in memory of Alice. Nowadays a large office building, Union House, occupies the corner of Union Street and Great Suffolk Street where the Chandler's house once stood.

Had Alice been a victim of the same fire today, her life might possibly have been saved. But what would be the point of going down this particular route? Except ... except that it helps us measure the progress of a branch of medicine on which we have come to rely heavily: Accident and Emergency. The first full time Casualty Consultant in England, Mr Maurice Ellis, was based at Leeds General Infirmary in 1952. By 1967 the Casualty Surgeons Association had been constituted. In due course it became the Royal College of Emergency Medicine. Its headquarters? At Octavia House, in Alice's Ayres Street, the street which was renamed to help us remember. It is just around the corner from Red Cross Hall – the place which first paid tribute to Alice's tragedy. A coincidence or perfect synchronicity?

Timothy Hyman, 'I open my heart to reveal London enshrined within', mixed media on prepared card, 2003.
(Private collection; © The artist)

Reconstructive surgery – urban design revisited

Reconstructive surgery is far older than the accident and emergency services just described, though serious progress in the former field was only really achieved in the twentieth century. Is reconstructive surgery in hospitals so very different from reconstructive surgery in urban planning and architecture? It is not as far apart as one might think.

Historian/philosopher Richard Sennett's thought-provoking book, *Flesh and Stone*, was published in 1994. There he pursued, through a wide range of historical examples, the argument that cities may be regarded as functioning like a human body: the author structured his book with cities' Voice and Eye, moving on to the Heart, before examining Arteries and Veins. He has a section on 'The Suffering Body' which is centred around a whole population affected by the plague – the world of epidemiology even more baffling then as it is now – but he never mentioned 'surgical interventions' or 'reconstructive surgery' to deal with defective parts of the city/body, to restore order and harmony where disorder reigned.

Inspired by the twelfth-century philosopher John of Salisbury –

among many others – Richard Sennett saw sense in the way John of Salisbury 'connected the shape of the human body and the form of the city: the city's palace or cathedral he thought of as its head, the central market as its stomach, the city's hands and feet as its houses' – Bankside and Borough forming a microcosmic version of this. For many years John worked for the Archbishop of Canterbury, including Thomas Becket; he travelled widely in Britain and abroad, so would have drawn some of his experience from real-life cities, including London.

One of our great contemporary painters, Timothy Hyman RA, has long understood this visceral connection between flesh and stone; he has handled it many times to show how London and Londoner were one and the same thing, for instance in 'I open my heart to reveal London enshrined within' (previous page); he has also painted London in his head, on his back, in his hand, all over his body, and latterly on the operating table – a map of London – with 'self' in pieces awaiting reconstructive surgery after the artist underwent three major operations.

But architects are the great city surgeons, and Allies and Morrison at 85 Southwark Street are not only ideally placed for interventions in this neighbourhood, they are also fully committed to the idea of regenerating and 'putting back the gaps'. Graham Morrison explains: '… buildings come and go … What remains is the space between the buildings and the spaces made by them. These spaces are the masterplan and will last. They become the bone structure of the city – the fabric of a place' (*Exploring Models of Urban Development*). Returning to Bankside he points out: 'You can now walk from Union Street to St Paul's in ten minutes, something that was not possible before'. Though this possibility comes with a warning: 'it's the capillaries which keep the life blood going. If you don't get the space, the links and the footfalls, all your reconstructive surgery will die. But Graham Morrison also challenges the idea of reconstructive surgery:

> It presupposes there was a condition that previously existed that you are trying to remake because it needs repair. The question of repair is irrefutable because the whole of Southwark and Lambeth were broken places … before 1939 the street patterns were functional and interesting … I would blame local councils as much as the Luftwaffe, because there was wholesale demolition of houses; more demolition done by the politicians than by the air raids during the war.

About the challenges of city making on the South Bank and elsewhere, Morrison adds, passionately:

> The thing I've been interested in throughout my career … the really interesting thing, it's the character of the place [which] is emerging. In terms of its reconstruction, it's the adolescence stage. It lacks confidence, it's not settled, it's not completely content with itself but it's going to grow into an area which is like no other. It is going to be itself.

Allies and Morrison regard Bankside Power Station as the 'heart' of their neighbourhood; they deplored its original isolation, even after the arrival of the Millennium bridge. Their project of greater connectivity is now almost complete – through sheer

Modern's turbine hall prior to its
conversion into an art gallery.
(Tate)

photograph of the Turbine Hall
Modern was taken by the Tate
photographers around 2000.
(Tate)

On the firm's philosophy (Bob Allies): Bob Allies co-edited with Di Haigh *The Fabric of Place*, published in 2014 'a book that explores how settlements of any scale can evolve and change by building on their historic form and identity. The book forms the foundation of the practice's approach to urbanism.'

On tall buildings (Graham Morrison): 'It's about getting the scale right. In the film *Zorba the Greek*, the principal actor, Anthony Quinn, is 6ft tall but he does this dance … it's almost on tiptoe! That's what I ask of our big buildings – you might be a giant but you can be part of the community, be graceful, dance on tiptoe and participate in the joy of the place …'

All photos courtesy of Allies and Morrison; 2 and 4: Dennis Gilbert/VIEW3
© Morley von Sternberg

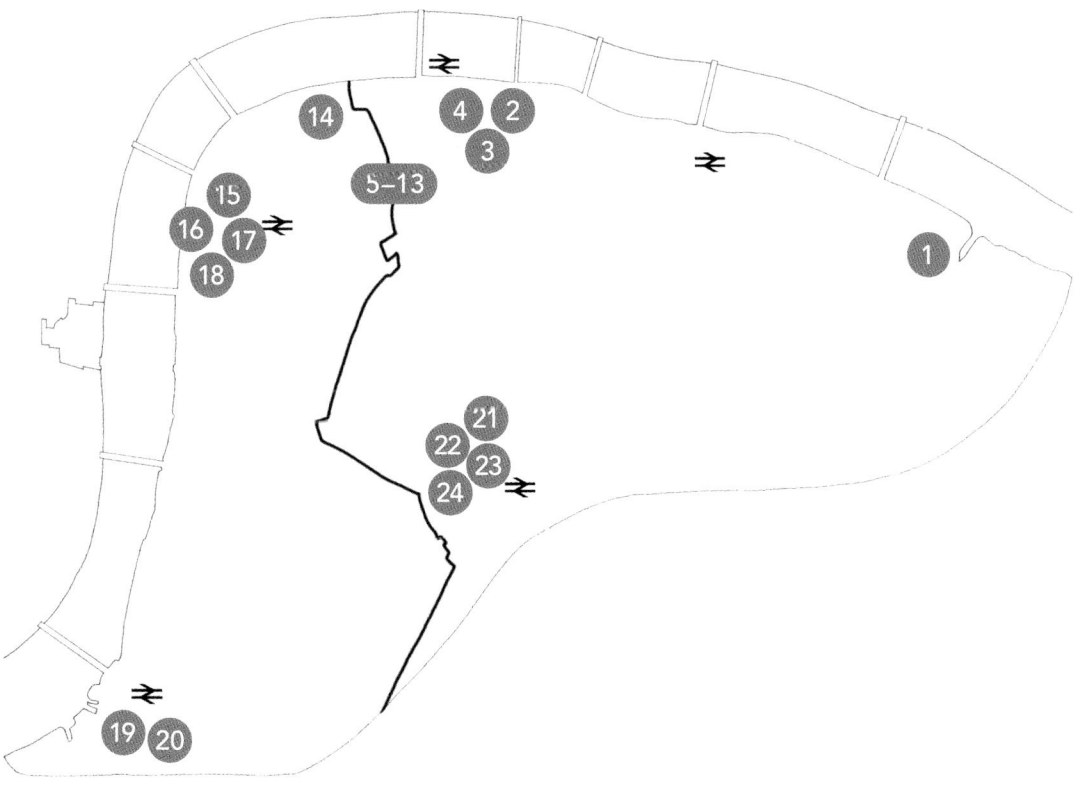

Key to Allies and Morrison

1. Clove Building
2. Shakespeare's Globe
3. Project Prospero
4. Bankside 123
5. Lavington Street Hotel
6. 67 Southwark Street
7. The Crane building
8. The Table
9. Southwark Street Studios
10. Farnham Place
11. Paris Gardens
12. Great Suffolk Street
13. Rosler Apartment
14. The Rambert
15. Temporary installation Southbank Centre
16. Royal Festival Hall (RFH)
17. Canteen at the RFH
18. Administration building
19. Vauxhall Square
20. Keybridge House
21. Two Fifty One
22. College of Communication
23. Elephant & Castle Masterplan
24. Contemporary Applied Arts

This 1947 photograph captures the old Bankside Power Station (1891–1947) with war damage buildings in the foreground: the Abercrombie plan of 1943 complained that 'on the south bank the dreary industrial scene, with its many damaged buildings, calls for drastic action'. Controversially, this was replaced by a new Bankside Power Station designed by Sir Giles Gilbert Scott (1880–1960), now the home of Tate Modern.
(The National Archives)

Waldemar Januszczak was not the only early doubter when he admitted:

> they needed to turn a blackened and enormous industrial cavity, 660ft long, filled with huge slabs of industrial junk from its previous role as a power station, with a useless chimney attached rising 325ft into the sky, into a state-of-the-art museum devoted pointedly to the state of the art. It was some ask …
>
> When they started the work, in 1995 … Nicholas Serota, the director of the Tate, took me on a personal tour of the vast, dripping, pigeon-filled blackness. It was so big, so damp. This was no place for an art gallery, surely? … The gigantic size that seemed to me to defeat the purpose of art, which was to achieve an intimate communication between an artwork and a viewer, was actually a big aesthetic plus … If you want to feel sublime, you need to feel small. (*Sunday Times*, 'Culture', May 2020)

When Michael Craig-Martin, one of the Tate's trustees, recounted the birth of Tate Modern on the South Bank, his input as an artist was to visit – with Bill Woodrow – several newly opened museums of modern and contemporary art on the Continent and report back on them.

> In general these modern museums seemed to serve the interests of architecture and architects more clearly than those of art and artists … Few architects seemed truly to understand or be interested in the needs of art … They tended either to create sequences of more or less identical and characterless neutral spaces or to make self-consciously over-designed spaces where art was barely necessary.

Surprisingly, when the concept of the 'white cube' was still prevalent, the two artists favoured the presentation of art in older buildings: 'None of the purpose-built museums could match the stimulating quality and variety of these exhibition spaces, nor the opportunity for interaction between the art and the space.' These findings were confirmed by most of the artists who completed a questionnaire prepared by Tate.

So, when, back in the 1980s, the Trustees of the Tate Gallery chose to expand their London activities by taking on a new site south of the river, they decided three things: that they would continue to develop the Collection as one, that

British Art would remain at Millbank and International Art would be found at Bankside, thereby creating a set of circumstances that would catapult Tate Modern and Bankside, into the forefront of the capital's cultural world! In 2020, on the occasion of the new gallery's twentieth anniversary, Januszczak declared that year 2000 had been

> a crappy year, except for one thing. In May, 2000, in London, Tate Modern opened its doors … the repurposed power station at Bankside had been a spectacular success. In the opening year, they were hoping for 2 million visitors. Instead, 5.25 million turned up … These days, Tate Modern is easily the most popular gallery of modern art in the world, regularly pushing an annual viewership of 6 million. (*Sunday Times*, 'Culture', May 2020)

Barely four years before the grand opening of the Tate in 2000, this is what architect Graham Morrison had to say about its immediate neighbourhood when his firm purchased the site for their current building:

> You could practically see tumbleweeds blowing down Southwark Street. Nothing happened here before the Millennium. Literally

Left:

This is a good example of the tradition for high and forbidding walls along the banks of the working river – narrow streets flanked on both sides by industrial buildings or warehouses – here Bear Gardens, photographed from Park Street in 1930, looking towards the Thames with Copper Wharf on the right and the Belfast and London Aerated Water Company on the left. The contemporary landscape in the same area strikes similar notes:
© London Metropolitan Archives (City of London)

Above:

This photograph, taken in 2021 shows how persistent certain 'traditions' are in the making of cities – here the Tate's tower extension and the Blue Fin building form a canyon style design which echoes the river bank's former days, though the use of glass and the punctuation of windows in the tower soften the impact of the buildings' height.
(© The author, 2022)

nothing [was] going on before the Tate, Southwark Station and the Millennium Bridge. Across the road [looking towards the Tate building] it was Britain's, well, Europe's largest office building at the time it was built [St Christopher's House]. It was occupied by the Ministry of Defence and it was like the MI5, people arrived and left. There were railings around it. It offered nothing back to the street.

There was, alas, a long tradition, going back to Victorian times, of giving nothing back to the street: narrow streets and tall forbidding walls on either side came about with the development of wharves and warehouse storage along the river – Shad Thames, which now seems so picturesque, ran into the now demolished Pickle Herring Street, then came Clink Street and Bear Gardens too (previous page), to name just a few examples.

Long after Shakespeare but before Bankside's return to culture

It was already clear by the 1840s that Bankside had become heavily industrialised (see pp. 222–223 Banks panorama). The site of Tate Modern was occupied by a power station as early as 1891, when the City of London Electric Lighting Company built a station next to Phoenix Gas Works. This supplied electricity to the City and parts of Southwark. The facility was regularly extended and improved as demand kept on growing. In 1934 it was in the hands of the Central Electricity Board and on 1 April 1948 electricity was nationalised and the London Electricity Board set up. By that stage the old power station (previous page) with its stacks of eighteen chimneys – one for each boiler – was being replaced by a brand-new power station, built in two stages – 1947–53 for the 'west end' and 1959–63 for the 'east end' after more land became available when the old power station was demolished in 1959. This 'cathedral of power', designed by Sir Giles Gilbert Scott, and defiantly facing St Paul's, continued the tradition of austere, tall and closed structures … but, arguably, with majesty.

The project was controversial, challenging the vision of the 1943 Abercrombie plan: 'The River Thames is the largest single open space in the country … an expanse of water with a contrasting setting of trees and buildings can be a great source of enjoyment'. Factories and industry had been forcefully rejected in Abercrombie's plan. Stephen Murray, who has extensively researched this topic explained that the arrival of Bankside B as it came to be known, 'was ultimately crisis-driven as a result of the national fuel supply problems of 1947'. The arguments for and against were rehearsed in the 1947 public enquiry and its chairman included in his report that the south bank 'is notoriously ugly and even a large new industrial building could not seriously affect it'. Coal shortage in 1947 encouraged the pursuit of the Bankside option, provided it could be oil rather than coal fuelled, which eliminated the problems of fly-ash (coal grit). But the move had not anticipated the mid-1970s increase in oil prices, and the station quickly became uneconomic, closing its doors for good in 1981, a year after Battersea power station, finally decommissioned in 1983, had been listed by English Heritage.

When the present embraces the past

The Tate purchased the site in 1994, work started in 1995, and it opened its doors in May 2000. From a 2020s perspective, it is easy to warm to the new mantra, described here by Artur Carulla from Allies and Morrison, a firm believer in the importance of 'retaining existing structures':

> This has always been the case with listed buildings because of statutory obligations but more and more we find masterplans are retaining structures not so much because of their architectural merit but because of their character, something that cannot be reproduced through new buildings. It is a character that infuses the masterplan with a patina of the organic, thus giving the illusion of historic continuum. (2019)

But if you cast your mind back to the 1990s when Tate Modern was being created, the situation was rather different. The architectural competition attracted nearly 150 architects and produced six distinguished finalists: Tadao Ando, Raphael Moneo, Renzo Piano, David Chipperfield, Jacques Herzog & Pierre de Meuron, and Rem Koolhaas. Michael Craig-Martin identified the central reason for selecting Herzog & de Meuron – their design was:

> The only proposal that completely accepted the existing building – its form, its materials and its industrial characteristics – and saw the solution to be the transformation of the building itself into an art gallery. They proposed a true union of their design with that of Giles Gilbert Scott, turning the box into a new building.

So, not only did Tate acquire land at Bankside, but they also meant to blend past and present into a seamless whole – the new 'historic continuum' spelt out by Artur Carulla above. There was a recent precedent in 1980s Paris, at the Orsay museum which was developed within the shell of the beautiful Orsay Station. The station may now be regarded as an Art Nouveau gem but came within inches of being demolished and its transformation into a museum was widely applauded.

This coming together of past and present structures may also be observed with the railways. They were found to be totally disfiguring in the 1940s and the Abercrombie plan effectively recommended them to be scrapped – the 'three railway bridges would eventually disappear' – insisting that 'successful replanning will be, in no small measure, conditioned by the extent to which these viaducts can be removed, especially those carrying the routes from London Bridge to Cannon Street and Charing Cross'. Prohibitively expensive of course, but nearly seventy years on a Bankside resident, David Stephens, inspired by the way the abandoned New York's 'High Line' had been turned into a green promenade, came up with a 'Low Line' concept – a walking route connecting London Bridge and Waterloo stations, running alongside the railway arches which can be used to shelter cafés, theatres, gyms etc. It is now time 'to celebrate the history and potential of the amazing Victorian railway arches' says the Southwark Council website (accessed on 27 December 2019). The scheme has been adopted by Southwark Council and Network Rail. One of the best examples of what may be achieved is found just off Union Street, close to the junction of three railway lines – those terminating at London Bridge, Cannon Street and Blackfriars stations (Old Union Yard Arches).

Olafur Eliasson
The weather project, 2003
Monofrequency lights, projection foil, haze machines, mirror foil, aluminium, scaffolding
26.7 x 22.3 x 155.44 m
Installation view: Tate Modern, London, 2003

This is arguably the most memorable of all Turbine Hall exhibitions – 'the weather project' by Icelandic-Danish artist Olafur Eliasson lasted six months in 2003-4, attracting two million visitors. The ceiling was fitted with mirrors which completed the semi-circular sun and reflected back the image of visitors. Very quickly people adapted their response to this display by lying on the floor to bask in the glow and look at themselves in the ceiling while so doing. The fine mist created by humidifiers was the final touch: 'eternal sunshine of the artist's spotless mind'.
(Photo: Andrew Dunkley & Marcus Leith. Courtesy of the artist; neugerriemschneider, Berlin; Tanya Bonakdar Gallery, New York / Los Angeles © 2003 Olafur Eliasson)

The intertwining of past and present as vital, creative threads, resonates deeply with an art pioneer connected to Bankside in his early formative years. In August 1969, **Derek Jarman (1942–1994)** was one of the first artists to move his studio into industrial premises at 51 Upper Ground, an old-corset factory – sculptor **Peter Logan (b. 1943)** was there too. A year later Jarman moved to 13 Bankside, 'the most beautiful room in London'. He was then twenty-eight and cut his teeth filming in Super 8 including an eight-minute film called *Studio Bankside*, shot in and around his studio. He wrote in his 1984 autobiography *Dancing Ledge*: 'no one took Super 8 particularly seriously … When I received my first film back and it was in focus, the whole thing seemed magical – an instrument to bring dreams to life … If independence was a form of purity, I had my hands on the philosopher's stone'. He also described his studio:

> In August 1969 I moved into the first of a series of warehouses on the river front. Upper Ground was at the end of Blackfriars Bridge. It was a large airy L-shaped room. After seven years in cramped Georgian terrace houses and basements, the change was exhilarating. There was space to spread out – to entertain – for friends to stay without falling over each other. Life could be a bit spartan in winter, but the summers were an idyll; and the old brick buildings – all of which have now disappeared under improvements – a delight.
>
> The area was deserted since the docks had been moved further down river. Returning home late at night down these empty streets you felt the city belonged to you. In the mornings you would be woken up by the tug *Elegance* towing the barges down river. The seagulls would desert them for a moment and come to catch the bread from your hand. The riverside was my world for another nine years, before the invasion I pioneered with Peter [Logan] turned the few remaining buildings into DES. RES.

In fact, according to Wedd, Peltz and Ross (see biblio), the first studio venture south of the river was when Richard Wentworth leased a redundant Mission Church in Dilston Grove, Southwark Park. For Jarman, the Bankside warehouse 'brought fun and laughter into our lives with a thousand events. People camped out, swung or slept in the white hammock suspended across the room. Andrew [Logan] kissed a thousand home-grown celebrities, and once Katie Hepburn came to tea'.

Soon the provision of artists' studios was put on firm footing with the creation of two 'housing/studios associations – SPACE (1968) and Acme (1972). As for Jarman, he had to move further east, to another warehouse

Applause for the actors at the end of 'The Knight of the Burning Pestle' by Francis Beaumont; both photographs taken during the Sam Wanamaker Playhouse's first season in 2014.
(Photo: Peter Le May/Shakespeare's Globe)

Right:
The Playhouse at the south east corner of the Globe complex. It is described by the Society for the Protection of Ancient Buildings, as a 'National Treasure'. It is a modern recreation, partly based on documents, of a seventeenth-century indoor theatre – archetypal rather than tied to a specific model. The candle-lit theatre, built in timber, creates 'a strange play of authenticity and illusion' remarks Rowan Moore in his review for The Guardian. Designed by Jon Greenfield in collaboration with Allies and Morrison, it represents, according to Moore, a tantalising experience: 'the auditorium itself becomes a kind of stage set, a fiction willingly entered into, that becomes more strange and fantastical the more realistic its historical reconstruction attempts to be'.
(Photos: Peter Le May/Shakespeare's Globe)

at Butler's Wharf (Warehouse A, see p. 514). He poignantly described the moment of departure from Bankside in September 1972:

> We closed the doors for ever at Bankside this evening after a showing of *A Midsummer's Nights Dream* and *The Wizard of Oz* … The demolition men, who have been tearing the buildings all around us, will be in next week. Before winter there will be just a hole in the ground and Horseshoe Alley will be no more'.

Jarman left the industrial south in 1979 – his last London address was Phoenix House in Charing Cross Road. Altogether he spent ten years along the South Bank, between 1969 and 1979.

Jarman was living at Bankside when he landed a fabulous job – designing the sets for Ken Russell's film 'The Devils' (1971). In 2020, in the course of the 'Save Prospect Cottage Campaign' – Jarman's Cottage at Dungeness – film critic Mark Kermode remarked that 'the sets had a key defining influence (along with the costumes) on how the film looked and how it had that modernity he [Russell, the film director] wanted. When you watch the film, you're not watching it as an ancient thing you're watching it as something modern'. Kermode pursued: 'later on in Jarman's career that intertwining of the ancient and the modern, of the historical and the futuristic, the past and the present actually become the key thing'.

This 'key thing' is also found in 'The Tempest' (1979) and 'Caravaggio' (1986), to limit ourselves to a couple of examples. This 'key thing' has also driven many cultural initiatives in Borough and Bankside.

If I were a planner … or a politician …

I would select projects which celebrate the fluent marriage of the past with the present – as a way of protecting the few islands of history which remain in this neighbourhood; and also as a way of revitalising the streetscape using a seamless blend of 'modernity' and old stones – or even brick for that matter. In particular I would nurture cultural projects; they are a perfect fit in this part of South London where they appear to thrive and address with ease, local and global issues– for instance the Globe, with its candle-lit progeny the Sam Wanamaker Playhouse and of course the appropriately named Tate Modern.

Sources (full references for abbreviated entries in bibliography)

MoLAS 1999; www.crossbones.org.uk/ accessed on 27 April 2021; Carlin 1983; Howard; Bowsher; Jan Piggott, *Dulwich College – A History 1616 to 2008*; Barker & Jackson 2008; *Survey of London* 22; Wendy Mathews, *My Ward – The Story of St Thomas', Guy's, and the Evelina Children's Hospitals and their ward names*, 2011; www.choleraandthethames.co.uk/ accessed on 26 April 2021; Price; Darley; Whelan; *Citymakers Exploring Models of Urban Development – Catalytic, Organic, Curated*, 2019, Allies and Morrison; Interview of Graham Morrison, June 2021; *Bankside London*, 2019, Allies and Morrison (pamphlet); Iwona Blazwick and Simon Wilson, *Tate Modern – the Handbook*, 2000; Murray; Michael Craig-Martin 'Towards Tate Modern' in *Tate Modern the handbook* (above); Roger Wollen, *Derek Jarman, A Portrait*, 1996; Wedd, Peltz & Ross.

SOUTHWARK AND BERMONDSEY
The highs and lows of a strategic neighbourhood

Southwark Fair	**486**
Babel in London – the Shard	**488**
Historical context	489
London and Babel	491
Babel in Southwark	492
How a star architect came to design the Shard	494
Towermania	497
The creation of London Bridge Quarter	500
The social 'pecking order'	501
The Manna Day Centre	**502**
London's larder	**504**
Antecedents	510
Inns and breweries	510
'Beere House'	511
Artists move into the empty shells of industry and commerce	**513**
The Southwark school of sculpture	**518**

Previous:
The Shard: its architect, Renzo Piano (b. 1937), sought an 'immaterial crystalline effect that would play with the light and the mood of the weather'.
(© The author, 2021)

Above:
(Cincinnati Art Museum; The Artchives/Alamy Stock Photo)

Southwark Fair – An artist's interpretation of the Fall

The American academic Ronald Paulson is rightly celebrated for his research into the London-based artist William Hogarth (1697–1764). He has described in great detail the engraving – after the painting reproduced here – writing that:

> Although Hogarth later referred to the print as 'Southwark Fair' he probably meant to generalize it, as his earliest title, simply 'A Fair' suggests.

And yet the accumulation of realistic details in this work, as in many other works by this artist, makes you feel you know the precise time, place, and mood of this annual event. And the details all seem to fit: the work was painted after 23 August 1733 and the fair was always held in September. Over time the original 7, 8, 9 September had grown into a fourteen-day event, much to the annoyance of the City authorities. The time is around 1.30 p.m. according to the clock of St George's; the medieval fair had developed around this landmark church prior to being granted permission to hold a fair in 1462 on and around the feast of the nativity of the Virgin, hence its name of Our Lady Fair. This painting offered a last glimpse of this church, since it was taken down in 1733 and rebuilding started the following year.

Hogarth's particular brand of realism seems to imply he was there and drew the scene as an eye-witness to the annual fun and chaos of this popular event. With the much older Bartholomew Fair (1133) on the other side of the Thames – at Smithfield – these were London's two major fairs. Hogarth is at pains to document his picture, naming proprietors, plays and other shows (more legibly in the engraving) – for instance [Elkanah Settle's] 'The Siege of Troy' at Lee & Harpers Great Booth; while 'Punches Opera' is on at a nearby booth; and at Cibber & Bullock's, it's 'The Fall of Bajazet'; other shows include 'Royal Wax Works', contortionists, a peep-show in the foreground and on the left Isaac Fawkes performing one of his tricks – he was famous for changing 'little Balls into Living Birds and Beasts'. According to Mrs Hogarth, her husband even made reference to a personal anecdote when depicting the handsome drummer-girl in the centre of the painting. In real life the artist had defended a beautiful drummer girl against being mistreated by her master. All these references and many others have been meticulously checked by Paulson and the conclusion

was that many of these 'real' characters and shows were drawn from a variety of sources – not just Southwark Fair and not just 1733 – in order to create one gigantic falling down. The fall of Troy, the fall of Adam and Eve, the fall of Joan – Punch's wife – into the mouth of hell, the fall of one of the rope-walkers from the top of the church, the fall of three women being groomed in the crowd, and on the right, 'The Fall of Bajazet' which is literally enacted with the collapse of the stage; soon it will crush the fragile tin-glazed earthenware on sale at the booth below. This particular play was not in fact performed at Southwark in 1733 and Paulson concludes 'it is evident that Hogarth transposed the fairs (and dates) partly to get as many "falls" as possible into his scene.'

The making of this image was closely connected with the making of the artist's famous 'Rake's Progress'. Hogarth was late delivering this work and appears to have used the Southwark Fair print as a way of pacifying his subscribers. 'The Rake's Progress', a series of eight paintings, engraved for subscribers, was about the life of the spendthrift, lazy, unprincipled Tom Rakewell … followed by his fall – a tale of immorality which finds echoes in this scene of general collapse!

Hogarth's painting would have reinforced the views of the City of London authorities who regarded Southwark as a place of lawlessness. As the fair kept on deteriorating, the Court of Common Council prohibited it in 1762; it was permanently suppressed by the City Corporation the following year. They had very similar problems with Bartholomew Fair though it benefited from greater tolerance and lasted until 1855 when it, too, was suppressed.

Babel in London – The Shard

This building is our new hierarchy, with its dim, sleazy restaurants in Imperial Chinese theme, with its menus for French bankers to slice their meat, with its apartments built for Russian oligarchs, with glass walls to press their fingers onto, with eyes looking into, but sealed away from, an immense vista of light. And like so much of London this huge, fragile piece of glass belongs to the Sheikh of Qatar.

From *This is London* by Ben Judah, 2016

The writer Will Self who has an ambivalent relationship with skyscrapers and the Shard in particular, writes about towers 'operating within the unified field of the same foundational myth: that of the tower of Babel, from Genesis, a tale of human hubris'. While the building of towers may still involve competitive pride, it no longer represents a challenge to God in our largely godless society. This is perhaps why the Shard is not more commonly associated with Babel: it is often seen as a rich man's game, and principally as the embodiment of dysfunctional finances and ethics.

Ben Judah, quoted above, writes with great originality and he has resisted a direct comparison with the Tower of Babel. And yet the Shard's very top, 'designed to look unfinished … [gives] the illusion that the building is disappearing into the clouds', echoing the Biblical text 'a tower, whose top may reach unto heaven' and a tower which is generally represented as being unfinished; while the Shard's multi-national visitors and residents have the flavour of the original Babel after God decided to 'confound their language, that they may not understand one another's speech'.

Historical context

But we ought to examine the sixteenth-century origins of the tower of Babel, because it has exercised a significant impact on European culture. It was an image dreamt up by painters at about the same time as the birth of the imaging of cities (the latter has been developed in 'The Eye of London' chapter 2).

Before Peter Brueghel the Elder's 1563 masterpiece (left), the Tower of Babel was a very unimpressive structure; in medieval art when scale and realistic depictions were not the order of the day, early Babel towers were not outlandishly large structures which dwarfed human beings. They were tall and thin, echoing the medieval towers which have survived in places like Bologna or San Gimignano in northern Italy but depicted on a miniature scale, in some instances dwarfed by humans and in great contrast to Brueghel's later interpretation (left).

Opposite

Pieter Brueghel the Elder (c. 1625/30–1569), 'The Tower of Babel' (detail), painted around 1563. This image is as extraordinary today as it was when first invented by the artist, to general public admiration. Brueghel, an artist of the northern Renaissance inspired by his visit to Rome, was able, for the first time, to master the scale of the tower versus that of the city lying below (based on Antwerp). (Kunsthistorisches Museum Vienna. Image in the public domain; Wikimedia Commons)

The building of the Tower of Babel, *Weltchronik in Versen*, c. 1370. Medieval manuscripts were mostly illuminated by anonymous hands. This artist follows the pictorial tradition of his time – a square and slender tower, without giving any sense of its immense size which should have dwarfed all the workers busy constructing it, in direct contrast to Brueghel's interpretation. (Bayerische Staatsbibliothek, Munich. Image in the public domain; Wikimedia Commons, for The Yorck Project (2002) 10.000 *Meisterwerke der Malerei* (DVD-ROM), distributed by DIRECTMEDIA Publishing GmbH. ISBN: 3936122202)

Martin van Valckenborgh (1535–1612), The Tower of Babel, oil painting. In the footsteps of Brueghel, this artist produced many different versions of the Tower of Babel – they included the work painted on the back of one of the copper plates which make up the 'London Copperplate Map'. This is one of his many versions on the theme. Dating from around 1600, it renders vividly the different building crafts in the foreground.
(Towneley Hall, Lancashire. Image in the public domain; Wikimedia Commons)

In the hands of Brueghel and his followers, the Tower became enormous and was generally found next to an urban settlement. The Bible is clear about this (but without reference to Nimrod or Babylon): 'Let us build us a city and a tower'. At times, however, the artistic Tower of Babel swallowed up the city and the Tower came to stand for the city, for example Marten van Valckenborgh's tower in Towneley Hall – the city is there but so insignificant that it almost looks like a village and has lost its purpose – to anchor the tower in an urban setting. Now, consider what the developer Irvine Sellar (1934–2017) asked of the architect of the Shard, Renzo Piano: a sky scraper which would be 'a vertical city'!

However, in the sixteenth century and just before the 1560s when the new muscular Tower of Babel emerged, artists were much involved with the mapping and other portrayals of cities. Brueghel himself based the city at the foot of his Tower on his native Antwerp. He is also believed to have painted his 'View of the Bay of Naples' around the same time as the Tower of Babel.

These sixteenth-century towers have been interpreted as standing for the folly and excesses of the Catholic Church and the Papacy, in a world which had just become divided along religious lines. The Tower which had been imagined by the first Christians and medieval man is not the Tower we have inherited from Pieter Brueghel the Elder (1525–1569) and the artists who followed in his footsteps. Its most overlooked symbolic interpretation is the Tower embodying the idea of the city in a world which was becoming urbanised and increasingly aware of the immense value and energy of cities. The Italian Renaissance provides the embodiment of this new realisation, with Florence, Siena, Venice, Bruges and Antwerp taking centre stage in art. And however unlikely this will seem, there is a direct link between this Tower of Babel and London itself.

Was Brueghel inspired by the grandiose ruins of the Colosseum which he would have seen when he travelled to Italy and stopped at Rome? Very possibly; it is also likely that he would have been aware of the most widely read histories in the sixteenth century: those of the Jewish people in *The Antiquities of the Jews*, written in AD 93 or 94 by Flavius Josephus. This text clearly associates the tower of Babel with the city-builder Nimrod and there too, this man's delusions of grandeur are punished with the subsequent destruction of the Tower. Although the remnants of the historic Tower in Babylon were not examined until the nineteenth century, there are accounts in 1583 and in the 1590s which compare the size of the ruins of the Tower of Babel in Persia to that of St Paul's Cathedral in London (see the work of Ton Hoenselaars in the bibliography).

To all art and urban historians, the sixteenth century is remarkable for at least one thing: it marks the emergence of cities in pictures – not just generalised background details as may be found in so many Renaissance religious paintings, but increasingly realistic depictions of actual towns and cities. This movement came out of the High Renaissance – Italian and Northern – in bird's eye views or pictorial maps of cities such as Florence (Rosselli's 'Chain' map c.1471–82), Venice (Jacopo de Barbari, 1500), Antwerp (anonymous woodcut, 1515), Bruges (Marcus Gheeraerts 1562), to name just a few. London's close links with Netherlandish trade and culture meant that it benefited from this in the shape of the earliest landscape painting to have been made in this country, the 'Fête at Bermondsey' in 1571 (see pp. 42–43) and the extraordinary Copperplate map – not as early as some of the examples cited above, but still dating from the 1550s. This Copperplate map has been mentioned on p. 40 but there is one further story which can now be revealed.

London and Babel

Two of the artists closely associated with Brueghel – brothers Martin and Lucas van Valckenborgh – followed in the master's footsteps and produced many versions of the Tower of Babel. Two of these versions are painted on the back of London's 'lost' Copperplate map – one section in the Museum of London, the other in Dessau Art Gallery in Germany. The word 'lost' is used because only three out of the original fifteen copper plates appear to have survived. All three have paintings on the smooth, non-engraved sides of the copperplates. The third copper plate, in the Museum of London, is painted with the Assumption of the Virgin.

There is an element of schizophrenia about the three surviving plates of the Copperplate Map. As objects, their identity is claimed by two separate worlds: that of the art historian for the painted sides, and that of the map/London historian for the engraved sides. Each side seems content to study half of these objects leaving the other half aside.

Notions of front and back when it comes to discuss the Copperplate Map are completely dependent on which of these two worlds engages with the plates. At Dessau the map is definitely on the back of the painting, whereas at the Museum of London the paintings are on the back of the map.

More than 100 works survive which depict the Tower of Babel between the 1560s and 1610s at exactly the same time that every European city was consolidating its image in maps and paintings. But these two precious sections from the Copperplate map – featuring the Tower of Babel on one side and London's map on the other – are in fact two sides of the same coin: the coin of urbanisation – giving shape to the city topographically and symbolically.

The copper plates depicting the South Bank have not come to light yet or have not survived. But they are not completely lost because several maps which derive from the Copperplate map have survived – particularly the Braun and Hogenberg map of 1572, a miniature version of the Copperplate map (see p. 40).

Research into Elizabethan texts confirms what is observable in pictures. The Dutch academic Ton Hoenselaars has written on the 'linguistic confusion in the shadow of St Paul's' and is very persuasive about the importance of the Tower of Babel in Elizabethan literature. He describes 'the unprecedented multiplication of languages' in London at that time and the way in which St Paul's Cathedral came to stand for the Tower of Babel. This is made explicit in a number of plays and publications including Thomas Dekker's 'Paule's Steeples Complaint' (in *The Dead Term*, 1607) as a result of the Cathedral losing its steeple in a 1561 storm. The steeple itself is given a voice, stating: 'I am the Tower of Babell newly to be builded vp, but presently despaire of euer being finished, because there is in me such a confusion of languages'. The steeple was never rebuilt.

When Margaret Aston was researching her book on the intriguing painting in the National Portrait Gallery 'Edward VI and the Pope: An Allegory of the Reformation', she came across a description of the

> revels for the young king's first Christmas which included the "makyng of a Towre Recemling the Tower of Babylon with all things belonging to the same" – a structure that was taken (together with the "maskyng garmentes" all the way from Blackfriars in London to Hampton Court and back.

On the topic of royal pursuits, Charles I, one of the greatest English art collectors of the seventeenth century, possessed no fewer than five paintings of the Tower of Babel, a significant number.

Babel in Southwark

Across the river from St Paul's and a little to the east stood a much smaller church, which to English ears contained much 'confusion of languages'. This was the church of St Olave in Tooley Street, bearing a Norwegian name and heading the parish of choice for the 'Doche' – the large community of men and women born in northern France, the Flemish provinces and northern Germany who took refuge in London before, during and after the Spanish governorship of this part of Europe.

And of course the Shard, with its Italian architect, its army of foreign cleaners, hotel and restaurant workers, with its rich foreign investors, stands on the very site which was home to many 'aliens' in times past and it takes on the Babel mantle with ease and charisma. It is, however, incredibly baffling to read some of the early published reactions to its appearance in Southwark:

> Jonathan Jones in *The Guardian* 19 August 2011: 'London has suffered an attack. The damage is ugly, and it is permanent.'

> Ian Dunt, 5 July 2012 at www.politics.co.uk: 'The problem with the Shard is that it is ugly, insecure and grotesque.'

Ugly? Seriously? I am on the side of Will Self's 'In Defence of the Shard', 25 May 2011 (Will Self's website):

> At dinner with a table of design professionals, including Terence Conran, I found myself defending the Shard, the 1,000ft incisor of a building currently being implanted in the rotten old gums of the Thames's banks to the immediate south of London Bridge. Not just defending the Shard but positively eulogising it.

Two years later in BBC Radio 4's 'Point of View' (18 January 2013) Will Self confessed:

> So taken am I by the spectacle of Renzo Piano's Shard lightsabering up into the London night, that I've taken to sleeping in the spare room, from where I have a good view of this, currently the loftiest building in Western Europe. I even leave the blind up, so that when I wake in the small hours I can contemplate the Shard under different light and weather conditions.

Nearby, there is a mini lookalike lightsabre (but lightless prototype) which forms part of the 'Southwark Gateway' project masterminded by Eric Parry Architects in 1999, thirteen years before the completion of the Shard. It consisted in making 'a new public space, a new tourist information centre and a stone marker' at the south eastern end of London Bridge. The stone marker or 'needle', by master mason André Vrona, was made of triangular shapes with steps to accentuate its elevated status. In the 2012 film which documents the project, Eric Parry describes the area as 'battle ground between the City and Southwark', the needle marking the site of the old Bridge Head; meanwhile the sculptor remarked on how much the 'Shard' echoed the 'Needle', the cameraman finding the perfect angle to demonstrate the closeness of the two designs despite, the dramatic difference in scale and orientation. Another claim has been made for closeness of design, published in *Private Eye's* 'Lookalikes', noted by Will Self in *The Guardian* (27 March 2015):

This 'needle', designed by Eric Parry, marks the entrance to London Bridge on the south side of the river.
(© The author, 2022)

The future site of the Shard was at Southwark Towers (on the left), opposite Guy's Hospital Tower (on the right). This cluster of high-rise buildings was often judged harshly, so there were few concerns when Southwark Towers was demolished in 2008. Photograph by Peter Marshall taken from the west, with Southwark Bridge in the foreground.
(© Peter Marshall; www.buildingsoflondon.co.uk/)

So it was that a postage stamp-sized photo of the Shard appeared, next to an equally grainy illustration of the four-pronged tower inhabited by the wizard Saruman in J R R Tolkien's *The Lord of the Rings*; and the reader's letter of course read: "has anyone else noticed the resemblance between the Shard and Isengard, I wonder if by any chance they may be related?"

In Peter Jackson's extraordinary films, the Orthanc tower and Isengard were based on Alan Lee's illustrations and modelled under the direction of Richard Taylor. Although the Tower is very impressive in the film, what was actually used was a 'very large miniature or "bigature" of Orthanc'. So, not a full-size monument either and one which is entirely black.

The original book cover of *The Tower of Glass*, the science fiction novel by Robert Silverberg (1970) is a more persuasive fit: the allusion to the shape, texture and colour are there. It belongs to the same visual family but not to the same narrative.

Beyond the biblical overtones mentioned above, the Shard has its own new millennial narrative which has been superbly told by Harold Watson in *The Shard – the vision of Irvine Sellar*, 2019. Despite being a eulogy of the developer Irvine Sellar, it is also a vivid, well researched contribution, written from within the world of architecture; the next section owes a great debt to Watson's work.

Southwark was not a stranger to towers. Its slightly 'distanced' cluster of towers was widely regarded as 'an architectural atrocity'. It comprised New London Bridge House – 1967, 94 metres high, by Richard Seifert, 'the king of the British high rise' but demolished in 2010 to make way for the News Building; then Guy's Hospital Tower, designed by Watkins Gray – the 134 metres Tower was extended to 149 metres in 2014; finally, Southwark Towers – 1975, 100 metres high, by Stephen Funnell from T P Bennett Architects.

How a star architect came to design the Shard

When the fashion entrepreneur turned property developer Irvine Sellar (1934–2017) purchased Southwark Towers in 1998, all he had in mind was 'to sit on it … and allow the rent cheques to come in'. The building had a single occupant: Price Waterhouse which had merged with Coopers Lybrand earlier in that year adopting the name Pricewaterhouse Coopers. However, shortly after making this acquisition Sellar became aware and inspired by a Government White Paper: *Planning Policy Guidance 1: General policy and principles* published in March 1998. He suddenly realised that he might be able to maximise the potential of the site through redevelopment. In the section dealing with 'Sustainable Development' the Paper encouraged 'the development of brownfield sites within built-up areas before considering the development of greenfield sites' also wishing to 'concentrate developments that generate a large number of trips in places well served by public transport' and finally advocating mixed-use schemes. Howard Watson points out in his book that at that time 'there were no multi-use skyscrapers in Europe, not a single one'.

The following year, Sellar talked to Pricewaterhouse Coopers and was told 'we don't have long term aspirations for this building'. Standing at the top of Southwark Towers and taking in the breath-taking view, 'Sellar made up his mind to build tall – very tall: four times the 328-foot (100 metre) high-rise on which he was standing'. He noted that the area was gathering cultural momentum with the Globe theatre which had opened in 1997, with Borough Market turning into a popular destination, the development 'More London' in the pipeline and Tate Modern about to open its doors (2000). Fred Manson, Head of Regeneration and Environment at Southwark Council, seemed ready to back such a project, frustrated by 'the City relying on Southwark's transport infrastructure to feed its offices across the water while there was no net benefit to the borough in terms of jobs and investment'. Manson suggested: 'Why don't you test the public appetite with some concepts?' Those early concepts were prepared by the firm Broadway Malyan architects (who were building their St George scheme at Vauxhall). In April 2000 Sellar announced his intention to build the tallest building in Europe at London Bridge. Manson was brutally frank: 'The likelihood of this going forward is 5 per cent, and the likelihood of this going forward with Broadway Malyan is zero'. The leading architectural critic Rowan Moore savaged the scheme in the *Evening Standard* (10 April 2000), lamenting: 'Oh spare us. A property developer with a bumpy history has joined forces with some mediocre architects to stick an upraised digit into the London air'; he concluded 'it is a developer trying out his luck. It is a poke in London's eye with a sharp stick. Please, future Mayor, save us from it'.

Sellar had heard enough. On 30 May he flew to Berlin to have lunch with leading architect Renzo Piano and after a shaky start when the Broadway Malyan design was immediately dismissed and Piano asserted: 'I don't like tall buildings … They are like fortresses', the two men actually got on and Piano responded to the idea of a mixed-use tower – 'a vertical city' – which he insisted should have public access. The architect admired London; he had lived there in the late 1960s, and early 70s: 'the place where I spent the most intriguing years of my life'. He attended the AA (Architectural Association School of Architecture) and set up a small office on Brook Street with Richard Rogers ('We were bad boys'). They made history when their design for the Centre George Pompidou in Paris (Beaubourg) was selected and then built between 1971 and 1977. But Piano had never built anything in this country. As developer and architect talked, Piano's enthusiasm grew and putting pen to paper he sketched on the menu a tapering tower in response to the multi-use brief (overleaf):

Top:
Antonio Canaletto (1697–1768), 'The Thames on Lord Mayor's Day' dates from the mid-1740s. For Renzo Piano this painting encapsulated a poetic picture of times past with its glorious forest of church spires. Just as the Shard was nearing completion Piano ordered a huge reproduction of this painting to go up near the entrance to London Bridge station (National Gallery of Prague. © AKG images)

Renzo Piano's first sketch for the Shard, when he first met the developer Irvine Sellar in Berlin in April 2000. Sellar's reaction to it has been recorded by Howard Watson: 'I thought, he's got it. I liked his thought process – the fact that it was like a sail coming out of the Thames, the elegance of it, the beauty of it … It had star-like quality even at that point'. (© RPBW)

If you want to make offices, you need a bigger plate at the bottom, then if you want a restaurant, you need a smaller plate, if you want a hotel you need a smaller plate and smaller again for apartments, and I liked the idea of a viewing platform at the top (Renzo Piano in Watson's book).

Almost immediately, the original plan for a 400 metre tower (September 2000) had to be revised down to 305 metres – the Civil Aviation Authority's recommended height of 1000 feet. Renzo Piano was well aware of the pitfalls: 'building a tower that could appear arrogant, a challenge to the city itself', but he described the tower as a 'building about gentleness'. Despite its dizzying height Piano wanted a tower 'light on its feet' and he wished to breathe air and light into its design: the windows were tilted to reflect the 'fluid northern sky'. Piano described his tower as a building which 'somehow manages to harness its soul and reflect it' … in perfect contrast to the site in Southwark which Piano liked to call 'the kingdom of darkness'.

The other key moment in the history of the Shard came when Deputy Prime Minister John Prescott ordered a public enquiry.

- Heavy-weight journalist Simon Jenkins who wrote unfailingly against the Shard used the following rallying call, in sympathy with English Heritage: 'Save our skyline from the Spike' (*Evening Standard* 17 April 2003).

- But Renzo Piano's cri de coeur must have resonated with the judge: 'I lived in Hampstead in the 1960s and used to take my children to Parliament Hill. It is a place I love. I will never do something that harms this view'. While John Hobson QC, acting for the Mayor of London, stated: 'The greatest benefit that the scheme will provide will be the addition to London's skyline of a world-class building of great and singular beauty. Far from causing any harm to St Paul's Cathedral or the Tower of London, it will positively enhance their setting.'

- English Heritage pursued a more local connection with its 'dagger through the heart of the Tower of London'. But the words of ace-lawyer Christopher Katkowski (acting for Irvine Sellar) spelt out irresistible common sense: 'The special qualities of the World Heritage Site do not depend in any way upon pretending that the world city outside does not exist … The ability to see the evolving world city around the Tower of London … only adds to the perception that the World Heritage site is different and special … a low-lying fortress embedded within an ever-evolving world city'.

- Unexpectedly, the Commission of Architecture and the Built Environment (CABE) was also against the project. Katkowski recalled: 'usually they [CABE] would side with the promoters of modern architecture, particularly if it was by a distinguished architect, as was the case with the Shard'. CABE was technically aligned with the opposition but contradicted their partners when they stated that 'London Bridge Tower will do no harm to London's historic environment'. While Kratkowski insisted that Southwark already had a cluster of skyscrapers but the London Bridge Tower would be replacing an 'utterly mediocre' building with a 'world-class tower'.

This much simplified account of an immensely complex project will, I hope, inspire readers to re-visit this amazing part of Southwark. Many may agree with the leading architectural commentator Peter Murray, Curator-in-Chief of New London Architecture, when he wrote in the *Financial Times* of 26 May 2012: '[The Shard] generates wonderful surprises in the cityscape … It is also, quite simply, one of the most beautiful tall buildings in the world'.

Towermania

With the benefit of hindsight, it seems that the judgement made by Tom Ball, a member of the public who had written in the press against the Shard, was prophetic when he wrote to the enquiry: 'If approved, it would set a precedent for a flood of huge and tall buildings and spell an end for London's much admired human scale'. Since the building of the Shard the following towers have appeared or threatened to appear on the South Bank:

- South Bank Tower (former IPC tower). The original tower of thirty storeys (111m) was designed by Richard Seifert and completed in 1972. In 2013 the building was redeveloped and completed two years later. It now has forty storeys (151m). The extension was designed by Make Architects. Hermes bought the building in 2015 and commissioned T P Bennett to redesign all the commercial areas (completed in 2017).

- No 1 Blackfriars, 2013–18 (see p. 328).

- St George Wharf Tower, Vauxhall, completed 2014 (see p. 317). The current development of Vauxhall represents a cluster of towers.

- In October 2015, Southwark Planning Department turned down a scheme for a rocket shaped tower and a Gagarin Square scheme for Southwark Street (*Evening Standard*, 9 October).

This aerial photograph, shot against the light in 2021, provides visual evidence of the sudden mushrooming of high-rise buildings on the South Bank. The picture is taken from the north bank, looking west in the direction of Battersea Power Station (in the centre). Floating in the early morning mist are from left to right: No 1 'boomerang' Blackfriars, the former IPC tower in its extended state, the Southbank Place cluster next to Waterloo station (now dwarfing the LWT tower below it), the London Eye. The very tall tower at the top left is St George Wharf, Vauxhall – nowadays surrounded by a forest of towers.

(© Jason Hawkes)

Opposite:

This diagram shows the heights of some of London's landmark buildings, two of them on the South Bank. From left to right: the Tower of London, Big Ben, St Paul's Cathedral, the London Eye, the Post Office Tower, the Gherkin, the Leadenhall building, Heron Tower, One Canada Square and the Shard.

(© Stephen Conlin)

- 18 Blackfriars Road: Wilkinson Eyre towers at Blackfriars secured planning permission in 2017 – the scheme was not followed up. They will now become Norman Foster's towers following the change of ownership of the land in 2021 (*Architects' Journal*, 21 October 2021).

- In 2020 two towers were proposed for the redevelopment of Vinegar Yard and the adjacent warehouse, Bermondsey. The CIT development, rejected by the Council in 2020 for being too high, has resubmitted a scheme (2021) with a tower even taller than the last one. The second tower, a Sellar development, was unveiled in 2019 for the site they have owned since 2008. According to *City A.M.* (29 June 2020): 'The council is set to approve Sellar's proposals, having considered they are "compliant overall"'. The scheme is controversial in conservation/heritage circles and the decision was delayed …

- Even a relatively small project such as the rebuilding of a school and library at Lower Marsh in Waterloo (Oasis Johanna Development Scheme) introduced a tower of fifteen storeys in its proposal as a way of financing the rebuilding. This scheme would be extremely damaging to the character of this precious historic bubble which has miraculously retained its original low-lying line of buildings with its remarkable visual connection to the City of London.

In truth, however, this new scale is not the prerogative of Southwark or even the South Bank. It is now to be found all over London.

Chronology of 'the tallest building in London' (in 2020)

1975	Completion of Southwark Towers at 32 London Bridge, designed by T P Bennett (100m high, 25 floors, 3 wings). The home of Price Waterhouse	2003	(November) Project received planning permission from John Prescott's office
1998	Price Waterhouse merged with Coopers & Lybrand	2007	Financial markets in difficulty and this raised concerns about the viability of the Shard
	Developer Irvine Sellar purchased Southwark Towers	2008	(early) Sellar announced new partners for the financing of the Shard: a consortium of Qatari banks and developer
1999	Government Bill encouraged planners to look favourably at high-rise buildings close to major transport hubs: Sellar's project for the site would be a major development and include London Bridge Station	2008	Demolition of Southwark Towers to make way for the Shard. Use of explosives too dangerous with the proximity of so many sensitive buildings, including Guy's Hospital. Southwark Towers was dismantled piece by piece
2000	Early scheme for a mixed-use tower ('vertical city'). Sellar was advised that a new tower would only win consent if it was an outstanding design	2009	(March) Construction began
	Spring: Sellar flies to Berlin to meet Renzo Piano	2012	The Shard was inaugurated on 5 July
2002	(March) Sellar's plan was approved	2013	The Shard opened (244m above ground, 310m in all, 95 floors – 72 habitable, viewing gallery at 72nd floor)
2002	(July) Deputy Prime Minister John Prescott ordered a public enquiry after several heritage bodies (including English Heritage) opposed the project	2017	(October) The Shard's offices were fully let

Above:

The Shard Quarter at London Bridge.
(© The author, 2020)

Opposite:

The 'backpack' is the name given to the building accretion (office space) on the east side of the Shard.

The News Building was built on the site of New London Bridge House.

'Shard Place' was the last piece of the 'Shard Quarter' puzzle: a luxury housing development at the foot of the Shard, completed in 2021.

(© The author, 2021)

The creation of London Bridge Quarter, later Shard Quarter

Irvine Sellar's original intention was simply a spectacularly tall tower – over 300 metres – which would be the embodiment of a 'vertical city'. It took over ten years to achieve this, with endless obstacles as well as opportunities along the way. The plan had to be adjusted at various critical times, in other words, the plan changed. The three most significant changes were recorded by Howard Watson:

- In 2002 'to improve the financial viability of the scheme, a sixteen-storey "backpack" of offices, projecting east along St Thomas Street, was added to the design' (top right).

- By April 2003, Sellar had settled the developer's contributions to the scheme (Section 106 of the 1990 Town and Country Planning Act) and they included a roof for the railway station to be designed by Piano and large sums to improve underground and bus facilities at London Bridge.

- In September 2003: 'the Sellar Property Group and its Shard development partner CLS announced they had bought New London Bridge House office block'.

At this point, if not before, Irvine Sellar's goal had changed: he could now afford to be a great deal more ambitious, and pursue a 'London Bridge Quarter' (he later settled on the 'Shard Quarter'). In due course, New London Bridge House was demolished (2010) and La Place, now known as the News Building, was built and ready in 2014, also designed by Piano (right, middle).

- In January 2014 Sellar announced that a 26-storey residential building was to be built on the sites of Fielden House and 21–27 St Thomas Street. It would become 'Shard Place' (bottom right).

Around the time of the Public Enquiry which John Prescott called for after Southwark granted planning permission to the Shard (April-July 2003), Renzo Piano and Irvine Sellar were faced with serious criticism from people and organisations concerned that the Shard would block strategic views of important historic buildings, particularly if, over time, one skyscraper attracted others leading to the formation of a cluster. Piano was insistent that the Shard 'was made to be lonely'. With the purchase and development of additional plots, the Shard is no longer 'lonely' and presides over the glass-glittering 'Shard Quarter'.

Renzo Piano explained: 'The concourse level, the new station and the combination of the Shard, the News Building and Shard Place altogether create a place of dignified urbanity. It is a bit frustrating that those things take a long time'. Indeed they do: Shard Place, due to open in 2018 was still unfinished in winter 2020. But delays will be forgotten when the construction workers hand over the site to new residents. Howard Watson's optimistic statement seems well deserved: 'Finally, London Bridge is a place rather than an accident of infrastructure'. But Sellar should be given the last word – he describes the complete transformation of London Bridge station: 'it's placemaking. And a tower should not be in splendid isolation, it should be part of the immediate facility, it should embrace it'. Placemaking is the new-ish buzzword that describes the role played by the places in-between buildings – they used to be neglected but now flourish in landscape design schemes, piazzas, gardens, public spaces for leisure and for establishing effective connections between buildings.

The social 'pecking order'

If we now return to the quotation by Ben Judah which opens this chapter, we can only measure its full impact with a little more context. In his book *This is London* it turns up on p. 233, well into the often harrowing accounts of life at the bottom of the social scale. By the time the Shard is mentioned – briefly – the context implied that the whole tower probably thrived off more exploitation, more badly paid staff and more struggling lives like those described in the rest of the book, with the added spice of poverty rubbing shoulders with disproportionate wealth.

One of Ben Judah's most telling interviews about the social hierarchy for immigrants is that of a Peckham policeman who arrived in London in 1989, believing in its 'streets paved with gold'. His first job, serving bankers in Liverpool Street, taught him everything he needed to know to survive in London:

There were a lot of Irish and Australian chefs … But the kitchen boys were all Nigerians and Ghanaians. That was when I realised, that's the pecking order …':

The room service and the waitresses, the people who touched the food, they were mostly white. Not from England, but the whites who were coming in. Australians, by and large. The receptionists, those who greeted the guests, and keyed things in for them, were Irish, with singsong voices, who swore at him there was no work for people like them back home. The cleaners, humming, always humming, between the floors and the corridors, with their trolleys and sprays, they were Africans, or a few that had very strange faces, which he thought must be South American.

Back to the policeman:

Y'see in London you've always had the Africans at the bottom of the pile along with the West Indians. I don't mean West Indians like who flew in yesterday from Jamaica but I mean the second generation of West Indians. They are the bottom too … Then you get some Afghans. Then the Eastern Europeans coming up. The East Europeans are above us Africans … because they are more acceptable. Because of the likeness of the race. There is a commonality in Europe of the ethnicity … you know? That's the way it is.

Then you get the Asians … Then you get the Irish. Then you get the white … And at the very top you get the rich …

Where there is no race.

In *This is London*, this 'pecking order' turns up in interview after interview: 'that's just the way it is'. Would things be so different in the Shard?

The Manna Day Centre/Society

Eventually, Ben Judah's policeman found a career, rather than just a job at the bottom of the social scale. For those who are not so lucky or hard working, it often means life on the streets with occasional respite at places catering for the homeless or the very poor. In the shadow of the Shard, at 12 Melior Street, is the Manna Day Centre. It has its finger directly placed on the pulse of struggling humanity. The Centre provides food, hot showers, housing and welfare advice, access to computers and social interaction daily between the hours of 8.00 a.m. and 1.30 p.m. These services are efficiently structured: the clothing store for instance is open three times a week for one hour only.

This Centre started in 1982 at No 6 Melior Street in St Joseph's disused infant

school. It was the tentative brainchild of a Catholic (Franciscan) nun, Nanette Ffrench who had gained the support of Bishop Henderson and soon after that of Ray Towey, a consultant anaesthetist at Guy's Hospital. She named it the Manna Centre, and early 'clients' came from the rough hostel set up at 147 Tooley Street – where George Orwell (overleaf) stayed to research his 1933 book *Down and Out in Paris and London* – but no longer in existence; and also, from the hostel in Great Guildford Street, still operating in the hands of St Mungo's. The Manna Society had its first annual general meeting in 1985 and in that year, Nanette left her religious order to become a lay person working for the Manna Society.

The Administrator, Paddy Boyle, has been at the helm of the Society since April 1986 and his brief is touching in its simplicity:

> Our philosophy is unconditional acceptance. Providing basic support to people in need. It's scandalous that people don't have food or shelter. People will only change their lives when they themselves have made the decision. We will facilitate as best we can when people are ready to change. There is no charge for any of our services and provisions.

In the words of the Lord Bishop of Southwark, Christopher Chessun: 'what happens here happens from the heart'.

When the Centre opened in 1986 there was a large number of Irish and Scottish men using the Centre. But ethnicity and countries of origin rise and fall in accordance with foreign policy, not local conditions. The once large number of eastern Europeans who replaced the Irish and the Scots is now waning.

The latest survey, on 19 October 2022 revealed that '17% of the 117 people who came last week were Africans. The number using our Housing

The Manna Day Centre at 12 Melior Street is open seven days a week, offering food, clothing and advice to homeless people or vulnerable local residents. These photographs were taken by former *Guardian* photographer Tricia de Courcy Ling in August 2011 and November 2015. Food preparation with Irena Boyle – inventiveness is the name of the game as Irena never knows what foods will be donated until the very last minute; drying clothes in the courtyard when the Centre was sited at 6 Melior Street (top); serving the food (middle); the clothes store run by volunteers (bottom). The impromptu wash day disappeared when the Centre moved to No 12.
(Courtesy of the Manna Society)

George Orwell (1903–1950) spent time in many tramps' hostels or 'spikes', 'researching' what would become his book *Down and Out in Paris and London* published in 1933. There he described the 'peculiarities' of English spikes: 'At A you are allowed to smoke but there are bugs in the cells; at B the beds are comfortable but the porter is a bully; at C they let you in early in the morning but the tea is undrinkable; at D the officials steal your money if you have any – and so on, interminably'. In 1931, when hop-picking in Kent, Orwell stayed at the Tooley Street 'spike' which he found particularly unpleasant. This photograph dates from around 1940.
(Photo in the public domain, Wikimedia Commons)

& Welfare advice service is even greater. In September, 35% of clients were of African heritage & 18% were refugees'.

It is not simply the client base which is shifting, the neighbourhood is changing too – from a somewhat forgotten corner of South London to a trendy part of 'Bermondsey Conservation Area'. In March 2014 Southwark Council Planning Department gave the go ahead to a controversial redevelopment scheme in Melior Street. It involved the demolition of part of St Joseph's School where the Manna Centre was located, and the Centre's move to new, smaller premises next door. The development of thirty-seven homes (eight of them 'affordable'), with two shop units – now occupied by high class restaurants, one with a Michelin star – is sited between Melior Street and Snowfields. The well informed *SE1 Community News* website lists ten eating and drinking places within 100 yards of the Manna Centre (Sollip, Horseshow Inn, Trivet, Café Link, Texas Joe's, Champor Champor, Petit Bleu, the Athenian, Bob's Lobster and the Rose) – the list is not exhaustive. The contrast between their kitchens and clientele and the Manna Centre could not be more striking, some would say, jarring; to which should be added the trendy practice of Newground Architects on the Weston Street corner. But perhaps it is the close cohabitation of people from worlds apart which makes London what it is.

London's larder

There is one place however, where being a foreign Londoner is positively a badge of honour, it is the world of food and markets: at nearby Borough market, exotic delicacies served by foreign nationals are all cheek by jowl and they seem to be winners: French cheeses, Spanish tapas, Indian spices, delicious toasties, pastei de nata or empanadas … The history of the market is one of developing its reach while controlling its chaotic impact on the streets of Southwark.

The fortunes of Borough market have been considered elsewhere; for many years it had thrived in Borough High Road before it was forced to either close or relocate. What now needs to be considered is the origin of the popular denomination of Southwark or Bermondsey as 'London's Larder'. Aytoun Ellis, who wrote a history of Hay's Wharf believes that it was the result of the business acumen of one of its Victorian owners, Hugh Colin Smith (1836-1910) who, in 1862, joined Alderman Humphery, former M.P. for Southwark, and Arthur Magniac, at the helm of the Hay's Wharf enterprise. Hugh Colin Smith became Governor of the Bank of England in the 1890s but before that came his association with Hay's Wharf that lasted for forty-eight years.

Hay's Wharf was in the heart of the Southwark stretch of the Port of London. It had been in existence for almost three hundred years – there was a dock at that site as early as 1501. In the late seventeenth century, the Pool of London had become seriously congested with all types of

ships which suffered long loading and unloading delays due to the limited number of legal quays. In 1663 Parliament had allowed the use of additional 'Sufferance' wharves and in 1789 the Sufferance Wharves Act created additional licensed wharves over and above the 'legal quays' on the north bank; at first the 'Sufferance Wharves' were reserved for goods of lower value – there were five on the north bank and eighteen on the south bank. In the late eighteenth century, the Port of London authorities recognised the essential role the sufferance wharves were playing in alleviating the chronic congestion of the Port's legal quays. These wharves were surveyed and mapped in 1789 by W. Fellows (overleaf). The sufferance wharves from London Bridge going east are thus listed in the correct sequence, from west to east (later additions shown in square brackets): [Fenning's Wharf and Topping's Wharf next to London Bridge were acquired by the Admiralty], then Chamberlain's Wharf, Cotton's Wharf, Hay's Wharf, [Depot Wharf], Beal's Wharf, [Carpenter Smith's Wharf], Griffin's Wharf, [Gun and Shot Wharf], Symon's Wharf, Stanton's Wharf, [Pickle Herring Upper Wharf, Pickle Herring Lower Wharf, Mark Brown's Wharf], Davis, Butt & Co Wharf, Hartley's Wharf, Pearson's Wharf, Holland's Wharf, Coles Wharf, [Butler's Wharf], Hogarth's Wharf. Beyond St Saviour's dock stood three more sufferance wharves – Meriton's, Carrington's and Scott's.

Although Hay's Wharf appears to be one of the smallest wharves, with a narrow river frontage, in terms of warehouse storage, it came second on the table published. In 1845 the Banks Victorian panorama (chapter 3.4) paid little attention to wharves at all; none

How Southwark and Bermondsey came to be known as London's Larder: these two wood engravings by the French artist Gustave Doré depict Southwark's busy wharves in 1872 – from the interior of a warehouse with St Paul's Cathedral in the background in 'Riverside Warehouse', showing the weighing and storing of goods; but also outside warehouses in 'Pickle Herring Street' with the discharging of goods from horse-drawn vehicles, hoisting them up all the way to the warehouses' upper storeys.
(From *London A Pilgrimage* by Blanchard Jerrold, 1872)

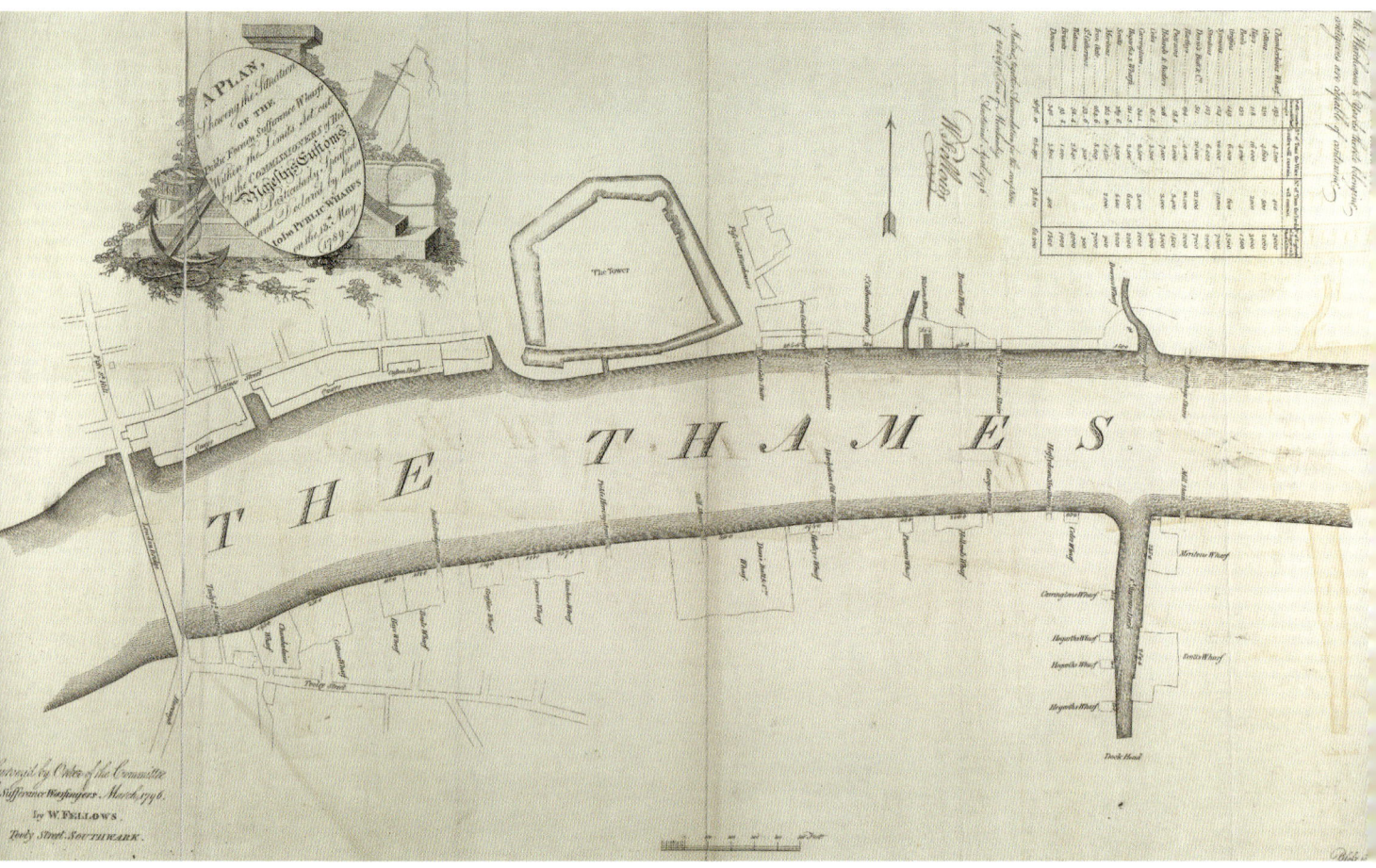

The Sufferance Wharves between London Bridge and St Saviour's Dock: 'A Plan showing the situation of the Public, Foreign Sufferance Wharfs Within the Limits Set out by the Commissioners of His Majestys Customs and Particularly Specified and Declared by them to be Public Wharfs, on the 13th May 1789.' This engraving was reprinted in 1796 and 1809.
(© British Library Board. All Rights Reserved/Bridgeman Images)

of them feature on the accompanying key. Eventually Hay's Wharf came to absorb most of the neighbouring wharves. But in the early days the overall sense of direction was far from being clear. Hay's Wharf owes its name to its 1651 leaseholder – Alexander Hay – although in his day the wharf was known as 'Pipe Borer's Wharf'. He took over the lease of a brewery called 'Goldings' (see p. 137). Members of the Hay family were then described as carpenter and joiner, primarily focused on supplying wooden pipes to water companies. Joseph Hay, Alexander's son, became involved instead in a fire insurance scheme – Ye Amicable Contributors (later assimilated into the Commercial Union Group). Pipe Borer's Wharf changed its name to Hay's Wharf around 1710. Three years later the brewhouse burnt down but was rebuilt.

A year later, in 1714, the year the 'Doggett's Coat and Badge Race for Watermen' was founded, Aytoun Ellis observed that:

> the warehousing system as we know it today came into being when, for the first time, the Customs authority allowed tobacco

to be warehoused on payment of a small portion of the import duty (repayable on exportation).

The Hay family mostly disappeared from the scene in the 1770s, choosing lighterage over warehousing. Hay's Wharf, then a relatively small pawn on the wharves chessboard, was mostly in the hands of William Humphery, a shipowner who had been one of Hay's clients. The over-riding lease however, covered a more substantial area – Pipe Borer's Wharf (i.e., Hay's Wharf), and the brewhouse and warehouses, plus the Bridge House (later renamed Cotton's Wharf) as well as ten acres in the Old Kent Road. In 1709 Charles Cox, MP for Southwark acquired this lease for sixty-one years and when it expired it went to Thomas Morgan. Meanwhile Thomas Cotton gave his name to the Bridge House Wharf in 1740. With the death of descendant Alexander Hay in 1796, Hay's Wharf was in the hands of J Humphery & Son. Increasingly, wharves operations would be placed in the hands of partners rather than those of a single owner or members of the same family, each partner providing a range of different experience, expertise, connections. We are finally able to catch a glimpse of the wharves' appearance and activities with the publication, in 1857, of *Loveday's London Waterside Surveys*. It includes descriptions of Chamberlain's (Joseph Barber), Cotton's (J H and J Scovell) and Hay's (J Humphery & Son) wharves, along many others. This is Hay's: 'the Warehouses constituting this Wharf are the most substantial Buildings represented in this work [publication]'. (Overleaf)

By that date, builder turned politician William Cubitt (1791–1863) had recently completed some of the warehouses around Hay's dock; two were still under construction, including the one above the entrance to the dock. Warehouses were commonly four or five floors above the cellars but at Hay's most reached six floors above the cellars. Their activities were described as:

> Trade, Foreign and Coasting. Goods hazardous and not hazardous landed; but the bulk of the merchandise consists of Sugars, Jute, Rice and Cotton. Locked lamps used when necessary. Hoisting by manual labour.

The traded goods involved foods but we are still a few years away from 'the Larder'; in the twentieth century 75% of London's butter, cheese and canned meat was stored at Hay's Wharf, according to Geoff Marshall.

The awful fire of 1861 (overleaf) devastated Hay's and Cotton's wharves and their list of losses confirms Loveday's description as well as completing the picture by giving some idea of the quantities stored on site: '18,000 bales of cotton; 10,000 barrels of tallow; 5000 tons of rice; 3000 tons of sugar; 1000 tons of hemp; 11000 tons of jute and immense quantities of bacon, tea, spices and other foodstuffs'. Tragically, Londoners also lost one of their heroes in that great fire of Tooley Street – James Braidwood, superintendent of the London Fire Engine Establishment which had been formed under his leadership in 1833. His death was so shocking, that the Surveyor for the Phoenix Fire Office included in his detailed map of the event, the following entry 'Here Mr Braidwood fell'; this was by the wall which separated Chamberlain's and Cotton's wharves. The wall crushed him, barely three hours into a fire which lasted two weeks and needed the help of several private fire brigades. The London Fire Engine Establishment was a private company funded by insurance companies and many argued this was an inadequate system. The catastrophic

These two images are artificially paired to show Hay's Wharf in the nineteenth century. On the left is G. Yates's informative watercolour, dated 1834, and taken from the street to show how the loading and unloading of goods was achieved; also note the charming details of two shops in the right foreground: 'Southwark Coffee House' and 'W.H. Chetwynd Oil and Colourman'. The print on the right shows Hay's Wharf from the Thames, labelled 'Alderman Humphery's Dock, Tooley Street, Southwark, 1857'. This lithograph was published in the same year as Loveday's *London Waterside Surveys*.

© London Metropolitan Archives (City of London)

Tooley Street fire was a prime mover in the passing of the 1865 Metropolitan Fire Brigade Act which gave birth to the publicly funded Metropolitan Fire Brigade.

Hay's Wharf was still in the hands of John Humphery & Sons, but it was now run by the son – Alderman Humphery, former MP and Mayor of Southwark. When he died in 1863, one of the firm's recently appointed partners, Hugh Colin Smith, took over the chairmanship. The other partner, Arthur Magniac, was extremely well connected within the China trade – he was the son of Hollingworth Magniac of the firm Jardine, Matheson & Co, the oldest and greatest of Merchant Adventurers in China and the Far East (their first steps in China had been eased by their neighbours, Beale's Wharf). Their ships, the famous tea clippers, were some of the best in the world and a familiar sight in the Pool of London – they chose Hay's Wharf for their London operations.

From then on, by pursuing a policy of innovation and acquisition, Hay's Wharf simply grew ever larger. After benefiting from the superior tea clippers of Jardine Matheson & Co which made the tea trade thrive, 'undoubtedly the foundation of the firm's prosperity' writes Aytoun Ellis, Hay's Wharf's owners purchased

equipment for husking and grading coffee, also expanding their cocoa trade. They equipped Cotton's Wharf, having purchased it in 1865, with the best cold storage facilities available. A number of external factors facilitated their rise – in the 1890s, the centre of gravity for the provision trade which had long been in Lower Thames Street on the north bank started shifting to the south bank, very possibly the outcome of Hugh Colin Smith's tenacious lobbying. The Egg Exchange came to Tooley Street, subsequently moving to the Hop Exchange and a new Provision Exchange was set up at Hibernia Chambers (No 2 London Bridge). In 1901 Hay's Wharf purchased Fenning's Wharf, later followed by Willson's Wharf which was where bottling of wine and spirits first started. 1909 saw them purchase property west of London Bridge – Old Hibernia, New Hibernia, Mann's & West Kent wharves; and later still, Pickford Wharf (1920). They acquired Mark Brown's Wharf in 1929 which had absorbed Davis Wharf. A 1921 List from the *London Street Directory* for Borough High Street west side shows how much food and drink business had permeated this area, listing out of a hundred or so entries: twenty-seven provision importers/merchants; eleven agents specializing in hop, and dealers in ham (1), eggs (2), oil (1), wine (1), potato (1), flour

The Tooley Street fire started at Cotton's Wharf on 22 June 1861 and lasted two weeks, destroying all of the warehouses alongside the Thames between Chamberlain's Wharf next to St Olave's church and Hay's Wharf Dock. This lithograph published by Louis Rocheford shows the scene on 23 June when the fire was at its most ferocious; it was described as the largest conflagration since 1666. The fire was fuelled by the high combustibility of the warehouse goods. Even London Bridge Station caught fire but the flames were quickly extinguished.
(London Metropolitan Archives. Image in the public domain, Wikimedia Commons)

Above:

St Olaf House, headquarters of the Hay's Wharf Company, 1932. Grade II listed, it was built on the site of St Olave's church after it became redundant and its nave demolished in 1926 – the tower following in 1928. The elegant Art Deco structure is six-storeys high, T-shaped with a wider frontage on the riverside, the most decorated part of the building with thirty-nine terracotta reliefs, gilded, by the artist Frank Dobson, on the theme of 'Capital, Labour and Commerce' (right). On the Tooley Street facade (left), Dobson designed a mosaic representing 'St Olaf, King of Norway' to whom the ancient church was dedicated. After the departure of the docks in the 1980s the building was purchased by the London Hospital.
(© The author, 2021)

(1), tea (1) and dairy (1), also naming one trader with Russia and one with West Africa.

The tall and elegant St Olaf House (left) which served as the firm's headquarters in the twentieth century was designed by H S Goodhart-Rendel. It testifies to the success and standing of the firm. It was ready in 1932 and by the Second World War, Hay's Wharf operations stretched from London Bridge to Butler's Wharf – London's Larder!

Antecedents

Despite the relatively recent description 'London's Larder' there is considerable continuity in the production and consumption of food in this part of the South Bank. Between 1598 and 1612, the year of his death, Robert Cecil, first Earl of Salisbury and a key administrator of the royal funds, was going through a period of intense estate building – he made numerous acquisitions of (mostly) royal land, turning 'the modest inheritance from his father into one of the great estates of the kingdom', according to the historian Lawrence Stone. Stone described how much of the Cecils' income came from two highly specialised types of property: urban housing (in the West End) and large pasture holdings. The Earl's property in Bermondsey, which included Grange Farm (below), catered to big London graziers and butchers who fattened their cattle for the London meat trade.

Inns and breweries

'We have Chaucer's authority for the fame of our inns', so begins the chapter on 'Ale and the Brewers' in Rendle and Norman's book on the inns of Southwark (1888). While the seventeenth-century antiquary John Aubrey points out that 'before the Reformation public inns were rare; travellers were entertained at religious houses for three days together if occasion served.'

But in the post-Reformation era, the rise of the inn as a place of hospitality is a noticeable feature of the Southwark/Bermondsey area, the greatest concentration is found on the east side of Borough High Street.

Rendle and Norman explain that in 1619 Southwark's inhabitants themselves stated that their neighbourhood consisted chiefly of inns. A few years later in 1631,

the question of too many alehouses came up; 228 were counted, and of these 43 had to be suppressed – 21 in Kent Street partly because of the plague, partly from their excessive number and evil repute … These old inns were the first places for theatrical entertainment.

Ale was the original drink – thus defined and regulated by a 1542 Act: 'Ale is made of malte and water, and they the whiche do put any oder thynge to ale than is rehersed except yest, barme or godes good doth sofysticat theyr ale.' Presumably John Crosse's brewery, recorded on the 1542 map of Southwark south of the church of St Saviour would have complied with the Act. Rendle and Norman believed hops were probably known in England long before that date, but not appreciated. One of the earliest places favoured by brewers was Pickle Herring Street, a centre for the herring trade.

At first beer or ale making was produced on a domestic scale as the brew made of malt could not be kept for long, but with the arrival of Flemings and other members of the 'Doche' community (see p. 136) the hospitality scene was transformed. Brewing establishments such as the 1572 'beere house' (overleaf), combined production and distribution on one and the same site. Flemings are generally credited with the introduction of hops and the scaling up of brewing operations.

'Beere House'

In John Fastolf's archives at Magdalen College, there are no less than 377 deeds which relate to his Southwark/Bermondsey possessions, including the Boar's Head Inn (east side of 'Long Southwark' see p. 134 and above). Another of his properties was connected with an earlier resident

Far left:

The façade of the Boar's Head inn on the east side of Borough High Street is reproduced on p. 134. This is Boar's Head Court at the back of the ancient inn, with two rows of tenements which were sublet to weekly tenants. Rendle and Norman noted that 'beneath the whole extent of the Court was a finely-vaulted cellar, doubtless the wine-cellar of the Boar's Head'.
(From *The Inns of Old Southwark* by William Rendle and Philip Norman, 1888)

left:

The White Hart was described in 1720 as 'very large and of a considerable trade, being esteemed one of the best inns in Southwark' (Stow 1720 in bibliography). This ancient inn was of the classic galleried type and survived well into the nineteenth century when it was drawn by Philip Norman for *The Inns of Old Southwark* book. It was vividly described by Charles Dickens in *The Pickwick Papers* published in 1836-37: 'In the Borough especially, there still remain some half dozen old inns, which have preserved their external features unchanged, and which have escaped alike the rage for public improvement, and the encroachment of private speculation. Great, rambling, queer old places they are, with galleries, and passages, and staircases, wide enough and antiquated enough to furnish material for a hundred ghost stories'.
(From *The Inns of Old Southwark* by William Rendle and Philip Norman, 1888)

Opposite:

This detail from a manuscript map of Bermondsey gives a very early depiction of one of its landmark sites – Grange Farm, which was originally attached to Bermondsey Abbey. The map was commissioned by William Cecil (1591-1668), second Earl of Salisbury who owned large tracts of Bermondsey – inland as in this example and on the river bank, stretching to Rotherhithe. He may have commissioned this survey when he became the second Earl of Salisbury in 1612, or indeed later. The yard is framed by groups of buildings including a long building, a row of smaller houses, timber barns and a tenter ground. There is a wooded area, and perhaps an orchard close to the houses.
(The Marquess of Salisbury, Hatfield House, Hertfordshire)

 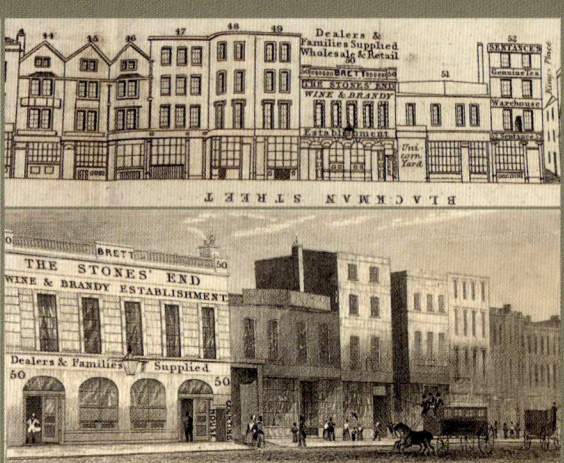

This section of Blackman Street (left), drawn by J C Buckler in 1827, would now be called Borough High Street (west side). It records an interesting group of buildings connected to drinking and hospitality in the 1830s. The easiest building to identify, and the oldest, is the King's Arms at No 44-46, in the middle. Its roof line and projecting bays date to the seventeenth century if not before. It stood very close to the Unicorn Inn which, many years later, was 'remembered' in Tallis's London (top right) – 'Unicorn Yard'. There is a detailed plan of this inn, dated 1676, in the Society of Antiquaries. Then it was a vast establishment which comprised alehouses (the Boar's Head and the Ship), stables (for up to fifty horses), wheelwrights, blacksmiths and small farms. Part of the site is No 50 on Tallis's *Street Views*. After the disappearance of the Unicorn Inn, it was replaced by businesses linked to the theme of drinking – No 50 was the premises of Alfred Brett, vintner & brandy merchant at The Stone's End. Right of its 'counting house' was the entrance to Unicorn yard. The taller building on the right, at No 52, is 'Sentence's genuine tea warehouse'. This arrangement is confirmed by the wood engraving reproduced on the same page as the map (bottom right).

(© London Metropolitan Archives (City of London) for the Buckler drawing; the other two from John Tallis's *London Street Views*, 1838–40)

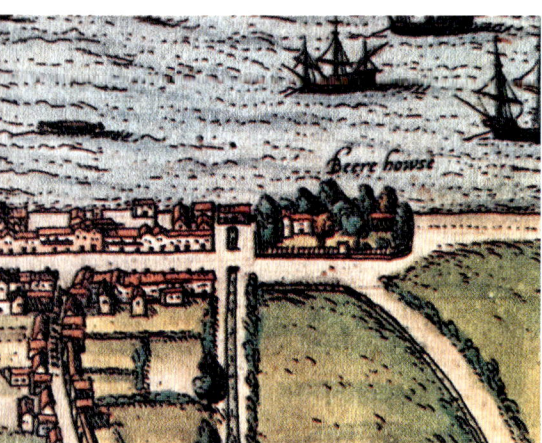

This detail from Braun & Hogenberg's 1572 map of London (see p. 40) shows the 'beere house' which took shape within the estate of Sir John Fastolf sometime after his death in 1459. By the late sixteenth century this was where two important Netherlandish brewers were based: Henry Leake and Wessel Webling.

– the celebrated architect Henry Yevele whom we encountered at Kennington Palace and London Bridge. In 1387 Yevele purchased the property around Morgan's Lane which had two water mills and a town house (the former inn of Malling Abbey). He rebuilt the water mills as a double mill, probably inspired by the nearby Battle Mills. These were pulled down in 1667. This estate was Fastolf's London residence, subsequently acquired by Flemish brewers (see p. 139). It was not, however, until the eighteenth century that beer brewing was pursued on an industrial scale with Calvert & Co, Whitbread and Truman the largest producers in 1760; Barclay & Perkins, Meux Reid & Co, Truman Hanbury & Co in 1815; and Barclay & Perkins, Truman Hanbury & Co, Whitbread & Co were major brewers by 1840.

The story of the vast Barclay & Perkins Brewery in Bankside – also known as the Anchor brewery – has been told elsewhere (p. 191); but their name spread to this neighbourhood which was the home of a rival landmark brewery: Courage. It was and continues to be one of the most striking buildings on the Bermondsey riverfront – its story starts at the end of the eighteenth century when John Courage, an Aberdeen shipping agent, founded a brewery in Horsleydown in 1787. It rapidly became known as the Anchor brewhouse and was

The Anchor brewery was set up by John Courage in Horsleydown in 1787 – now sited at the foot of Tower Bridge. The (later) building still exists, captured at night time by Mike Seaborne in 1981, just before its closure and redevelopment.
© Mike Seaborne,
www.mikeseaborne.co.uk

in the ownership of Courage & Donaldson between 1797 and 1851. In the twentieth century, with the decline of the docks, it merged with the Barclay & Perkins brewery (1955). Brewing stopped in 1962.

Artists move into the empty shells of industry and commerce

In 1952 When Aytoun Ellis wrote his book about Hay's Wharf, this organisation seemed solid and the future bright. But within just over a decade the Thames working wharves and the docks gradually turned into ghost quarters. The Port of London reached its peak in 1964 when it handled 61 million tons of goods. After that date, the size of the ships slowly became unmanageable and the advent of containerisation killed the activities of a port sited so close to central London. One after the other the docks closed between 1967 and 1981 while the Port shifted further east. Tilbury Docks, the last of the Port of London Authority's docks was privatised in 1992.

Butler's Wharf became a magnet for artists in search of cheap premises. Its early history is unclear but Geoff Marshall writes that in 1794, a Mr Butler and a Mr Holland formed a partnership and were

Top:
This print by Michael Heindorff (born 1949) depicts the studio of the sculptor Stephen Cripps at Warehouse D, Butler's Wharf. While Derek Jarman adopted a greenhouse for a bedroom, Cripps had a garden shed instead, seen here to the left of the composition. This drypoint comes from a set of seven called 'For S.C.', 1980.
(© Michael Heindorff)

Bottom:
Michael Heindorff described Stephen Cripps' studio at Warehouse D, Butler's Wharf, as 'a metal junkyard with bits of helicopter, machinery and all sorts'. This drypoint comes from a set of seven called 'For S.C.', 1978.
(© Michael Heindorff)

wharfingers. Mr Butler's Wharf is clearly shown on Horwood's map of 1799. By 1857 Butler's Wharf featured in *Loveday's London Waterside Surveys*; it had become a very substantial establishment but Loveday records a blend of mostly old buildings with a few new warehouses. It was then a sufferance wharf, in the hands of Messrs Curtis and Brandon; this is what Loveday recorded:

> the whole Warehouse portion may be considered as four separate parts … The business is extensive and well regulated. Goods hazardous and not hazardous landed, warehoused, and covering the whole extent, as convenience may determine. All approved for bonding. Oil and Palmer's Candle Lamps, locked, and kept in charge, used when required. A Fire Engine and buckets kept ready for use in the event of a fire happening.

There was also a dwelling house on the site with a W.C. and a large open yard. Loveday lists six buildings as 'recently erected' but otherwise the remaining fourteen buildings were 'old' or 'very old'. In 1872 Butler's Wharf became a registered public company and new warehouses were commissioned from James Tolley and Daniel Dale. This state-of-the-art warehouse accommodation closed a hundred years later in 1972. Regeneration came in the 1980s, masterminded by Terence Conran and Partners – it was their first large-scale project in London. The concept was a 'mixed-use approach' with restaurants and retail at ground level. Today Butler's Wharf survives in three distinct units: the Clove building, Allies and Morrison's first major work, converting a mid-twentieth century warehouse into office accommodation (1987); followed by the main warehouse at 34 Shad Thames which was turned into luxurious apartments designed by Conrad Roche (1989); finally, the Tea Trade Wharf was converted to a design by OSEL Architecture (2003).

The artist and film maker Derek Jarman was one of the first, along with the Logan brothers – Peter and Andrew – to move to the derelict wharves of a once thriving riverfront. In 1973 he moved into Warehouse A at Butler's Wharf and he gives us a glimpse of the house/studio in his autobiography *Lancing Ledge*:

> The studio is furnished; the greenhouse is up [Jarman's bedroom]. There is a Baby Belling to cook on, carpets from the Lots Road auction-rooms – and furniture collected from the empty offices of Butlers and Colonial Wharfs. Since there is no one else working at the Wharf I close and padlock the huge iron gates: now we have our own 1,000-feet terrace on the Thames where we can film, undisturbed in the sun.

Michael Heindorff also captured the interior of Mr Cripps' engineering workshop at Mill Street near Butler's Wharf. This print comes from a series of ten drypoints called 'Affirmations', inspired by Piranesi's *Carceri* series (prisons) and dated 1980.

(© Michael Heindorff)

Another artist who documented life at Butler's Wharf was Michael Heindorff (born 1949); he lived there between 1977 and 1979. He left the Royal College of Art on a high note – the great art collector Charles Saatchi had visited the College's final degree show and had bought everything Michael exhibited. That year Michael also landed a teaching job at St Martin's College of Art as Head of First Year Painters and found cheap accommodation at Butler's Wharf – he lived in Warehouse D6 on the top floor, sharing with several artists two of whom became friends: the printer Alan Cox (1942–2021) and the sculptor Stephen Cripps (1952–1982). Stephen's studio was next to Michael's and formed the subject of a series of seven prints called 'For S.C.'. Stephen was a very gifted artist who, tragically, died at the age of thirty. At first Stephen was drawn to industry (previous page), but later he turned to pyrotechnics which must have been somewhat alarming for the Butler's Wharf authorities!

By some extraordinary coincidence the other subject Michael Heindorff developed when he was based at Butler's Wharf, was a series of ten prints, 'Affirmations', based on another, totally unrelated Cripps, the owner of an engineering workshop sited in nearby Mill Street. When shipping life moved to Tilbury, Mr Cripps' job came to a standstill, but he continued to show up every morning at his 'place of work' (left). These two sets of prints are remarkable for apart from being objects of beauty, they chronicle a period of transition between industry and creativity – a situation which became commonplace in many cities at the end of the twentieth century. Both sets are in the collection of the Museum of London precisely for those reasons.

Just as Jarman had captured in words the deeds of the 'demolition men' at Bankside (see p. 482), the artist has used even more dramatic language to describe what was happening to Docklands. It is August 1973 and the heading reads 'Burning for Profit':

> Butlers Wharf: All through the summer the buildings burn on the river, bringing a glint to the speculators' eyes. The first to go was the beautiful Regency building that John Betjeman had listed after I showed it to him last year. Then the huge ice storage warehouse at Hays went, followed by St Catherine's Dock. Some of the finest buildings in London – then Mary's Wharf opposite, and a warehouse just beyond St Saviour's Dock – Not a bad tally for one summer's speculation.

The artists at Butler's Wharf, described as 'possibly the largest colony of artists in London at the time' (Wedd), always knew their days were numbered. But the end was brutal and Jarman gave an eye witness account of the serious fire which engulfed the warehouse on 14 August 1979.

> Three floors of the building had already been gutted, down to our studio roof, and the building was surrounded by a mass of hoses pumping water onto the flames … Jean Marc, who has lived and worked at Butlers Wharf for the last two years … arrived at 9.30 and on the verge of tears the two of us tramped up the stairs against a cascade of oily water to find a sodden, smoke-stained ruin … Peter Logan lost everything … there was no insurance.

Michael Heindorff takes up the story:

> I remember that shortly after the fire … we had a visit from the Fire Brigade notifying all residents that we had four days to move out of our tinder boxes … but it was not a deadline that could have been met. I recall that A-Block burnt to the ground while the building was thought to be completely unoccupied that morning. The fire was said to have started in a wood workshop on an upper floor – 3rd floor I think. No one came to harm, a massive fire without casualties.

Did any of these artists realise that history was repeating itself? that these wharves had known one of London's greatest fires in 1861 and many other fires on either side of that date? And that there was once a remarkable colony of artists on these shores in the sixteenth and seventeenth centuries? The Bermondsey group of artists – painters, glaziers – who thrived there in the sixteenth century has been discussed in the 'Eye of London' chapter two. Here we examine a group of sculptors who have been labelled 'the Southwark School' by art historian Margaret Whinney.

A detail of the tomb of Bishop Lancelot Andrewes (1555–1626) at Southwark Cathedral. The effigy has been attributed to Gerard Johnson from the 'Southwark School of sculptors'. The head of the dead bishop is realistic and the eyes are open but increasingly, sculptors and their patrons favoured the subject being depicted fully alive, as is exemplified in the monument in the background of this picture – Alderman Richard Humble (d. 1616) and his two wives, also reproduced here, and ascribed to William Cure the Younger.

(© The author, 2022)

The Southwark School of sculpture

This label hides the fact that in the absence of an established artistic tradition in this country, Netherlandish artists filled the gaps, many of them based around the parishes of St Saviour's, St Olave's or St Thomas'. They easily dominated the lucrative tombs and memorial monuments' market. Several workshops have been identified, the best documented being that of Gerard Johnson (i.e., Janssen); he came over from Amsterdam around 1567 and died in 1611; he is buried at St Saviour's church.

According to Margaret Whinney, the Southwark style adopts specific patterns and motifs such as the use of recumbent effigies – men in armour lie on a plaited straw mattress which is rolled up under their head while women rest their heads on embroidered pillows with their cloaks open to show hands. The facial features are generalised while the clothing is very detailed. The tombs may include allegorical references in large and complex compositions such as small figures of nude boys, one with a spade, the other with an inverted torch to represent Labour and Rest (it is the case with the Sutton tomb below), with inscriptions framed in strapwork with bunches of ribbons. The material of choice was alabaster. However, the recumbent figure was gradually replaced by representations of people in life rather than in death, adopting such compositions as figures praying on either side of a fald-stool or figures propped up on one elbow. Whinney also admits 'it is unfortunately hard to say precisely what designs the Netherlanders brought to England' though one thing was certain 'the refugee sculptors owned patterns which they prized and passed on to their sons' as is clear when examining their wills.

Other workshops have been identified but they are not necessarily in Bankside as is generally assumed – for instance those of William Cure the Elder (i.e., Cuer) born in Amsterdam and invited to come to England to work for Henry VIII at Nonsuch Palace. He was based in the parish of St Thomas the Apostle from 1559, as was his grandson William Cure the Younger whose reputation suffered setbacks, notably criticism by the architect Inigo Jones – the attractive monument to Richard Humble and his family in Southwark Cathedral has been attributed to him. Richard Stevens (1542–1592), a German speaker from Brabant, moved around three of Southwark parishes from 1568. His documented work is very limited unlike that of Isaac James (real name Hawstert), born in Holland – perhaps the son of William James in the parish of St Mary Overie – and the author of the large and magnificent tomb of Henry, 1st Baron Norris of Rycote in Westminster Abbey (overleaf). The famous Nicholas Stone (1586–1647), though born in Devon, was closely connected to Netherlandish artists and to Southwark. He trained under Isaac James who came to England in the reign of Henry VIII; he also met and followed the distinguished architect-sculptor Hendrick de Keyser back to Amsterdam and married his daughter. His tomb of Thomas Sutton at Charterhouse is a very memorable piece.

A remarkable sculpture from the eighteenth century, made for Southwark and by a Southwark born artist provides a coda to this discussion. You will find it inside the chapel of Guy's Hospital – the wall monument pays homage to the hospital's founder, Thomas Guy, and was placed over his tomb in 1779. The author of the piece was John Bacon (1740–1799); he was thirty-nine when he carved what many regard as his masterpiece.

Bacon was a precocious student: he was apprenticed at Mr Crisp's China factory in Lambeth at the age of fourteen. He was very gifted, collecting awards and promotions throughout his early years before becoming an associate of the Royal Academy at the age of thirty. Like his sixteenth-and seventeenth-centuries predecessors, John Bacon's career was centred on the South Bank where his day job at Lambeth was supervising design and production at Mrs Coade's Artificial Stone Manufactory (see p. 170) from 1771 until his death; he also dealt with a wide variety of commissions. His virtuoso technique and his temperament for bravura gestures antagonised some but there is general agreement about the moving tribute he paid to Thomas Guy, as recorded in Cherry and Pevsner's guide *The Buildings of England* (South London volume):

… one of the noblest and most sensitive of its date in England. It still has the compositional flourish and technical mastery of the Baroque and [Jean François] Roubiliac, yet shows the genuine warm feeling of the new age.

Above:

The monument to John Stow (1525–1605), London's first historian, is in the church of St Andrew Undershaft in the City of London; it has been described as belonging to 'the scholar type' by art historian Margaret Whinney, along with its more famous counterpart; the tomb of William Shakespeare in Stratford upon Avon – they were judged to be 'the best-known work of the Johnsons and also the worst'. The two monuments have been attributed to Gerard Johnson the Younger, with the John Stow dating from around 1606.
Watercolour by Philip Norman, around 1900.
© London Metropolitan Archives (City of London)

Monument to Henry, first Baron Norris of Rycote (1525-1601), and his wife Margaret by Isaac James. This monument is in St Andrew's Chapel (off the north transept) at Westminster Abbey (the couple are buried at Rycote chapel in Oxfordshire). The kneeling men in armour are their sons, three on either side; only one of them is looking up – the third son, and the only one still alive at his father's death, but not alas visible in the photograph. (© 2023, Dean and Chapter of Westminster)

The large tomb of Thomas Sutton at London's Charterhouse was the outcome of a collaboration between Nicholas Stone, Nicholas Johnson (son of Gerard the Elder) and Edmund Kinsman – the latter in charge of building alterations to Charterhouse. It was installed in the chapel at Charterhouse in November 1615. Stone was responsible for the carving, Johnson for the design. The dense overall programme includes the recumbent figure of Sutton framed by captains in armour who hold the monument's inscription and recall Sutton's times with the army. The scene in low relief above the canopy shows pensioners and officers of the charity gathered in the chapel. Sutton's arms crown the composition and various allegorical figures – Faith, Hope and Charity accentuate the verticality of the monument.

(Photo: Nicholas Jackson. Image in the public domain, Wikimedia Commons)

Funerary marble monument to Thomas Guy, founder of Guy's Hospital, by John Bacon, 1779. Sited in the hospital chapel, the life-sized memorial is generally regarded as Bacon's masterpiece and described in Pevsner as 'one of the noblest and most sensitive of its date in England'. Simply dressed, Thomas Guy, standing, holds the hand of a seated sick man encouraging him to make his way to the hospital behind him which another sick patient is entering on a stretcher. Thomas Guy's face and body, filled with quiet compassion, are treated with restraint but great sensitivity.
(© The author, 2022)

The 'warm feeling of the new age' is perhaps the spirit of charity which was either endured – the terrible workhouses – or which benefited the South Bank with its influx of charitable institutions, often on the doorstep of poverty itself.

If I were a planner … or a politician

Two themes stand out in this chapter. First the establishment of a corporate identity, slick, even flashy, born out of the grime and dark energy along the riverbank: Shard Quarter, London Bridge City, More London; this has also been examined in chapter 3.5. Second the revival and continuity of the area as London's Larder – for the large breweries of times past, substitute the beer mile and impromptu cider making, foodies' corners – Maltby market and other delicious eateries. They seem to be wholly separate, but perhaps they are not. A collaboration between the two worlds could benefit both this area and Londoners at large … provided the corporate world willingly collaborates, without insisting on exclusivity.

Sources (full references for abbreviated entries in bibliography)

Ben Judah, *This is London*, 2016; *London's Lost Map*, Museum of London pamphlet, 1998; Watson; http://www.skyscrapernews.com/index.php; London Bridge City website; Rendle & Norman; Ellis; Marshall; the website Thrale.com; Lawrence Stone, *Family and Fortune – Studies in Aristocratic Finance in the Sixteenth and Seventeenth Centuries*, 1973; Wedd; Margaret Whinney, *Sculpture in Britain 1530 to 1830*, revised by John Physick, 1988; 'A Biographical Dictionary of London Tomb Sculptors c. 1560 – c. 1660' by Adam White in *Walpole Society*, vol. 61 (1999); 'Afterword: Stow's Remains' in Gadd & Gillespie.

ANSWERS TO THE QUEST

Dialogue with the past — **527**
- Twenty-first century versus seventeenth century – surprising links — 527
- Panorama of London: where the sixteenth century comes face to face with our present times — 531
- Synchronicity — 536
- Urban memory: short term versus long term — 536
- The architect and the archaeologist — 537

Becoming increasingly disconnected from the environment — **544**
- The disconnect between science and human emotions — 544
- Mental paralysis in the face of multi-culturalism — 544
- Disconnected: the trees exhibition — 545

Looking for the soul of London — **546**
- German thinkers — 546
- Soullessness — 549
- Soulfulness — 550
- The art of healing — 554
- Honouring the lives of the desperate — 556

South Bank a mirror of the north bank? Concluding remarks — **557**
- Endpiece — 561

This book has covered a considerable amount of ground about the history and personality of the South Bank, from topographical, social, artistic and spiritual standpoints. It is now time to take stock, widen the perspective and draw a few conclusions. Before embarking on this more meditative part of the book, I should remind the reader that in my search for answers, I was driven by two principal questions – one concerned the nature of the relationship between north and south banks, the other, perhaps more elusive, concerned the soul or essence of London. Both involve scrutinising the dialogue between the past and the present.

Dialogue with the past

Twenty-first century versus seventeenth century – surprising links

Previous and above:

Sarah Medway, 'Flow State', oil on linen, 2021. 'We do not see things as they are, we see things as we are' wrote the artist in her 2022 book *The River Series* – a body of work that came out of lockdown. Sarah has always been fascinated by water and living in London, she is naturally drawn to the Thames: 'The reflective qualities of water ... are endlessly surprising. They never repeat. Water is a mirror to us, to landscape, the cityscape and the sky. And an element in which to carry the emotions as well.' Sweet or mighty, brown or blue, the Thames is also the unspoken frontier between London's north and south banks (© The artist)

The decision to focus on 'big' human stories for each area of the South Bank, allowed something fascinating to emerge – the personalities of neighbourhoods. Their distinctive features were made up of inhabitants' passions – those which somehow succeeded in being significant to the places where they developed. This is how Vauxhall and Lambeth came to be associated with gardens. Downtrodden Waterloo swapped its reputation for vice for better housing and education, then the arts. Borough and Bankside embraced theatre and later art, overcoming tragedies caused by sin, fire and death. While Southwark and Bermondsey, gateway to London and also its 'larder', now resplendent with its guardian tower glittering in the sky, blends with ease its medieval past and high-tech architecture.

Because I have long had a passion for London in the seventeenth century – the century of disasters and rebirth – it did not take me long to notice that some of this century's significant symbols, so elegantly described in an Oxford exhibition, found strong echoes in the histories of the South Bank. In 1998, on the eve of the new millennium, the Bodleian Library mounted a show called 'The Garden, the Ark, the Tower, the Temple'. This assemblage of biblical themes set out to tell 'a coherent story of the growth and decline of knowledge' which played such a critical role in English culture of the sixteenth and seventeenth centuries. The catalogue which accompanied the exhibition explained:

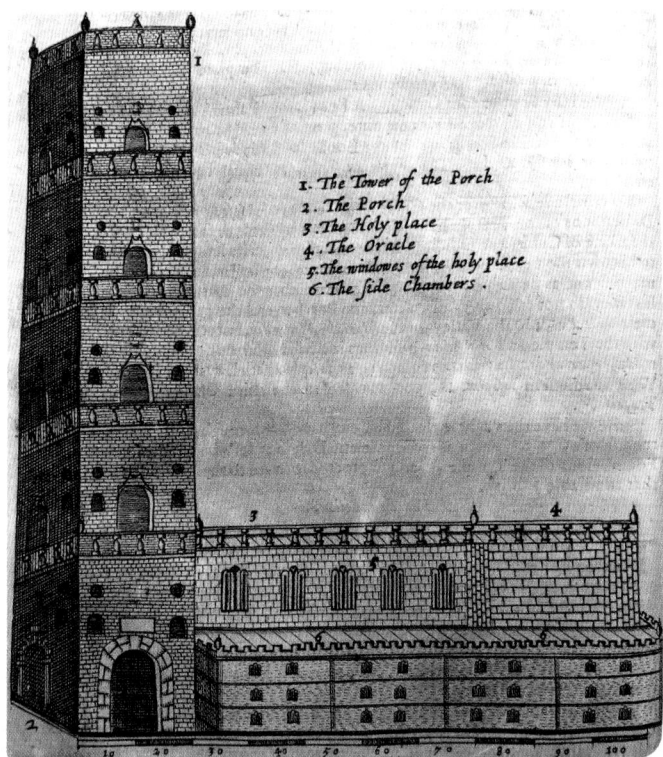

This imagined rendering of the Jerusalem Temple has been described as 'a very English interpretation' of the lost ancient structure. It even bears some resemblance to the church of St Olave in Tooley Street! It comes from Samuel Lee's *Orbis miraculum; or, the Temple of Solomon Pourtrayed by Scripture-Light* (1659). It contrasts with other very elaborate reconstructions but Lee argued his version was practical and grounded unlike those which were directly inspired by the description of the visionary Ezekiel.

Opposite top:
William Curtis's botanical garden in Waterloo, watercolour by James Sowerby, mid to late 1780s. It occupied a site framed by Ufford Street (south east), Webber Street (south west) and Mitre Road (north west). Local historian Graham Gibberd successfully linked the content of this watercolour painting to the Ordnance Survey plan of the 1870s. (Private collection; Photo: © Christie's images/ Bridgeman images)

Opposite bottom:
Caption overleaf

As metaphors of knowledge, the four stories gave information about … the ideal state of human understanding. But they also issued warnings about the … difference between human and divine knowledge … The image that they conjured up was … both hopeful and threatening.

The Garden is a metaphor for the original garden, Eden or Paradise, the setting of the original sin which has made humanity yearn to find a way back to this special place (see p. 360 for image). The Ark refers to Noah's heroic adventure – saving humanity from God's vengeful Flood. So it represents hope and salvation … but only for some! The Tower is the defiant Tower of Babel which aimed to reach the sky but remained unfinished – a contradictory symbol of spiritual aspiration and despicable ambition (see p. 488 for image). The Temple refers to the most sacred of them all in Judeo-Christian history and beliefs, Jerusalem's – all three incarnations of this splendid building have been lost, but their reputation has continued to fuel human desire to recover its form and the sacred geometry which underlined its construction (above).

The Oxford project went on to connect these stories and their themes to Samuel Hartlib (1600–1662), a polymath interested in science, politics and education. I have found that all four stories underpin important aspects of the past and present history of the South Bank. At Oxford they concluded that 'stories from the Bible provided coherent explanations for the human condition … they also seemed to offer plans for escape into a better world'. What lessons can be drawn from the presence of these Biblical images within the South Bank context?

In this book you will find the archetypal **Garden** in Vauxhall and Lambeth, distinctly echoing Paradise, alongside an attempt to create a universal garden filled with plants from around the world – a cornucopia of fruit, trees, flowers, medicinal plants and others – in the South Lambeth property of the Tradescants, whose garden was a living museum. It is clear that this garden made a lasting impression on its neighbourhood, with more memorable gardens clustering in that part of Lambeth up to modern times – some very well-known like Vauxhall Gardens, others more modest such as Cumberland Gardens. It was also in Lambeth's Waterloo that the second botanical garden to grace the South Bank could be found – William

Curtis' (above). Waterloo sheltered William Blake's very own garden of Eden as well (see p. 377). In recent times, the small and energetic community of Bonnington Square in Vauxhall practiced aspects of 'guerilla gardening' with marvellous results – paradise at your fingertips! Lambeth is also where the Museum of Garden History, renamed the Garden Museum, was born, and the outcome of a private pilgrimage to the extraordinary Tradescant tomb in the grounds of its home, St Mary's Lambeth.

You will find the **Ark** in Vauxhall too, next to the well documented Tradescant garden. This country's earliest 'museum', the Ark was a repository of all manner of natural and man-made artefacts. By way of contrast, Bankside offered a live, dysfunctional Ark – with bears, monkeys, bulls and dogs fighting to death for the thoughtless pleasure of gamblers. Nowadays the animals of city farms (Vauxhall City Farm and Oasis Farm Waterloo) invite a more positive response to animals with their nurturing and preservation programmes (overleaf).

In the nineteenth century, White Hind Alley in Bankside changed its name to Noah's Ark Alley, presumably inspired by the eponymous pub which stood at the junction of this narrow lane with Park Street (overleaf). On the 1873 Ordnance Survey map the street was labelled Noah's Ark Alley and its continuation, White Hind Alley; in 1799 it was simply named White Hind Alley (Horwood). Noah's Ark was the name of the pub on the south west corner of Park Street and the tiny Noah's Ark Lane (92 Park Street); it was open from around 1788 until at least 1938. It is worth noting that

Previous:

James Sowerby (1757–1822), whose watercolour is reproduced on the previous page, was the distinguished naturalist and botanical illustrator employed by William Curtis for his pioneering *Botanical Magazine*. He published several landmark books including *Sowerby's Botany*. He was Lambeth born and lived at 2 Mead Place on the site of the present Morley College. There he amassed a large collection of natural history material with the aim of founding a museum. He kept this material around his house, eventually building an additional room at the back of his property. The collection received visitors but after James's death, his son tried to realise his father's dream of a proper museum; he failed and the collection was put up for sale in 1831. This lively oil portrait by Thomas Heaphy dates from 1817 when Sowerby was sixty. It includes the collector's pride and joy: a meteorite which fell near Wold Cottage in Yorkshire in 1795 and is now in the British Museum.
(Image in the public domain; Wikimedia Commons)

there were in fact very few pubs named Noah's Ark in London. Did the original pub landlord regard his establishment as an island of life and jollity in a sea of industrial living and grimy surroundings?

The **Tower** is found at the Shard in Southwark. In the late 1990s the Museum of London considered commissioning a 'Millennium Painting' and proceeded to raise money to enable the artist Ben Johnson to produce a great London panoramic painting. As the curator of paintings at that time, I promoted and co-ordinated this project. Since the importance of the South Bank in creating the first portrait of London has been discussed in chapter two, it is worth revisiting the issue of viewpoints in this context. Ben researched twelve different viewpoints for his panorama, including one from the west (Millbank Tower), one from the east (Canary Wharf tower), one from the north (one of the Barbican towers) and one from the south (Guy's Hospital tower). I favoured a viewpoint from the south as this would have created a direct parallel to London's seventeenth century 'prospects' described in the Eye of London chapter. The tallest building in Southwark and Lambeth at that time was Guy's hospital tower at just over 148 metres. The Museum of London painting did not proceed and even if it had, the viewpoint from the south had been ruled out in favour of one from east London. But it is fascinating to think that at exactly the time we were discussing the best viewpoint for this new panorama of London, developer Irvine Sellar was working on a building which would give London the

ultimate viewpoint, the 'View from the Shard' (244m above ground, 310m in all) supplanting with ease its historic neighbour – the tower of Southwark Cathedral. Serendipitous synchronicity … If you had to decide which viewpoint, which one would you choose?

Like the historic temples of Jerusalem, the south bank **Temple** or even **Temples** are now lost; but they have been brought back to life by archaeology. These former Romano-Celtic structures are now well hidden in Southwark – one, on the east side of Borough High Street, under the News Building (see p. 75), the other two, discovered in 2004, stood side by side at Tabard Square, underneath a group of storage sheds which have now made way for a residential development (see p. 75). The church of St George-the-Martyr stands right against this former sacred enclosure, so that this area is still connected to spiritual practices echoing the men and women who communicated with their gods using a different set of beliefs but pursuing the same aim. In Colijnsplaat in Holland they discovered a similar temple, dedicated to the goddess Nehalennia and they simply reconstructed it – not just on paper but physically. It was known to have stood in the immediate neighbourhood and the reconstruction bears close similarities to that of the Southwark temples.

Each of the areas which make up the South Bank is linked to a powerful symbol from the ancient past. Does this symbolism evoke long term memory; or the long-term reach of spiritual beliefs, or even the absence of alternative beliefs, powerful enough to displace tradition and history? But in our story, there is another link between the past and the present which is remarkable – this time in the sixteenth century, when the image of London was first created.

Panorama of London: where the sixteenth century comes face to face with our present times

In the print room of the Ashmolean Museum, there is a mid-sixteenth century 'long view' of London which has been unfairly neglected (overleaf). Like many other early long views, it is taken from the South Bank. It was believed to be by the renowned topographical artist Anthonis van den Wyngaerde and reproduced by the London Topographical Society in 1944, thus labelled and with the following commentary – 'important for its detailed study of the river bank'. But when it was catalogued by David Blayney Brown in 1982 it was judged 'too wooden and awkward' to be by the Master himself. However, the paper on which it was drawn appeared to have 'two watermarks which, although cut, seem to be the pot and hand types present on Wyngaerde's own [panorama] sheets'. Thus, the link with Wyngaerde could not be completely dismissed. The two long views are in fact very different – Wyngaerde adopting a high viewpoint produced a bird's eye view of the north and south banks (see pp. 36–37), while the anonymous artist adopted a rare low-level viewpoint, eliminating

Opposite left:

This somewhat surreal scene combines gentle animal domesticity with the mighty outline of London's MI6 building, designed by Terry Farrell and ready in 1995. Vauxhall City Farm is the unlikely neighbour of Britain's Secret Intelligence Service – created in 1909 and on the South Bank since 1966, previously at Century House, 100 Westminster Bridge Road).
(© The author, 2018)

Opposite right:

A view of Noah's Ark Alley at Park Street, Southwark, with the Noah's Ark pub on the left – the word '[Mer]chant' indicating an inscription such as Spirit or Wine Merchant; this pub is clearly marked on the 1873 Ordnance Map. The photograph, taken by LCC photographers in 1923, also enables us to catch a glimpse of Bankside Power Station in the background. It was the gradual extension of this facility which dictated the fate of this street and its local shops – they disappeared around 1938 when last listed in the Post Office Directory.
(© London Metropolitan Archives (City of London)

Opposite:

A section from the anonymous mid-sixteenth century view of London has been placed side by side with Jiro Osuga's 2019 working drawing for the same section of the river. The only recognisable landmark is St Paul's Cathedral but it is remarkable to be able to draw such a close comparison between two drawings which are separated in time by almost 500 years.
(© Ashmolean Museum, University of Oxford/© Jiro Osuga)

Below and bottom right:

The City of London is viewed from the South Bank and drawn by an anonymous artist, perhaps from the circle of Anthonis van den Wyngaerde, mid-sixteenth century. It is unusual for adopting a ground level viewpoint when most artists sought to present bird's eye views of cities.
(© Ashmolean Museum, University of Oxford)

the south bank altogether and concentrating on a much smaller section of the north bank. There is a vivid immediacy in the latter drawing which is missing from the more calculated drawing by Wyngaerde intent on making sense of the spatial arrangement of buildings and city. The anonymous drawing is finished – a life rendering of what was in front of the artist, while Wyngaerde's composition, more ambitious in scope, is unfinished.

The approach of the anonymous artist is revealed by placing the panorama side by side with a contemporary drawing (2019) by the London-based artist Jiro Osuga (top right). Jiro, completely unaware of the sixteenth-century drawing, explains: 'I spent the summer of 2019 walking along the stretch of the river, the south bank, looking north, drawing basically every single building, every single bridge, every kind of boat that you see on the river'. He ignored the south bank entirely – along with so many of his predecessors – and he also ignored the people. The outcome of Jiro's project was a series of paintings – 'River' – exhibited at the Flowers Gallery in 2021; they record but also distort the river as a way to celebrate its vast presence in London, from Barnes to the Thames Barrier (overleaf).

The French poet Baudelaire wrote a poem called 'Correspondences' where ideas, memories, experiences connect through the physical world of the senses and beyond all notion of time and place. Through the physical act of sketching, Jiro's drawing connects magically with the almost five hundred years old Ashmolean long view; of course, all the buildings have changed but the viewpoint and the act of drawing share a sense of continuity and it would be difficult to find a more appropriate manifestation of Baudelaire's 'Correspondences'.

> Like those deep echoes that meet from afar
> In a dark and profound harmony,
> As vast as night and clarity,
> So perfumes, colors, tones answer each other.

(Geoffrey Wagner, *Selected Poems of Charles Baudelaire*, NY: Grove Press, 1974)

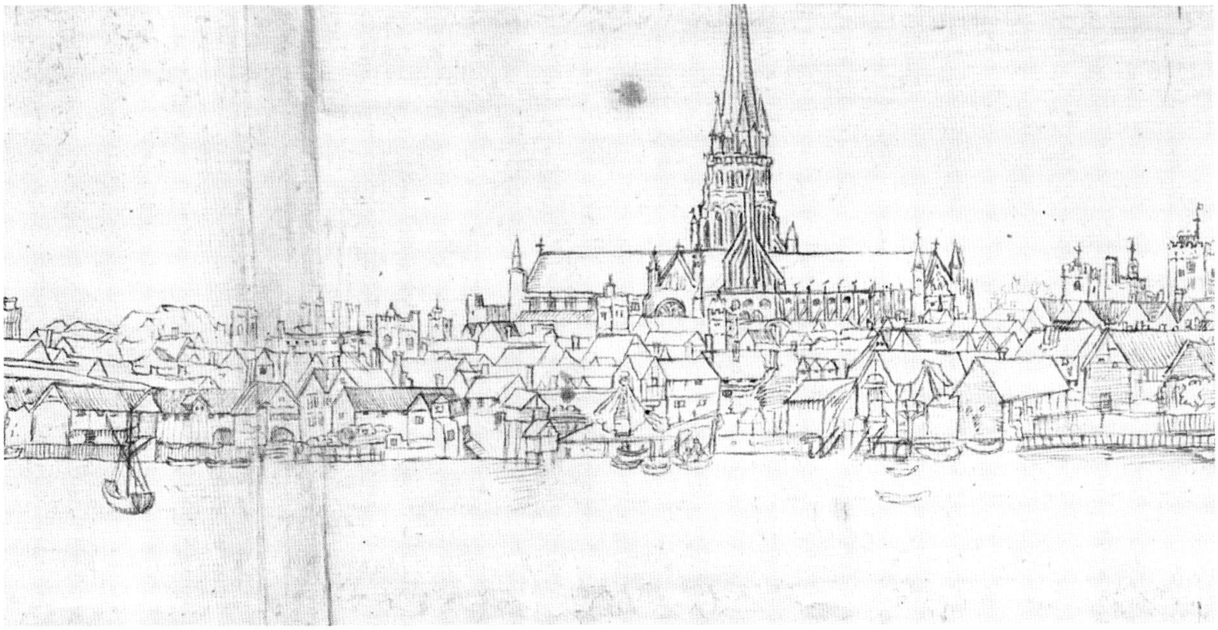

ANSWERS TO THE QUEST 533

ANSWERS TO THE QUEST 535

Jiro Osuga, 'River 6', Blackfriars Bridge to Tower Bridge, 2019, oil on canvas. This is the painted outcome of the research drawing made by the artist on p. 533. It represents a breakthrough because it has found a way of dealing with the southern end of bridges. Instead of finishing abruptly they fly over the pedestrians' heads lifting the whole composition with their dynamism.
© The artist/Flowers Gallery

Synchronicity

The Thames has always been a magnet for Londoners, and artists in particular. Just as the painter Jiro Osuga was unknowingly walking in the footsteps of the anonymous author of the sixteenth-century panorama, it is possible to identify 'hot spots' or 'centres of meaning' in London, places which are more conducive to ambitious visions, thoughts or ideas. I was struck for instance, by the realisation that the very first inscription to refer to 'Londoners' was found near St George's church in Southwark – a Roman stone fragment bearing an inscription partially visible which defined London by its citizens rather than its walls (see p. 76). In that very location Hogarth produced his exuberant 'Southwark Fair' – a melting pot of human endeavours, ranging from the extraordinary to the pathetic, with a ready audience of 'Londoners' to lap it all up (see p. 486).

Urban memory: short term versus long term

These unspoken dialogues across centuries, are often overlooked and these 'correspondences' inevitably bring up the notion of memory. When neighbourhoods develop a theme, such as the ones highlighted at the beginning of this chapter, do people exercise free will when, time and time again, they follow the same patterns of thought and creativity, often in similar locations? Or is long-term memory at work even when there is no awareness of it?

To the ethereal and poetic connections across time we have just witnessed, we must now oppose the resilience of memory in urban settings. We saw at Cross-Bones Yard how the ancient cemetery on that site was 'forgotten' within a few decades – a state of affairs which was duly exploited in 1883 by the leaseholders of the site. They proposed to build 'a block of industrial dwellings' much to the horror of Lord Brabazon, who had researched this site's history (see p. 444),

In the sixteenth century, people worried so much about what would happen to their souls after death that those who could afford it, made arrangements for prayers in perpetuity – a thoroughly unrealistic interpretation of the concept of long-term memory. To give an example, the antiquary William Maitland deplored what happened to the great London historian John Stow in 1732:

> That truly worthy, laborious and excellent Antiquary, to whom the City is so greatly indebted … neither that, nor any other Consideration, was sufficient to protect his Repository from being spoil'd of his injured Remains by certain Men [gravediggers] in the Year 1732. Who removed his corpse to make way for another.

This took place 127 years after Stow's death and would have been no surprise to Stow's contemporaries, including Shakespeare, who penned the following inscription to safeguard his own remains:

> Cvrsed be he yt move my bones

Interference with the sacred peace of death is still much feared, encouraging many people to regard burials as sacrosanct. On the whole, due respect has been adhered to but there has been plenty of burial interference, for development reasons but also academic reasons. The following extract comes from a government report (DCMS) entitled 'Guidance for the Care of Human Remains in Museums':

> In the United Kingdom, there is a long tradition of excavating historic and prehistoric human remains, normally skeletons, studying them and including them in museum collections and displays … The vast majority of work on human remains in the United Kingdom is uncontroversial and has wide popular and academic support. Research into human remains and their context are an important source of direct evidence about the past.

This is interesting because 'research' and 'science' now make it acceptable to breach a deeply ancient taboo concerning the inviolability of corpses and tombs. Spiritual practices involving the dead rest on the belief that souls can only thrive if the remains of their material incarnations are respected and if the places of burial also remain untouched. This, however, usually only applies to corpses of high social or religious status. From the eighth century onwards, Christians had been offering mass and prayers for the souls of the dead. The rise of monasteries in the eleventh century, encouraged the creation of chantry chapels amongst the wealthy classes. They were often created within parish churches but could also be private free-standing chapels; they were endowed so as to ensure permanent support for departed souls, for instance the chapel of St Thomas Becket on Old London Bridge. Have all these deeply felt practices disappeared for ever or do they survive in some form or other, across time and beyond changing attitudes? The new interest in dispersing ashes in the Thames echoes back through the centuries to prehistoric and Roman practices of appeasing gods with offerings of all kinds.

Although the world of sixteenth- and seventeenth-centuries London bears very little relationship to our world today, there are constant reminders of it. When the contemporary American artist Mark Dion was commissioned to 'record' the Thames at the sites of both London Tate Galleries – Pimlico and Bankside – he chose a very similar approach to that of the Tradescants in the seventeenth century who created repositories of live and 'dead' artefacts at their Lambeth Garden and Ark. 'Tate Thames Dig' (1999) and its follow-up 'Tate Thames Dig – Locker' (2000) exploit the thrill of the cabinet of curiosity and the treasure chest, with found objects from the Thames shore which the viewer finds 'in seemingly unhistorical and largely uninterpreted arrangements.' (Overleaf)

The architect and the archaeologist

An architect, Graham Morrison, comes face to face – metaphorically – with an archaeologist, Chris Constable. The latter, Borough Archaeologist for Southwark, is steeped into the culture of the past while the former is preoccupied by the present and builds for the future. Graham Morrison founded Allies and Morrison (with Bob Allies) in 1984, while Chris has been working for Southwark for over ten years.

In his 'Tate Thames Dig' the contemporary American artist Mark Dion (born 1961) chose the cabinet of curiosities, the ancestor of museums, to organise his display of found objects on the Thames shore of both Tate Galleries – Millbank and Bankside. The project relied on a team of local volunteers, in the words of the artist people 'witnessing the process rather than coming to see an object'. Dion explained that finds were 'not stratified, everything is jumbled together and just spilled out … things in transition and we are showing this alchemical process … garbage from the beach is taking meaning as we take it through institutional levels'. The project benefited from the input of staff from the Museum of London, Thames River Police and ecologists. This work was first displayed as an Art Now installation between October 1999 and January 2000.
(© Mark Dion, Photo: Tate)

Both were asked to answer exactly the same questionnaire. Will their worlds be poles apart and irreconcilable as were those of John Stow and Thomas Dekker in the early years of the seventeenth century (see p. 453)? Or is the dialogue between past and present robust, healthy and open to breakthroughs?

1. Could you describe your institution/company's goals in a few sentences?

Graham Morrison (GM): *You think it's a simple question but it's sort of saying what's your reason for being on this earth really? (laughing) No, I think it's very simple: we want to produce buildings that are worthy, that fit well in their context, are derived from a sense of place – from where they are located; and that have a long life because they are flexible and well made.*

Chris Constable (CC): *Southwark Council's Archaeology unit is found within the Planning and Building Control Department – under Design and Conservation. The Council's goals are spelt out on their website: 'We champion Southwark's archaeology and have dedicated planning policies and an expert archaeology officer to ensure it's identified, protected and managed for future generations.' (Accessed August 2021)*

2. Could you describe your personal job description in a few sentences?

GM: *I am a partner of an architectural firm. I've started this firm Allies and Morrison with Bob Allies with the aim of doing exactly the answer to the first question.*

CC: *To protect the archaeology of Southwark means two things – the physical protection of sites and encouraging the public knowledge of archaeology amongst the local community and London at large. The level of my involvement will depend on the importance of the site. There are:*
- *'Strategic major sites' where the environmental impact will be substantial and will generally involve a public consultation, such as Landmark Court in Southwark Street (2021–22)*
- *'Major sites' – such as the Pickle Factory in Trinity Church Square (2006)*
- *'Smaller sites' in the hands of smaller, less experienced developers; sometimes there can be issues with these … for instance the small development north of Brandon House at Lyon House in Borough High Street (August 2016)*

3. But of course, your job description may not account for what 'makes you tick'. Could you explain what you find deeply satisfying about the job you are doing?

GM: *Yes, there is a unique pleasure in seeing change happen for the good; secondly it is working with colleagues that are really great to work with. And then employing young people throughout our career who then go on to be better than us. As an aside, our employment motto was always employing people who are really better than you, just don't tell them that.*

CC: *My initial interest was in medieval architecture of northern England. There is little of that in Southwark but I am still driven by the prospect of new discoveries and being able to expand my knowledge of the past.*

4. You have been working in SE1 for many years, what is the most memorable project you have been working on and why? Name one only

GM: *The Royal Festival Hall. It was a building that represented its time – it opened in 1951 – and then almost within a decade, it was pretty much rejected by the architectural fraternity; then it was surrounded by a concrete coat in the 1960s. And our job was not only to restore the building but to return the Festival Hall to a kind of happy urban place.*

CC: *Thameslink – and specifically what was discovered near London Bridge: Roman baths and the thirteenth-century foundations of St Thomas' Hospital below a small office building which had to be rebuilt (next to the Post Office). Nearby, below the News Building, we uncovered the foundation of a Roman temple and a column base.*

5. Briefly, could you name your top three most important projects – either for personal or corporate reasons

GM: *I think the Royal Festival Hall is one of the three. The second one would be the new Abbey Mills Sewage Pump station in the east end, the third one this office [at 85 Southwark Street].*

CC: *Bermondsey Abbey – a major medieval landmark; Brandon House, in the High Street, opposite St George's church. The elaborate terracotta decorations which covered*

Portrait of Borough Archaeologist for Southwark, Chris Constable, with a photograph (right) of the excavation at Landmark Court – one of the most extraordinary projects he supervised. (Photo: Andy Chopping/MOLA)

part of this building were a surprise find; finally, Thameslink again, this time the site at the back of the Wheatsheaf pub in Stoney Street – the archaeology was spectacular with the full range of layers, from prehistory to the Victorian period.

6. Bearing these projects in mind (and others too) was there ever any tension between the demands of the past versus those of the present? Give one example only if applicable

GM: *Well, without wanting to sound like a broken record, the Royal Festival Hall would be the example. Because it's a Grade 1 listed building and effecting considerable change within the building was a challenge to its heritage values – we changed quite a lot in the auditorium for acoustic reasons and then we made quite a few changes externally in order to fulfil the ambition of reconnecting the building to its urban context. So the fact that it worked out – and was incredibly popular when finished, and is still popular – I feel gives us a great deal of satisfaction; the challenge worked out but there was extraordinary tension.*

It was quite frightening to be dealing with the building, to have that kind of responsibility. We felt more like a heart surgeon I think … it could have gone wrong. Changing the stage in the auditorium and the canopy over the stage. To me it was a piece of iconic 50s design but it actually didn't work acoustically; it was very beautiful visually but it was quite wrong in the way the building performed. So much so that Simon Rattle used to say 'Rehearsing in the Royal Festival Hall was like losing the will to live'.

Portrait of architect Graham Morrison with, above, a photograph of the project he holds close to his heart: the Royal Festival Hall viewed from the river.
(Allies and Morrison)

And when we finished, he said playing there was now a privilege. Basically, changing the canopy allowed all the orchestra to hear each other because the sound just went bang to the auditorium but now they could work as a team.

CC: *Yes, compromise is the rule of the game and tension may arise in the process. Perhaps the best example is at Brandon House. The developer undertook a very limited evaluation, and the design of the building continued, increasing its impacts upon archaeology. This had a knock-on effect on the design they proposed for their building which included a basement. The more significant archaeology was that of the sixteenth-century palace rather than the Roman period. The planning conditions specified that should the Renaissance palace – known as Brandon House or Suffolk Place – be revealed, it would necessitate a full excavation and appropriate measures of preservation. And this is what happened, though the office building on the site was kept operational right to the very end – creating a somewhat fraught scenario. The location of each pile had to be agreed to ensure the preservation of remains of the Renaissance palace. In the end the developers lost half of their basement and the foundation piles all had to fit within the delicate conservation work surrounding the palace remains, leading to a redesign of the modern basement.*

[A few months after this interview, the already important site of Landmark Court, with its excellent mosaics (see previous page), grew into a major site which in Chris Constable's mind superseded the Brandon House site].

7. When you become aware of exciting archaeological discoveries, do you ever catch yourself thinking – how thrilling it would be to reconstruct past landmarks on the site where they were found?

GM: *No. Generally, no. And I imagine that sounds like a rather heartless answer. But I think the sediments of history are so complete that we are simply another layer on top. For example, we found just at the end of Southwark Street a Roman mosaic floor and of course all the work stops. The archaeologists go in and whatever is done in order to make it work; I think in this case it's been removed but had that not been the case we would have adjusted the design to acknowledge it. But we would have never rebuilt a Roman villa on top of it because we are in the middle of the city of London – it would have been an impossible thought – the reality of land values but also the needs of the city. I think we could have accommodated it within the design but we wouldn't stop what we were doing and then rebuild the original building; I can't see an intellectual basis for that, let alone a practical one. (see above)*

CC: *Yes. This was very present at Tabard Square (see p. 75). The discovery of two Roman temples there represented such a dramatic development in the archaeological fortunes of Southwark. One of the theories circulating then was that the ancient part of the sculpture of King Alfred which now stands on the green at Trinity Church Square, may well have come from the temples' sacred enclosure. (See opposite).*

8. Struggling or unrealised projects – What are the lessons? (for example the Rose for archaeology, the 2000 failed revamping of the South Bank Centre for architecture)

GM: *Thank goodness for the dropping of the Richard Rogers masterplan for the*

South Bank. He was going to put a huge glass enclosure over it and the idea at the time was that it would feel the same as being in Barcelona. We just thought it was wrong. We were right through to the last two and the jury took six hours to decide between Richard Rogers and us. [Richard Rogers was selected]. Then Richard Rogers got dropped and when it came to the revamping of the Royal Festival Hall they appointed us.

Failed projects – yes, all the time, lots. There are lessons … I never regard it as being entirely negative. When we were starting out, when we were young, we were doing competitions all the time. We came second in a whole string of competitions. We got our first major break for a site behind the Design Museum at Butler's Wharf [Clove Building]. The main thing is I regard any project as piano practice to rehearse how to do something. You are constantly developing your thinking, you are learning all the time.

CC: *The Rose theatre is a good case in point. It is lucky that the temporary preservation work could be done. The whole site needs to have proper access and be sustainable. There is great interest in the project amongst archaeologists – I am a trustee – and theatre professionals but what is needed now is a massive injection of cash.*

9. Would you like to add anything to what has been said already on the theme of architecture v archaeology?

GM: *Only that I think that we absolutely do base our thoughts when we are planning anything on what went before. We can't look at the future without first knowing about the past, so for an archaeologist the past is about preservation and rightly so; for us it's being correctly informed by it. So, understanding the place, understanding how it got there is absolutely significant to understanding where you should then go. We are not the architects who come up with a concept that's never been thought of before, we are the architects absolutely rooted to the place and one reason I put this building in my top three [their architectural practice at 85 Southwark Street] is because it's probably the best example of that in Southwark.*

CC: *Most projects are reactive and developer-led. Other projects emerge from the ongoing conservation work – for instance the restoration of the statue of Alfred the Great, financed by Trinity House estate and the Heritage of London Trust. It was installed in the square by 1830. Most unusually, it combines a fragment of antique statuary (the draped bottom half) with Coade stone.*

That architect and archaeologist share a healthy respect towards the past can be seen in the answer to question 6, but answers to the following question provide divergent views, reflecting the two men's very different roles. Although neither mentioned it, the extraordinary reconstruction and success of the Globe theatre springs to mind but came from a non-archaeological commitment. However, this building contributed as positively to regenerating Bankside as the Royal Festival Hall in Waterloo.

The statue of King Alfred standing in Trinity Church Square, Southwark, looks pristine after its restoration scaffolding was removed in August 2021
(© The author, 2021)

Becoming increasingly disconnected from our environment

The disconnect between science and human emotions

In *This is London*, Ben Judah recounts his meeting with 'the Sectioner', a Nigerian 'mental health officer who sections the most people in London':

I imagine London as two buildings …
The first building is the one that accommodates London's science and technology: in this building we have moved from gliders to supersonic. We have moved from typewriters to the most high-powered computer systems, even voice controlled ones … This building contains all sorts of chemicals and biologicals and weapons and everything. The building has become a skyscraper. We can see its glory … But now the other building.
This other building deals with … London's emotion. It controls the feelings. The emotion that makes up our social interaction. But unfortunately this building is still at the foundation level … They are working by candlelight … The building is staffed by cavemen. In fact nobody has done any building for thousands of years. And there is rising damp.

The Sectioner concludes: 'Unless we develop our emotions … London is very unstable'. He is also a man who is deeply sceptical about multiculturalism: 'a recipe for disaster … Even in London where people are more enlightened'. The Sectioner believes that multiculturalism only works when the economy is good and there are no crises looming on the horizon. But as soon as there is any significant upheaval, the equilibrium collapses and 'foreigners' be they 'white' in Africa or 'brown' in the UK will turn into casualties.

Mental paralysis in the face of multi-culturalism

The Sectioner provides a striking visualisation of the problem and he may or may not be aware that he shares some of his conclusions on multi-culturalism with those of an American academic, Robert D Putnam from Harvard University. In a 2007 ground-breaking article Putnam writes:

Ethnic diversity is increasing in most advanced countries, driven mostly by sharp increases in immigration … New evidence from the US suggests that in ethnically diverse neighbourhoods residents of all races tend to 'hunker down'. Trust (even of one's own race) is lower, altruism and community cooperation rarer, friends fewer.

Putnam regards diversity as 'a valuable national asset' but recognises that, and he is not alone, it is also a challenge, at times seemingly insurmountable. He describes how creativity, economic growth and the injection of vital new blood go hand in hand with immigration. His research sample is 30,000, across forty-one different communities – primarily in metropolitan areas; his survey was carried out in 2000. He further describes how 'in the theoretical toolkit of social science we find two diametrically opposed perspectives on the effect of social connections'. The first, 'contact hypothesis', encourages the shedding of prejudices through regular contact. The other, 'conflict theory', sees limited resources and other factors affecting diversity negatively: people distrust the 'out-group' while finding solidarity in the 'in-group'. However, led by data, Putnam's research showed clearly that neither described the situation accurately – 'constrict theory' was a more appropriate label. In other words, 'diversity, at least in the short run, seems to bring down the turtle in all of us', a form of instability and social isolation with the following results: 'Inhabitants of diverse communities tend to withdraw from collective life, to distrust their neighbours, regardless of the colour of their skin … to expect the worst from their community …' – the 'hunker down' effect.

Despite this oversimplification of Putnam's deeply researched reasoning, the academic remains optimistic because 'in the long run … successful immigrant societies have overcome such fragmentation by creating new, cross-cutting forms of *social solidarity* and *more encompassing identities*' (my italics). He gives as examples the military, religious institutions and earlier waves of American immigration. In London we witnessed the Grenfell Tower effect – the pulling together of communities in the aftermath of the devastating fire ('forms of social solidarity') and the 'I am Charlie' effect in the aftermath of the Paris attack on Charlie Hebdo ('more encompassing identities'). Can such an agenda exist without being tragedy-led? Can London find a permanent way of becoming truly comfortable with its multi-cultural society, and this without exploitation?

Disconnected: the trees exhibition

To the multi-cultural uncertainties, we need to add the sense, increasingly, of being disconnected from the environment. In 2020 I was invited to the private view of an exhibition entitled 'Being with Trees', shown at Bermondsey Project Space Gallery, 183–185 Bermondsey Street. This gallery was set up with sponsorship money, based on a proposal by State/F22 Magazines; its strapline is 'A not-for-profit creative platform promoting the fusion of art, photography, and culture'.

I walked to the gallery from Redcross Street where I was revisiting the Cross-Bones Yard, now a charming memorial garden. I picked my way through the back streets and to my surprise discovered a string of small and charming open spaces with an abundance of trees. It was a moment of perfect synchronicity I thought – making my way to an exhibition about trees with the unexpected opportunity of seeing so many trees while walking through an area of dense urban fabric. I was enchanted by the following gardens: Guy Street Park, the extensive Leathermarket Gardens and abandoning briefly my gallery mission, Tanner Street Park, also noting that the gallery itself was sandwiched between the latter and the churchyard of St Mary Magdalen church to the south. When I finally reached my destination, and mentioned my discovery to one of the (London) artists in the show I was greeted with a blank expression. The work on show had been submitted by artists from all walks of life and all parts of England and even Europe. The geographical context for the show was never really considered, except perhaps its accessibility by public transport and the fact it was in the art capital, London. The art connection superseded that of nature. It also did so in the 2020 Hayward Gallery's 'Among the Trees' exhibition where the Finnish artist Eija-Liisa Ahtila presented 'Horizontal, 2011', a 'projected installation', the portrait of an extremely tall spruce tree shown … horizontally.

It is of course exceedingly common to feel disconnected in very large cities. It takes a lifetime to actually know a city reasonably well and most people – especially those who are just passing through – learn to navigate urban life around a relatively small number of venues and places. They also tend to pay little attention to their own immediate environment – the places where they live – pursuing Central London venues for 'special occasions'; though the COVID pandemic has forced everyone to revisit this issue and reconnect with their neighbourhood.

Looking for the soul of London

Following on from the prologue of this book, could the soul of London rest close to its geographic centre in Waterloo, as it does in Auroville, India? If its site was linked to the number of souls resting in its earth, Southwark would be the best contender. If it was linked to attempts to recreate the garden paradise of the Bible, the obvious candidate would be Vauxhall and Lambeth. But where might it be?

German thinkers

Some might argue that we have enough trouble sensing, recognising and feeding our own souls without embarking on a quest to identify the soul of a city! Maybe, but just as we know that certain acts and behaviours antagonise or damage our private souls, we might equally benefit from a greater awareness of what is not good for the larger souls of cities, increasingly our dearest and closest environment. This chapter opened with parallels between our own times and the sixteenth and seventeenth centuries. The Garden, the Ark, the Tower and the Temple are still significant today despite their Biblical origins and laments that our society has in fact turned its back on spirituality to embrace a world of materialism. They continue to be significant because nothing powerful enough has come to supplant them. So, if there are strong biblical undertones to our urban lives, why should we not examine the nature of the city's soul? Two German philosophers of the first half of the twentieth century did exactly that. They could sense the meteoric rise of cities in human consciousness and lives, so were remarkably prescient about current dilemmas:

> I see, long after A.D. 2000, cities laid out for ten to twenty million inhabitants, spread over enormous areas of countryside, with buildings that will dwarf the biggest of today's and notions of traffic and communication that we should regard as fantastic to the point of madness.

This was written and published between 1918 and 1922, in *The Decline of the West*, a two-volume text by Oswald Spengler (1880–1936). It presents a somewhat pessimistic history of the world and its civilisations – the end, inevitably, is always death. It stresses that 'world-history is the history of civic man' and one of its chapters is boldly labelled 'The Soul of the City'. Spengler begins with towns: 'the real miracle is the birth of the *soul* of a town'. Having drawn a firm line between town and country he asserts: 'It goes without saying that

what distinguishes a town from a village is not its size, but the presence of a soul'. The soul appears when the town or city becomes:

> a place from which the countryside is henceforth regarded, felt, and experienced as "environs", as something different and subordinate. From now on there are two lives, that of the inside [town] and that of the outside [countryside], and the peasant understands this just as clearly as the townsman ... the man of the land and the man of the city are different essences.

Robert Morden was the first mapmaker to produce a centralised map of London in the 1680s. For the first time London was placed at the centre of its 'environs', making it perfectly clear that the environs now existed in relation to London. Morden's collaborator, Philip Lea, copied and published this map on his own account around 1690; 'A Mapp containing the Townes Villages Gentlemens Houses Roads Rivers Woods and other Remarks for 20 Miles Round London', reproduced here.
(© British Library Board. All Rights Reserved/ Bridgeman Images)

'We are the city', oil painting by Jiro Osuga, 2017. This is one from a series of paintings where the artist plays with Londoners' headdresses. The series shows mostly single heads with architectural headdresses whereas this work is unusual in tackling the idea of crowd. Medieval and classical church towers jostle with the Leadenhall building, 'the Gherkin', 'the Walkie-Talkie', the Old Bailey, 'the Shard' (on the right). This direct and humorous way of relating Londoners to their buildings is a fitting way to illustrate the complex relationship between living souls and the fabric of the city.
(© The artist. Flowers Gallery)

Map historian Peter Barber uses cosmic imagery to express the impact London had on its environs; in the world of maps, towns and villages 'were shown like stars surrounding the central sun of London', adding that 'despite their increasing integration with London, most of the villages were still surrounded by fields in 1850'; though this was not the case with the South Bank which by then was a largely urban environment (see chapter 3.4). The first mapmaker to place London at the centre of the surrounding countryside was Robert Morden in the 1680s. (previous page)

Southwark and Lambeth had certainly started life as 'the environs of London' – the title of a seminal work by Daniel Lysons published between 1792 and 1796. Both shared the same 'subordinate' status – to the City for Southwark, to the Church and Duchy of Cornwall estate for Lambeth. They have now been absorbed by the great city but their identity has been shaped by the idea of being at the service of a greater power. Both neighbourhoods are notable for their charitable work, hospitals, fire service and ambulance service; even Southwark's 'London's larder' is linked to the idea of a service industry – feeding the masses on home ground and beyond. At Lambeth, recent discussions about rebuilding Johanna School and the local library were briefly framed within the concept of pursuing the establishment of a 'charitable quarter' in Waterloo – as expressed by Rev. Steve Chalke, founder and Leader of Oasis Academy.

Having explored the moment when a town/city acquires a soul, Spengler goes on to describe its characteristics. The soul has its own language 'tantamount to the language of the Culture itself'. It has a 'facial expression' or 'visage … almost the spiritual history of the Culture itself'. The city's 'stone visages have incorporated the humanness of the citizen himself … all eye and intellect'. In this description, Spengler implies that the city soul looks like us, as we all represent the city where we live.

Spengler does not mention the heart of a town or city – possibly because it might be argued that cities have more than one. But in the late 1970s when all the artists based at Butler's Wharf were threatened with being moved on in favour of the gentrification of the area on the model of St Katherine's Dock, artist Maurice Agis is quoted in the *Evening News* of 14 December 1979 as saying: 'This is the heart of the area and we aren't going to have it torn out'. It was the heart of the area because they were there! Prior to their arrival, the place was deserted but the gradual colonisation by artists built its own momentum. This suggests that both heart and soul are linked directly to human energy and endeavours.

City life is rarely static and having meshed people and cities together, Spengler concluded: 'the birth of the City entails its death'. He explained that at first, the country town 'confirms the country, is an intensification of the picture of the country'. But the trajectory of the town will lead to the larger city, and finally to the 'gigantic megalopolis, the city-as-world, which suffers nothing beside itself. And sets about annihilating the country picture'.

> Long, long ago the country bore the country-town and nourished it with her best blood. Now the giant city sucks the country dry … They take the City with them into the mountains or on the sea. They have lost the country within themselves and will never regain it outside.

The contemporary painter Julian Cooper captured the widening gap between city and country in his 'Paris Texas' painting (overleaf). In his notes the artist described the scene as showing 'that particular modern form of split consciousness and suspension between two realities' – inescapably present since 'it is in the day turning into night, the city in the country, and turbulence and calm in the same sky'. The film 'Paris Texas' by Wim Wenders was released in 1984 and the artist also noted: 'the film is about dislocation from any home place, and television itself seems to have the effect of undermining the sense of the local in favour of a general fictional space'.

The German author Georg Simmel (1858-1918) defined a little more precisely the nature of urban materialism: 'city life has transformed the struggle with nature for livelihood into an inter-human struggle for gain, which here is not granted by nature but by other men'. He described the battle between the individual and the city: 'the individual has become a cog in an enormous organization of things and powers', this leading to the atrophy of individual culture.

Soullessness

Having described the birth of cities and that of their souls, Spengler also considered the soullessness of certain types of urban developments. Of the cities created by the city-architect, Spengler wrote uncompromisingly: 'in all Civilizations alike, these cities aim at the chessboard form, which is the symbol of soullessness. Regular rectangle-blocks astounded Herodotus in Babylon and Cortez in Tenochtitlan.' London of course had started life on the north bank as a chessboard town, though the rigid formula was limited to the area between the bridge and the forum with greater freedom for other parts of the walled city. Spengler considered the final stage of cities prior to their death as places and seats of civilisation: 'for the history of these Civilisations is merely apparent, like their great cities, which constantly change in face, but never become other than what they are. In these cities there is no soul. They are land in petrified form'.

Simmel discussed the 'inner life' of the metropolis. He made the point that the metropolis was characterised by 'its essential independence even from the most eminent

The artist Julian Cooper (born 1947) painted 'Paris Texas' in 1990. He was then based at Ambleside in the Lake District, the setting for the work. A woman is watching a scene from the film 'Paris Texas', hence the title, but what is particularly memorable is the clash of two cultures – the polished city on TV (Houston) and the rugged, wild mountain in the background. The city may appear in a fiction film, on a small screen and disembodied from its regular context, but its power remains undeniable, stealing the show from one the most spectacular landscapes on earth, as if it had already won the battle between town and country. (Private collection, © Julian Cooper)

individual personalities'; he gave the example of Weimar – 'its significance was hinged upon individual personalities and died with them'. Although it could be argued that the fortunes of Stratford-upon-Avon and Bankside were revived with the help of William Shakespeare … a relatively recent and deliberate piecing together of the great writer's myth, which in many ways has totally regenerated the places themselves. The association of great figures of history with certain cities or some of their neighbourhoods is definitely able to ensure a regenerating process, though in most cases, it has to be engineered.

Soulfulness

But I set out to try and find the soul of the South Bank and it would be disappointing if the answer was only made up of generalities; so, lifting my head over the parapet, I will now make a suggestion – with tentative 'proofs'. Not only does Waterloo hold London's geographic centre (see p. 19), it is also in the centre of the area under review. It is articulated around two major landmarks – Waterloo Bridge (1817) and Waterloo Station (1848). In terms of size the station is the largest in the country and one of the busiest, while the bridge is the only one to command London's most complete panorama, taking in Westminster at the south west, the City at the east and the West End ahead (see p. 24).

The other extraordinary character trait of Waterloo should be noted here – it is the determination to fight for local issues and local people; there is an ability to resist fiercely those outside forces which would be detrimental to the community. It was described in a *Guardian* article as 'How David took on Goliath and won', but I prefer the image of Asterix and Obelix defending the values of their village against interfering Roman rule attempting to impose and subjugate. Just as Asterix's village was the guardian of Gaul's customs and traditions, Waterloo is the guardian of community values and interests, and this is descriptive of the neighbourhood's own history.

The Guardian article of 31 May 1986, written by Tim Roberts, spelt out Waterloo's successes at Coin Street: 'The victory by well organised, well briefed and well-motivated local people in the face of seemingly insurmountable odds'. While Colin Ward, who chronicled the events at Coin Street, spelt out the issue in his book *Welcome, Thinner City*: 'No one has yet been willing to tell me to my face that people with low incomes and no chance of a mortgage have no right to occupy valuable space in the city.' So it is about class, valuable property and developers with deep purses driven by profit.

The LCC, partly driven by the spirit of the 1951 Festival of Britain and partly for reasons only known to them, had acquired in the 1950s most of the land between Waterloo and Blackfriars Bridges. The area's main income generator was clearing sites for car parking. Colin Ward recounts the impact on local residents: 'the surviving residents found its emptiness dangerous and menacing. It had turned into a land bank, a commodity like gold in a vault: too valuable to be useful.' Local groups were able to convince the GLC to build housing and a park but following the 1977 elections, the GLC dropped the three housing schemes its architects had been developing to open their door to large scale developers who were hovering around the 'gold', principally the Heron Corporation and Commercial Properties (Vestey family) with the Greycoat Estates (McAlpine family). Public enquiries and elections followed and the two main developers joined forces to become the Greycoat Commercial Estates purchasing key sites from the GLC. In 1983 the Secretary of State announced he was giving planning consent both to the housing scheme for the community and the hotel/offices wanted by the developers.

> By this time the Association of Waterloo groups [who had been fighting the community corner] was supported by the GLC, and

This view of the award-winning Palm Coop development was taken from Bernie Spain Gardens. Both schemes were realised by Coin Street Community Builders; the first was completed in 1988, the second in 1994. Palm has twenty-seven homes: ten family houses with gardens, five two-bedroom flats and ten one-bedroom flats. (© The author, 2022)

by both Lambeth and Southwark councils, who went to the High Court and the Court of Appeal, arguing that the approval for the Greycoat proposal was not legal. They lost. (Source: Colin Ward)

But the impasse was short-lived as Greycoat Commercial Estates withdrew from the scheme, selling the land back to the GLC. The GLC itself faced extinction but before its abolition, part of the land was leased (for £1) to the Society for Co-operative Dwellings and its freehold sold to a newly formed non-profit making company – Coin Street Community Builders for £750,000.

The results are impressive. Waterloo has a formidable array of organisations keeping an eye on local interests – Waterloo Action Centre (WAC), Waterloo Community Development Group (WCDG), the South Bank Employers' Group (SBEG), the South Bank Waterloo Neighbourhood Forum (SOAN), the Bankside Open Spaces Trust (BOST) and of course Coin Street ('creating an inspirational neighbourhood') (previous page); some of these come under the Association of Waterloo Groups (AWG). Readers may think that this was a one-off fight, unlikely to be repeated. But Waterloo's guardian dragon has raised its head once again in the face of another unwelcome development – what 'they' threatened to build on the site of the LWT tower site, next to the National Theatre. The leaflet posted in winter 2022 throughout Waterloo argues:

> This is not just a local issue – it's a national issue: South Bank's riverside walkway is currently one of the most visited areas of London. The proposed over-development of ITV's former home threatens the special qualities and success of London's Cultural Quarter on South Bank.

The scheme's visualisation looks inappropriate and overly dense.

However, for years Waterloo was the home of 'Cardboard City' – a ghostly community of homeless people who took refuge in the Bullring, the vacant 'hole in the ground' immediately south of Waterloo Bridge – this is the sunk pedestrianised roundabout, currently the site of Imax cinema, but soon to be redeveloped again. The writer Peter Conrad went there in 1989, observing the shocking 'architectural' contrast from Waterloo Bridge:

> To the east, you look at a spider's web of steel and glass; down below, you find a city of cardboard inhabited by those whose risks no one thinks it worthwhile to insure. The urine-perfumed alleys and stairwells under the South Bank concert halls house people who have fallen through society's floor.

Homeless people started drifting to this weather-proof location in 1978 and this community was finally evicted by Lambeth Council in 1998, after offering its 'residents' alternative accommodation. I am irresistibly reminded of 'Buddleia', the Dublin play by Paul Mercier which has been described at p. 63. There the accidental death of the young homeless teenager signals the final demise of the house he was repeatedly drawn to and its neighbourhood. Over and over again, journalists, commentators and writers have expressed respect and compassion towards the dispossessed whose tough lives have

The Chapel at Magdalen House, St George's Circus. This establishment cared for prostitutes and has been described on p. 175. Religion was an important weapon in the armoury of social rehabilitation and the accompanying text to this print published in *The Microcosm of London* (1808–1810) reads: 'the chaplain attends to them [the penitent prostitutes] daily to promote and encourage their good resolutions, and to exhort them to religion and virtue'.

been so often looked down upon. What if, the soul could shine a brighter light still when the body has been entirely stripped of all the comforts of 'civilised life'. What if the bad or indifferent treatment of homeless people and the embarrassment they cause us at the sight of society's 'fallen', only reflected badly on all those 'well-adjusted' members of society?

> Blessed are you who are poor, for yours is the Kingdom of God
> (Luke 6)

What if the homeless community was a poignant reminder of the human condition – raw, unpolished by society, on the verge of tragedy. In his biography of Dickens, Peter Ackroyd comes close to the same intuitive conclusion. Dickens was once confronted with 'five bundles of rags', all women 'who had just been refused entry to a workhouse'. Dickens tried unsuccessfully to intervene on their behalf. He ended up giving one of them a shilling - she had not eaten for a day and a night. He noted: 'she never thanked me, never looked at me - melted away into the miserable night', Ackroyd adding: 'it is as if in these worn and silent creatures he [Dickens] was beginning to see the soul of London itself.'

Waterloo is comparatively young, clinging to its rural character

'School for the Indigent Blind And Bethlehem Hospital St George's Fields, Southwark', engraving after T H Shepherd from *The World's Metropolis, or, Mighty London* (ed. H S Brooke, 1855). This view confirms the point made in *The Microcosm of London* that 'Her [London's] Hospitals are Palaces'. The building on the left is the School for the Indigent Blind which stretches along London Road and in the distance, grander still, stands Bethlehem Hospital, in neo-classical style.

until well into the nineteenth century. It took various wrong turns which made it 'notorious' in the purely negative sense of the word, but also, as if to compensate, it attracted idealists – Emma Cons, Lilian Baylis, garden lovers ... including the great poet William Blake, who created there his own paradise on earth (see p. 377).

Although I have tried to give 'proofs' for this tentative choice, I cannot claim it is based on scientific evidence at all, more of a gut feeling after five years of work on the South Bank.

The art of healing

Looking back again, another important strand emerges from the South Bank as a whole.

The meeting of four men in St Dunstan's Coffee House, Fleet Street on 14 January 1716 may be regarded to this day as a turning point in the history of London's hospitals. There were only two hospitals then, both outside the City walls: St Bartholomew's on the edge of the City and St Thomas's in Southwark. These four men were a banker (Henry Hoare), a vintner (Robert Witham), a religious writer (William Wogan) and a clergyman (the Rev Patrick Coburn). They founded 'The Charitable Society for relieving the Sick Poor and Needy'. The Society vanished after three months, possibly because initial fundraising efforts were disappointing; but

three years later it was back and soon the first hospital to be maintained by voluntary contributions was born – the small Westminster Infirmary in Petty France (1720). Disagreement between staff and Board of Governors led to a staff walk out which would eventually lead to the creation of a second hospital – St George's (1733). The infirmary continued, renamed Westminster Hospital. Other hospitals followed, operating on the new voluntary general hospital model or relying on individual philanthropy – Guy's Hospital in Southwark (1721) was amongst those. This meant there were two hospitals operating within a stone's throw of each other!

Within a few decades, this account was published in *The Microcosm of London* (1808–1810), in the section dealing with St Luke's Hospital:

> London … possesses an exclusive circumstance in her description, which belongs to no other city in the world; and it is this – that her Hospitals are Palaces … stately edifices arise for the relief of every evil, corporeal, moral, and intellectual, that afflicts the human species: diseases of every name, accidents of every kind, helpless infancy, friendless youth, decrepid [sic] age, moral infirmity, and mental derangement, find alleviation, restoration, reception, instruction, support, improvement, and renovation … within these splendid receptacles , which the

Graeme Miller exhibited his 'Beheld' installation at Southwark Dilston Grove in 2006. The 'people who fell from the sky' were those hidden in the under carriage of planes in search of a better life; each was represented by a film with soundtrack of the places where they fell. The impact of the fall may have created a small crater which finds an echo in the shape of the glass vessel visitors were encouraged to lift from their pedestal – 'on lifting these bowls they resonate with the sound of their location'. Photos courtesy of the artist (© Graeme Miller)

Reflections: Cannon Street Station viewed from London Bridge, and the same reflected in the glass of No 1 London Bridge.
(© The author, 2022)

piety of kings, the beneficence of individuals, and the charitable associations of the people at large, have erected for the most benign offices of humanity.

Chapter 3.3 [1770] and Chapter 3.4 [1845] cover a good number of these compassionate organisations, but perhaps one of the most effective images to illustrate this quote is the engraving by T H Shepherd reproduced on the previous spread: it shows two major charitable organisations – the School for the Indigent Blind and Bethlehem Hospital which both make the point of 'palace' architecture. There were no less than four more charitable establishments within a minute's walk of these: Magdalen Hospital in Blackfriars Road, the Philanthropic Society, The Freemasons' School for Girls (it is shown on Horwood's map of 1813), and the Asylum for Female Orphans – a historic cluster of good intentions which in due course will turn the South Bank into a place where charitable work and charitable service hold a prominent place.

Honouring the lives of the desperate

However, compassion needs to function at its highest level when faced with 'the anonymous' and there are no better places than cities for dealing with anonymity. Consider how compassion struggles to surface when we walk past the pavement shadows of homeless people or when the cries of a child break the silence of the street or when a drunk shouts uncontrollably at the wickedness of the world. Shouldn't we all feel enormous gratitude towards the teams of people whose lives are daily spent on trying to alleviate the miseries of cities.

Today, in the face of so many anti-emigrant rules and behaviour, many choose mostly to turn their backs to people who have fled desperate situations and countries. For all their shortcomings, are cities the last bastions of systematic solidarity, mindfulness and compassion? I feel a deep gratitude to sound artist Graeme Miller for his heart-rending installation 'Beheld' and for bringing silently tragic lives to our attention. I saw the exhibition at Dilston Grove, formerly known as Clare College Mission Church and located on the edge of Southwark Park – believed to be the first concrete church to be built in this country and an extraordinary exhibition venue. Miller's exhibition paid homage to the tragic lives of ten souls desperate enough to flee their countries and their miserable lives there, by taking refuge in the under carriage of a plane (previous page). Stripped of their proper context, their story sadly became that of 'people who fell from the sky'. If they managed to survive the agonisingly cold temperatures of the flight, their bodies would just drop like stones when the pilot lowers the wheels prior to landing.

Since 2006 Graeme has visited places around the world where migrants have fallen from aircraft – stowaways who have hidden in the wheel bays of commercial airlines. As the planes approach airports and lower their wheels, so their bodies fall to the ground … the migrant meets the settled, the living meet the dead. https://www.artsadmin.co.uk/project/beheld/ (accessed 15 January 2022)

This project is ongoing – an immensely moving gesture towards those who seemingly failed to reach their destination alive, including the fourteen-year-old boy who fell in the Black Forest. It is especially fitting that this special show was showcased in Southwark given its long-term dedication to healing and being of service

The south bank – a mirror of the north?

> The ancients built Valdrada on the shores of a lake … Thus the traveller, arriving, sees two cities: one erect above the lake, and the other reflected, upside down … Valdrada's inhabitants know that each of their actions is, at once, that action and its mirror image … At times the mirror increases a thing's value, at times denies it … The twin cities are not equal, because nothing that exists or happens in Valdrada is symmetrical … The two Valdradas live for each other, their eyes interlocked; but there is no love between them.
>
> From Italo Calvino's *Invisible Cities*

In London, the 'lake' is the mighty, tidal Thames – a formidable force which has seemingly been tamed by multiple human interventions – embankments, bridge and a Barrier, now close to the end of its life. William Blake, who wrote his upbeat 'Songs of Innocence' on the north bank (Westminster) and his gloomier 'Songs of Experience' on the south bank (Waterloo) must have felt a deep connection between the two since he chose to attach the same title to two of the poems, one from the first collection, the other from the second: 'Holy Thursday'. In the first poem, Blake is in awe of the vitality and beauty of the flow of charity children flocking to St Paul's Cathedral on Ascension Day, their singing rising to the heavens and filling the air with incredible optimism. The counterpart poem focuses instead on the bleak reality and the 'eternal winter' of the 'babes' lives' wondering the streets of London, in rags. Both poems were clearly deeply felt and both are true – two sides of the same coin, with awareness sitting in between. The South Bank is a vital component of the city as a whole. It encourages those with an open mind to form a more complete picture of urban men and women, young or old.

Chapter 3.4 presents an in-depth investigation of J H Banks' 1845 balloon view of London, hovering over the South Bank. However, there is not just one but two balloon views of London by Banks. The second was taken from Hampstead and hovering over Regent's Park in 1851, the year of the Great Exhibition. It is this later, more sophisticated version which struck me most for the way the configuration of the City and the South Bank seem to coincide (overleaf and p. 560). It is interesting too, because just as the north bank is better understood from the south bank (see the Eye of London chapter), so the south bank is far more legible when viewed from the north bank, as is so clearly demonstrated with the 1851 balloon view: I have included a handful of examples to illustrate this point.

1. Lion Brewery and shot tower (Waterloo)

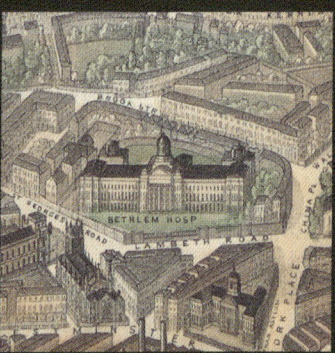

2. Bethlehem Hospital and St George's Catholic church

3. London Bridge Station

J H Banks' 'A Balloon View of London' was published in 1851, six years after 'A Panoramic View of London' which is reproduced in detail in Chapter 3.4. This later view taken from Hampstead, is more accomplished, more vivid too, and the section of the South Bank between Waterloo Bridge and the [future] Tower Bridge reads like the inverted shape of the City of London (overleaf). Some of the South Bank's landmarks are worth reproducing here as they offer a more detailed rendering than the 1845 panorama.

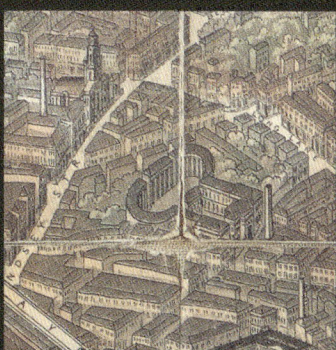

4. Bermondsey Leather Market

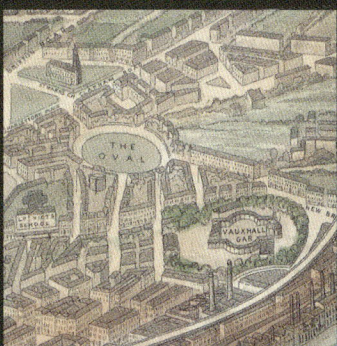

5. Vauxhall Gardens and the Oval

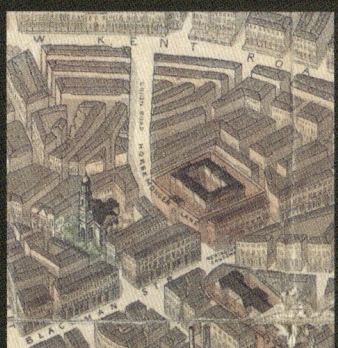

6. Trinity Church Square and County Gaol in Horsemonger Lane

The way in which the South Bank appears to echo the shape of the City leads me to ask whether the subconscious mission of the South Bank has been to produce a reversed form of the original model. The 'nerve centres' for each correspond well enough: Bank of England/Royal Exchange on the north bank, with the star-shaped road pattern at St George's church/Borough station on the south bank. The first represents the most significant financial institutions in the City while its opposite number on the south bank is an important spiritual centre as well as a key junction for road communication – a neighbourhood which would benefit from drawing attention to itself through a sensitive regeneration programme.

If we now focus on the 'City shape' on the south bank, it is created by a series of roads which starting from the west are: Waterloo Road, St George's Circus, London Road, Elephant & Castle, New Kent Road, Bermondsey New Road and Bermondsey Street. We are reminded of the key position of Waterloo Bridge and the magnetic need to connect Lambeth to Southwark and the City. Waterloo Station was never meant to be a terminus, but a mere cog in the vision of connecting Nine Elms to the City. This eastward pulling force was already at work in the 1740s when Westminster Bridge was built, opening up new opportunities for development in Lambeth but also weighted towards the City: Westminster Bridge Road to St George's Circus etc. When Waterloo Bridge was built sixty years later, the same eastern direction was at work.

With the City exerting such a gravitational pull on the South Bank, it is legitimate to question the satellite effect on the South Bank, particularly as we chart, in the introductory chapter, the City's efforts from medieval times onwards to control Southwark. City government in Southwark never followed the rightful procedure, since the Alderman for the 'Bridge Without' ward was appointed by the City, not by the locals with a right to vote. The City of course, represented an unrivalled economic magnet but the South Bank succeeded in retaining its separate identity and London as a whole is the richer for it.

We can all think of examples where north and south are spurred on by a sense of competition – Elizabethan theatres thrived on both sides of the river, albeit outside the City where they were not wanted, the Royal Institution on the north bank found a southern echo in the Leverian Museum in Great Surrey Street (Blackfriars Road) and the London to Greenwich railway, London's first in the 1830s, was too good an invention to remain a local feature – it rapidly spread to the whole of London.

Endpiece

In a city in flux, within a diverse and sometimes intimidating context, where each individual wages a constant battle to find and feed itself, a neighbourhood has grown which embraces art, compassion and healing. This is not simply a physical affair – it has metaphysical, philosophical, artistic and spiritual undertones; from the sixteenth century when theatre outings shaped Londoners' sense of their city, to the artists who gave a face to London at around the same time; also the achingly sad end of 'Alice' and fireman James Braidwood in 1861 – the latter spurred on the establishment of emergency services worthy of their name; while the tragic loss in 1866 of Evelina, the young wife of Baron Ferdinand de Rothschild, hours after giving birth to a still-born baby, gave the South Bank its Evelina Children's Hospital.

We should salute 'patron saints' Octavia Hill and Emma Cons for restoring housing to a place of long-lasting dignity, Irvine Sellar for pursuing doggedly his impossible Shard, William Shakespeare and Lilian Baylis for being so devoted to the theatre, Sam Wanamaker for not giving up on the Shakespeare-Globe dream and the many others, famous, barely remembered or forgotten in this pantheon of healing force. Because in the end WE are the city and therefore responsible for its failures as well as its breakthroughs. Perhaps a neighbourhood can be 'played' like a piece of music, by all of us, joining in the full orchestra of the city. Harmony or cacophony? It will depend on the residents' ability to care for one another and for their environment.

Sources:

https://www.flowersgallery.com/exhibitions/520-jiro-osuga-the-river/, accessed on 2 June 2021; Gibberd for William Curtis and James Sowerby; Robert D. Putnam, 'E *Pluribus Unum*: Diversity and Community in the Twenty-first Century' in *Scandinavian Political Studies*, Vol. 30, No 2, 2007; For Baudelaire, see https://fleursdumal.org/poem/103 (accessed on 22 December 2021); https://www.pubology.co.uk/pubs/9770.html for Noah's Ark, also found at https://www.pubwiki.co.uk/LondonPubs/SouthwarkStSaviour/NoahsArk.shtml; Oswald Spengler, 'The Soul of the City' in Sennett (see biblio); Georg Simmel, 'The Metropolis and Mental Life' in Sennett; Barber 2012; Lysons; 'Lost Hospitals of London' at https://ezitis.myzen.co.uk/alphabeticallist.html (accessed 9 January 2022); Colin Ward, *Welcome, Thinner City – Urban survival in the 1990s*, 1989; https://www.tate.org.uk/art/artworks/dion-tate-thames-dig-t07669; https://www.tate.org.uk/art/artworks/dion-tate-thames-dig-t07669/digging-thames-mark-dion; https://www.artsadmin.co.uk/wp-content/uploads/2020/05/Graeme-Miller_Beheld_Ed.pdf (accessed on 16/01/2022);

List of Subscribers

1. Christine ALBRECHT
2. Caroline BARRON
3. Graham BAUGH
4. Alexandra BLUM
5. Nicholas COLLINS
6. Julian COOPER
7. Anne COUDRAIN LAUNAY
8. Christine COWDRAY
9. Frank CREBER
10. John CUMMING
11. Valerie CUMMING
12. Mark EASTMENT
13. Anne EATWELL
14. Karen EYRE
15. Ferha FAROOQUI
16. Joan FUGLESANG
17. Kristian FUGLESANG
18. Annick GALINOU
19. Lesley GIBBS
20. Philippa GLANVILLE
21. Michael HEINDORFF
22. Mary-Elizabeth HELLYER
23. David HEPHER
24. Janet HEPHER
25. David HOGARTH
26. Rosalind HOLT
27. Terry HUNT
28. Desislava ILIEVA
29. Judith KING
30. Dominique LAUNAY
31. Vivienne LOREN
32. Ed MARCHANT
33. Sarah MEDWAY
34. Christine MEZARD
35. Simon MORRIS
36. Camilla NEWBEGIN
37. Shelagh NORRIS
38. Jiro OSUGA
39. John PERRY
40. Andy POOLE Christine
41. Oliver PROBYN
42. Edith RAMBURE-LAMBERT
43. Cathy ROSS
44. Eva RUPPRECHT
45. David J SCHAER
46. Elizabeth SCOTT
47. Hazel WATSON
48. Alex WERNER
49. Harriet and Toby WOOLLARD
50. Richard and Vicky WOOLLARD

Select bibliography & other sources

Maps and panoramas (in chronological order)

Londinium – a new map and guide to Roman London, Museum of London Archaeology, 2011

1542 Map of Southwark, reproduced on p. 129

VAN DEN WYNGAERDE – See LTS 1996 under Books

A map of Tudor London – The city in 1520, British Historic Towns Atlas, 2018

COPPERPLATE MAP – see Saunders & Schofield under Books; also LTS 1979

BRAUN & HOGENBERG: see LTS 1979 under Books

NORDEN: John Norden's 1600 long view of London is reproduced on pp. 38-39

AGAS – see LTS 1979 under Books

HOLLAR 1647 – Wenceslaus Hollar, *Long View of London 1647*, London Topographical Society, 1906–7

HOLLAR: Wenceslaus Hollar, *The Prospect of London and Westminster taken from Lambeth* (two versions before 1666 and 1707), London Topographical Society, 1988

MORGAN 1682 – see LTS 2013 under Books

ROCQUE 1747 – see LTS 1982 under Books

HORWOOD 1799: Richard Horwood's map 1791–1799 is at http://www.romanticlondon.org/explore-horwoods-plan

RHINEBECK PANORAMA, *c.* 1810, published by the London Topographical Society in 1998. Introduction by Ralph Hyde. With detailed key

HORWOOD 1813: this Horwood edition has been published by the London Topographical Society – see LTS 1985 under Books

LEIGH: Samuel Leigh, Panorama of the Thames from Vauxhall to Richmond, 1829

BANKS 1845: see this book's chapter 3.4

BANKS 1851: 'A Balloon View of London as seen from Hampstead', London, published by Banks & Co, 1851. See pp. 558–559 in this book's last chapter

BACON 1888: this map has been published by the London Topographical Society – see LTS 1987

O/S: THE GODFREY EDITION of Old Ordnance Survey Maps, 1872–74 (Waterloo & Southwark sheet 76; The Borough sheet 7.85; London Bridge Station sheet 7.86)

London Large Scale: Bankside sheet 7.75; Waterloo Bridge & the South Bank 7.74; Waterloo & Lambeth Marsh 7.84; Lambeth Road 7.94; Elephant & Castle 7.95)

O/S the 1893-1896 edition is available on the 'Layers of London' website.

BOMB DAMAGE MAPS: *The London County Council Bomb Damage Maps 1939°–1945*, London Topographical Society, 2005. Republished by Thames & Hudson in 2015

Books and articles

ACKROYD: Peter Ackroyd, Blake, 1995

ALLDERIDGE: Patricia Allderidge, *Bethlem Hospital 1247–1997 A Pictorial Record*, Phillimore & Co, 1997

ALLEN: Thomas Allen, *A New and Complete History of the County of Surrey*, two volumes, 1830

ALTICK: Richard Altick, *The Shows of London*, 1978

ART AND CITIES (The London Arts Café Magazine):

'Towards Jerusalem – Ben Johnson on Painting the Holy City', issue 12, Spring/Summer 2003

'Timothy Hyman: Taking on London', issue 15, Autumn/Winter 2004

(copies in the British Library)

ASTON: Margaret Aston, *The King's Bedpost*, 1993

AUBREY: John Aubrey, *The Natural History and Antiquities of the County of Surrey*, 1718–1719

AUERBACH: Erna Auerbach, *Tudor Artists – A study of Painters in the Royal Service and of Portraiture on Illuminated Documents from the accession of Henry VIII to the death of Elizabeth I*, 1954

BAIGENT & COWELL: Elizabeth Baigent and Ben Cowell (eds), *'Nobler imaginings and mightier struggles' – Octavia Hill, social activism and the remaking of British Society*, 2016

BANHAM & HILLIER: Mary Banham and Bevis Hillier, *A Tonic to the Nation – The Festival of Britain 1951*, 1976

BARBER 1995: Peter Barber, 'A Glimpse of the Earliest Map View of London?', *London Topographical Record*, No 27, 1995

BARBER 2012: Peter Barber, *London A History in Maps*, The London Topographical Society and the British Library, 2012

BARKER & JACKSON 1974: Felix Barker and Peter Jackson, *London – 2000 years of a city and its people*, 1974

BARKER & JACKSON 2008: Felix Barker and Peter Jackson, *Pleasures of London*, London Topographical Society, 2008

BARTON: Nicholas Barton, *The Lost Rivers of London*, 1962

BENNETT & MANDELBROTE: Bennett and Scott Mandelbrote, *The Garden, the Ark, the Tower, the Temple – Biblical metaphors of knowledge in early modern Europe*, 1998

BESANT: Walter Besant, *South London*, 1898

BOWSHER: Julian Bowsher, *Shakespeare's London Theatreland – Archaeology, History and Drama*, Museum of London Archaeology, 2012

BRAYLEY & BRITTON: E W Brayley and John Britton, *A History of Surrey*

BROOKE: Christopher Brooke, *London 800–1216: the shaping of a city* in The History of London series, 1975

CARLIN 1983: Martha Carlin, *The Urban Development of Southwark c. 1200 to 1550*, PhD thesis, University of Toronto, 1983

CARLIN: Martha Carlin, *Medieval Southwark*, 1996

CARRINGTON: R C Carrington, *Two Schools – A Short History of St Olave's and St Saviour's Grammar School Foundation*, 1962

CHERRY & PEVSNER: Bridget Cherry and Nikolaus Pevsner, *London 2: South*, The Buildings of England, 1983 & 2002

CLARK: John Clark, '"Brut sett Londen Ston": London and London Stone in a 14th-century English *Metrical Chronicle*' in *London & Middlesex Archaeological Society Transactions*, Volume 69, 2018

CLARK: Kath Clark, 'William Curtis's London Botanic Gardens and "*Flora Londinensis*"' in The London Gardener, 2009-10

COKE & BORG: David Coke and Alan Borg, *Vauxhall Gardens – A History*, 2011

COLEMAN: Terry Coleman, *The Story of a Great Theatre from Kean to Olivier to Spacey*, 2014 [The Old Vic]

DARLEY: Gillian Darley, *Octavia Hill social reformer and founder of the National Trust*, 1990

DODD: George Dodd, *Days at the Factory*, 1843

DYOS: H J Dyos, 'Railways and Housing in Victorian London', Part I and II in *Journal of Transport History*, Vol. II, 1955–56

DYOS & WOLFF: H J Dyos & Michael Wolff (eds), *The Victorian City – Images and Realities* Vol I Past and Present/Numbers of People, 1977

EDMOND: Mary Edmond, 'Limners and Picture Makers – New Light on the lives of miniaturists and large-scale portrait painters working in London in the sixteenth and seventeenth centuries' in *Walpole Society*, 1978–80

EDWARDS: David L Edwards, *Lambeth and the Archbishops*, 1998

ELLIS: Aytoun Ellis, *Three Hundred Years on London River – The Hay's Wharf Story 1651–1951*, 1952

FOISTER: see LTS 1996

GADD & GILLESPIE: Ian Gadd & Alexandra Gillespie (eds), *John Stow (1525–1605) and the making of the English Past*, British Library, 2004

GALINOU & HAYES: Mireille Galinou & John Hayes, *London in Paint, Oil Paintings in the Collection at the Museum of London*, 1996

GALINOU 1990: Mireille Galinou (ed), *London's Pride – A History of the Capital's Gardens*, 1990

GALINOU 2010: Mireille Galinou, *Cottages and Villas – The Birth of the Garden Suburb*, 2010

GERHOLD 2016: Dorian Gerhold, *London Plotted – Plans of London Buildings c.1450–1720*, London Topographical Society, 2016

GERHOLD 2019: Dorian Gerhold, *London Bridge and its houses, c.1209–1761*, London Topographical Society, 2019

GIBBERD: Graham Gibberd, *On Lambeth Marsh – The South Bank and Waterloo*, 1992

GRENADE: L. Grenade, *The Singularities of London, 1578*, edited by Derek Keene and Ian W Archer, 2014, The London Topographical Society

HARRIS: Judy Harris, *The Roupells of Lambeth – Politics, Property and Peculation in Victorian London*, 2001, Streatham Society

HEARN: Karen Hearn (ed), *Dynasties – Painting in Tudor and Jacobean England 1530–1630*, Tate exhibition catalogue, 1995

HIND: Arthur M Hind, *Engraving in England in the sixteenth and seventeenth centuries: Part I, The Tudor Period*, 1952

HIGGINBOTHAM: Peter Higginbotham, The workhouse http://www.workhouses.org.uk

HIGGINBOTHAM 2019: Peter Higginbotham, *Workhouses of London and the South East*, 2019

HOENSELAARS & BUNING: A J Hoenselaars & M Buning, *English Literature and the Other Languages*, 1999

HOWARD: Jean Howard, *Theater of a City – the Places of London Comedy 1598–1642*, paperback edition 2009

HUELIN: Gordon Huelin, *Lambeth Palace – A Short History*, 1974

HUGH ALLEY: Ian Archer, Caroline Barron, Vanessa Harding (eds), *Hugh Alley's Caveat, The Markets of London in 1598*, London Topographical Society, Publication No 137, 1988

HUMPHREY: Stephen Humphrey, *Elephant and Castle – A History*, 2013

HYDE 1994: Ralph Hyde, *A Prospect of Britain – The Town Panoramas of Samuel and Nathaniel Buck*, 1994

HYDE 1985: *Gilded Scenes and Shining Prospects – Panoramic Views of British Towns 1575–1900*, Yale Center for British Art, 1985

HYDE 1988: Ralph Hyde, *Panoramania! The Art and Entertainment of the 'all-embracing View'*, 1988

INGLIS: Simon Inglis, *Played in London – Charting the heritage of a city at play*, English Heritage, 2014

JACKSON: Peter Jackson, *London Bridge – A Visual History*, 2002 (first published 1971)

KELLY: Alison Kelly, *Mrs Coade's Stone*, 1990

LEITH-ROSS: Prudence Leith-Ross, *The John Tradescants – Gardeners to the Rose and Lily Queen*, 1984

LOVEDAY: James Thomas Loveday, *Loveday's London Waterside Surveys. For the use of Fire Insurance Companies, merchants, brokers, agents, wharfingers, granary-keepers etc.*, 1857

LTS 1906: see Hollar 1647 under 'Panoramas'

LTS 1979: The A to Z of *Elizabethan London*, compiled by Adrian Prockter and Robert Taylor, London Topographical Society, Publication No 122

LTS 1982: *The A to Z of Georgian London* – Introductory Notes by Ralph Hyde; London Topographical Society, Publication No 126, 1982

LTS 1985: *The A to Z of Regency London*, London Topographical Society, Publication No 131, 1985

LTS 1987: *The A to Z of Victorian London*, London Topographical Society, Publication No 136, 1987

LTS 1988: see Hollar under 'Panoramas'

LTS 1996: Howard Colvin and Susan Foister, *The Panorama of London circa 1544 by Anthonis van den Wyngaerde*, London Topographical Society, 1996

LTS 2013: *The A to Z of Charles II's London 1682 – London &.c. Actually Survey'd by William Morgan.* Introductory Notes by Peter Barber and Ralph Hyde; London Topographical Society, Publication No 174, 2013

LYSONS: *Daniel Lysons, Environs of London: Volume 1 The County of Surrey*, 1792

MANNING & BRAY: Owen Manning and William Bray, *The History and Topography of the County of Surrey*, 1847

MARSHALL: Geoffrey Marshall, *London's Docklands – An Illustrated History*, 2018

MAUGHAM: Somerset Maugham, *Liza of Lambeth*, 1897

MOLA 2009: Carrie Cowan, Fiona Seeley, Angela Wardle, Andrew Westman, Lucy Wheeler, *Roman Southwark Settlement and Economy: Excavations in Southwark 1973–91*, Monograph Series 42, Museum of London, 2009

MOLA 2009: Simon Blatherwick, Richard Bluer, *Great houses, moats and mills on the south bank of the Thames: medieval and Tudor Southwark and Rotherhithe*, Monograph Series 47, Museum of London, 2009

MOLA 2011: Tony Dyson, Mark Samuel, Alison Steele, Susan M Wright, *The Cluniac priory and abbey of St Saviour Bermondsey, Surrey – Excavations 1984–95*, MOLA Monograph Series 50, Museum of London, 2011

MOLA 2012: Adrian Miles with Brian Connell, *New Bunhill Fields Burial Ground, Southwark: excavations at Globe Academy, 2008*, Archaeology Studies Series 24, Museum of London

MoLAS 1999: Megan Brickley, Adrian Miles, Hilary Stainer, *The Cross-Bones burial ground, Red Cross Way, Southwark, London: archaeological excavations (1991-1998) for the London Underground Limited Jubilee Line Extension Project*, Monograph Series 3, Museum of London, 1999

MoLAS 2002: Jane Sidell, Jonathan Cotton, Louise Rayner, Lucy Wheeler, *The prehistory and topography of Southwark and Lambeth*, Monograph Series 14, 2002

MoLAS 2005 (A): Kieron Tyler and Hugh Wilmott, *John Baker's late 17th-century glasshouse at Vauxhall*, MoLAS Monograph Series 28, Museum of London, 2005

MoLAS 2005 (B): Kieron Tyler, *The Doulton stoneware pothouse in Lambeth: excavations at 9 Albert Embankment, London*, MoLAS Archaeological Studies Series No 15, Museum of London, 2005

MoLAS 2006, Christopher Phillpotts, Mark Samuel, Derek Seeley, *Winchester Palace: excavations at the Southwark residence of the Bishops of Winchester*, Monograph Series 31, Museum of London, 2006

MoLAS 2008: Kieron Tyler, Ian Betts, Roy Stephenson, *London's Delftware industry: the tin-glazed pottery industries of Southwark and Lambeth*, Monograph Series 40, Museum of London, 2008

MULLETT: Michael Mullett, *Sources for the History of English Non-Conformity 1660–1830*, British Records Association, 1991

MURRAY: Stephen Murray, 'The Rise, Fall and Transformation of Bankside Power Station 1890–2010' in the *Journal of the Greater London Industrial Archaeology Society* (GLIAS), 2010. At https://leicester.figshare.com/articles/thesis/Bankside_Power_Station_Planning_Politics_and_Pollution/10127297

NEW: Elizabeth New 'The Common Seal and Communal Identity in Medieval London' in S. Solway's *Medieval Coins and Seals* (ed), 2015

NEWMAN: Jon Newman, *Lovely Lambeth – South London Walks*, 2017

NEWMAN & WESTERN: Jon Newman and David Western, *Death on the Brighton Road*, 2017

PCA 2015: Douglas Killock, *Temples and Suburbs – Excavations at Tabard Square, Southwark*, Pre-Construct Archaeology Ltd No 18, 2015

PCA 2013: Victoria Ridgeman, Kathelen Leary & Berni Sudds, *Roman Burials in Southwark Excavations at 52–56 Lant Street and 56 Southwark Bridge Road, London SE1*, Pre-Construct Archaeology Ltd No 17, 2013

PHILLIPS: Hugh Phillips, *The Thames about 1750*, 1951

PINDER: John William Pinder, *St George-the-Martyr church, Southwark – A short history*, [1965]

PLEASURE GARDENS OF SOUTH LONDON (THE), two volumes of cuttings and images, partly based on the work of Warwich Wroth's *London Pleasure Gardens* volume (see below), but precious for additional texts and pictures. Museum of London Library

POTTER: Jennifer Potter, *Strangle Blooms – The Curious Lives and Adventures of the John Tradescants'*, 2006

PRAGNELL: Hubert J Pragnell, *The London Panoramas of Robert Barker and Thomas Girtin circa 1800'*, London Topographical Society, 1968

PRICE: John Price, *Heroes of Postman's Park – sacrifice in Victorian London*, 2017

PUGIN & ROWLANDSON: Rudolph Ackermann (publisher) *Microcosm of London*, with plates by Augustus Pugin and Thomas Rowlandson, 1808–1810

PUTTEVILS: Jeroen Puttevils, *Merchants and trading in the sixteenth century: the golden age of Antwerp*, 2015

RENDLE 1878: William Rendle, *Old Southwark and its People*, 1878

RENDLE and NORMAN: William Rendle and Philip Norman, *The Inns of Old Southwark*, 1888

ROSS & CLARK: Cathy Ross & John Clark, *London – The Illustrated History*, 2008

ROWELL: George Rowell, *The Old Vic Theatre A History*, 1993

SACKS: Janet Sacks (ed), *Morley College – A 125th anniversary portrait*, 2015

SADLEIR: Michael Sadleir, *Forlorn Sunset*, 1947

SADLEIR: Michael Sadleir, *Fanny by Gaslight*, 1940

SAUNDERS & SCHOFIELD: Ann Saunders and John Schofield (eds), *Tudor London: a map and a view*, London Topographical Society, 2001

SCHOFIELD: John Schofield, *London 1100–1600 The Archaeology of a Capital City*, 2011

SCOULOUDI: Irene Scouloudi, *Panoramic Views of London 1600–1666*, Corporation of London, 1953

SENNETT: Richard Sennett (ed), *Classic Essays on the Culture of cities*, 1969

SHARP: Tony Sharp, '*Southwark ca 1542: The Duchy of Lancaster Plan newly annotated*', published online at https://www.academia.edu/, 2020

SMITH: Greg Smith, *A 'Connoisseur's Panorama' Thomas Girtin's Eidometropolis and Other London Views, c.1796–1802*, London Topographical Society, 2018

SOUTH BANK: *Designing the future of the South Bank*, South Bank Centre, 1994

STOW 1598: John Stow, *A Survey of London written in the year 1598*, revised 1603 (also includes William Fitzstephen's late twelfth-century's *Description of London*), paperback edition 1999 (first edition 1994). The text is also available online at 'British History Online'

STOW 1720: *A survey of the cities of London and Westminster … very much enlarged … and the survey and history brought to the present time by John Strype*, 1720

STOW 1755: *A survey of the cities of London and Westminster … very much enlarged … and the survey and history brought to the present time by John Strype*, 1755

SURVEY OF LONDON 22: *Survey of London: Volume 22, Bankside (The Parishes of St. Saviour and Christchurch)*, edited by Howard Roberts and Walter H Godfrey, 1950

SURVEY OF LONDON 23: *Survey of London: Volume 23, Lambeth: South Bank and Vauxhall*, edited by Howard Roberts and Walter H Godfrey, 1951

SURVEY OF LONDON 25: *Survey of London: Volume 25, St George's Fields (The Parishes of St. George the Martyr Southwark and St. Mary Newington)*, edited by Ida Darlington, 1955

SURVEY OF LONDON 26: *Survey of London: Volume 26, Lambeth: Southern Area*, edited by F H W Sheppard, 1956

TALLIS: John Tallis's *London Street Views 1838–40*, re-published by the London Topographical Society, Publication No 160, 2002

TANSWELL: John Tanswell, *The History and Antiquities of Lambeth*, 1858

TATTON-BROWN: Tim Tatton-Brown, *Lambeth Palace, A History of the Archbishops of Canterbury and their houses*, 2000.

TINDALL: Gillian Tindall, *The House by the Thames and the people who lived there*, 2007

TOWN 2014: Edward Town, 'A Biographical Dictionary of London Painters' in *Walpole Society*, 2014 (volume 66)

TOWN 2015: Edward Town, 'A Fête at Bermondsey': an English landscape by Marcus Gheeraerts the Elder' in the *Burlington Magazine*, vol. CLVII, No 1346, May 2015

TRADES: *Dictionary of Traded Goods and Commodities 1550–1820*, Wolverhampton, 2007 (available at British History Online)

VCH 4 (Victoria County History Surrey): H E Malden (editor) *A History of the County of Surrey – Volume 4*, 1912

WALKER: Hope Walker, 'Netherlandish immigrant painters and the Dutch reformed church of London, Austin Friars 1560–1580' in *Netherlands Yearbook for History of Art*, 2013 (Volume 63)

WATSON: Howard Watson, *The Shard – The Vision of Irvine Sellar*, 2017

WEINREB & HIBBERT: Ben Weinreb and Christopher Hibbert, *The London Encyclopaedia*, first published in 1983, several reprints

WHELAN: Robert Whelan, 'The poor, as well as the rich, need something more than meat and drink': the vision and work of the Kyrle Society' in *'Nobler imaginings and mightier struggles': Octavia Hill, social activism and the remaking of British society*, edited by Elizabeth Baigent and Ben Cowell, 2016

WILKINSON: Robert Wilkinson, *Londina Illustrata*, 1819

WINCHESTER: Simon Winchester, *The Surgeon of Crowthorne*, 1998

WEDD, PELTZ and ROSS: Kit Wedd, with Lucy Peltz and Cathy Ross, *Creative Quarters – the art world in London 1700–2000*, Museum of London, 2001 (also published under the title Artists' London – Holbein to Hirst)

WOLFF: Michael Wolff, '*The Metropolis on Stage*' in *The Victorian City – Images and Realities* (Vol. I) edited by H J Dyos & Michael Wolff, 1976

WROTH: Warwick Wroth, *The London Pleasure Gardens of the Eighteenth Century*, 1896

Websites

British History online: for the Survey of London volumes – useful for the text but some images missing https://www.british-history.ac.uk/

Layers of London – very useful for maps and map comparisons https://www.layersoflondon.org/

British Museum and Museum of London: collections online

London Picture Archive for the picture collection of the London Metropolitan Archives https://www.londonpicturearchive.org.uk/

Diocese of Southwark: 'Find a church', including 'Former Places of Worship' at https://southwark.anglican.org/find-a-church/

Mapping the Practice and Profession of Sculpture in Britain and Ireland 1851-1951, University of Glasgow History of Art and HATII, online database 2011 http://sculpture.gla.ac.uk/

https://database.theatrestrust.org.uk/resources/theatres/show/3182

http://www.arthurlloyd.co.uk for theatres and music halls

Dictionary of Victorian London by Lee Jackson https://www.victorianlondon.org/

History of Parliament online https://www.historyofparliamentonline.org/

INDEX

Numbers in bold indicate a main entry.

Numbers in italics indicate a picture.

Abbey Street 211

Abbot of Battle's Inn 88, 124-125, **137**

Abbot of Hyde 133

Abbot of St Augustine's House 124-125, **137**

Abercrombie, Patrick 438; – Plan 438, 476, 479

Acanthus WSM Architects 313

Ackroyd, Peter (author) 17, 18, 52, **133**, 285, 553

Albert Embankment 227, 232, 235, 308, 313, **317-318**; the Corniche 317-318; the Dumont 317; Merano building 317-318

Albion Flour Mills 57, 58, 177, 182, **185-187**

Albion Place (Great Surrey Street) 57, 166-167, **178-179**, 186

Alleyn, Edward (actor) 95, 108, 109, 115, 116, 196, 449, 450

Allford Hall Monaghan Morris (architects) 326

Allies and Morrison (architects) 10, 302, 315, 325, 335, 346, 347, **472-475**, *482*, 514; Bob Allies 474-475, 537, 539; Alfredo Caraballo 315, Artur Carulla 479; Graham Morrison 472, 474-475, 537-543

ALMSHOUSES: Drapers' – 182-183, **199**, 167, *275*; Fishmongers' – 150-151, **162-163**; Hopton's – 182-183, **188**, *336*; Overman's – 193; Rowland Hill's (or Surrey almshouses) – 267, *275*, 277. Also see Cure's College

Anchor Terrace 273

Angel Place (Southwark) 132

Angell, William 184

Animal baiting 109; bear 108, **114**, **116**, 448; bull 114

Antwerp *33-35*, 37, 38, *46-47*, 55

ARCHBISHOP OF CANTERBURY: 79, 87, 88, 89, 97-100, 128, 133, 159, 252, 255, 390-391; Augustine (first Archbishop of Canterbury) 79; Baldwin of Forde 98; Richard Bancroft, 97, 100, 390; Henry Chichele 99, 100; Thomas Cranmer 99, 106; William Juxon 157; William Howley 237; Stephen Langton 98-99; William Laud 32, 99; Matthew Parker 99, 391; Archibald Campbell Tait 398; Hubert Walter 98; William Warham 99; John Whitgift 97

Archbishop's Park 394, 398

ARCHAEOLOGY: 138, 195, *445*, 454, 531, 454; archaeologist v architect 537-543; Bermondsey Abbey 539; Brandon House 539, 542; Landmark Court 539,*540*, 542; Lyon House 539; MOLA (Museum of London Archaeology) see bibliography; News Building 539; Pickle Factory Trinity Church Square 539; PCA (Pre-Construct Archaeology) 75, 78, 79; Thameslink 539, 540

Architects Co-Partnership 311

Arnout, Jules (printmaker) *224-225*, – Jean Baptiste 225

Arundel estates 99, 134

Ashmole, Elias (antiquarian) 95, 152, 371-372, 390; – Deed of Gift 371-372; – House 150-151, **152**

Ashmolean Museum 10, 387, 388, 389, *391*

Astley's 150-151, **158**-*159*, 174, 230-231, *240-241*, 438; Philip Astley 159, 240, 378, 421

Asylum for the Deaf and Dumb **159**-*161*, 204-205, *212*

Asylum for Female Orphans 150-151, 230-231, **241-242**, 379, 404, 556

Aubrey, John (author) 94, 95, 97, 451, 510

Auroville, India 17-*18*, 546

Ayloffe, Sir John (knight) 83

Ayres, Alice 18, **464-471** ; – Street 464, 471

Bacon, John (sculptor) 171, 519, 522

Ballooning 198, 200-201, 222-223, *224-225*, 264-265, 289, 557, *558-559*

Banks J H (artist/publisher) 67, *222-223*, 224-225, 557; 1851 panorama 225, 557-560

Banks, Sir Joseph (botanist) 177

BANKSIDE: 51, 63, 83, 114, 139, 299, **445-448**; 550; – one two three 333, *335*, 474-475; Neo – 299, 333, **335-336**, *336*; Nos 49-52 Bankside 188; – power station 302, 472-473, 476, *530*, 531; – St Christopher's House 335, 474-475, 478. Also see Theatres, Globe, Hope, Rose, Winchester House

Barclay, Robert 191

Barge 454; – builders 166-167, **172**; ceremonial – 154; Prince Frederick's 172

BARGEHOUSES: 101, 150-151, *150-151*; Armourers' – 101; Barber-Surgeons' – 108; Clothworkers' – **154**; Fishmongers' – **154**; Goldsmith's – 101; Grocers' – 108; Mercers' – **154**; Skinners' – 154; also see Old Barge House

Barham Street 210

Barker, Robert (artist) *56-57*, 58, 162, 424; Henry Aston – 57

'Barons', The 178, 184; George Baron 184

Barry, Charles the elder (architect) 310

Bartholomew Street 130

Battle Bridge 125, **137**

Baudelaire, Charles (poet) 25, 358, 534, 532

Bawden, Edward (artist) *429*, 430

Baylis, Lilian (theatre impresario) **426-429**

Bazalgette, Joseph William (engineer) 227, 353

BDP Architects 342

Beaconsfield Contemporary Arts 235

Bear Garden 112-113, 115, **116**, 449, 450. Also see animal baiting

Bear Gardens (street) *477*, 478

Bear Lane (Southwark) 402-403

Beaufoy, Henry 234-235, John Hanbury – 240, Mark **169**, 383-386; Mrs – 234. Also see vinegar manufactories

Beaumont, Francis (playwright) 451, 482

Beavan, Sharon (artist) 10, *58-61*

Becket, Thomas see St Thomas Becket

Bede (historian) 79

Bedford, Francis 235, 255, 287, 288

Bell, Julian (artist) *8-9*, 10

Belvedere/Belvidere House 168, 252, 253. Also see Breweries

Belvedere Road 250-251, 252, 253, 255, 431

Benevolent Society of St Patrick 251, 255, **258**, 259

Bennet Street 260

Bennet, T P Architects 494, 497, 499

Bentham, Jeremy 217; – Sir Samuel 232

Berkeley Homes 75, 245, 317

BERMONDSEY: 41, *42-43*, 45, 70-71, 81, 89, 225, 261, 510; – artillery ground *42*, 44; – Clove building 474-475, 514, 543, *543*; – Conservation Area 504; – Cross 125, **139**; – eyot 76; – Lake 70; – Maypole *42*, 44; – New Road 560; – Spa 204-205, **212**; – Square 281, **289-291**. Also see Jacob's Island

Bermondsey Street 125, 139, 211, 284, *285*, 286, 289, 354, 545

Bermondsey Abbey 21, 88, *122*, *125*, 131, 139, *140-141*, 204-205, **211**, 511; Long Walk 291; – remains *290-291*

Bermondsey Project Space Gallery 545

Bethlehem/Bethlem Hospital 162, 230-231, ***242-244***, 263, 407, 554, *558*; State Criminal Lunatic Asylum 243, 407; Hospital for Nervous Diseases 263

Bevans, James (architect) 217

BFLS (formerly Hamiltons Architects) 344

Binnie, Sir Alexander (engineer) 232

BISHOPS – of Bethlem 242; – of Carlisle 101, 120, 398; – of Hereford's Diamond Hall *235*; – of London 79 (Mellitus), 117, 263; – Tenison 156, 462

Bishop Bonner 131; – house(s) 104-105, **106-107**, 166-167, *173*

Bishop of Rochester 100, 101, 192; – Inn 98, **120**, 192, 193

Bishop of Winchester 89, 115, 119, 120, 134, 196, 445, 447; Lancelot Andrews 191, *518*; Henry Beauford 119, 120; Richard Foxe 117; Stephen Gardiner 119; William Gifford 119; Peter des Roches 135; St Swithun 117; Charles Sumner 270, 271; Thomas Wolsey 120, – Manor see Clink

BLACKFRIARS: 57; – Bridge 59-61, 182, **185**, *267*, **270**, 332, **334**; – Circus 333, **336**; – Road 260, No 1 – 323, 328, 497; No 18 – 323, 329, 498; No 142 – **336**; No 251 – 328

Black Prince 95; Edward of Woodstock (1st Duke of Cornwall) 95; Joan of Kent 95; – Court 95

Black Prince Road 235, 238, 311

Blackman Street (Borough High Street) 115, 197

Blake, William (poet and artist) 18, **377-380**, **403-404**, 512, 557; – house 13, 150-151, *377-378*; London poem 378-379

Bleaching see Industries

Bligh, William (Vice-Admiral) 157

Blore, Edward (architect) 237, *239*

Blue Boar Court 218

Bol, Cornelis (artist) 53, *54-55*

Bonnington Partnership (architect) 352

Bonnington Square **391-394**, *395*

Booth, Charles *410*, 411, 418-419, 426, *462*

Borough & Bankside **110-121, 180-201, 266-293, 442-483**, 527

Borough High Street 37, 51, 75, 78, 134, 135, 196, 213, 219, *282-283*, 284, 287, 504, 510, 539; Nos 170-192 – 121, 129; Nos 201-205 – 132

Borough market 13, 182-183, **192-193**, 271, 333, **336**, 495, 504

Borough Road 197-198; No 103 – 342

Borough station 78, 199

Boulton, Matthew 186

Bourgeois, Louise (artist) 444

Brabazon, Lord 194, 444, 536

Braidwood, James (fireman) 463, 507, 561

Brandon family landowners Sir William – 120; Sir Thomas – 120; Charles – 120

Brandon House, Southwark see Suffolk Place

BREWERIES: 146, **510-513**; Anchor **191**, 271, 281, 289; Barclay's – 280-281, **288-289**; Barclay Perkins 186, 191, 209, 268, *272-273*, 303, 512, 513; Beere House 125, **138-139**, 209, **511-513**; Belvedere 166-167, **172**; Castle 230-231, **244**, 253; Clowes & Co **209**; Coombe & Co 276; Courage **210**, 289, 512, 513; Courage & Donaldson 210, *513*; Dolphin and the Beare 137; Goldings 137, 506; John Crosse 511; (Red) Lion – *171*, 172, 250, **252-253**, 406-407, 431, *558*; Henry Meux & Co 209; Horn 166-167, **172**; Martineau 166-167, **170**; Phoenix **209**; Southwark – 182-183, 188; Stoney Lane – 205, **209**; Watney Coombe, Reid & Co 276; Whitbread brewery 170

Bricklayer's Arms station 280, 289

Bridewell prison 182-183, **196**, 214

Bridge House 124-125, **137**, 204-205, **209**, 507; – estates 115, **137**, 197, 208, 209, 355; New London – 494, 500, 501

Bridge Ward Without 83

Broad Street (Lambeth) 236-237

Broadwall 326

Broadway Malyan architects 315-316, 495

Brome, Richard (playwright) 107

Brookwood cemetery *412*, 458

Brothels see prostitution

Browker, Hugh (landowner) 120; Thomas and Mary – 184

Browne, Sir Anthony 118; – Junior (1st Viscount Montague) 118

Brueghel, Jan the Elder (artist) *361*, 362, 366

Brueghel, Pieter (artist) *488*-492

Brunel, Isambard Kingdom (engineer) 252

Brunswick House 150-151, **153**, 230-231, **246**-*247*,

Bryce, John (artist) 10, *442-443*, *444*,

Buck, Samuel and Nathaniel 52, 196, 197

Buckler, J C (artist) *57*, 140, *218*, 244-245, *512*

Bunyan, John 188-189

Burbage, James 116, 449, 451, 453

Burton, James (architect) 177

BURIAL GROUNDS: 456-457; with funeral *207*; Christ church 260; College ground 456; Quaker's – 212; Roman – **75**-79, 455, 458; St John Horsleydown 286; St Mary's (Newington) 244; St Saviour's churchyard 456. Also see Cross-Bones Yard, Death, Flemish burial ground

Butler, Richard (glass-painter) 32, 34, 45

Cabanel, Rudolph (architect) 175, 258, 424

Cade, Jack 17

Calvert's Buildings 112-113

Calvino, Italo (author) 73, 557

Camp, Jeffery (artist) *441*

Campbell, Colen (architect) 159

Canaletto, Antonio (artist) 52-*54*, *147*, 159, *160*, *169*, 375, 402, *496*

Canterbury pilgrimage 30, *133*; pilgrim badges *127*, 128

Capon, William *158*, *402*-403, 440

Carbuncle Cup 315, 344, 354, 344, 354

Cardinal's Hat House 112-113, 182-183, **188**

Carlisle House 92-93, 97, **100-101**, 146, 150-151. Also see Pottery

INDEX

Carlisle Street 101

Caron, Noel (ambassador) 95, 246; – House 92-93, *94*, **95, 96**, 246, 373; – estate 385

Caroon House 246, *384*, 385

Cartwright, Thomas (master mason) 217

Caruso St John (architects) 310-311

Casper Mueller Kneer (architects) 355

Cary, Henry (landowner) 109

Casson Square (Waterloo) 436

Cemeteries – see burial grounds

Chadwick, Edwin 226, 227

Chadwick, William 288

Chaplin, Charlie 312

Charitable giving 132, 137, 548; (bread for the poor), 139, 367; Charitable Society for relieving the Sick Poor and Needy 554; Vaughan Charity 276

Charlotte Street (now Union Street) 184

Chase, John (photographer) 10, *334*, 335

Chaucer, Geoffrey 30, *133*, 139

CHILDREN: 83, 155, 190, 210, 211, 212, 240, 254, 369, 379, 410-411, 557; child mortality 463, 462, 464 ff; – infanticide 405; – orphans 159-160; – playground 288, 387, 391, 393. Also see Evelina Hospital and Lambeth Ragged School, Philanthropic institution

Cholera *455*, 458

Chopping, Andy (photographer) 11, *540*

CHURCHES: Act for Building New Churches 255; Commissioners for Building 50 New Churches 210, 215; Independent – 188; All Saints church (Vauxhall) 315; All Saints church (Waterloo) 250, 257, **264**; Christ Church (Blackfriars) 57, 166-167, **175**, 251, **259-260**; Christ Church (Waterloo); Clare College Mission Church 556; St Anne, church of 315; St George's Catholic church 243, 250-251, **262-263**, *558*; St George-the-Martyr 77, 89, 106, 124, **130-131**, 136, 204-205, **214-215**, 280, 284, 531; St James's, Rotherhithe/Bermondsey 281, **289**; St John (Waterloo) 235, 251, **255**; St John Horsleydown 204-205, *207*, **210**-**211**, 280, **286**, with funeral *207*; St Margaret 117, 120, 132, 133, New churchyard 118-119; St Mary-at-Lambeth 13, 89, 92-93, **97**, 150-151, **157**, 230-231, 235, **239**, 366-368, 391; St Mary Magdalen (Bermondsey) *42-43*, 44, 89, 125, **139**, 204-205, **211**, 280, **289**; St Mary Magdalen (Southwark) 117; St Mary Newington, church of 89, 92-93, 94, 150-151, *162-163*, 230-231, **244**; St Mary Overie (Priory) 25, 88, 126, 128, 135; St Mary-the-Less, church of 230-231, **235-237**, *238*; St Olave (Tooley Street) 89, 122, 124-125, 136, 139, 204-205, **208-209**, 280, **283-284**, 492; St Peter's church, Sumner Street 267, **270-271**; St Peter's church Vauxhall 236, 314; St Saviour's 38-39, 47, 48, 56, 88, 89, 112-113, **117**, 120, **136-137**, 182-183, *193*, 268, **274**, 467; St Thomas Becket chapel 30-*31*, 127-128, 135, 537; St Thomas, church of 89, 124-125, **135**, 136, 204-205, **217**, 219, 280-281, **288**; Waterloo St Andrew with St Thomas 264

CITY COMPANIES Apothecaries' 156; Armourers' 107; Barber-Surgeons' 108; Brewers' 191; Drapers' 199; Fishmongers' 162; Glasssellers' 153; Goldsmiths' 107; Grocers' 108, 131; Skinners' 131

City Corporation of London 33, 158, 199, 260, 273, 275, 335, 378, 487; City of London Common Seal 30-*31*

City Hall 139, 299, 351, **353**, 354

City & Guilds of London Art School 236

City & Guilds of London Institute 430

Clayton, Sir Robert (City merchant) 217; Sir William – 380, 381

Clayton Street 380-381

Clink, Liberty of the 115; – prison **119, 192**; – Street 62, 192, 478

Clove Building, see Bermondsey

Coade, Eleanor (Senior and Junior) **170-171**

Coade's manufactory 166-167, **170-172**; William Croggon 171; Edward Sealey 171; Routledge & Co 172. Also see John Bacon

COIN STREET: 257, 322, **326-327**, 551; – Community Builders 324, **326-327**, 551, 552; Iroko Housing Co-op 326; Mulberry Housing Cooperative 326; Palm Coop Development 326, 551

Cole Street 288

Colechurch, Peter 126, 128, 137

Collingwood Street 217

College Street 255, 431

Commercial Road (now Upper Ground) 168

Commons Preservation Society (now Open Spaces Society) 385

Commonwealth 98

Conlin, Stephen (illustrator) *12-13*, *67*, *71*, *81*, *84*, *86-87*, *140-141*, *142*, *144-145*, *148*

Conran, Terence **352-353**; – and Partners 353, 514

Cons, Emma (housing worker) *417*, 418, 421, **426-428**, 439

Constable, Chris (archaeologist) 10, 537-543

Constable, John (artist) *413*, 414

Constable, John (writer) see John Crow

Cooper, Julian (artist) 10, 549, 550

Copt or Copped Hall (Vauxhall) 66, 96

Corbusier, Le 325, 343

Cornwall Road 406

Cottingham, L N (architect) *415*-416

Cottons Centre 352. Also see Cotton's Wharf

Cottmansfield (Lambeth) 157

County Gaol (Southwark) – two sites 204-205, **213-214**, 216. Also see White Lyon prison

County Hall *60-61*, 68, 253, 431

Coverdale, Miles 136

Cox, Alan (printer) 516

Cox, Maggie (photographer) 11, *445*

Crane, Walter (artist) **468-470**

Cripps, Stephen (artist) *515-516*

Crisp, Stephen (garden designer) 388, 396-397

Critz, John de (the Elder) 367; Thomas de – *368*, 369

Cromwell, Thomas 136

Cross-Bones Burial Ground/Yard 112-113, **115**, 182 183, **194-195**, 276, 444 (builder's yard), *445*, 454, *456*, **458-461**, 536

Crow, John 460

Crowther, John (artist) *213*

Crucifix Lane 139, 204-205, **210**

Cubitt, Joseph 270, 334

Cubitt, William 507

Cuper's Garden 166-167, **169**, 173, 404; Cuper's Bridge 403

Cure, Thomas senior 97, 109, **118-119**, 120; – junior 109

Cure's College 112-113, **118-119**, 182-183, **193-194**; – burial ground 193-194

Curtis, William (botanist) 172; – garden 166-167, **172**, *529*, 530

Cut, The /New Cut 159, 172, 251, **255-256**, 258, 414, *419*, 439

Dadd, Richard (artist) 244

Dalton, Chris (photographer) cover, 5, 10

Dance, George (architect) 198, 208, 381

DANISH/SCANDINAVIAN RULERS: 80; Cnut and Harthacnut (Hardicanute/Canute) 80; Olav Haraldsson (king of Norway) 80

Deadman's Place (now Park Street) 112-113, 118, **119-120**, 192, 272

Deane, Charles (artist) *400*, *402*

DEATH: 'city of the dead' 77, 454-461; Necropolis Company 412, 458; also see Brookwood cemetery, burial grounds, cholera, tragic deaths

Dekker, Thomas (playwright) 453, 538

Demolition 311, 344, 385, 417, 482, 517

Denham, John (poet) 25, 107

DEVELOPERS now: Barratt homes (developer) 311, 336; Canary Wharf Group 436, Delancey 346; Laing Management 352; Regalian Properties plc (developer) 313; Irvine Sellar 490, 494-501, 530, 561; Qatari Diar 436; Squire & Partners 437, St George 328, 497; St James Group 317; St Martin's Property Group 355

DEVELOPERS in history: William Angell 104; James Hedger 162, 199; Thomas Kendall 162; Samuel Short 257; John Roupell 257, 402-403

DEVELOPMENTS recent: 301, 302; Elephant and Castle 302, 342-347; London Plan 301; Opportunity Areas (OAs) 301; 2012 Opportunity Area Planning Framework (OAPF) 314; Southbank Place **436-437**; Southwark Towers 494-495, 499; Vauxhall/Nine Elms 302, **314**, 318; Visioning Vauxhall 314; See Chapter 3.5

Dibdin, Charles (composer and singer) 174

Dickens, Charles (author) 240, 285, 286, 288, 291, 511, 553

Digby, Sir Kenelm 192

Dilston Grove 480, 555, 556

Dion, Mark (artist) 11, 537, 538

Dingley, Robert (philanthropist) 175

Dirty Lane 182-183

Dissolution of the monasteries 25, 32, 36, 83, 88, 119, 120, 136, 140

Di Stefano, Arturo (artist) 10, 413, *414*, 415

Doche 34, 136, 492, 511. Also see Flemings

Dodd, George (author) 246, 257, *258*, 270, 273

Dodd, Dr William 175

Dog and Duck tea gardens 150-151, **160-162**, 260

Doggett's Coat and Badge Race 506

Doré, Gustave (artist) *234*, *420*, *506*

Domesday survey **80-81**; 89, 117, 140

Doon Street 326

Doulton, Henry 233, 236, 387; H Lewis – 254; – John 233, 235

Doulton's pottery 230-231, **233-234**, 236; – & Watts 233; – & Co 233; Henry – & Co 233

Dow Jones architects 388

Drury, Alfred (sculptor) 232

Duchy of Cornwall 87, 95, 246, 382

Dugard Way 312

Duke of Berri (John) 95

Duke of Bedford 386

Duke Street 257, 464

Dung Hill (Lambeth) 236-237; also see Harrow Dung Hill (Southwark)

Dunley Place 138

Earl of Arundel: Richard Fitzalan, 4th – 97;

Earl of Salisbury Robert Cecil 369, 510, 511

Earl of Shaftesbury: 'Lord Ashley' (Anthony Ashley Cooper) 234

Earl of Sussex: – Thomas Radcliffe 44-45, 140

Earl's Sluice (river) 70

Effra, The (river) 244

ELECTRICITY: 234, 460; Central Electricity Board 478; City of London Electric Lighting Company 478; London Electricity Board 478. Also see Bankside Power Station

ELEPHANT & CASTLE 9, 21, 71, 94, 299, 302, **342**; Elephant Park 342; Highpoint, 340, **345**; Metro Central Heights (Alexander Fleming House) 341, **343-344**; One the Elephant 341, *345*; Perronet House 340, **347**; – pub **244-245**; – Shopping Centre (demolished) 303, **345-346**; – station 342; Strata 13, 302, 313, 341, **344-345**; Town Centre 340; Two Fifty One **347**

Eliasson, Olafur (artist) 10, 480-*481*

Elizabeth Baxter Hostel for Distressed Women and Girls 263

Erasmus, Desiderius (Dutch scholar) 99

Eric Parry Architects *493*

Evans, Gethin (artist) 11, 325

Evelina Children's Hospital 395, 462

Evelyn, John (diarist) 53

Ewer Street 225, 226, 227

Eworth, Hans (painter) 34, 35

Fair Street 286

Falcon glassworks 182-183, **187**, 267, **270**, *271*

Falcon tavern 182-183, **187**

Falmouth Street 287

Falstaff, John 138

Farmer and Brindley (stone masons) 236

Farrell, Terry (architect) 66, **313**, *530*, 531

Fastolf, Sir John (landowner) 134, 219; – Hall 125, **138-139**, 146, 209, 511-512

Faux Hall /Fox Hall (or Fulke's Hall) 66, 88, 92-93, **96-97**, 146, 150-151, **154**

Fawcett, Henry M P 383-*386*; – House & Garden **384**-*385*

Fentiman Road 246

Ferry crossings 68, 70, 100, 101, 107; – men 117, 126, 186; horse – 100, 107, 159

Festival of Britain 253, 302, 325, **431-435**, 437, 551; Skylon 434; Dome of Discovery 431, 435

Fielden Clegg Bradley (architects) 315

Fielding, Sir John (magistrate) 160, 208

Finch, George (architect) 311

Findlay, James (artist) *374*, 375

FIRE BRIGADE: 517 London Fire Engine Establishment 507; London Fire Brigade 259, 463, ; Metropolitan Fire Brigade Act

508; Metropolitan Fire Brigade 508

FIRE STATIONS: Renfrew Road 312; Waterloo 329

FIRES: **463-471** (Southwark); 1212 Southwark fire 117, 127; Great Fire of London (1666) 55-56, 464; 1613 Globe fire 117; 1676 fire 55-56, 118, 133, 134, 135, 137, 193; 1689 fire 56, 215; 1713 Hay's Wharf 506; 1725 London Bridge 208; 1780 Gordon riots 192; 1791 Albion Mills **185-187**; 1794 fire Astley's 159; 1803 fire Astley's 159; 1805 fire Royal Circus 463; c. 1810 Rhinebeck panorama 206; 1814 Mustard manufactory; 1825 Cumberland Gardens 153; 1826 Shot tower 255, 256; 1841 Astley's 240; 1843 Southwark shot tower (and St Olave's) 283, 284; 1861 Tooley Street 507, *509*; 1865 Surrey Theatre 260, 1885 'Alice's fire' 464-470; 1979 Butler's Wharf 517

Fitzroy Robinson & Partners (architects) 329

Fletcher, John (playwright) 451

Flemings/Flemish 34, 45, 55, 95-96, *139*, 445, *446*, 492, 512; – burial ground 135, 137, *219*, 461. Also see Doche

Flitcroft, Henry (architect) 209

Flood 70, 73, 136, 232, 528

Fore Street 230-231, *232*, 235

Foster + partners (architects) 317-318, 328, **334-335**, *353-355*; Norman Foster 300

Fowler and Hill (architects) 313

Frampton, George (sculptor) 237

Freeman's Lane 210

Fry, Roger (artist) 343

Gage, Sir Thomas (artist) *107*

Garden Museum 13, 239, **387-391**, 388, 372; Garden 388, 395; Museum of Garden History 387-391

GARDENS: – of Eden 361, *362*, 366, 377, 379, 528; Apollo – 166-167, 404; Asparagus – 104-105, **107**; Bernie Spain Gardens 60, 326, 551; Botanical – 166-167, **172**, 362, 363 ff; Cumberland (Smith's) – 150-151, **153**, *381*; Flora Tea – (or Mount Gardens) 150-151; Dr James's medicinal garden **172**; Fawcett's – 384-386; Guy Street Park 545; Kennington Palace – 95; Leathermarket – 545; Marble Hall 153; New Spring – 372-373; Norfolk House – 97; Old Paradise – 395; Tanner Street Park 545; Temple of Flora – 166-167. Also see Curtis' garden, Bermondsey Spa, Dog and Duck, Garden Museum, Market Gardens, Metropolitan Public Gardens Association, Tradescants' garden, U S Embassy, Vauxhall Gardens

Garth, Richard (artist) 50

GAS SUPPLY: 245; Phoenix Gas Company 245, 271, 382, 478; Western Gas 247

Geographic centre 19-*20*

Geographic realism 107

Geographic school 40, 107

George, Sir Ernest (architect) 335

Gerard, John (herbalist) 364

Gheeraerts, Marcus (painter) – the Elder 37, 41, *42-43*, 44-45, *139*; – the Younger 367

Girtin, Thomas (artist) *58-59*

Glagget, Walter **174**

Glasshill Street 275

Glasshouse Street 154

GLASSMAKING: *186*, 232, *270*, 271; crystal 119; John Baker *94*, 150-151, **153-154**; John Bellingham 153; Edward Salter 119; John Straw 175. Also see Falcon glassworks, Old Barge Stairs glasshouse, Stained Glass, Vauxhall plate glasshouse, Winchester House glass factory

GLC – see Greater London Council

GLOBE theatre **around 1600** 112-113, **116-117**, 188, 303, 449, 450, 452, 453; **now** 13, 302, 332, 335; *452*, 543; Shakespeare's Globe Trust 302; Sam Wanamaker playhouse 302, 335, 474-475

Goda, Countess 97

Godwin, George 226, 227

Golden Jubilee bridges **324**

Goldfinger, Erno (architect) 343

Gordon, Lord George 184, **198-199**; – riots 192, 197, 198-*199*

Gormley, Antony (sculptor) 11, 26, 27-30

Goscombe John, W (sculptor) 237

Gower, John (poet) 136

Granby Street (Waterloo) 264, 409-411, 418

Grange, The 204-205, **211-212**, *510*, 511; – Road 211; – Walk 212, 291

Grant, Duncan (artist) *343*

Gravel Lane (Great Suffolk Street) 196, 464, 467, 470

Gray's Walk 156

Great Dover Street 75, 77, 78, 82, 213, 214, 287

Great Guildford Street 270

Great Suffolk Street 196, 213, 287

Great Surrey Street (later Blackfriars Road) 57, 175, **178-179**, 185, 267, *270*; No 1 – **328-329**; No 18 – **328**. Also see Rotunda

Greater London Council 254, 326, 551, 552; GLC Architects 304, 325, 329, 347

Green Dragon Court 118

Greenfield, Jon (designer) 482

Greenwood, James (journalist) 238-239

Grenade, L (chronicler) 83, 114, 128

Grenfell tower 311, 545

Gresham, Sir Richard (Mayor of London) 82

Greycoat estates 551

Grimshaw Architects 342

Gun-House Stairs 154

Guy, Thomas (philanthropist) 216, **217**, 522

Guy's channel 73

Guy's Hospital 204-205, **216-217**, 280-281, **288**, 460, 503, 555; – Cancer Centre 73; – 'Mad House' 204-205, 217, *522*; – Tower 494

Gwilt family, 194; George – the elder (architect) 195, 214; George – the younger (architect) 193, 274, *456*, 457; Mrs – 457

Halfpenny Hatch 159

Hanway, Jonas (philanthropist) 175

Hardwick, Philip Charles (architect) 239

Harleyford Street 380; – Road Community Gardens 391-394

Harper Road 78

Harrow Street 196 ; Harrow Dung Hill (Southwark) **196**, *197*

Harvard, John 118, 137; – Robert 112-113, **120**, 137,

Harvey, Dean Monroe (architect) *431*

Hastings, Sir Edward 131

Hastings, Selina (Countess of Huntingdon) 184

Hawksmoor, Nicholas (architect) 159, 210

Hawkstone Hall (Waterloo) 242

Haworth Tompkins 326

Hay's Galleria 71, 350, 352; Wharf 137, 146, 209, *355*, **504-510**

Hayle's estate 115, 156, 254

Hayman, Francis (artist) 374-375

Hayward Gallery *26, 27, 28*, 60-61, 545-546

Heaphy, Thomas (artist) 529, 530

Hedger family, 199; James – (developer) 162; Mrs – 160

Heere, Lucas de (artist) 37, 44

Heindorff, Michael (artist) 11, **515-517**

Henslowe, Philip (entrepreneur) 95, 108, 115, 116, 448, 449, 450, 452

Hepher, David (artist) 11, *312*, 313, *316*

Hercules Buildings (now street) 150-151, 377-380, 404; Hercules Hall 150-151, *378*; Hercules Inn 159-160

Heron Corporation and Commercial Properties 551

Herzog and de Meuron (architects) 300, 302

Heywood, Thomas 453

HIGH RISE buildings 301; – at bridge heads 301; London Tall Buildings Survey 301

Hill, Octavia (philanthropist) 304, 383, 385, 418, 427, 467-470; Miranda – 383, 418, 467-470

Hill, Rowland (preacher) 242, 275

Hill Street (now Glasshill Street) 275

Hirst, Damien (artist) 310-311

Hoefnagel, Jacques (Antwerp merchant) 41, 45

Hoefnagel, Joris (artist) 41-42, 44

Hogarth, William (artist) 373-374, 446, *486-487*

Holbein, Hans the Younger (artist) 99

Holford, Lord 355

Hollamby, Edward (architect) 304, 311

Holland Street 270, 273, 335

Holland's Leaguer see Paris Garden

Hollar, Wenceslaus (artist) 47, *48-49, 52-53*, 88, *117, 363, 392-393*

Homelessness 290, 416, 502-504, 553; Cardboard city (Bullring) 552

Hood, Thomas (author) 405-406

Hooke, Robert (architect) 242

Hopes, The 97, 429

Horsleydown 139; – Lane 289

Horsemonger Lane (now Harper Road) 287; – prison 196, **213-214**, 280, **288**, 407, *559*

HOSPITALS: 554-555 see Evelina, Guy's, St Thomas', Locke, London Hospital, (Westminster) New Lying-in

HOTELS: Bankside 328; The Hoxton 324; Mondrian 305, **327-328**, Park Plaza 305, Riverbank Park Plaza 317; Sea Containers UK 323, **327-328**; Shangri-La 305

HOUSING: 301, **303-305**; – estates: Draper 302, 340, *345*; Ethelred 303, 309, **311**; Heygate 302, 303, 341, 342, **344**, *346*; Elephant Park 302; Lambeth Towers 309, **311**-*312*; Wellington Mills 304; General Society for Improving the Dwellings of the Working Classes 227; Queen's Buildings 276; Society for Improving the Condition of the Labouring Classes 227; South London Dwellings Company 427; squatting 392; Surrey Lodge housing 427; Sydney Waterlow's Improved Industrial Dwellings Company 227. Also see Peabody

Howard family 97, Catherine – 97; Sir John – 120; St Philip – 97; Thomas – (4th Duke of Norfolk) 97; Thomas – (14th Earl of Arundel) 52

Howard, John (prison reformer) 197, 215, 217

Howes, Edmund (historian) 25

Hungerford (or Charing Cross) Bridge 226, 250, **252**, 430

Hungerford pedestrian bridge 300, 322

Hunter Robert 383, 385

Hyman, Timothy (artist) 11, *22-23*, 24-5, *29*-30, *471*, 472

Ibbetson, Julius Caesar (artist), *200-201*

IBM building 322, **326**

Iconoclasm 32

IMAX 63

Imperial Court 309, 313

India Stores Depot 170, 431

INDUSTRIES 138, 146; candle works (John Field) 416; chainsmith's (Crip's) 516; carpentry 192; China factory (Mr Crisp's) 519; emery paper at Wellington Mills (J Oakey & Sons) 241; glaziers 136, glue 212; gun manufactory 146, 154; hat and cap manufactory 258-259; industrial and sanitary ceramics 233; ironmonger and manufactory 270, 271, 403; jam & pickle factory (Crosse & Blackwell) 431; lead-works 403; mustard manufactory 175, 192 (Lingard and Sadler/Wardale); pickle factory 78; sealskin works 271; soap manufactory 196; starch manufactory (Messrs Stonard & Watson) 175; stone 168; timber yards 159, *168* (also see Searle's); turpentine (Flockton's) 204-205, **210**; whitening/bleaching 45, 168, 184; zinc manufacturer (Barton Lawrence) 158. Also see breweries, Coade's, glassmaking, leather, pottery, printing, tenter grounds, vinegar.

INNS/TAVERNS: **Lambeth** – the Artichoke *173*, *257*; Canterbury Arms 241; Founder's Arms 109; The George 13; The Bell 97; James Head 115; the Windmill 172. **Southwark** – *133*, **510-513**; Alfred's Head 267, **276**, 289; Boar's Head 120, 124, **134**, 204-205, *218*, *219*, *511*; Bricklayers' Arms 280, **289**; Cardinal Hat's inn **120**; Elephant & Castle 230-231, 289; Falcon 187; Flower de Luce 138; The George 55-56, 124-125, **134**; Goat Inn (later Brew House) 118; Green Dragon 56, 118; King's Arms 194, 512; Kings John's Head 291; Noah's Ark 529-530; Queen's Head 56; Rockingham Arms 280, **289**; Tabard/Talbot Inn 56, 124-125,**133**, **289**; Waterman's Arms Tavern 212; Wheatsheaf pub 540; White Hart *511*; White Lyon inn 131-132. Also see Beere House

IPC tower *60-61*

Jackson, Peter (historian and illustrator) 67, *208*

Jacob Street 291

Jacob's Island (Bermondsey) *225*, *226*, **291**-*293*, 324, 455

James, John (architect) 210

James, Robert (doctor) **172**,

Jarman, Derek (artist) 388, 480, 482, 514,

Jesus College (Cambridge) 170

Jesus College, Oxford 431

JLE Architects 300

Johnson, Ben (artist) 107, 116

Johnson, Dr 160, 175, 191, 373

Johnson, Joel (carpenter/architect) 175

Johnson, Michael (artist) *Preface*, 5,*377*

Jones, Horace (architect) 353

Jones, Inigo (architect) *51*, 519

Jonson, Ben (playwright) 107, 109, 116

Jubilee Gardens *60-61*, 436

JUBILEE LINE 299-*300*; London Bridge 300; Southwark *300*; Waterloo 300

Judah, Ben (author) 489, 502, 544

Jupp, Richard (architect) 217

Kennington 81, 89; – Lane 232, 240; – Park Square 311; – Palace 88, 92-93, **95**; – Road 155

Kent Street (now Tabard Street) 124, **130**, 204-205, **214**, 289

Kent, William (architect) 172, 374

Kiefer, Anselm (artist) *355*

Kieran Timberlake (architects) 397

King Alfred (sculpture) 276, 287, 542, 543

King Street 464

King's Arms Stairs 170

King's Bench prison (Southwark) 56, 119, 120, 124, **132**, 194, 197, 204-205, 213, **215**; New – 182-183, **197**, *198*, 213; the 'Rules' **197**, *198*

King's Bench Street 347

Kings – see Monarchs

Kingston Road 232

Kubrick, Stanley (film maker) *346*

Kuwait 299, 355

Kyrle Society 383-386, 467-470

Labelye, Charles (engineer) 159

Lafone Street 71

Lambert, Water (artist/artiste) *419*

LAMBETH: *58-59*, 70-71, 81, 83, 324; – Baths 250, **263-264**; – Bridge *235*, 308, **318**; – Council 311, 383, 388, 552; – Lambeth High Street 89, 233, 395, 461; – Hospital 312; – Manor 89; – Marsh (the area) 87, 89, 104-105, **106-107**, 166-167, **169**, *402-403*, 407; – Marsh (the street) 107, 169, 172, *173*, 174, 175 (also see Lower Marsh); – Road 115, 160, 237; – Walk 150-151, **156**; also see South – and Water –

Lambeth Delftware see pottery

Lambeth House/Palace 13, 32, 51, 88, 92-93, **97-101**, 150-151, *153*, **157**, 230-231, **237**, 388, **391**; – gardens 92-93, 99, 391; Laud's tower 99; library *98*-100, 308, **310**, 395; Lollards' tower 99, 100; Morton's Tower 99-101, 150-151; prisons 92-93, **99-100**

Lambeth Palace Road 310

Lambeth School of Art 234, **236-237**, *238*, 387, 421, 429

Lambeth Village Green 394

Lambeth Water Tower 309, *312-313*

Langley, Francis (developer) 89, 109

Lant Street (Southwark) 77-79

Lanteri, Edouard (sculptor) *303*

La Place (Lambeth) see Carlisle House

La Place (Southwark) see Shard Quarter

Laroon, Marcellus (artist) *132*

Lasdun, Sir Denys (architect) 326

LASSCO 153

Lawson, Andrew (photographer) 11, *394*, 395

LCC – see London County Council

Leake, Henry (brewer) 137, 139

Leake, John (doctor) 173

LEATHER INDUSTRY: 204-205, **212**; Barrow Hepburn and Gale 212; fire engine maker improved leather (Tilley) 270; Sadler & Harness manufacturer (Chequer) 270

Leathermarket *226*, 280, **286**, 302, *559*; – Gardens 545

Le May, Pete (photographer) 11, *452*, *482*

Leper hospitals 130. Also see Lock Hospital.

Lethbridge family 184,

Lever, Sir Ashton 176. Also see Museums

Lewes priory (Sussex) 140

Lifschutz Davidson Sandilands (architects) 324, 326-327

Llewelyn Davies (architect) 352

Lock Hospital 82, 124, **130**, *131*, 204-205, **213**, 214

Logan brothers (artists) 514 Peter 480, 517; Andrew 480

London Ambulance Service Headquarters 323, **329**

LONDON BRIDGE 80; OLD – 31, *50*, *122*, *124*, **126-128**, 137, 155, 193, 204-205, *208*, 282, *284*; chapel of St Thomas Becket 47, *124*, *128*; Drawbridge 126, 127, 129; House with the many windows *122*, *124*, **129**; shooting the arches *208*; traitors' heads 126, 128; NEW – 226, 280, *282-283*, *284*; – NOW 350, **355**; – station 137, 225, 280, **284**, 286, *499*, *558*. Also see Nonsuch House

London Bridge City 19, 350, **352**; No 1 London Bridge 72, 352; More London 13, 299, 351, *352*, **353-355**

London Bridge Tower, see Shard

London College of Communication 346

London County Council 240, 252, 255, 329, 386, 407, 430, 437, 438, 551; – Parks Dpt 383; Architects Dpt 288, 304, 325

London Eye 62, 297, *298*, 299, 322, **324**

London Hospital 352. Also see
St Olaf House

London's Larder **504-513**

London South Bank University (LSBU) 341, **342**-*343*; Borough Polytechnic Institute 342

London stone 17-*18*

London to Greenwich Railway 225, 226, 281, **289-291**

London Transport 300; see Jubilee line

Long Lane 73, 75, 124-125, 211

Long Southwark (now Borough High Street) *36*, 116, 119, 124, **129-130**

Lottery 176-177

Low line 479

Lower Marsh 104-105, *106*, *176*, 264, 411, 498; Nos 17-18 – 166-167, **172**, *174*; No 19 – 106

LWT tower (London Weekend Television) *60*, 301, 552

Maccreanor Lavington (architects) *336*

Magdalen Hospital 166-167, **175**, 251, **260**, 379, *553*, 556

Magdalen College (Oxford) 138, 209

Maid/Maiden Lane (now Sumner Street) 182-183, 188-189, 190, 446

Manna 11, **502-504**

MANORS (Lambeth) 89, *94*; also see South Lambeth; Lambeth; Kennington; Paris Garden, Vauxhall

MANORS (Southwark) *81*, 89; Great Liberty –

89; Guildable – 82, 89; King's – 89; Liberty of the Clink 89; Walworth 89

Mansell, Sir Robert (glassmaking) 154

Marmion, Shackerley (playwright) 109

MAPS (references from the main text only): 1542 map of Southwark 88, 116, **129**, 130, 133; Copperplate map 40-41, 491, 492; 1572 Braun & Hogenberg **40**, 101, 119, *512*; 1658 William Faithorne 391; 1681 map of Vauxhall manor *94*; 1680s Robert Morden London and its environs 547-548; 1682 William Morgan 88, 119, 146, 168, 168, 169, 209, 211, 373; 1747 Rocque 146, 153, 155, 157, 168, 169, 175, 187, 188, 190, 191, 209, 211, 255, 362-363; 1799 Richard Horwood 146, 153, 155, 156, 168, 191, 196, 211, 212, 244, 256, 289, 290, 529; 1806 enclosure map 106; 1813 edition of Horwood map 146, 189, 196, 256, 258, 385; 1828 C & J Greenwood 393; 1873 Ordnance Survey 271

Marble Hall (Vauxhall) 150-151, **153**

Margaret's Hill 130, 192, 193

Market gardens 169, *362-363*, 381

Marks Barfield (architects) 324

Marlborough Street 190, 258

Marlowe, Christopher (playwright) 116, 352

Marquess of Worcester: Edward Somerset (2nd Marquess of Worcester) 370

Marshall, Peter (photographer) 11, 494

Marshalsea prison (Southwark) 106, 116, 119, 124, **132**, 204-205, 214, **215-216**, 276, 285

Marshalsea Road 274

Martin, Leslie (architect) 325

Mary Duggan architects 395

Maugham, Somerset (author) 411, 412, 421

Mawbey, Sir Joseph 153, 240

Mayhew, Henry (journalist) 256, 286, 288, 291, 421

Maze, The 125, **138**; – Pond estate 217

McAlpine family – see Greycoat estates

McCormac Jamieson Prichard (architects) 300

Mead Place 530

Medway, Sarah (artist) 11, *524*, 527

MEETING HOUSES: Maiden Lane (Charles Skelton) – 182-183, **188-189**; Wesleyan – 175; Zoar Street – 182-183, *189*

Melancholy Walk (now Surrey Row) 184

Melior Street 502-504

Mercier, Paul (playwright) 63, 414

Metropolitan Public Gardens Association 383, 398

Meunier Gallery 9

Mill Lane 137, 217

Mill Street 516

Millennium Bridge 300, 332, **334**

Miller, Graeme (artist) 11, *555*, 556

MILLS: Bone/stone grinding *188*; drug – 156; tide – 137; water – 209, 512; wind – 172

Minor, Dr William Chester (criminal) **406-409**

Mint, The 267; royal mint 120-121; – neighbourhood 225, 226, **274**, 416-417, 462, 463; – Street 182-183, *416*, 417. Also see workhouses

Mitre Road 172

MONARCHS: 371, Aethelberht 79; Aethelred 80; Alfred 276, 287; Charles II 219; Edward I 82, 137; Edward II 82, 138; Edward III 2, 87, 89, 95, 130; Edward VI 31, 82-83, 115, 119, 135, 136, 492; Elizabeth I *42-43*, 44-45, 88, 95, 106, 109, 118, 119, 132, 369, 452, 454; Elizabeth II 313; George III 153, 159, 243, 375; George IV 153; James I *51*, 96, 193, 390; Henry III 96; Henry VI 17; Henry VIII 25, 31, 33,95, 96, 97, 100, 106, 242, 274, 447, 519; Jane 120; Mary I ('Bloody Mary') *35*, 36, 106, 119, 120; Philip II (of Spain) 35, 36; Olaf II of Norway 80, 136, 510; Richard II 95; Richard III 33, 109; Victoria 243, 270, 276, 334; William I 80; William II 89, 97; also see Danes

Monnox, George (Alderman) 137

Montague Close 112-113, 117, 182-183, **193**; Montague House 118

Morgan, Edmund 209; Morgan's Lane 204-205, **209**, 512

Morley College **428-430**, 439, 530; – murals 429

Morley, Samuel 427, 429

Moro, Peter (architect) 325

Morris, Peter (Dutch engineer) 127; John – (brother) 365

Morrison, Herbert (politician) 432, 437

Morton Charles (impresario) 241, 420

MPs for Southwark – see Thomas Cure

Murphy Street 425, 426

MUSEUMS: 195, 274; Cinema – 312; Cottingham's – 415; Design – 353; Docklands – 78, 455; – of Garden History ; – of London 8, 46, 73, 75, 128, 138, 153, 240, 270, 272, 398, 460, 491-492, 517, 530, 538; Gwilt's – 415; Imperial War – 13, 300, 311; Leverian – 166-167, **176-178**, 376; Sowerby's – (Waterloo) 530

MUSIC HALL: 416, **418-421**; Canterbury – 230-231, *241*, 420; Great Harmonic Hall 420; Raglan – 464; Surrey – 420. Also see the Old Vic (Royal Victoria Palace)

Mylne, Robert (architect) 185, 198, 270

Narrow Wall (later Belvedere Road) 170, 252, 255

Nashe, Thomas (playwright) 116,

National Sunday School Union 189

National Theatre 13, *60-61*, 322, **326**, 437

Neckinger, The (river) 70, 139, 291

Newcomen Street 464

New Cut see Cut

NEWINGTON 89; – Butts 162, 198, 199, 244; – Butts playhouse 92-93, **94-95**, 449, 452; – Causeway 276, 288, 289; – Road 190

New Kent Road 190, 198, 213, 245, 342

Newport Street 234, 236; – Gallery 309, **310-311**

Nicholson, Rosemary and John 239, 388

Noah 528; – Ark 360, 362, 529-530; – Ark Lane/Alley 529

Nonsuch House *122*, 124-125, 126, **129**, 208

Norden, John (artist) *38-39*, 116, *126*, *128*

Norfolk House (Lambeth) 52, 92-93, **97**, 106, 150-151, **156-157**. Also see Pottery

Oasis Academy 548

Obelisk see St George's Circus

O'Dwyer, Mike (photographer) *345*

Old Barge House 104-105, 107, 184

Old Barge Stairs glasshouse 166-167, **168**

Old Kent Road 70, 198, 289, 507; No 155 – 204-205, **212-213**, 280

Old Vic theatre 13, 260, **424-429**, 437, 439; Royal Coburg 260, *422-423*, 438; Royal

Victoria Palace 260, *417*, 418, 419, 421; Victoria theatre 251, **258**. Also see Morley College

Olivier, Laurence (actor) 437

Orwell, George (author) 238, 503, *504*

Osuga, Jiro (artist) 11, *14-16*, *24*, 25, *64-67*, *358*, *359*, 532-535, 536, 548

Oval, The 150-151, 244, 245, 309, **380-382**, *559*; – Ambulance Station 329

Oxford English Dictionary **408-409**

Oxo tower 13, 60-61, 62, 302, 323, 327

Panoramas of London – see the Eye of London chapter and chapter 3.4

Paradise 363 ff, 366, 392, 528; – Row/Street 150-151, **156**, 157. Also see Gardens for Old Paradise Gardens

Paragon, The 204-205, 212, 213, 280, 289

Paris Garden 89, *109*, 116, 120, 175, **184**; Holland's Leaguer 104-105, 107, **109**, 184, 445

Parish Street 210

Park Street 119-120, 302, 477

Peabody – estates 260; – Square 260; – Trust 227, 245

Pearman Street 21, *329*, 393

Pearson, Dan (garden designer) 11, 310, 388, 392, **394-395**

Pearson, John L (architect) 236-237, 314

Pedlar's Acre 171

Pellatt and Green/Apsley Pellatt (glassmakers) 186, 270

Pepper Street 189, 258

Pepys, Samuel (diarist) 39, 107, 132, 157, 367, 368, 463

Philanthropic Society/Institution 251, **260-262**, 556

Piano, Renzo (architect) 9, 479, *485-486*, 490, 493, 495, 496, 499, *500-501*

Pickle Herring Street 139, 204-205, 288, 478, 505, 511. Pickleherring mill 209

Pike, Jonathan (artist) *403*

Pillory *130*

Piper, John (artist) *432-433*, 434

Pitt Street 230-231, 244

Plague 100, 291, 449, 451, 471, 511

Platner, Warren (architect) 327

Pocock Street 109

Pole, Cardinal Reginald 99

Police 407, 411, 465, 538

Pomeroy, Frederick (sculptor) 232

Pope, Sir Thomas 45, **140**-*141*

Portland Place (Bartholomew Street) 213

Potter's Fields 139, 210

POTTERY: 57, 146, 232; Carlisle – **154-155**; Delftware – 118, *138*, *154*, 155; Glass House – 150-151, 155 (John Sanders); James Stiff pothouse 234; John de Wilde 155; Montague Close – *117*-118, *118* (Jacob Prynn); Norfolk House – **154-155**; Pickleherring – *138*, 139; porcelain – 155; stoneware – 154, 155; tin-glazed – *118*, 139, 154, 15, *486-487*; Union – 233; Vauxhall pothouse 155. Also see Doulton's

Powhattan 370, *371*; (daughter) Pocahontas 370

Prehistory **70-72**, 75

Prescott, John (politician) *316*, 317, 496, 499

Prior of Lewes House 124-125, *136*, **137**, 146

Pratt, Joseph 153; Richard – 153

Price, John (architect) 215

PricewaterhouseCoopers (professional services) 352, 353, 494, 495, 499

Prince Albert (consort) 227

Prince of Wales (royalty) 159, 314, 373, 374, 375, 386

Prince of Wirtemberg Lewis Frederick

Prince's Meadows 97

Prince's Road (now Black Prince Road) 235, 238

Prince's Street 232

Princess Street 347

PRINTING: 136, 251 262; William Clowes & Sons 251, **257**; London School of – & Graphic Arts 255; bookbinding 262

PRISONS: see Bridewell; County Gaol; Horsemonger Lane; see Bridewell for House of Correction; King's Bench; Marshalsea; Queen's Bench; Southwark Compter; White Lyon Inn. Also see Prison cells at Lambeth House/Palace and Lambeth workhouse

Prostitution 81, 109, 115, **175**, 193, 254, 264, 373, 379, 404, 405-406, 409-411, 416, **445-448**, *553*; first prostitute 445; 'Winchester geese' 115, 447, 460

PUBLIC SPACE 'pseudo public space' 298-299

Pugin, A W (architect) 243, 262-263; Pugin & Rowlandson 31

Qatar 436, 489, 499

Queen Street 464

Queen Elizabeth Street 286

Queens – see Monarchs

Queen's Bench prison (later Queen's prison) 267, **276**

Quest 6, 17-19; answers 524-561

Rackham, Arthur (artist) 237

RAILWAYS: **414-418**, Baker Street and Waterloo – 260; Charing Cross – 242, 252, 288, 324, 414, 416-417; South Eastern – 289; South Western – 234, 247, 384, 412; Spa Road Station *290-291*; Waterloo and City line 412. Also see Bricklayers' Arms station, London and Greenwich railway, Low Line

Rambert Dance Company 326, 474

Ravilious, Eric (artist) *429*, 430

Red Cross Street (now Redcross Way) 276, 418, 464, **468-469**; – Hall **468-469**

Redcross Way 115; – Cottages 464, 470

Regent's Bridge. See Vauxhall Bridge

RELIGION Calvinistic – 184; Catholic Relief Act 199; Methodists 184; Non-conformism 189, Premonstratensian order 98, Presbyterians 188, Unitarian Chapel 254, 259, Wesleyan chapel (Waterloo) 166-167, **175**, *176*; John Wycliffe (Lollards) 99, 100

Renfrew Road 312

Rennie, John (architect) 186-187, 226, 232, 252, 254, 273, 282-283, 335, 355; – the Younger 255, 282-283

Rennie Street 260

Rhinebeck Panorama 57, *206-207*, 208, 287

RIBA awards 336, 344, 354; Stirling prize 310, 335, 355

Richard Rogers Partnership (architects) 300, 317-318, 495, 542-543; also see RSHP

Robertson, Sir Howard (architect) 436

Rolls' estate 115

ROMAN era **72-78**; – boat 68, 70, 73; – mausoleums *78*; – roads (Stane and Watling streets) 75, 77; – sarcophagus 78, *80*; – temples 72, 74-77, 531; – artefacts 74

Rosary (la Rosere) 138

Rose, Henry (architect) 240

Rose theatre, around 1600 112-113, 115, **116**, 449, 450; now 302, 543

Rotunda, The (3 Great Surrey Street) **176-178**

Roupell Street 402-403

Rowland Hill's chapel see Surrey chapel

Rowlandson, Thomas (artist) *373*; Also see Pugin & Rowlandson

Royal Circus 166-167, **174**, 251, 260, 423, 438

Royal Festival Hall 13, *60-61*, 322, **325**, 437, 474-475, 539, 541-542; poetry library 325

Royal Shakespeare Company 437

Royal South of London Dispensary 250-251, **263**

Royal Universal Infirmary for Children 250-251, **254**

RSHP architects 317-318, 335; Graham Stirk 318

Ruskin, John (author) 380

Russell Street (now Tanner Street) 211, 212; Upper – 212

Sadleir, Michael (author) 264, 409-411, 416, 417

Salisbury Lane 45

Salter, Ada 418

Sandby, Paul (artist) *156*, 168, 173

Savage, Jerome (actor) 449

Scheemakers, Peter (sculptor) 217

Schnebbelie, Robert (artist) *189*, *290-291*

School of Historical Dress 263

SCHOOLS: Boys Charity – (Union Street) *195*; Freemasons' – for Girls 556; graveyard – *461*, 556; – for the Blind 251, 260, 554, 556; Johanna School 548; Lambeth – **156-157**, 461; Lambeth Ragged – 230-231, **234-235**, **236-237**; Licensed Victuallers School 230-231, **240**, 313; National Free – for Girls 195; Nautical – 254-255; St Mary-the-Less Schools 236-238, 314; St Saviour's Charity – *195*, 461; Sunday – 184-185, **189**, 235, 272; Yorkshire Society's – *428*, 430. Also see St Saviour's grammar school, St Olave's grammar school

Scott, Sir Giles Gilbert (architect) 326, 476, 478, 479

Sea Containers House, see Hotels

Seaborne, Mike (photographer) 11, 513

Searle, Michael (architect) 212; – home/office 204-205, **212**; also see Paragon

Searle's timber yard 159

Second World War 237, 241, 257, 260, 263, 271, 273, 288, 326, 391, 398, 428, 430

Seifert, Richard (architect) 494, 497

Serres, John Thomas (artist) 424,

SEWAGE 227; 'the 'Great Stink' 227;

Shad Thames 204-205, **209-210**, 289, **352-353**, 478

Shakespeare, William (actor, playwright) 28, 115, 116, 138, 428-429, **450-453**, 519, 550; – Reading Society of London *303*, – Memorial National Theatre Committee 438

Shand Street 210

Shard (The) 13, 25, 301, 316, 350-351, 355, **494-497**, *499*, 530; News Building (La Place) 75, 494, 501; – Quarter 13, 350-351, 355, **500-501**; View from the – 62

Shell estate 303, **435-436**; tower 437

Shepherd, Jack (criminal) 274

Shepherd, T H (draughtsman) *225*, *261*, *273*, *275*, 554; George – *171*, *209*

SHOPS: butcher's 112-113, **120**, 510; Moser's hardware merchants 121. Also see Trades

Short Southwark (now Tooley Street) *122*, 124-125, **129-130**, 137

Short Street 264

SHOT TOWERS: Lambeth: *168*, *224*, 250-251, **253-254**, **255**, *256*, 431; Southwark 280, *282*-**283**,

Simmel, Georg (philosopher) 549

SimpsonHaugh (architects) 328

Skelton, Charles (Reverend) 188

SLUMS: 342, 409-411; Borough – 416-417, *462*; see Ewer Street, Granby Street, Jabob's Island, Mint

Smirke, Sydney (architect) 243

Smith, Captain John (explorer) 365, 370, 388,

Social welfare – 1601 statute 132

Soden Robert (artist) 11, *298*, *300*

Soul (of London) 62-63, 546, 553

South Bank c. 1600 **84-141**; c. 1770 **142-219**; c. 1845 **220-293**, *224*; now **294-355**, **324-326**; as *terra incognita* 29. Also see National Theatre

South Bank Centre 21, *60-61*, 300, 322, **325-326**; Hayward Gallery 325; Purcell Room 325; Queen Elizabeth Hall 254, 325

Southbank Place 13, 323, 328, 329

South Lambeth 89, *246*, 375; – Road 95, 232, 363, 366, 385

South Sea Court 462

SOUTHWARK: 48-49, 51, 70-71, 80-81; – Bridge 226, 268, *273*, 333, **335**; – Castle Leisure Centre 71; – Compter 56, 112-113, **120**, **194**, 204-205, **217**; – Council 328, 344, 346, 347, 479, 538; – Fair 192, *486-487*; – market 82, 124-125, *130*; – market bell *130*; – Manors *81*; – Marsh 119; – Park 480, 556; – Place see Suffolk Place; – Sessions House **120**, **194**; – Town Hall 182-183, *192*-**194**, 268

Southwark & Bermondsey **122-141**, **202-219**, **278-293**, **348-355**, **484-523**, 527

Southwark Bridge Road 77, 78, 270, 273, 276, 340, 347

Southwark Cathedral 13, 25, 75, 225, 282; also see St Mary Overie's and St Saviour's churches

Southwark School of Glaziers 136

Southwark School of Sculpture 517, *518-522*; Isaac James 519, 520; Gerard Johnson 518, 519; Nicholas Stone & Nicholas Johnson 519, *521*

Southwark Street 73, 78; No 85 – 332, **334**, *472*, 474-475; No 89 – 332, **334**, 497; – Landmark Court 539, *540*, 542

Southwell, Sir Robert 140

Sowerby, James (botanist) *529*, 530

Spa Road 291; – station *290-291*

Sparkes John C L (educator) 236, 429

Spengler, Oswald (philosopher) 546-547, 548-549

SPORT: Bowling greens 166-167, **168**; Lambeth Baths, 250, **263-264**; Oval for cricket

St Alphege parish *462-463*

St George's Circus 174, 197, 185, **197-198**, **197-201**, 227, 260, 336; Obelisk 166-167, 174, 198, 199, *201*, 260

St George's Fields 57, 97, 104-105, 112-113, **115**, 132, 175, 182-183, 196, **197-201**, 227, 242, 260, 261, 262

St George Inn – see the George under Inns

St George's Road 115, 245, 262

St George's Spa **160-162**

St Mary's Gardens (Walcot estate) 155

St Olaf House 352, *510*

St Olave's (grammar school) 112-113, **118**, 122, 124-125, **137**, 204-205, **219**, 272, 280, 284-**285**, 461,

St Peter's Hospital, see Fishmongers' Almshouses

St Saviour's Dock 13, 21, 125, **139**, 209, 281, 506

St Saviour's (grammar) school 112-113, **118**, 182-183, **193**, 267, **271**, 286, *461*

St Thomas' Hospital 56, 82, 83, 88, 124, 130, **135-136**, 204-205, 211, **216**, **217**, 219, 280-281, **288**, 407, 411, 554

St Thomas Street 78, 130, 216, 217, 219, 500, Nos 21-27 501

STAINED GLASS: Frederick Walter Cole 260. See Richard Butler

Stamford Street 250-251, **254-255**, 258, 326

Stane Street 75, 77

Stangate 92-93, **101**; – Stairs 92-93, **101**, 150-151; – Street 240

Steam power 233, 257

Stoney Lane (Bermondsey) 192, 288

Stoney Street (Borough) 204-205, 209, 540

Stow, John (historian) 25; 153, 519, 536, 538. See also *Survey of London* references under individual entries

Strand Bridge 226, **252**; – Company 169. Also see Waterloo Bridge

Strudwick, William (photographer) *235*

Suffolk Place (or House) *36-37*, 82, 88, 112-113, **120-***121*

Sumner Street 189, 270, 272

SURREY: 21; – chapel 182, **184-***185*, 242, 267, 276; – Chapel Centenary Fund 241-242; – Dispensary 464; – Institution **177-178**; –

justices of the peace 120; – Row 184

Swan Street 78, 288

Tabard Square **72-77**; *299*

Tabard Street 82, 289

Tanner Street 211, 212; – Gardens 208-*209*. Also see Russell Street

Tanneries, see leather industry

Tate Britain 537; – Modern 13, 300, 302, 332, 334, 335, *473*, 476-479, 481, 537; Blavatnik tower 336

Tate, Henry 386

Telegraph *244*

Temperance 427

Tenison Street 406

Tenter grounds 166-167, **175**

THAMES 30, 52, 70-71, 79-80, **100**, 109, *126*, 137, *152*, 464, 514, *524*, *527*, 537, 557; – 'illuminated river' 324; – Path 62; – Riverside Walkway 327, 534-535, 536; suicides; – Valley 71

Thameslink 539, 540

THEATRES: 88, 112, **115-117**, 302, **448-449**; closure of – 450; Companies of actors: Admiral's Men 116 449, Chamberlain's Men 449, Pembroke's Men 450, King's Men 450, Warwick's Men Company 95; Hope theatre 107, 108, 115, 448, 450; Penny gaffs **420-421**; Surrey theatre 175, 251, 258, **260**, 423, 438; Sadler's Wells 429, 437; Swan theatre 109, 112-113, 450; scenery painters 424-426. Also see Globe, Hope, Old Vic, Rose, Winchester House

Thrale, Hester – 160, 191; Ralph – 191; Henry – 191

Three Coney Walk 150-151, 157; also see Lambeth Walk

Tinker, Jim (architect) 344

Tinworth, George (sculptor) 237, *386*

Tite, William (architect) 412

Tooley Street 51, 80, *129*, 130, 136, 137, 139, 194, 208, 217, 219, 280, 282, 284, **285**, 299, 352, 503, 504, 509. Also see Short Southwark and Fires.

Tower Bridge 13, 210, 351, **353**; – Road 211, 286

TOWERMANIA: Babel 488-494, 497-499, 528;. Also see Shard, Shot towers

Townsend, Charles Harrison (architect) 386, 387

TRADES: **504-513**; coffee shop/trade *508*; cocoa trade 509; farrier's 342; food shops 257; herring 511; linen drapers 270; oil & colourman *508*; porters *168*, 257; rope-making 262; shoemakers 262; silk mercers 270; tailors 262; street sellers *245*, *272*, 286; tea dealer and grocer 270, *508*, *512*, 514

Tradescants (The) John – the Elder 95, 363-372; John – the Younger 95, 152, 364-372; Hester – 152, 367-368, 371

Tradescant House 92-93, 94, **95-96**, 150-151; **152**; the Ark: 366, 369-372, 387-390

Tradescant garden 362-366

Tradescant tomb 366-368, 391

TRAGIC DEATHS: drowning at 'suicide bridge' 405-406; Alice's fire 464-470. See James Braidwood

TRANSPORT 438 'battle of the bridges' 438, 439; Tram 438. Also see Jubilee Line; Railways

Trenet Lane 130

Trinity Church **286-288**; – Square 78, 280, **286-288**, 559

Trinity House estate 286-288, 543

Trinity Street 287

Tyers, Jonathan (entrepreneur) 372-375

Uffenbach, Conrad von (German diarist) 168, 404

Ufford Street 172, 528

Union Jack Club 323, **329**

Union Street 78, 115 444, 457, 464-467, 470, No 194 – 464-465, ; No 8 – 182-183, **195-196**

Upper Ground 112-113, **114-115**, 168, 188, 326, 327, 480

Upper Marsh 107, 241

U S Embassy 13, 308, 317, **396-397**, 408

Vaccination 184

Valckenborg brothers 491; Martin van – 490

Vanderbank, John (painter) *216*

VAUXHALL: 70-71, 89, 370; Atlas building 308, 315, *316*, – Bridge 153, 154, 226, 230-231, **232**, 244, 308, 317, 382; – City Farm *530*, 531; – Escheat 95, 152, 153, 376;– jetty

13, 21, 66, *71*; Keybridge 308; MI6 66, 309, **314-315**, *530*, 531; – The Lawn *381*, 384-385 ; – Pleasure Gardens 314; St George Wharf 301, 308, **315-317**, 497; – Station 384; – Walk 233, – water works 244, 245

Vauxhall & Lambeth 12-13, **90-141, 148-179, 228-247, 306-319**, 527

Vauxhall Gardens 13, *94*, 150-151, 240, 309, 313-314, 372-375, *381*, 391, 398, 404, *559*

Vauxhall Park 246, 381, **382-387**

Vauxhall plate glasshouse 150-151, **153**

Vauxhall Square 154 (1600s), 475 (2020s)

Vestey Family – see Heron Corporation

Vine Street, 172

Villiers, George (2nd Duke of Buckingham) **154**

VINEGAR MANUFACTORIES: 146, 150-151, 271; Beaufoy – **169**, *170*, 230, **246**, 385; Fassett & Burnet – 153; Messrs Potts – 182-183, **190-191**, 70, 270, 271; Rushe's – 182-183, **190-191**; Sarson's 302

Viner Street 253

Vinopolis 300

Walkers, Parker & Company (shot tower operators) 255

Walcot, Edmund 155; – Richard 157

Walcot Place (now Kennington Road) 150-151, **155-156**

Walcot estate 115, 155-156, 157, 254

Wale, Samuel (artist) 375, *376*

Walnut Tree Walk 155

Walters, Sir Roger (architect) 347

Walworth 89

Wanamaker, Sam 302, 335

Wandsworth Road 246

Warenne family 89, 136, 137

Watch house 263

Water Lambeth 51, 89, 100-*101*, *232*

Water Lane 291

WATERLOO: **102-109, 164-179, 248-265, 320-329, 400-441**, 527, 551-554; – Bridge *60-61*, *224*, 226, 250, **252**, *253*, 322, **326**, 405, 406, *413*-414; – helmet *70*; – Ring 63; – Road 242, 254, 254, 329, 409, 414, 415, 416, *419*; – Station 63, 224, 264, 409, 411, **412-414**

'Waterloo churches' (or Commissioners' churches) 255, 289

Watermen 506

Water supply 127, 208, **244-245**, 250, **252**, *381*, *382*, 431

Watt, James (inventor) 186

Watts, G F (artist) *405*, 406, 467

Watts, William 255; Messrs – 256

Waverley House 118, 120

Webber Street 172

Webling, Wessel (brewer) 139, 210; Nicholas – 139

Wellington Mills 241

Wesley, John 175

West family 115, 199; Catherine – 197; Temple – 162; Col Templeton – 424

West Square *57*, 150-151, **162**, 230-231, *244*, 424

Westminster Bridge *147*, 150-151, 159, **159**, *160*, 224, 230-231, 250, 308, 342; – Lion 13, *171*; – Road 160, 171, 172, 236, 252, 395, 412, 421, 430, 458

Westminster Hospital (formerly – Infirmary) (Westminster) New Lying-in Hospital 166-167, **173**, 250, **252**, 254, 379

Westmoreland Road 259

Weston Street 286

Weston Williamson (architects) 300

WHARVES: Butler's 351, **352-353**, 482, **504-510, 513-517**, 548-549; Cotton's – 507, 505, 509; Drainpipe Wharf (Lambeth) 233, *235*; Fenning's 72, Gabriel's 60-61; Hartley's 210, 289; Liddard's 289; Phoenix 71; Stanton's 288; Sufferance – 505-*506*; Tea Trade Wharf 514; Topping's 283; Wilson's 71. Also see Hay's Wharf

White brothers 172; Gilbert – **375-377**; Thomas – 376; Benjamin – 376

White Cross Street *464*, Also see Ayres Street

White Cube Gallery 351, **354-355**

White Lyon prison 124, 131-132, *213*, 216

Whittington, Richard (Dick) (Lord Mayor) 136

Wild, Jonathan (criminal) 274

Wilhelm, Christian (potter) 139

Wilhelm, Friedrich (Duke of Brunswick) **153**

Wilkinson Eyre (architects) 328

Wilkinson, Fanny 386

William Street 233

Willow Walk (Bermondsey) 172

Willows (Wilys) 89

Winchester Geese see prostitution

Winchester House/Palace/Place 88, 112-113, **119**, 182-183, **191-192**; – glass factory **119**, 146, 192; – park 196; pottery 146

Windmill Street 172

Wingfield, James Digman (artist) **236-*237***

Witt, Johannes de (humanist) 116

Wolseley Street 71

Wood, John (father and son) 381

Workhouse Lane 155

WORKHOUSES: 405, 553; Bermondsey – 204-205, **211**; Christchurch – 166-167, 175, **189**, 251, **258**; Gilbert Unions 190; Lambeth – 150-151, **155**, 190, 230-231, **237-239**, 312, 313, 455, ; Mint Street – 190, 259, *274*, 463; Newington's 259; St Olave's – 204-205, **210**; St Saviour's – 182-183, **189-190**

Wren, Christopher (architect) 217, 252

Wright and Wright (architects) 310

Wyatt, James and Samuel (architects) 186

Wyngaerde, Anthonis/Antony van den (artist) *36-37*, 41, 44, 47, 51, 88, 120, 531, 532

Yevele, Henry (architect) 95, 128, 512

York Road 252, 254, 329, 412, 418, 458

Zoar Street 182-183

Zouch, Sir Edward (glassmaking) 119, 154